Seeing

Handbook of Perception and Cognition
2nd Edition

Series Editors
Edward C. Carterette
and **Morton P. Friedman**

Seeing

Edited by
Karen K. De Valois

Departments of Psychology and Vision Science
University of California at Berkeley
Berkeley, California

A Harcourt Science and Technology Company

San Diego San Francisco New York
Boston London Sydney Tokyo

To Russ

This book is printed on acid-free paper. 

Academic Press
A Harcourt Science and Technology Company
525 B Street, Suite 1900, San Diego, California 92101-4495, USA
http://www.academicpress.com

Academic Press
24-28 Oval Road, London NW1 7DX, UK
http://www.hbuk.co.uk/ap/

Library of Congress Catalog Card Number: 99-68017

International Standard Book Number: 0-12-443760-5

PRINTED IN THE UNITED STATES OF AMERICA
00 01 02 03 04 05 EB 9 8 7 6 5 4 3 2 1

Contents

Contributors

Numbers in parentheses indicate the pages on which the authors' contributions begin.

Duane G. Albrecht (79)
Psychology Department
University of Texas
Austin, Texas 78712

Andrew Derrington (259)
School of Psychology
University of Nottingham
Nottingham NE7 2RD, England

Karen K. De Valois (129)
Departments of Psychology and Vision Science
University of California at Berkeley
Berkeley, California 94720

Russell L. De Valois (129)
Departments of Psychology and Vision Science
University of California at Berkeley
Berkeley, California 94720

Jack L. Gallant (311)
Department of Psychology
University of California at Berkeley
Berkeley, California 94720

Wilson S. Geisler (79)
Department of Psychology
University of Texas
Austin, Texas 78712

Clifton M. Schor (177)
School of Optometry
University of California at Berkeley
Berkeley, California 94720

Robert Shapley (55)
Center for Neural Science
New York University
New York, New York 10003

Larry N. Thibos (1)
School of Optometry
Indiana University
Bloomington, Indiana 47405

Jeremy M. Wolfe (335)
Harvard Medical School and
Center for Ophthalmic Research
Brigham and Women's Hospital
Boston, Massachusetts 02115

Foreword

The problem of perception and cognition is in understanding how the organism transforms, organizes, stores, and uses information arising from the world in sense data or memory. With this definition of perception and cognition in mind, this handbook is designed to bring together the essential aspects of this very large, diverse, and scattered literature and to give a précis of the state of knowledge in every area of perception and cognition. The work is aimed at the psychologist and the cognitive scientist in particular, and at the natural scientist in general. Topics are covered in comprehensive surveys in which fundamental facts and concepts are presented, and important leads to journals and monographs of the specialized literature are provided. Perception and cognition are considered in the widest sense. Therefore, the work treats a wide range of experimental and theoretical work.

The *Handbook of Perception and Cognition* should serve as a basic source and reference work for those in the arts or sciences, indeed for all who are interested in human perception, action, and cognition.

Edward C. Carterette and Morton P. Friedman

Preface

Of all the things that humans can do, seeing is arguably what we do best. The eyes encode and transmit enough information to allow the brain to construct a vivid representation of the three-dimensional structure of the external world, including estimates of the relative intensity and spectral composition of the light at every visible point, all within a fraction of a second. We detect and identify objects, and determine where they are and the direction and speed with which they are moving, with extraordinary sensitivity and precision. The most remarkable thing about seeing, however, is that it appears to be effortless. We are rarely aware of the complex computational tasks our visual systems are accomplishing, and we do not experience seeing as difficult. When we open our eyes, the world simply appears. The apparent ease with which we accomplish vision makes it difficult to recognize just how complicated the visual system is.

In this volume, several specific aspects of seeing are considered. Their selection was based in part on the state of our current knowledge. Some are classical topics, for example, color vision, spatial vision, binocular vision, and visual receptive fields for which there is a broad and deep pool of knowledge. Others (motion vision, image formation, and sampling) are traditional problems about which there has been a relatively recent explosion of new information and understanding. Still others (neural representation of shape, visual attention) have more recently become prominent, in part because only now do we have the tools necessary to begin to understand the mechanisms responsible. Each of these topics could be—indeed, has been—the subject of dedicated volumes. Here we attempt to describe some of the problems attendant upon each topic, to give a useful overview of the current state of our knowledge, and to introduce the interested reader to the modern literature.

I am indebted to my colleagues who wrote the various chapters of this book and to the publisher and series editors who decided to bring out a new, expanded version of the *Handbook of Perception,* now the *Handbook of Perception and Cognition.* I am grateful to the various authors and publishers who have given permission for the reprinting of figures from earlier publications. They are individually acknowledged and credited where the figures appear. My friends—colleagues, staff, and students—at Berkeley have been immensely helpful and supportive, and I am grateful. Finally, Russell De Valois has been deeply involved at every stage—writing, reading, editing. Without his help and support, this undertaking would never have been completed.

Karen K. De Valois

CHAPTER 1

Formation and Sampling of the Retinal Image

Larry N. Thibos

I. INTRODUCTION

Vision begins with the formation of an optical image of the external world upon the retinal mosaic of light-sensitive photoreceptors. Because image formation is the very first step in the visual process, imperfections in the eye's optical apparatus have the potential for affecting every aspect of visual perception, from color to motion, space, and form. Even if the focusing components of the eye's optical system were perfect, the retinal image would still be degraded by the diffraction of light as it passes through the pupil. Another potential limiting factor for vision is the scattering of light as it traverses the ocular media and retina before being absorbed by the visual pigment molecules inside photoreceptors. Thus the study of visual perception must logically begin with the imaging properties of the eye to uncover those optical factors which constrain the quality of vision.

The second step in the visual process is the sampling of the optical image by the retina, a thin layer of neural tissue at the back of the eye. The light-sensitive rod and cone photoreceptors are the transducers of the retina that convert the optical image into a discrete, neural representation of the retinal image. This discrete "neural image" is then resampled by an array of interneurons (called bipolar cells), and this intermediate neural image is then resampled yet again by the output cells of the retina (called ganglion cells) for transmission through the optic nerve to the brain. These multiple sampling operations are of fundamental importance to vision because they limit the fidelity of the neural representation of the external world. Just as a coarse layer of light-sensitive crystals on photographic film produces a coarse picture, so too will a coarse array of light-detecting neural elements represent a visual image coarsely. Consequently, it is physically impossible for a sparse neural array, such as exists in the peripheral parts of the retina, to faithfully represent fine visual patterns. This is not to say that fine patterns fail to produce a useful neural image. To the contrary, it is possible for fine patterns to generate visual signals which yield viable percepts, but these percepts must necessarily misrepresent the stimulus as a coarse pattern. This phenomenon, called *aliasing,* represents an irretrievable loss of fidelity in the neural image that has the potential for affecting many aspects of visual perception.

The aim of this chapter is to succinctly review our current understanding of the formation and sampling of the retinal image in the human eye and the visual limitations imposed by these initial stages of the visual process. For the benefit of readers unfamiliar with the physical and mathematical description of image formation, a brief review is provided of the main optical concepts needed to understand how the retinal image is formed and how the quality of that image is characterized. These concepts are then embodied in an optical model of the eye which is useful for qualitative as well as quantitative thinking about retinal images. Similarly, the mathematical concepts needed to formulate the intuitive notion of neural sampling limits on vision are summarized before presenting a model of the sampling process. When taken together, this neuro-optical model of the eye provides a conceptual framework for interpreting empirical studies of the optical and sampling limits to visual perception and the impact these two factors have in daily life.

II. FORMATION OF THE RETINAL IMAGE

A. Optical System of the Eye

The optical components of the adult human eye are shown in anatomical cross-section in Figure 1 (Walls, 1942). In its resting state, two-thirds of the optical power of the eye is provided by refraction of light by the cornea and the remaining third is provided by the internal lens of the eye. However, the internal lens of the eye is capable of changing shape to provide additional focusing power when looking at close objects. An eye is said to be *emmetropic* if it produces a clearly focused retinal image of distant targets when the lens has minimum power. At birth the human eye is small, but it grows rapidly over the first 3 years of life, and by 3 years of age it is nearly adult size (Bennett & Rabbetts, 1989). During this period a coordinated growth process called *emmetropization* aims to keep the eye clearly focused for distant targets when the eye is in its resting state (Gwiazda, Thorn, Bauer, & Held, 1993; Wallman, Adams, & Trachtman, 1981). Although the mechanism of emmetropization is not fully understood, it appears to function independently of

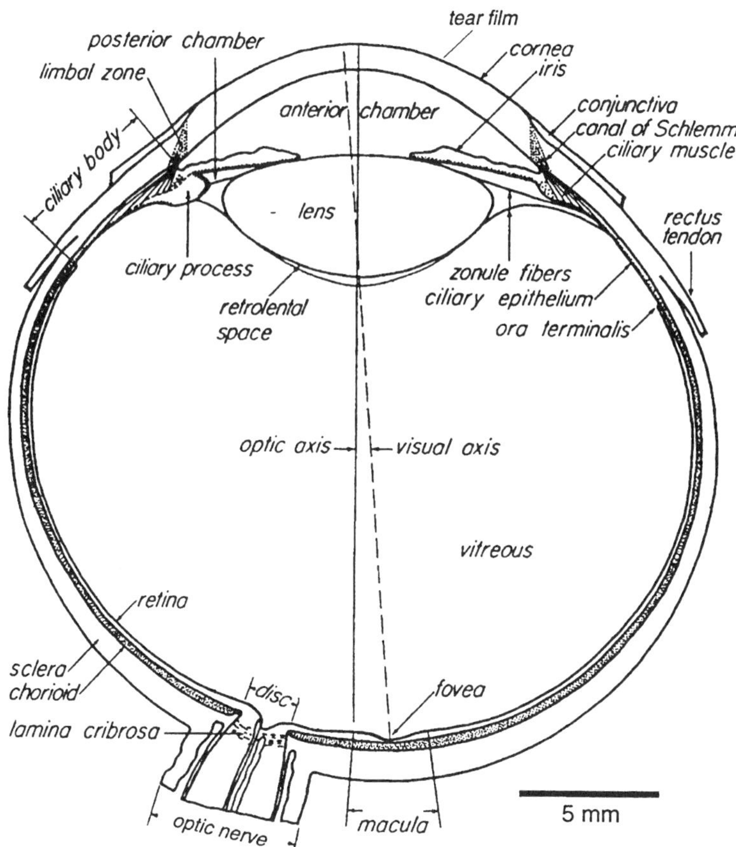

FIGURE 1 An anatomically correct drawing of a human eye in cross-section. (Redrawn from Walls, 1942.)

the brain, since cutting of the optic nerve in experimental animals does not alter the pattern of eye growth (Raviola & Wiesel, 1985; Troilo, Gottlieb, & Wallman, 1987).

During childhood and early adulthood the internal lens of the eye is flexible so its anterior surface can bulge forward to make the lens more powerful optically, thus focusing the eye on closer targets. These changes in shape occur as tension on the supporting zonule fibers is released in response to forward movement of the ciliary processes caused by contraction of the ciliary muscle (Glasser & Campbell, 1998; Helmholtz, 1909/1924). This ability of the human eye to increase its focal power, called *accommodation,* provides an operating range for focusing that extends from infinity to less than 10 cm from the eye in a young person. The physical unit of focusing power is the diopter (D), which is computed as the inverse of the distance (in meters) from the eye to a target which is clearly focused on the retina. The accommodative range is more than 10 D in a young eye, but this value declines steadily throughout adulthood (Duane, 1922) and eventually disappears (a condition called *presbyopia*) as about 55 years of age when the lens has become completely inflexible (Glasser & Campbell, 1998).

In addition to changes with age that occur in all eyes, there are other changes that occur in a significant minority of eyes. For example, many eyes grow excessively in the axial direction during childhood or early adulthood, which causes the retinal image of distant objects to be formed in front of the retina. As the target is brought closer to the eye, the optical image will move backwards towards the retina and eventually come into focus on the photoreceptors. Such eyes are called "near-sighted" (*myopic*), a condition which is easily corrected by weakening the optical power of the eye by wearing a spectacle or contact lens with negative power. The opposite condition of "far-sightedness" (*hyperopia*) results when the eye lacks sufficient power in the resting state to focus distant objects on the photoreceptor layer. The young eye easily overcomes this condition by exerting some accommodative effort, but a presbyopic eye requires corrective lenses. Other eyes may have a cornea or lens which is not radially symmetric, which causes contours of different orientations to produce images at different distances. This condition of *astigmatism* is corrected by spectacle lenses which have the same asymmetry, but opposite sign. Although other defects in the eye's optical system occur in the human population, the only optical defects which are routinely corrected by spectacle or contact lenses are myopia, hyperopia, presbyopia, and astigmatism. This traditional practice is likely to change in the near future, however, as new technologies for measuring and correcting the eye's aberrations mature (Liang, Grimm, Goelz, & Bille, 1994). The fascinating potential for supernormal visual performance resulting from comprehensive optical correction of all the optical imperfections of the eye is but one intriguing spin-off from current research in this area (Liang, Williams, & Miller, 1997).

B. Physics of Image Formation

If an eye could be fitted with a perfect optical system, it would focus all rays of light from a distant point source into a single image point on the retina, as shown in Figure 2a. In this case the only optical question to be answered is, Where is the image point located? To answer this question we may apply the basic laws of paraxial (Gaussian) optical theory to describe the idealized case of perfect imaging. Real eyes, on the other hand, suffer from three types of optical imperfection which are not treated by paraxial theory: *aberrations, diffraction,* and *scattering.* While the mechanism is different in each case, the common effect of these imperfections is to spread light across the retina, as illustrated in Figure 2b. Thus a second, and more difficult, question to be answered is, What is the spatial distribution of light intensity in the image? To answer this question will require the concepts and computational tools of Fourier analysis.

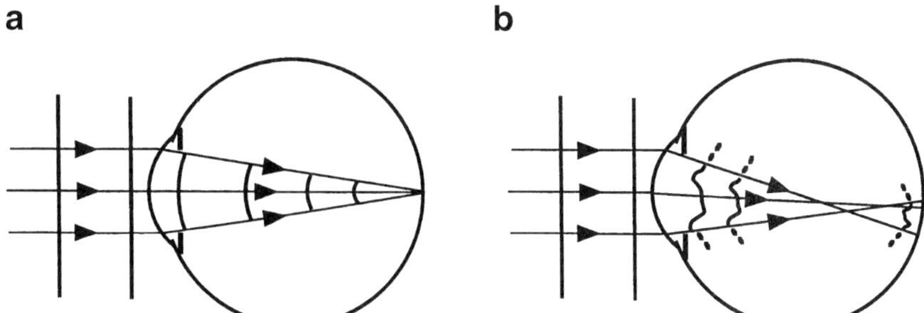

FIGURE 2 Formation of the retinal image depicted as change in curvature of incident wavefronts or as bending of light rays, assuming the eye's optical system were perfect (a) or imperfect (b).

1. Geometrical Optics in the Paraxial Domain

Light is an electromagnetic field which propagates energy through space as a traveling wave. At any given point in space the amplitude of the electromagnetic field modulates sinusoidally in time, like the height of a bubble on the surface of a pond waxes and wanes sinusoidally following the impact of a pebble. Just as a falling pebble causes the water to rise and fall synchronously in such a way that energy propagates outwards in the form of traveling waves, so light propagates in waves. The direction of propagation of the advancing wavefront at any given point in space is specified by a ray drawn perpendicular to the wavefront at that point. Some examples of this dual representation of light propagation are shown in Figures 2 and 3.

In the paraxial domain of perfect imaging, wavefronts of light are assumed to have spherical shape characterized by a center of curvature and a radius of curvature. Since

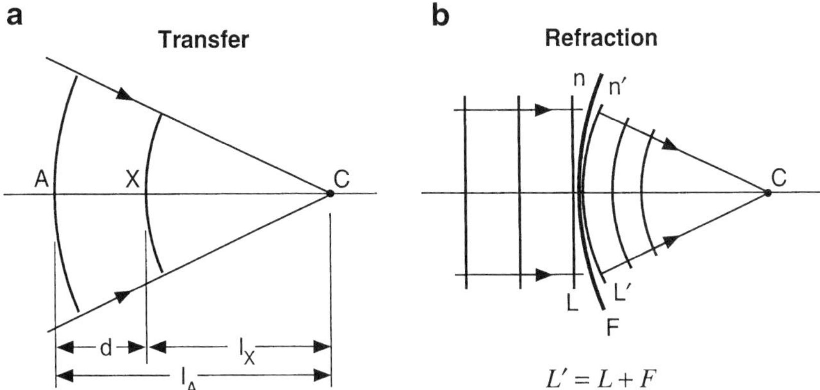

FIGURE 3 Geometrical optics rules for the change in wavefront vergence due to propagation in a homogeneous medium (a) or refraction by an interface between two media of different refractive indices (b).

the image formed by a collapsing spherical wavefront is a single point at the center of curvature, determining image location is the same problem as locating the center of curvature of a refracted wavefront. Such problems are more easily solved if we describe wavefronts in terms of their curvature (i.e., inverse of radius of curvature), and for this reason we define the *vergence* L of a spherical wavefront as

$$L = n/r \tag{1}$$

where n is the refractive index of the medium in which the wavefront exists, and r is the radius of curvature of the wavefront.

Two rules illustrated in Figure 3 govern the imaging process: the *transfer rule* and the *refraction rule.* The transfer rule describes how the vergence of a wavefront changes as the wavefront propagates from a starting point A through the distance d to any later point X on route to the center of curvature C. To derive the transfer rule we simply express the linear relationship

$$l_X = l_A - d \tag{2}$$

in terms of vergence by substituting $L_A = n/l_A$ and $L_X = n/l_X$ to get

$$L_X = \frac{L_A}{1 - (d/n)L_A} \tag{3}$$

In words, the transfer rule of Equation 3 says that the vergence "downstream" at some point X is given by the vergence "upstream" at A, divided by 1 minus the product of the upstream vergence and the "reduced" distance traveled by the wavefront. The term *reduced distance* denotes the physical distance traveled by a light ray, divided by the refractive index of the medium.

The refraction rule describes how the vergence of a wavefront changes when entering a new medium. The interface between the two media can be any shape, but in the paraxial domain the shape is approximated by a spherical surface with radius of curvature r. By definition, the refracting power F of the surface is

$$F = \frac{n' - n}{r}, \tag{4}$$

where n is the refractive index of the medium the wavefront is leaving, and n' is the index of the medium the wavefront is entering. If the wavefront incident on such a surface has vergence L immediately prior to entering the new medium, then immediately after entering the new medium the wavefront has vergence L' given by the refraction equation

$$L' = L + F \tag{5}$$

In words, Equation 5 says that the wavefront vergence after refraction is equal to the vergence prior to refraction plus the power of the refracting surface.

The refraction rule expresses in quantitative terms the net result of two factors acting to change the curvature of the wavefront. These two factors are the wavelength of light, which varies with refractive index of the medium, and the curvature of the refracting surface. This interaction is most easily understood for the case of an incident plane wave, as illustrated in Figure 3b. The incident plane wave is analogous to a marching band of musicians traveling across an open field. The musicians all march to the same beat and their cadence (i.e., temporal frequency of light oscillation) never varies. The curved surface separates the dry marching field where the musicians have a long stride (i.e., wavelength is relatively long) from a muddy field where the musicians must shorten their stride to avoid slipping (i.e., the wavelength of light is reduced). Since the musicians near the middle enter the muddy field first, that part of the line slows down first. As time progresses, more and more of the marching line enters the slower medium, but because the interface is curved, those musicians farthest from the centerline stay on dry land the longest and therefore travel the farthest before they too must enter the slower field. By the time the entire marching line has passed into the new medium, the end of the line has advanced farther than the center and so the line is curved. So it is with light. The incident wavefront is delayed more near the centerline than at the edges, and thus the wavefront becomes curved. This is the phenomenon of refraction. The alternative description of refraction as the bending of light rays by an amount which depends upon the angle of incidence relative to the surface normal is known as Snell's Law.

Given the above rules and definitions, the paraxial location of the image of an axial point source formed by an arbitrary number of refracting surfaces may be found by repeated application of the refraction and transfer equations. To begin, one uses the definition of vergence (Equation 1) to determine the wavefront vergence of incident light immediately prior to refraction by the first surface. The refraction rule (eq. 5) then yields the wavefront vergence immediately after refraction. The transfer rule (Equation 3) is then applied to determine the new vergence of the wavefront after propagating from the first surface to the second surface. The "refract and transfer" process is repeated as many times as necessary until all surfaces have been encountered. After the final surface, the definition of vergence yields the center of curvature (i.e., the image point) of the exiting wavefront.

To determine the image of object points which are off axis but still within the paraxial image domain, the simplest method is to apply a magnification formula derived from Snell's Law. Consider the ray of light shown in Figure 4 emanating from the tip of the arrow object and intersecting the refracting surface at the vertex (i.e., where the surface intersects the optical axis of symmetry). The incident ray makes an angle u with the optical axis, and after refraction the same ray makes angle u'. Snell's Law is a law of angular magnification

$$n \sin u = n' \sin u' \tag{6}$$

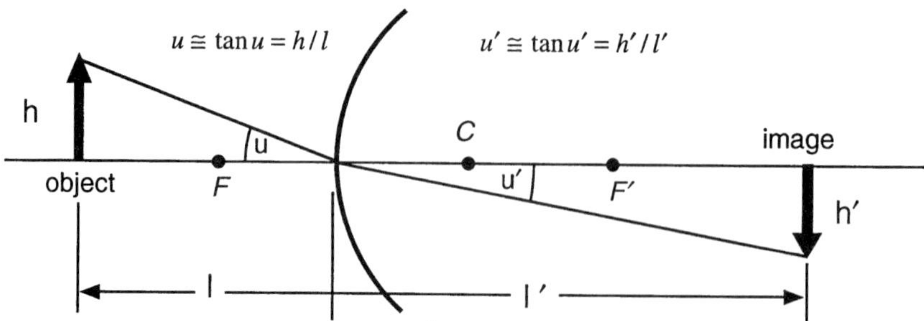

FIGURE 4 The geometry of Snell's law for refraction of the chief ray from an off-axis object point yields the paraxial formula for image magnification.

which, in the paraxial domain where the small angle approximation sin $u = u$ is appropriate, becomes

$$n \cdot u = n' \cdot u' \tag{7}$$

Replacing the angles of incidence and refraction with their trigonometrical equivalents, and applying the small angle approximation tan $u = u$, Equation 7 becomes

$$n \cdot h/l = n' \cdot h'/l', \tag{8}$$

and by the definition of vergence, this result simplifies to

$$h \cdot L = h' \cdot L'. \tag{9}$$

The ratio of image height to object height is called the linear magnification of the optical system. Thus the lateral location of a paraxial object point is found by application of the linear magnification formula

$$\textit{magnification} = \frac{h'}{h} = \frac{L}{L'} \tag{10}$$

2. Geometrical Optics in the Nonparaxial Domain

Ouside the paraxial domain of perfect imaging, aberrations are said to exist when refracted light rays from a single object point intersect the image plane at different locations, causing the light to spread out over an area. This distribution of light intensity in the image of a point source, called a *point spread function* (PSF), is a fundamental characterization of the system. The PSF also has great practical utility because it allows the computation of the image of an arbitrary object as the superposition of individual PSFs from every point in the object.

Two general methods for determining the PSF of any optical system are (a) direct observation of the image formed by the system for a point object, and (b) computational modeling of the system. Direct observation of the PSF of the human eye is complicated by the inaccessibility of the retinal image, which forces us to use the eye's optical system a second time to make the observation. For this reason, the computational approach using an optical model of the eye has played an especially important role in understanding the optical imperfections of the eye. Many such models have been proposed over the last century or more, and most modern schematic eye models have been implemented with computer programs. Given such programs, one common method for determining the PSF is to introduce a uniform bundle of rays that fills the model eye's pupil and then to trace all the rays to their destination on the imaging screen (retina). Each ray intersects the screen at a single spot, so the image as a whole may be visualized by a diagram of spots for the entire bundle. With elementary trigonometry and Snell's law of refraction, it is not difficult to write a computer program to perform such ray tracing and so determine numerically a spot diagram rendition of the PSF for the eye.

Unfortunately, ray tracing fails to account for diffraction, the second major source of image degradation in the eye. Diffraction is the name given to any deviation of light rays from straight lines which cannot be interpreted as reflection or refraction. If the phenomenon of diffraction did not exist, then when a wavefront of light passes through an aperture (such as the eye's pupil), the marginal rays would define a sharp boundary between light and shadow, as suggested by the dashed lines in Figure 5. In fact, light does penetrate the shadow and the effect is not insignificant. For an eye with a pupil diameter about 2 mm or less, diffraction is the primary factor which prevents the formation of a perfect point image of a point source (Campbell & Green, 1965; Liang & Williams, 1997). Since the pupil diameter of the normal eye spans the full range from diffraction-dominated performance to aberration-dominated performance, we require an optical theory of image formation which takes account of both factors. For this reason we will now set aside the ray theory of image formation in favor of the wave theory.

3. Wave Theory of Image Formation

According to the wave theory of image formation, the perfect image of a point object is formed by a collapsing hemispherical wavefront with center of curvature

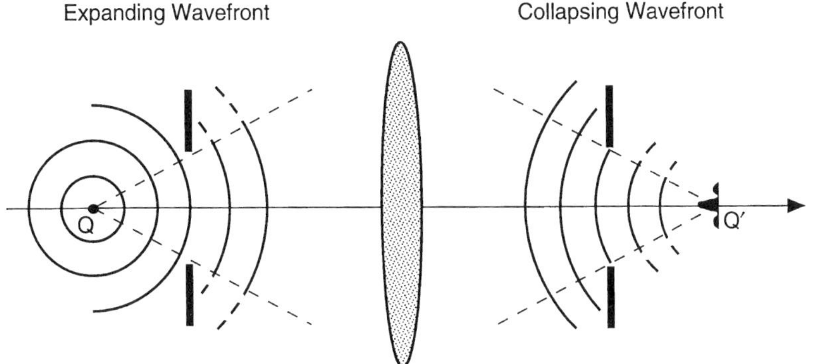

FIGURE 5 Diffraction by an aperture is the propagation of light into the geometrical shadow region shown by broken lines.

located in the image plane. An aberrated wavefront, therefore, is characterized by its deviation from this perfect wavefront. Even without defects of this kind, however, the image of a point source through a circular pupil will still be spread out across the retina as a diffraction pattern consisting of a bright central disk surrounded by unevenly spaced concentric circles known as the Airy pattern (after G. B. Airy, who first derived its analytical form). The underlying reason for this diffractive imperfection in the image is that the wavefront emerging from the eye's pupil is only a small part of the complete wavefront needed to form a perfect point image.

The necessity of having a complete wavefront for perfect imaging follows logically from Helmholtz's principle of reversibility: what is true for waves diverging from a point is also true for waves converging towards the point. If an ideal point *source* produces spherical waves *expanding* symmetrically in all directions of three-dimensional space, then to produce an ideal point *image* requires spherical waves *collapsing* symmetrically from all directions of three-dimensional space. By a similar argument (C. Williams & Becklund, 1989), to mimic the effect of an aperture which transmits only a segment of a diverging hemispherical wavefront propagating towards the plane of the aperture (Figure 6a) would require an extended source in order to cancel the wavefront everywhere except where the segment persists (Figure 6b). Therefore, by the principle of reversibility, a converging segment of a spherical wavefront passed by an aperture must produce an extended image. This is the phenomenon of diffraction.

To take the next step and quantitatively describe the nature of the diffraction pattern produced by a wavefront after passing through an aperture, we require some help from diffraction theory. Diffraction theory is not for the faint-hearted, as diffraction problems have a reputation for being amongst the most difficult ones encountered in optics. Nevertheless the basic ideas are not difficult to understand if we leave rigorous mathematical proofs for the standard reference works (Born & Wolf, 1999; Goodman, 1968). As a bonus reward for this effort we will have laid the foundation for Fourier optics, which is the primary computational method for modern image analysis.

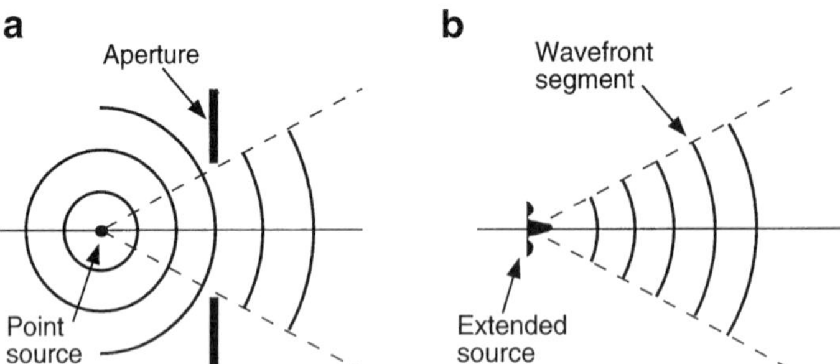

FIGURE 6 To replicate the creation of a wavefront segment by an aperture (a) would require an extended source in the absence of the aperture (b).

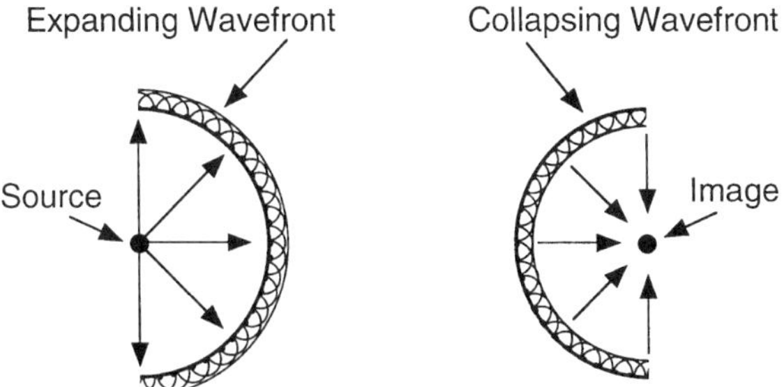

FIGURE 7 Huygens's theory of wavefront propagation.

A framework for thinking quantitatively about the diffraction of propagating waves is illustrated in Figure 7. To understand how an expanding or collapsing wave propagates, Huygens suggested in 1678 that if every point on the wavefront were the center of a new, secondary disturbance which emanates spherical wavelets in the direction of propagation, then the wavefront at any later instant would be the envelope of these secondary wavelets. In 1818 Fresnel advanced Huygens's intuitive notions by incorporating Young's discovery in 1801 of the phenomenon of interference to propose a quantitative theory now known as the Huygens–Fresnel principle of light propagation. By this principle, Huygens's secondary wavelets are directed (i.e., the amplitude is strongest in a direction perpendicular to the primary wavefront) and they mutually interfere to re-create the advancing wavefront. Consequently, when a wavefront encounters an opaque aperture, the points on the wavefront near the obstruction are no longer counter-balanced by the missing Huygen wavelets, and so light is able to propagate behind the aperture. Subsequently, Kirchoff demonstrated in 1882 that critical assumptions made by Fresnel (including the nonisotropic nature of Huygens's wavelets) were valid consequences of the wave nature of light. In 1894 Sommerfeld rescued Kirchoff's theory from mutually inconsistent assumptions regarding boundary values of light at the aperture. In so doing Sommerfeld placed the scalar theory of diffraction in its modern form by establishing that the phenomenon of diffraction can be accurately accounted for by linearly adding the amplitudes of the infinity of Huygens's wavelets located within the aperture itself. Mathematically this accounting takes the form of a superposition integral known as the Rayleigh-Sommerfeld diffraction formula (Goodman, 1968, Equations 3–26, p. 45). For a fuller account of the history of the wave theory of light, see Goodman, p. 32, or Born & Wolf, 1970, pp. xxv–xxxiii).

To express the diffraction formula requires a mathematical description of Huygens's wavelets and a way of summing them up at an observation point R beyond the aperture as shown in Figure 8. Although a rigorous theory would describe light as a vector field with electric and magnetic components that are coupled according to Maxwell's equations, it is sufficient to use a much simpler theory that treats light

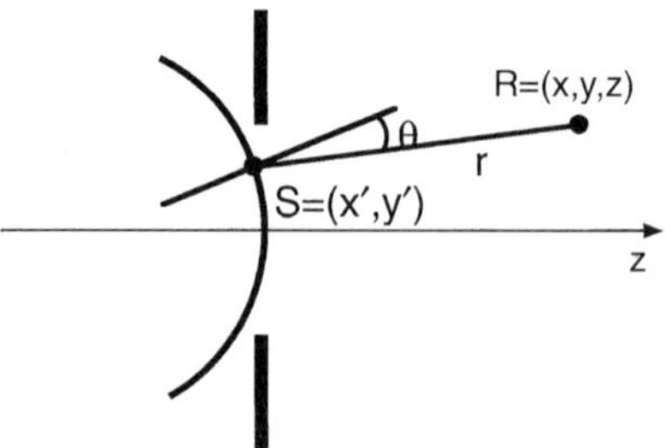

FIGURE 8 Geometry for computing the contribution of Huygens's wavelet at point S to the amplitude of light at point R.

as a scalar phenomenon, the strength of which varies sinusoidally in time. Thus, for a monochromatic wave, the field strength may be written as

$$u(R,t) = U(R)\cos[2\pi\nu t + \phi(R)], \tag{11}$$

where $U(R)$ and $\phi(R)$ are the amplitude and phase, respectively, of the wave at position R, while ν is the optical temporal frequency. For mathematical reasons it is more convenient to express the trigonometric function as the real part of a complex exponential by writing Equation 11 as

$$u(R,t) = \mathrm{Re}[\mathbf{U}(R)\exp(-i2\pi\nu t)], \tag{12}$$

where $i = \sqrt{-1}$ and $\mathbf{U}(R)$ is a complex valued function of position only:

$$\mathbf{U}(R) = U(R)\exp[-i\phi(R)]. \tag{13}$$

The temporal oscillation of the field is not essential to the diffraction problem, and for this reason we concentrate on the phasor $\mathbf{U}(R)$ as a description of a wavefront. Accordingly, we seek such a phasor description of Huygens's wavelets. The required function for an arbitrary point S on a wavefront of unit amplitude is

$$\mathbf{H}(S,R) = \frac{1}{i\lambda} \cdot \frac{\exp(ikr)}{r} \cdot \cos\theta, \tag{14}$$

where

$\mathbf{H}$ = complex amplitude of light at R due to Huygen wavelet at S
r = radial distance from source point S to observation point R
k = $2\pi/\lambda$, wave number, converts r to phase shift in radians
λ = wavelength of light
θ = angle between line RS and the normal to wavefront at S

Each of the three factors on the right-hand side of Equation 14 relates to an essential feature of Huygens's wavelets. The middle factor is the standard expression for a spherical wavefront due to a point source. The numerator of this factor accounts for the phase shift that results when the wavelet propagates from S to R, and the denominator accounts for the loss of amplitude needed to keep the total energy constant as the wavefront expands. This spherical wavelet is modified by the first factor, which says that the amplitude of the secondary source is smaller by the factor $1/\lambda$ compared to the primary wave, and the phase of the secondary source leads the phase of the primary wave by 90°. The third factor in Equation 14 is the obliquity factor, which states that the amplitude of the secondary wavelet varies as the cosine of the angle θ between the normal to the wavefront at S and the direction of the observation point R relative to S.

Equation 14 describes the secondary wavelet produced by a primary wavefront of unit amplitude. Applying the actual wavefront amplitude $\mathbf{U}(S)$ as a weighting factor, the wavelet at point S is the product $\mathbf{U}(S)\mathbf{H}(S,R)$. The total field at point R is then found by linearly superimposing the fields, due to all of the secondary wavelets inside the aperture A. The result is a superposition integral over the aperture

$$\mathbf{U}(R) = \iint_{Aperture} \mathbf{U}(S)\mathbf{H}(S,R)dA, \tag{15}$$

which is known as the Rayleigh–Sommerfeld diffraction integral. (Goodman, 1968, p. 45, Equations 3–28).

4. Fourier Optics

Under certain restricted circumstances, the superposition integral of Equation 15 reduces to a convolution integral. This immediately suggests an application of the convolution theorem of Fourier analysis (Bracewell, 1969), which transforms the given quantities **U** and **H** into a corresponding pair of new quantities, which provides a complementary view of diffraction and optical image formation. This is the domain of Fourier optics.

To begin, erect a coordinate reference frame centered on the aperture as shown in Figure 8, with the x, y plane coinciding with the plane of the aperture. The observation point at R has the coordinates (x, y, z), and an arbitrary point in the aperture plane has the coordinates $(x', y', 0)$. The initial simplifying assumptions are that the observation point R is far from the aperture and close to the z-axis, in which case the obliquity factor $\cos\theta$ in Equation 14 is approximately 1. Under these assumptions the distance r in the denominator of Equation 14 may be replaced by z. However, this is *not* a valid substitution in the numerator because any errors in this approximation are multiplied by a large number k. To deal with this problem we need to investigate in more detail how r depends on the coordinates of S and R. By the Pythagorean theorem,

$$r = \sqrt{(x' - x)^2 + (y' - y)^2 + z^2}, \tag{16}$$

which may be approximated, using the first two terms of a binomial expansion, as

$$r \cong z + \frac{(x' - x)^2 + (y' - y)^2}{2z}. \tag{17}$$

Applying these approximations to Equation 14 yields the following approximate formula for Huygens's wavelets

$$\mathbf{H}(x', y', x, y, z) = \frac{1}{i\lambda z} \cdot \exp\left\{ik\left(z + \frac{(x' - x)^2 + (y' - y)^2}{2z}\right)\right\}. \tag{18}$$

The important point to note about this formula is that although **H** is a function of the (x, y) coordinates of the observation point and the (x', y') coordinates of the source point, that dependence is only upon the *difference* between coordinates, not on their absolute values. This is the special circumstance needed to interpret the Rayleigh–Sommerfeld superposition integral of Equation 15 as a convolution integral. The underlying simplifying assumptions are known as the Fresnel (near field) approximations.

To simplify the convolution integral even further, we expand Equations 17 and group the individual terms in a physically meaningful way.

$$r \cong z + \frac{(x'^2 + y'^2)}{2z} + \frac{(x^2 + y^2)}{2z} - \frac{(xx' + yy')}{z}. \tag{19}$$

If we assume that the aperture is small compared not only to z, the observation distance, but small even when compared to z/k, then the second term in Equation 19 may be omitted. This assumption is known as the Fraunhofer (far field) approximation, and it is evidently a severe one given that k is a very large number on the order of 10^7 m for visible light. Nevertheless, under these conditions the Rayleigh–Sommerfeld diffraction integral simplifies to

$$\mathbf{U}(x, y) = \mathbf{C} \iint\limits_{Aperture} \mathbf{U}(x', y') \exp\left(-\frac{ik}{z}(xx' + yy')\right) \cdot dx'dy', \tag{20}$$

where C is the complex constant

$$\mathbf{C} = \frac{1}{i\lambda z} \cdot \exp\left\{ik\left(z + \frac{x^2 + y^2}{2z}\right)\right\}. \tag{21}$$

To put this result in a more convenient form we normalize the (x,y) coordinates by introducing a substitution of variables $\hat{x} = x/\lambda z$ and $\hat{y} = y/\lambda z$. We also introduce a *pupil function* $P(x',y')$ which has value 1 inside the aperture and 0 outside.

Using this pupil function as a multiplication factor in the integrand allows us to define the integral over the whole plane of the aperture, in which case Equation 20 becomes

$$\mathbf{U}(\hat{x},\hat{y}) = \mathbf{C}\int_{-\infty}^{\infty}\int_{-\infty}^{\infty} \mathbf{P}(x',y')\mathbf{U}(x',y')\exp[-2\pi i(\hat{x}x' + \hat{y}y')] \cdot dx'dy'. \tag{22}$$

If this last integral doesn't look familiar, think of x', y' as spatial frequency variables in the plane of the pupil, and think of $\hat{x}$, $\hat{y}$ as spatial variables in the image plane. Now, except for the scaling constant C in front, *the Fraunhofer diffraction pattern is recognized as a two-dimensional inverse Fourier transform of the incident wavefront as truncated by the pupil function*. This seemingly miraculous result yields yet another astonishing observation when the incident wavefront is a plane wave. In this case the field amplitude **U** is constant over the aperture, and thus the diffraction pattern and the aperture are related by the Fourier transform. A compact notation for this Fourier transform operation uses an arrow to indicate the direction of the forward Fourier transform

$$\mathbf{U}(\hat{x},\hat{y}) \xrightarrow{F} \mathbf{P}(\hat{x},\hat{y}). \tag{23}$$

In words, Equation 23 says that *the amplitude U of the light distribution in a distant plane due to diffraction of a monochromatic plane wave by an aperture is proportional to the inverse Fourier transform of the aperture's pupil function P.*

Equation 22 has had a major impact on optics, including visual optics, in the latter half of the 20th century because it brings to bear the powerful theory of linear systems and its chief computational tool, the Fourier transform (Bracewell, 1969; Gaskill, 1978; Goodman, 1968; Williams & Becklund, 1989). Although cast in the language of diffraction patterns, Equation 22 is readily applied to imaging systems by generalizing the concept of a pupil function to include the focusing properties of lenses. By thinking of the pupil function as a two-dimensional filter which attenuates amplitude and introduces phase shifts at each point of the emerging wavefront, a *complex-valued pupil function* $\mathrm{P}(x',y')$ may be constructed as the product of two factors

$$\mathbf{P}(x',y') = D(x',y')\exp(ikW(x',y')), \tag{24}$$

where $\mathrm{D}(x', y')$ is an attenuating factor, and $\mathrm{W}(x', y')$ is a phase factor called the *wave aberration function,* which is directly attributable to aberrations of the system. This maneuver of generalizing the pupil function captures the effect of the optical system without violating the arguments which led to the development of Equation 23. Thus, the complex amplitude spread function $\mathbf{A}(x,y)$ in the image plane of an aberrated optical system, including diffraction effects, for a distant point source of light equals the inverse Fourier transform of the pupil function of the system,

$$\mathbf{A}(x, y) \xrightarrow{F} \mathbf{P}(x', y'). \tag{25}$$

A graphical depiction of this important relationship is shown in Figure 9a,c.

Ordinary detectors of light, such as retinal photoreceptors, are not able to respond fast enough to follow the rapid temporal oscillations of light amplitude. Instead, physical detectors respond to the *intensity* of the light, which is a real-valued quantity defined as the time average of the squared modulus of the complex amplitude. Consequently, the intensity PSF is given by

$$I(x, y) = |\mathbf{A}(x, y)|^2 = \mathbf{A}(x, y) \cdot \mathbf{A}^{\star}(x, y), \tag{26}$$

where $\mathbf{A}^{\star}$ denotes the complex conjugate of **A.** A graphical depiction of this important relationship is shown in Figure 9c,d.

Taken together, Equations 25 and 26 say that the intensity PSF, which is a fundamental description of the imaging capabilities of the eye's optical system, is the squared modulus of the inverse Fourier transform of the eye's pupil function. The next section shows that the pupil function may also be used to derive another fundamental descriptor of the eye's imaging system, the optical transfer function. As

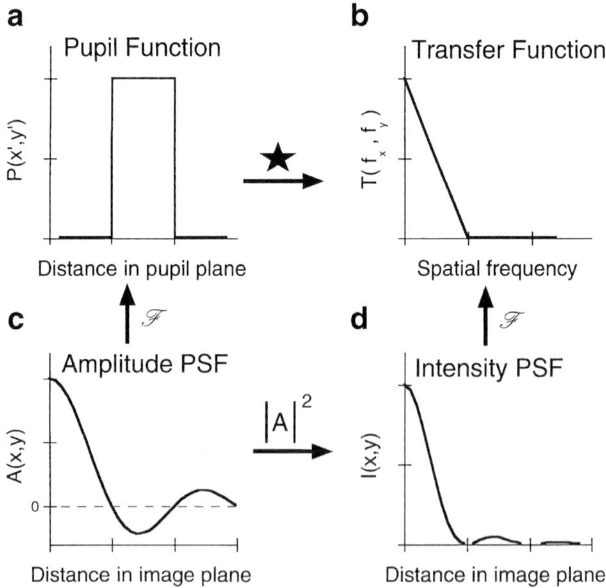

FIGURE 9 Fourier relationships between fundamental quantities associated with an optical imaging system.

will be shown, both of these descriptors can be used to compute the retinal image of an arbitrary object in a straight forward manner.

C. Linear Systems Description of Image Formation

One of the major paradigm shifts in optics this century has been the treatment of imaging systems, including the eye, as a linear system characterized in the spatial domain by the PSF. (For an historical account, see Williams & Becklund, 1989). It doesn't matter whether the image is well focused or blurred, diffraction-limited or aberrated. The key assumption is simply that the PSF is invariant to lateral (i.e., orthogonal to the optical axis) translations of the point source. In the theory of linear systems, this property is called *space-invariance,* but in optics it is called *isoplanatism.* The special significance of the linear systems approach to the eye is that it allows us to easily compute the actual retinal image (which is normally inaccessible to an outside observer) from knowledge of the PSF and the spatial distribution of intensities in the object.

Although the eye's PSF varies significantly across the visual field, it is not unreasonable to assume spatial invariance over small patches of the retinal image. Within such a patch the image is conceived as the superposition of a myriad PSFs, one for each point in the object and scaled in intensity according to the intensity of the corresponding point in the object. For ordinary objects there is no fixed relationship between the phases of light waves emitted from different points on the object. Such light sources are called *spatially incoherent,* and for such sources the intensities of elementary PSFs in the retinal image are real-valued quantities which add linearly. Thus the retinal image may be represented by a superposition integral that is equivalent, under the assumption of spatial invariance, to a convolution integral. Using $*$ to denote the convolution operation, we can summarize the imaging process by a simple mathematical relationship

$$\text{spatial image} = \text{spatial object} * \text{PSF} \tag{27}$$

An example of the application of Equation 27 to compute the retinal image expected for an eye with a 4-mm pupil suffering from 1 diopter of defocus is shown in the upper row of Figure 10. For computational purposes, the upper-case letter in this example was assumed to subtend $\frac{1}{3}$ degree of visual angle, which would be the case for a 3.3-mm letter viewed from 57 cm, for ordinary newprint viewed from 40 cm, or for letters on the 20/80 line of an optometrist's eye chart. Additional examples of computed retinal images of this sized text viewed by an eye with a 3-mm pupil and various amounts and combinations of optical aberration are shown in the lower row of Figure 10. To make these calculations, Van Meeteren's power series expansion of the wave aberration function in dioptric terms was used (van Meeteren, 1974). These results demonstrate that the effect of optical aberrations can be to blur, smear, or double the retinal image depending on the types of aberration present and their magnitudes.

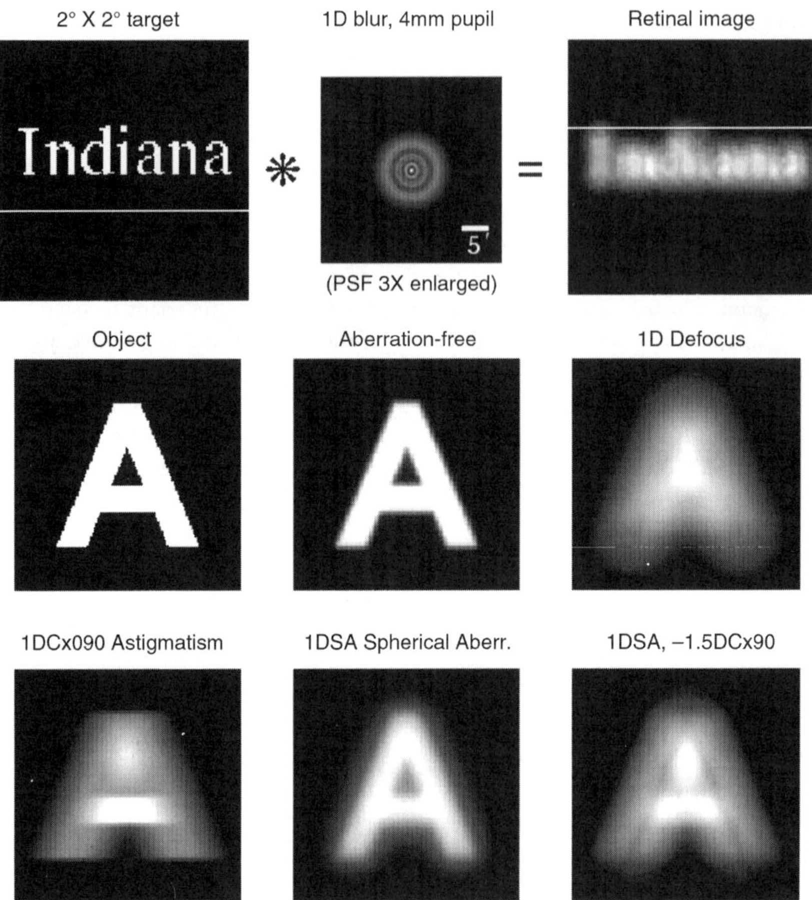

FIGURE 10 Top: An example of the computation of the retinal image (including diffraction effects) as the convolution of an object and the point-spread function of the eye. To perform the computation, the square field was assumed to subtend 2° × 2° visual angle, the eye defocused by 1 diopter, and pupil diameter = 4 mm. The spread function is enlarged threefold to show detail. Bottom: Additional examples of the blurring of an individual letter of the same angular size as above. Letter height = $\frac{1}{3}$ degree of visual angle, pupil diameter = 3 mm. D = diopters of defocus, DC = diopters of cylinder (astigmatism), DSA = diopters of longitudinal spherical aberration.

In the general theory of Fourier analysis of linear systems, any input function (e.g., an optical object), output function (e.g., an optical image), or performance function (e.g., an optical PSF) has a counterpart in the frequency domain. In optics, these correspond respectively to the frequency spectrum of the object, the frequency spectrum of the image, and the optical transfer function (OTF). By definition the OTF is a complex-valued function of spatial frequency, the magnitude of which is equal to the ratio of image contrast to object contrast, and the phase of which is equal to the spatial phase difference between image and object. These two components of the OTF are called the modulation transfer function (MTF) and phase transfer function (PTF), respectively.

The link between corresponding pairs of spatial and frequency functions is forged by the Fourier transform. For example, the intensity PSF and the OTF are a Fourier transform pair

$$\mathbf{I}(x,y) \xrightarrow{F} \mathbf{T}(f_x, f_y). \tag{28}$$

A graphical depiction of this important relationship is shown in Figure 9b,d. The physical basis of Equation 28 derives from the fact that in the frequency domain the elemental object is not a point of light but a sinusoidal grating pattern. In this way of thinking, a visual target is defined not by the arrangement of many points of light but by the superposition of many gratings, each of a different spatial frequency, contrast, and orientation. Given that a single point of light has a flat Fourier spectrum of infinite extent, forming the image of a point object is equivalent to simultaneously forming the image of an infinite number of gratings, each of a different frequency and orientation but the same contrast and phase. Forming the ratio of image spectrum to object spectrum is trivial in this case, since the object spectrum is constant. Therefore, the variation in image contrast and spatial phase of each component grating, expressed as a function of spatial frequency, would be a valid description of the system OTF. Thus the PSF, which expresses how the optical system spreads light about in the image plane, contains latent information about how the system attenuates the contrast and shifts the phase of component gratings. According to Equation 28, this latent information may be recovered by application of the Fourier transform.

A frequency interpretation of the input–output relationship of Equation 27 requires an important result of Fourier theory known as the convolution theorem. This theorem states that the convolution of two functions in one domain is equivalent to multiplication of the corresponding functions in the other domain (Bracewell, 1969). Applying this theorem to Equation 27 summarizes the imaging process in the frequency domain as a multiplication of the complex-valued object spectrum and complex-valued OTF,

$$\text{image spectrum} = \text{object spectrum} \cdot \text{OTF}. \tag{29}$$

Given the above result, two important conclusion may be drawn. The first is a Fourier transform relationship between the PSF and the pupil function. As a preliminary step, evaluate the squared modulus of the amplitude spread function in both domains by using the convolution theorem and the complex conjugate theorem (Bracewell, 1969) in conjunction with Equation 25:

$$\begin{aligned} &\mathbf{A}(x,y) \xrightarrow{F} \mathbf{P}(x',y') \\ &\mathbf{A}^*(x,y) \xrightarrow{F} \mathbf{P}(-x',-y') \\ &\mathbf{A}(x,y) \cdot \mathbf{A}^*(x,y) \xrightarrow{F} \mathbf{P}(x',y') * \mathbf{P}(-x',-y'). \end{aligned} \tag{30}$$

It is customary to translate this convolution relationship into an auto-correlation relationship, denoted by the pentagram (★) symbol (Bracewell, 1969, pp. 112, 122), using the rule

$$\mathbf{P}(x',y') * \mathbf{P}(-x',-y') = \mathbf{P}(x',y') \star \mathbf{P}(x',y'). \tag{31}$$

Combining Equations 26, 30, and 31 gives

$$I(x,y) \xrightarrow{F} \mathbf{P}(x',y') \star \mathbf{P}(x',y'). \tag{32}$$

In words, Equation 32 says that the intensity PSF is the inverse Fourier transform of the auto-correlation of the pupil function.

The second conclusion we may draw from the preceding development completes the matrix of relationships diagrammed in Figure 9. Because the OTF (Equation 28) and the autocorrelation of the pupil function (Equation 32) are both Fourier transforms of the PSF, they must be equal to each other

$$\begin{aligned} &I(x,y) \xrightarrow{F} \mathbf{T}(f_x, f_y) \\ &I(x,y) \xrightarrow{F} \mathbf{P}(x',y') \star \mathbf{P}(x',y') \\ &\therefore \mathbf{T}(f_x, f_y) = \mathbf{P}(x',y') \star \mathbf{P}(x',y'). \end{aligned} \tag{33}$$

A graphical depiction of this important relationship is shown in Fig. 9a,b. This last result puts the pupil function at the very heart of the frequency analysis of imaging systems, just as for the spatial analysis of imaging systems. It also lends itself to an extremely important geometrical interpretation, since the autocorrelation of the pupil function is equivalent to the area of overlap of the pupil function with a displaced copy of itself.

On a practical note, to use the preceding results requires careful attention to the scale of the (x',y') coordinate reference frame in the pupil plane (see Goodman, 1968, p. 117). The simplest way to deal with this issue is to normalize the pupil coordinates by the pupil radius when formulating the analytical expression for the pupil function. Then, after all computations are completed, the frequency scale may be converted into physical units by appealing to the fact that the cutoff spatial frequency f_c set by diffraction is

$$f_c = d/\lambda \text{ cyc/radian (subtended at the pupil center)}, \tag{34}$$

where d is pupil diameter and λ is wavelength. By convention, the magnitude of the OTF is always unity at zero spatial frequency, which is achieved by normalizing the magnitude of the pupil function by pupil area. For example, in an aberration-free system, the pupil function has value 1 inside the pupil and 0 outside. For a system with a circular pupil, such as the eye, the OTF by Equation 33 is simply the area of overlap of two circles as a function of their overlap, normalized by the area of the circle. By symmetry, the result varies only with the radial spatial frequency $f_r = \sqrt{f_x^2 + f_y^2}$ (Goodman, 1968; Equation 6–31):

$$\mathbf{T}(f) = \frac{2}{\pi}\left[\cos^{-1} f - f\sqrt{1-f^2}\right], \quad f = f_r / f_c . \tag{35}$$

In summary, the pupil function (Figure 9a), the PSF (Figure 9d), and the OTF (Figure 9b) are interrelated characterizations of the incoherent imaging characteristics of an optical system such as the eye. Of these, the pupil function is the most fundamental, since it may be used to derive the other two. However, the reverse is not true in general because the lack of reversibility of the autocorrelation operation and the squared-modulus operation indicated in Figure 9 prevents the calculation of a unique pupil function from either the PSF or the OTF. It should also be kept in mind that the theory reviewed above does not take into account the effects of scattered light, and therefore is necessarily incomplete.

D. Empirical Evaluation of the Eye as an Imaging System

1. Point Spread Function

All three of the optical performance metrics described above have been used to evaluate the imaging performance of the human eye experimentally. Historically, the first measures were of the line-spread function (LSF), the one-dimensional analog of the PSF (Flamant, 1955; Krauskopf, 1962; Westheimer & Campbell, 1962). The technique was to use the eye's optical system to image a white line source onto the retina, and the light that is reflected out of the eye is imaged by the eye a second time onto a photodetector. Because the light that forms the aerial image captured by the detector has been imaged twice by the eye, the technique is known as the double-pass method. In order to make inferences about the single-pass behavior of the system from double-pass measurements, it is necessary to make assumptions about the nature of the fundus as a reflector. Early evidence suggested the fundus acts as a perfect diffuser that does not contribute a further spread of the image (Campbell & Gubisch, 1966), but this point continues to be debated (Burns, Wu, Delori, & Elsner, 1995; Gorrand & Bacom, 1989; Santamaria, Artal, & Bescós, 1987).

These early experiments indicated that the white-light LSF of the eye for foveal vision has the narrowest profile for a pupil diameter of approximately 2.5 mm, which is about one-third the maximum physiological pupil diameter attainable under dim illumination. For smaller pupils, the LSF closely matched the wider profile of a diffraction-limited system, whereas for a larger pupil the LSF was much broader. Taken together, these results indicated that diffraction dominates the LSF for small pupils, and aberrations dominate for large pupils, with the optimum tradeoff occurring for a medium-sized pupil. Similar measurements in the peripheral visual field revealed a loss of image quality attributed to oblique astigmatism and the transverse effects of chromatic aberration.

The main technical difficulty of the early experiments was in recording the extremely faint aerial image of the fundus reflection from a source that was kept dim for safety reasons, so as not to risk damaging the retina. Subsequently, the invention of lasers and microchannel light intensifiers allowed the development of instrumentation sensitive enough to record the monochromatic, two-dimensional PSF by the double-pass method (Santamaria et al., 1987). These results indicated a lack of circular symmetry in the PSF, as would be expected of an eye with some degree of astigmatism. With the new technology it became possible to reliably survey the eye's PSF across the visual field. When the eye is left in its natural state, the PSF varies dramatically from central to peripheral vision due to the presence of oblique astigmatism plus additional defocus, which varies depending on the particular location of the fundus relative to the midpoint of the astigmatic interval (Navarro, Artal, & Williams, 1993). However, when these focusing errors are corrected with spectacle lenses, then the quality of the peripheral optics are much improved (Williams, Artal, Navarro, McMahon, & Brainard, 1996).

Scattered light from the ocular media adds a broad tail to the PSF, which is difficult to measure experimentally. Nevertheless, despite uncertainty about the height and extent of this tail of the double-pass image measurements, Liang and Westheimer have demonstrated that reliable information on PSF shape in the central 7-arcmin radius can be obtained (Liang & Westheimer, 1995). When these data are coupled with psychophysical techniques for estimating the background retinal illumination due to widely scattered light, it was possible to synthesize the complete PSF, which takes into account all three factors of diffraction, aberrations, and scatter.

2. Optical Transfer Function

Given the Fourier transform relation between the PSF and the OTF (Equation 28), it might be thought that the OTF could be derived computationally from empirical measurements of the PSF. Unfortunately, the double-pass through the eye's optics forces the light distribution in the aerial image to have even symmetry regardless of any asymmetry in the single-pass PSF. As a result, the simple double-pass technique is not capable of recording odd aberrations such as coma, or transverse chromatic aberration. This implies that although the modulation component (i.e., MTF) of the OTF can be inferred from PSF measurements, the phase component (i.e., PTF) cannot (Artal, Marcos, Navarro, & Williams, 1995). Given this limitation, Figure 11a shows MTFs calculated by Williams, Brainard, McMahon, and Navarro (1994) from PSFs recorded by the double-pass method in the central field using a 3-mm artificial pupil. These results indicated that for foveal vision in an eye with a medium-sized pupil, optical imperfections reduce retinal contrast for most spatial frequencies by a factor of from 3 to 5 compared to retinal contrast when diffraction is the only limiting factor. Similar experiments performed in the peripheral field (Williams et al., 1996) yielded the MTFs shown in Figure 11b. These results show that image contrast is reduce by an additional factor of 2 or

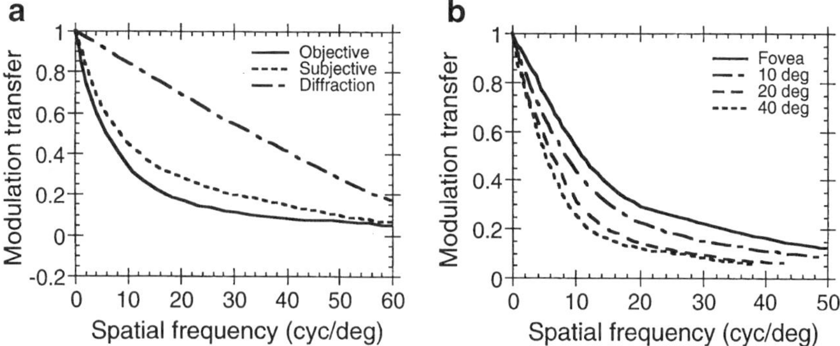

FIGURE 11 Empirical modulation transfer functions (MTF) for the human eye with 3-mm pupil (0.633 μm light). (a) Comparison of the diffraction-limited MTF with the interferometric (subjective) and double-pass (objective) MTFs averaged for three observers. (Redrawn from Williams et al., 1994). (b) MTFs of eyes for various eccentric locations in the visual field when astigmatic and defocus refractive errors are corrected. (Redrawn from D. Williams et al., 1996.)

3 as objects move farther into the midperipheral field. Modifications of the double-pass method to make it more sensitive to asymmetric aberrations indicate the existence of significant amounts of coma and other odd-symmetric aberrations in some individuals (Artal, Iglesias, Lopez-Gil, & Green, 1995; Navarro & Losada, 1995).

One of the awkward features of the double-pass method is that light used to make the measurements is reflected from the fundus, which means the measurement light is *not* the light absorbed by photoreceptors for vision. Therefore, it is useful to have another technique available for measuring the MTF, which has a closer connection to vision. A technique based on the principle of Young's interference fringes consists of imaging a pair of mutually coherent points of light in the pupil plane of the eye (Le Grand, 1935; Westheimer, 1960). Once inside the eye, the coherent sources produce high-contrast, sinusoidal interference fringes directly on the retina. Because the optical system of the eye is not required to form a retinal image in the conventional sense, the interferometric method is often said to "bypass the optics of the eye." Although this may be true for monochromatic fringes, the eye's optics can have a major affect on fringe contrast for polychromatic interference fringes (Thibos, 1990).

Campbell and Green were the first to use the interferometric method to measure the MTF of the eye psychophysically (Campbell & Green, 1965). In this classic technique, the human observer is asked to adjust the contrast of the fringes until they are just visible. Next, the observer repeats this judgment for sinusoidal gratings generated on the face of an oscilloscope or computer monitor. Since the visual stimulus is imaged on the retina by the optical components of the eye in the second experiment, but not in the first, the ratio of threshold contrasts in the two experiments is the modulation transfer ratio (i.e., the loss of contrast due to imperfect imaging). Replication of this experiment at different spatial frequencies thus produces an estimate of the eye's MTF. D. Williams et al. have compared the results obtained by this interferometric technique with those from the double-pass method on the same individuals viewing under carefully matched stimulus conditions (Williams et al., 1994). This comparison of monochromatic MTFs is drawn in Figure 11A. The double-pass method produced MTFs that were similar to but slightly lower than those of the interferometric method. This additional loss in modulation transfer was attributed to light reflected from the choroid and captured in the aerial image of the double-pass method, which could be reduced by a different choice of wavelength. The mean PSF computed from the interferometric data for three observers had an equivalent width of 0.97 min of arc, where *equivalent width* is defined as the width of the rectangular function, which has the same height and area as the given function (Bracewell, 1969).

For analytic work it is useful to have available a mathematical description of the shape of the MTF and PSF. Several such formulas are available for central vision (IJspeert, van den Berg, & Spekreijse, 1993; D. Williams et al., 1994) and for peripheral vision (Jennings & Charman, 1997; D. Williams et al., 1996).

3. Pupil Function

According to Equation 24, the complex-valued pupil function of the eye has two components: an attenuation factor $D(x',y')$ and a phase factor $W(x',y')$ known as the wave aberration function. Shading of the pupil to attenuate light differentially across the pupil is called *apodization*. Although cataracts in the eye would seem to be the obvious candidate for apodization studies, the main experimental work has been on a phenomenon discovered by Stiles and Crawford in the 1930s now known as the Stiles–Crawford Effect (SCE). They discovered that the visual effectiveness of light entering the eye varied systematically with the point of entry in the pupil plane (Stiles & Crawford, 1933). In other words, the observer behaves as if the eye has a filter in the pupil plane which attenuates light near the margin of the pupil more than light passing through the center, as illustrated in Figure 12 (Bradley & Thibos, 1995). Experiments show a large change in sensitivity η to light entering the eye through different parts of the pupil, which can be described by the equation

$$\eta(r) = \eta_{\max} \cdot 10^{-\rho(r - r_{\max})^2}, \tag{36}$$

where r is the radial distance from the point of maximum sensitivity, and ρ is a space constant which affects the rate of change in sensitivity. For example, rho values are typically around 0.05 mm^{-2}, which means that sensitivity for light entering the pupil 4 mm from the peak of the SCE is about 16% of the peak sensitivity (Applegate & Lakshminarayanan, 1993).

Although an apodization model can account for the SCE by using Equation 36 as the transmission factor D in the pupil function (Artal, 1989; Carroll, 1980; Metcalf, 1965), the phenomenon has a retinal basis in the optical behavior of cone pho-

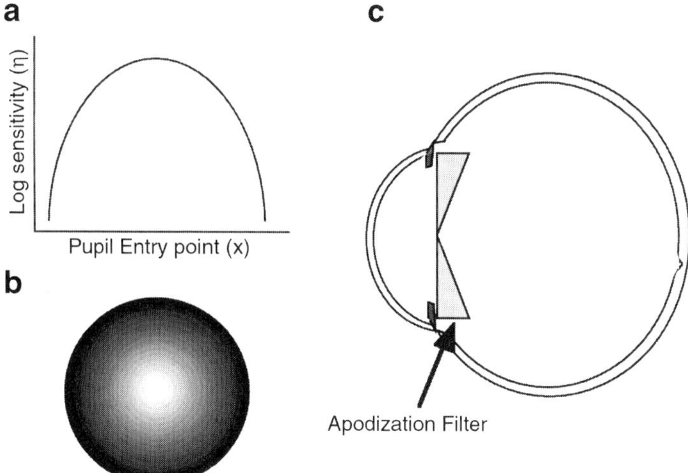

FIGURE 12 Schematic representation of the Stiles–Crawford Effect (SCE). Visual sensitivity η is dependent upon the radial distance between the point x at which light passes through the eye's pupil and the peak of the SCE (a). In the equation relating sensitivity to pupil location, ρ determines the steepness of this function. Although the origin of the SCE is retinal, it can be modeled with an apodizing filter (b), which behaves as a radially symmetric neutral density wedge in the pupil plane (c). (Redrawn from Bradley & Thibos, 1995.)

toreceptors (Enoch & Lakshminarayanan, 1991). Because the photoreceptor inner and outer segments are short thin cylinders with a higher refractive index than the surrounding tissue, they act as small optical fibers and exhibit typical waveguide properties. For example, light entering along the fiber axis will be totally internally reflected, and light entering from peripheral angles can escape into the surrounding tissue. Consequently, light entering near the receptor axis will pass through the entire length of the outer segment and therefore will have an increased probability of being absorbed by a photopigment molecule, thereby generating a visual signal. Because the photoreceptors are phototropic, the SCE can shift in response to a chronic change in pupil centration (Applegate & Bonds, 1981) but otherwise is surprisingly stable over the life span (Rynders, Grosvenor, & Enoch, 1995). The same phenomenon is responsible for nonuniform retro-illumination of the pupil by reflected light from a point source imaged on the retina, which has led to new objective methods for measuring the apodization function for the eye (Burns et al., 1995; Gorrand & Delori, 1995).

Most of the experimental effort aimed at defining the pupil function of the eye has been directed towards measuring the wave aberration function, $W(x',y')$. According to optical theory (Hopkins, 1950; Welford, 1974), an analytical formula for W may be synthesized from knowledge of the optical aberrations of the system, regardless of whether the aberrations are conceived in terms of deviant rays or misshapen wavefronts (Figure 2). Traditional optical theory distinguishes between chromatic and monochromatic aberrations, the former caused by the dispersive nature of the ocular media and the latter by structural defects and the nonlinear laws of refraction. Analytically this division can be handled by allowing W to vary also with wavelength, and then integrating over wavelength when computing the polychromatic PSF or OTF. A further subdivision and classification of the monochromatic aberrations is made possible by representing W as a Taylor or Zernike polynomial and then identifying each of the terms of the polynomial with one of the five classical Seidel aberration types (spherical, coma, oblique astigmatism, field curvature, distortion). Although the Seidel classification scheme has been used extensively in visual optics, it assumes rotational symmetry and therefore can only be an approximation to the actual situation in eyes.

A variety of experimental techniques have been used to measure the wave aberration function of the eye. The early work was done with three main methods (see the reviews by Charman, 1991, for references to the literature): (a) successive determination of the aberration at different points in the pupil either by subjective or objective means; (b) the Foucault knife-edge method of optical engineering adapted for the eye as a double-pass technique; (c) an aberroscope method that traces rays by projecting on to the retina the shadow of a grid placed near to the eye. These early studies showed considerable intersubject variability in the wave aberration function. The aberration function is rarely symmetric about the pupil center, but over the central 2 to 3 mm most eyes have such little aberration as to qualify as a diffraction-limited system according to the Rayleigh criterion ($W < \lambda/4$).

Liang et al. (1994) introduced a promising new technology for measuring the wave aberration function called the Hartmann–Shack technique. Developed extensively in astronomy for monitoring aberrations introduced into telescopes by the turbulence of the earth's atmosphere, this new technology provides a rapid, objective, detailed assessment of the wave aberration function in eyes. The principle of operation of the technique is shown in Figure 13. A laser beam is directed into the eye with a half-silvered mirror and focused by the eye's optical system to a small spot on the retina. For an eye free from aberrations, the light reflected back out of the eye will be a plane wave, but for an aberrated eye the wavefront will be distorted. To measure this distortion, the light wave is broken down into a large number of separate beams by an array of small lenses that focus the light into a corresponding array of dots on the surface of a CCD sensor. For a plane wave the array of dots will match the geometry of the lens array, but for a distorted wavefront the dots will be displaced because the position of each dot depends on the slope of the wavefront when it encounters a lenslet. Thus by comparing the array of dots with a standard reference array, it is possible to work out the slope of the wavefront in both the x and y directions at each point across the pupil. Integration yields the shape of the wavefront which, when compared to the perfect plane, gives the wave aberration function. An example of a wavefront aberration function determined by the Hartmann–Shack technique for the author's right eye is shown in Figure 13b in the form of a contour map (Salmon, Thibos, & Bradley, 1998). The vertical contours

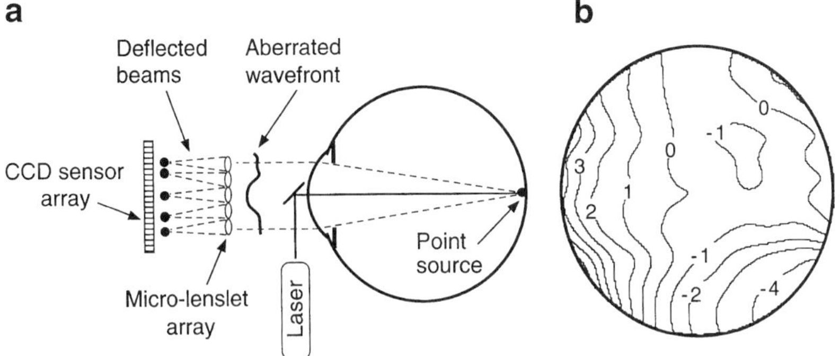

FIGURE 13 (a) Principle of Hartmann-Shack method of sensing aberrations of wavefronts reflected from a point source imaged on the retina. (b) The two-dimensional wavefront aberration function for the author's right eye is shown as a contour map (numbers indicate number of wavelengths of aberration for 0.633 μ light). (Redrawn from Salmon et al., 1998.)

on the left side of the map indicates the presence of astigmatism, whereas the irregular contours on the right side reveal the presence of asymmetrical aberrations, which are common in human eyes (Walsh, Charman, & Howland, 1984), as might be expected of an optical system made from biological components.

Liang and Williams have used the wavefront sensor technique to measure the irregular as well as the classical aberrations of the eye for foveal vision (Liang & Williams, 1997). They found that the wave aberration function of eyes with a dilated (7.3 m) pupil reveal substantial local, irregular aberrations that were not evident with smaller (3 mm) pupils. MTFs computed from the measured aberration functions are shown in Figure 14. When plotted on absolute scales (Figure 14a), the MTF was

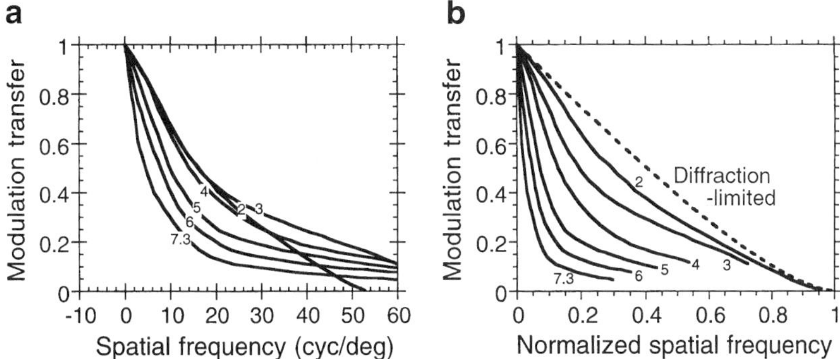

FIGURE 14 Mean modulation transfer function (MTFs) determined by the Hartmann-Shack method for 12–14 eyes. Number on each curve indicates pupil diameter in millimeters. MTFs were computed assuming that defocus and astigmatism were fully corrected. (a) Spatial frequency is plotted in physical units to show the absolute performance of the eye for various pupil sizes. (b) Spatial frequency is normalized by the diffraction cutoff frequency to show performance of the eye relative to a diffraction-limited system. (Redrawn from Liang & Williams, 1997.)

optimal for an intermediate pupil diameter of about 3 mm. However, when the frequency axis is normalized by the cutoff frequency set by diffraction (Equation 34) the results indicate that the 3-mm MTF is already significantly worse than expected of a diffraction-limited system (Figure 14b). The 3-mm MTF computed from the wave aberration function indicated slightly higher optical performance than was measured by the double-pass or the interferometric technique on the same observers. When analyzed in terms of Zernike polynomials, their results indicated that the irregular aberrations beyond defocus, astigmatism, coma, and spherical aberration (i.e., Zernike orders 1–4) do not have a large effect on retinal image quality in normal eyes when the pupil is small. Consequently, correcting the lower-order aberrations would be expected to bring the eye up to nearly diffraction-limited standards for a 3-mm pupil. However, the higher order, irregular aberrations beyond the fourth Zernike order have a major effect on retinal image quality for large pupils, reducing image contrast up to threefold for a 7-mm pupil. Although the root-mean-squared (RMS) wavefront error fell monotonically with Zernike order, the RMS value nevertheless exceeded the diffraction-limited criterion of $\lambda/14$ for Zernike orders 2 to 8.

4. Chromatic Aberration

In addition to the monochromatic aberrations described above, the eye suffers from significant amounts of chromatic aberration caused by the dispersive nature of the eye's refractive media. (Dispersion is the variation in refraction that results from the variation of refractive index n with wavelength λ.) Chromatic dispersion causes the focus, size, and position of retinal images to vary with wavelength as illustrated in Figure 15. In theory, these forms of chromatic aberration are related by the following approximate relationships (Thibos, Bradley, & Zhang, 1991).

$$\Delta Focus = K_\lambda = \frac{n'(\lambda_1) - n'(\lambda_2)}{r n_D} \tag{37}$$

$$\Delta\ Magnification = \mathrm{z}K_\lambda \tag{38}$$

$$\Delta\ Position = \tau = K_\lambda \mathrm{z} \sin \omega, \tag{39}$$

where $n_D = 1.333$ is the refractive index of the ocular medium at the reference wavelength 589 nm, $r = 5.55$ mm is the radius of curvature of a single-surface model of the eye's chromatic aberration, z is the axial location of the pupil relative to the eye's nodal point, and ω is the field angle of an off-axis object point.

The variation of focal power of the eye with wavelength has been widely studied in human eyes and the results are summarized in Figure 16a. Various symbols show the refractive error measured in human eyes in 13 different studies over the past 50 years using a wide variety of experimental methods (Thibos, Ye, Zhang, & Bradley, 1992). The sign convention is best illustrated by example: the human eye

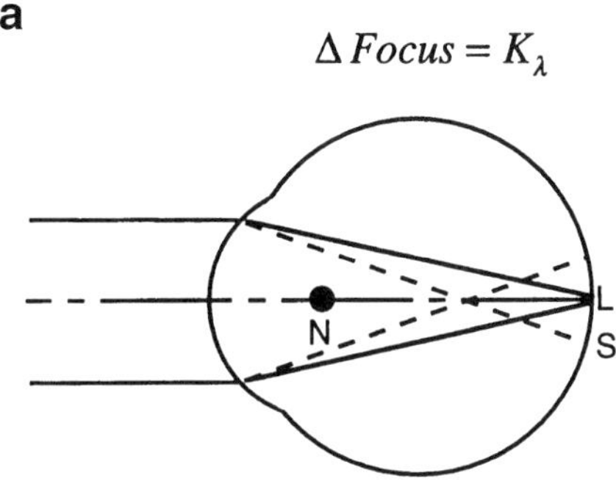

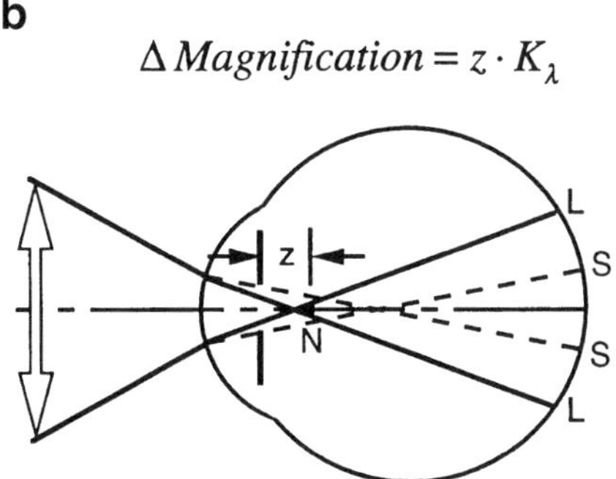

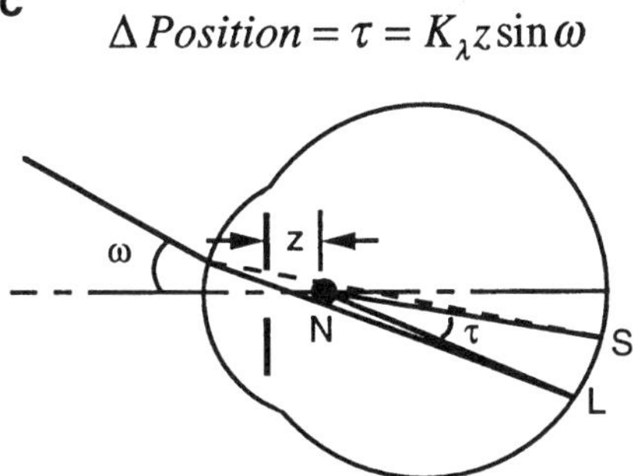

FIGURE 15 Ocular chromatic aberration takes the form of chromatic difference of focus (a), magnification (b), and position (c). Rays of short-wavelength (S) light are shown with broken lines, rays of long-wavelength (L) light are shown with solid lines.

has too much power (i.e., is myopic) for short wavelengths, and so a negative spectacle lens is required to correct this focusing error. The good agreement between these various studies is testimony to the fact that, unlike other ocular aberrations,

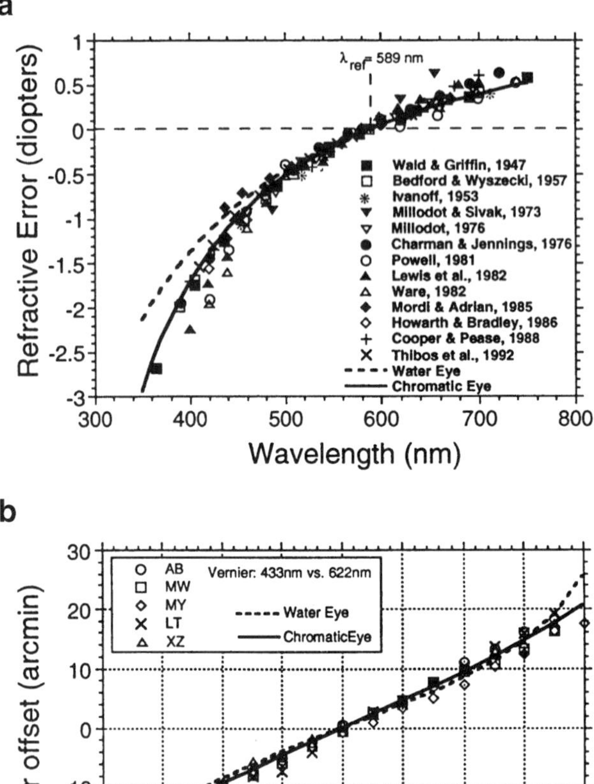

FIGURE 16 Comparison of published measurements of longitudinal (a) and transverse (b) chromatic aberration with predictions of the reduced-eye model. (Redrawn from Thibos et al., 1992.)

there is little variability between eyes with regard to chromatic aberration. Likewise, chromatic aberration does not change significantly over the life span (Howarth, Zhang, Bradley, Still, & Thibos, 1988).

The variation of retinal image size with wavelength is strongly affected by axial pupil location. For example, if the pupil is well in front of the nodal point then the rays admitted by the pupil from an eccentric point of the object will enter the eye with greater angle of incidence and therefore will be subjected to stronger chromatic dispersion and a larger chromatic difference of magnification. Measurements indicate the difference in size is less than 1% for the natural eye, but can increase significantly when viewing through an artificial pupil placed in front of the eye (Zhang, Bradley, & Thibos, 1993).

If attention is focused upon a single point of the extended object, then chromatic dispersion causes the image of an off-axis point to be spread out across the retina as a colored fringe, as illustrated in Figure 15c. The same phenomenon occurs also when viewing a foveal target through a displaced pinhole. Figure 16b shows experimental measurements of the angular spread on the fovea between the wavelength limits of 433 and 622 nm as a function of the displacement of the artificial pupil from the visual axis (Thibos, Zhang, & Bradley, 1992). At the margin of the pupil the spread is about 20 min of arc, which is more than two orders of magnitude larger than visual threshold for detecting the displacement of two points.

E. Schematic Models of the Eye

A schematic eye is a functional model of the average, or typical, eye. Early schematic eyes formulated in the 19th century aimed to match the gross anatomy of the eye and to predict simple paraxial attributes of the eye, such as focal length and image size (Gullstrand, 1909). In the 20th century the trend has been towards increasing anatomical accuracy by including such features as aspherical refracting surfaces and nonuniform refractive media (Lotmar, 1971; Navarro, Santamaria, & Bescos, 1985). However, the increasing complexity of such models has made them less tractable mathematically, and less accessible to the nonspecialist. An alternative approach favored by students, teachers, and a minority of researchers has been to simplify the schematic eye drastically, paying less attention to anatomical accuracy than to creating a useful tool for thinking about imaging and computing the quality of images in the eye.

Given the empirical evidence reviewed above of large amounts of variability between eyes, the thought of constructing a model eye that is truly representative may seem to be a case of wishful thinking. Indeed, caution rings loudly in the words of Walsh, Charman, and Howland (1984) who said,

> There is a rich variety of higher-order aberrations of the human eye, with the eyes of no two persons being exactly alike. The variety is so great and exists in so many dimensions that no single set of aberration coefficients can meaningfully be said to be typical. (p. 991)

Aside from this natural, biological variability, recent surgical developments have introduced new sources of variance into the human eye population. For example, although myopic eyes result from excessive ocular growth, they are sometimes treated by surgically reducing the optical power of the cornea, but at the same time this surgery may introduce unwanted aberrations (Applegate, Hilmantel, & Howland, 1996). Nevertheless, despite these various sources of individual variability, schematic eye models have proven useful in a variety of contexts, from the prediction of visual function to the design of visual instrumentation (Thibos & Bradley,

1999). These success stories are testament to the fact that there are many features of the eye that are common to virtually all human eyes and therefore may be represented by a schematic model.

Of all the aberrations of the eye, chromatic aberration seems to show the least amount of individual variability between eyes, as may be seen from the close agreement of the many studies compared in Figure 16. The simplest model which can account for these data has a single refracting surface separating the ocular media from air. Performance of the classic model of this type, consisting of a volume of water inside a spherical refracting surface, is shown by the dashed curve in Figure 16. An even better account of the experimental data is obtained by increasing slightly the dispersion of the medium and using an elliptical (rather than spherical) refracting surface. A schematic diagram of this new model, dubbed the "Chromatic Eye," (Thibos et al., 1992) is given in Figure 17. The predictions of the Chromatic Eye are shown by the solid curves in Figure 16. The close match of the model to the data suggests that a more complicated model is not required to model the chromatic aberration of the eye.

Pupil location controls the obliquity of those rays which pass on to stimulate the retina and thus the magnitude of the eye's aberrations. A study of a population of young adult eyes determined that the mean angle ψ between the visual and achromatic axes of the eye is zero, which means that the eye's pupil is, on average, well centered on the visual axis (Rynders, Lidkea, Chisholm, & Thibos, 1995). With this justification, all four reference axes of the schematic eye shown in Figure 17 collapse into a single axis to make an even simpler model called the "Indiana Eye." The Indiana Eye model has been tested against experimental measurements of the spherical aberration (Thibos, Ye, Zhang, & Bradley, 1997) and oblique astigmatism (Wang

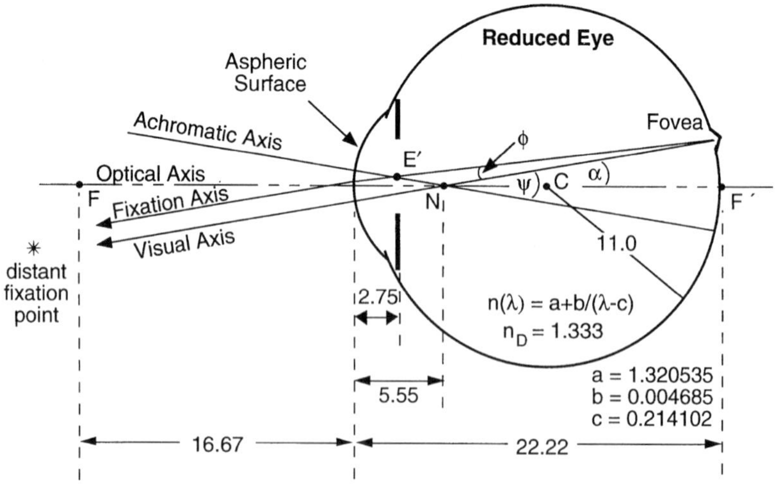

FIGURE 17 The Chromatic Eye schematic model of the eye's optical system.

& Thibos, 1997) of human eyes reported in the literature. Analysis revealed that by slightly adjusting the shape of the refracting surface and the axial location of the pupil, it becomes possible for this simple optical model to simultaneously account for the chromatic, spherical, and oblique-astigmatic aberrations of typical human eyes.

III. NEURAL SAMPLING OF THE RETINAL IMAGE

A. Retinal Architecture

Neural processing of the retinal image begins with the transduction of light energy into corresponding changes of membrane potential of individual light-sensitive photoreceptor cells called rods and cones. Photoreceptors are laid out across the retina as a thin sheet that varies systematically in composition as shown schematically in Figure 18a. This cartoon is only intended to convey a sense of the relative size and spacing of rods and cones, not their true number, which is of the order 10^8 and 10^6, respectively, per eye. At the very center of the foveal region, which corresponds roughly to the center of the eye's field of view, the photoreceptors are exclusively cones. Because cone-based vision is not as sensitive as rod-based vision, the central fovea is blind to dim lights (e.g., faint stars) that are clearly visible when viewed indirectly. At a radial distance of about 0.1–0.2 mm along the retinal surface (= 0.35–0.7° field angle) from the foveal center, rods first appear, and in the peripheral retina rods are far more numerous than cones (Curcio, Sloan, Kalina, & Hendrickson, 1990; Polyak, 1941). Each photoreceptor integrates the light flux entering the cell through its own aperture which, for foveal cones, is about 2.5 μ in diameter on the retina or 0.5 arcmin of visual angle (Curcio et al., 1990; W. Miller & Bernard, 1983). Where rods and cones are present in equal density (0.4–0.5 mm from the foveal center, = 1.4–1.8°), cone apertures are about double their foveal diameter and about three times larger than rods.

Although rod and cone diameters grow slightly with distance from the fovea, the most dramatic change in neural organization is the increase in spacing between cones and the filling in of gaps by large numbers of rods. For example, in the mid-periphery (30° field angle) cones are about three times larger than rods, which are now about the same diameter as foveal cones, and the center-to-center spacing between cones is about equal to their diameter. Consequently, cones occupy only about 30% of the retinal surface and the density of rods is about 30 times that of cones. Given this arrangement of the photoreceptor mosaic, we may characterize the first neural stage of the visual system as a sampling process by which a continuous optical image on the retina is transduced by two interdigitated arrays of sampling apertures. The cone array supports *photopic* (daylight) vision, and the rod array supports *scotopic* (night) vision. In either case, the result is a discrete array of neural signals called a *neural image.*

Although the entrance apertures of photoreceptors do not physically overlap on

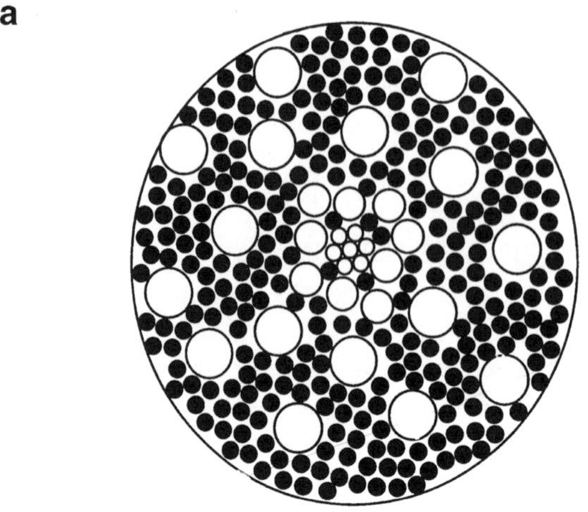

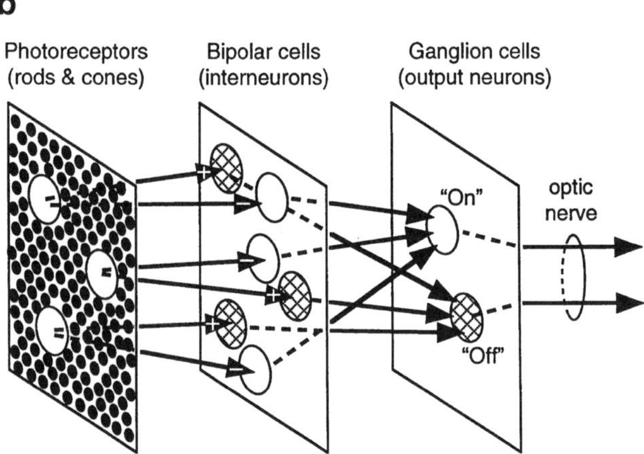

FIGURE 18 Schematic model of neural sampling of the retinal image. (a) Photoreceptor mosaic showing the relationship between cones (open circles) and rods (filled circles) across the visual field. (b) Neural architecture of the P-system of retinal cells, which carry the neural image to the brain via the optic nerve. At the second and third stages open circles represent on-neurons; hatched circles represent off-neurons.

the retinal surface, it is often useful to think of the cone aperture as being projected back into object space, where it can be compared with the dimensions of visual targets as illustrated in Figure 19a. This back-projection can be accomplished mathematically by convolving the optical point-spread function of the eye with the uniformly weighted aperture function of the cone, as illustrated in Figure 19b. For this illustration the optical system of the eye was assumed to be diffraction-limited (2.5-mm pupil, 550-nm light), and the aperture function of a foveal cone was assumed to be a uniformly weighted circular disk 0.5 arcmin in diameter. (This latter assumption ignores the effects of diffraction at the cone aperture that would increase the cone aperture still further.) The result is a spatial weighting function called the *receptive field* of the cone. Since foveal cones are tightly packed on the retinal surface, this illustration shows that the receptive fields of foveal cones must overlap when plotted in object space. Furthermore, these receptive fields will be optically dominated because even under optimum viewing conditions the width of the optical PSF of the normal eye is greater than the aperture of foveal cones (Williams et al., 1994). Just the opposite is true in the periphery, where cones are widely spaced and larger in diameter than the optical PSF, provided off-axis astigmatism and focusing errors are corrected with spectacle lenses (D. Williams et al., 1996).

The neural images encoded by the rod-and-cone mosaics are transmitted from eye to brain over an optic nerve which, in humans, contains roughly one million individual fibers per eye. Each fiber is an outgrowth of a third-order retinal neuron called a ganglion cell. It is a general feature of the vertebrate retina that ganglion cells are functionally connected to many rods and cones by means of intermediate, second-order neurons called bipolar cells. As a result, a given ganglion cell typically responds to light falling over a relatively large receptive field covering numerous rods and cones. Neighboring ganglion cells may receive input from the same receptor, which implies that ganglion cell receptive fields may physically overlap. Thus in general the mapping from photoreceptors to optic nerve fibers is both many-to-one and one-to-many. The net result, however, is a significant degree of image compression since the human eye contains about five times more cones, and about 100 times more rods, than optic nerve fibers (Curcio & Allen, 1990; Curcio et al., 1990). For this reason the optic nerve is often described as an information bottleneck

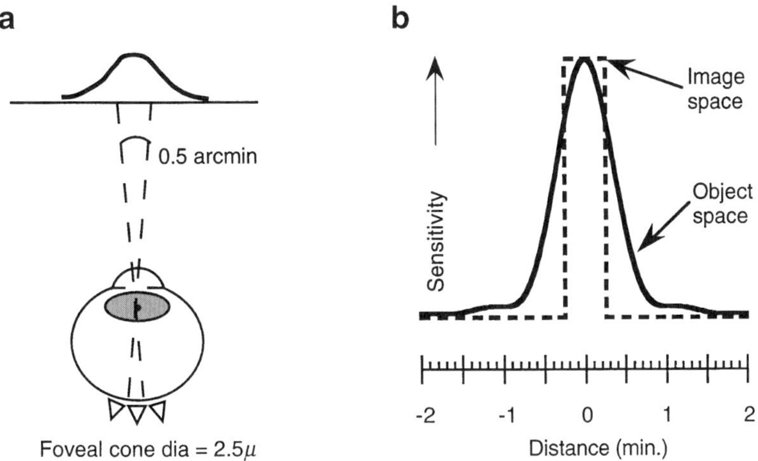

FIGURE 19 Receptive fields of cone photoreceptors in the fovea. (a) Cone apertures on retina are blurred by the eye's optical system when projected into object space. (b) Spatial sensitivity profile of foveal cones in object space (solid curve) is broader than in image space (broken curve).

through which the neural image must pass before arriving at visual centers of the brain where vast numbers of neurons are available for extensive visual processing. To cope with this bottleneck, retinal neurons have evolved sophisticated image compression algorithms, similar to those used in computer graphics programs, which eliminate spatial and temporal redundancy, passing signals only when the scene changes between neighboring points in space or time (Werblin, 1991).

It would be a gross oversimplification to suppose that the array of retinal ganglion cells form a homogeneous population of neurons. In fact, ganglion cells fall into a dozen or more physiological and anatomical classes, each of which looks at the retinal image through a unique combination of spatial, temporal, and chromatic filters. Each class of ganglion cell then delivers that filtered neural image via the optic nerve to a unique nucleus of cells within the brain specialized to perform some aspect of either visually controlled motor behavior (e.g., accommodation, pupil constriction, eye movements, body posture, etc.) or visual perception (e.g., motion, color, form, etc.). Different functional classes thus represent distinct subpopulations of ganglion cells that exist in parallel to extract different kinds of biologically useful information from the retinal image.

In humans and other primates, one particular class of retinal ganglion cell called P-cells (by physiologists) or midget cells (by anatomists) is by far the most numerous everywhere across the retina (Rodieck, 1988). This P-system has evolved to meet the perceptual requirements for high spatial resolution by minimizing the degree of convergence from cones onto ganglion cells (Wässle & Boycott, 1991). The ultimate limit to this evolutionary strategy is achieved in the fovea, where individual cones exclusively drive not just one, but two ganglion cells via separate interneurons (bipolar cells). These bipolar cells carry complementary neural images, analogous to positive and negative photographic images. One type of bipolar cell ("On" cells) signals those regions of the retinal image that are brighter than nearby regions, and the opposite type of bipolar cell ("Off" cell) signals those regions that are darker. Farther into the periphery, beyond about 10–15° field angle, there are more cones than ganglion cells, so some convergence is necessary. Nevertheless, even in the midperiphery the retina preserves high spatial resolution through the bipolar stage, thereby delaying convergence until the output stage of ganglion cells (Wässle, Grünert, Martin, & Boycott, 1994).

A schematic diagram of the neural organization of the P-system is shown in Figure 18b. Individual cone photoreceptors make exclusive contact with two interneurons, one ON-bipolar and one OFF-bipolar, through synaptic connections of opposite sign. In general, signals from several ON-bipolars are pooled by a given ON-ganglion cell, and similarly for OFF-cells, thus preserving the complementary neural images for transmission up the optic nerve to the brain (Kolb, 1970; Polyak, 1941). In the fovea, each ganglion cell connects to a single bipolar cell (Kolb & Dekorver, 1991; Kolb, Linberg, & Fisher, 1992), which connects in turn to a single cone, thus producing a ganglion cell with a receptive field the size of an individual cone. In an eye of an individual with normal color vision, the cone population that drives the P-system consists of two subtypes (L- and M-type) with slightly different spectral sensitivities. Since a foveal ganglion cell is functionally connected to a single cone, the ganglion cell will inherit the cone's spectral selectivity, thereby preserving chromatic signals necessary for color vision. In peripheral retina, P-ganglion cells may pool signals indiscriminately from different cone types, thus diminishing our ability to distinguish colors.

B. Functional Implications of Neural Sampling

1. Contrast Detection and the Size of Sampling Elements

The neural architecture of the retina outlined above has important functional implications for the basic visual tasks of contrast detection and spatial resolution. The finest spatial pattern for which contrast is detectable depends ultimately upon the size of the largest receptive fields in the chain of neurons that supports contrast perception. Since ganglion cell receptive fields can be no smaller than that of individual cones, and are generally expected to be larger, the retinal limit imposed on contrast detection will be set by the spatial filtering characteristics of ganglion cell receptive fields. To first approximation, the cutoff spatial frequency for an individual cell is given by the inverse of its receptive field diameter. For example, a ganglion cell connected to a foveal cone of diameter 2.5 μm would have a cutoff frequency of about 120 cyc/deg, which is about twice the optical bandwidth of the human eye under optimum conditions and about three times the visual acuity of the average person. Although this is an extremely high spatial frequency by visual standards, this prediction has been verified experimentally by using interference fringes to avoid the eye's optical limitations (Williams, 1985). However, under natural viewing conditions the optical bandwidth of the retinal image is typically about 60 cyc/deg (Williams et al., 1994), which is approximately half the bandwidth of individual foveal cones. This implies that the cutoff spatial frequency for signaling contrast by ganglion cells in foveal vision is determined more by optical attenuation than by cone diameter.

The situation is a little more complicated in peripheral retina, where a ganglion cell's receptive field may be the union of several disjoint, widely spaced, cone receptive fields. It can be shown that ganglion cells of this kind will have secondary lobes in their frequency response characteristics which extend the cell's cutoff spatial frequency up to that of individual input cones (Thibos & Bradley, 1995). Thus as 30° field angle where cones are three times larger than in the fovea, cutoff frequency would be expected to be three times smaller, or 40 cyc/deg. This is also a very high spatial frequency, which approaches the detection cutoff for normal foveal vision and is an order of magnitude beyond the resolution limit in the midperiphery. Nevertheless, the prediction has been verified using interference fringes as a visual stimulus (Thibos, Walsh, & Cheney, 1987). Under natural viewing conditions with refractive errors corrected, the cutoff frequency for contrast detection is slightly lower (Thibos, Still, & Bradley, 1996; Wang, Thibos, & Bradley, 1997c), indicating that optical attenuation of the eye sets a lower limit to contrast detection than does neural filtering in peripheral vision, just as in central vision.

2. Spatial Resolution and the Spacing of Sampling Elements

More than a century ago Bergmann (1857) and Helmholtz (1867) laid the foundation for a sampling theory of visual resolution when they argued that for two points to be discriminated, at least one relatively unstimulated photoreceptor must lie between two relatively stimulated photoreceptors. Although this rule was formulated in the context of resolving two points of light, it applies equally well to the case of resolving the individual bars of a sinusoidal grating as illustrated in Figure 20. For a grating stimulus, the sampling rule states that there must be at least two sample points per cycle of the grating so that individual dark and light bars can be separately registered. It is of some historical interest to note that the Bergmann-Helmholtz rule for adequate spacing of neural sampling elements on the retina predates by more than half a century the celebrated sampling theorem of communication theory formulated in the 20th century by Whittaker and Shannon (D'Zmura, 1996; Zayed, 1993).

Figure 20 illustrates the penalty for disobeying the sampling theorem because of

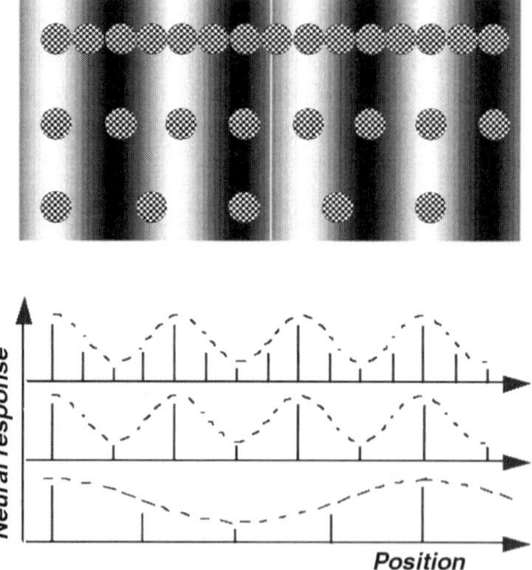

FIGURE 20 Three schemes for one-dimensional neural sampling of the retinal image. Upper diagram shows location of three rows of neural receptive fields relative to the image of a sinusoidal grating. Top row, oversampled; middle row, critically sampled; bottom row, undersampled. Lower diagram shows strength of response of each neuron (bar graph). Interpolation of neural responses (broken curves) faithfully reconstructs the original image in the top two rows, but misrepresents the grating's frequency in the bottom row.

insufficient sampling density. The top half of the figure depicts a sinusoidal grating being sampled by three rows of visual neurons, each with a different spacing between their receptive fields. The corresponding spatial pattern of neural responses shown on the bottom half of the figure constitutes a neural image that represents the stimulus within the visual system. The neurons in the top row of neurons are packed so tightly that the requirements of the sampling theorem are exceeded, a condition called oversampling. The middle row of neurons illustrates the critically sampled condition in which the neurons are as widely spaced as possible while still satisfying the requirement for at least two samples per cycle of the stimulus. The spatial frequency of the grating in this critical case is called the *Nyquist frequency*. The bottom row of neurons are too widely spaced to satisfy the sampling theorem, a condition called undersampling. As described below, undersampling causes the neural image to misrepresent the retinal image because there aren't enough sample points to register each and every bar in the pattern.

Although the neural image is meant to be a faithful representation of the retinal image, these two kinds of images are fundamentally different: the optical image formed on the retina is spatially continuous, whereas the neural image is discrete. This difference between the stimulus and its neural representation is central to the sampling theory of visual resolution, and it raises an important theoretical question. Is information lost by converting a continuous light image into a discrete neural image? To answer this question, it is helpful for the reader to mentally interpolate between sample points in Figure 20 to form an envelope of modulation, as illustrated by the dotted curve. Clearly this envelope accurately represents the spatial frequency of the visual stimulus for the upper and middle neural images illustrated. In fact, given the proper method of interpolation, Shannon's rigorous sampling theorem states that the envelop will *exactly* reconstruct the retinal image provided that the sampling process is error-free and that the sampling density is sufficient to provide at least two samples per cycle of the highest spatial frequency component in the image. However, if these preconditions are not satisfied, as indicated in the bottom row of neurons in Figure 20, then information will be irretrievably lost and the stimulus will be misrepresented by the neural image as a pattern of lower spatial frequency. This false representation of the stimulus due to undersampling is called *aliasing*.

The one-dimensional analysis presented in Figure 20 oversimplifies the problem of neural undersampling of a two-dimensional signal such as the retinal image. The penalty of undersampling a two-dimensional image is that the neural image may misrepresent the orientation of the stimulus pattern as well as its spatial frequency. Furthermore, if the pattern is moving then the direction of motion may also be misrepresented. The static features of two-dimensional visual aliasing are illustrated in Figure 21 for a more naturalistic visual scene. In this computer simulation of neural undersampling, the original image (Figure 21a) was first undersampled and then the empty spaces between samples were filled in by interpolation (Figure 21b). Notice how the zebra's fine stripes are transformed by undersampling into the

FIGURE 21 Comparison of two methods for limiting resolution of a natural object: (a) was undersampled to yield (b); (c) was created by blurring the original image in (a). The degree of undersampling and blurring was chosen so that the finer stripes in the animal's coat would be unresolved.

coarse, irregular, splotchy pattern of the leopard. The important point is that although the finer stripes are distorted and nonveridical, they remain visible because of the relatively high contrast that persists in the neural image. This illustrates the important point made earlier that spatial patterns can remain visible even though they are misrepresented in the neural image.

In summary, according to the sampling theory of visual resolution, the spectrum of visible spatial frequencies is partitioned into two regions by the Nyquist frequency of the neural array. Frequencies below the Nyquist limit are perceived veridically, whereas frequencies above the Nyquist limit are misperceived as aliases of the stimulus. Thus *aliasing is the proof that neural undersampling is the limiting mechanism for spatial resolution.*

Surprisingly, although the Bergmann-Helmholtz rule has been a popular fixture of visual science for more than a century (Helmholtz, 1911; Ten Doesschate, 1946; Weymouth, 1958), until relatively recently there was little evidence that the rule actually applies to human vision. Despite thousands of scientific experiments since the mid-19th century, and countless numbers of clinical measurements of visual acuity by optometrists and ophthalmologists, only a few scattered publications prior to 1983 mentioned the telltale signs of aliasing appearing when the visual resolution limit is exceeded (Bergmann, 1857; Byram, 1944). In the absence of compelling evidence of neural undersampling, a competing theory rose to prominence, which suggested that the theoretical sampling limit is never attained in real life because a lower limit is imposed by spatial filtering mechanisms in the eye. According to this filtering theory, spatial resolution fails not because of undersampling, but because of contrast insufficiency. In other words, contrast sensitivity falls below the absolute threshold of unity for high spatial frequencies beyond the neural Nyquist limit, thus preventing aliasing. This is the scenario depicted in the simulated neural image in Figure 21c, which was prepared by blurring the original image with a low-pass spatial filter. Notice how the finer stripes of the zebra's coat have vanished altogether as filtering reduces their contrast to below our visual threshold. This is the familiar experience we all share in central vision: fine patterns disappear rather than mutate into coarse, aliased patterns that remain visible. In central vision it is contrast insufficiency, not the ambiguity of aliasing, which limits resolution and justifies the common practice of taking the endpoint of the contrast-sensitivity function as a definition of the resolution limit (De Valois & De Valois, 1988). As will be described next, the situation is just the reverse in peripheral vision.

C. Evidence of Neural Sampling in Perception

The widespread acceptance of filtering theories of visual resolution reflects the dominance of our foveal visual experience in shaping our thinking about the visual system (Hughes, 1996). However, over the past decade of research into parafoveal and peripheral vision we have come to realize that the fovea is the only part of the optically well-corrected eye which is ordinarily *not* sampling-limited. The reason sampling-limited performance is not normally achieved in foveal vision is because the extremely high packing density of adult cone photoreceptors and ganglion cells causes the Nyquist frequency to be higher than the optical cutoff of the eye. Thus, central vision is protected from aliasing by the low-pass spatial-filtering action of the eye's optical system. We know that the limiting filter is optical in nature rather than neural because aliasing will occur in central vision if a special interferometric visual stimulator is used to bypass the optical system of the eye (D. Williams, 1985). In fact, even foveal vision is sampling-limited under optimal conditions in some individuals with eyes of exceptionally high optical quality (Bergmann, 1857; Miller, Williams, Morris, & Liang, 1996).

Outside the central fovea the sampling density of retinal cones and ganglion cells declines rapidly (Curcio & Allen, 1990; Curcio et al., 1990), whereas the optical quality of the eye remains excellent, provided that off-axis refractive errors are corrected (D. Williams et al., 1996). Despite these favorable conditions for undersampling, perceptual aliasing in the periphery was reported for the first time only relatively recently (Thibos & Walsh, 1985). Subsequent experiments have shown that visual resolution in the parafovea is well predicted by photoreceptor density (D. Williams & Coletta, 1987). Beyond about 10–15° of eccentricity, however, human resolution acuity is much lower than can be accounted for by the density of cones, but closely matches anatomical predictions based on the density of P-type retinal ganglion cells (Thibos & Bradley, 1995; Thibos, Cheney, & Walsh, 1987).

Perhaps the most compelling evidence of neural undersampling in human vision comes from drawings of what gratings look like when carefully scrutinized by trained observers. Figure 22a illustrates a series of such drawings obtained in the course of experiments reported by Thibos et al. (1996). The stimulus was a patch of vertically oriented grating displaced from the fixation point by 20° along the horizontal meridian of the nasal visual field. When the spatial frequency of the grating was below the resolution cutoff, the stimulus appeared veridically. That is, the sub-

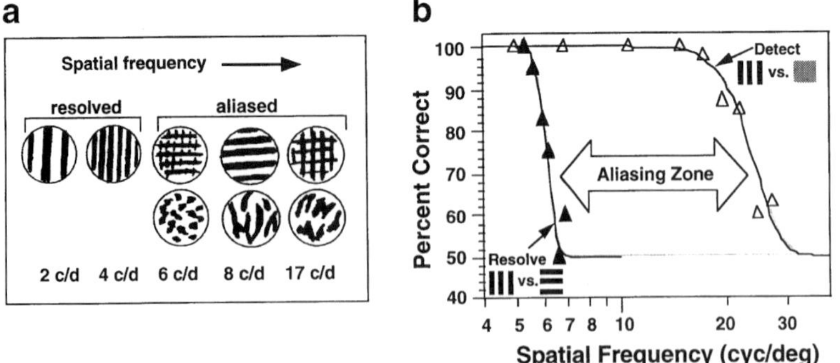

FIGURE 22 Aliasing in human peripheral vision. (a) Drawings of subjective appearance of gratings in peripheral vision. (b) Comparison of visual performance for resolution and detection of spatial contrast. Target eccentricity = 20° in horizontal nasal field.

ject reported seeing a patch of vertical grating containing a few cycles of the pattern. However, when the spatial frequency exceeded the resolution limit, which in this case was about 5.5 cyc/deg, the perceived stimulus looked quite different from the actual stimulus. The pattern was distorted, the orientation was frequently wrong, and the spatial scale of the visible elements was much coarser than the actual stimulus. These features of aliased perception were remarkably similar to the simulated neural image of Figure 21b. Another characteristic of visual aliasing is the unstable nature of the percept. The two rows of drawings in Figure 22a illustrate the changing appearance from moment-to-moment of the fixed stimulus. This characteristic of aliasing is probably due to small fixational eye movements which continually alter the position of the retinal image relative to the neural sampling array, thus introducing instability into the alias and ambiguity into the perceived pattern. Although cortical mechanisms normally compensate for eye movements to produce a stabilized perception of the external world, these mechanisms would be defeated by the lack of correlation between eye movements and the misrepresented spatial position of an undersampled neural image.

Quantitative measurements of visual performance in the periphery are shown in Figure 22b for the contrast-detection task of discriminating a grating from a uniform field and the resolution task of discriminating a horizontal from a vertical grating (Thibos et al., 1996). Whereas acuity for the resolution task is about 5.5 cyc/deg at this location in the visual field, acuity for the detection task is nearer 20 cyc/deg. These results lend strong support to the hypothesis that resolution in the peripheral visual field is limited by undersampling. At the same time, the data are inconsistent with an alternative hypotheses based on neural or optical filtering because the filtering model predicts that resolution acuity and detection acuity will be equal and that perceptual aliasing will not occur.

Today a large body of psychophysical evidence supports the sampling theory of spatial resolution everywhere in the visual field except the central few degrees where optical filtering dominates (S. Anderson, Drasdo, & Thompson, 1995; R. Anderson, Evans, & Thibos, 1996; S. Anderson & Hess, 1990; S. Anderson et al., 1991; Artal, Derrington, & Colombo, 1995; Coletta, Segu, & Tiana, 1993; Coletta & Williams, 1987; Coletta, Williams, & Tiana, 1990; Galvin & Williams, 1992; He & MacLeod, 1996; Thibos & Bradley, 1993; Thibos, Cheney, & Walsh, 1987; Thibos et al., 1996; Thibos, Walsh, & Cheney, 1987; Wang, Bradley, & Thibos, 1997a, 1997b; Wang, Thibos, & Bradley, 1996; Wilkinson, 1994; Williams, 1985; Williams & Coletta, 1987). Qualitative evidence includes subjective reports by several different research groups of spatial and motion aliasing under a variety of test stimuli and viewing conditions. Quantitative support for the sampling hypothesis includes evidence that detection acuity can exceed resolution acuity by up to an order of magnitude in peripheral vision, and that contrast sensitivity is much greater than unity at the resolution limit (Thibos et al., 1996). Saturation of resolution acuity as contrast increases is definitive evidence that peripheral resolution of high-contrast retinal images is not limited by the contrast insufficiency predicated by filtering models (Thibos et al., 1996).

Further evidence that retinal undersampling is responsible for perceptual aliasing effects comes from the close correlation between psychophysical and anatomical estimates of sampling density of the cone mosaic in the parafoveal retina (Williams & Coletta, 1987) and the ganglion cell mosaic in the periphery (Thibos, Cheney, & Walsh, 1987). Given that the visual system consists of a series of anatomically distinct stages (e.g., photoreceptors, bipolars, ganglion cells), each of which sample the preceding stage, it stands to reason that the lowest sampling limit will be set by the coarsest array of the visual pathway. Over most of the retina, excluding the foveal and parafoveal region, cone photoreceptors and midget bipolar cells greatly outnumber midget ganglion cells, which implies that peripheral ganglion cells subsample the photoreceptor array. Consequently, if retinal undersampling is the limiting factor for spatial resolution, rather than optical or neural filtering mechanisms, then human resolution acuity should match the Nyquist frequency of the cone array in central vision but the ganglion cell array for peripheral vision.

Results of a systematic exploration of the limits to contrast detection and resolution across the visual field in human vision are summarized in Figure 23a. Cutoff spatial frequency was measured for two different tasks (contrast, detection, pattern resolution), for two different types of visual targets (interference fringes, sinusoidal grating displayed on a computer monitor with the eye's refractive error corrected by spectacle lenses), at various locations along the horizontal nasal meridian of the visual field (Thibos, Cheney, & Wash, 1987; Thibos, Walsh, & Cheney, 1987). These results show that for the resolution task, cutoff spatial frequency was the same regardless of whether the visual stimulus was imaged on the retina by the eye's optical system (natural view) or produced directly on the retina as high-contrast, interference fringes. This evidence supports the view that, for a well-focused eye, resolution of high-contrast patterns is limited by the ambiguity of aliasing caused by undersampling, rather than by contrast attenuation due to optical or neural filtering. Aliasing occurs for frequencies just above the resolution limit, so the triangles in Figure 23a also mark the lower limit to the aliasing portion of the spatial frequency spectrum. This lower boundary of the aliasing zone is accurately predicted by the Nyquist limit calculated for human P-ganglion cells in peripheral retina beyond about 15° of eccentricity (Curcio & Allen, 1990).

The upper limit to the aliasing zone in Figure 23a is determined by performance on the contrast-detection task. Detection acuity is significantly lower for natural viewing than for interferometric viewing at all eccentricities. Consequently, the spectrum of frequencies for which aliasing occurs is narrower for natural viewing than for interference fringes. This difference is directly attributable to imperfections of the eye's optical system, since all else is equal. In both cases the neural system is faced with identical tasks (contrast detection) of the same stimulus (sinusoidal gratings). Notice that for natural viewing the aliasing zone narrows with decreasing field angle and vanishes completely at the fovea, where contrast sensitivities for detection and for resolution of gratings are nearly identical. Thus we may conclude that under natural viewing conditions, the fovea is protected from aliasing by optical

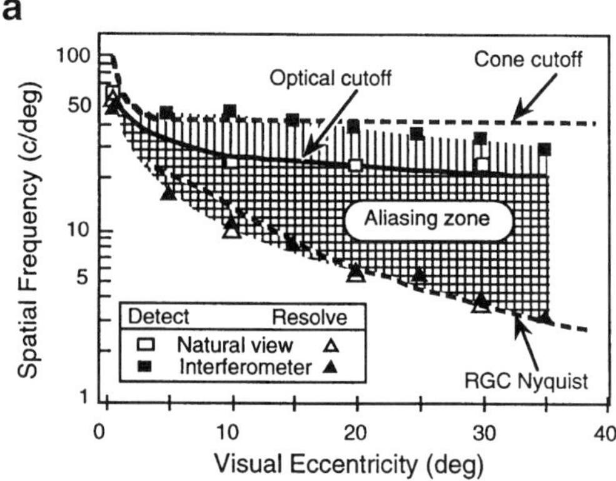

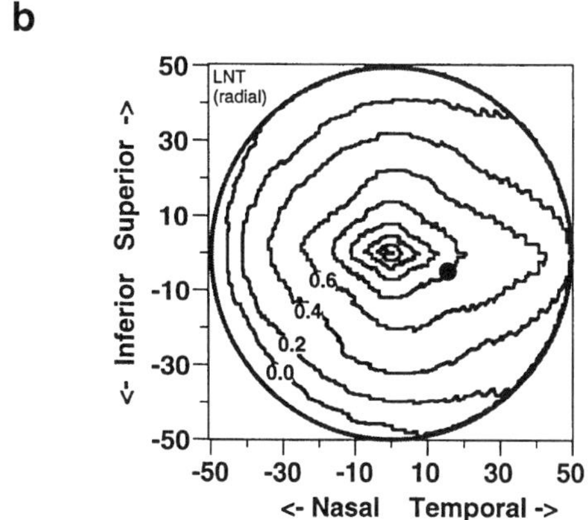

FIGURE 23 Summary of optical and neural limits to pattern detection and pattern resolution across the visual field in humans. (a) Symbols show psychophysical performance (mean of three subjects from Thibos et al., 1987) for grating detection (squares) and resolution (triangles) tasks under normal viewing conditions (open symbols) or when viewing interference fringes (closed symbols). The aliasing zone extends from the resolution to the detection limits. Solid curve drawn through open squares indicates the optical cutoff of the eye and marks the upper limit to the aliasing zone for natural viewing (horizontal hatching). The expanded aliasing zone observed with interference fringes (vertical hatching) extends beyond the optical cutoff to a higher value set by neural factors. Dashed curve shows computed detection limit of individual cones (from Curcio et al., 1990), and dotted curve shows computed Nyquist limit of retinal ganglion cells (RGC; from Curcio & Allen, 1990). (b) Topography of visual resolution for radially oriented interference fringes. Iso-acuity contour lines were interpolated from measurements at eight eccentricities along eight meridia. Contours are spaced at 0.2 log cyc/deg intervals as indicated by numbers on curves. Black spot indicates location of optic nerve head in the visual field.

low-pass filtering. However, in the periphery, the optical bandwidth of the retinal image exceeds the neural Nyquist frequency (assuming refractive errors are corrected), and so the eye's optical system fails to protect the relatively coarse sampling array of the peripheral retinal ganglion cells against undersampling.

If it is true that resolution acuity in peripheral retina is determined by the sampling density of retinal ganglion cells, then we should expect to see a close similarity between the topography of visual resolution and the topography of retinal ganglion cells determined anatomically. An example of a resolution topographic map obtained using the interference fringe method is shown in Figure 23b. This map, obtained for the author when viewing through his right eye (Wilkinson, 1994), contains all of the major features of the anatomical topographic map of ganglion cells described by Curcio and Allen (1990). The isodensity contours are elongated along the horizontal meridian, the contours are displaced into temporal field by an amount which increases with eccentricity, and the contours are displaced inferiorly in the visual field. The visual streak (an anatomical feature of retinas from many different species in which cell density on the horizontal meridian is slightly higher than in neighboring areas just above or just below the horizon) is clearly evident along the horizontal meridian, and the nasal/temporal asymmetry expected for retinal ganglion cell density is also apparent psychophysically. In the central portion of the visual field (inside 15° of eccentricity), these characteristic asymmetries are not as strong in either the topographic map of resolution or the corresponding map of photoreceptor density (Curcio et al., 1990).

In summary, recent evidence indicates that not only does neural sampling limit visual resolution everywhere in the visual field (provided optical limitations are avoided), but the limiting neural array is in the retina itself. Thus, the long-standing theory of visual resolution as a sampling-limited process is now well substantiated experimentally, thus providing a clear link between the neural architecture of the retina and visual perception.

IV. OPTICAL VERSUS SAMPLING LIMITS TO VISION

The evidence reviewed herein indicates that despite the declining optical quality of the peripheral retinal image due to off-axis aberrations, the quality of the retinal image is much higher than the corresponding neural resolution limit, provided the off-axis astigmatism and defocus of the eye are corrected. However, in daily life this is an unlikely circumstance because peripheral refractive errors are not routinely corrected with spectacles or contact lenses. If an individual wears corrective lenses, they are prescribed for the refractive errors of central vision, not peripheral vision. The distinction here is important because the appropriate prescription for different parts of the visual field varies systematically over a range of several diopters, including large changes in astigmatism, depending on the angle of eccentricity of peripheral targets (Ferree, Rand, & Hardy, 1931). Furthermore, in our three-dimensional world objects may lie at various distances relative to the foveal stimulus which drives the accommodative reflex to focus the eye. For these reasons, we must conclude that the retinal image will be habitually out-of-focus over most of the visual field most of the time. Since defocus reduces the quality of the retinal image, it is important to inquire how much optical defocus is required to abolish aliasing from our perceptual experience.

A systematic investigation of the effect of retinal defocus on visual performance for the contrast detection and spatial resolution tasks indicates that although the former is very sensitive to defocus, the latter is remarkably robust, as illustrated in Figure 24a (Wang, Thibos, & Bradley, 1997). The aliasing zone of spatial frequencies for which detection acuity exceeds resolution acuity is diminished by defocus, but nevertheless persists over a range of 6 diopters or more in the midperiphery. This is an extremely large range which, under favorable conditions, may encompass nearly all of visual space from 16 cm in front of the eye to infinity. In general, however, the range of viewing distances encompassed by depth-of-field will depend upon the eye's state of accommodation, central refractive error, and peripheral refractive error.

To visualize how depth-of-field for resolution changes across the visual field, it is convenient to use a dioptric scale for object distances so that distances beyond optical infinity can be represented. Figure 24b represents such a depth-of-field plot for the horizontal nasal field for the same subject as in Figure 24a. The data are plotted relative to the central refractive error, which is tantamount to assuming the refractive error of the eye has been corrected with prescription lenses appropriate for central vision. The thick line indicates the locus of object distances which are conjugate to the retina for a centrally corrected eye. Since this particular individual is hyperopic in his peripheral field when his eye is optimally corrected for central vision, the thick line lies beyond optical infinity in the figure. Thin lines in this illustration indicate the blurring lens power that reduces detection acuity to the level of resolution acuity at any given eccentricity. Thus, the shaded region bounded by thin lines is the depth-of-field for resolution and corresponds to the range of distances over which high-contrast gratings just beyond the resolution

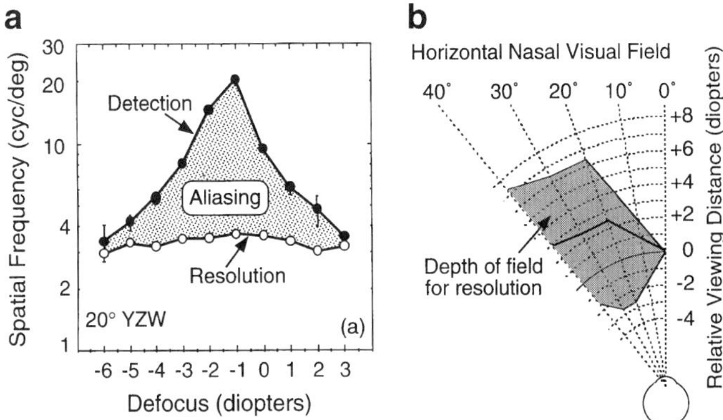

FIGURE 24 Effect of optical defocus on spatial resolution and detection. (a) Detection varies strongly with defocus, but resolution is unaffected over a large dioptric range. Target was a vertical grating located 20° in horizontal nasal field. (b) Depth of focus for resolution for vertical gratings at various locations. Shaded region shows dioptric range for which resolution acuity remains constant and sampling-limited. (Redrawn from Wang et al., 1997.)

limit can be positioned without affecting their resolvability. Although resolution acuity is constant throughout the shaded region, detection acuity varies significantly, being maximum at the retinal conjugate distance marked by the thick line. Outside the shaded region, gratings at the resolution limit are so badly blurred that they are not detectable, which prevents aliasing and reduces resolution acuity below the retinal sampling limit.

A great deal of individual variability would be expected in the position of the shaded area in Figure 24b along the dioptric viewing distance axis because of differences in peripheral refractive errors of different eyes. However, the dioptric extent of the depth of field for resolution would be expected to be similar across individuals because it is primarily an optical consequence of defocus. Since the mean refractive error of eyes varies by less than 3 D for eccentricities up to 40° (Ferree et al., 1931), which is less than half of the depth of focus for resolution, we may conclude that for the average person the depth of focus is likely to include a large range on either side of the fixation distance. Thus, contrary to the expectation that aliasing might be abolished in daily life by optical defocus, the evidence suggests that perceptual aliasing of high-contrast patterns is to be expected of peripheral vision.

For low-contrast targets the moiré effects of undersampling are not as conspicuous for several reasons. First, the optical depth of focus for peripheral vision illustrated in Figure 24 will be shorter because reducing the contrast of the target adds to the contrast-attenuating effects of defocus. Second, natural scenes have continuous contrast spectra which fall inversely with spatial frequency (Barton & Moorehead, 1987; Field, 1987), and therefore the higher frequency components that are eligible for undersampling may produce too little contrast on the retina to cause perceptual aliasing. This happens for bar patterns and edges, for example, partly because the contrast threshold for detection is relatively high in peripheral vision, but also because of masking of high-frequency patterns by low-frequency patterns (Galvin & Williams, 1992; Wang, Bradley, & Thibos, 1997a).

The neural effects of undersampling described above are primarily a feature of peripheral vision, which is commonly regarded as inferior to central vision. Yet, in many regards just the opposite is true. Night vision is an obvious example for which the central blind spot is attributed to the lack of rods in the retinal fovea. Another broad area in which peripheral vision excels is in the sensing and control of self-movement. For example, the visual control of posture, locomotion, head, and eye movements are largely under the control of motor mechanisms sensitive to peripheral stimulation (Howard, 1986; Matin, 1986). Many of these functions of peripheral vision are thought of as reflex-like actions which, although they can be placed under voluntary control, largely work in an "automatic-pilot" mode with minimal demands for conscious attention. This suggests that information regarding body attitude, self-motion through the environment, and moving objects are ideally matched to the natural ability of the peripheral visual system to extract such information. The cost of retinal undersampling, therefore, is the possibility of erroneous perception of space, motion, or depth, which may have unintended or undesirable consequences. Evidently this risk of occasional misperception is outweighed by the pressure to maximize the quality of vision by maximizing retinal image contrast over a large visual field, which has led to the evolution of eyes of remarkable high quality over a panoramic field of view (Snyder, Bossomaier, & Hughes, 1986).

Acknowledgments

This manuscript was prepared with the support of the National Eye Institute (grant R01 EY05109) of the U.S. National Institutes of Health. A. Bradley provided valuable suggestions and critical comments. Y. Wang created the computer programs for illustrating retinal images in the presence of optical aberrations.

References

Anderson, R. S., Evans, D. W., & Thibos, L. N. (1996). Effect of window size on detection acuity and resolution acuity for sinusoidal gratings in central and peripheral vision. *Journal of the Optical Society of America, A, 13,* 697–706.

Anderson, S. J., Drasdo, N., & Thompson, C. M. (1995). Parvocellular neurons limit motion acuity in human peripheral vision. *Proceedings of the Royal Society of London, B, 261,* 129–138.

Anderson, S. J., & Hess, R. F. (1990). Post-receptoral undersampling in normal human peripheral vision. *Vision Research, 30,* 1507–1515.

Anderson, S. J., Mullen, K. T., & Hess, R. F. (1991). Human peripheral spatial resolution for achromatic and chromatic stimuli: Limits imposed by optical and retinal factors. *Journal of Physiology, 442,* 47–64.

Applegate, R. A., & Bonds, A. B. (1981). Induced movement of receptor alignment toward a new pupillary aperture. *Investigative Ophthalmology and Visual Science, 21,* 869–873.

Applegate, R. A., Hilmantel, G., & Howland, H. C. (1996). Corneal aberrations increase with the magnitude of radial keratotomy refractive correction. *Optometry and Vision Science, 73,* 585–589.

Applegate, R. A., & Lakshminarayanan, V. (1993). Parametric representation of Stiles–Crawford functions: Normal variation of peak location and directionality. *Journal of the Optical Society of America, A, 10,* 1611–1623.

Artal, P. (1989). Incorporation of directional effects of the retina into computations of optical transfer functions of human eyes. *Journal of the Optical Society of America, A, 6,* 1941–1944.

Artal, P., Derrington, A. M., & Colombo, E. (1995). Refraction, aliasing, and the absence of motion reversals in peripheral vision. *Vision Research, 35,* 939–947.

Artal, P., Iglesias, I., Lopez-Gil, N., & Green, D. G. (1995). Double-pass measurements of the retinal-image quality with unequal entrance and exit pupil sizes and the reversibility of the eye's optical system. *Journal of the Optical Society of America, A, 12,* 2358–2366.

Artal, P., Marcos, S., Navarro, R., & Williams, D. R. (1995). Odd aberrations and double-pass measurements of retinal image quality. *Journal of the Optical Society of America, A, 12,* 195–201.

Barton, G. J., & Moorehead, I. R. (1987). Color and spatial structure in natural scenes. *Applied Optics, 26,* 157–170.

Bedford, R. E., & Wyszecki, G. (1957). Axial chromatic aberration of the human eye. *Journal of the Optical Society of America, 47,* 564–565.

Bennett, A. G., & Rabbetts, R. B. (1989). *Clinical visual optics* (2nd ed.) London: Butterworths.

Bergmann, C. (1857). Anatomisches und Physiologisches uber die Netzhaut des Auges. *Zeitschrift fur rationelle Medicin, 2,* 83–108.

Born, M., & Wolf, E. (1999). *Principles of optics* (7th ed.). Cambridge: Cambridge University Press.

Bracewell (1969). *The Fourier transform and its applications.* New York: McGraw Hill.

Bradley, A., & Thibos, L. N. (1995). Modeling off-axis vision—I: the optical effects of decentering visual targets of the eye's entrance pupil. In E. Peli, (Ed.), *Vision models for target detection and recognition* (pp. 313–337). Singapore: World Scientific Press.

Burns, S. A., Wu, S., Delori, F., & Elsner, A. E. (1995). Direct measurement of human-cone-photoreceptor alignment. *Journal of the Optical Society of America, A, 12,* 2329–2338.

Byram, G. M. (1944). The physical and photochemical basis of visual resolving power. Part II. Visual acuity and the photochemistry of the retina. *Journal of the Optical Society of America, 34,* 718–738.

Campbell, F. W., & Green, D. G. (1965). Optical and retinal factors affecting visual resolution. *Journal of Physiology, 181,* 576–593.

Campbell, F. W., & Gubisch, R. W. (1966). Optical quality of the human eye. *Journal of Physiology 186,* 558–578.

Carroll, J. P. (1980). Apodization model of the Stile-Crawford effect. *Journal of the Optical Society of America, 70,* 1155–1156.

Charman, W. N. (1991). Wavefront aberrations of the eye: A review. *Optometry and Vision Science, 68,* 574–583.

Charman, W. N., & Jennings, J. A. M. (1976). Objective measurements of the longitudinal chromatic aberration the human eye. *Vision Research, 16,* 99–1005.

Coletta, N. J., Segu, P., & Tiana, C. L. M. (1993). An oblique effect in parafoveal motion perception. *Vision Research, 33,* 2747–2756.

Coletta, N. J., & Williams, D. R. (1987). Psychophysical estimate of extrafoveal cone spacing. *Journal of the Optical Society of America, A, 4,* 1503–1513.

Coletta, N. J., Williams, D. R., & Tiana, C. L. M. (1990). Consequences of spatial sampling for human motion perception. *Vision Research, 30,* 1631–1648.

Cooper, D. P., & Pease, P. L. (1988). Longitudinal chromatic aberration of the human eye and wavelength in focus. *American Journal of Optometry & Physiological Optics, 65,* 99–107.

Curcio, C. A., & Allen, K. A. (1990). Topography of ganglion cells in human retina. *The Journal of Comparative Neurology, 300,* 5–25.

Curcio, C. A., Sloan, K. R., Kalina, R. E. & Hendrickson, A. E. (1990). Human photoreceptor topography. *Journal of Comparative Neurology, 292,* 497–523.

De Valois, R. L., & De Valois, K. K. (1988). *Spatial vision.* Oxford: Oxford University Press.

Duane, A. (1922). Studies in monocular and binocular accommodation with their clinical applications. *American Journal of Ophthalmology, 5,* 865–877.

D'Zmura, M. (1996). Bergmann on visual resolution. *Perception, 25,* 1223–1234.

Enoch, J. M., & Lakshminarayanan, V. (1991). Retinal fiber optics. In W. N. Charman (Ed.), *Vision optics and instrumentation* (pp. 280–308). London: MacMillan Press.

Ferree, C. E., Rand, G., & Hardy, C. (1931). Refraction for the peripheral field of vision. *Archives of Ophthalmology, 5,* 717–731.

Field, D. J. (1987). Relation between the statistics of natural images and the response properties of cortical cells. *Journal of the Optical Society of America A, 4,* 2379–2393.

Flamant, F. (1955). Étude de la répartition de lumière dans l'image rétinienne d'une fente. *Revue d'optique théorique et instrumentale, 34,* 433–459.

Galvin, S. J., & Williams, D. R. (1992). No aliasing at edges in normal viewing. *Vision Research, 32,* 2251–2259.

Gaskill, J. D. (1978). *Linear systems, Fourier transforms, and optics.* New York: John Wiley & Sons.

Glasser, A., & Campbell, M. C. W. (1998). Presbyopia and the optical changes in the human crystalline lens with age. *Vision Research, 38,* 209–229.

Goodman, J. W. (1968). *Introduction to Fourier optics.* New York: McGraw-Hill.

Gorrand, J. M., & Bacom, F. (1989). Use of reflecto-modulometry to study the optical quality of the inner retina. *Ophthalmic and Physiological Optics, 9,* 198–204.

Gorrand, J. M., & Delori, F. (1995). A reflectometric technique for assessing photoreceptor alignment. *Vision Research, 35,* 999–1010.

Gullstrand, A. (1909). Appendix II.3. The optical system of the eye. In H. von Helmholtz, *Physiological optics.* Southall, J. P. C. (Trans. and Ed.) (pp. 350–358). Washington, DC: Optical Society of America.

Gwiazda, J., Thorn, F., Bauer, J., & Held, R. (1993). Emmetropization and the progression of manifest refraction in children followed from infancy to puberty. *Clinical Vision Sciences, 8,* 337–344.

He, S., & MacLeod, D. I. A. (1996). Local luminance nonlinearity and receptor aliasing in the detection of high frequency gratings. *Journal of the Optical Society of America, A, 13,* 1139–1151.

Helmholtz, H. v. (1867). *Handbuch der physiologischen Optik.* Leipzig: Leopold Voss.

Helmholtz, H. v. (1909). *Treatise on physiological optics* (3rd ed.). Washington: Optical Society of America. (1924).

Helmholtz, H. v. (1911). *Treatise on physiological optics* (3rd ed.) Washington: Optical Society of America.

Hopkins, H. H. (1950). *Wave theory of aberrations.* London: Oxford University Press.

Howard, I. (1986). The perception of posture, self motion, and the visual vertical. In K. R. Boff, L. Kaufman, & J. P. Thomas (Ed.), *Handbook of perception and human performance* (Ch. 18). New York: John Wiley & Sons.

Howarth, P. A., & Bradley, A. (1986). The longitudinal chromatic aberration of the human eye, and its correction, *Vision Research, 26,* 361–366.

Howarth, P. A., Zhang, X., Bradley, A., Still, D. L., & Thibos, L. N. (1988). Does the chromatic aberration of the eye vary with age? *Journal of the Optical Society of America, A, 5,* 2087–2092.

Hughes, A. (1996). Seeing cones in living eyes. *Nature 380,* 393–394.

IJspeert, J. K., van den Berg, T. J. T. P., & Spekreijse, H. (1993). An improved mathematical description of the foveal visual point spread function with parameters for age, pupil size, and pigmentation. *Vision Research, 33,* 15–20.

Ivanoff, A. (1953). *Les Aberrations de l'Oeil.* Paris: Editions de la Revue D'Optique Theorique et Instrumentale.

Jennings, J. A. M., & Charman, W. N. (1997). Analytic approximation of the off-axis modulation transfer function of the eye. *Vision Research, 37,* 697–704.

Kolb, H. (1970). Organization of the outer plexiform layer of the primate retina: Electron microscopy of Golgi-impregnated cells. *Philosophical Transactions of the Royal Society Ser. B, 258,* 261–283.

Kolb, H., & Dekorver, L. (1991): Midget ganglion cells of the parafovea of the human retina: A study by electron microscopy and serial section reconstructions. *The Journal of Comparative Neurology, 303,* 617–636.

Kolb, H., Linberg, K. A., & Fisher, S. (1992). Neurons of the human retina: A Golgi study. *The Journal of Comparative Neurology, 318,* 147–187.

Krauskopf, J. (1962). Light distribution in human retinal images. *Journal of the Optical Society of America, 52,* 1046–1050.

Le Grand, Y. (1935). Sur la mésure de l'acuité visuelle au moyen de franges d'intérference. *C.R. Seances Academic Science, 200,* 400.

Lewis, A. L., Katz, M., & Oehrlein, C. (1982). A modified achromatizing lens. *American Journal of Optometry and Physiological Optics, 59,* 909–911.

Liang, J., Grimm, B., Goelz, S., & Bille, J. (1994). Objective measurement of the wave aberrations of the human eye using a Hartmann-Shack wavefront sensor. *Journal of the Optical Society of America A, 11,* 1949–1957.

Liang, J., & Westheimer, G. (1995). Optical performance of human eyes derived from double-pass measurements. *Journal of the Optical Society of America A, 12,* 1411–1416.

Liang, J., & Williams, D. R. (1997). Aberrations and retinal image quality of the normal human eye. *Journal of the Optical Society of America, A, 14,* 2873–2883.

Liang, J., Williams, D. R., & Miller, D. T. (1997). Supernormal vision and high-resolution retinal imaging through adaptive optics. *Journal of the Optical Society of America, A, 14,* 2884–2892.

Lotmar, W. (1971). Theoretical eye model with aspherics. *Journal of the Optical Society of America, 61,* 1522–1529.

Matin, L. (1986). Visual localization and eye movements. In K. R. Boff, L. Kaufman, & J. P. Thomas, (Eds.), *Handbook of perception and human performance* (Ch. 20). New York: John Wiley & Sons.

Metcalf, H. (1965). Stiles-Crawford apodization. *Journal of the Optical Society of America, 55,* 72–74.

Miller, D. T., Williams, D. R., Morris, G. M., & Liang, J. (1996). Images of cone photoreceptors in the living human eye. *Vision Research, 36,* 1067–1079.

Millodot, M. (1976). The influence of age on the chromatic aberration of the human eye. *Graefe's Archive for Clinical and Experimental Ophthalmology, 198,* 235–243.

Millodot, M., & Sivak, J. G. (1973). Influence of accommodation on the chromatic aberration of the eye. *British Journal of Physiological Optics, 28,* 169–174.

Miller, W. H., & Bernard, G. D. (1983). Averaging over the foveal receptor aperture curtails aliasing. *Vision Research, 23,* 1365–1369.

Mordi, J. A., & Adrian, W. K. (1985). Influence of age on the chromatic aberration of the human eye. *American Journal of Optometry and Physiological Optics, 62,* 864–869.

Navarro, R., Artal, P., & Williams, D. R. (1993). Modulation transfer of the human eye as a function of retinal eccentricity. *Journal of the Optical Society of America A, 10,* 201–212.

Navarro, R., & Losada, M. A. (1995). Phase transfer and point-spread function of the human eye determined by a new asymmetric double-pass method. *Journal of the Optical Society of America, A, 12,* 2385–2392.

Navarro, R., Santamaria, J., & Bescos, J. (1985). Accommodation-dependent model of the human eye with aspherics. *Journal of the Optical Society of America A, 2,* 1273–1281.

Polyak, S. L. (1941). *The retina.* Chicago: University of Chicago Press.

Powell, I. (1981). Lenses for correcting chromatic aberration of the eye. *Applied Optics, 29,* 4152–4155.

Raviola, E. R., & Wiesel, T. N. (1985). An animal model of myopia. *New England Journal of Medicine, 312,* 1609–1615.

Rodieck, R. W. (1988). The primate retina. *Comparative Primate Biology, 4,* 203–278.

Rynders, M. C., Grosvenor, T. P., & Enoch, J. M. (1995). Stability of the Stiles-Crawford function in a unilateral amblyopic subject over a 38 year period: A case study. *Optometry & Vision Science, 72,* 177–185.

Rynders, M. C., Lidkea, B. A., Chisholm, W. J., & Thibos, L. N. (1995). Statistical distribution of foveal transverse chromatic aberration, pupil centration, and angle psi in a population of young adult eyes. *Journal of the Optical Society of America A, 12,* 2348–2357.

Salmon, T. O., Thibos, L. N., & Bradley, A. (1998). Comparison of the eye's wavefront aberration measured psychophysically and with the Shack-Hartmann wavefront sensor. *Journal of the Optical Society of America, A, 15,* 2457–2465.

Santamaria, J., Artal, P., & Bescós, J. (1987). Determination of the point-spread function of human eyes using a hybrid optical-digital method. *Journal of the Optical Society of America, A, 4,* 1109–1114.

Snyder, A. W., Bossomaier, T. R. J., & Hughes, A. (1986). Optical image quality and the cone mosaic. *Science, 231,* 499–501.

Stiles, W. S., & Crawford, B. H. (1933). The luminous efficiency of rays entering the pupil at different points. *Proceedings of the Royal Society of London (B), 112,* 428–450.

Ten Doesschate, J. (1946). Visual acuity and distribution of percipient elements on the retina. *Ophthalmologica, 112,* 1–18.

Thibos, L. N. (1990). Optical limitations of the Maxwellian-view interferometer. *Applied Optics, 29,* 1411–1419.

Thibos, L. N., & Bradley, A. (1993). New methods for discriminating neural and optical losses of vision. *Optometry and Vision Science, 70,* 279–287.

Thibos, L. N., & Bradley, A. (1995). Modeling off-axis vision—II: The effect of spatial filtering and sampling by retinal neurons. In E. Peli (Ed.), *Vision models for target detection and recognition* (pp. 338–379). Singapore: World Scientific Press.

Thibos, L. N., & Bradley, A. (1999). Modeling the refractive and neuro-sensor systems of the eye. In P. Mouroulis (Ed.), *Optical design for visual instrumentation* (pp. 101–159) New York: McGraw-Hill.

Thibos, L. N., Bradley, A., & Zhang, X. X. (1991). Effect of ocular chromatic aberration on monocular visual performance. *Optometry and Vision Science, 68,* 599–607.

Thibos, L. N., Cheney, F. E., & Walsh, D. J. (1987). Retinal limits to the detection and resolution of gratings. *Journal of the Optical Society of America, A, 4,* 1524–1529.

Thibos, L. N., Still, D. L., & Bradley, A. (1996). Characterization of spatial aliasing and contrast sensitivity in peripheral vision. *Vision Research, 36,* 249–258.

Thibos, L. N., & Walsh, D. J. (1985). Detection of high frequency gratings in the periphery. *Journal of the Optical Society of America, A, 2,* P64.

Thibos, L. N., Walsh, D. J., & Cheney, F. E. (1987). Vision beyond the resolution limit: Aliasing in the periphery. *Vision Research, 27,* 2193–2197.

Thibos, L. N., Ye, M., Zhang, X., & Bradley, A. (1992). The chromatic eye: A new reduced-eye model of ocular chromatic aberration in humans. *Applied Optics, 31,* 3594–3600.

Thibos, L. N., Ye, M., Zhang, X., & Bradley, A. (1997). Spherical aberration of the reduced schematic eye with elliptical refracting surface. *Optometry and Vision Science, 74,* 548–556.

Troilo, D., Gottlieb, M. D., & Wallman, J. (1987). Visual deprivation causes myopia in chicks with optic nerve section. *Current Eye Research, 6,* 993–999.

van Meeteren, A. (1974). Calculations on the optical modulation transfer function of the human eye for white light. *Optica Acta, 21,* 395–412.

Wald, G., & Griffin, D. R. (1947). The change in refractive power of the human eye in dim and bright light. *Journal of the Optical Society of America, 37,* 321–336.

Wallman, J., Adams, J. I., & Trachtman, J. (1981). The eyes of young chicks grow toward emmetropia. *Investigative Ophthalmology and Visual Science, 20,* 557–561.

Walls, G. L. (1942). *The vertebrate eye and its adaptive radiation.* Bloomfield Hills, Michigan: Cranbrook Institute of Science.

Walsh, G., Charman, W. N., & Howland, H. C. (1984). Objective technique for the determination of monochromatic aberrations of the human eye. *Journal of the Optical Society of America, A, 1,* 987–992.

Wang, Y. Z., Bradley, A., & Thibos, L. N. (1997a). Aliased frequencies enable the discrimination of compound gratings in peripheral vision. *Vision Research, 37,* 283–290.

Wang, Y. Z., Bradley, A., & Thibos, L. N. (1997b). Interaction between sub- and supra-Nyquist spatial frequencies in peripheral vision. *Vision Research, 37,* 2545–2552.

Wang, Y. Z., & Thibos, L. N. (1997). Oblique (off-axis) aberration of the reduced schematic eye with elliptical refracting surface. *Optometry and Vision Science, 74,* 557–562.

Wang, Y. Z., Thibos, L. N., & Bradley, A. (1996). Undersampling produces non-veridical motion perception, but not necessarily motion reversal, in peripheral vision. *Vision Research, 36,* 1737–1744.

Wang, Y. Z., Thibos, L. N., & Bradley, A. (1997). Effects of refractive error on detection acuity and resolution acuity in peripheral vision. *Investigative Ophthalmology and Visual Science, 38,* 2134–2143.

Ware, C. (1982). Human axial chromatic aberration found not to decline with age. *Graefe's Archive for Clinical and Experimental Ophthalmology, 218,* 39–41.

Wässle, H., & Boycott, B. B. (1991). Functional architecture of the mammalian retina. *Physiological Review, 71,* 447–480.

Wässle, H., Grünert, U., Martin, P., & Boycott, B. B. (1994). Immunocytochemical characterization and spatial distribution of midget bipolar cells in the macaque monkey retina. *Vision Research, 34,* 561–579.

Welford, W. T. (1974). *Aberrations of the symmetrical optical system.* London: Academic Press.

Werblin, F. S. (1991). Synaptic connections, receptive fields, and patterns of activity in the tiger salamander retina. *Investigative Ophthalmology and Visual Science, 32,* 459–483.

Westheimer, G. (1960). Modulation thresholds for sinusoidal light distributions on the retina. *Journal of Physiology, 152,* 67–74.

Westheimer, G., & Campbell, F. W. (1962). Light distribution in the image formed by the living human eye. *Journal of the Optical Society of America, 52,* 1040–1045.

Weymouth, F. W. (1958). Visual sensory units and the minimal angle of resolution. *American Journal of Ophthalmology, 46,* 102–113.

Wilkinson, M. O. (1994). *Neural basis of photopic and scotopic visual acuity.* Unpublished doctoral dissertation thesis, Indiana University, Bloomington, IN. UMI #AAC 9518591.

Williams, C. S., & Becklund, O. A. (1989). *Introduction to the Optical Transfer Function.* New York: John Wiley & Sons.

Williams. D. R. (1985). Aliasing in human foveal vision. *Vision Research, 25,* 195–205.

Williams, D. R., Artal, P., Navarro, R., McMahon, M. J., & Brainard, D. H. (1996). Off-axis optical quality and retinal sampling in the human eye. *Vision Research, 36,* 1103–1114.

Williams, D. R., Brainard, D. H., McMahon, M. J., & Navarro, R. (1994). Double pass and interferometric measures of the optical quality of the eye. *Journal of the Optical Society of America, A, 11,* 3123–3135.

Williams, D. R., & Coletta, N. J. (1987). Cone spacing and the visual resolution limit. *Journal of the Optical Society of America, A, 4,* 1514–1523.

Zayed, A. I. (1993). *Advances in Shannon's Sampling Theory.* Boca Raton: CRC Press.

Zhang, X., Bradley, A., & Thibos, L. N. (1993). Experimental determination of the chromatic difference of magnification of the human eye and the location of the anterior nodal point. *Journal of the Optical Society of America, A, 10,* 213–220.

CHAPTER 2

The Receptive Fields of Visual Neurons

Robert Shapley

I. INTRODUCTION

An outstanding scientific problem is how to account for mental activity in terms of the activity of nerve cells in the brain. Among the many, many different paths of scientific effort in this direction, one of the most well traveled has been the science of visual neurophysiology. The visual neurophysiologist aims to link neurons to visual perception. But he or she also wants to explain neural activity in terms of the cellular properties of neurons, and of the functional connectivity of neurons in neural networks. Thus visual physiology has two separate scientific goals: looking upward to explain visual behavioral performance in terms of neurons, and looking downward to explain how the patterns of visual activity in the neurons arise from the neurons' cellular properties, or functional connections in neural networks. It is likely that these two different sets of questions are related. Biological evolution probably caused visual neural networks to have particular specializations to serve perception. But the reverse course of influence is also likely: biological constraints on signal processing by nerve cells may limit visual performance.

Throughout the study of visual properties of visual neurons, one constant organizing principle is the concept of the Receptive Field. More precise definitions will follow, but basically, one can say that the receptive field is the region of space in which stimuli affect the activity of a neuron. One may wonder why this is so interesting to neurophysiologists. In my opinion, the reason is that it has been thought

Seeing

that measurements of the receptive field provide a clear picture of the spatial mapping of receptor inputs to a sensory neuron. Once one knows the receptive field, so it has been thought, one can predict how the neuron will react to an infinite variety of stimuli. It is important now to realize that this is an implicit commitment to a particular view of how the nervous system works.

The concept of a visual receptive field originally came with the implication that the neuron combines signals by linear summation, and that its inputs are coming via a feedforward neural network. As I aim to show, departures from this linear feedforward conceptual framework require stretching the idea of "receptive field" until it hardly means anything definite at all. In the application to cortical neurophysiology, where nonlinear mechanisms abound, the receptive field concept begins to break down until there is nothing left of the original idea, though the term is still used. In the description and analysis of many cortical cells, it is my belief that one needs to change the analytical framework and abandon receptive fields as a conceptual tool in favor of nonlinear dynamical systems theory. My aim in this chapter is to make the case for a new organizing principle—the neural network as a spatiotemporal, dynamical system. Some illustrations will come later, when we discuss the major findings of cortical neurophysiology.

One should also ask, before embarking on a detailed review of the visual receptive fields of single neurons, what is the use of this concept in understanding perception? This is a very difficult question to answer at this point in time. The main positive outcome one can identify is that the nature of receptive fields can be related to limits of perception. For example, the spatial scale of the smallest receptive fields is believed to be a most important factor in limiting spatial resolution (see for example, Hawken & Parker, 1990; Parker & Newsome, 1998). Second, if it were true that the spatial layout of the receptive fields of simple cells in the cortex determined their orientation tuning selectivity, then the limits of angular discrimination could be explained in terms of receptive field structure (cf. Vogels & Orban, 1991). This second example is problematic, however, as discussed below. Another possibly important consequence of understanding neuronal receptive fields is that it could give insights into how the brain works, how it represents the sensory world, how it decides to act based on evidence. That is, in studying and learning to understand how receptive fields work, we might learn about fundamental rules of structure–function correlation, or synaptic physiology, that generalize to all aspects of brain function. However, if it is true that the analytical framework for understanding the neural network of the cerebral cortex requires a new organizing principle, then the receptive field concept will turn out to have been only a first step in the direction of understanding the true complexity of the brain. Before we can judge, we must go through the evidence and the explanations together.

II. RECEPTIVE FIELDS OF RETINAL GANGLION CELLS

The original idea of visual receptive fields came from H. K. Hartline in his studies of the visual properties of retinal ganglion cells in the frog retina (Hartline, 1940).

This was an idea Hartline derived from E. D. Adrian, who in turn had used a term invented by C. S. Sherrington (cf. the scholarly review of the history of retinal ganglion cell physiology by Enroth-Cugell, 1993). The frog ganglion cells from which Hartline recorded had no maintained discharge of nerve impulses in the absence of stimulation, so the only nerve impulses they fired were either responses to spots of light that Hartline flashed on the frog's retina, or responses to the turning off of the light. The area on the retina from which he could evoke nerve impulses from a ganglion cell Hartline termed the receptive field of that ganglion cell. Figure 1, a reproduction of Hartline's classic figure, shows the compact, approximately elliptical receptive field of a frog's retinal ganglion cell.

Later work by Stephen Kuffler on cat retinal ganglion cells (Kuffler, 1953) required a modification of Hartline's definition of receptive field because cat ganglion cells have a maintained impulse rate in the absence of stimulation. The modified definition was that the receptive field was the region on the retina where stimulation could cause a *modulation of the impulse rate* around the average level of firing in the absence of stimulation.

It is also important that because of the maintained activity, Kuffler could observe stimulus-dependent modulations in spike rate above and below the maintained activity. For this reason, Kuffler was the first to recognize center-surround antagonism in the cat retinal ganglion cell: stimuli in the periphery of the receptive field caused a response modulation of the spike rate opposite in sign to that evoked by central stimuli (Kuffler, 1953).

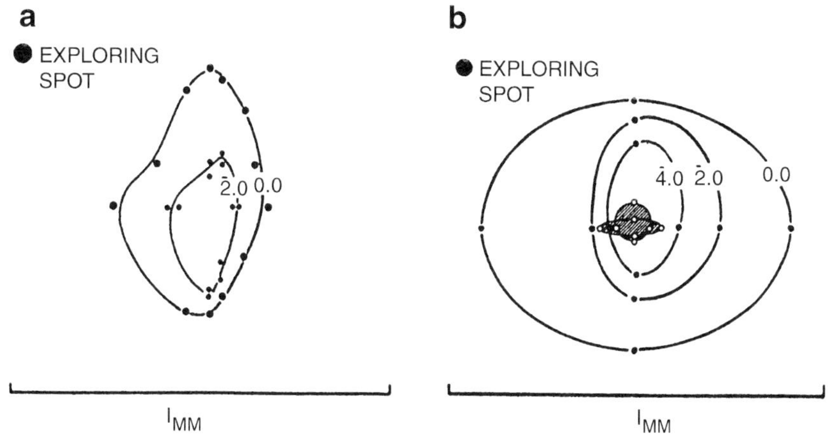

FIGURE 1 The original visual receptive fields (Hartline, 1940). These are maps of the threshold response contours from two different retinal ganglion cells of a bullfrog, *R. catesbiana*. (a) The data are from an "on–off" retinal ganglion optic nerve fiber, the activity of which was recorded with a wick electrode after microdissection of the nerve fiber on the surface of the retina in an excised eye. The log units of attenuation of the light source are drawn on the threshold contour. The unattenuated light source had a luminance of $2 \star 10^4$ cd/m^2. The exploring spot had a diameter of 50 μm on the retina. It was flashed on from darkness for several seconds. (b) Similar experiment on an "on" type frog ganglion cell. The central shaded region is where a sustained "on" response was obtained.

From the beginning, it was clear that the receptive field was not an invariant characterization of the spatial, visual properties of a neuron. This is because, as defined, it varies in size with stimulus size, intensity, color, and any other stimulus variable that determines the effectiveness of the stimulus in exciting the neuron. Hartline stated explicitly that the receptive field varied in size with size or intensity of stimulus spot (Hartline, 1940). For example, if one uses a stimulus spot with light intensity 1 unit, and then a second stimulus spot with light intensity 100, the receptive field mapped out with the second spot may be ten times bigger (or perhaps more!) than the field mapped out with the first spot. However, from his work on spatial summation, it is reasonable to suppose that already in the 1930s, Hartline had the idea of spatial invariants of the visual properties of the ganglion cells he studied. These are the spatial distributions of sensitivity. For instance, in Figure 1, the closed curves connect points in the visual field of equal sensitivity because there are the boundaries at which a threshold response was elicited with the stimulus intensity indicated in the figure. If one defines sensitivity as 1/threshold intensity, these are thus equal sensitivity contours. A collection of equal sensitivity contours, one for each intensity of stimulus spot, will trace out the 2-dimensional (2-D) distribution, a surface, of sensitivity for the neuron studied. Hartline further predicted the sensitivity for a compound stimulus, which was the sum of two simpler stimuli. He found reasonably good agreement with linear summation of sensitivity (Hartline, 1940), the first result consistent with the concept of linear spatial summation weighted by the spatial sensitivity distribution.

A. The Two-Mechanisms Model: Center and Surround

Rodieck (1965) was the first to state explicitly the idea of spatial distributions of sensitivity and the linear combination of signals weighted by the sensitivity distributions. Rodieck and Stone (1965) demonstrated that the way in which to extract the spatial distributions of sensitivity was to map sensitivity with small spots, just as Hartline did originally. They presented their data as 1-D slices, termed *sensitivity profiles,* through the 2-D sensitivity distributions. But then they went further to account for the measured sensitivity profiles with a two-mechanism model, the Difference of Gaussians (DOG) model (Rodieck, 1965). Figure 2 (Rodieck, 1965) is a drawing of the DOG model for a cat retinal ganglion cell's sensitivity profiles. The two mechanisms were the receptive field Center mechanism, and the receptive field Surround mechanism. Let us call $S_c(r)$ the Center's sensitivity distribution as a function of position relative to the receptive field middle, and $S_s(r)$ the Surround's sensitivity distribution. Each of these mechanisms was assumed to be well fit by Gaussian function of position, so that

for the Center $\quad S_c(r) = k_c \exp\{-(r/\sigma_c)^2\}$

for the Surround $\quad S_s(r) = k_s \exp\{-(r/\sigma_s)^2\}$

Receptive field $\quad S(r) = S_c(r) - S_s(r) \qquad \{A\}$

Because total sensitivity, S(r), is the difference between $S_c(r)$ and $S_s(r)$, this is a DOG model. In these formulae, k_c is the peak local sensitivity of the Center; k_s is the peak local sensitivity of the Surround; σ_c is the spatial spread of the Center, the distance from the receptive field middle at which sensitivity declines by 1/e; and σ_s is the spatial spread of the Surround.

Rodieck (1965) also included a temporal response component, making his DOG model truly a spatiotemporal model. He assumed that the step response of the Center mechanism was a delayed (delay $= t_{dc}$) sharp transient followed by an exponential relaxation to a steady state value, and that the Surround temporal response was similar with a similar time constant of relaxation but with a longer delay to response onset, t_{ds}.

Therefore, the complete DOG model for the total sensitivity S(r,t) is:

$$S(r,t) = S_c(r,t) - S_s(r,t) \qquad \{B\}$$

Center: $S_c(r,t) = k_c \exp\{-(r/\sigma_c)^2\} \star \exp(-[t-t_{dc}])/\tau_c)$, when $t > t_{dc}$;

$S_c(r,t) = 0$; when $t \leqq t_{dc}$

Surround: $S_s(r,t) = k_s \exp\{-(r/\sigma_s)^2\} \star \exp(-[t-t_{ds}])/\tau_s)$; when $t > t_{ds}$;

$S_s(r,t) = 0$; when $t \leqq t_{ds}$

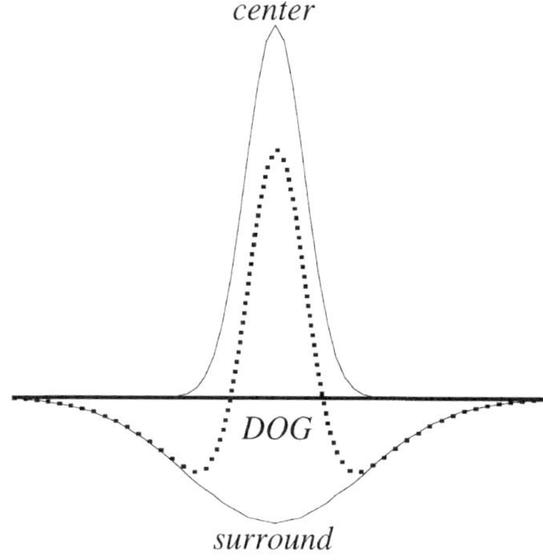

FIGURE 2 The DOG model of the receptive field of cat ganglion cells (after Rodieck, 1965). Two mechanisms overlap in space: a Center Mechanism and an antagonistic Surround Mechanism (both indicated with solid lines). Each mechanism has a sensitivity as a function of position that is a Gaussian function (see text). Their summed response (the DOG or Difference of Gaussians) produces the response of the retinal ganglion cell, and it is drawn as a dotted line. Each mechanism has a spatial sensitivity distribution that is a Gaussian function of space. The spread of the center is smaller than that of the Surround. In this drawing, the line-weighting function of the model is depicted: the response as a function of position for a thin line stimulus. The Center and Surround are set equal in summed effect on the cell, and the surround is drawn as three times wider than the Center.

Rodieck (1965) was explicit that his model was a linear model of the receptive field of cat retinal ganglion cells. The point of making such a model was to synthesize (and therefore to predict) the response to arbitrary stimuli by means of convolution, a standard technique of linear systems analysis. He applied this conceptual tool to synthesize the ganglion cell responses to drifting bars. Convolution means, basically, linear summation of the effects of the moving bars, point by point within the receptive field. The qualitative agreement between theory and experiment supports the notion of approximate linear summation within the retina (at least for the neurons Rodieck studied).

One fundamental idea of the DOG model for receptive fields is that the Center and Surround mechanisms are feed-forward, converging with their separately computed signals onto the ganglion cell in parallel. This idea is consistent with many of the data on signal summation of center and surround signals in the cat retina (Enroth-Cugell & Pinto, 19792; Enroth-Cugell et al., 1977).

The work of Enroth-Cugell and Robson (1966) is a more elaborate study of linearity and receptive field properties of retinal ganglion cells. These authors introduced the idea of spatial frequency analysis of the sensitivity distributions of a retinal ganglion cell's receptive field. Using Rodieck's DOG model, they were able to account for the shape (both qualitatively and quantitatively) of the spatial frequency response of many cat retinal ganglion cells (the X cells). Figure 3, a summary figure from their Friedenwald lecture (Enroth-Cugell & Robson, 1984), illustrates (in b) the fact that the spatial spread of the receptive field Center is much smaller than

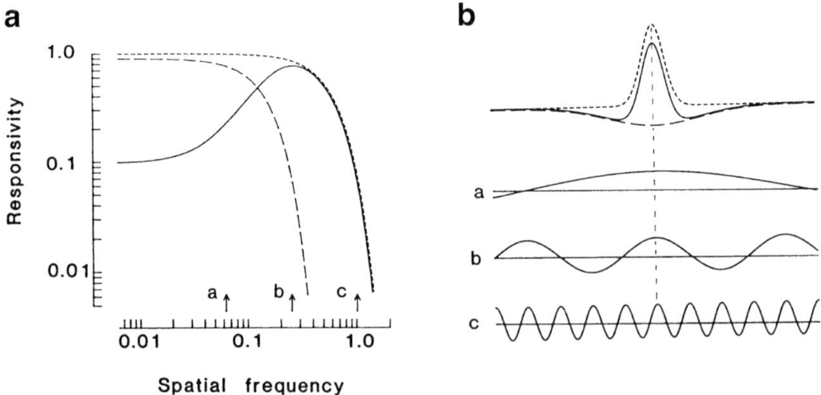

FIGURE 3 Spatial frequency analysis of the receptive field (Enroth-Cugell & Robson, 1984). (a) Spatial frequency response functions for Center, Surround, and their sum (the ganglion cell's net response). The Center's spatial frequency response is drawn with small dashes, the Surround's with broader dashes, and the sum is the solid curve. Three different illustrative spatial frequencies are indicated as a,b,c; respectively, these are in the Center-Surround antagonistic regime, at the peak of the cell's spatial frequency response and at a high spatial frequency at which the Center's response is unopposed by Surround response. (b) The DOG model in the space domain, with spatial sinusoids at spatial frequencies a, b, c also drawn.

that of the Surround. This (as illustrated in a) causes the spatial frequency range of the Center to be much broader than the spatial frequency range of the Surround. In other words, the spatial frequency resolution of the Center exceeds greatly the resolution of the Surround, so that in these cells at high spatial frequency, the response comes from one mechanism only: the Center mechanism. At lower spatial frequencies, the response is a linear subtraction of the Surround's response from the Center's. The typical bandpass shape of the spatial frequency response is thus accounted for by the Center–Surround model and linear spatial summation.

An important technical simplification that enables one to "see" the spatial frequency consequence of the DOG model is the following: the Fourier Transform of a Gaussian function of spatial location is a Gaussian function of spatial frequency. The standard deviation of the Gaussian of spatial frequency is the reciprocal of the standard deviation of the spatial Gaussian. Thus the defining equations for the DOG model become, in the dimension of spatial frequency, v:

for the Center $S_c(v) = K_c \exp\{-(v\sigma_c)^2\}$

for the Surround $S_s(v) = K_s \exp\{-(v\sigma_s)^2\}$

Receptive field $S(v) = S_c(v) - S_s(v)$ $\{C\}$

This set of equations $\{C\}$ are what is illustrated graphically in Figure 3.

Although the results of Rodieck and Stone (1965), and Enroth-Cugell and Robson (1966), are impressive in their rigor and predictive power, it is worth being critical and worth asking how many of their results are crucial for understanding receptive fields. For instance, is it important that the DOG model uses Gaussian functions to account for receptive field mechanisms? What is the significance functionally to the nervous system of linear summation within the receptive fields?

Later work has revealed that the Gaussian shape of a receptive field mechanism in the DOG model is only an approximation to the true spatial profile. In the case of the receptive field center of X cells in the cat retina and lateral geniculate nucleus (LGN), the overall sensitivity profile of the center mechanism appears to be the envelope of a number of smaller subprofiles, each of which is smaller than the total center (Soodak, Shapley, & Kaplan, 1991). Furthermore, the receptive field surround mechanism seems to be constructed out of multiple subregions, each of them bigger in spatial extent than the receptive field center (Shapley and Kaplan, unpublished results). However, the essence of the DOG model seems to be the idea that you will obtain a concentric Center–Surround organization even if the antagonistic Center and Surround mechanisms overlap in space, as long as the Surround is larger in spatial extent than is the Center mechanism. And this basic idea has been confirmed unequivocally in studies of Center–Surround organization of color-opponent retinal ganglion cells and LGN cells of the monkey visual system (Reid & Shapley, 1992). In monkey ganglion cells of the P-type, the M(530 nm) cones and the L(560 nm) cones are almost always connected with opposite signature to the ganglion cell, so that, for example, a cell may be M+, L−, or M−, L+. The M cone input may be to the smaller Center mechanism, or to the broader Surround mechanism. Reid and Shapley (1992) used spatial stimuli for receptive field mapping that were also cone-isolating (so that only, say, M cones were mapped out in one experimental run; only L cones in a subsequent run). As shown in Figure 4, they found that, for example, an M cone Surround always overlapped in space an L cone Center; in general, Surround and Center always overlapped in space. This is strong confirmation of the basic idea of the DOG model of Center–Surround receptive fields.

The question of the functional significance of linearity is much more general, and there is no definite answer to this question, though candidate answers have been proposed. I believe the biological evidence is very convincing that there must be some important advantage to linear summation because the retina goes to some trouble to produce it. It is known that until one reaches the retinal ganglion cells, retinal intercellular signaling is by slow potentials not spike trains. The slow potentials in bipolar cells must be a linear function of the receptors' intracellular potentials in order for linear signal summation to work. This implies that the synapses between photoreceptors and bipolar cells must be linear transducers, and this makes them special synapses. How this is done is still an outstanding problem in synaptic biophysics. Nevertheless, that it is done seems to imply that there must be an important functional reason for the nervous system to depart from its default synapses (which are quite nonlinear). Speculations for the perceptual reason for preserving linearity are concerned with the accuracy of the computation of brightness, color, and direction of motion, all of which require precise computations across spatial locations.

B. A Third Mechanism: Nonlinear Subunits

That the nervous system does not always preserve linear signal summation in the visual pathway is indicated by another major finding in the Enroth-Cugell and Rob-

FIGURE 4 Receptive field map of a macaque Parvocellular lateral geniculate nucleus (LGN) cell with cone-isolating stimuli (Reid & Shapley, 1992). The response was measured by reverse correlation with a spatiotemporal m-sequence. This gives a map of locations that excited the neuron under study, as a function of time. Here the time of peak response was chosen (at 48 ms after a stimulus) and the spatial sensitivity distributions plotted for this peak time. When an increment of intensity causes excitation of the neuron, the picture element is made brighter than the mean gray; when a decrement causes excitation, the pixel is made darker than mean gray. Strength of excitation is encoded as amount of lightness or blackness of the pixel. Three different spatial distributions are shown. (a) The spatial sensitivity map for black/white stimuli. This corresponds to the Center-Surround maps of Kuffler (1953). This cell was excited by decrements in its Center, so it would classically be called an "off" center neuron. (b) The spatial sensitivity map for L cone-isolating stimuli. The pixels in the stimuli were shades of red and green that were equally effective for M and S cones, so only L cones responded. This is the map of L cone input to the neuron. (c) The spatial sensitivity map for M cone-isolating stimuli. The pixels in the stimuli were shades of red and green that were equally effective for L and S cones, so only M cones responded. This is the map of M cone input to the neuron.

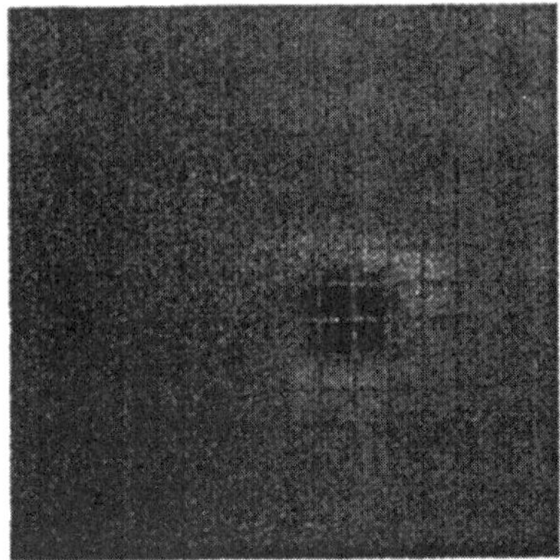

b
L cone

c
M cone

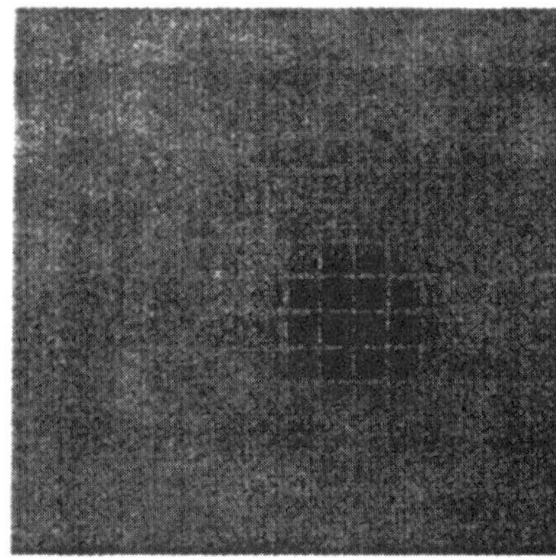

son (1966) paper: the existence of a class of nonlinearly summing retinal ganglion cells, the Y cells. Y cells have a classical Center–Surround organization but also receive mainly excitatory input from another retinal mechanism. This third mechanism is excitatory but nonlinear. That is, a Y cell receives a broadly spatially distributed excitatory input from spatial subregions within which there is linear spatial summation but between which signals are added together only if the signals exceed a threshold. Thus these many mechanisms can be thought of as nonlinear subunits within the Y cell's receptive field (Hochstein & Shapley, 1976). The multiplicity of nonlinear subunits confers upon the Y cell the unusual property of *spatial phase invariance* at high spatial frequencies. This means that a Y cell's response to a flashed (or contrast reversed) sine grating is invariant with the spatial phase, the position, of the grating with respect to the receptive field midpoint. A sketch of the array of nonlinear subunits, and a Y cell's receptive field organization is shown in Figure 5. The nonlinear subunits make a Y cell very sensitive to temporal contrast variation and motion of textured backgrounds. Understanding the nonlinear subunit mechanism in Y-type retinal ganglion cells is useful because similar sorts of nonlinear subunit mechanisms appear also in the visual cortex, in the receptive fields of "complex" cells.

C. Measuring Receptive Fields—Systems Analysis

The alert reader will have noticed that I have used a few equations to *describe* the spatial distributions of sensitivity in ganglion cells, but that I have not yet addressed the issue of the theoretical *analysis* of receptive fields. Analysis and measurement go hand in hand, and so one needs also to address the question, are there preferred stimuli with which to measure the receptive field properties of neurons? This is a controversial and somewhat emotional issue, for reasons that seem to have more to

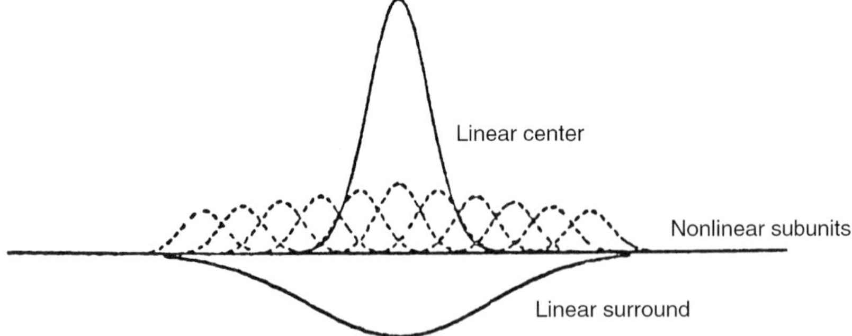

FIGURE 5 Model of the receptive field of a cat Y-type retinal ganglion cell (Hochstein & Shapley, 1976). There is a conventional Center–Surround receptive field like the DOG model of Figure 2, but also there is an array of nonlinear subunits that excite the Y cell. Within each subunit there is linear spatial and temporal summation of light-evoked signals, but between subunits there is nonlinear summation.

do with human history than with science. Perhaps we can lighten up a little. In Molière's play, *Le Bourgeois Gentilhomme,* the title character is surprised when he learns that he has been speaking prose all his life! There is an analogy with neurophysiologists who use intuitively simple stimuli like flashing spots, or drifting bars, to study visual receptive fields. Perhaps unknown to themselves, they have been doing systems analysis all their lives! Usually, by counting spikes, or measuring response waveforms averaged with respect to the stimulus, they are implicitly performing a kind of linear systems analysis because, as I show below, they are measuring a first-order correlation with the stimulus. One cannot escape some kind of systems analysis technique if one is attempting to characterize a receptive field—it is like trying to speak without speaking in prose.

The major theoretical question in the area of analyzing receptive fields is how to characterize the way signals are combined by visual neurons. One major question is whether there is linearity of signal summation within receptive fields—whether the elegant equations of the DOG model have any predictive validity. The classical measurements of Hartline (1940), Rodieck and Stone (1965), and Enroth-Cugell and Robson (1966) were all designed to ask whether the ganglion cells summed signals linearly, but they were not stringent tests of the hypothesis of linearity. There have been several studies that have used more rigorous methods derived from Wiener analysis (reviewed in Victor, 1992). In general such studies are based on the use of "dense" stimuli like white noise. To measure the spatial as well as the temporal signal transfer properties, spatiotemporal white noise (like the "snow" on a television set that is receiving no broadcast signal), or some convenient variant, has been used as a stimulus. Cross-correlation of such a white-noise stimulus and the neural response has led to estimates of the spatial and temporal transfer characteristics of the neurons (see for example, Reid et al., 1997; Sakuranaga, Ando, & Naka, 1987; Sakai & Naka, 1995). This technique rests on the theory that in a linear system, the impulse response of the system can be recovered by cross-correlation with white noise. In fact, if we write that the white noise input is $\mathrm{W}(\mathbf{x},\mathrm{t})$ and the response of the system(neuron) is $\mathrm{R}(\mathrm{t})$, and the spatiotemporal impulse response that characterizes the system (neuron) is $\mathrm{h}(\mathbf{x},\mathrm{t})$, then the following equation is true:

$$h(\mathbf{x},t) = < W(\mathbf{x}, t')\,\mathrm{R}(t'+t) >, \qquad \{\mathrm{D}\}$$

where $< \ldots >$ is the average over t'.

The governing equation {D} for characterizing receptive fields with white noise can be generalized to nonrandom, nonwhite stimuli. In general, the transfer properties of a neuron can be characterized by cross-correlating stimulus with response, even if the stimulus is a flashing spot, or a drifting bar, or a drifting or contrast modulated sine grating. (Technically, one has to take into account the autocorrelation of the stimulus.) This is the reason for writing that all measurements of receptive fields are a kind of systems analysis, whether intentional or not.

Spekreijse (1969) was among the first to use noise correlation techniques to study the visual system, and he used it to characterize the temporal response properties of retinal ganglion cells in the goldfish. In general, such measurements indicate large first-order correlations between stimulus and response, consistent with a mainly linear transduction system. However, the responses of Y cells, and other nonlinear ganglion cell types, cannot be accounted for simply by this first-order analysis, and the full power of nonlinear system identification theory is required to say anything meaningful about the responses of Y cells or similarly nonlinear cells. The reason is that responses in these neurons are not simply the result of processing one stimulus at a time independently of all others, as in a linear system. Rather, nonlinear interaction—for example, coincidence of stimuli, crosstalk between two or more stimuli, and distortion of stimulus waveforms—is characteristic of such neurons. The concept of receptive fields begins to break down here, because the receptive field for a given stimulus is not well defined without specifying the entire stimulus context (Victor & Shapley, 1979; Shapley & Victor, 1979; Victor, 1988, 1992). Volterra or Wiener functional expansions may be of some use in identifying the nature of the nonlinearity and in testing models of functional architecture of such nonlinear systems (Victor, 1992).

D. Lateral Geniculate Nucleus Cell Receptive Fields

The extension of these ideas to neurons in the LGN has shown to what a great extent the LGN neurons' visual properties are inherited from their retinal excitors (Cleland, Dubin, & Levick, 1971; Derrington & Lennie, 1984; Kaplan & Shapley, 1984). What I would like to emphasize in the space available is how the same ideas that worked so well for retinal ganglion cells have been applied to neurons in the visual cortex. This leads naturally to a discussion of the validity of the use of the receptive field concept in the cerebral cortex.

III. VISUAL CORTEX

Modern neurophysiology of the visual cortex begins with Hubel and Wiesel's study of visual receptive fields of neurons in cat primary visual cortex (Hubel & Wiesel, 1962). There are three main functional results of this study: (a) cortical neurons respond most vigorously to the motion of elongated contours or bars aligned with a particular orientation in space; (b) there are classes of cortical cells, simple and complex, with simple cells obeying at least qualitatively the rules of linear spatial summation, while complex cells are fundamentally nonlinear; (c) the receptive fields of simple cortical cells, mapped with small flashing spots as Hartline (1940) did in frog retinal ganglion cells, are elongated along the preferred orientation axis. Many of these original findings were extended to the monkey's striate cortex, and are presumably relevant to the function also of human primary visual cortex, which seems a lot like the monkey's (DeValois, Morgan, & Snodderly, 1974; De Valois, Albrecht, & Thorell, 1982; Hubel & Wiesel, 1968; Skottun et al., 1991).

A. Simple and Complex Cells

The explanation of the functional importance of the simple–complex classification remains a difficult unsolved problem. Simple cells exhibit qualitative properties of linear summation (DeValois et al., 1982; Maffei & Fiorentini, 1973; Movshon, Thompson, & Tolhurst, 1978; Skottun et al., 1991; Spitzer and Hochstein, 1985), responding, for example, mainly at the fundamental frequency of modulation of the contrast of a pattern. Complex cells are nonlinear in several different ways, mainly in responding to drifting patterns with an elevated mean spike rate, and in responding in a frequency-doubled ("on–off") manner to contrast modulation (DeValois et al., 1982; Movshon et al., 1978; Spitzer & Hochstein, 1985). These specific characteristics of complex cell responses have been accounted for by fairly simple network models that include a threshold nonlinearity after some spatial filtering. In fact, models of complex cells resemble qualitatively the model of cat retinal ganglion cells of the Y-type, discussed before, in that they all postulate summation of responses from nonlinear subunits of the receptive field. However, the complex cell models have to account also for orientation selectivity and spatial position effects that are more complicated than those observed in Y cells. It certainly must be the case that the neural network that produces the complex cells is a cortical network, but it has some resemblance to the Y cell's retinal network in its architecture. Much more could be written about what has been done to comprehend complex cells, but for simplicity's sake, I will focus on what is known about simple cells.

Though I write "simple cells for simplicity's sake," in reality there is nothing simple at all about simple cells in the visual cortex. As has been discussed previously (Jones & Palmer, 1987; Tolhurst & Dean, 1990; Shapley, 1994), both in cat and monkey cortex the linear spatial summation that characterizes simple cells cannot be inherited simply from convergence of excitation from many LGN cells onto a single simple cell. The reason is that LGN cells' responses to effective spatial patterns of moderate contrast are distorted, clipped at zero, by the threshold nonlinearity of the spike-encoding mechanism. They cannot modulate as much below their mean rate as they modulate above it. Therefore, the excitatory input to simple cortical cells from the LGN is highly nonlinear. One possible way to deal with this problem is to postulate direct LGN → cortex inhibition that will linearize the simple cell's response by a "push–pull" mechanism (Jones & Palmer, 1987; Tolhurst & Dean, 1990). Another is by disynaptic cortico-cortical lateral inhibition (Shapley, 1994). This latter mechanism has already been involved to explain in part the phenomenon of orientation selectivity in the cortex (Ben-Yishai, Bar-Or, & Sompolinsky, 1995; Bonds, 1989; Sillito, 1975; Somers, Nelson, & Sur, 1995, among others). Whatever the explanation, one should keep in mind the fact that the linearity, or quasi-linearity of simple cortical cells is the emulation of a linear system by a nonlinear system with a highly nonlinear input from the LGN. One important question for which there is yet no completely satisfactory answer is, why does the cortex go to such lengths to emulate a linear transducer? This is related to the sim-

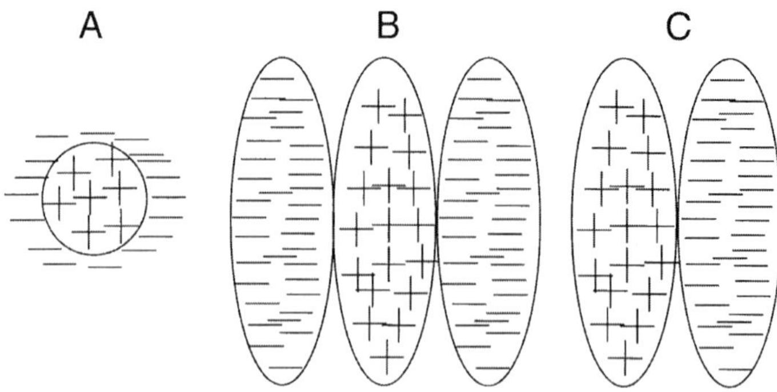

FIGURE 6 Receptive field maps in cat area 17 neurons (after Hubel & Wiesel, 1962). Cortical cells in area 17 of the cat cortex were mapped with small flashing spots in the manner of Hartline (1940) and Kuffler (1953). (A) Map of an LGN response as a function of position. (B, C) Maps of cortical receptive fields of simple cells. Points marked with a + sign indicate regions where incrementing the spots excited the neuron; those marked with a − sign indicate that decrements excited the neuron at that location.

ilarly unanswered question about the retina I raised previously, and may be answered by one of the speculations offered there about color and motion computations.

B. Orientation Selectivity

Orientation selectivity and its relation to receptive field organization remains an outstandingly important issue in cortical neurophysiology. In simple cells one should expect a direct relationship between receptive field structure and orientation tuning. If simple cells were linear, one would be able to predict orientation tuning selectivity from measurements of the receptive field sensitivity distributions—just as Rodieck (1965) predicted the responses to drifting bars from the sensitivity profiles of retinal ganglion cells' receptive fields. It was the qualitative agreement of receptive field maps with orientation tuning selectivity that inspired the Hubel–Wiesel feed-forward model (Hubel & Wiesel, 1962). As shown in Figure 6, these maps derived from responses elicited when flashing spots were elongated and aligned with the preferred axis of orientation selectivity of the neuron. But the question is, can linear summation of sensitivity explain not just the preferred axis

→

FIGURE 7 Reverse correlation maps of receptive fields of cat visual cortical neurons (Jones & Palmer, 1987). Reverse correlation maps of cortical receptive fields in cells of cat area 17. (a,b,c) Data from three different neurons. Data are shown in the left-hand column. The "fit" in the middle column is the best fitting 2-D Gabor function (see text). The column on the right-hand side of the figure is the difference between the fit and the data. The data in this figure were measured with a reverse correlation procedure. Every 50 ms a small square of light was flashed in the visual field at random positions with respect to the midpoint of the neuron's receptive field. Cross-correlation of the spike trains with the stimulus yielded the receptive field maps indicated in the left-hand column (as 3-D projection plots and beneath them, in the boxes, as contour plots).

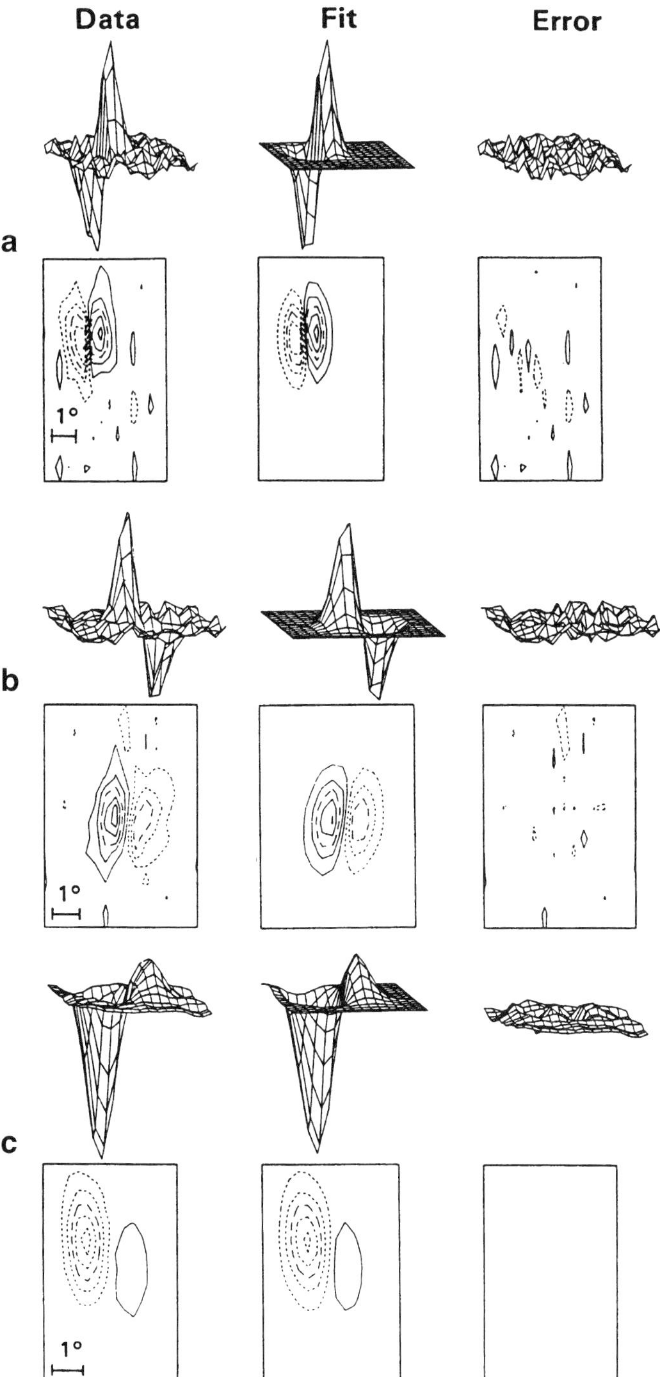
Data
Fit
Error
a
1°
b
1°
c
1°

but the observed orientation tuning? This question was asked directly by Jones and Palmer (1987) using a sophisticated quantitative technique.

Jones and Palmer (1987) performed a detailed quantitative test of linearity in cat simple cells by measuring 2-D receptive field properties and predicting the orientation and spatial frequency tuning. They cross-correlated the neuron's response with a quasi-random input signal as in equation {D}, in order to calculate the neuron's 2-D spatial impulse response. In these experiments the time variable was suppressed—they took the peak spatial response as characterizing the neuron's response. In terms of equation {D}, they measured $h(\mathbf{x}, t_{max})$, at the time t_{max} that gave maximum response. This experiment was done to test the hypothesis that the neuron was acting as a linear transducer of contrast signals, so the test came when Jones and Palmer attempted to account for the spatial frequency versus orientation tuning surfaces they measured independently on the same neurons with drifting grating patterns. The comparison was done by fitting $h(\mathbf{x}, t_{max})$, the neural spatial sensitivity distribution, with what they called a 2-D Gabor function, which was an elliptical Gaussian function of space, that is,

$$\exp\{-[(x - x_0)/a]^2 + [(y - y_0)/b]^2\},$$

multiplied by a sinusoidal function of space. They also fit the spatial frequency versus orientation tuning surfaces with the Fourier transform of a 2-D Gabor function. Then they compared the parameters of the fitted functions to test the linearity hypothesis. Though in some cells there was good agreement between the fitted curves, in a majority of their cells there was a clearly visible discrepancy that indicated a significant nonlinearity of spatial summation (this is contrary to the authors' conclusions from the same data, so I encourage readers to go back to the original paper). Jones and Palmer's data were replicated by DeAngelis, Ohzawa, and Freeman (1993) for the preferred orientation only; they found what I believe to be a significant discrepancy in many cells between the shape of the predicted (from spatial sensitivity distribution) versus measured spatial frequency responses. There was a systematic narrowing of the spatial frequency response in the data measured with drifting gratings compared with the linear prediction from the spatial impulse response. Thus, although the cortex attempts to emulate a linear system with the neural network that drives a simple cell, it cannot hide the nonlinearity of the cortical network from these very precise experimental tests. This is a second indication that simple cells are not so simple. A third indication comes from the different time courses of cortical responses from different parts of the receptive field, and this is related to the cortical cell property of directional selectivity.

C. Direction Selectivity

The specificity of cortical cells for *direction of motion* is also an emergent property of the visual cortex that could be due to specific receptive field properties. It has been shown that visual neurons can give directionally selective responses if different spatial locations within the receptive field have different time courses of response. Technically, this means that the spatiotemporal impulse response h(**x**,t) is not factorable into two parts h_x(**x**) and h_t(t) but rather cannot be separated—hence it is called spatiotemporally inseparable. Spatiotemporal inseparability does cause direction selectivity in completely linear neural models (Watson & Ahumada, 1985; Adelson & Bergen, 1985; Burr, Ross, & Morrone, 1986; Reid, Soodak, & Shapley, 1987, 1991). Because simple cells in visual cortex are often direction selective, it is natural to ask whether spatiotemporal inseparability in the receptive field causes direction selectivity in these neurons. McLean, Raab, and Palmer (1994) answered this directly for cat cortical cells using a reverse correlation approach just like Jones & Palmer's (1987), with the following improvements: they used a briefer stimulus presentation, and they measured the time evolution of h(**x**,t) instead of just measuring h(**x**,t_{max}). Their results are displayed in Figure 8, which shows h(**x**,t) for two different cells: a spatiotemporally separable, nondirection-selective neuron, and a spatiotemporally inseparable, directionally selective neuron. Separability is indicated in an x-t plot like Figure 8 as vertical symmetry of the main envelope of h(**x**,t). Inseparability is indicated by an oblique axis of symmetry in the x-t graph. In general, McLean et al. found direction selectivity and inseparability were associated in cat directional simple cells. This confirmed the previous work of Reid et al. (1987), who demonstrated spatiotemporal inseparability's correlation with direction selectivity by means of experiments with contrast reversal sine gratings (rather than with the reverse correlation measurements of h(**x**,t) as was done by McLean et al., 1994).

The relation of the receptive field properties of visual neurons to their direction selectivity is analogous to the relation of orientation tuning to receptive field properties discussed above. There is a qualitative association between a receptive field property—in this case spatiotemporal inseparability—and a visual property, namely direction selectivity. But again, a true test of linearity would be the prediction of the quantitative characteristics of directional selectivity from first-order sensitivity distributions [in this case, the spatiotemporal sensitivity distribution h(**x**,t)]. When this is done, the preferred direction can be accounted for from measurements of h(**x**,t), but the measured directional selectivity is usually quite a bit more than that predicted from linear synthesis (McLean et al., 1994; Reid et al., 1987, 1991; Tolhurst & Heeger, 1997). Thus, some nonlinearity in cortical processing is needed to account for the discrepancy, and this is reminiscent of orientation and spatial frequency tuning. It has been proposed in the case of direction selectivity that known cortical nonlinearities (which are known but hardly understood) could account for the nonlinear stage that is needed (Tolhurst & Heeger, 1997). However, as argued below with respect to orientation tuning, it seems that an adequate understanding requires a distributed network model of intracortical interactions and cannot simply be explained by the sort of fairly simple nonlinear box models proposed previously.

In general, all explanations offered so far for the nonlinearities of cortical visual processing include a major role of lateral interaction or feedback interaction. Non-

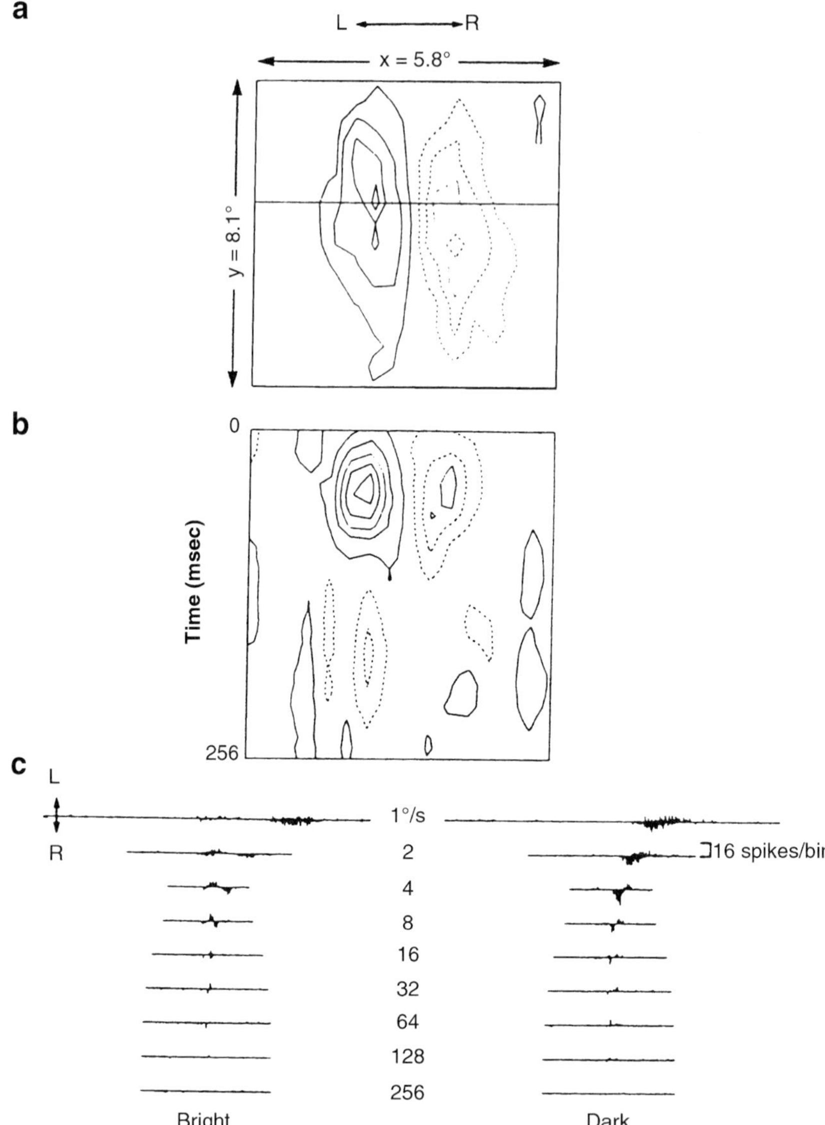

FIGURE 8 Space-time coupling in cat cortical cell receptive fields (McLean, Raab, & Palmer, 1994). Reverse correlation maps of cortical receptive fields in cells of cat area 17, as in Figure 7, but here briefer stimuli (usually 20 ms in duration) were used, so the time evolution of the sensitivity distribution was measured. The sensitivity distributions are represented as contour plots. In (a) and (b) the data are from a nondirectionally selective neuron, whereas (d) and (e) are data from a directionally selective cell. (a) and (d) are x-y plots of sensitivity as a function of position, at the peak time about 50 ms after stimulus onset. B and E are x-t plots of the sensitivity as a function of x position (averaged over the y-dimension) as a function of time after stimulus onset. The point of the figure is to show that the directionally selective cell [data from it are in (d), (e), and (f)] has a slanted x-t plot, indicating spatiotemporal inseparability in the directional neurons.

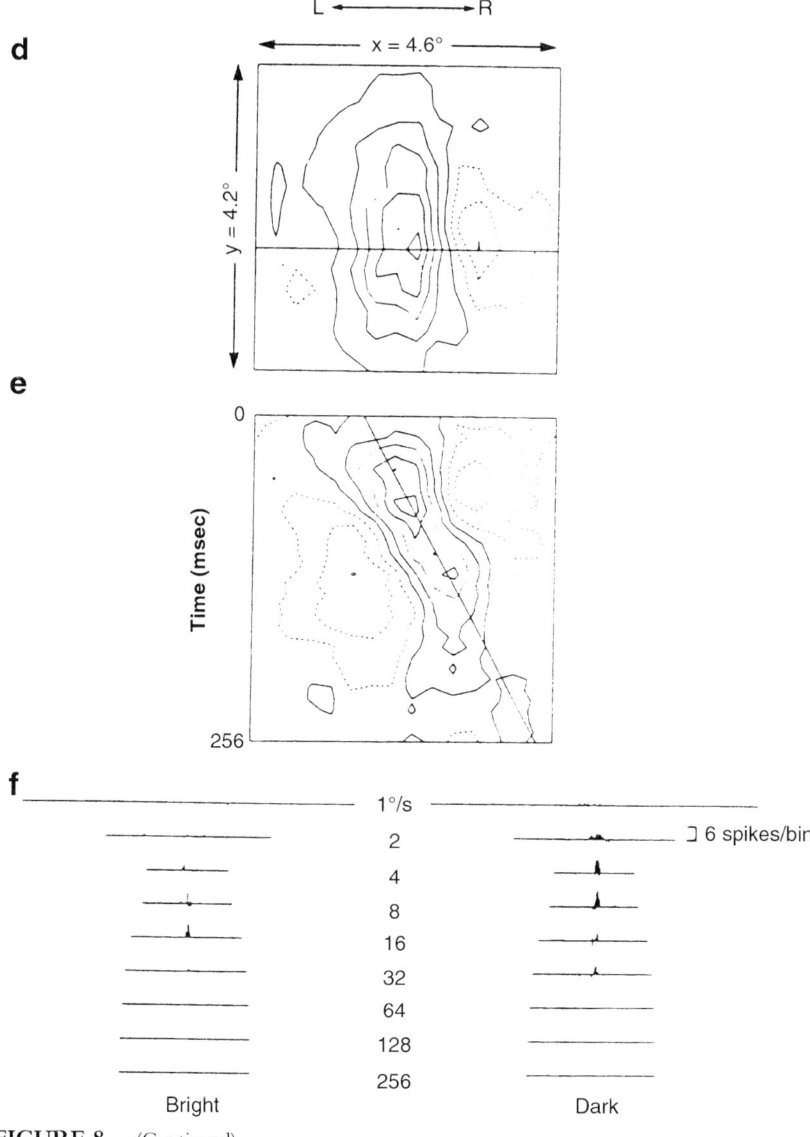

FIGURE 8 (Continued)

linear feedback models cannot be accommodated easily within the usual concepts of receptive fields because a nonlinear feedback is usually adaptive in a complex manner. With such a feedback term added, the "receptive field" becomes less useful as an explanatory concept, because which receptive field is meant—the one under condition A or the one under condition B? So, to the degree that nonlinear

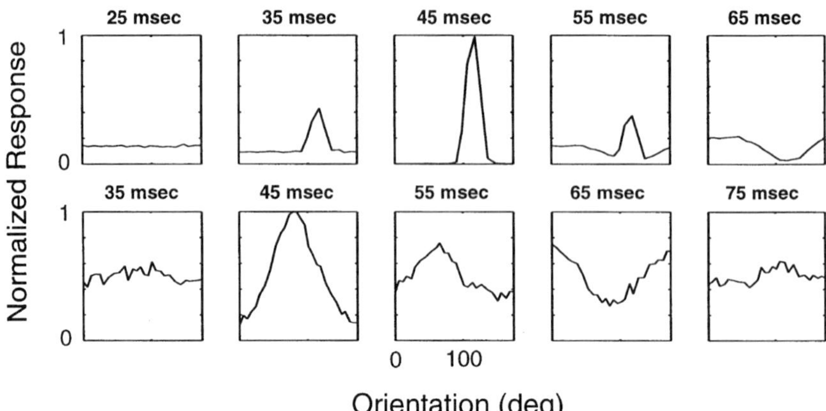

FIGURE 9 Reverse correlation measurements of the time evolution of orientation tuning in macaque V1 neurons (Ringach, Hawken, and Shapley, unpublished results). Here the results are obtained by reverse correlation in the orientation domain. To study dynamics of orientation tuning we used as stimuli the set of sine gratings of optimal spatial frequency at many orientations (around the clock in 10° steps). The dynamical stimuli used consisted of a rapidly changing sequence of sinusoidal gratings. The responses of the neurons are the cross-correlations of their spike trains with the sequence of images—this gives the neurons' orientation-tuning functions, as functions of time. In each graph, the horizontal axis goes from 0–180° orientation. This figure displays orientation tuning function for two neurons in macaque V1 layer 4B. Results for each cell occupy a different row, as marked. The five different panels for each neuron correspond to give different delays between neural response and stimulus onset. Note that already in layer 4B there is evidence for complex interactions in the orientation domain: rebound inhibition in both cells can be observed around 65-ms delay, and in cell 1, there is clear evidence for flanking inhibition around the peak at 55 ms. In cell 2's response, there is an especially clear indication of an elevated response orthogonal to the main peak, at a later time, at 65 ms in this case.

feedback changes the neural activity of cortical cells significantly, to that same degree we are forced to question whether the idea of a receptive field is adequate to describe the behavior of a cortical cell. This then is the reason for considering recent work on the dynamics of orientation tuning (Ringach, Hawken, & Shapley, 1997), in which the importance of nonlinear cortical feedback has become evident.

D. Orientation Dynamics

To study dynamics of orientation tuning in simple cells, we (Ringach et al., 1997) used as stimuli sine gratings of optimal spatial frequency at many orientations (around the clock in 10° steps) and at several spatial phases (responses were averaged over spatial phase). The dynamical stimuli used consisted of a rapidly changing sequence of sinusoidal gratings. The responses of the neurons are measured as the cross-correlations of their impulse train outputs with the sequence of images—this gives the neurons' orientation tuning functions, as functions of time. Thus the method used permitted the measurement of orientation tuning when the test stimuli are embedded within a rich stimulus set of temporally adjacent stimuli. We also could check linearity of spatial summation directly by creating images that were linear combinations of the original set, and measuring whether the spatiotemporal correlation functions were changed by the process of superposition of stimuli—for a linear system, there would be no change. We studied neurons in all layers of macaque V1, keeping track of their locations through standard methods of track reconstruction (Ringach et al., 1997).

Our preliminary results indicate that most cells in the input layers 4Cα and β have simple dynamics and are relatively broadly tuned for orientation. By simple dynamics I mean that after a time delay, the response simply has a single peak in time and, after the peak, simply relaxes back to baseline. However, cells in layers 2, 3, 4B, 5, and 6 showed complicated dynamics: rebound responses, sharpening of the orientation tuning with time, and/or transient peaks of activity at off-optimal orientation. Furthermore, we found that these neurons with complicated dynamics are usually much more sharply tuned in orientation. Examples of more sharply tuned cells with complicated dynamics are given in Figure 9, which displays orientation tuning functions, derived from subspace correlation measurements, for two neurons in macaque V1 layer 4B. Results for each cell occupy a different row, as marked. The five different panels for each neuron correspond to five different delays between neural response and stimulus onset. Note that already in layer 4B there is evidence for complex interactions in the orientation domain: rebound inhibition in both cells can be observed around 65-ms delay, and in cell 1, clear evidence for flanking inhibition around the peak at 55 ms. In cell 2's response, there is an especially clear indication of an elevated response orthogonal to the main peak, at a later time, at 65 ms in this case. When we compare these measurements to orientation tuning curves obtained by conventional methods on the same neurons, we find good qualitative agreement on the peak orientation, but conventional measurements completely miss the dynamic aspects of the orientation tuning: rebound suppression at the peak orientation, and off-peak excitation later in the response. These results indicate that lateral interaction in the orientation domain is prevalent. The nature of this interaction is not yet understood, but peaks far from the main tuning peak, so evident in cell 2 at 65 ms, for instance, suggest that we must consider recurrent or feedback inhibitory mechanisms in a model for the cortex.

This work has implications about the importance of "the receptive field" as a valid way of understanding cortical function. The implication is that lateral interactions in the cortex shape all aspects of cellular functions. Much work supports this view but uses a very different paradigm: the study of cortical visual interactions across space, also known as "contextual effects." This includes the work on Center–Surround interactions (reviewed by Allman, 1985), orientation contrast (Knierim & Van Essen, 1992; Sillito, Grieve, Jones, Cudeiro, & Davis, 1995; Levitt & Lund, 1997), and figure–ground effects (Lamme, 1995; Zipser, Lamme, & Schiller, 1996), among others. The work of Bullier and colleagues (reviewed in Salin & Bullier, 1995) indicates the importance of feedback connections from extrastriate areas into V1. This body of work suggests that the cells in the primary visual cortex are influenced by lateral and feedback interactions in a very significant way, much more than was imagined when the receptive field concept was first applied to cortex. In perception of natural scenes, even more than in laboratory experiments on simplified stimuli, the effects of context may play an important role in visual cortical cell responses. This must be quantified in future experiments.

It was a good first approximation to see whether we could treat the visual cortex like the retina, as a passive filter of visual information, which is how I view the receptive field concept. However, as researchers learn more and more about how the cortex works, this approximation seems less useful. It is not a lost cause, and we don't have to give up the scientific analysis of the cortex just because the concept of "receptive field" that works well in the retina does not apply to cortex. Rather, we need to use other tools, perhaps nonlinear dynamical system theory, perhaps some different analytical tools, to comprehend what is going on in the cortex. It is also important to realize that understanding the network architecture of the cortex is critical for building models. In the future, theory and experiment, structure and function will all have to be integrated in a concerted scientific probe of the cortex's contribution to visual perception.

References

Adelson, E. H., & Bergen, J. R. (1985). Spatiotemporal energy models for the perception of motion. *Journal of the Optical Society of America, Series A, 2,* 284–299.

Allman, J. (1985). Stimulus-specific responses from beyond the classical receptive field: Neurophysiological mechanisms for local-global comparison in visual neurons. *Annual Review of Neuroscience, 8,* 407–430.

Ben-Yishai, R., Bar-Or, R. L., & Sompolinsky, H. (1995). Theory of orientation tuning in the visual cortex. *Proceedings of National Academy of Sciences, 92,* 3844–3848.

Bonds, A. B. (1989). Role of inhibition in the specification of orientation selectivity of cells in the cat striate cortex. *Visual Neuroscience, 2,* 41–55.

Burr, D. C., Ross, J., Morrone, & M. C. (1986). Seeing objects in motion. *Proceedings of the Royal Society of London, series B, 227,* 249–265.

Cleland, B. G., Dubin, M. W., & Levick, W. R. (1971). Simultaneous recording of input and output of lateral geniculate neurones. *Nature, New Biology, 9,* 191–192, 231.

DeAngelis, G. C., Ohzawa, I., & Freeman, R. D. (1993). Spatiotemporal organization of simple-cell receptive fields in the cat's striate cortex. II. Linearity of temporal and spatial summation. *Journal of Neurophysiology, 69,* 1118–1135.

Derrington, D. M., & Lennie, P. (1984). Spatial and temporal contrast sensitivities of neurones in lateral geniculate nucleus of macaque. *Journal of Physiology, 257,* 219–240.

De Valois, R. L., Albrecht, D. G., Thorell, L. G. (1982). Spatial frequency selectivity of cells in macaque visual cortex. *Vision Research, 22,* 545–559.

De Valois, R. L., Morgan, H., & Snodderly, D. M. (1974). Psychophysical studies of monkey vision. 3. Spatial luminance contrast sensitivity tests of macaque and human observers. *Vision Research, 14,* 75–81.

Enroth-Cugell, C. (1993). The world of retinal ganglion cells. In D. K. Lam & R. M. Shapley (Ed.), *Contrast sensitivity* (pp. 149–179). Cambridge, MA: MIT Press.

Enroth-Cugell, C., & Pinto, L. H. (1972). Properties of the surround response mechanism of cat retinal ganglion cells and centre-surround interaction. *Journal of Physiology, 220 (2),* 403–439.

Enroth-Cugell, C., Hertz, B. G., & Lennie, P. (1977). Convergence of rod and cone signals in the cat's retina. *Journal of Physiology (London), 269,* 297–318.

Enroth-Cugell, C., & Robson, J. G. (1966). The contrast sensitivity of retinal ganglion cells of the cat. *Journal of Physiology (London), 187,* 517–552.

Enroth-Cugell, C., & Robson, J. G. (1984). Functional characteristics and diversity of cat retinal ganglion cells: Basic characteristics and quantitative description. *Investigative Ophthalmalogy and Visual Science, 25,* 250–267.

Hartline, H. K. (1940). The receptive fields of optic nerve fibers. *American Journal of Physiology, 130,* 690–699.

Hawken, M. J., & Parker, A. J. (1990). Detection and discrimination mechanisms in the striate cortex of the Old World monkey. In C. Blakemore (Ed.), *Vision: Coding and efficiency.* Cambridge, UK: Cambridge University Press.

Hochstein, S., & Shapley, R. (1976). Quantitative analysis of retinal ganglion cell classification. *Journal of Physiology (London), 262,* 237–264.

Hubel, D. H., & Wiesel, T. N. (1962). Receptive fields, binocular interaction and functional architecture in the cat's visual cortex. *Journal of Physiology (London), 160,* 106–154.

Hubel, D. H., & Wiesel, T. N. (1968). Receptive fields and functional architecture of monkey striate cortex. *Journal of Physiology (London), 195,* 215–243.

Jones, J. P., & Palmer, L. A. (1987). An evaluation of the two-dimensional Gabor filter model of simple receptive fields in cat striate cortex. *Journal of Neurophysiology, 58,* 1233–1258.

Kaplan, E., & Shapley, R. M. (1984). The source of S(slow) potentials in the mammalian LGN. *Experimental Brain Research, 55,* 111–116.

Knierim, J. J., & van Essen, D. C. (1992). Neuronal responses to static texture patterns in area V1 of the alert macaque monkey. *Journal of Neurophysiology, 67,* 961–980.

Kuffler, S. W. (1953). Discharge patterns and functional organization of mammalian retina. *Journal of Neurophysiology, 16,* 37–68.

Lamme, V. A. (1995). The neurophysiology of figure-ground segregation in primary visual cortex. *Journal of Neuroscience, 15,* 1605–1615.

Levitt, J. B., & Lund, J. S. (1997). Contrast dependence of contextual effects in primate visual cortex. *Nature, 387,* 73–76.

McLean, J., Raab, S., & Palmer, L. A. (1994). Contribution of linear mechanisms to the specification of local motion by simple cells in areas 17 and 18 of the cat. *Visual Neuroscience, 11,* 271–294.

Maffei, L., & Fiorentini, A. (1973). The visual cortex as a spatial frequency analyser. *Visual Neuroscience, 13,* 1255–1267.

Movshon, J. A., Thompson, I. D., & Tolhurst, D. J. (1978). Receptive field organization of complex cells in the cat's striate cortex. *Journal of Physiology (London), 283,* 79–99.

Parker, A. J., & Newsome, W. T. (1998). Sense and the signal neuron: Probing the physiology of perception. *Annual Review of Neuroscience, 21,* 227–277.

Reid, R. C., & Shapley, R. M. (1992). Spatial structure of cone inputs to receptive fields in primate lateral geniculate nucleus. *Nature, 356,* 716–718.

Reid, R. C., Soodak, R. E., & Shapley, R. M. (1987). Linear mechanisms of directional selectivity in simple cells of cat striate cortex. *Proceedings of the National Academy of Sciences, 84,* 8740–8744.

Reid, R. C., Soodak, R. E., & Shapley, R. M. (1991). Directional selectivity and spatiotemporal structure of receptive fields of simple cells in cat striate cortex. *Journal of Neurophysiology, 66,* 509–529.

Reid, R. C., Victor, J. D., Shapley, R. M. (1997). The use of m-sequences in the analysis of visual neurons: linear receptive field properties. *Visual Neuroscience, 14,* 1015–27.

Ringach, D. L., Hawken, M. J., & Shapley, R. M. (1997). The dynamics of orientation tuning in the macaque monkey striate cortex. *Nature, 387,* 281–284.

Rodieck, R. W. (1965). Quantitative analysis of cat retinal ganglion cell response to visual stimuli. *Vision Research, 5(11),* 583–601.

Rodieck, R. W., & Stone, J. (1965). Analysis of receptive fields of cat retinal ganglion cells. *Journal of Neurophysiology, 28,* 832–849.

Sakai, H. M., & Naka, K. (1995). Response dynamics and receptive-field organization of catfish ganglion cells. *Journal of General Physiology, 105,* 795–814.

Sakuranaga, M., Ando, Y., & Naka, K. (1987). Dynamics of the ganglion cell response in the catfish and frog retinas. *Journal of General Physiology, 90,* 229–259.

Salin, P. A., & Bullier, J. (1995). Corticocortical connections in the visual system: Structure and function. *Physiology Review, 75,* 107–154.

Shapley, R. M. (1994). Linearity and non-linearity in cortical receptive fields. In *Higher order processing in the visual system: Ciba Symposium* (vol. 184, pp. 71–87). Chichester: Wiley.

Shapley, R., & Victor, J. D. (1979). Nonlinear spatial summation and the contrast gain control of cat retinal ganglion cells. *Journal of Physiology (London), 290,* 141–161.

Sillito, A. M. (1975). The contribution of inhibitory mechanisms to the receptive field properties of neurones in the striate cortex of the cat. *Journal of Physiology (London), 250,* 305–329.

Sillito, A. M., Grieve, K. L., Jones, H. E., Cudeiro, J., & Davis, J. (1995). Visual cortical mechanisms detecting focal orientation discontinuities. *Nature, 378,* 492–496.

Skottun, B. C., De Valois, R. L., Grosof, D. H., Movshon, J. A., Albrecht, D. G., Bonds, A. B. (1991). Classifying simple and complex cells on the basis of response modulation. *Vision Research, 31,* 1079–1086.

Somers, D. C., Nelson, S. B., & Sur, M. (1995). An emergent model of orientation selectivity in cat visual cortical simple cells. *Journal of Neuroscience, 15,* 448–465.

Soodak, R. E., Shapley, R. M., & Kaplan, E. (1991). Fine structure of receptive field centers of X and Y Cells of the cat. *Visual Neuroscience, 15,* 5448–5465.

Spekreijse, H. (1969). Rectification in the goldfish retina: Analysis by sinusoidal and auxiliary stimulation. *Vision Research, 9,* 1461–1472.

Spitzer, H., & Hochstein, S. (1985). Simple- and complex-cell response dependences on stimulation parameters. *Journal of Neurophysiology, 53,* 1244–1265.

Tolhurst, D. J., & Dean, A. F. (1990). The effects of contrast on the linearity of spatial summation of simple cells in the cat's striate cortex. *Experimental Brain Research, 79,* 582–588.

Tolhurst, D. J., & Heeger, D. J. (1997). Contrast normalization and a linear model for the directional selectivity of simple cells in cat striate cortex. *Visual Neuroscience, 14,* 19–25.

Victor, J. D. (1988). The dynamics of the cat retinal Y cell subunit. *Journal of Physiology (London), 405,* 289–320.

Victor, J. D. (1992). Nonlinear systems analysis in vision: Overview of kernel methods. In R. Pinter & B. Nabet (Eds.), *Nonlinear vision: Determination of neural receptive fields, function and networks* (pp. 1–37). Cleveland, OH: CRC Press.

Victor, J. D., & Shapley, R. (1979). Receptive field mechanisms of cat X and Y retinal ganglion cells. *Journal of General Physiology, 74,* 275–298.

Vogels, R., & Orban, G. A. (1991). Quantitative study of striate single unit responses in monkeys performing an orientation discrimination task. *Experimental Brain Research, 84,* 1–11.

Watson, A. B., & Ahumada, A. J., Jr. (1985). Model of human visual-motion sensing. *Journal of the Optical Society of America, Series A, 2,* 322–341.

Zipser, K., Lamme, V. A., & Schiller, P. H. (1996). Contextual modulation in primary visual cortex. *Journal of Neuroscience, 15,* 7376–7389.

CHAPTER 3

Spatial Vision

Wilson S. Geisler
Duane G. Albrecht

I. INTRODUCTION

The topic of spatial vision concerns the fundamental mechanisms within the eye and the brain that analyze and represent the distribution of light across the visual field, with the ultimate goal of understanding how these mechanisms contribute to object recognition and scene interpretation in general.

A wealth of psychophysical and physiological research supports the view that stimulus selectivity plays a fundamental role in spatial vision. Psychophysical studies have provided evidence that the human visual system is selective along a number of stimulus dimensions including orientation, size, position, wavelength (color), speed of motion, direction of motion, and binocular disparity. These studies have shown that there are mechanisms ("channels") selective to different regions along each of these stimulus dimensions. Similarly, neurophysiological and anatomical studies have demonstrated that neurons in the visual pathway are selective along a number of stimulus dimensions, and that this selectivity increases from the retina to the primary visual cortex. For example, photoreceptors are selective along a few stimulus dimensions (spatial position, wavelength, temporal frequency), whereas cortical neurons are selective along many stimulus dimensions (spatial position, wavelength, temporal frequency, orientation, spatial frequency, direction of motion, disparity, etc.). Concomitant with this increase in stimulus selectivity, there is an increase in the heterogeneity; that is, there is an increase in the complexity and diversity of the cells along all of the stimulus dimensions. Thus, for example, the intensity response functions of cones are all very similar from cell to cell, whereas the contrast response functions of cortical neurons are quite different from cell to cell.

A number of different explanations have been proposed for this emergence of stimulus selectivity along the visual pathway. One explanation is that this progressive selectivity is part of a hierarchical process, ultimately leading to single neurons that respond uniquely to specific real-world objects (Barlow, 1972, 1995): "The Neuron Doctrine." A second explanation is that this selectivity reflects a low redundancy code that is well matched to the statistics of natural images (Barlow, 1961, 1989; Field, 1987; Olshausen & Field, 1997): "Sparse Coding."

A third explanation is that this selectivity is a critical step in segregating objects from their context: "Object Segregation." Objects of interest within the natural environment are generally located within a very complex context of other objects. In order to recognize an object of interest, the parts of the object must be separated from the parts of other objects. For example, to recognize a longhorn bull behind a barbed wire fence, it is necessary to separate the image features that define the wire fence from those that define the bull. Fortunately, context is much less of a problem on a local scale; it is relatively easy to identify the orientation, position, and color of local image contours. The selectivity of visual cortical neurons permits recognition of these local image properties, thus allowing subsequent grouping mechanisms to bind together the contours that define the fence separately from those that define the bull.

These three different explanations for stimulus selectivity are not necessarily incompatible. Object segregation or sparse coding could be a first step in producing single neurons tuned to real-world objects. On the other hand, the processing following object segregation or sparse coding could be highly distributed. Further, having neurons matched to the statistics of the natural environment must surely be advantageous for both sparse coding and object segregation, given the constraint of limited resources. However, the goals of sparse coding and object segregation are quite different; hence, the specific selectivities, and how they are implemented, could well be different. It is important to keep all three explanations in mind, given that one's theoretical viewpoint can substantively influence the direction of future research.

In this chapter we will rely upon a wealth of psychophysical and physiological research to develop the topic of spatial vision with two themes in mind. The first theme concerns how stimulus selectivity develops along the visual pathway. The second theme concerns how the anatomical and physiological mechanisms of stimulus selectivity contribute to visual performance, and ultimately, object recognition and scene interpretation.

II. SINGLE NEURONS AND BEHAVIOR

A. Levels of Analysis

Research in perception and cognition has been performed at many different levels of analysis: the organism as a whole, the subregions of the brain, the individual neurons, and the components of individual neurons. The main focus in this chapter will be on the responses of the organism as a whole (i.e., visual psychophysics) and on the responses of the individual neurons (i.e., single neuron electrophysiology).

Focusing on the behavioral responses of the organism as a whole is justified because the ultimate goal of perception and cognition research is to understand behavior. Indeed, behavioral abilities define the phenomena of interest in perception and cognition, and hence provide the groundwork for directing and interpreting the measurements at all the other levels.

Specifically, behavioral findings often serve as a guide to neurophysiological and anatomical studies. To begin with, note that there is an enormous amount of information available in the visual stimulus. The visual system is not capable of transmitting and utilizing all of this information because it has finite neural resources. Some of this information will be used by the nervous system and some of this information will be lost. Behavioral performance can tell us what information is used and what is lost. If behavioral performance indicates that a certain kind of information is lost, then there should be some stage in the neural processing where the loss occurs, and neurophysiological measurements should be able to demonstrate this loss. If behavioral performance indicates that a certain kind of information is not lost, then the information must be preserved at every sequential level of the nervous system between the stimulus and the behavior, and neurophysiological measurements should be able to demonstrate the presence of the information.

Consider, for example, the task of color discrimination. There is an enormous number of different wavelength distributions that can be presented to a human observer. Behavioral studies have shown that most of these wavelength distributions cannot be distinguished. This fact indicates that substantial chromatic information has been lost in the nervous system. Neurophysiological measurements have demonstrated that most of this loss occurs at the level of the photoreceptors. On the other hand, behavioral studies have also shown that sufficient chromatic information is transmitted to support trichromacy. Neurophysiological studies have used this fact as a basis for designing chromatic stimuli and locating the neural systems responsible for trichromatic color discrimination.

The justification for focusing on the responses of individual neurons is somewhat more involved. All of the information transmitted by a neuron is contained in the temporal sequence of action potentials generated by the neuron; this information represents the net sum of all the synaptic inputs to the neuron, plus all of the prior neural information processing that those inputs represent. Because of the all-or-none property of action potentials and their short duration, it is relatively easy to accurately measure the temporal sequence (with a resolution finer than milliseconds) and hence all of the transmitted information (the noise in the recording instrument has little or no effect on the accuracy of the measurements). This fact makes it possible to quantitatively relate physiological responses to perception and cognition in a way that is not possible by current methods for measuring the responses of subregions of the brain or subcomponents of individual neurons.

When measuring the responses of a subregion in the brain using one of the neuroimaging techniques, the responses from the individual neurons are measured indirectly through metabolic activity, with relatively poor spatial and temporal resolution. Although certain questions can be answered with these techniques, it is very difficult to know how to relate the measurements to behavioral performance in a quantitative fashion.[1] Similarly, although the responses of some particular subcomponents of individual neurons can be measured (such as the activity of a single synapse), a complete characterization of all the components is not possible at this point in time, and thus it is difficult to relate the responses of the subcomponents to the responses of the neuron as a whole or to behavioral responses.

There are, of course, limitations to the inferences that can be drawn about visual information processing by measuring action potentials from single neurons. To begin with, not all neurons at all levels of the visual system produce action potentials. However, these neurons are generally local circuit neurons. Neural communications that extend over distances greater than a few millimeters are carried via action potentials. Thus, measurement of action potential responses should be sufficient to characterize the output of the information processing that is transmitted from one region of the brain to another. Further, using intracellular recording (and similar techniques) it is generally possible to measure the information transmitted by the voltage potential responses of nonspiking neurons, with reasonable accuracy. A second limitation concerns the variation in sampling probabilities that may occur with different cell sizes and different subpopulation densities. However, anatomical measurements of subpopulation densities can help to lessen this uncertainty; and, increasing the sample size of measured neurons can increase the probability of obtaining measurements from small subpopulations. A third limitation is that it is not possible to record the individual responses of many neurons simultaneously. However, by measuring the responses of many neurons, one at a time, to the same set of stimuli, it is possible to make inferences about the information processing of

[1] Neuroimaging techniques are useful because they allow simultaneous measurement of large populations of neurons and they can be performed on human beings (without invasive procedures). However, there are a number of factors which make neuroimaging data difficult to interpret. First, there is considerable uncertainty about the degree to which the measurements correspond to neural activity, because most techniques measure neural responses indirectly via the level of metabolic activity. Second, because the signals are summed over a relatively long temporal interval (on the order of seconds) it is difficult to obtain useful measurements of the rapid neural information processing that ordinarily occurs during perception and cognition (on the order of milliseconds). Third, because the signals are summed over space and time, many different patterns of neural activity within a given region could produce exactly the same summed level of metabolic activity, and thus it is impossible to quantitatively characterize the information transmitted by the population of neurons. Fourth, neural circuits for a given behavioral information-processing task are identified when the difference in metabolic activity between a baseline condition and a test condition exceeds a certain criterion level. Thus, to the extent that the neural circuits for a given information-processing task are distributed throughout different regions of the brain, or to the extent that the neural circuits for different information-processing tasks are intermingled, the changes in metabolic activity will fail to exceed the criterion. (For further discussion of this issue see Wandell, 1999.)

the population as a whole. These inferences depend upon knowing the degree of statistical independence of the responses across neurons. New techniques that allow recording from two or three neurons simultaneously suggest that the responses are relatively uncorrelated.

B. Linking Hypotheses

The ultimate goal of measuring the anatomical and physiological properties of the neurons in the visual pathway is to understand behavioral performance. For example, it is possible to measure the responses of visual cortex neurons as a function of spatial frequency and contrast, but ultimately we would like to understand how the responses of these neurons contribute to spatial frequency discrimination, contrast discrimination, and other behavioral performances. To understand how neural responses contribute to behavioral performance, it is necessary to have a *linking hypothesis* so that predictions for behavioral performance can be generated from the responses of the neurons at a particular level of the visual system (Brindley, 1960; Teller, 1984). A linking hypothesis can be regarded as a specific model of the neural processing which occurs subsequent to the selected level.

Two general categories of linking hypotheses have been widely considered. One consists of the Bayesian ideal-observer models; these models assume that all of the information available in the responses of the neurons is extracted and optimally combined with knowledge about stimulus probabilities. The other consists of simple pooling models; these models assume that the responses of the neurons are combined using a simple operation such as simple summation, Minkowski summation, or "winner take all."

An advantage of the Bayesian ideal-observer models is that all of the available neural information is used, and hence if the behavioral performance exceeds the predicted performance, then one can be certain there is something missing in the neurophysiological data (e.g., an undetected subpopulation of neurons). Conversely, if the behavioral performance falls below that of the ideal observer, then either there must be something inaccurate about the neurophysiological data, or there must be some loss of information in subsequent neural stages. For some situations, the ideal combination of the neural responses is relatively simple but in general, it is complex and varies from situation to situation. Although the human visual system is sophisticated, it has many complex tasks to perform (with limited resources) and hence it probably does not perform any individual task in *the* optimal fashion.

An advantage of the simple pooling rules is that they are easy to understand, and they could be implemented with simple neural circuits. However, for many situations, the simple pooling rules probably do not adequately represent the complexity of later neural processing.

Given a linking hypothesis, it is then possible to compare neural performance and behavioral performance along stimulus dimensions of interest. For some linking hypotheses it is possible to compare absolute levels of performance. One example is the "winner-take-all" rule, where the behavioral performance for each stimulus condition is determined by the neuron with the best performance. However, it is generally not possible to compare absolute levels of performance because of uncertainty about the number of neurons that are combined. In these cases, only the shapes of the behavioral and neural performance functions can be compared. Nonetheless, if the two performance functions have the same shape (i.e., if they only differ by a scale factor) then it suggests that subsequent brain mechanisms are equally efficient in processing the information along the stimulus dimension, and hence that the variations in the behavioral performance are the result of the variations in the neural responses at the selected level (or at a lower level). Of course, matching shapes for the neural and behavioral performance functions could be the result of a fortuitous cancellation of effects in subsequent neural levels, but such a cancellation would be improbable.

As is clear from this discussion, there is uncertainty about what the appropriate linking hypothesis might be in any particular comparison of neural and behavioral performance. Because of this uncertainty it is necessary to consider a range of possible linking hypotheses, and to evaluate, for each linking hypothesis, how accurately the predicted behavioral performance matches the measured behavioral performance. In some situations the choice of linking hypothesis has relatively little effect on the predicted behavioral performance (e.g., assumptions about subsequent neural processing have little effect on the predictions of behavioral color matching performance based upon the spectral sensitivity of the photoreceptors). In other situations, the choice of the linking hypothesis may have a substantial effect on the predictions. In these cases, the large differences in the predictions might be sufficient to exclude some linking hypotheses.

III. WINDOW OF VISIBILITY

The stimulus for vision is completely specified by describing light intensity as a function of position, time, and wavelength. The limits of what can be seen along these dimensions define the selectivity of the visual system as a whole: the so-called *window of visibility.*

A. Space and Time: Retinal Coordinates

The window of visibility has been measured using spatiotemporal sine waves (patterns that vary sinusoidally in intensity or wavelength over space and time). Each contour in Figure 1 represents the spatiotemporal frequencies that define the window of visibility for a given luminance contrast. These curves are based upon contrast thresholds (i.e., the smallest contrast that can be reliably detected) measured at phototopic (daylight) mean luminances. All spatiotemporal frequencies that fall within a contour would be visible, and all those outside would be invisible. For example, the central pair of contours defines the set of stimuli that would be visible at 0.5% contrast, and the outer pair of contours defines the set of stimuli that

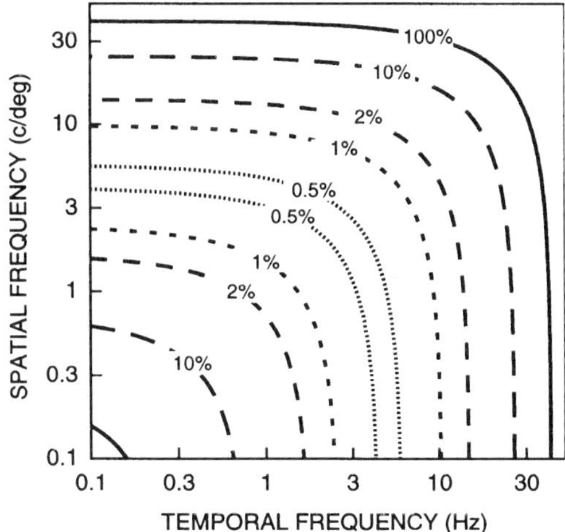

FIGURE 1 Window of visibility for spatial frequency and temporal frequency. Each contour represents the locus of stimuli that have the same contrast threshold (in percent). (Based upon Robson, 1966.)

would be visible at 100% contrast, the maximum contrast. Note that all spatiotemporal frequencies outside of the 100% contour would be invisible, regardless of contrast.

B. Space and Time: Environmental Coordinates

The contours in Figure 1 describe the overall selectivity of the visual system in retinal coordinates. Although this is a very concise and general description, it is nevertheless useful to translate these limits into environmental coordinates (i.e., into objects moving in the natural environment). Each contour in Figure 2 represents the smallest size object that can be detected at a given speed, as a function of viewing distance. For stationary objects (the lowest contour), the smallest size that can be detected increases in direct proportion to distance; at one quarter of a meter, the nearest distance for good focus, the smallest size is approximately 0.06 mm; at 100 m the smallest size is approximately 20 mm. As physical speed increases, the smallest detectable size increases (the contours shift vertically). As viewing distance increases, the effect of speed decreases (the contours converge). Finally, note that at near viewing distances the effect of speed on spatial acuity decreases at higher speeds (the contours compress).

C. Naturalistic Viewing Conditions

In the laboratory, the detectability of spatiotemporal sine waves is often measured during steady fixation, where the duration of the stimulus can be quite long. Under these conditions, there is a substantial increase in contrast threshold for low spatial

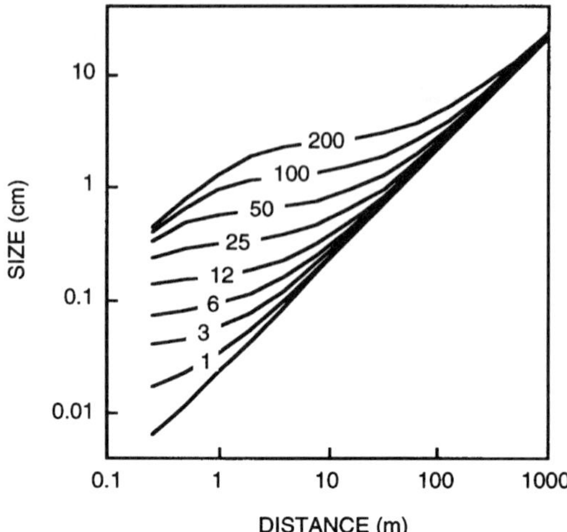

FIGURE 2 Window of visibility for size and distance. Each contour represents the locus of stimuli that have a contrast threshold of 100% for the indicated physical velocity (cm/sec). In other words, all size–distance combinations lying below a contour are invisible, even at 100% contrast, when they are moving at the physical velocity indicated on the contour.

frequencies at low temporal frequencies. However, under normal viewing conditions the eyes are almost always moving, and thus low temporal frequencies are relatively uncommon. When inspecting a static scene, the eyes jump from location to location quite frequently (saccadic eye movements), with fixation durations of approximately 200–500 ms (Carpenter, 1991). When tracking objects, the eyes move continuously (smooth pursuit eye movements), interspersed with saccadic corrections. Under these conditions, the most relevant region of the spatiotemporal visibility window is the region above 2–5 Hz (periods less than 200–500 ms). In this region there is little or no increase in threshold at low spatial frequencies. Similarly, when contrast thresholds are measured using short discrete presentations, with durations comparable to those of single fixations, there is little or no increase in threshold at low spatial frequencies (Arend, 1976; Banks, Sekuler, & Anderson, 1991; Robson & Graham, 1981). Figure 3 compares contrast threshold as a function of spatial frequency for short and long presentation durations.

D. Retinal Eccentricity, Luminance, and Color

The description of the window of visibility given above applies to stimuli centered on the point of fixation (i.e., at the fovea, on the visual axis). Although the temporal limits of visibility remain relatively constant across the entire visual field, the spatial limits decrease markedly away from the point of fixation (Wertheim, 1894). Figure 4 illustrates this decrease in spatial resolution for briefly presented stimuli; each contour represents the spatial frequencies that define the window of visibility across

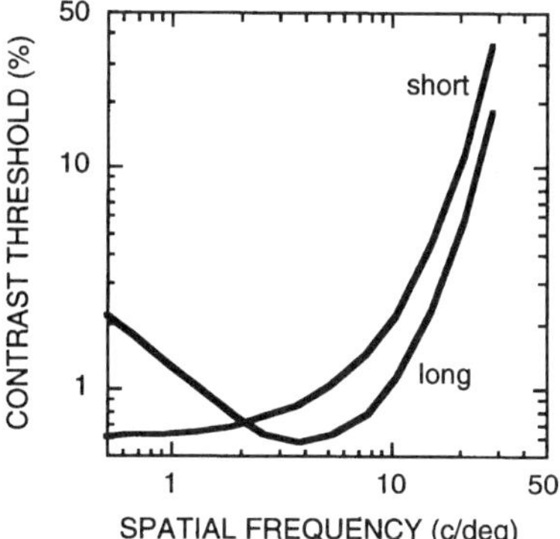

FIGURE 3 Contrast threshold as a function of spatial frequency for short- and long-duration stimuli.

the visual field for a given contrast. These contours show that 40° away from the point of fixation the spatial limit of visibility has decreased by a factor of 16 (from 37 cpd to 2.3 cpd). Because of this decrease in spatial resolution away from the line of sight, eye movements are required to bring the high-resolution region of the system onto objects of interest.

The window of visibility changes continuously with light level (mean luminance). As the light level decreases, the overall sensitivity decreases with relatively

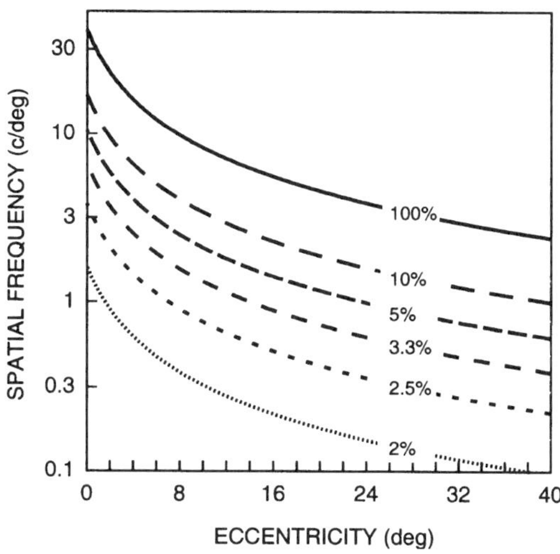

FIGURE 4 Window of visibility for spatial frequency and eccentricity. Each contour represents the locus of stimuli that have the same contrast threshold, in percent. (Based upon Robson & Graham, 1981.)

greater loss in sensitivity at high spatial and high temporal frequencies. This decrease in sensitivity translates into a significant loss in real-world performance in terms of the visibility of moving objects at different distances.

The window of visibility for purely chromatic modulations in space and time differs from the window of visibility for purely luminance modulations. In comparison to the photopic luminance contours in Figure 1, there is a loss of sensitivity at high spatial and temporal frequencies, and an increased sensitivity at low spatial and temporal frequencies; that is, no low-frequency falloff (for a review see Mullen, 1985). However, under normal viewing conditions, where the eyes are moving and very low temporal frequencies are uncommon, the spatiotemporal chromatic sensitivity will generally be less than or equal to the luminance sensitivity.

IV. OPTICS AND PHOTON NOISE

The optics of the eye (the cornea, the pupil, and the lens) form an image on the retina that is a two-dimensional projection of the three-dimensional visual environment. The size, position, and shape of the retinal image can be determined by tracing rays from points in the environment through the center of the optics (the nodal point) until they intersect the retina.

The quality of the retinal image can be summarized with a point-spread function (a spatial impulse response function), which describes the two-dimensional distribution of light produced on the retina by a single point in space (e.g., a distant star). The visual environment can be regarded as a dense collection of discrete point sources. Thus, given knowledge of the point-spread function, and the center of the optics, it is possible to determine the retinal image for any arbitrary visual scene. The light from each source produces a distribution on the retina; the shape of the distribution is given by the point-spread function, the position by ray tracing, and the amplitude by the intensity of the source. The retinal image as a whole is then determined by summing these distributions.

Equivalently, the quality of the retinal image can be summarized with an optical transfer function, which describes the change in the amplitude and the phase of spatial frequency sine waves as they pass through the optics. Within this framework, the visual scene is decomposed into a collection of spatial frequency components. The amplitude and phase of each component are adjusted according to the optical transfer function. The retinal image as a whole is then determined by summing the adjusted components.

Point spread functions and optical transfer functions have been measured in the living human eye (Campbell & Green, 1965; Charman, 1993; Westheimer & Campbell, 1962). The results of these studies have shown that the quality of the retinal image is dependent upon many different factors; for example, pupil size, state of accommodation, eccentricity, wavelength, and individual differences. The best optical quality occurs on the optic axis, in a well-accommodated eye, with pupil sizes in the range 2–3 mm (the size of the pupil under normal daytime light levels).

Under these conditions, the optical quality approaches what would be expected from an ideal optical system. Nonetheless, even under these conditions, the optics are the major factor limiting the visibility of fine spatial detail (Banks, Geisler, & Bennett, 1987; Sekiguchi, Williams, & Brainard, 1993). For example, the highest spatial frequency transmitted by the optics is in the range of 50–60 cpd, which corresponds approximately to the highest visible spatial frequency (see Figure 1). Under other conditions (e.g., off the visual axis or at low light levels), other factors become more important in limiting the visibility of fine spatial detail.

Even with a perfect optical system, the quality of the image is ultimately limited by photon noise. By way of analogy, the pattern of photons falling on the retina through time is similar to the random pattern of raindrops falling on a dry surface. Specifically, the number of photons incident at a given point in the image, in a given amount of time, is random; as the average number of photons increases the variance increases in direct proportion.

It is important to keep in mind that optics and photon noise are the first factors limiting visual processing, thus their effects are seen all along the visual pathway; for example, it is impossible to recover the fine detail that is lost due to optical blur. The information-processing limits set by any given stage of the visual system will propagate to all subsequent stages.

V. RETINA AND LATERAL GENICULATE NUCLEUS

The image formed by the optical system is transduced by the photoreceptors (cones and rods), processed by the neurons of the inner nuclear layer (horizontal, bipolar, and amacrine cells) and then transmitted to subsequent brain regions via the axons of the ganglion cells, which comprise the optic nerve. The vast majority of ganglion cell axons project to the lateral geniculate nucleus (LGN), which in turn sends most of its axons to the primary visual cortex.

A. Selectivity

The retina does not encode and transmit all of the information available in the retinal image; it is selective to a limited range of wavelengths, luminances around the mean, and temporal frequencies. Furthermore, over most of the visual field, the retina encodes a limited range of the available spatial frequencies (only in the fovea is the full range encoded). Within these broad limits, there are subpopulations of neurons that are even more selective, subdividing the information into narrower ranges.

1. Space

The optics of the eye create a high-quality retinal image over much of the visual field. However, it is not possible to encode all of the information available in the entire image, given the limited resources of the visual system. To solve this problem, the image is encoded with high resolution in the fovea and then the resolution decreases with eccentricity; eye movements are utilized to direct the fovea to points of interest. At each eccentricity, the spatial information is relayed from the retina to the visual cortex via separate and parallel neural systems, each performing a slightly different analysis.

The photoreceptors sample the retinal image at discrete locations. The cones, which are specialized for daytime light levels, are concentrated in the central retina, but present throughout the visual field. The rods, which are specialized for nighttime light levels, are more evenly distributed throughout the retina, but are absent in the fovea.

There are approximately 120 cones per degree of visual angle in the center of the fovea; this sampling density is sufficient to represent the full range of spatial frequencies transmitted by the optics (for a review see Williams, 1988). However, the sampling density of the cones decreases rapidly with eccentricity, reaching approximately 20 cones per degree, 10° away from the fovea. The optics of the eye degrade very gradually with eccentricity, and thus the peripheral cone sampling density is not sufficient to represent the full range of spatial frequencies present in the image. Further, the diameter of the cones, and hence their attenuation of high spatial frequencies, increases with eccentricity.

The responses of the cones are relayed to the cortex along a pair of parallel pathways that are first established at the level of the bipolar cell. In the central retina, the dendrites of midget bipolar cells make synaptic connections with a single cone, and the dendrites of diffuse bipolar cells make synaptic connections with a small cluster of cones. As eccentricity increases, the dendritic field diameter for both classes increases such that the ratio of the diameters between them remains approximately constant. Midget and diffuse bipolar cells appear to make synaptic connections with midget and diffuse ganglion cells. The midget ganglion cells project to the parvocellular (P) layers of the LGN, the diffuse ganglion cells to the magnocellular (M) layers. Sampling density (cells/deg) is about three times greater for the cells in the P pathway than in the M pathway, and this ratio remains approximately constant over eccentricity. The decrease in the density of M and P cells is more rapid than the decrease in the density of cones; thus, in the peripheral retina there is a further loss of high spatial frequency information, beyond that imposed by the cones.

Single neuron electrophysiological measurements of ganglion cells and LGN cells have shown that the receptive field center sizes of neurons in the P and M pathways increase with eccentricity in a fashion similar to the diameters of the dendrites of the bipolar cells. Further, the ratio of the receptive field center sizes remains approximately constant (3:1) with eccentricity. In the central retina, the receptive field center size of P cells is primarily determined by the optical point spread function, because a single P cell appears to be driven by a single cone. The diameter of the surround is approximately four to six times the size of the center, and the strength of the surround is approximately half that of the center, at all eccentricities, for both P and M cells (Croner & Kaplan, 1995; Derrington & Lennie, 1984).

Neurons in the P and M pathways are selective for spatial position and spatial frequency. The P and M pathways only encode and transmit spatial frequency information from a highly localized region of the visual field. The size of the center determines the highest spatial frequency that can be resolved (the spatial resolution), and the size of the surround determines the attenuation at lower spatial frequencies. Because the ratio of the surround size to the center size is large, and the ratio of the surround strength to the center strength is small, both P and M neurons are selective to a broad range of spatial frequencies. Because the receptive fields of M cells are larger than P cells, at any given eccentricity, the M cells are selective to an overlapping but lower band of spatial frequencies. Because the receptive field sizes of both P and M cells increase with eccentricity, their spatial frequency tuning curves shift to lower frequencies with eccentricity. In sum, for each location in space, the information transmitted to the cortex is subdivided into two spatial frequency bands by the P and M pathways.

The P and M layers of the LGN are separated by layers of very small cells, the koniocellular (K) layers (Kaas, Huerta, Weber, & Harting, 1978; for a review see Casagrande, 1994). These layers receive inputs from small ganglion cells including the bistratified ganglion cells that appear to carry chromatic information from the S (blue) cones (Dacey, 1996; for a review see Rodieck, 1998).

The responses of the rods are transmitted to the midget and diffuse ganglion cells (and hence into the P and M pathways) through a specialized sequence of neurons: the rod bipolar followed by the AII amacrine; rod responses may also be transmitted via small ganglion cells to the K layers of the LGN (for reviews see Rodieck, 1998; Sterling, 1998). Although the sampling density of the rods in the periphery is nearly as great as that of the cones in the central fovea, there is substantial spatial pooling by the bipolar and amacrine cells. The combination of dense sampling and spatial pooling optimizes sensitivity to low light levels, at the expense of decreased spatial resolution. However, this is a reasonable trade-off because, at low light levels, high spatial resolution information is not available in the stimulus due to photon noise.

2. Contrast and Luminance

Objects of interest in natural visual scenes generally consist of surfaces that are illuminated by primary light sources, such as the sun. These surfaces reflect a certain percentage of the incident light, typically 10 to 90%. Thus, to obtain useful information about the environment, the visual system must be sensitive to small reflectance differences within this range. These small reflectance differences produce small differences in luminance around a mean level. Further, a specific reflectance difference produces a specific luminance contrast independent of the mean luminance. Thus, the crucial information that must be encoded by the retina and LGN is the spatial distribution of local contrast.

During a 24-h period, the intensity of natural light outdoors varies over an enormous range, approximately 12 orders of magnitude, and thus the visual system must be able to encode small contrasts over an extraordinarily wide range of mean luminances. This poses a serious encoding problem, given the limited response range of neurons. The visual system partially solves this problem by encoding contrast information in two separate and parallel neural pathways, the rod (scotopic) and cone (photopic) systems. In addition, within each pathway, there are a variety of different adaptation mechanisms for adjusting luminance sensitivity to compensate for the variations in mean luminance.

As light level increases, the response of a photoreceptor increases linearly and then gradually saturates. In a cone, absorption of approximately 2000 photons, during a brief presentation, will produce a response equal to half the maximum; whereas in a rod, absorption of approximately 30 photons will produce a response equal to half the maximum. The temporal integration time for a cone is approximately 50 ms, and for a rod it is approximately 150 ms. The rods and the cones show only a small amount of light adaptation, except at very high light levels where photopigment depletion occurs (for reviews see Hood, 1998; Walraven, Enroth-Cugell, Hood, MacLeod, & Schnapf, 1990). These facts, combined with the known changes in pupil size with background luminance, imply that rods respond linearly up to nearly 1 cd/m^2 (a cloudy sky just after sunset) and cones respond linearly up to nearly 1,000 cd/m^2 (a cloudy sky at noon). Thus, over most of the light levels encountered in the natural environment, one of the two systems will be operating in an approximately linear range: over the scotopic range the rods respond linearly, and over most of the photopic range the cones respond linearly.

To increase sensitivity to small changes in reflectance around a given mean luminance, the bipolar and ganglion cells amplify the photoreceptor responses. (Purpura, Tranchina, Kaplan, & Shapley, 1990; Virsu & Lee, 1983). The slopes of the intensity response functions (on linear axes) for bipolar and ganglion cells are steeper than they are for the photoreceptors, and they saturate at lower intensities. For example, under dark-adapted conditions, foveal ganglion cells (both P and M) reach half their maximum response for brief presentations that produce a small number of photons absorbed by a single cone. Similarly, under dark adapted conditions, peripheral ganglion cells reach half their maximum response for brief presentations that produce less than one photon absorbed per rod. This amplification is produced through a variety of different mechanisms, which include both electrochemical mechanisms and spatial summation mechanisms. For example, there is a great deal of spatial pooling of photoreceptor responses in the peripheral ganglion cells and bipolar cells (especially over the rods).

The high amplification of photoreceptor responses seen in the ganglion cells results in saturation at relatively low intensities. Thus, light adaptation mechanisms are required in order for small changes in reflectance to be signaled at higher mean luminance levels. In general, as mean luminance increases, the adaptation mechanisms (both multiplicative and subtractive) adjust the response characteristics of post-receptor neurons so that the neurons become less sensitive to absolute intensity differences but more sensitive to relative intensity ratios (luminance contrasts).

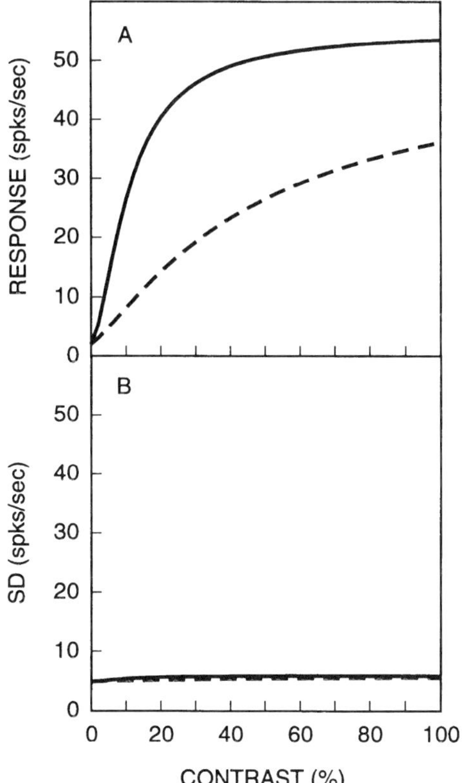

FIGURE 5 Schematic illustration of response means (A) and standard deviations (B) for magnocellular cells (solid curves) and parvocellular cells (dashed curves) as a function of the contrast of a sine wave grating. (Based upon average values reported by Croner et al., 1993, and Sclar et al., 1990.)

At higher mean luminance levels the sensitivity of the neurons to intensity ratios is constant, and there is little or no change in the maintained activity with mean luminance; thus the response to the mean luminance is largely removed. In other words, at higher mean luminances post-receptor neurons respond primarily to the contrast of the stimulus. Figure 5 shows the typical responses of M and P cells as a function of the contrast of sine wave gratings. As can be seen, M cells have higher contrast gain and larger maximum response (Kaplan & Shapley, 1986; Sclar, Maunsell, & Lennie, 1990).

Diffuse and midget bipolar cells come in two varieties, on-cells and off-cells. The responses of on-bipolars increase to increments of light on the center (white), and the responses of off-bipolars increase to decrements of light in the center (black). On-cells and off-cells make synaptic contacts with the very same cones. The separation of contrast information into on-and-off pathways, which continues up to the cortex, has a number of potential benefits. First, having two independent neurons sample in exactly the same retinal location increases sensitivity. Second, separate on and off pathways make it possible to encode increases and decreases around the mean luminance level with low maintained activity. Low maintained activity results in substantial savings in metabolic resources, and also allows the full dynamic range of a neuron to be devoted to half of the intensity range. These advantages of on and off pathways are particularly evident in the visual cortex, where the number of neurons increases dramatically and the maintained discharges are quite small.

The amount of information that can be transmitted along the visual pathway is limited by the amount of noise (random variability) in the neural responses. The noise in the neural responses is a combination of noise within the stimulus (e.g., photon noise) and noise within the nervous system (for a review see Pelli, 1990). As the intensity of the light increases, the variability in the number of photons in the retinal image increases in direct proportion to the intensity (the variance is equal to the mean). Near scotopic threshold, a small number of absorbed photons can produce a reliable response in a ganglion cell (Barlow, 1981), and thus under these stimulus conditions the effect of photon noise must be substantial. Under photopic conditions, measurements of the intensity response functions of ganglion cells have shown that although the mean of the response increases with the intensity, the variance of the response remains nearly constant (Croner, Purpura, & Kaplan, 1993)—the variance increases in proportion to the mean response with a slope of only 0.2 (see Figure 5).[2] This suggests that under most photopic conditions the neural noise is considerably larger than the photon noise, and thus it dominates, or hides, the effect of the photon noise.

3. Time

In order to react quickly to events that occur in the environment, neurons in the visual system must be able to respond quickly to changes in intensity or wavelength. The response latency of the visual system is limited by the time interval over which light is integrated: the shorter the interval, the shorter the response latency. Two of the important factors that determine the temporal integration interval are light adaptation and compensation for neural and photon noise.

As described earlier, the light adaptation mechanisms are utilized to keep neural responses within a dynamic range across variations in mean luminance. One of the mechanisms that the visual system utilizes is to shorten the temporal integration interval as mean luminance increases. The effects of this can be seen in the temporal contrast sensitivity of ganglion cells. As light level increases, the high temporal frequency resolution increases.

The amount of noise (both neural noise and photon noise) sets strong constraints on the temporal integration interval. As light level decreases, the signal-to-noise

[2] This result holds even when the analysis is restricted to increases above the maintained activity (unpublished observations).

TABLE 1 Average Constrasts of Natural Surfaces

	From the surface (%)	After the receptors (%)
Luminance	40	40
Chromatic	12	2
Increase	30	5

level in the retinal image decreases. Thus, to the extent that neural responses are dominated by photon noise, light must be summed over longer periods of time to obtain a reliable representation. In comparison to the photopic system, the scotopic system has a longer integration time, which results in slower reaction times and lower temporal frequency resolution. For example, the integration time for a rod is approximately three times longer than the integration time for a cone, the peak response occurs approximately 100 ms later, and the highest temporal frequency that can be resolved is approximately three times lower. This difference in the photopic and scotopic systems is probably due at least in part to the fact that the relative importance of photon noise (in comparison to neural noise) increases as light level decreases.

4. Color

In general, surfaces of objects in natural visual scenes differ simultaneously in both the overall amount of light that is reflected, and the relative amount of light that is reflected at different wavelengths. Thus, surface boundaries can be detected on the basis of either luminance or chromatic differences. The luminance contrast is usually quite a bit larger than the chromatic contrast.

As analysis of the responses of photoreceptors to natural scenes has shown that the amount of information available for contour detection from the luminance differences is generally much greater than the amount of information from chromatic differences (Geisler, 1995). Although the chromatic contrasts in the natural environment can be substantial, the chromatic contrasts are greatly reduced after the photoreceptors, due to the overlap of the absorption spectra of the photopigments.[3] The first two rows of Table 1 show the average chromatic and luminance contrasts that can be found in a random sample of natural surfaces at the cornea and then after the photoreceptors. The third row shows that the effective increase in total contrast due to chromatic information is only 5% after the photoreceptors. Nonetheless, chromatic information is crucial for a variety of tasks (other than contour detection), such as texture segregation, grouping, visual search, and so on. Further, spatial discriminations that are based solely upon chromatic differences can be quite good when the chromatic contrasts are high (for a review see De Valois, 1994).

[3] The overlap of absorption spectra of the long and middle wavelength cones reduces the possibility of undersampling the retinal image, and it also reduces the effects of chromatic aberration.

The major goal of color vision is to help identify objects and materials on the basis of the spectral reflectance of surfaces. Unfortunately, the distribution of wavelengths that reaches the eye is the product of the spectral distribution of the surface reflectance and the light source. Furthermore, the eye contains only three classes of cone, each selective to a different band of wavelengths. Nonetheless, the visual system is often able to determine the approximate spectral reflectance of the surfaces because the spectral distributions of natural surface reflectances can be characterized quite well with only three parameters, and because in any given scene the light source remains relatively constant over all of the different surfaces. Although the light source is not known, it can be estimated by comparison of the photoreceptor responses from the different surfaces. (For example, retinal adaptation mechanisms help to compensate for the light source by averaging the reflected light over many fixations). Thus, three classes of photoreceptor are often sufficient to estimate approximately the spectral reflectance of the surface. (For a general discussion of the issues see Wandell, 1995.)

The neurons in the P pathway carry both luminance and chromatic information. Most P cells are chromatically opponent across space, with their centers dominated by one range of wavelengths and their surrounds by another. In comparison, the M cells carry primarily luminance information. Most M cells are not chromatically opponent across space; their centers and surrounds are dominated by the same range of wavelengths. Recent evidence suggests that the koniocellular pathway plays an important role in color vision (Dacey, 1996; De Valois & De Valois, Chapter 4, this volume; Rodieck, 1998).

B. Performance

All of the visual information extracted by the eye is represented in the responses of the retinal ganglion cells, which number approximately one million in each eye. However, this same information is represented in the responses of 200 to 500 million neurons at the level of the primary visual cortex. Thus, a reasonable hypothesis would be that much of the information contained in the ganglion cell responses is reliably represented in the primary visual cortex, and hence that much of the information lost during visual processing is lost in those anatomical and physiological mechanisms lying between the cornea and the optic nerve. In other words, it would seem plausible that optical and retinal mechanisms are the major factors limiting visual performance in many tasks. The evidence suggests that, indeed, optical and retinal mechanisms are dominant for some basic visual tasks, such as pattern detection against uniform backgrounds. However, the evidence also suggests that cortical mechanisms become major limiting factors in other basic visual tasks, such as pattern discrimination and identification.

As described earlier, a Bayesian ideal-observer model can serve as a useful linking hypothesis for evaluating how anatomical and physiological mechanisms (as well as the physical properties of the stimulus) limit behavioral performance (e.g.,

Geisler, 1989). An ideal observer analysis consists of three components: (a) a precise physical description of the stimuli; (b) a description of how the stimuli are modified by the relevant anatomical and physiological mechanisms; and (c) an optimal decision rule for the specific task under consideration. Such an ideal observer specifies the best possible performance that could be obtained given the stimuli, the task, and the mechanisms included in the analysis. The difference in performance between the human and ideal observers is a precise measure of the information lost in the nervous system following the anatomical and physiological mechanisms included in the ideal-observer analysis. The degree to which human performance is predicted by the ideal observer shows the degree to which overall visual performance is limited by the physical properties of the stimuli and by the anatomical and physiological mechanisms included in the ideal observer.

Ideal-observer analyses have suggested that optical and retinal factors are largely responsible for limiting the detectability of sine wave stimuli along the dimensions of spatial frequency, eccentricity, and wavelength (Arnow & Geisler, 1996; Banks et al., 1987; Banks et al., 1991; Sekiguchi et al., 1993). For example, Arnow and Geisler (1996) compared the detection performance of an ideal observer, which incorporated optical and retinal factors, to the detection performance of humans, for the dimensions of spatial frequency, eccentricity, and target size. The optics were represented using the point-spread function reported by Campbell and Gubisch (1966) for a 3-mm pupil. The retinal factors were represented by current estimates of the properties of retinal ganglion cells. The sampling density of the ganglion cells was taken from the measurements of Curcio and Allen (1990) for the adult human retina. Based upon electrophysiological studies in the monkey (Croner & Kaplan, 1995; Derrington & Lennie, 1984), the center diameter of the receptive field was made equal to the spacing between the ganglion cells; the surround diameter was six times the diameter of the center; and the surround strength was 75% of the center strength. Only the P cells were included in the analysis because of evidence from lesion studies that M cells contribute little to sine wave grating thresholds in monkeys except for low spatial frequencies presented at high temporal frequencies (Merigan & Maunsell, 1993).[4]

The symbols in Figure 6 (connected by dashed lines) show the contrast threshold data reported by Robson and Graham (1981), and the solid curves show the performance of the ideal observer. The symbols connected by dashed lines plot contrast sensitivity (1/contrast threshold) as a function of retinal eccentricity for five different spatial frequencies. The grating target width decreased with spatial frequency such that the target contained four cycles, and the length was set equal to

[4] Two relevant properties of the neural responses in the cortex were also included in the analysis. First, near detection threshold cortical cell responses grow with contrast according to a power function with an exponent that averages 2.5 in the monkey. Thus, an exponent of 2.5 was applied to the final output. Second, the variance of cortical cell responses increases in proportion to the mean response with a proportionality constant of 1.5 (the average for neurons in primary visual cortex). Thus, the variance of the final output was made equal to the mean times 1.5.

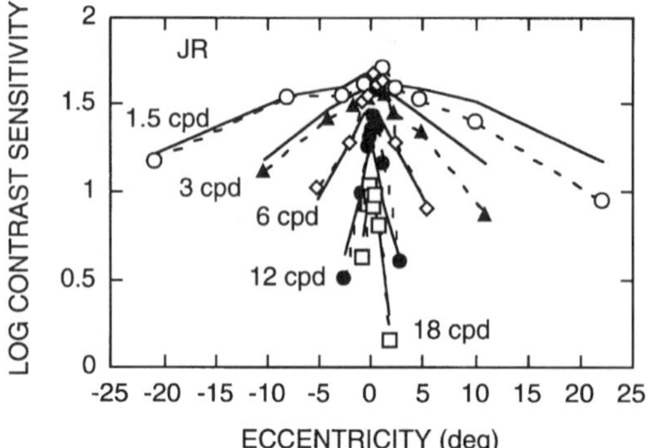

FIGURE 6 Contrast sensitivity as a function of eccentricity and spatial frequency for a briefly presented target with a width and height of four cycles. The symbols connected by dashed lines show the measured contrast sensitivity for a single observer (JR). The solid curves show the ideal-observer predictions incorporating optical and retinal factors. (Data from Robson & Graham, 1981.)

the width. The symbols in Figure 7 plot contrast sensitivity as a function of target size for three different spatial frequencies; the left panel is for targets located in the fovea, and the right panel is for targets located in the periphery. The solid curves show the predictions of the ideal observer.

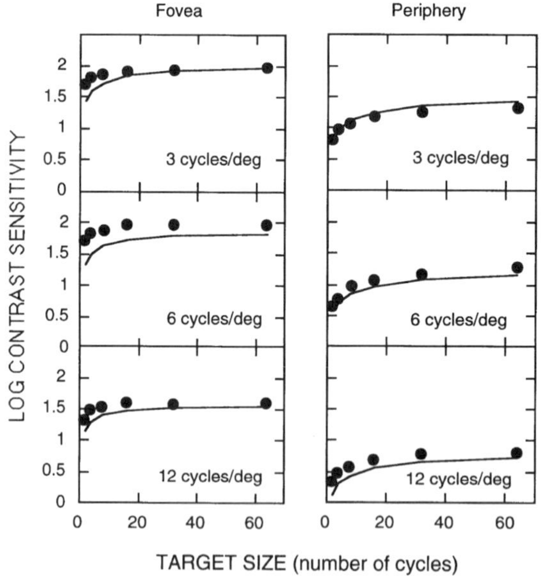

FIGURE 7 Contrast sensitivity as a function of target size and spatial frequency for briefly presented targets in the fovea and in the periphery (42 periods from the fovea). The symbols show the measured contrast sensitivity for a single observer. The solid curves show the ideal-observer predictions incorporating optical and retinal factors. (Data from Robson & Graham, 1981.)

As noted above, the performance of the ideal observer was based upon current anatomical and physiological measurements with only one free scaling parameter, and thus the close correspondence between the human and ideal performance suggests that the visibility window for the dimensions of spatial frequency and eccentricity is largely determined by optical and retinal factors.

VI. PRIMARY VISUAL CORTEX

The output neurons of the LGN project to the primary visual cortex.[5] The number of neurons in the primary visual cortex is on the order of 200 to 500 times greater than the number of neurons projecting from the LGN. Thus, it would be possible (according to sampling theory) to have 200 to 500 complete, yet different, independent representations of all of the information contained in the LGN output. In spite of this incredible potential for representing all of the information, some information is lost due to various nonlinear mechanisms, such as response expansion and contrast gain control. Although these nonlinear mechanisms limit suprathreshold discrimination performance, they nevertheless enhance and maintain the stimulus selectivity of cortical cells. We will argue that these nonlinearities play an essential role in higher level processes, such as object recognition.

In addition to the nonlinearities, it is crucial to consider the variability of the neural responses because noise characteristics also play an important role in determining performance.

A. Selectivity

Single neuron electrophysiology has shown that neurons in the primary visual cortex generally respond to a narrower range of stimuli than neurons in the retina and LGN (De Valois, Albrecht, & Thorell, 1982; De Valois, Yund, & Hepler, 1982; Hubel & Wiesel, 1962, 1968; Movshon, Thompson, & Tolhurst, 1978a,b,c). Among other things, it has been shown that they are often simultaneously selective along the dimensions of spatial position, orientation, spatial frequency, contrast, temporal frequency, direction of motion, and color. Selectivity along these fundamental dimensions makes it possible for the visual cortex to represent the position, size, and orientation of the local image structure produced by surfaces and objects in the environment. Because most cortical neurons are simultaneously selective along many dimensions, a typical cortical neuron is generally much less active than a neuron in the retina or the LGN. For example, during normal saccadic inspection of a

[5] The P, M, and K cell projections terminate in separate target regions; however, the clear segregation maintained in the retina, the LGN, and these cortical regions is more difficult to discern in the subsequent neural circuitry (for a review see, Callaway, 1998). Nonetheless, there is some evidence for functionally different pathways in the primary visual cortex and in extrastriate visual cortical areas that are linked to these pathways originating in the retina and LGN (Felleman & Van Essen, 1991; Merigan & Maunsell, 1993; Van Essen & DeYoe, 1994).

complex natural scene, a large fraction of the ganglion cells and LGN cells would respond during each fixation because of their broad tuning in space and time, whereas only a very small fraction of cortical cells would respond during a single fixation.

The selectivity of neurons in the visual pathway has often been characterized in terms of linear mechanisms which perform simple addition and subtraction of the light falling on the receptive field (Enroth-Cugell & Robson, 1966; Hartline, 1974; Rodieck, 1965). The receptive field map indicates the magnitude of the excitatory and the inhibitory responses of the cell to a spot of light placed at each location within the receptive field. To the extent that the neuron is linear, it is then possible to predict the neuron's response to arbitrary spatial patterns of light from this map. This is because an arbitrary spatial pattern can be decomposed into small spots of light and then the total response of the neuron can be found by adding up the responses to each of the small spots according to the weights given by the receptive field map. These linear models have been able to account quantitatively for many of the response properties of visual neurons.

However, there are a number of response properties of neurons in the primary visual cortex that can only be explained by nonlinear mechanisms. For example, it is well established that the neurons which Hubel and Wiesel classified as "complex cells" cannot be described by simple addition and subtraction of the light falling on the receptive field (Skottun et al., 1991). For these cells, it is not possible to predict the responses to arbitrary spatial patterns from the receptive field map. In general, complex cells show excitatory responses to small spots of light everywhere within the receptive field, and thus one would predict that the best stimulus would be a uniform distribution of light covering the receptive field. However, this pattern produces little or no response. The optimal stimulus is typically an oriented bar that is much narrower than the width of the receptive field map; further, the bar will generally produce a large response no matter where it is positioned within the receptive field.

In comparison to complex cells, the neurons classified by Hubel and Wiesel as "simple cells" are better characterized by linear mechanisms, in that it is possible to qualitatively predict the optimal stimulus based upon the receptive field map. Nevertheless, simple cells display several fundamental nonlinear response properties. Further, these nonlinear response properties are also observed in complex cells. First, the responses of cortical neurons as a function of stimulus contrast are nonlinear (Albrecht & Hamilton, 1982): at low contrasts the responses increase with a power function exponent greater than one, and at high contrasts the responses approach an asymptotic maximum (that is, the responses saturate at a maximum value). Second, the response saturation generally occurs at the same contrast for all stimuli (both optimal and nonoptimal); as a consequence, the asymptotic response maximum is different for optimal and nonoptimal stimuli, even though the power function exponent remains the same (Albrecht & Hamilton, 1982). Third, most cortical cells have little or no maintained spontaneous discharge and thus the effects of inhibitory stimuli cannot be directly observed (i.e., the responses are rectified).

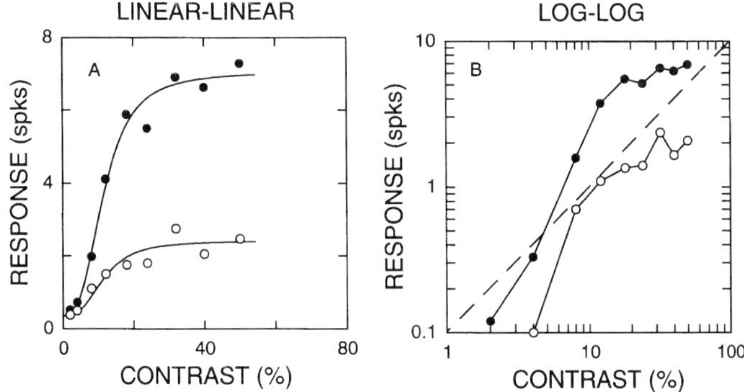

FIGURE 8 Contrast response functions of a typical monkey cortical cell for an optimal stimulus (solid circles) and for a nonoptimal stimulus (open circles) plotted in linear coordinates (A) and in logarithmic coordinates (B).

These nonlinear properties have a profound effect in determining the selectivity of simple and complex cortical cells.

1. Contrast

As noted above, a specific reflectance difference in the natural environment produces a constant luminance contrast independent of the level of the illumination. Thus, the crucial information that must be encoded is the spatial distribution of local contrast. Cortical neurons are selective to local contrast; this selectivity is the culmination of a process begun in the retina.

a. Nonlinearities

The response of a typical cortical cell as function of stimulus contrast is plotted in linear coordinates in Figure 8A and in logarithmic coordinates in Figure 8B. As the stimulus contrast increases, the response increases rapidly in the range of 0 to 10% and then reaches a maximum saturated response beyond 15%. The contrast at which the response reaches half of the maximum value, the "half-saturation contrast," is approximately 7% for this cell. Across the population of cells as a whole, the half-saturation contrast varies over the full range of possible values, with some cells saturating at a contrast as low as 5% and others saturating beyond 50%, with a median value of approximately 30%.

Figure 9A shows the responses of a cortical neuron as a function of stimulus contrast measured for five different spatial frequencies. Note that the responses saturate at different levels depending upon the spatial frequency of the stimulus. For example, the response saturates at 10 spikes/second for the optimal spatial frequency of 4.0 cycles/degree but saturates at 3 spikes/second for the nonoptimal spatial frequency of 1.5 cycles/degree. On the other hand, the half-saturation contrast remains approximately constant for the different spatial frequencies. These response

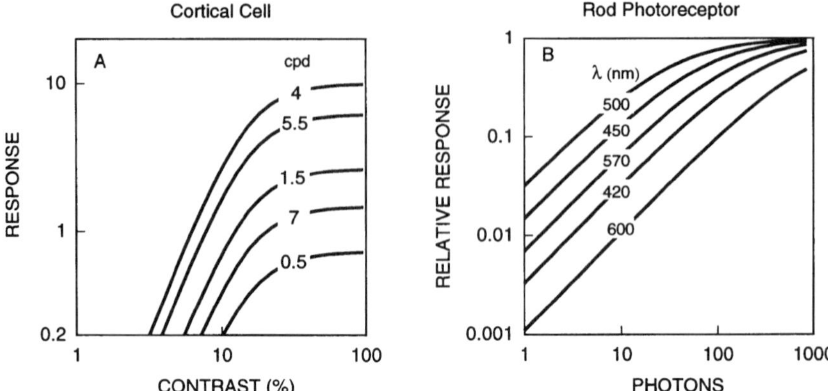

FIGURE 9 Schematic illustrations of response functions of a cortical cell for different spatial frequencies and of a rod photoreceptor for different wavelengths.

properties are not what would be expected from simple response saturation or compression of the type often found in sensory neurons and routinely proposed in psychophysical models. Simple response saturation often reflects some neurophysiological limit, such as the maximum level of depolarization, or the maximum spike rate. For example, the response saturation observed in photoreceptors is quite different from that observed in cortical cells. Figure 9B illustrates the responses of a photoreceptor as a function of intensity for several different wavelengths of light. Note that, unlike cortical cells, the responses saturate at the *same* level for all of the different wavelengths and that the half-saturation intensity *changes* with wavelength.

The nonlinear saturation observed in the photoreceptors is determined by a limit in the maximum response (a hyperpolarization limit); this type of saturation, "response saturation," has negative consequences for color selectivity, as well as color identification and discrimination. At high intensities, nonoptimal wavelengths (those away from the peak of the spectral-sensitivity function) produce the same maximum response as near optimal wavelengths. In comparison, the nonlinear saturation observed in cortical neurons is not determined by a limit in the maximum response rate, but instead is determined by the local contrast. This type of saturation, "contrast saturation," has a number of beneficial consequences for stimulus selectivity, as well as for identification and discrimination performance, because only near optimal stimuli can produce the maximum response. With contrast saturation, the selectivities along all the various stimulus dimensions remain invariant with contrast.

Interestingly, note that the responses shown in Figures 8 and 9A do not increase in a linear fashion even at low contrasts, but instead increase in a nonlinear accelerating fashion. As illustrated by the dashed line in Figure 8B, a linear relationship appears as a straight line with a slope of 1.0, when plotted in log-log coordinates (a power function with an exponent, or power, equal to 1.0). However, the measured responses follow a line with a slope closer to 3.0 (a power function with an exponent equal to 3.0). Across cells, the slope, or power function exponent, varies over a wide range, from less than 1.0 to greater than 5.0, with a median value of 2.5 (Albrecht & Hamilton, 1982; Geisler & Albrecht, 1997; Sclar, Maunsell, & Lennie, 1990). This accelerating nonlinearity enhances stimulus selectivity and eases the structural requirements for producing high degrees of selectivity. For example, high degrees of orientation tuning can be obtained with relatively short receptive fields. This accelerating nonlinearity also has beneficial consequences for discrimination and identification performance because responses to near optimal stimuli are enhanced relative to the responses to nonoptimal stimuli.[6]

In sum, measurements of the contrast response function at different spatial frequencies (and other stimulus dimensions) have revealed two important nonlinear characteristics of cortical neurons: a saturation controlled by the local contrast that manages to preserve stimulus selectivity, and an accelerating response (revealed at low contrasts) which enhances stimulus selectivity. There is considerable evidence that the saturation is produced by a contrast normalization network (Albrecht & Geisler, 1991, 1994; Albrecht & Hamilton, 1982; Bonds, 1991; Carandini & Heeger, 1994; Geisler & Albrecht, 1997; Heeger, 1992b; Li & Creutzfeldt, 1984; Robson, 1991; Sclar & Freeman, 1982; Tolhurst & Heeger, 1997) and that the accelerating response is due to a final expansive response exponent (Albrecht & Geisler, 1991, 1994; Albrecht & Hamilton, 1982; DeAngelis, Ohzawa, & Freeman, 1993; Geisler & Albrecht, 1997; Heeger, 1992a; McLean & Palmer, 1994; Sclar et al., 1990).

b. Variability

Visual performance is limited by the amount of noise (random variability) in the neural responses. Unlike the retina and LGN, the variability of cortical neuron responses increases substantially as the magnitude of the responses increases. Figure 10A illustrates the change in both the mean and the variability of the response as a function of contrast for a typical cortical neuron; the measurements are shown for an optimal and a nonoptimal spatial frequency. Note that as the response increases the variability increases in a parallel fashion. Further, the magnitude of the variability is not determined by the magnitude of the contrast, per se, but rather by the magnitude of the response; thus, the variability is smaller for a nonoptimal stimulus, even at very high contrasts. Systematic measurements from many different laboratories are consistent with the hypothesis (represented by the solid curves in Figure 10A) that the variance of the response is directly proportional to the mean of the response (Geisler & Albrecht, 1995, 1997; Snowden, Treue, & Andersen, 1992; Softky & Koch, 1993; Tolhurst, Movshon, & Dean, 1983; Vogels, Spileers, & Orban, 1989).

2. Spatial Frequency

The selectivity of cortical cells to stimulus size has been quantitatively investigated by varying the spatial frequency of sinusoidal grating stimuli (for general reviews

[6] Current evidence suggests that this accelerating power function exponent could be a consequence of a nonlinear relationship between the intracellular voltage and the number of action potentials (see Figure 1, McCormick, Connors, Lighthall, & Prince, 1985).

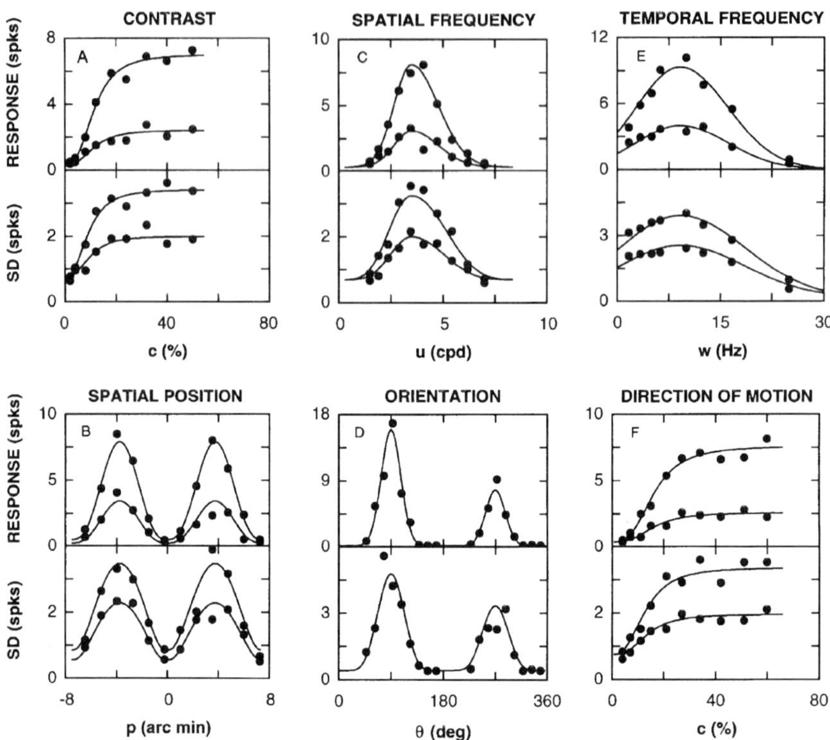

FIGURE 10 Response means and standard deviations of representative neurons recorded from the primate visual cortex, along six stimulus dimensions for stimulus durations of 200 ms. (Taken from Geisler and Albrecht, 1997.)

see De Valois & De Valois, 1990; Palmer, Jones, & Stepnoski, 1991). Figure 10C shows the mean and the variability of the response of a typical cell as a function of spatial frequency; the measurements are shown for a low contrast and a saturating contrast. This neuron responds best to a spatial frequency of 4.0 cpd. The optimal (critical) spatial frequency varies widely across neurons, even for those neurons sampling the same location in visual space; the physiological range of critical frequencies is roughly consistent with the behavioral range of detectable frequencies.

As is typical of cortical cells, the neuron shown in Figure 10C responds to only a limited range of spatial frequencies (approximately 2.5–5.0 cpd at half-height). This range of spatial frequencies corresponds to a bandwidth of 1.2 octaves. There is considerable heterogeneity in the bandwidth across cells, from less than 0.7 octaves to greater than 3.0 octaves. The average bandwidth reported in the literature is approximately 1.5 octaves. This average bandwidth is smaller than the average bandwidth of ganglion cells or LGN cells (3 to 5 octaves) and corresponds to only a small portion of the overall behavioral range (for a general review see Shapley & Lennie, 1985).

The spatial frequency tuning of cortical cells remains relatively invariant when measured at different contrasts. Remarkably, even at saturating contrasts the critical frequency and the bandwidth do not change. For example, the solid curves in the upper panel of Figure 10C have the same critical frequency and bandwidth; they only differ by a scale factor. As described above (see section VI.A.1.a), this contrast-invariant tuning is consistent with a saturation that is determined by the local contrast (a contrast normalization mechanism).

The spatial response properties of cortical cells have been characterized by measuring spatial frequency tuning functions and receptive field maps. If the spatial response properties were the result of simple summation of excitation and inhibition then the two characterizations would be equivalent (one would be the Fourier transform of the other). Cells with broad spatial frequency tuning would be expected to have receptive field maps with only a few excitatory and inhibitory regions, whereas cells with narrow tuning would be expected to have maps with many excitatory and inhibitory regions. Although this is approximately true for some cells, for many cells the receptive field maps have fewer excitatory and inhibitory regions than would be expected from their spatial frequency tuning.

This mismatch could potentially be accounted for by the expansive nonlinearity revealed in measurements of the contrast response function (see section VI.A.1.a). An expansive nonlinearity simultaneously narrows the spatial frequency tuning and reduces the number of excitatory and inhibitory regions in the receptive field map. The solid curves in Figure 11 show the receptive field map (A) and the spatial frequency tuning (B) of a hypothetical linear cortical neuron which performs simple

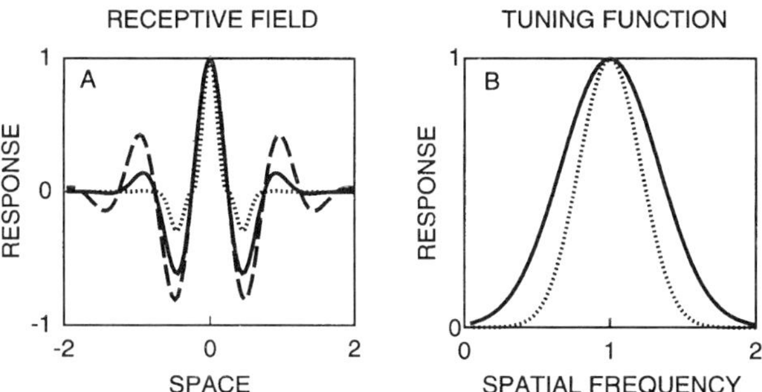

FIGURE 11 The effect of an expansive response exponent on the receptive field map and the spatial frequency tuning function. The solid curves show the receptive field map (A) and the corresponding spatial frequency tuning function expected given a linear receptive field (B). The dotted curves show the effect of an expansive response exponent of 2.5 on the receptive field map and tuning function. The dashed curve in A shows the receptive field predicted (dotted curve) in B under the assumption of linearity. The difference between the dashed and dotted curves in A shows the expected mismatch between the receptive field map measured in the space domain and the one predicted from measurements of the tuning function in the frequency domain.

summation of excitation and inhibition. The dotted curves show the receptive field map and the spatial frequency tuning function that would be measured given an expansive exponent of 2.5. If the spatial frequency tuning indicated by the dotted curve in 11B were measured in an experiment, then the receptive field map, predicted given linear summation of excitation and inhibition, would be the dashed curve in 11A. This figure demonstrates that because of the expansive nonlinearity, high degrees of spatial frequency selectivity can be obtained with a structurally simple receptive field.

Note that the variability of the response, as a function of spatial frequency, for the cell shown in 10C, mirrors the mean of the response. This is a consequence of the fact that the variance increases in direct proportion to the mean; the solid curves through the mean and variance data were generated under the hypothesis that the variance is proportional to the mean.

3. Orientation

Figure 10D shows the mean and the variability of the response of a typical cell as a function of orientation; the measurements are shown for two directions of motion. As Hubel and Wiesel (1962, 1968) first demonstrated, the optimal (critical) orientation differs from cell to cell, and is distributed across the full range (De Valois, Albrecht, & Thorell, 1982). The orientation bandwidth for this cell is 22°. The orientation bandwidth also differs from cell to cell; the average bandwidth is 40°. Like spatial frequency tuning, orientation tuning remains relatively invariant with contrast; this is true even at contrasts which produce response saturation (Sclar & Freeman, 1982). The degree of orientation tuning is determined by the elongation of the receptive field; the greater the length, the smaller the orientation bandwidth. However, for many cells, the receptive field maps are shorter than what would be expected from their orientation tuning. Once again, this mismatch could potentially be accounted for by an expansive nonlinearity (see section VI.A.1.a), which narrows the measured orientation tuning without requiring a longer receptive field. The solid curves through the mean and variance data were generated under the hypothesis that the variance is proportional to the mean.

4. Position

The selectivity of cortical cells to spatial position has been quantitatively investigated by varying the phase, or position, of spatial frequency stimuli (De Valois, Albrecht, & Thorell, 1982; Movshon et al., 1978c). Figure 10B shows the mean and the variability of the response of a typical cell as a function of the spatial position of a grating pattern that was turned on and off, reversing in contrast. The optimal position differs from cell to cell, such that the population of cells as a whole covers the entire visual field. The width of the position tuning function at half-height, for the cell shown in Figure 10B, is approximately 4 min of arc. The width varies depending upon the cell's receptive field as well as the spatial frequency of the stimulus. Like spatial frequency and orientation, the spatial position tuning remains invariant with contrast (Albrecht & Geisler, 1991). If the spatial response properties were the result of simple summation of excitation and inhibition, then the spatial position tuning functions should be exactly sinusoidal in shape (Enroth-Cugell & Robson, 1966; Hochstein & Shapley, 1976). Although the functions appear approximately sinusoidal, they are in fact narrower than would be expected, and are more similar to a sine wave taken to an exponent greater than one. Again, this could potentially be accounted for by an expansive nonlinearity and is, in fact, converging evidence for the existence of such a nonlinearity. Comparable to other stimulus dimensions, the effect of the expansive nonlinearity is to enhance selectivity, in this case position selectivity. The solid curves through the mean and variance data were generated under the hypothesis that the variance is proportional to the mean.

5. Temporal Frequency

The temporal integration properties of cortical cells have been quantitatively investigated by varying the temporal frequency of sine wave grating patterns (Foster, Gaska, Nagler, & Pollen, 1985; Hamilton, Albrecht, & Geisler, 1989; Hawken, Shapley, & Grosof, 1996; Movshon et al., 1978b). Figure 10E shows the mean and the variability of the response of a typical cell as a function of the temporal frequency of a drifting sine wave grating with the optimal spatial frequency and orientation; the measurements are shown for a low contrast and a saturating contrast. This neuron responds best to a temporal frequency of 8.0 Hz. The optimal (critical) temporal frequency varies across neurons. The physiological range of temporal frequency tuning measured in the cortex is roughly consistent with the behavioral range of detectable frequencies. In general, temporal frequency tuning is relatively broad in comparison to spatial frequency tuning, with nearly half of the cells showing little or no attenuation to frequencies as low as 0.25 Hz. For those cells that do show low-frequency attenuation, the average bandwidth is approximately 3.0 octaves at half-height. The bandwidth for the cell in Figure 10E is 3.1 octaves. The solid curves through the mean and variance data were generated under the hypothesis that the variance is proportional to the mean.[7]

6. Direction of Motion

Many of the cells in the primary visual cortex are selective for the direction of stimulus motion (Hubel & Wiesel, 1962, 1968). M and P cells in the retina and LGN

[7] Unlike the other dimensions, the tuning function for temporal frequency changes shape somewhat with contrast. As contrast increases, the critical frequency increases, and the temporal phase of the response decreases (Albrecht, 1995; Carandini & Heeger, 1994; Reid, Victor, & Shapley, 1992). Similar effects are observed in the retina (Shapley & Victor, 1978) and LGN (Sclar, 1987). These effects are consistent with what could be expected from a dynamic contrast normalization mechanism. Also, unlike the other dimensions, the variance proportionality constant is affected by temporal frequency: the value of the constant increases at lower temporal frequencies (see Appendix B, Geisler & Albrecht, 1997).

are not direction selective; the visual cortex is the first level in which direction-selective neurons are found. Figure 10F shows the responses of a representative single neuron as a function of contrast for a sine wave grating moving in the optimal and the nonoptimal directions. In the optimal direction the average maximum response was 7.5 spikes (in 200 ms); in the nonoptimal direction the average maximum was 2.5 spikes. The response in the preferred direction is approximately 2.5 times larger than the response in the nonpreferred direction, and this ratio remains the same at all contrasts, even in the saturated region. The solid curves through the mean and the variance data were generated under the hypothesis that the variance is proportional to the mean.

The degree of direction selectivity varies from cell to cell. For approximately 30% of simple cells and complex cells the magnitude of the response in the preferred direction is more than twice the magnitude of the response in the nonpreferred direction (De Valois, Yund, & Hepler, 1982). The average direction selectivity for the population as a whole (one minus the ratio of the nonpreferred to preferred response) is slightly less than 0.5.

Barlow and Levick (1965) demonstrated that direction selectivity could be produced by neural summation of inputs that are displaced in space and delayed in time. Others have described direction selectivity in terms of "spatiotemporal" receptive fields, where one axis represents space and the other axis represents time (e.g., Adelson & Bergen, 1985; Watson & Ahumada, 1985). They demonstrated that direction selectivity can be obtained through strictly linear summation of excitation and inhibition over the spatiotemporal receptive field. The degree of direction selectivity is determined by the degree to which the spatiotemporal receptive field has a single dominant orientation off the temporal axis. The dominant orientation determines the preferred direction of motion.

It has been shown that the spatiotemporal orientation of the receptive fields measured in the visual cortex correctly predicts the preferred direction of motion. However, there is a mismatch between the spatiotemporal receptive field and the degree of direction selectivity, which is greatly reduced when the response exponent is taken into consideration (DeAngelis et al., 1993; McLean & Palmer, 1989; McLean, Raab, & Palmer, 1994). Although high degrees of direction selectivity require rather precise wiring in space and time, cortical cells apparently achieve high degrees of direction selectivity by combining a less precise receptive field structure with an expansive response exponent (Albrecht & Geisler, 1991, 1994).

7. Surround Suppression and Facilitation

The responses of cortical neurons are often affected by stimuli which fall outside of the classical receptive field (e.g., De Valois, Thorell, & Albrecht, 1985; DeAngelis, Freeman, & Ohzawa, 1994; Gilbert & Wiesel, 1990; Levitt & Lund, 1997; Li & Li, 1994; Sengpiel, Baddeley, Freeman, Harrad, & Blakemore, 1998; Sillito, Grieve, Jones, Cudiero, & Davis, 1995; Zipser, Lamme, & Schiller, 1996). The classical receptive field is defined operationally; typically, a small patch of grating (of the optimal spatial frequency, orientation, and direction of motion) is centered on the receptive field and then expanded in size until the response of the neuron increases no further. Stimuli presented outside of the classical receptive field produce little or no response when presented alone. However, when presented in conjunction with stimuli inside the classical receptive field, surround stimulation can sometimes suppress or facilitate responses. The magnitude and sign of the effect vary from cell to cell and depend upon a variety of different stimulus factors (e.g., contrast, orientation, spatial frequency). In general, the magnitude of the reduction in response that is produced by the suppressive effect varies across cells from 0 to 100%, with an average value of approximately 30%. Facilitatory effects have been observed less frequently and are generally smaller in magnitude. There have been many different suggestions for the role of these surround effects in cortical functioning (e.g., gain control, texture segregation, etc.). Nonetheless, at this point in time, it appears as though the responses of V1 cortical cells are dominated by the effects of stimulation within the classical receptive field and modulated by the effects of stimulation within the surround.

8. Continuous and Heterogeneous Distribution of Properties

The neurons illustrated in Figure 10 are representative of neurons in the primate visual cortex. However, there is a great deal of heterogeneity from cell to cell: the cells vary widely in their particular preferences along all of the stimulus dimensions. For example, each cell has a different preferred orientation, spatial frequency, temporal frequency, direction of motion, and spatial phase. The bandwidths of the cells also vary along all of the stimulus dimensions. In addition, there is a great deal of heterogeneity from cell to cell in the contrast response function, the maximum firing rate, the spontaneous firing rate, the noise characteristics, the color tuning, the AC/DC index (for the simple–complex dimension) and so on.

Throughout the history of vision science there has been a tendency to organize the complexity of the visual system by segregating and classifying neural mechanisms into a small manageable number of discrete types: four types of photoreceptors, three types of opponent mechanisms (two color and one luminance), two spatial phase pathways (on and off pathways), P and M pathways, simple and complex cells, discrete spatial frequency tunnel channels, sustained and transient temporal channels, direction-selective and nondirection-selective cells, and so on. Although such simple taxonomies may be appropriate for classifying the various mechanisms in the retina and LGN, they seem less appropriate at the level of the visual cortex, where the properties of the neurons are heterogeneous and distributed continuously.

However, even though the properties of cortical neurons are heterogeneous and distributed continuously, the neurons are very regular in a certain way. For example, their tuning functions and contrast response functions generally have a characteristic shape. Thus, in general, it is possible to summarize the stimulus–response relationships of each cortical cell using a small set of relatively simple descriptive functions, where each descriptive function has only a few free parameters. For example, Geisler and Albrecht (1997) found that a set of simple descriptive functions could account for approximately 90% of the variation in both the means and standard deviations of cortical cell responses (across a large population of neurons in both monkey and cat), for the dimensions of contrast, spatial frequency, spatial position, temporal frequency, orientation, and direction of motion. This suggests that a better way to organize the complexity of cortical neurons might be based upon the frequency distributions of the various cell properties.

9. Contrast–Gain Exponent Model

The response properties of cortical cells described in the sections above can be summarized with the model illustrated in Figure 12 (see also, Albrecht & Geisler, 1991; Geisler & Albrecht, 1997; Heeger, 1991, 1992a,b). The model consists of four components: (a) a linear filter, which establishes the neuron's stimulus selectivity, (b) a contrast normalization mechanism, which maintains selectivity in spite of response saturation, (c) an expansive nonlinearity, which enhances selectivity, and (d) a noise source, which makes the variance proportional to the mean. This figure shows the hypothesized processing, as a function of contrast, for two different sinusoidal stimuli; one that is optimal for the cell (the solid curves) and one that is nonoptimal (the dashed curves). The nonoptimal stimulus could be nonoptimal along any dimension (e.g., spatial frequency, orientation, position, direction of motion, etc.). The four upper boxes represent the four major stages of the model. The five lower boxes illustrate contrast response functions measured before and after each stage.

Measured at the input, the amplitude of the sinusoidal stimulus increases in proportion to contrast, by definition. If amplitude and contrast are plotted on log–

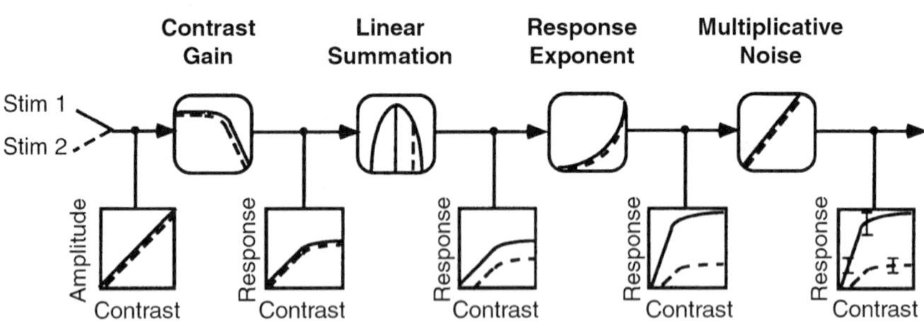

FIGURE 12 Contrast-Gain/Exponent (CGE) model of cortical cell responses. This model applies to both simple and complex cells; however, for complex cells, two or more rectified linear filter outputs are summed before the response exponent.

log coordinates, as they are here, the slope is 1.0. Next, the contrast normalization mechanism (contrast gain) scales the input amplitude by a factor that decreases with increasing contrast. This is a fast-acting gain control which is set by the local spatiotemporal contrast. Thus, the gain does *not* depend upon the response rate of the cell. As a consequence, both the optimal and nonoptimal stimulus are attenuated equally. According to this model, response saturation occurs because at higher contrasts the decrease in gain cancels the increase in input amplitude.

Next, the gain-adjusted signals are passed through a linear filter (summation of excitation and inhibition), which gives the cell its fundamental selectivities. The response to the nonoptimal stimulus, Stim 2, is attenuated more than that to the optimal stimulus, Stim 1. Next, the response exponent takes the output of the linear filter, or filters (after half-wave rectification) to an exponent greater than 1.0. Note that the exponent does not eliminate response saturation, but it does increase the stimulus selectivity of the neuron (notice the bigger difference in response to optimal vs. nonoptimal stimuli). Finally, a multiplicative noise source causes the variance of the response to be proportional to the mean of the response. It is important to emphasize that this model is meant to provide a functional description of single cortical neuron responses and should not be taken as a hypothesis about the detailed anatomy and physiology. For example, contrast normalization is probably occurring at many levels, starting in the retina (Albrecht, 1995; Albrecht & Geisler, 1991; Sclar, 1987; Shapley & Victor, 1978). This model is consistent with the descriptive functions which have been used to summarize the responses of cortical neurons and hence it can account for 90% of the variability in both the means and standard deviations of cortical cell responses across a wide array of stimulus dimensions.

B. Performance

There is considerable psychophysical evidence for multiple pathways or channels in the visual system that are selective for the stimulus dimensions of size (spatial frequency), orientation, direction of motion, and binocular disparity (for reviews see Braddick, Campbell, & Atkinson, 1978; De Valois & De Valois, 1990; Graham, 1989; Regan, 1991; Sekuler, Pantle, & Levinson, 1978; Wilson, Levi, Maffei, Rovamo, & De Valois, 1990). Much of this evidence is based upon masking and adaptation studies, which demonstrate selective threshold elevations for stimuli that are similar to the masker or adapting pattern. For example, adapting to a specific spatial frequency raises the threshold for detecting that particular spatial frequency and similar spatial frequencies, but it has little effect on the detection of dissimilar spatial frequencies. Neurophysiological evidence has demonstrated that the primary visual cortex is the first level in the visual pathway where neurons exhibit high degrees of selectivity along these stimulus dimensions (see section VI.A). Thus, the response properties of neurons in the primary visual cortex are particularly important to consider in trying to understand the relationship between neural mechanisms and visual performance, which involve these stimulus dimensions.

To compare the performance of single neurons to behavior it is necessary to measure the responses of individual neurons along the same stimulus dimensions that are used to measure behavioral performance. The performance of the neuron can then be assessed by applying an optimal decision rule to the measured responses (which is equivalent to assuming that subsequent brain mechanisms are able to make use of all of the information in the responses). Using this approach it has been demonstrated (a) that the sensitivity of single neurons sometimes approaches that of the organism, (b) that the shape of the neural performance function sometimes resembles that of the organism, but (c) that no single neuron matches the performance along the entire stimulus range to which the organism is sensitive (see for example, Barlow, Kaushal, Hawken, & Parker, 1987; Bradley, Skottun, Ohzawa, Sclar, & Freeman, 1985; Geisler & Albrecht, 1997; Geisler, Albrecht, Salvi, & Saunders, 1991; Hawken & Parker, 1990; Newsome, Britten, & Movshon, 1989; Parker & Newsome, 1998; Tolhurst et al., 1983).

The standard method of measuring single-neuron performance is to essentially run a psychophysical experiment on the individual neuron. However, this method is quite time consuming, and thus it greatly restricts both the number of neurons that can be measured and the number of stimulus conditions that can be run on an individual neuron. For example, discrimination performance is often measured using a two-alternative forced choice task, where a minimum of 100 stimulus presentations is required for each point on the discrimination function. Thus, only a handful of discrimination points can be measured during the typical time available for recording from a given neuron.

An alternative method, the *descriptive-function* method, is to measure the response of the neuron (both the mean and the variance) along the stimulus dimension of interest and then summarize the responses as a whole with a descriptive function. With this method, entire performance functions can be measured along several different stimulus dimensions during the time available for recording from a given neuron (Geisler & Albrecht, 1995, 1997). Furthermore, because the descriptive function method makes it practical to measure the performance of large populations of individual neurons, it becomes possible to estimate the performance of a population of cells as a whole and compare this population performance to behavioral performance. Control experiments have shown that the discrimination performance obtained using the descriptive function method is equivalent to the discrimination performance obtained using the standard method (see Appendix D, Geisler & Albrecht, 1997).

When making comparisons of neural and behavioral performance it is important to take into consideration the fact that behavioral discriminations typically occur within the time frame of a single fixation (approximately 200 ms), or less: psychophysical estimates of temporal integration intervals typically range from 50 to 200 ms. Thus, it is important to measure neural performance using comparable stimulus durations.

In what follows, we first describe the detection and discrimination performance of single neurons for brief stimulus presentations. Next, we describe the detection and discrimination performance of the primary visual cortex as a whole based upon measurements from large populations of single neurons. Finally, we consider the relationship of the population performance of cortical neurons to psychophysical models of performance.

1. Single Neuron Performance

a. Discrimination Performance

In order to encode surface reflectances the visual system must be able to discriminate contrasts. Figure 13A shows the contrast discrimination performance (contrast threshold as a function of the background, or base, contrast) for a typical neuron in the primary visual cortex. This discrimination function was obtained by applying an optimal decision rule (from signal-detection theory) to the descriptive functions that were fitted to the responses in Figure 10A. The trial duration was 200 ms. Note that the neuron can only discriminate contrasts over a narrow range of background contrasts (0–12%); the absolute detection threshold was 7% contrast; the threshold decreased to a minimum value of 4% and increased thereafter. Similar to behavioral

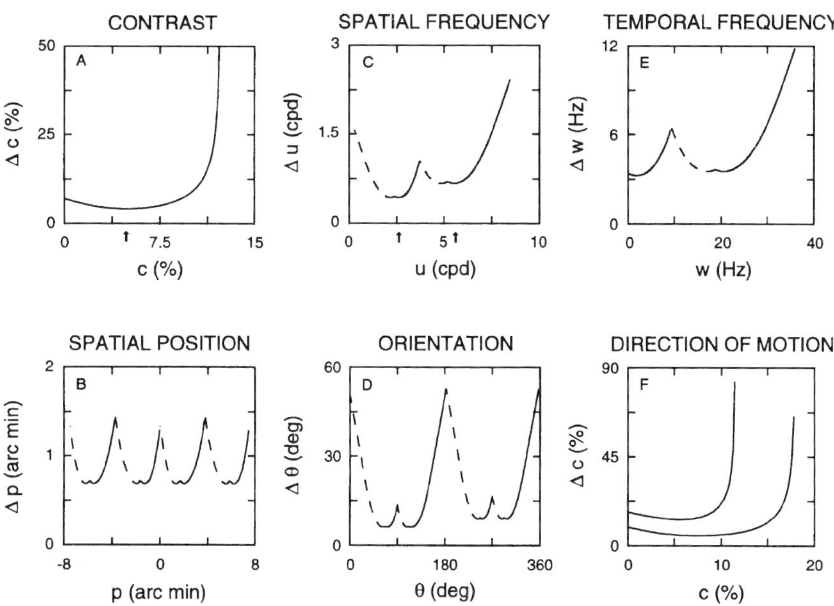

FIGURE 13 Discrimination performance of single neurons in monkey visual cortex.

contrast discrimination functions, this cell shows a "dipper effect" (the thresholds initially decrease as a function of contrast). However, behavioral contrast discrimination functions extend across the full range of contrasts (0–100%). Most neurons in the primary visual cortex show the dipper effect and can only discriminate over a limited range of background contrasts; those cells that can discriminate over a wide range are very insensitive (see for example, Barlow et al., 1987; Bradley et al., 1985; Geisler & Albrecht, 1997; Geisler et al., 1991).

In order to encode different shapes and sizes, the visual system must be able to discriminate differences in spatial frequency. Figure 13C shows the spatial frequency discrimination performance (frequency threshold as a function of the base frequency) for a typical neuron. This discrimination function was obtained by applying an optimal decision rule to the descriptive functions that were fitted to the responses in Figure 10C. Note that there are two minima on either side of the characteristic frequency (at 2.5 cpd and 6 cpd). The minima occur where small changes in frequency produce big changes in response; that is, where the slope of the selectivity function is steep. These discrimination functions were determined for both frequency increments (dashed curves) and decrements (solid curves); for ease of viewing, only the lower of the two thresholds at each frequency is plotted. For some cells, the minimum of the frequency discrimination function approaches that of behavioral performance. However, the shape of the behavioral discrimination function is very different; it is a straight line that corresponds to Weber's law.

In order to encode the location, shape, and motion of objects we must be able to discriminate spatial position, orientation, temporal frequency, and direction of motion. The discrimination performance of representative neurons along these stimulus dimensions are also shown in Figure 13.

In sum, although there is heterogeneity in the discrimination functions from cell to cell, there are general trends: (a) the neural discrimination functions often share some properties with behavioral discrimination functions; (b) for most neurons the discrimination functions only cover a fraction of the behavioral range; and (c) those few cells whose discrimination functions cover most of the behavioral range are very insensitive, relative to behavioral performance.

The discrimination performance illustrated in Figure 13 is for stimulus durations of 200 ms, a duration similar to the duration of fixations during saccadic inspection. If the stimulus duration were longer than 200 ms, one would expect performance to improve. However, longer stimulus durations would not be representative of the normal functioning of the visual system because the behavioral temporal integration intervals for similar discrimination tasks are less than 200 ms. As mentioned above, psychophysical estimates of temporal integration intervals typically range from 50 to 200 ms. If the stimulus duration were shorter than 200 ms, then one would expect performance to decrease. Interestingly, the discrimination performance of cortical neurons does not decrease dramatically when the stimulus duration decreases from 200 to 50 ms, because the variance proportionality constant decreases in the shorter intervals (Frazor, Albrecht, Geisler, & Crane, 1998).

b. Identification Performance

In order to perform object recognition it would be useful if neurons in the early visual system were able to identify local image features along various stimulus dimensions. This would permit subsequent brain mechanisms to begin the process of segregating objects from their context on the basis of local feature similarity. Although cortical cells are simultaneously selective along several different stimulus dimensions, they may not be capable of identifying local image features because they are rather broadly tuned, they have low firing rates, and they have high response variability. However, quantitative measurements of the identification performance indicates that individual cortical neurons can reliably signal the presence of specific local image features.

The identification task can be conceptualized as follows. One must identify which stimulus was presented on a trial, when the stimulus is randomly selected from a wide range of possibilities. Suppose as an observer (or as a subsequent brain mechanism), that the only information available on each trial is the total number of action potentials from a given neuron (plus some implicit knowledge of the neuron's tuning functions and variability). What could be known about the stimulus given a particular spike count during a single trial? This question can be answered using the descriptive functions for the mean and variance to determine a *certainty function* (an *a posteriori* probability density function), which is the probability of each possible stimulus given that particular spike count. From the certainty function it is possible to determine a 95% confidence region in stimulus space. If the 95% confidence region is small it means that the neuron's identification performance is good (i.e., the stimulus can be localized to a small region of stimulus space).

Figure 14 shows representative certainty functions for the dimensions of contrast, spatial position, spatial frequency, orientation, temporal frequency, and direction of motion, given that the stimulus is random and free to vary along the entire axis (i.e., a uniform prior probability distribution for the stimulus). These probability distributions were obtained from the descriptive functions shown in Figure 10, for the case where a maximum response has occurred in a 200-ms trial (e.g., a count of seven spikes for the dimension of contrast). The arrows along the stimulus dimensions indicate the 95% confidence region.

The certainty functions in Figure 14 are for single dimensions. In the natural environment, cortical neurons are confronted with simultaneous uncertainty along many stimulus dimensions. Interestingly, the certainty function along any given dimension is little affected by uncertainty along other stimulus dimensions. For example, the certainty functions for spatial frequency and orientation are unaffected even when the contrast is random and free to vary.

In general, the following statements are true:

1. Identification performance improves with increasing response, reaching fairly impressive levels at 5–10 spikes in a 200-ms interval. For these response levels, the width of the 95% confidence region along a particular stimulus dimension is

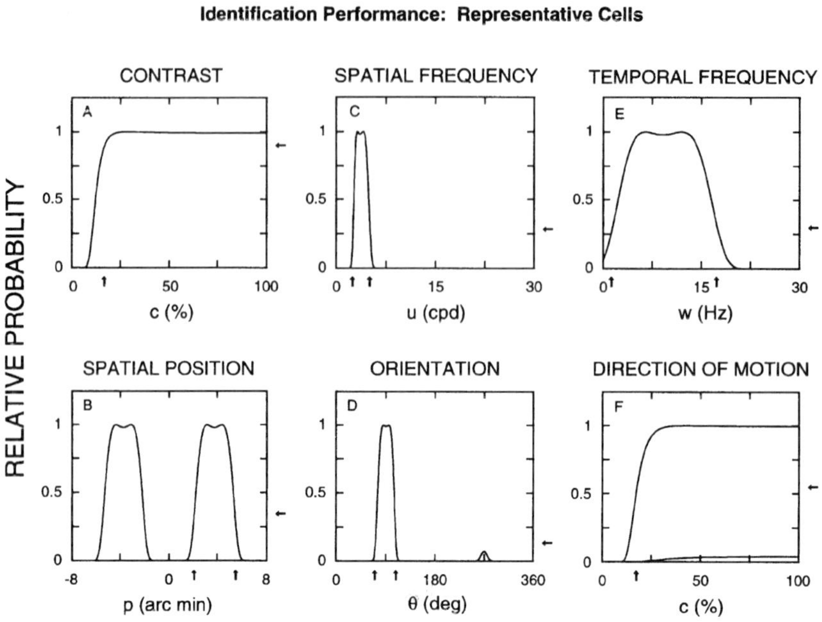

FIGURE 14 Identification performance of single neurons in monkey visual cortex.

approximately equal to the half-height bandwidth of the cell's tuning along that dimension.

2. At low spike rates, identification performance becomes quite poor (the confidence regions become large and complex).

3. Because many cortical neurons saturate at low contrasts (i.e., between 5 and 20% contrast) without losing their tuning, good identification performance is often reached at very low contrasts.

The remarkable ability of a cortical neuron to respond uniquely to a relatively specific local image feature is a consequence of the linear filtering combined with the nonlinear response expansion and the contrast normalization. The linear filtering and the response expansion are essential for establishing the selectivity; however, the contrast normalization plays the crucial role of transforming cortical neurons so that they behave less like linear filters and more like feature detectors. Because of the special kind of saturation that is introduced by contrast normalization, a cortical cell will produce a large response to a very low contrast image feature of the correct size, orientation, and position, but will produce a weaker response to a high-contrast image feature that differs only slightly from the preferred stimulus along any dimension. This is very different from what would be expected from a linear filter.

2. Neural Population Discrimination Performance

Although the discrimination performance of individual neurons is similar to the behavioral discrimination performance in some respects, the performance of any single neuron is generally restricted to a much smaller stimulus range. Behavioral performance across the entire range of any stimulus dimension must involve the pooled activity of more than one neuron. Therefore, to understand behavioral performance, it is necessary to go beyond an analysis of the single neuron and to consider the performance of neural populations.

One method for evaluating the discrimination performance of neural populations is to combine the measurements from individual neurons. In order to do this, it is first of all necessary to measure the responses of a large representative sample of neurons along the stimulus dimensions of interest. (As shown earlier, the measured responses along the stimulus dimensions can be summarized using simple descriptive functions.) It is then necessary to combine the measured responses of each neuron using an appropriate pooling rule (i.e., a linking hypothesis). There are many possible pooling rules, and thus one sensible strategy to consider both "minimum pooling," where the performance at each stimulus level is determined by the most sensitive neuron, and "optimum pooling," where the performance at each stimulus level is determined by optimally combining the responses of all the neurons in the sample. These two pooling rules represent the end points of a continuum of possible pooling rules and hence set the boundaries of behavioral performance that might be expected based upon the responses of the neurons in the sample.

Figure 15 shows the population discrimination performance for a sample of neurons recorded from monkey cortex, along the stimulus dimensions of contrast and spatial frequency, using these two pooling rules. Consider first the minimum pooling rule. Each solid symbol in the upper panels shows the minimum of the discrimination function for one of the neurons in the population (see arrows in Figure 13A, 13C). As can be seen, for the dimension of contrast, the best performance points are widely scattered at each background contrast, and they span most of the contrast axis. All points that fall on the vertical axis at 0% contrast represent cells for which the best discrimination threshold was the absolute threshold; all other points represent cells for which the threshold initially decreased with contrast (i.e., they showed the dipper effect). It is interesting to note that as contrast increases, the thresholds of the most sensitive cells increase monotonically. Specifically, those cells with the lowest thresholds are bounded by an envelope that is approximately constant at lower contrasts and linear (in log–log coordinates) at higher contrasts. For the discrimination of spatial frequency, the best performance points are also widely scattered at each base frequency, and they span most of the frequency axis. As frequency increases, $\Delta f/f$ initially decreases and then becomes approximately constant (Weber's law). The open symbols in Figure 15 plot behavioral discrimination functions for monkeys and humans; each function is for a different published study or

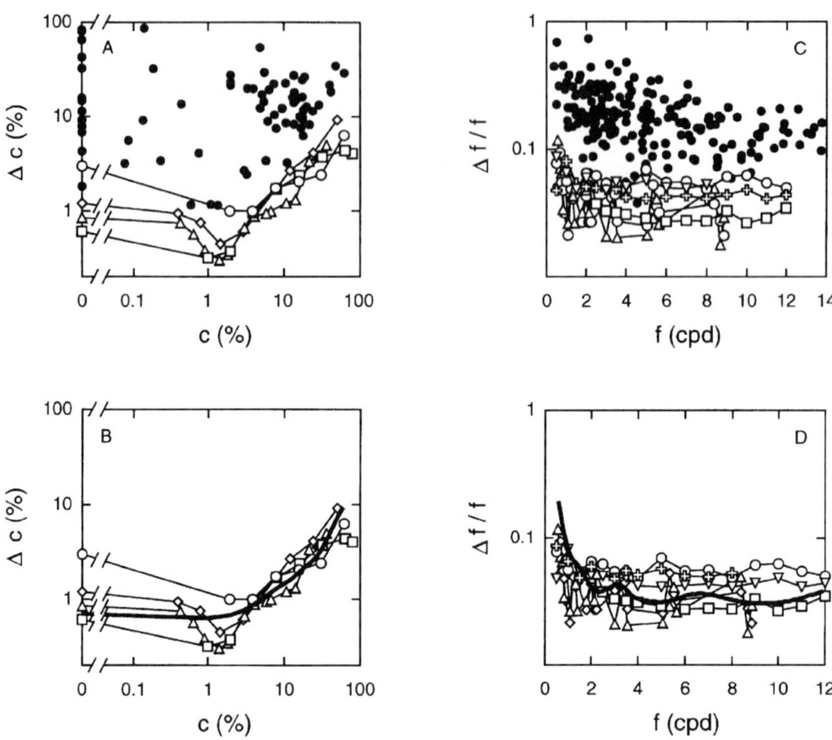

FIGURE 15 Comparison of neural population discrimination performance in monkeys with behavioral discrimination performance in monkeys and humans.

subject. Interestingly, the general shape of the behavioral functions is quite similar to the shape of the envelope of the most sensitive cells.[8] However, the behavioral thresholds are somewhat lower.

Consider next the optimum pooling rule. The thick curves in the lower panels of Figure 15 show the discrimination functions that result from pooling all of the discrimination information from all of the cells in an optimal fashion. As can be seen, the shapes of the population discrimination functions are very similar to the shapes of the behavioral discrimination functions. These curves were obtained as follows. First, we used the descriptive functions for each neuron to find the mean responses and standard deviations to the base stimulus (contrast or frequency) and

[8] Like the behavioral performance, the contrast discrimination functions for most individual cortical neurons show a dipper effect; however, the contrast discrimination function for the neural population does not. This is a consequence of the fact that the minima of the contrast discrimination functions for the individual neurons are widely scattered along the contrast axis.

to the base-plus-increment. Second, we used these means and standard deviations to obtain the signal-to-noise ratio, d′, for each cell. Third, the d′ summation formula from Bayesian decision theory was used to find the signal-to-noise ratio for the entire population. Fourth, the threshold was obtained by varying the increment until the population d′ equaled 1.0 (i.e., 75% correct discrimination). Finally, we shifted the population function vertically, using an efficiency parameter (which was the same for contrast and spatial frequency), to allow comparison of the shapes of the behavioral and neural population discrimination functions.

These two methods of comparing behavioral and neural performance represent two extremes in psychophysical linking hypotheses. At one extreme, behavioral performance is determined by assuming no pooling across neurons—the threshold for each stimulus condition is determined by the most sensitive cell (Barlow, 1972, 1995; De Valois, Abramov, & Mead, 1967; Talbot, Darian-Smith, Kornhuber, & Mountcastle, 1968). At the other extreme, behavioral performance is determined by assuming optimal pooling of the responses across all the neurons (Geisler, 1984, 1989; Watson, 1983). The results show that both pooling rules account for the data about equally well, and presumably, pooling rules between these two extremes could also account for the data reasonably well. Because of this, it may prove difficult to distinguish between different decision models (pooling rules) for discrimination tasks, even when both behavioral and neurophysiological data are available (Parker & Newsome, 1998). Nonetheless, the fact that the neural population performance matches the shape of the behavioral psychophysical performance regardless of the pooling rule suggests that the mechanisms up to and including area VI are largely responsible for limiting contrast and spatial frequency discrimination performance.

Finally, note that the heterogeneity of the contrast response functions and the spatial frequency tuning functions in cortical neurons appears to be the critical factor in determining the behavioral discrimination functions. Different cells are most sensitive to different regions along the stimulus dimensions and hence at each point along the stimulus dimension, different cells are determining the overall behavioral performance. Although population performance has not yet been determined for other stimulus dimensions, this principle, in which behavioral performance is dependent upon the continuous and heterogeneous distribution of cell properties, may prove to be general.

3. Psychophysical Models of Performance

a. Traditional Models

There are many aspects of spatial pattern discrimination that cannot be explained by the response properties of neurons in the retina. For example, in pattern adaptation experiments, a sine wave grating adaptor only elevates thresholds for spatial frequencies and orientations that are similar to that of the adapting grating. In pattern masking experiments, a sine wave grating masker only elevates thresholds for spatial frequencies and orientations similar to that of the masking grating. Furthermore, retinal properties cannot explain interocular pattern masking and adaptation, or the complex effects of maskers with multiple frequency components. Finally, it is unlikely that either the contrast discrimination function or the spatial frequency discrimination function can be explained by retinal mechanisms.

Early models of spatial vision combined linear spatial frequency and orientation tuned channels with a simple pooling mechanism, such as selecting the most sensitive channel (Campbell & Robson, 1968) or probability summation (Brindley, 1960; Graham, Robson, & Nachmias, 1978; Wilson & Bergen, 1979). These models are able to qualitatively account for pattern adaptation and pattern masking. More recent models incorporated a final nonlinear response function prior to the pooling mechanism (Foley & Legge, 1981; Legge & Foley, 1980; Wilson, 1980; Wilson & Gelb, 1984). These models are able to quantitatively account for contrast discrimination, frequency discrimination, and pattern masking under limited conditions. The most recent models have replaced the final nonlinear response function with nonlinear mechanisms similar to the contrast normalization and response expansion found in the primate visual cortex (Foley & Boynton, 1994; Teo & Heeger, 1994; Thomas & Olzak, 1997; Watson & Solomon, 1997; Wilson & Humanski, 1993). These models are able to quantitatively account for a wider array of pattern masking effects. However, there remain a number of effects that cannot be explained, such as the strong masking effects that can occur when two weak maskers are presented simultaneously (see, for example, Derrington & Henning, 1989).

Most of these recent models of spatial vision consist of a small number of discrete channels, each tuned to a different range of spatial frequency and orientation, along with some nonlinear response mechanism. The parameters for these models are generally estimated by fitting psychophysical data. The sensitivities of the channels are estimated by fitting contrast sensitivity functions; the bandwidths of the channels and the nonlinearities are estimated by fitting masking data. The models are best able to account for the masking data when the bandwidths of the spatial frequency and orientation channels are similar to the average bandwidth of neurons in the primary visual cortex. However, for most of the models the estimated parameters of the nonlinearity are different from the average values for neurons in the primary visual cortex.

b. Neuron Sampling Models

The traditional models were designed to account for psychophysical data, and hence there is no requirement that they be consistent with all aspects of cortical neurophysiology. Nonetheless, there are important ways in which they are not consistent, and it may be valuable to consider models that more closely approximate the properties of the visual cortex. First, there is little neurophysiological evidence for a small number of discrete channels. Cortical neurons appear to be continuously variable in preferred spatial frequency, preferred orientation, spatial frequency bandwidth, and orientation bandwidth. Second, the spatial vision models have generally assumed a single nonlinear contrast response function. In fact, cortical neurons appear to be continuously variable in their contrast response functions, just as they are in their spatial frequency and orientation tuning functions. These discrepancies with the physiology could be reduced by expanding the number of spatial channels and nonlinearities. Unfortunately, the cost is reduced parsimony and more free parameters. Each new channel or nonlinearity would add more parameters to already complex models.

However, even though cortical neurons are heterogeneous in their response properties, they are very regular in a different way. As we have seen (Section VI.A), it is possible to summarize the stimulus–response relationships of each cortical cell using a small set of relatively simple descriptive functions, where each descriptive function has only a few free parameters. This suggests that it would be useful to consider quantitative models of spatial vision that are defined in terms of probability distributions of descriptive function parameters (i.e., cell properties) rather than in terms of discrete channels or pathways. Specifically, the early visual system might be modeled as a large collection of neurons whose spatial-frequency tuning, orientation tuning, contrast response functions, and noise characteristics are randomly sampled from frequency distributions. We term this class of models *neuron sampling models* (Geisler & Albrecht, 1997). In a neuron sampling model, the frequency distributions for the descriptive function parameters replace the discrete channels as the fundamental construct of the model.

Neuron sampling models consist of three major components: (a) a functional model of single cortical neuron responses, which generates a predicted response mean and variance (e.g., the contrast-gain exponent model shown in Figure 12), (b) a set of frequency distributions, or histograms, for each key parameter in the functional model (taken from empirical measurements of the neurons or estimated from fitting psychophysical data), and (c) a pooling/decision rule (e.g., optimal pooling). To generate predictions for any stimulus of interest, a large population of model neurons is created by randomly sampling a value for each of the key parameters. (Any measured correlations that might exist between parameters can be incorporated in the sampling process.) The receptive field spacing (and average size) at each eccentricity is proportional to the cortical magnification at that eccentricity. The mean and variance of each neuron's response is then determined for the given stimulus. Finally, a pooling/decision rule is applied to the population as a whole.

This class of model can generate predictions for simple patterns such as sine wave gratings as well as complex natural images.

VII. IMPLICATIONS FOR OBJECT RECOGNITION AND SCENE INTERPRETATION

The overall goal of the visual system is to provide an accurate three-dimensional description of the environment over time which includes the identification of objects and events. The retina contributes to this overall goal by (a) measuring the intensity and wavelength information in the retinal image, (b) encoding small contrast variations independent of the ambient light level, (c) enhancing local image contours, and (d) compressing the information to a manageable size. The primary visual cortex contributes to this overall goal by representing the visual scene in terms of local image features/attributes,[9] including (a) local orientation, (b) local size, (c) local spatial phase, and (d) local motion. This local representation is crucial for identification of objects and events by subsequent cortical regions.

Following the representation in terms of local image features/attributes, the next crucial step toward the overall goal is organizing the local image features into larger coherent groups, which form the basis for segregating individual objects from their context (i.e., solving the problem of "Object Segregation"). Once the features are organized into coherent wholes and the objects are segregated, object recognition becomes feasible. (For a recent review of this literature see Ullman, 1996.)

The linear and nonlinear receptive field properties of primary visual cortex neurons produce responses that are particularly well suited for grouping and segregation by subsequent brain mechanisms. The spatiotemporal receptive field shape makes each neuron selective to a specific local image feature. The expansive response exponent enhances this selectivity. The contrast normalization ensures that each neuron will only respond when a particular image feature is present—only a near optimal stimulus can produce a near maximum response. Finally, in the case of complex cells, the rectification nonlinearities produce phase-invariant responses.

These linear and nonlinear response properties create a population of cells with three particularly useful characteristics for object segregation. First, there are many different neurons selective to many different local image features (i.e., there is a wide range of narrow selectivities across the population of neurons as a whole). Second, each neuron only responds when a particular feature is present in the image (i.e., each neuron has a unique stimulus–response relationship). Third, there is a subpopulation of neurons (the complex cells) that respond invariantly to local spatial phase (i.e., they respond equivalently to the same stimulus anywhere within the receptive field). These three characteristics make it possible to find *global* similarities and differences within and between image regions along the dimensions of orientation, size, motion, contrast, and so on, which ultimately permits simple grouping (similarity grouping). Furthermore, these properties also make it possible to find smooth transitions in *local* similarities along the dimensions of orientation, size, motion, and so on, which ultimately permits contour integration and region integration.

[9] The local image feature to which a cortical cell responds is not a single spatiotemporal pattern (such as a bar, or an edge, or sine wave grating) but is instead a collection, or set, of similar local spatiotemporal patterns. This collection of patterns defines the local image feature to which the cell responds. An appropriate method for quantifying the local image feature is to measure the confidence region in stimulus space when the stimulus is random and free to vary: specifically, the 95% confidence region in the space of all possible local two-dimensional spatiotemporal patterns that might occur in the natural environment (see section VI.B.1.b).

References

Adelson, E. H., & Bergen, J. R. (1985). Spatiotemporal energy models for the perception of motion. *Journal of the Optical Society of America A, 2,* 284–299.

Albrecht, D. G. (1995). Visual cortex neurons in monkey and cat: Effect of contrast on the spatial and temporal phase transfer functions. *Visual Neuroscience, 12,* 1191–1210.

Albrecht, D. G., & Geisler, W. S. (1991). Motion selectivity and the contrast-response function of simple cells in the visual cortex. *Visual Neuroscience, 7,* 531–546.

Albrecht, D. G., & Geisler, W. S. (1994). Visual cortex neurons in monkey and cat: Contrast response nonlinearities and stimulus selectivity. In T. Lawton (Ed.), *Computational vision based on neurobiology* (Vol. 2054, pp. 12–37). Bellingham, WA: SPIE.

Albrecht, D. G., & Hamilton, D. H. (1982). Striate cortex of monkey and cat: Contrast response function. *Journal of Neurophysiology, 48*(1), 217–237.

Arend, L. E., Jr. (1976). Temporal determinants of the form of the spatial contrast threshold MTF. *Vision Research, 16,* 1035–1042.

Arnow, T. L., & Geisler, W. S. (1996). Visual detection following retinal damage: Predictions of an inhomogeneous retino-cortical model. *SPIE Proceedings: Human Vision and Electronic Imaging, 2674,* 119–130.

Banks, M. S., Geisler, W. S., & Bennett, P. J. (1987). The physical limits of grating visibility. *Vision Research, 27,* 1915–1924.

Banks, M. S., Sekuler, A. B., & Anderson, S. J. (1991). Peripheral spatial vision: Limits imposed by optics, photoreceptors, and receptor pooling. *Journal of the Optical Society of America A, 8,* 1775–1787.

Barlow, H. B. (1961). Possible principles underlying the transformations of sensory messages. In W. A. Rosenblith (Ed.), *Sensory communication* (pp. 217–234). Cambridge, MA: MIT Press.

Barlow, H. B. (1972). Single units and sensation: A neuron doctrine for perceptual psychology? *Perception, 1,* 371–394.

Barlow, H. B. (1981). Critical limiting factors in the design of the eye and visual cortex. *Proceedings of the Royal Society of London, B 212,* 1–34.

Barlow, H. B. (1989). Unsupervised learning. *Neural Computation, 1,* 295–311.

Barlow, H. B. (1995). The neuron doctrine in perception. In M. S. Gazzaniga (Ed.), *The cognitive neurosciences* (pp. 415–435). Cambridge: The MIT Press.

Barlow, H. B., Kaushal, T. P., Hawken, M., & Parker, A. J. (1987). Human contrast discrimination and the threshold of cortical neurons. *Journal of the Optical Society of America A, 4*(12), 2366–2371.

Barlow, H. B., & Levick, W. R. (1965). The mechanism of directionally selective units in rabbit's retina. *Journal of Physiology, 178,* 477–504.

Bonds, A. B. (1991). Temporal dynamics of contrast gain in single cells of the cat striate cortex. *Visual Neuroscience, 6,* 239–255.

Braddick, O., Campbell, F. W., & Atkinson, J. (1978). Channels in vision: Basic aspects. In R. Held, H. W. Leibowitz, & H.-L. Teuber (Eds.), *Handbook of sensory physiology* (Vol. VIII: Perception, pp. 3–38). Berlin: Springer-Verlag.

Bradley, A., Skottun, B. C., Ohzawa, I., Sclar, G., & Freeman, R. D. (1985). Neurophysiological evaluation of the differential response model for orientation and spatial-frequency discrimination. *Journal of the Optical Society of America A, 2,* 1607–1610.

Brindley, G. S. (1960). *Physiology of the retina and the visual pathway.* London: Edward Arnold.

Callaway, E. M. (1998). Local circuits in primary visual cortex of the macaque monkey. *Annual Review of Neuroscience, 21,* 47–74.

Campbell, F. W., & Green, D. G. (1965). Optical and retinal factors affecting visual resolution. *Journal of Physiology, 181,* 576–593.

Campbell, F. W., & Gubisch, R. W. (1966). Optical quality of the human eye. *Journal of Physiology, 186,* 558–578.

Campbell, F. W., & Robson, J. G. (1968). Applications of Fourier analysis to the visibility of gratings. *Journal of Physiology, 197,* 551–566.

Carandini, M., & Heeger, D. J. (1994). Summation and division by neurons in primate visual cortex. *Science, 264,* 1333–1336.

Carpenter, R. H. S. (Ed.). (1991). *Eye movements.* London: MacMillan Press.

Casagrande, V. A. (1994). A third parallel visual pathway to primate area V1. *Trends in Neuroscience, 17,* 305–310.

Charman, W. N. (1993). Optics of the eye. In M. Bass (Ed.), *Handbook of optics* (Vol. I, pp. 24.3–24.54). Washington: Optical Society of America.

Croner, L. J., & Kaplan, E. (1995). Receptive fields of P and M ganglion cells across the primate retina. *Vision Research, 35,* 7–24.

Croner, L. J., Purpura, K., & Kaplan, E. (1993). Response variability in retinal ganglion cells of primates. *Proceedings of the National Academy of Sciences, 90,* 8128–8130.

Curcio, C. A., & Allen, K. A. (1990). Topography of ganglion cells in human retina. *The Journal of Comparative Neurology, 300,* 5–25.

Dacey, D. M. (1996). Circuitry for color coding in the primate retina. *Proceedings of the National Academy of Sciences, 93,* 582–588.

DeAngelis, G. C., Ohzawa, I., & Freeman, R. D. (1993). Spatiotemporal organization of simple-cell receptive fields in the cat's striate cortex. II. Linearity of temporal and spatial summation. *Journal of Neurophysiology, 69,*1118–1135.

DeAngelis, G. C., Freeman, R. D., & Ohzawa, I. (1994). Length and width tuning of neurons in the cat's primary visual cortex. *Journal of Neurophysiology, 71,* 347–374.

Derrington, A. M., & Henning, G. B. (1989). Some observations on the masking effects of two-dimensional stimuli. *Vision Research, 28,* 241–246.

Derrington, A. M., & Lennie, P. (1984). Spatial and temporal contrast sensitivities of neurones in lateral geniculate nucleus of macaque. *Journal of Physiology, 357,* 219–240.

De Valois, K. K. (1994). Spatial vision based upon color differences. In T. Lawton (Ed.), *Computational vision based on neurobiology* (Vol. 2054, pp. 95–103). Bellingham, WA: SPIE.

De Valois, R. I., Abramov, I., & Mead, W. R. (1967). Single cell analysis of wavelength discrimination at the lateral geniculate nucleus in the macaque. *Journal of Neurophysiology, 30,* 415–433.

De Valois, R. L., Albrecht, D. G., & Thorell, L. G. (1982). Spatial frequency selectivity of cells in macaque visual cortex. *Vision Research, 22,* 545–559.

De Valois, R. L., & De Valois, K. K. (1990). *Spatial vision.* New York: Oxford University Press.

De Valois, R. L., Thorell, L. G., & Albrecht, D. G. (1985). Periodicity of striate-cortex-cell receptive fields. *Journal of the Optical Society of America A, 2,* 1115–1123.

De Valois, R. L., Yund, E. W., & Hepler, N. (1982). The orientation and direction selectivity of cells in macaque visual cortex. *Vision Research, 22,* 531–544.

Enroth-Cugell, C., & Robson, J. G. (1966). The contrast sensitivity of retinal ganglion cells of the cat. *Journal of Physiology, 187,* 517–552.

Felleman, D. J., & Van Essen, D. C. (1991). Distributed hierarchical processing in the primate cerebral cortex. *Cerebral Cortex, 1,* 1–47.

Field, D. J. (1987). Relations between the statistics of natural images and the response properties of cortical cells. *Journal of the Optical Society of America A, 4,* 2379–2394.

Foley, J. M., & Boynton, G. M. (1994). A new model of human luminance pattern vision mechanisms: Analysis of the effects of pattern orientation, spatial phase and temporal frequency. *SPIE, 2054,* 32–42.

Foley, J. M., & Legge, G. E. (1981). Contrast detection and near-threshold discrimination in human vision. *Vision Research, 21,* 1041–1053.

Foster, K. H., Gaska, J. P., Nagler, M., & Pollen, D. A. (1985). Spatial and temporal frequency selectivity of neurones in visual cortical areas V1 and V2 of the macaque monkey. *Journal of Physiology, 365,* 331–363.

Frazor, R. A., Albrecht, D. G., Geisler, W. S., & Crane, A. M. (1998). Discrimination performance of V1 neurons in monkeys and cats for different intervals of integration. *Investigative Ophthalmology & Visual Science Supplement, 39/4,* S238.

Geisler, W. S. (1984). Physical limits of acuity and hyperacuity. *Journal of the Optical Society of America A, 1,* 775–782.

Geisler, W. S. (1989). Sequential ideal-observer analysis of visual discriminations. *Psychological Review, 96,* 267–314.

Geisler, W. S. (1995). Discrimination information in natural radiance spectra. In E. Peli (Ed.), *Vision models for target detection and recognition* (pp. 117–131). New York: World Scientific Publishing Co. Inc.

Geisler, W. S., & Albrecht, D. G. (1995). Bayesian analysis of identification in monkey visual cortex: Nonlinear mechanisms and stimulus certainty. *Vision Research, 35,* 2723–2730.

Geisler, W. S., & Albrecht, D. G. (1997). Visual cortex neurons in monkeys and cats: Detection, discrimination, and identification. *Visual Neuroscience, 14,* 897–919.

Geisler, W. S., Albrecht, D. G., Salvi, R. J., & Saunders, S. S. (1991). Discrimination performance of single neurons: Rate and temporal-pattern information. *Journal of Neurophysiology, 66,* 334–361.

Gilbert, C. D., & Wiesel, T. N. (1990). The influence of contextual stimuli on the orientation selectivity of cells in the primary visual cortex of the cat. *Vision Research, 30,* 1689–1701.

Graham, N. (1989). *Visual pattern analyzers.* New York: Oxford.

Graham, N., Robson, J. G., & Nachmias, J. (1978). Grating summation in fovea and periphery. *Vision Research, 18,* 815–825.

Hamilton, D. B., Albrecht, D. G., & Geisler, W. S. (1989). Visual cortical receptive fields in monkey and cat: Spatial and temporal phase transfer function. *Vision Research, 29,* 1285–1308.

Hartline, H. K. (1974). *Studies on excitation and inhibition in the retina.* New York: The Rockefeller University Press.

Hawken, M. J., & Parker, A. J. (1990). Detection and discrimination mechanisms in the striate cortex of the Old-World monkey. In C. Blakemore (Ed.), *Vision: Coding and efficiency* (pp. 103–116). Cambridge: Cambridge University press.

Hawken, M. J., Shapley, R. M., & Grosof, D. H. (1996). Temporal frequency selectivity in monkey lateral geniculate nucleus and striate cortex. *Visual Neuroscience, 13,* 477–492.

Heeger, D. J. (1991). Computational model of cat striate physiology. In M. S. Landy & J. A. Movshon (Eds.), *Computational models of visual perception* (pp. 119–133). Cambridge: The MIT Press.

Heeger, D. J. (1992a). Half-squaring in responses of cat striate cells. *Visual Neuroscience, 9,* 427–443.

Heeger, D. J. (1992b). Normalization of cell responses in cat striate cortex. *Visual Neuroscience, 9,* 191–197.

Hochstein, S., & Shapley, R. M. (1976). Quantitative analysis of retinal ganglion cell classifications. *Journal of Physiology, 262,* 237–264.

Hood, D. C. (1998). Lower-level visual processing and models of light adaptation. *Annual Review of Psychology, 49,* 503–535.

Hubel, D. H., & Wiesel, T. N. (1962). Receptive fields, binocular interaction, and functional architecture in the cat's visual cortex. *Journal of Physiology, 160,* 106–154.

Hubel, D. H., & Wiesel, T. N. (1968). Receptive fields and functional architecture of monkey striate cortex. *Journal of Physiology, 195,* 215–243.

Kaas, J. H., Huerta, M. F., Weber, J. T., & Harting, J. K. (1978). Patterns of retinal terminations and laminar organization of the lateral geniculate nucleus of primates. *The Journal of Comparative Neurology, 182,* 517–554.

Kaplan, E., & Shapley, R. (1986). The primate retina contains two types of ganglion cells, with high and low contrast sensitivity. *Proceedings of the National Academy of Sciences, 83,* 125–143.

Legge, G. E., & Foley, J. M. (1980). Contrast masking in human vision. *Journal of the Optical Society of America, 70,* 1458–1470.

Levitt, J., & Lund, J. S. (1997). Contrast dependence of contextual effects in primate visual cortex. *Nature, 387,* 73–76.

Li, C., & Creutzfeldt, O. (1984). The representation of contrast and other stimulus parameters by single neurons in area 17 of the cat. *Pflugers Archiv, 401,* 304–314.

Li, C.-Y., & Li, W. (1994). Extensive integration field beyond the classical receptive field of cat's striate cortical neurons—classification and tuning properties. *Vision Research, 34,* 2337–2355.

McCormick, D. A., Connors, B. W., Lighthall, J. W., & Prince, D. A. (1985). Comparative electrophysiology of pyramidal and sparsely spiny stellate neurons of the neocortex. *Journal of Neurophysiology, 54,* 782–806.

McLean, J., & Palmer, L. A. (1989). Contribution of linear spatiotemporal receptive field structure to velocity selectivity of simple cells in area 17 of cat. *Vision Research, 29,* 675–679.

McLean, J., & Palmer, L. A. (1994). Organization of simple cell responses in the three-dimensional (3-D) frequency domain. *Visual Neuroscience, 11,* 295–306.

McLean, J., Raab, S., & Palmer, L. A. (1994). Contribution of linear mechanisms to the specification of local motion by simple cells in areas 17 and 18 of the cat. *Visual Neuroscience, 11,* 271–294.

Merigan, W. H., & Maunsell, J. H. R. (1993). How parallel are the primate visual pathways? *Annual Review of Neuroscience, 16,* 369–402.

Movshon, J. A., Thompson, I. D., & Tolhurst, D. J. (1978a). Receptive field organization of complex cells in the cat's striate cortex. *Journal of Physiology, 283,* 79–99.

Movshon, J. A., Thompson, I. D., & Tolhurst, D. J. (1978b). Spatial and temporal contrast sensitivity of neurones in area 17 and 18 of cat's visual cortex. *Journal of Physiology, 283,* 101–120.

Movshon, J. A., Thompson, I. D., & Tolhurst, D. J. (1978c). Spatial summation in the receptive fields of simple cells in the cat's striate cortex. *Journal of Physiology, 283,* 53–77.

Mullen, K. T. (1985). The contrast sensitivity of human colour vision to red-green and blue-yellow chromatic gratings. *Journal of Physiology, 359,* 381–400.

Newsome, W. T., Britten, K. H., & Movshon, J. A. (1989). Neuronal correlates of a perceptual decision. *Nature, 341,* 52–54.

Olshausen, B. A., & Field, D. J. (1997). Sparse coding with an overcomplete basis set: A strategy by V1? *Vision Research, 37,* 3311–3325.

Palmer, L. A., Jones, J. P., & Stepnoski, R. A. (1991). Striate receptive fields as linear filters: Characterization in two dimensions of space. In A. G. Leventhal (Ed.), *The neural basis of visual function* (pp. 246–265). Boston: CRC Press.

Parker, A. J., & Newsome, W. T. (1998). Sense and the single neuron: Probing the physiology of perception. *Annual Review of Neuroscience, 21,* 227–277.

Pelli, D. G. (1990). The quantum efficiency of vision. In C. Blakemore (Ed.), *Vision: coding and efficiency* (pp. 3–24). Cambridge: Cambridge University Press.

Purpura, K., Tranchina, D., Kaplan, E., & Shapley, R. M. (1990). Light adaptation in the primate retina: Analysis of changes in gain and dynamics of monkey retinal ganglion cells. *Visual Neuroscience, 4,* 75–93.

Regan, D. (Ed.). (1991). *Spatial vision.* New York: Macmillan.

Reid, R. C., Victor, J. D., & Shapley, R. M. (1992). Broadband temporal stimuli decrease the integration time of neurons in cat striate cortex. *Visual Neuroscience, 9,* 39–45.

Robson, J. G. (1966). Spatial and temporal contrast sensitivity functions of the visual system. *Journal of the Optical Society of America, 56,* 1141–1142.

Robson, J. G. (1991). Neural coding of contrast in the visual system. *Journal of the Optical Society of America, Technical Digest Series, 17,* 152.

Robson, J. G., & Graham, N. (1981). Probability summation and regional variation in contrast sensitivity across the visual field. *Vision Research, 21,* 409–418.

Rodieck, R. W. (1965). Quantitative analysis of cat retinal ganglion cell response to visual stimuli. *Vision Research, 5,* 583–601.

Rodieck, R. W. (1998). *The first steps in seeing.* Sunderland, MA: Sinauer.

Sclar, G. (1987). Expression of "retinal" contrast gain control by neurons of the cat's lateral geniculate nucleus. *Experimental Brain Research, 66,* 589–596.

Sclar, G., & Freeman, R. D. (1982). Orientation selectivity in the cat's striate cortex is invariant with contrast. *Experimental Brain Research, 46,* 457–461.

Sclar, G., Maunsell, J. H. R., & Lennie, P. (1990). Coding of image contrast in central visual pathways of macaque monkey. *Vision Research, 30,* 1–10.

Sekiguchi, N., Williams, D. R., & Brainard, D. H. (1993). Efficiency in detection of isoluminant and isochromatic interference fringes. *Journal of the Optical Society of America A, 10,* 2118–2133.

Sekuler, R., Pantle, A., & Levinson, E. (1978). Physiological basis of motion perception. In R. Held, H. W. Leibowitz, & H.-L. Teuber (Eds.), *Handbook of sensory physiology* (Vol. VIII: Perception, pp. 67–96). Berlin: Springer-Verlag.

Sengpiel, F., Baddeley, R. J., Freeman, T. C. B., Harrad, R., & Blakemore, C. (1998). Different mechanisms underlie three inhibitory phenomena in cat area 17. *Vision Research, 38,* 2067–2080.

Shapley, R. M., & Lennie, P. (1985). Spatial frequency analysis in the visual system. *Annual Review of Neuroscience, 8,* 547–583.

Shapley, R. M., & Victor, J. D. (1978). The effect of contrast on the transfer properties of cat retinal ganglion cells. *Journal of Physiology, 285,* 275–298.

Sillito, A. M., Grieve, K. L., Jones, H. E., Cudiero, J., & Davis, J. (1995). Visual cortical mechanisms detecting focal orientation discontinuities. *Nature, 378,* 492–496.

Skottun, B. C., De Valois, R. L., Grosof, D. H., Movshon, J. A., Albrecht, D. G., & Bonds, A. B. (1991). Classifying simple and complex cells on the basis of response modulation. *Vision Research, 31*(7/8), 1079–1086.

Snowden, R. J., Treue, S., & Andersen, R. A. (1992). The response of neurons in areas V1 and MT of the alert rhesus monkey to moving random dot patterns. *Experimental Brain Research, 88,* 389–400.

Softky, W. R., & Koch, C. (1993). The highly irregular firing of cortical cells is inconsistent with temporal integration of random epsps. *The Journal of Neuroscience, 13,* 334–350.

Sterling, P. (1998). Retina. In G. M. Shepherd (Ed.), *The synaptic organization of the brain* (pp. 205–253). New York: Oxford University Press.

Talbot, W. P., Darian-Smith, I., Kornhuber, H. H., & Mountcastle, V. B. (1968). The sense of flutter-vibration: Comparison of human capacity with response patterns of mechano-receptive afferents from the monkey hand. *Journal of Neurophysiology, 31,* 301–334.

Teller, D. Y. (1984). Linking propositions. *Vision Research, 24,* 1233–1246.

Teo, P. C., & Heeger, D. J. (1994). Perceptual image distortion. *SPIE Proceedings, 2179,* 127–139.

Thomas, J. R., & Olzak, L. A. (1997). Contrast gain control and fine spatial discriminations. *Journal of the Optical Society of America A, 14,* 2392–2405.

Tolhurst, D. J., & Heeger, D. J. (1997). Comparison of contrast-normalization and threshold models of the responses of simple cells in cat striate cortex. *Visual Neuroscience, 14,* 293–309.

Tolhurst, D. J., Movshon, J. A., & Dean, A. F. (1983). The statistical reliability of signals in single neurons in the cat and monkey visual cortex. *Vision Research, 23,* 775–785.

Ullman, S. (1996). *High-level vision.* Cambridge, MA: MIT Press.

Van Essen, D. C., & DeYoe, E. A. (1994). Concurrent processing in the primate visual cortex. In M. S. Gazzaniga (Ed.), *The cognitive neurosciences* (pp. 383–400). Cambridge, MA: MIT Press.

Virsu, V., & Lee, B. B. (1983). Light adaptation in cells of macaque lateral geniculate nucleus and its relation to human light adaptation. *Journal of Neurophysiology, 50,* 864–878.

Vogels, R., Spileers, W., & Orban, G. A. (1989). The response variability of striate cortical neurons in the behaving monkey. *Experimental Brain Research, 77,* 432–436.

Walraven, J., Enroth-Cugell, C., Hood, D. C., MacLeod, D. I. A., & Schnapf, J. L. (1990). The control of visual sensitivity: Receptoral and postreceptoral processes. In L. Spillman & J. S. Werner (Eds.), *Visual perception: The neurophysiological foundations* (pp. 53–101). San Diego: Academic Press.

Wandell, B. A. (1995). *Foundations of vision.* Sunderland, MA: Sinauer.

Wandell, B. (1999). Functional imagery of human visual cortex. *Annual Review of Neuroscience, 22,* 145–173.

Watson, A. B. (1983). Detection and recognition of simple spatial forms. In O. J. Braddick & A. C. Sleigh (Eds.), *Physical and biological processing of images* (pp. 110–114). Berlin: Springer-Verlag.

Watson, A. B., & Ahumada, A. J. (1985). Model of human visual-motion sensing. *Journal of the Optical Society of America A, 2,* 322–342.

Watson, A. B., & Solomon, J. A. (1997). Model of visual contrast gain control and pattern masking. *Journal of the Optical Society of America A, 14,* 2379–2391.

Wertheim, T. (1894). Über die indirekte Sehschärfe. *Zeitschrift für Psychologie und Physiologie der Sinnesorgane, 7,* 172–189.

Westheimer, G., & Campbell, F. W. (1962). Light distribution in the image formed by the living human eye. *Journal of the Optical Society of America, 52,* 1040–1045.

Williams, D. R. (1988). Topography of the foveal cone mosaic in the living human eye. *Vision Research, 28,* 433–454.

Wilson, H. R. (1980). A transducer function for threshold and suprathreshold human vision. *Biological Cybernetics, 38,* 171–178.

Wilson, H. R., & Bergen, J. R. (1979). A four mechanism model for threshold spatial vision. *Vision Research, 19,* 19–32.

Wilson, H. R., & Gelb, D. J. (1984). Modified line-element theory for spatial-frequency and width discrimination. *Journal of the Optical Society of America A, 1,* 124–131.

Wilson, H. R., & Humanski, R. (1993). Spatial frequency adaptation and contrast gain control. *Vision Research, 33,* 1133–1149.

Wilson, H. R., Levi, D., Maffei, L., Rovamo, J., & De Valois, R. (1990). The perception of form: Retina to striate cortex. In L. Spillmann & J. S. Werner (Eds.), *Visual perception: The neurophysiological foundations* (pp. 231–272). San Diego: Academic Press.

Zipser, K., Lamme, V. A. F., & Schiller, P. H. (1996). Contextual modulation in primary visual cortex. *The Journal of Neuroscience, 16*(22), 7376–7389.

CHAPTER 4

Color Vision

Karen K. De Valois
Russell L. De Valois

I. INTRODUCTION

Color vision is the ability to discriminate changes in the wavelength composition of a visual stimulus independently of its effective intensity. It is an ability that humankind shares with many other species, including insects, amphibians, reptiles, fish, and birds, as well as other mammals. Because color vision apparently evolved independently several times, and the range and limitations of color vision differ significantly among different animals (Jacobs, 1981), the underlying neural mechanisms are not identical in different species. For this reason, we shall restrict our discussion of the relevant anatomy and physiology to data derived primarily from humans and the Old World primates, which have been shown to have color vision essentially identical in every measured aspect to that of humans (De Valois, Morgan, Polson, Mead, & Hull, 1974).

A. Trichromacy

A complete physical description of the spectral composition of a stimulus requires specifying its location in a space of many dimensions. A human observer with normal color vision, however, can provide a match for every possible test light by approximately combining and adjusting just three variable lights. This trichromatic limitation reflects a huge loss of information in the human visual system. The

Seeing

trichromatic nature of color vision was postulated as early as the 18th century (Palmer, 1777; Young, 1802), and it was empirically demonstrated during the 19th century (Maxwell, 1860). Trichromacy implies that at some processing stage, color information is limited by being transmitted through a three-channel pathway. It does not identify the point at which the three-channel bottleneck occurs, despite many suggestions that trichromacy implies the existence of only three cone types. Indeed, recent evidence (*vide infra*) clearly implicates not the receptors, but rather a later, postreceptoral site as the source of the trichromatic limitation.

The three variable lights which, when mixed, can produce a match for any test light, can be selected from an infinite set of possible primaries. The only restriction is that no two primaries can be mixed (in any proportion) to match the third. Thus, the three primaries can be all drawn from similar colors or from very different colors. There is no requirement that they be red, blue, and yellow, or any other particular set. In color matching, one of the primaries must often be added to the test light to be matched, while the other two are combined.

In a standard color-matching experiment, the test light (which the subject is asked to match) is displayed on one side of a bipartite field, usually a circle divided into halves. The subject may combine any or all of the three primaries in the other half field, or he may add a primary to the half field containing the test light. In this case, of course, the appearance of the test light itself will generally be altered. The subject controls the radiance as well as the half-field position of each of the three primaries. The results are described in the form of an equation, such as:

$$\alpha \mathbf{A} + \beta \mathbf{B} - \gamma \mathbf{C} \equiv \mathbf{T}$$

where **A, B,** and **C** are the three primaries; α, β, and γ are the radiances of primaries **A, B,** and **C,** respectively; **T** is the test light to be matched; the symbol $\equiv$ denotes a complete visual match; and a minus sign indicates that the primary so designated was added to the half field containing the test light. The strong form of the trichromatic generalization (Grassmann, 1853) also states that adding any other light to both sides of a color match will not disturb the match (the additivity property), and that multiplying the radiances of both sides of a color match by the same factor will not disturb the match (the proportionality property).

The quantitative data generated by color-matching experiments and the strong implication of a three-channel limiting stage combined to drive research and theory in color vision for many decades. Models proposing three largely independent channels that began at the receptor stage and continued with little or no interaction through most of the visual system were based on the undeniable demonstrations of trichromacy. Among the best known of such models was that of Helmholtz (1867), who postulated three receptors with somewhat overlapping spectral absorption functions but widely separated peaks centered in the regions of the spectrum typically identified as red, green, and blue by a normal observer adapted to an achromatic background. We now know that both of these postulates—widely separated spectral peaks and independent channels from the different cone types to the brain—are quite wrong. Nonetheless, attention to the trichromatic nature of color vision is essential to an understanding of many anomalies of color vision, as well as of normal color matching. For example, the reduced chromatic discrimination of a dichromat can be understood as the behavior of a system in which only two, not three, channels are present.

B. Color Spaces and the Representation of Color

Because color vision is trichromatic, all visible colors can be adequately represented in a three-dimensional space. There are an infinite number of possible spaces, and insofar as color mixing in the visual system is linear (and it is), any one space can be linearly transformed to any other. Thus the characteristics of the space used can be selected for convenience or for their ability to represent more or less directly the processing stages in the neural color system. Several color spaces have been devised over the years. We briefly describe three of the most useful.

1. Perceptual Color Space

A consideration of the perceptual dimensions of color led to the representation of color in a three-dimensional space in which each dimension corresponds to one of the three main perceptual dimensions of color. It is most commonly illustrated (in a nonquantitative, diagrammatic way) as two cones of equal size with their round bases abutting, as illustrated in Figure 1. The vertical axis (running lengthwise through the two cones) is the locus of all achromatic lights and corresponds to lightness or brightness, with bright, achromatic lights being represented near the peak, intermediate grays arrayed in order along the middle of the axis, and dark, achromatic stimuli near the bottom. The lateral distance of a point from the achromatic axis indicates its saturation, the perceived amount of hue in the stimulus. Thus, the light pastel colors would plot to points above the middle and near the vertical axis; the dark desaturated colors such as navy and brown would be represented near the vertical axis and below the middle; and the most highly saturated colors would be arranged around the perimeter of the midlevel of the double cone. At any vertical level, the hues vary in sequence around any horizontal plane through the space. The hues are arranged in such a way that nearest neighbors are those hues that appear most similar. Thus green, for example, would gradually shade into yellowish-green, which would gradually turn into yellow, and so on. Generally, such an ordering reflects spectral ordering, with adjacent wavelengths appearing most similar. The one exception results from the fact that while wavelength varies along a single dimension and can be represented along a straight line, the color appearance of spectral lights has a circular organization, with the long wavelengths curling back to meet the shortest visible wavelengths. Thus very short-wavelength violets appear reddish. This space also illustrates the fact that greatly increasing the intensity of a light reduces its saturation, so that the brightest lights appear white (Parsons, 1915). Sim-

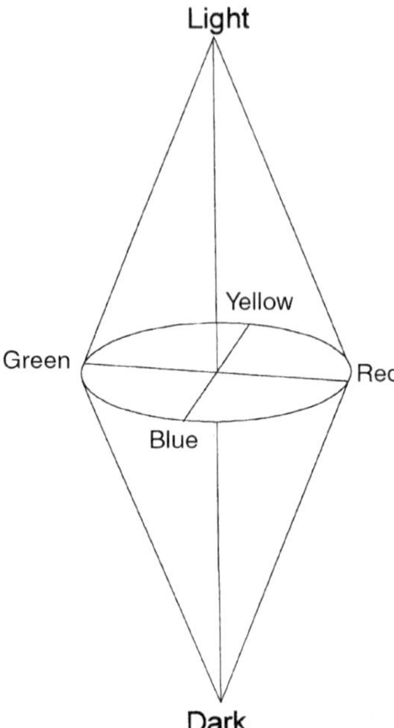

FIGURE 1 A perceptually based color space, in which the vertical axis represents lightness or brightness, the angle around a circular cross-section at any level represents hue, and the distance along any radius represents saturation. All colors that lie along the central vertical axis, thus, are achromatic, and all colors that lie along any vertical axis have the same hue.

ilarly, even monochromatic stimuli much darker than the adaptation level appear black.

2. CIE xyz Color Space

Although a perceptually defined color space well represents the relationships in appearance across the broad gamut of visible colors, it has proven less useful as a scientific tool, though a modified version of such a space, the Munsell color space, is still widely used in industry. A more widely used color space is the 1931 xyz chromaticity diagram defined by the Commission Internationale de l'Eclairage (CIE). This is based upon color-matching data generated early in the 20th century using several observers in different laboratories, making color matches using different sets of primaries. The data were combined and averaged to produce color-matching functions for a standard observer.

Recall that in color-matching experiments, one primary often must be added to the test light, and that the amount of this primary is represented by a negative coefficient. If any set of three physically realizable primaries were used to define the three dimensions of the space, many points would plot outside the first quadrant. In order to eliminate negative values, the color-matching data defining the standard observer were transformed to a set of imaginary primaries. These were selected such that all realizable colors could be represented using only positive coefficients. One of the three imaginary primaries was defined as matching the photopic spectral sensitivity function (known as V_λ) of the standard observer. The absolute values representing the amounts of each of the three primaries used for a particular color match (called distribution coefficients) were also transformed into ratios. Each distribution coefficient was represented as a proportion of the sum of the three distribution coefficients. With the transformation from absolute values to ratios, if two of the transformed values (known as chromaticity coordinates) are given, the third is implicitly known, since the three proportions must sum to 1. Thus, any point in this three-dimensional space can be shown in the two-dimensional representation shown in Figure 2. The z coefficient, which is not shown directly, equals $1-(x+y)$.

In the CIE 1931 xyz chromaticity diagram, the monochromatic lights are represented on the curved spectral locus bounding most of the space. The wavelengths corresponding to several points are shown on the figure. The straight line connecting the longest wavelengths with the shortest wavelengths is the locus of the most saturated purples. A region in the middle of the space contains the loci of points

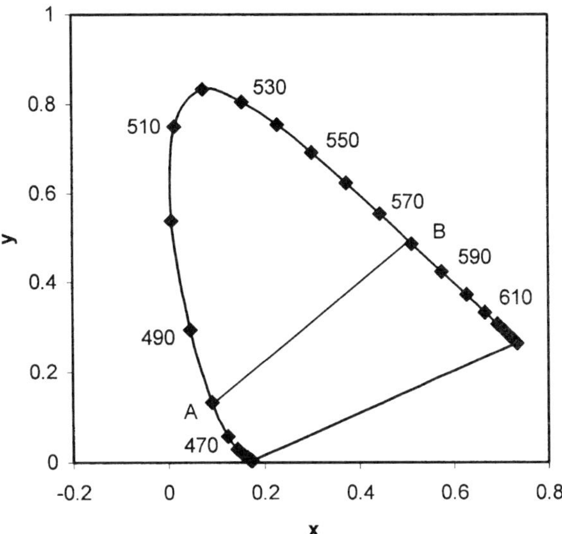

FIGURE 2 The Commission Internationale de l'Eclairage (CIE) 1931 xyz chromaticity diagram, in which the third (z) dimension is implicitly represented. The sum of x+y+z is constrained to equal 1. Monochromatic lights are represented on the curved spectral locus, whereas the straight line segment connecting the longest and shortest wavelengths is the locus of the most saturated purples. A central region of the diagram represents the points a normal observer in a state of neutral adaptation will see as white.

seen as white under neutral adaptation. This color space has several very useful properties. For example, a mixture of any two lights in any proportions will lie somewhere along the straight line connecting the two mixture components. A normal observer in a state of neutral adaptation will generally see the point labeled A as blue, and the point labeled B as yellow. If the two lights represented by those points are mixed, the chromaticity of the resulting light will lie on the line AB. This line passes through the region most observers see as white under neutral adaptation. Thus, this intuitively unlikely result—that blue and yellow can mix to produce white—can be deduced from inspection of the color space. An excellent discussion of the development and the characteristics of the CIE 1931 xyz chromaticity space is given by Kaiser and Boynton (1997).

3. MBDKL Physiological Color Space

The third color space that we will describe briefly was derived not from color appearance (like the double-cone space) or from color matching (like the CIE 1931 xyz space), but from physiological data. We now have a quite precise knowledge of cone photopigment spectral sensitivity curves (see Figure 4) and of the neural transformations of the cone outputs in the retinal processing (see Figure 5). This color space is based on such data. A cone-based color space was initially developed by MacLeod and Boynton (1979). It was later elaborated, on the basis of different chromatic cell types seen in the path through the lateral geniculate nucleus (LGN) to the cortex, into a three-dimensional space by Derrington, Krauskopf, and Lennie (1984). We will refer to it as the MBDKL color space. A version of this is shown in Figure 3. The outputs of the cone photoreceptors, with peak spectral sensitivities in the short (S), medium (M) and longer (L) wavelengths, respectively, are compared at later neural levels by neurons that sum and difference their outputs (De Valois, 1965; De Valois, Abramov, & Jacobs, 1966; Derrington et al., 1984), as discussed below. The three axes of this color space correspond to the three types of neurons in the retina and LGN that carry the information to the cortex about these sums and differences. The vertical axis represents luminance (light intensity weighted by the spectral sensitivity function of the visual system, modeled as the sum of 2L+M cone outputs). Two orthogonal axes lying in a horizontal plane of the sphere represent the difference of L and M cone absorptions (the LM axis), and the variation in S-cone absorption, with L and M cone absorptions held constant (the S or tritan axis). In this space, any point can be specified by its azimuth (representing the angle in a horizontal plane, with the LM axis defining the 0°–180° directions, and the S-varying axis defining the 90°–270° directions) and its elevation, where the elevation represents luminance with respect to the midpoint. Within any horizontal plane, all points represent stimuli that are equated for luminance (thus, an isoluminant plane), with different horizontal planes representing different luminance levels.

Below we shall briefly discuss first the anatomy and physiology underlying color

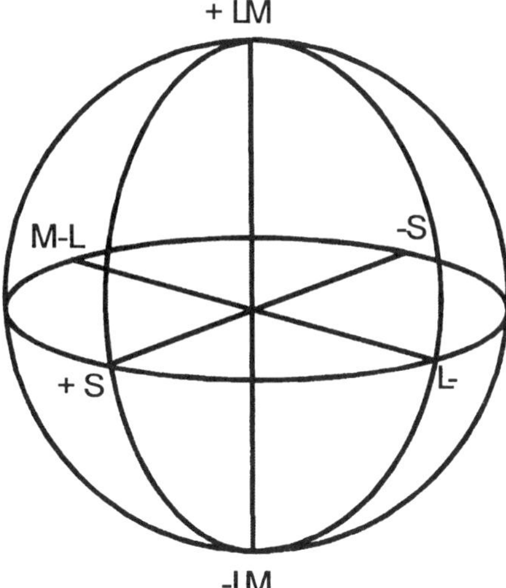

FIGURE 3 The MBDKL physiologically based color space in which the vertical axis represents luminance (defined as the sum of long [L] and medium [M] cone outputs), and the two spectrally opponent axes seen at an early neural level are orthogonally represented on the horizontal plane. All points that lie on a common horizontal plane represent isoluminant stimuli; hue varies with angle around the horizontal plane; saturation increases along any radius in a given horizontal plane. The point L-M is by convention defined as 0°; +S is 90°; M-L is 180°; and −S is 270°.

vision, including the photopigments and their spectral sensitivities, the distribution of different receptor types across the retina, receptor function, types of retinal computations, and color processing in the cortex. Then we shall discuss several behavioral (or psychophysical) aspects of color vision, including chromatic opponency, perceptual dimensions of color, chromatic discriminations, spatial and temporal contrast sensitivity, color appearance, and color motion. In each case, we shall attempt to relate the behavioral aspects of color vision to the underlying physiology.

II. PHYSIOLOGY

A. Photopigments and Spectral Sensitivity

The initial stage in the visual response is the absorption of light by the photopigments in the receptors. The cones are the most relevant receptors for color vision, indeed for all vision at high light levels. The absorption of light by a cone photopigment triggers a complex series of reactions, leading ultimately to synaptic transmission at the cone pedicle. Here we discuss briefly some characteristics of the photopigments that are relevant in determining whether a given photon will be absorbed when it encounters a photopigment molecule.

The receptor outer segment is filled with about 500–1000 disks, each containing millions of photopigment molecules. The photopigments in our rods (the receptors used for vision at low light levels) and in all the different types of cones are built on a very similar plan: a chromophore, retinal (Vitamin A aldehyde) is attached to a large protein molecule called an opsin. Such photosensitive pigments (called rhodopsin in rods) are found in the eyes of all animals and have been highly conserved in the course of evolution, having arisen a billion or more years ago in bacteria. Rhodopsin and the similar cone opsins are uniquely useful for vision for two reasons. One is that the capture of just one photon is sufficient to break the molecule apart into its separate retinal and opsin components, so it has attained ultimate photosensitivity. The other reason is that when the retinal breaks away from the opsin, it reveals an enzymatic site. The opsin now acts as an enzyme to initiate a cascade of chemical reactions, providing the amplification of the tiny energy of a few photons to the much larger energy required to activate neurons and transmit information through the nervous system. Although the cone transduction sequence has not been as exhaustively studied as that in rods, there are good reasons to assume that it is similar.

The basic shape of the spectral sensitivity curve of rhodopsin and the various cone opsins is determined by retinal, which is common to all receptor photopigments. All receptors therefore have similarly shaped spectral sensitivity curves. But the spectral region to which the molecule is most sensitive is also affected by parts of the opsin in the vicinity of the retinal attachment site, and each different receptor type, rods and three (or more) cone types, has a somewhat different opsin. The substitution of one amino acid for another at a particular point in the opsin molecule can shift the spectral sensitivity curve to longer or to shorter wavelengths. Amino acid substitutions that produce major shifts in spectral sensitivity have created three primary regions of receptor peak sensitivities (Schnapf, Kraft, & Baylor, 1987; Schnapf, Kraft, Nunn & Baylor, 1988) (see Figure 4). These are found in the S cones (with greatest sensitivity at about 430 nm), in rods (which peak at about 500 nm), and in L and M cones (with peaks ranging from about 530 to 565 nm). Amino acid substitutions in L and M opsins that produce smaller spectral shifts have created a variety of L and M photopigment types among the normal and color-defective human population (Neitz, Neitz, & Jacobs, 1991). For example, there are M cones with peak absorption at 530 and others at 535 nm, and L cones with peak sensitivities at 555 or 560 or 565 nm.

All humans appear to have the same S-cone and rod photopigments, but they differ somewhat in their L and M cone pigments. About 8% of human males and about 1% of females have color vision deficiencies, most of which are the so-called red–green deficiencies. The prevalence of this particular type of color-vision defect can be accounted for by the chromosomal location of the various photopigment genes. The rod photopigment gene is on chromosome 3; the S cone pigment gene is on chromosome 7; and both the M and the L cone photopigment genes are side-

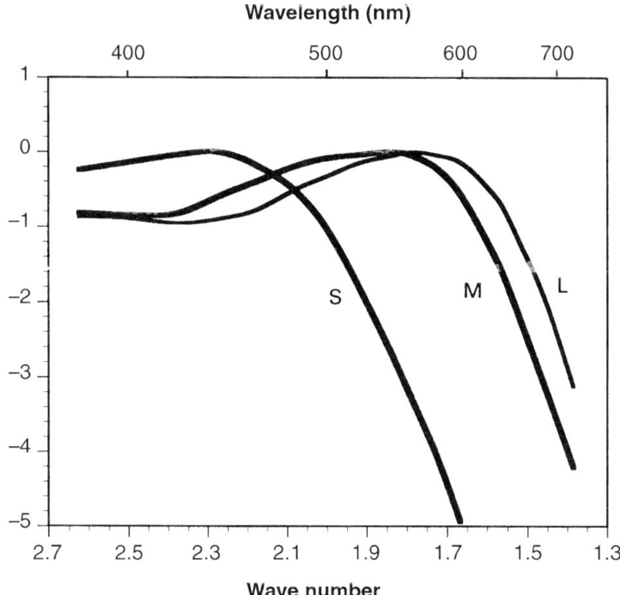

FIGURE 4 Three representative cone pigments in primates, based on the report of Baylor, Nunn, and Schnapf, 1987. (S, short; M, medium; L, long).

by-side on the X chromosome (Nathans, Thomas, & Hogness, 1986). Because they are adjacent to one another on the same chromosome, the L and M photopigment genes are subject to interchanging parts in the process of crossing over during meiosis, resulting in a variety of L and M gene types (alleles) in the population. The extreme case is one in which the two genes end up being identical, thus specifying only one longer wavelength (either M or L) photopigment. Because males only inherit one copy of the X chromosome, whereas females inherit two, a female would have to inherit defective genes from both parents (but a male only from his mother) to be color-defective. An interesting corollary of this is that many females appear to have more than just two LM pigments, and thus more than three different cone types (Neitz & Jacobs, 1990), but females with more than three cone types nonetheless have only a trichromatic color vision system (Nagy, MacLeod, Heyneman, & Eisner, 1981). Presumably, the two L cones that such a woman might possess are treated as being identical by the retinal organization and thus do not lead to an additional chromatic dimensionality. This strongly suggests that the trichromatic limit to human color vision is the result of only three types of analyses in the retina, and/or of only three paths from the retina to the cortex, not, as was long supposed, because of the presence of only three cone types.

2. Receptor Distribution

Color vision is not uniform across the retina. Important sources of the nonuniformity are variations in the numbers and distributions of different cone types across the retina. Corresponding to the three main photopigment types, in the rods, the S cones, and the L and M cones, are three different patterns of receptor distribution and number. There are about 100,000,000 rods in each human (and Old World monkey) eye, about 4,000,000 L and M cones, and perhaps 300,000 S cones (Curcio, Sloan, Kalina, & Hendrickson, 1990). Rods are absent in the central 30° or so of the eye, reach their highest density at about 20° eccentricity, and drop off in density from there to the periphery (Curcio et al., 1990; Østerberg, 1935).[1] The L and M cones are extremely tightly packed in the center of the fovea (the foveola) where their density is highest. They fall off in density rapidly from the center but are present throughout the retina. The S cones taper off in density from the edge of the fovea to the periphery at about the same rate as do the L and M receptors. Their distribution *within* the fovea, however, is quite different from that of the L and M cones. The S-cone density falls from the edge of the fovea toward the center (while the density of L and M cones rises rapidly), and approaches zero in the very center of the foveola (Anhelt, Kolb, & Pflug, 1987; Curcio et al., 1991; de Monasterio, McCrane, Newlander, & Schein, 1985).

3. Receptor Function

Receptors are similar to neurons elsewhere in the nervous system; the retina is in fact part of the brain that just happens to lie some distance away, in the eye. Receptors respond to stimuli by either a depolarization or a hyperpolarization of their outer dendritic membranes, and they communicate the results of the computation they carry out by releasing synaptic chemicals in proportion to the amount of depolarization in the synaptic region. Although ordinary neurons respond to external transmitter chemicals from other neurons, photoreceptors respond to chemicals generated within the receptor itself, triggered by a change in the number of photons absorbed.

At a steady illumination level, the receptor outer segment membrane is maintained at a certain intermediate level of polarization by a balance between opposing sets of chemical interactions briefly summarized below. The effect of increases and decreases in the amount of light absorbed by the receptor photopigment molecules (due to a change in either the intensity or the wavelength of light reaching it) is to shift the polarization balance momentarily in one direction or the other. This polarization change in the outer segment is conducted in one direction or the

[1] It is customary to specify the sizes of visual objects and of retinal images in terms of the visual angle, in degrees, minutes, and seconds, that they subtend at the eye. Thus your fingernail at arm's length subtends about 1° visual angle, approximately the diameter of the foveal center.

other. This polarization change in the outer segment is conducted to the synaptic region, where it produces a change in the rate of synaptic chemical release. A *decrement* in light absorbed shifts the balance towards *depolarization* and leads to an increase in synaptic transmitter release to activate the next neurons in the chain to the brain; an *increment* in light absorption shifts the balance towards *hyperpolarization* and produces a decrease in transmitter release. As we move our eyes around in a scene, as we do constantly, the amount of light absorbed by each receptor oscillates up and down, as the intensity or the wavelength of light being absorbed varies. The receptors faithfully transduce these oscillating increases and decreases in light absorption into oscillating amounts of synaptic transmitter release.

The receptor outer segment membrane is maintained at a certain level of polarization (roughly −40 mV) by a balance between the action of $_c$GMP, which opens pores in the cell membrane allowing Na^+ and Ca^{++} ions to enter and depolarize the cell, and a metabolic pump that expels these ions and hyperpolarizes the cell. The polarization varies as the level of $_c$GMP varies, and that in turn is determined, moment by moment, by the changes in absorption of light in the outer segment disks. $_c$GMP is constantly being produced, but it is broken down by phosphodiesterase, which in turn is produced by a chemical, transducin, activated by the breakdown of rhodopsin or the cone opsin by light. With a decrease in light being absorbed by the receptor, less phosphodiesterase will be produced, the level of $_c$GMP will go up, the membrane will be depolarized, and the receptor will secrete transmitter chemicals to the next neurons in the chain. An increase in light being absorbed by the receptor will produce more phosphodiesterase, the level of $_c$GMP will go down, and the membrane will be hyperpolarized, resulting in a decrease in the amount of receptor transmitter chemical being released.

A second set of reactions also plays an important role in the responses of receptors. As $_c$GMP opens membrane pores, Ca^{++} ions flow in and inhibit, with a brief time delay, the production of $_c$GMP; conversely, when the pores are closed, the internal Ca^{++} level falls and the production of $_c$GMP increases. This negative feedback has the effect of making the receptor responsive to transient increments and decrements but less so to the steady-state illumination level. It thus forms the second stage, after the variations in pupil size, in the process by which the visual system minimizes responses to the illuminant in order to concentrate on capturing information about visual objects.

B. Retino-Geniculate Processing

1. Retinal Connectivity

There are two levels of synaptic interaction in the retina: among receptors, bipolar cells, and horizontal cells in the outer plexiform layer, and among bipolar cells, amacrine cells and ganglion cells in the inner plexiform layer. The path from receptors to bipolar cells to ganglion cells leads towards the brain; horizontal and amacrine cells form lateral connections and provide for data processing within their respective plexiform layers.

Anatomists have identified many different subtypes of each of the various neural elements in the retina, for example, as many as 25 different varieties of amacrine cells. However, the function of many of these subtypes, and indeed whether or not some of the slight anatomical differences have any functional significance at all, is unknown. What we present here is a simplified version of the anatomical arrangement, based on the currently well understood cell types and connections, including only those clearly relevant to color vision.

It is equally important for the visual system to detect increments and decrements in light intensity, and to detect changes in wavelength toward longer and toward shorter wavelengths. Receptors presumably depolarize and hyperpolarize symmetrically about the mean depolarization level, and can thus signal changes in these opposite directions equally well. When the form of the information is changed from variations in graded potentials of receptors and bipolar cells to variations in spike firing rate at the level of ganglion cell axons (a transformation that is needed to transfer the information the long distance to the thalamus and from there to the cortex), this symmetry is lost. Cells can fire bursts of spikes at rates up to about 400/sec, but rapid firing rates are very expensive metabolically. For a single cell to carry information equally well about increments and decrements from the mean adaptation level, it would have to fire an average of 200 spikes/sec, day and night. The visual system has instead divided the task between two cells in each location, each with a low maintained rate (of perhaps 10 spikes/sec), with one responding from 10 to 400 spikes/sec to various sizes of increments in absorption, and the other responding from 10 to 400 spikes/sec to decrements in absorption. This division of labor takes place at different levels, and with different organizations, for rods as compared to L and M cones, and seemingly almost not at all for S cones.

Receptors contact bipolar and horizontal cells with two different sorts of connections. The receptor synaptic region has a number of pouches, and receptors contact bipolar and horizontal cell processes that invaginate the pouches. All receptors, rods and all types of cones, make this sort of connection. In addition, L and M cones make synaptic contact with a different class of bipolars outside the pouches, on the basal parts of the synaptic region (Missotten, 1965). The important fact is that invaginating and basal bipolars respond in opposite ways to the receptor transmitter, and thus in opposite ways to increments and decrements in the amount of light absorbed by the receptor (Famiglietti & Kolb, 1976). Receptors depolarize, and thus increase synaptic transmitter release, in response to decrements in light absorption. The basal bipolars are depolarized by the receptor transmitter and thus also depolarize to decrements. Invaginating bipolars, however, invert the receptor signal and thus depolarize to increments in light absorption.

Two different types of bipolar cells, midget and diffuse bipolars, pick up from L and M cones, and each of these is one of a pair, with one making invaginating contacts and one making basal contacts (Kolb, Boycott, & Dowling, 1969; Mariani,

1981). Each L and M cone, therefore, feeds into at least four different bipolars, two of which depolarize to increments and two to decrements. The L and M cones thus have separate, symmetrical systems for responding to increments and decrements starting at the bipolar level. This separate, symmetrical arrangement is continued up to the cortex. The midget bipolars contact midget ganglion cells, which in turn project up to the parvocellular (Pc) layers of the LGN. The diffuse bipolars contact parasol ganglion cells, which project to the magnocellular (Mc) layers of the LGN. Within each of these midget-Pc and parasol-Mc systems, there are separate cells responding primarily to increments and decrements in light.

The circuitry for S cones and for rods, however, is quite different. S cones contact a special type of invaginating bipolar (Mariani, 1984), which has no basal mate (there are some reports of certain different types of bipolars making basal contacts with S cones, but the circuitry involved is not known). The S-bipolar in turn contacts a different ganglion cell from those contacted by L and M cones, a bistratified ganglion cell that depolarizes to S-cone increments (Dacey & Lee, 1994). These S-ganglion cells appear to project to the koniocellular (Kc) layers of the LGN. The S-cone system is thus unbalanced, with ganglion cells and LGN cells that fire to S-cone increments, but few if any that respond to S-cone decrements.

Rods have still a third type of retinal organization and projection pattern to central levels. Rods do not have a separate path to the brain, but rather feed up through the same paths as the L and M cones. Although there is only an invaginating rod bipolar (which, like other invaginating bipolars, responds to light increments), the rods generate symmetrical incremental and decremental systems at a later level, through an intermediate type of rod amacrine cell. The rod bipolars contact rod amacrine cells, which in turn contact diffuse and midget ganglion cells. The rod amacrine cells each make two different types of connections, one a direct excitatory contact with an incremental ganglion cell, and a second sign-inverting connection with a decremental ganglion cell. The rod signals are thus similar to those of cones in being divided into separate paths that carry information about increments and decrements of light. They would therefore be expected to *reinforce* cone responses to intensity variations when both rods and cones are active. However, insofar as the rods feed up the Pc pathway, they would be sending the same signal to opposite sides of mirror-image opponent cell types (see discussion of opponent cells below), and would then have the effect of *decreasing* information about color variations. In fact, colors become quite desaturated as light levels decrease.

The discussion above refers only to the straight-through connections from receptors to bipolars to ganglion cells. However, critical to the functioning of the whole system are the lateral interactions made at each synaptic level, through the action of horizontal cells and amacrine cells. In the absence of such interactions, the retinal processing would simply consist of directly relaying the receptor outputs to the brain. This would be pointless because the output of a receptor contains no useful information by itself. It does not identify the color or the brightness in that region; it does not distinguish between a white and a black object or anything about shape or motion. Everything of interest to the visual system is contained in the relative activity of different receptors, and this is what the neural processing detects and encodes at all visual levels, starting with the receptor-bipolar-horizontal cell synapse.

Horizontal cells interconnect groups of nearby cones, picking up from a group of cones and feeding back into the same group. The horizontal cell processes within the pouches are stimulated by the receptors and also release synaptic transmitters back into the pouches. Each horizontal cell process that connects two or more receptors conducts graded potentials in both directions along its extent, allowing each of the receptors to influence and be influenced by each of the other receptors. The horizontal cell, by that mechanism, responds to the average light level in its local region. Horizontal cells, like receptors, depolarize to decrements and release synaptic transmitters in proportion to their level of depolarization. However, the transmitter released has the effect of hyperpolarizing the contacted membrane. With this feedback from the horizontal cells, then, the output of a given receptor is *not* just related to how many photons it is receiving, but rather is proportional to how many photons it is receiving relative to the number being absorbed by the other cones in the near neighborhood. Horizontal cells clearly feed back onto receptors. To what extent they also feed forward onto bipolar cells is not clear. If they do, it poses something of a problem to understand, since the invaginating bipolars, closely juxtaposed to the horizontal cell endings, would presumably be much more affected than the basal bipolars.

There are two main types of horizontal cells connected with cones in the primate retina. One type interconnects all the L and M cones within a region, but may largely bypass S cones (Anhelt & Kolb, 1994; Wässle, Boycott & Röhrenbeck, 1989). The other type contacts mainly S cones, but some L and M cones, as well. Thus there is no evidence for any specificity in the L/M connectivity (e.g., the feedback to an L cone appears to come from both L and M cones in the region). There appears to be little specificity in the S cone connectivity, as well. A rather similar type of connectivity is present in the inner plexiform layer, where amacrine cells interconnect groups of nearby bipolar cells and feed back to the bipolars, but also feed forward onto ganglion cells.

The receptive field (RF) of a cell is defined as all those receptors which, when stimulated, will activate the cell, or, alternatively, as that region in visual space within which stimuli will activate the cell (see Shapley, chapter 2, this volume). Typically, some stimuli depolarize a cell and lead to an increase in firing; other stimuli hyperpolarize a cell and produce a decrement in firing. The RF organization of a cell, then, is the arrangement of these opposing inputs within the RF extent. The RFs of ganglion cells consist of two opposing inputs: a "center" mechanism and an antagonistic "surround" mechanism. Despite the terms, both of these mechanisms are overlapping and centered on the same receptors. The primary difference between center and surround is the size of the two regions, the center (generally) being smaller in extent than the surround. The center mechanism in ganglion cells is produced by the direct connections of receptors to bipolars to ganglion cells. The surround mechanism is produced by some combination of the connections made by both horizontal and amacrine cells. The larger size of the surround reflects the fact that horizontal and amacrine cells pick up laterally over larger regions.

2. Types of Retinal Computations

The neural organization discussed above results in the visual system's carrying out three main types of computation in relation to color vision: a sum of receptor outputs, and two differences between cone outputs. To examine this, we will consider the RF characteristics of these various types of cells.

a. Summation of L and M Cone Outputs

The pathway from L and M cones to diffuse bipolars to parasol ganglion cells, with inputs from rods, and from horizontal and amacrine cells at the two synaptic levels, computes the sum of the outputs of a small group of L and M cones (and rods, when they are functional) minus the sum of the outputs of a larger, overlapping group of L and M cones (and rods). These cells thus have spatial opponency but not spectral opponency. That is, they respond in opposite directions to light intensity changes in different spatial locations, but not to lights of different spectral compositions.

Ignoring the rod input, and given the mirror-image arrangement of invaginating and basal bipolar types, the cells in this pathway can be characterized as $+(L+M)_c - (L+M)_s$ and $-(L+M)_c + (L+M)_s$, where $_c$ and $_s$ refer to RF center and surround, respectively. Such cells report not the amount of light in an area, but the extent to which there is more or less light in this region (center area) compared with the mean level over a somewhat larger region (surround area), that is, the local contrast. These cells feed up to the Mc layers of the LGN and from there to layer IVα[2] of the striate cortex, with a weaker projection to lower layer VI. Because these cells are summing the outputs of different cone types, and color information lies not in the sums but in the differences between the outputs of different cone types, they presumably make no contribution to our perception of different hues. They may well have an input into the black–white color system, however.

b. Difference of L and M Cone Outputs

The pathways from L and M cones to midget bipolars and midget ganglion cells, with lateral inputs from horizontal and amacrine cells, computes the *difference* between the absorptions by the L and M cones within their RFs. They thus have spectral opponency, but they also have spatial opponency, because the L and M cones that feed into their RFs do not lie in the same locations. The midget ganglion cells feed up to the 2–4 Pc layers of the LGN and from there to layer IVβ of the striate cortex, with weaker projections to layers IIIBβ and upper layer VI.

[2] The terminology for the different layers of the striate cortex appears to be in transition from the older Brodmann terms to a more recent nomenclature suggested by Hässler (1967), in which the input layers are designated by IVα and β rather than IVcα and IVcβ.

Within the foveal region, the RF center of each midget ganglion cell receives input from just a single L or M cone, with input into the surround from the other cone type (Wässle, Grünert, Martin, & Boycott, 1994). There are thus four subtypes of L/M opponent cells: $+L_c-M_s$, $-L_c+M_s$, $+M_c-L_s$ and $-M_c+L_s$. To understand the functional role of these cells, note that these four subtypes fall into two different combinations of pairs, on the basis of similarity of the polarity of the L and M inputs (whether L−M or M−L), or the polarity of RF center and surround (whether + or − center). Two of these subtypes ($+L_c-M_s$ and $-M_c+L_s$) are +L−M, with excitatory input from L cones and inhibitory input from M cones in the RF as a whole; and two ($+M_c-L_s$ and $-L_c+M_s$) are +M−L. Two of the subtypes ($+L_c-M_s$ and $+M_c-L_s$) are $+_c-_s$, with excitatory center input and inhibitory surround input; and two ($-L_c+M_s$ and $-M_c+L_s$) are $-_c+_s$. It is not certain whether RF surrounds are cone-type specific, as suggested above, or made up of a combination of L and M cone inputs (De Valois & De Valois, 1993; Reid & Shapley, 1992). It makes surprisingly little difference which is the case. Since the center mechanism is much stronger than the surround, the presence in the surround of some of the center-type cones would merely slightly diminish the effective strength of the center.

Outside the foveal region, each midget bipolar still picks up from only one cone, but the midget ganglion cells receive input from more than one midget bipolar (Wässle et al., 1994). It is not known to what extent a given midget ganglion cell in this region picks up just from L-center bipolars, or just from M-center bipolars. Overall, the output of some 4,000,000 cones must feed into some 800,000 midget ganglion cells, so considerable convergence must be present in the retinal periphery. Finally, in the far periphery of the eye, there is no anatomical indication of specificity of connectivity to the bipolar cells; rather, a bipolar cell appears to connect to all the neighboring cones in a small region (Wässle et al., 1994); it would thus have a combination of L and M cones in both RF center and surround. It thus appears likely that there is a loss in cone-type opponency with increasing retinal eccentricity, but the opponency between different locations should be maintained. The peripheral Pc cells thus start to resemble Mc cells in their spectral properties. However, at all eccentricities, Mc cells have considerably larger RFs than Pc cells at the corresponding eccentricity (Rodieck, Binmoeller, & Dineen, 1985).

c. *Difference of S and LM Cone Outputs*

The pathway from S cones to S-bipolar cells and to S-ganglion cells computes the difference between the absorption of the S cones and the sum of the absorptions of L and M cones. The "center" and "surround" mechanisms are about the same size, but the center is stronger. As a result, these cells have only spectral opponency with no spatial opponency. In contrast to the paths discussed previously that signal the sum and difference of the L and M cone responses, the S-cone pathway is very unbalanced. There are many more $+S_c-(L+M)_s$ cells than there are $-S_c+(L+M)_s$ (de Monasterio, 1979; Derrington et al., 1984; Valberg, Lee, & Tidwell, 1986). In fact, by some accounts the latter do not even exist (Malpeli & Schiller, 1978). Also in contrast to the L/M path, the S-cone bipolars and ganglion cells appear to maintain their specificity, picking up in their RF centers just from S cones, all the way to the retinal periphery (Kouyama & Marshak, 1992). The S-ganglion cells appear to feed into the Kc layers of the LGN (Hendry & Yoshioka, 1994; Martin, White, Goodchild, Wilder, & Sefton, 1997), and from there to layer IIIBα in the cytox-blob regions (see later discussion of cytox blobs) of the striate cortex (Ding & Casagrande, 1997).

3. Summary of Connectivity

There are three main types of retinal processing and three main paths to the cortex, the Mc, Pc, and Kc paths. None of the cells in these three paths signals the amount of light in its region of the retina; rather, they signal the differences between different distributions of light within their RFs. None of the cells in these three paths signals the outputs of just one cone type, either; instead, they signal the sums of or the differences between the activity of different cone types. The cells in the Mc path, in a *spatially opponent* organization, signal changes in the amount of light absorbed by a small group of L and M cones relative to the amount absorbed by the L and M cones in a larger, overlapping area. Their responses would correspond to the vertical, luminance axis in MBDKL color space (shown in Figure 3). The cells in the Kc path, in a *spectrally opponent* organization, signal changes in the amount of light stimulating one or more S cones relative to the amount stimulating the neighboring L and M cones. Their outputs correspond to the S or tritan axis in MBDKL space; see Figure 5. Finally, cells in the Pc path (about 80% of the total) have both a *spatially and a spectrally opponent* organization, at least in the central retina. They signal the difference between the activity of L and M cones in a small region, in a spectrally opponent organization; but they also signal the changes in the amount of activation of one cone relative to that in the surrounding cones, in a spatially opponent organization. Thus, the cells in the predominant channel from the eye to the cortex, the Pc cells, carry both color and intensity information. In response to full-field or very low spatial frequency stimuli, their outputs would constitute the LM axis in MBDKL color space; see Figure 5. In response to high spatial frequency stimuli, their outputs would contribute to the luminance axis in MBDKL color space.

C. Cortex

1. Striate Cortex

The three main retino-cortical paths have separate projections to the striate cortex (V1), as described above, but within the cortex the paths are no longer discrete. Rather, striate cortex cells combine the outputs of the different cell types in various ways. Most of the cortical processing involves building RFs to detect various spatial characteristics (e.g., spatial frequency, orientation, depth) of the pattern

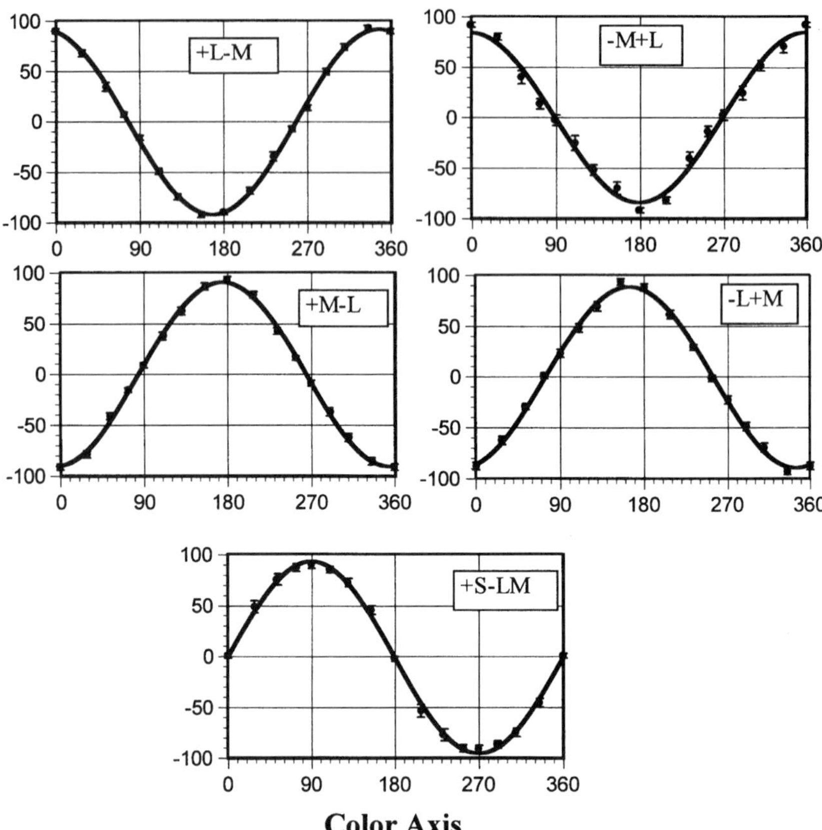

FIGURE 5 Responses of a sample of each of the various types of macaque lateral geniculate nucleus (LGN) opponent cells to stimuli that consist of a shift from a white background to various isoluminant stimuli arranged in a circle in MBDKL space. L, M, and S refer to the long, medium, and short wavelength sensitive cones, respectively. The (LM) opponent cells give their peak responses to 0° or 180°, and the S-opponent cells to 90°. The contrasts of these stimuli were chosen to produce sinusoidal variations in absorption by each of the cone types. It can be seen from the sinusoidal fits to the data (with error bars of +/− 1 SEM) that the processing up to the LGN is very linear.

within a local cortical region (see Geisler & Albrecht, chapter 3, this volume). With respect to color vision per se, the primary processing involves separating color and luminance information, and constructing cells whose color selectivity corresponds to perceptual color appearance.

Figure 6 shows a cortical organization proposed by De Valois and De Valois (1993) that would separate color and luminance information and also construct cells whose chromatic selectivities correspond to the way in which normal human observers under neutral adaptation divide the spectrum into the primary colors of red, yellow, green, and blue. There are two main features to this proposed organization. One is that the output of the Kc path, the S_o (S-opponent) cells, would be combined with the output of cells in the Pc path, the L_o and M_o cells in various ways to produce not just some, but *all* the different cortical chromatic cell types. The second main feature is that the different subtypes of Pc cells would be combined in specific ways to produce cortical cells responsive mainly to color or mainly to luminance, respectively. We have direct evidence for the existence of cells with the postulated response properties in monkey striate cortex.

One aspect of this cortical interaction is the separation of the luminance and color information that is multiplexed in the responses of the primary input to the cortex, that of the Pc LGN cells. Recall that there are four subtypes of Pc cells, considering inputs to RF center and surround. As pointed out also by Lennie, Haake, and Williams (1991), if the responses of these cells were summed in pairs by cells in the striate cortex in one way, the luminance components to their responses would sum and the color components would cancel. Combined in a different proportion, the color would sum and the luminance cancel.

Consider a striate cortex cell (see Figure 7a) that combines superimposed inputs from one or more $+L_o$ $(+L_c-M_s)$ and $+M_o$ $(+M_c-L_s)$ LGN cells in a region. It

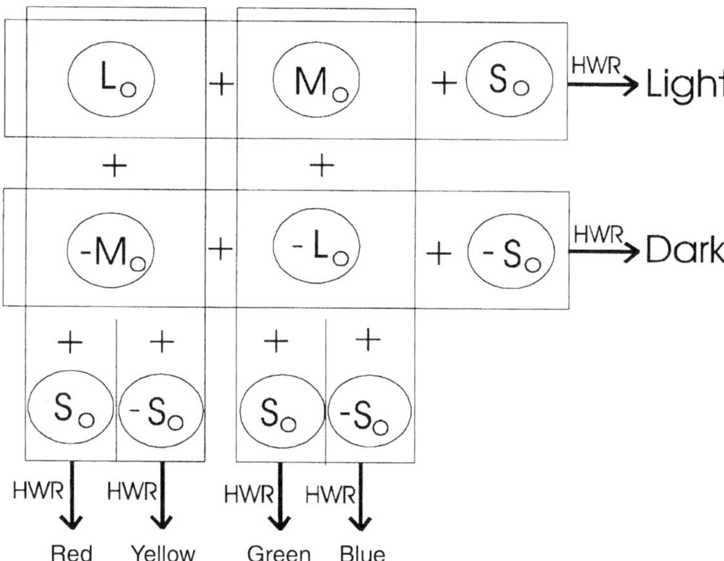

FIGURE 6 The third (cortical) stage of a three-stage model of color processing proposed by De Valois and De Valois (1993). In this model, the outputs of lateral geniculate nucleus (LGN) L_o, M_o, and S_o cells are combined in various ways to form the perceptual black, white, red, yellow, green, and blue systems. The L_o and M_o cell outputs are either added together to form the achromatic systems, canceling the color information, or subtracted from each other in the chromatic systems, canceling the intensity information. Note also that all three cell opponent cell types are combined in each chromatic and achromatic system. HWR refers to half-wave rectification.

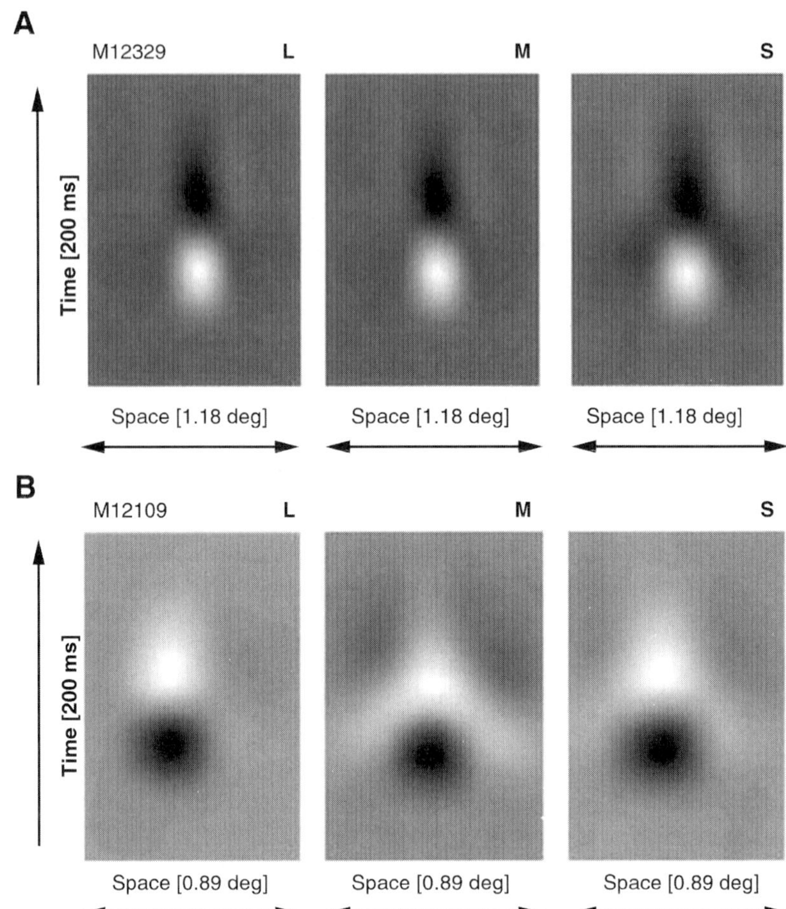

FIGURE 7 Space–time receptive fields (RF) of two nonopponent macaque striate cortex cells. For each cell, the RFs are shown for responses to cone-specific stimuli that activate just the (L), (M), and (S) cones, and thus the L-opponent, M-opponent, and S-opponent lateral geniculate nucleus (LGN) cells, respectively, as well as the nonopponent cells. In white are shown responses to increments in cone-specific stimuli, and in black responses to decrements in the cone-specific stimuli. The RFs are shown side-by-side, but cover the same spatial region, so the three maps are aligned spatially. From these RFs, one can also see how the responses change over time. There is initially no response (grey), but after about 50 ms the cell starts to respond, reaching its peak at about 75 ms, and then reverses polarity after about 90 ms. (A) This cell (a +L+M+S cell) responds in the same location to increments of L, M, or S-cone stimulation, and thus would respond optimally to a white luminance increment. (B) This cell is also spectrally nonopponent, but it responds to decrements in activations of each cone type rather than to increments, and thus is a −L−M−S cell, which would fire optimally to black. (Data collected from N. P. Cottaris, S. D. Elfar, and L. E. Mahon.)

responds well to luminance but not color variations. Both of its input cells fire to luminance increments in the RF center and to decrements in the surround, but their color organizations are opposite to each other, one being L-M and the other M-L.

Combined with input from a $+S_o$ ($+S_c-LM_s$) cell, this would produce a striate cell that fires to white and inhibits to black, but responds poorly if at all to pure color variations, as diagrammed in the top row of Figure 6. Similarly, as shown in the second row of Figure 6, a striate cortex cell (Figure 7b) that sums $-L_o$, $-M_o$, and $-S_o$ cells fires to black and inhibits to white because it has a $-c+s$ luminance RF. It would, however, be unresponsive to pure color variations, because the color RFs are opposite and thus would cancel.

Cortical cells receiving input from $+L_o$ ($+L_c-M_s$) and $-M_o$ ($-M_c+L_s$) cells, or from $+M_o$ and $-L_o$ cells, would respond well to color but not luminance variations, since their color responses would add while their opposite luminance RFs would cancel. This organization by itself would produce L-M color cells that would fire to warm colors (red and yellow) and inhibit to cool colors (blue and green), and M-L cells that fire to cool colors and inhibit to warm colors, respectively. As shown in Figure 6, the further addition of $+S_o$ or $-S_o$ cells would split these into separate red and yellow, and separate blue and green systems, respectively. Examples of these are shown in Figure 8.

If the inputs to cortical cells as diagrammed were perfectly balanced (e.g., if the weights to the $+L_o$ and $+M_o$ inputs to the cells shown in Figure 8 were precisely equal and thus completely canceled the chromatic components of their responses), this cortical organization would produce cells of six distinct classes, corresponding to the orthogonal axes in the *perceptual* color space shown in Figure 1. However, the weights of the various LGN-cell inputs are not always balanced, with the result that striate cortex cells are tuned to a variety of color axes, and many respond to both color and luminance patterns to variable extents (Thorell, De Valois, & Albrecht, 1984; Lennie, Krauskopf, & Sclar, 1990). Many functions are carried out in the striate cortex, and surely only a minority of the cells are actually involved in the processing of color. It is clear that certain cells in the striate cortex (cells not present at earlier levels) that respond just to color and are tuned to the perceptual color axes, and others that respond just to white or to black. It is possible, but by no means certain, that only these few cells contribute to our perceptual color organization, with the other cells merely using color as well as intensity information to compute various aspects of the spatial and temporal properties of visual stimuli.

2. Color beyond the Striate Cortex

Early reports (Zeki, 1973) stated that a prestriate region (termed area V4) was specialized for color, all of the cells being color-selective and apparently involved in color processing. It appears, however, that V4 is the major path to the temporal lobe, which is involved in all aspects of form vision, and that no larger a proportion of V4 cells than striate cortex cells are color-selective (Schien, Marrocco, & de Monasterio, 1982). Furthermore, lesions to V4 in monkeys produces only a slight impairment in color discrimination (Schiller, 1993). However, many clinical studies have identified a syndrome of cerebral achromatopsia in humans, a loss of color vision resulting from a prestriate cerebral lesion (Meadows, 1974). Such patients see the

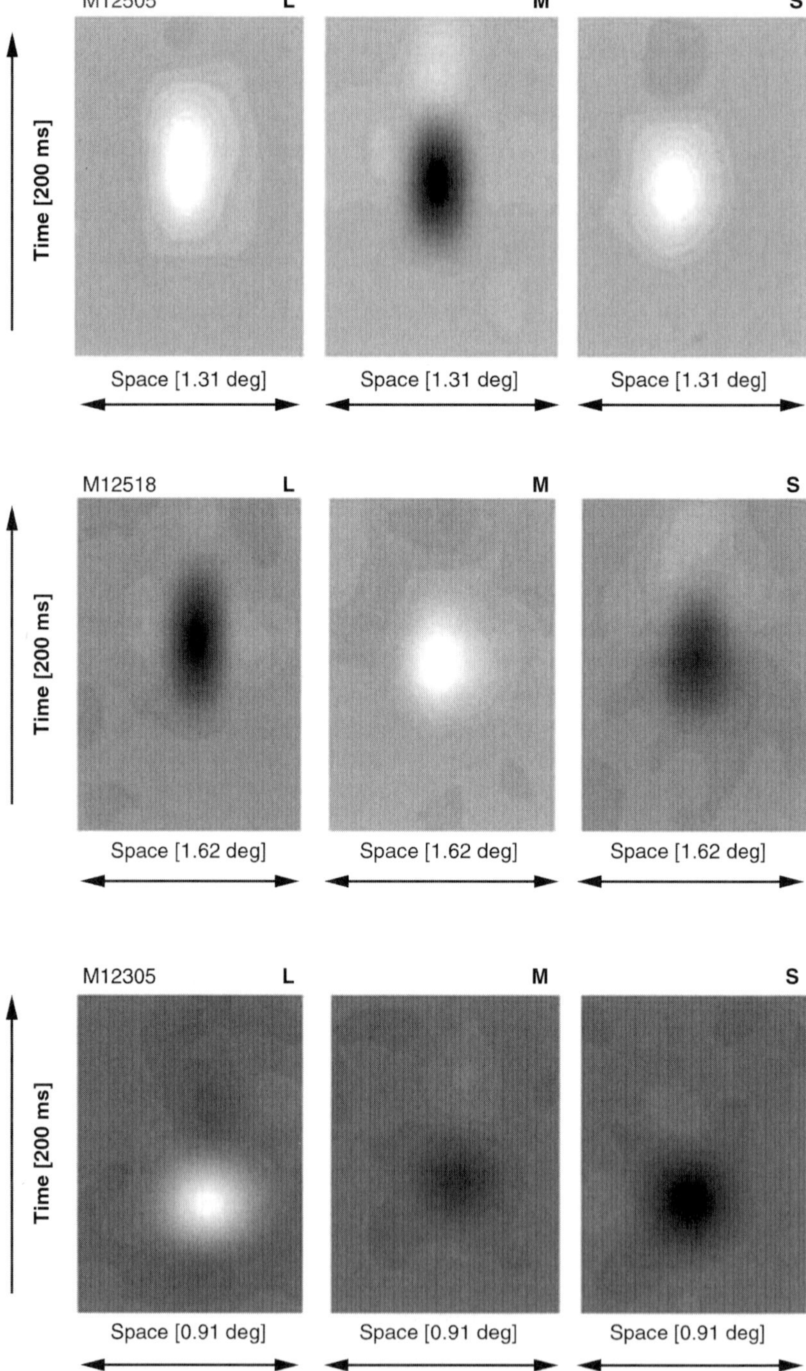
M12505
L
M
S
Time [200 ms]
Space [1.31 deg]
Space [1.31 deg]
Space [1.31 deg]
M12518
L
M
S
Time [200 ms]
Space [1.62 deg]
Space [1.62 deg]
Space [1.62 deg]
M12305
L
M
S
Time [200 ms]
Space [0.91 deg]
Space [0.91 deg]
Space [0.91 deg]

world just in shades of grey (only on one side of the field in the case of those with unilateral lesions). Imaging studies (Tootell, Hadjikhani, Liu, & Cavanagh, 1998) have identified a critical color region in human subjects anterior to the striate cortex, in a region that appears not to be homologous with monkey V4. It is thus possible that in humans, but not in monkeys, a prestriate region is critical for color perception.

It is not clear what transformations of color information per se take place past the striate cortex, although one likely possibility is that of interactions with surrounding regions to enhance color constancy. The visual system must compensate for the changing color of the illumination in the course of the day, from yellowish at dawn and dusk to bluish at noon on a clear day, in order to correctly identify the color of objects. Most of this compensation takes place at the level of the receptors, in the adaptation processes described above. However, longer distance interactions are involved as well, as seen in the familiar demonstrations of color contrast, in which, for instance, a red surround makes a central patch of gray appear greenish. The processing up and through the striate cortex is local, and such color-contrast effects are not seen at these levels (De Valois, Snodderly, Yund, & Hepler, 1977). Grouping together cells of similar selectivities in different prestriate areas (e.g., to motion or color) would allow interactions over longer distances. Such appears to be the case in prestriate area V4, where long-distance color contrast effects are found: the responses of cells to chromatic patterns in the centers of their RFs are modified by the color of the surround (Schein & Desimone, 1990).

III. CHROMATIC DISCRIMINATIONS AND THEIR PHYSIOLOGICAL BASES

A. Chromatic Discrimination of Uniform Stimuli

Many studies over the years have measured the basic chromatic capabilities of human observers for lights presented as large homogeneous or bipartite fields (2° or more in diameter). These experiments examine just chromatic discriminations, largely ignoring the spatial characteristics of the stimuli.

1. Wavelength Discrimination

A wavelength discrimination experiment determines the smallest difference in wavelength between two monochromatic lights (e.g., in a bipartite field) that an

FIGURE 8 The receptive fields (RFs) for cone-specific stimuli for three cortical cells that receive spectrally opponent LGN inputs. Note that each of these cells combines inputs from all the LGN opponent cell types. The cell at top combines $+L_o$, $-M_o$ and $+S_o$ and would thus respond preferentially to red, with little response to luminance variations, since the L and M receptive field centers for luminance are in opposite directions. The cell in the middle has just the opposite organization, $-L_o$, $+M_o$, and $-S_o$, and would thus respond to green. The cell at bottom has inputs of $+L_o$, $-M_o$, and $-S_o$ and would thus respond best to yellow. (Data collected with N. P. Cottaris, S. D. Elfar, and L. E. Mahon.)

observer can discriminate, examining this for lights in different parts of the spectrum. The observer usually has control of both the wavelength and the intensity of the test field. She or he is instructed to change the wavelength until the standard and test stimuli are just discriminably different, then to try to eliminate the perceived difference by adjusting the intensity of the test light. The latter step is necessary to ensure that the discrimination is based upon a wavelength difference rather than a change in effective intensity. The absolute values obtained depend upon adaptation level, field size, and retinal eccentricity, among other things. The function obtained for wavelength discrimination in the fovea at phototopic light levels is roughly W-shaped. The minimal discriminable wavelength change, $\Delta\lambda$, passes through two shallow minima—at about 490 and 590 nm, respectively—where a change in wavelength of 1 nm can reliably be detected under optimal conditions (Wright & Pitt, 1934, and many others). Making the field smaller, moving it into the retinal periphery, or reducing the mean light level will all increase the measured thresholds, though not necessarily uniformly. Lowering the luminance level, for example, will tend to increase $\Delta\lambda$ more at the spectral extremes than for midspectral lights (Bedford & Wyszecki, 1958).

It is clear that hue discrimination in general is primarily limited by the characteristics of the receptor photopigments and by the processing that takes place in the retino-geniculate path. The visual stimulus contains much more information than we can perceive and discriminate, and it appears that almost all of this loss occurs early in the path, due to the presence of a very limited number of receptor types and of only three paths from each region of the retina to the cortex. There appears to be little additional loss once the information reaches the cortex, presumably reflecting the fact that there are an effectively unlimited number of cells to process color information at that level.

The normal human wavelength discrimination curve, showing two spectral regions of best discrimination, reflects the characteristics of the cone photopigments and the presence of just two opponent-cell types in the retina and LGN. The region of good discrimination in the long wavelengths at about 570 nm is where the rate of change in the L minus M (or M minus L) signal is highest, and where the LM opponent cells show the largest change in firing with a change in wavelength (De Valois, Jacobs, & Abramov, 1964). The second region of good discrimination, at short wavelengths in the region of 490 nm, is attributable to the fact that the S-LM opponent cells show the best wavelength discrimination in this region (De Valois et al., 1964), where the slope of the S-cone pigment curve differs most from that of the combined L and M cones.

This explanation of the two regions of best discrimination in the wavelength discrimination function of normal observers is supported by data from dichromats (see discussion of color defects below). These color-defective observers, missing one of the cone types, and thus necessarily one of the opponent cell types, each show only one region of good color discrimination, at only short wavelengths for those missing L or M cones, and at only long wavelengths for those missing S cones.

2. Purity Discrimination

When a white light is added to a monochromatic light, the excitation purity of the monochromatic light is reduced. Excitation purity is defined (in the CIE chromaticity diagram, see Figure 2) as the ratio between the distance from the white point to the test point and the distance from the white point to the corresponding point on the spectral locus. Reducing excitation purity corresponds perceptually to a reduction in a light's saturation (see Figure 1). The ability to discriminate changes in purity is determined most commonly by measuring the purity change required to produce the first discriminable step from white towards various spectral loci (i.e., how much monochromatic light has to be added to white for it to be seen as colored). Other measures are the number of discriminable steps in purity between the monochromatic point and white, or the size of the first discriminable step from monochromatic light towards white. With a photopic, foveal stimulus, the purity (or saturation) discrimination function shows a sharp minimum at about 570 nm, a spectral locus seen as a slightly greenish yellow by a normal observer under neutral adaptation (Priest & Brickwedde, 1938; Wright & Pitt, 1937). In this region of the spectrum, a large amount of monochromatic light must be added to white in order for a subject to detect a change. The function rises sharply (implying better discrimination) in the long wavelengths and somewhat less precipitously in the shorter wavelengths. Both spectral extremes appear very highly saturated, very different from white.

Since spectrally opponent LGN cells clearly carry chromatic information to the brain, and spectrally nonopponent cells carry achromatic information, one would expect that the relative saturation of various spectral regions would be proportional to the relative sensitivities of these different cells types to lights of different wavelengths. The ratio of opponent to nonopponent LGN cell responses to various isoluminant monochromatic lights (De Valois et al., 1966) shows close agreement with the human purity-discrimination function. The minimum saturation of lights in the region of 570 nm is accounted for by the fact that this spectral region is that to which the nonopponent cells are most responsive, and is the region to which the LM opponent cells are the least responsive, since both the L-M and the M-L opponent are crossing over from excitation to inhibition in this region, leaving only the relatively few S-opponent cells responding here. The spectral extremes, on the other hand, produce little output from the nonopponent cells, but large responses from the opponent cells and are thus very saturated. Direct tests of the responses of various opponent cell types to monochromatic lights of different purities (De Valois & Marrocco, 1973; Valberg, Lee, & Tryti, 1987) confirms this conclusion.

3. Intensity, Luminance, and Brightness

A spot of light has a certain chromatic component related to its hue and saturation, but it also has an intensive component. To measure the intensive dimension of lights of various wavelengths, one must somehow eliminate the contribution from purely chromatic variations. A spectral sensitivity measure that shows linear additivity would also be useful. Such a linear measure, however, does not necessarily correspond to any or all perceptual intensity dimensions.

The human visual system, like all photosensitive biological systems, is not equally sensitive to increments and decrements of light from different spectral regions. Under photopic conditions, we are most sensitive to light in the midspectral region from 500–600 nm, with sensitivity falling off towards both spectral extremes. Spectral sensitivity under scotopic (dim-light) conditions is invariant and reflects the spectral absorption characteristics of the rods, which are the sole functioning receptors at these low light levels. However, the shape of the spectral sensitivity function at photopic levels, when multiple cone types are involved, depends on how it is measured; that is, the contribution of the different cone types to the intensive measure depends on the visual task involved.

There are several ways of comparing the effective intensities of light of different wavelengths that yield linear additivity for lights of any spectral distribution. The most widely used of these is heterochromatic flicker photometry, which takes advantage of the fact that our ability to resolve rapid temporal changes in color is decidedly inferior to our ability to follow rapid changes in intensity. If one rapidly alternates two lights (at, say, 15 Hz) in the same location, a significant luminance difference between the two will be visible and will appear as a brightness flicker. Any change in hue, however—even one as dramatic as an alternation between red and green—will be invisible. The two hues will blend, and the observer will perceive their additive mixture color (generally yellow or white in the case of red-green flicker). Under these conditions an observer can now adjust the intensity of one of the two flickering lights until the perception of brightness flicker is minimized. If various monochromatic lights are flickered against a standard white light in this way, a spectral sensitivity curve that has the property of additivity will be obtained.

A linearly additive measure of spectral sensitivity can also be derived from the minimally distinct border technique (Boynton & Kaiser, 1968). Subjects are presented with a bipartite field in which the radiance of one half is fixed. The subject controls the radiance of the test light in the other half field, and the two halves abut. The subject is asked to adjust the test radiance until the border between the two appears minimally distinct. At that point, the two lights will be equated in effective intensity, and the equation will be identical to that determined by flicker photometry for the same two lights.

The CIE combined data from multiple laboratories to arrive at a standardized, linear, effective intensity measure for the standard observer, officially called a spectral luminous efficiency function, abbreviated V_λ. (As there are individual differences between normal observers in photopigments and in lens and macular pigmentation, for visual studies in which it is crucial to have isoluminant stimuli, one should determine the effective luminance for the particular observer being tested. Such a measure is referred to as sensation luminance [Kaiser, 1988], to differentiate it from luminous efficiency for the standard observer.) Luminous efficiency is highest for wavelengths at about 555 nm and falls off rapidly at both longer and shorter wavelengths. If luminance were only a convenient engineering measure, it would have little relevance to visual perception, but it is more than that. It can be modeled very well as a sum of the spectral absorption curves of the L and M cone pigments (Vos & Walraven, 1971; Smith & Pokorny, 1975; Schnapf et al,. 1988). The luminosity function is also well fit by the sum of the outputs of the spectrally nonopponent LGN cells (De Valois et al., 1966; Lee, Martin, & Valberg, 1988*), indicating that the cells in the Mc path are computing this sum of L+M.

A quite different intensity measure from luminous efficiency, although sometimes confused with it, is brightness. This is a perceptual measure determined by having an observer adjust two lights until they appear equally bright. Similar spectral sensitivity curves are obtained for the increment threshold for large, long-duration monochromatic lights presented on a white background (Sperling & Harwerth, 1971). For any given light under invariant viewing conditions, brightness varies monotonically with luminance, but lights of different wavelengths equated in luminance are by no means necessarily equal in brightness. For example, monochromatic lights near the spectral extremes typically appear much brighter than midspectral monochromatic lights of the same luminance. Also, spectrally complex lights containing multiple wavelengths typically appear less bright than monochromatic lights equated for luminance, the Helmholtz-Kohlrausch effect. The failure of additivity is such that the sum of two monochromatic lights can even appear to be less bright than one of the separate lights alone (Guth, 1967).

The spectral brightness function is typically three-humped, with highest sensitivity in the regions of 430, 540, and 630 nm, as opposed to the single region of highest luminance at about 555 nm. These three regions of highest brightness correspond closely to the regions of peak responses from +S−LM, +M−L, and +−M opponent LGN cells to incremental flashes of monochromatic light. Although only the nonopponent cells contribute to luminance, brightness appears to be contributed to by all the LGN cells, both opponent and nonopponent (Abramov, 1968; Sperling & Harwerth, 1971).

B. Spatial Contrast Sensitivity

To the extent that the visual system behaves linearly, the detectability of any spatial pattern can be predicted from knowledge of the observer's spatial contrast sensitivity function (CSF). A discussion of such an approach to spatial vision can be found in De Valois and De Valois (1988) and in Geisler and Albrecht (chapter 3, this volume). Although an infinite number of possible basis functions could be used to measure an observer's CSF, the most common is a grating pattern that various sinusoidally in one spatial dimension while remaining invariant in the orthogonal dimension. The experimenter determines the minimum contrast that an observer can detect at a particular spatial frequency, defined in terms of cycles per degree visual angle (c/deg). The grating pattern can vary either in luminance contrast (e.g., a black-white grating) or in color contrast (e.g., a red-green grating).

The foveal spatial CSF for luminance-varying gratings measured at photopic light levels is bandpass. Contrast sensitivity is greatest for spatial frequencies of about 2–4 c/deg, with reduced sensitivity to both higher and lower spatial frequencies. When spatial frequency is represented on a logarithmic scale, as it usually is, the falloff in sensitivity is quite rapid and pronounced at the higher spatial frequencies, and more gradual in the low spatial frequencies.

To make comparable measures for color-varying patterns that contain no luminance variation is difficult. In theory, such a pattern can be produced by adding together two colored luminance-varying patterns out of phase (e.g., a red luminance grating interlaced with a green luminance grating to produce a red-green color grating). If the two are matched in space-averaged luminance and in luminance contrast, then their superposition should produce an isoluminant color-varying sinusoid. However, chromatic aberration produced by the eye's optics tends to produce luminance artifacts in the retinal image of such a pattern. (See Thiros, chapter 1, this volume, for a discussion of chromatic aberration.) Although there are ways to minimize the effects of these unintended luminance variations, it is probably wise never to assume that a retinal image is truly isoluminant. Luminance artifacts are a particular problem because of the great sensitivity of the visual system for even miniscule amounts of luminance contrast. Nevertheless, the differences that are seen when comparing spatial CSFs for luminance-varying patterns with those for nominally isoluminant patterns suggest that standard methods of producing isoluminant stimuli are at least reasonably adequate at low-to-middle spatial frequencies. Because the problem of chromatic aberration grows increasingly severe as spatial frequency increases, measurements made with higher frequencies become increasingly problematic.

A second problem arises in comparing contrast sensitivity for luminance and chromatic patterns, namely, the choice of a contrast metric. Many have been used, though they have often been selected out of expediency, not principle. For the current discussion, it is sufficient to note that all such metrics should be simply related, and the only one that provides an obvious point of comparison with luminance contrast metrics is that of cone contrast (Cole & Hine, 1992), which is derived by calculating the variation in light absorptions in each of the cone classes. Most studies of chromatic spatial contrast sensitivity have used other simple but less satisfactory measures of contrast. For example, the contrast of a red–green isoluminant grating can be defined as being equivalent to the luminance contrast of either the red or the green component gratings alone.

When the test pattern is a set of isoluminant red–green sinusoids of different spatial frequencies, the foveal spatial contrast sensitivity function of a normal observer is low-pass, not band-pass as it is for luminance. Sensitivity either continues to increase as the spatial frequency of the test becomes increasingly lower, or it reaches an asymptote at some low spatial frequency (van der Horst & Bouman, 1969; van der Horst, de Weert, & Bouman, 1967; Kelly, 1983; Granger & Heurtley, 1973; Mullen, 1985). At higher spatial frequencies, contrast sensitivity falls quite rapidly, not extending to the high frequencies that are readily seen when the test grating is defined by luminance variations.

The implication of the differences between the luminance and the chromatic CSFs is that color differences alone, in the absence of corresponding luminance variations, cannot support fine spatial acuity. In a red–green world without luminance variations, for example, written material would have to be printed in much larger letters, and the fine resolution to which we are normally accustomed (which reflects sensitivity to luminance-varying patterns) would not exist.

Spatial resolution is even more severely compromised when the test pattern produces differential absorption only in the S cones (a tritanopic confusion axis, the 90°–270° axis in MBDKL space). S cones alone cannot support spatial discriminations as good as those achieved by the LM cone mosaic, because they are so few in number and so widely spaced on the retina. Several attempts have been made to measure the spatial contrast sensitivity function using stimuli that are restricted to the S cones (e.g., Cavonius & Estévez, 1975; Green, 1972). In general, researchers agree that contrast sensitivity for S-cone-isolating gratings begins to fall once the spatial frequency exceeds 1 c/deg, and the ability to resolve gratings disappears for patterns higher than about 10 c/deg.

Although the decision as to how to compare *absolute* contrast sensitivity for luminance versus chromatic patterns is somewhat arbitrary, a comparison of the *shapes* of their respective CSFs is straightforward. At low temporal frequencies, as usually measured, the spatial CSF for luminance is bandpass, with considerable high-spatial-frequency and some low-spatial-frequency attenuation. The color CSF, on the other hand, is low-pass, with little or no low-frequency attenuation (at least down to very low spatial frequencies). This can be understood in the differing ways that Pc LGN cells, which multiplex color and luminance information, respond to chromatic versus luminance variations, respectively (De Valois & De Valois, 1975; De Valois et al., 1977). Information about very high spatial frequencies is lost due to optical imperfections and the finite spacing of the photoreceptors (see De Valois & De Valois, 1988, for discussion). This is reflected in the high-frequency attenuation of both the color and the luminance CSFs. However, information about low spatial frequencies is not lost due to either the eye's optics or the receptor spacing, but rather results from inhibitory lateral neural interactions.

For low spatial frequency patterns, which produce fairly uniform illumination across the entire RF of a retinal or geniculate Pc cell, the center and surround regions are *antagonistic* for luminance variations, but *synergistic* for chromatic variations. Thus LGN cells show decreased sensitivity to low spatial frequency luminance variations, but increased sensitivity to low spatial frequency color variations. Perhaps the easiest way to understand this is to consider that an intensity change drives the L and M cones in the same direction, but a color change drives them in opposite directions; however, L and M cone outputs are combined in Pc LGN cells in an opponent way. A uniform luminance increment, then, would result in an excitatory input from the L cones and an inhibitory input from the M cones to a +L−M cell, and thus little total response. But a color change toward long wavelengths would produce excitation from L cones and a decrease in inhibition from M cones. The combination would therefore produce a large response.

C. Temporal Contrast Sensitivity

A moving or flickering pattern produces a temporal change in light in a given retinal area. One can ask how sensitive we are to different temporal frequencies (specified in Hz = cycles per second) of color changes versus luminance changes. Historically, the temporal sensitivity of the chromatic system has been assessed using a homogeneous flickering field alternating in time between two different colors. That of the luminance system has been studied using a black–white flickering stimulus. When the flicker modulation depth (i.e., the amplitude of the chromatic or luminance difference between the two) is held constant and the flicker frequency is varied until the flicker can no longer be seen, the measure is referred to as the critical flicker frequency (CFF). The CFF depends upon such factors as mean luminance and stimulus size, but when the two stimuli that are alternated are chromatic stimuli equated for luminance, the CFF will rarely exceed 12–14 Hz. This stands in marked contrast to the CFF for luminance variations, which may easily reach 60 Hz or higher under photopic conditions.

Temporal contrast sensitivity measures can be used (assuming linearity) to derive temporal impulse response functions for color and luminance, an estimate of the temporal response sequence that follows a single brief stimulus impulse. For an increment in luminance at a photopic adaptation level (90 cd/m^2, for instance), the derived temporal impulse response function is biphasic, with an excitatory response that peaks at about 40 ms, drops to zero by about 70 ms, then becomes negative, returning to the baseline only after 170 ms or so. At the same luminance level, however, the derived temporal impulse response function for an isoluminant color change is monophasic. It reaches its positive peak only after approximately 70 ms, has no negative lobe, and falls slowly to zero after 250 ms or so (Swanson, Ueno, Smith, & Pokorny, 1987). These different impulse-response functions for color and luminance appear to be directly related to the different temporal properties of cells in the Pc and Mc paths. Macaque Pc cells produce monophasic temporal responses to a flash of light, whereas Mc cells give quite biphasic temporal responses (Schiller & Malpeli, 1978).

Another way to characterize the temporal properties of the visual system is to examine sensitivity to stimuli varying sinusoidally in time. For stimuli of very low spatial frequencies or for uniform illumination, the temporal CSF functions for luminance and for color are very similar to their respective spatial CSFs, bandpass for luminance, and low-pass for color. Very high temporal frequency attenuation for both color and luminance patterns is primarily attributable to the random diffusion characteristics of the intrareceptor cascade intervening between the capture of a photon of light and the initiation of a change in permeability of the receptor outer membrane. Synaptic neural processes also contribute to this loss in high temporal frequency information, since the highest temporal frequencies to which cells respond decrease at each successive synaptic level. These processes decrease sensitivity to high temporal frequencies for both luminance and color. *Low* temporal frequency attenuation, which is seen for luminance but not color variations, must have a different explanation, perhaps in the differential latency of the RF center versus surround inputs to ganglion and LGN cells. As in the case of the difference between luminance and color spatial CSF functions, the presence of low-temporal-frequency attenuation for luminance but not color can be explained by the opposite changes in receptor output produced by variations in intensity versus color.

For very low temporal and spatial frequencies, the RF center and surround inputs to a Pc LGN cell are antagonistic for luminance patterns and synergistic for color patterns, as discussed above. At such low temporal frequencies, the slightly longer latency of the surround relative to the center is an insignificant proportion of a total cycle, and the center and surround would essentially coincide in time. However, as the temporal frequency increases, the fixed center/surround latency difference would increasingly shift the relative phases of the center and surround until at some temporal frequency they would be out of phase rather than in phase. At this higher temporal frequency, center and surround would now be *synergistic* for luminance and *antagonistic* for color. Luminance sensitivity thus increases while sensitivity to color decreases with increasing temporal frequency up to a point, so that the luminance temporal CSF is bandpass whereas the color temporal CSF is low pass.

D. Color Vision Defects

Approximately 8% of males and 1% of females differ significantly from the majority of the population in their color vision abilities. A very small proportion of these, called monochromats, can make no discriminations based solely on spectral differences. They are truly color blind. Most of these are rod monochromats, who appear to have no functioning cones or to be incapable of using whatever signals their cones might provide. A larger (but still small) group of observers are dichromats. They can match any light with a combination of only two primaries, unlike the normal observer who requires three primaries to match many test lights. Dichromats appear to lack one of the three basic classes of cones and are classified in terms of which cone type is believed to be missing. Protanopes are missing their L cones, deuteranopes their M cones, and tritanopes their S cones. Their spectral sensitivity, wavelength discrimination, and other color vision functions differ in ways that are predictable from the loss of one cone type. The most dramatic difference from normal trichromats in the visual capabilities of the various classes of dichromats is that each has a narrow spectral region (known as a neutral point) in which even a monochromatic light cannot be discriminated from white.

The third and most common class of color vision anomalies occurs in observers who are trichromatic, like the majority of the population, but make color matches that may differ quite dramatically from those a "normal" trichromat would set. Anomalous trichromats, like dichromats, are classified by the cone system that appears to be affected. Thus, there are protanomalous, deuteranomalous, and tritanomalous observers. Anomalous trichromats appear to have a cone class that contains a photopigment different in its spectral absorption function from that found in normal trichromats (Neitz & Neitz, 1998).

IV. COLOR APPEARANCE AND ITS PHYSIOLOGICAL BASES

The various discrimination functions described above all reflect the degree to which an observer can tell that two stimuli differ along some specified dimension. They do not represent the appearance of stimuli, except in the most minimal sense of the distinction between "same" and "different." As Hering realized, however, an understanding of color vision must encompass the more complex aspects of color appearance, as well as color discriminations.

A. Opponency

Following the early suggestions of trichromacy from Palmer (1777) and Thomas Young (1802), its quantitative demonstration by Maxwell (1860), and Helmholtz's popularization and extension (1867) of Young's theory, the nature of color mixture and its explanation formed the central topic in the study of color vision. The work of Ewald Hering (1878) helped shift scientific concern back to the perceptual appearance of color, not just the discrimination and matching of colors. Hering noted that among the chromatic hues (here ignoring the achromatic range of blacks, whites, and greys), four hues, red, green, blue, and yellow, are perceptually unique. Each of them exists in a pure form that appears to contain no tinge of any other hue, unlike the intermediate or mixture colors such as purple (which appears to contain both red and blue), cyan (which appears to contain both blue and green), or orange (which appears to contain both red and yellow). Further, he noted, the unique hues exist in two opponent pairs that have a special, mutually exclusive relationship. Red and green, Hering said, cannot be seen in the same place at the same time. Though there are reddish blues and reddish yellows, there is no reddish green or greenish red. Similarly, blue and yellow are an opponent pair. Chromatic opponency provides a useful framework within which to consider complementary colors (two colors that, when added in proper proportions, combine to produce an achromatic white or grey), negative afterimages, and the Bezold-Brücke Effect (a change in hue produced by a change in the luminance of a monochromatic light), among other phenomena.

Quantification of the spectral response functions associated with the four unique hues identified by Hering awaited the development by Jameson and Hurvich (1955, 1956; Hurvich & Jameson, 1955, 1956) of a psychophysical hue cancellation technique. In this procedure, a subject is presented with a sequence of test lights of various wavelengths and told to cancel or eliminate all the greenness, say, by adding an appropriate amount of red to the test light. This method exploits the opponent relationship between, in this case, red and green, and allows one to define precisely the extent to which a given unique hue contributes to the percept of various nonunique hues. As Hering's analysis would predict, and Jameson and Hurvich demonstrated, the addition of red can completely cancel the appearance of green in any stimulus over the whole range of wavelengths that have any greenish appearance. With the red and the green canceling each other out, the test light will now appear blue, yellow, or achromatic. Similarly, the addition of blue can completely cancel the appearance of yellow, and vice versa, leaving the test light appearing red, green, or achromatic. When the unique hue spectral response functions (or chromatic valence functions) for monochromatic lights are defined by the color cancellation method, red, which is most prominent in the long wavelengths, is seen also at the very short wavelengths. This reappearance of red poses a challenge to physiological models of color encoding and will be discussed further below.

The work of Hurvich and Jameson forced a serious reexamination of color models based on independent paths from three cones to the brain. Zone models (which typically begin with a trichromatic initial stage followed by one or more opponent interaction stages) were initially proposed more than a century ago (e.g., von Kries, 1905). However, it was the work of Hurvich and Jameson along with the supporting physiological evidence from LGN recordings in the monkey that brought them to the fore in modern studies of color vision. Thus, the observations of Young and Helmholtz, on one hand, and those of Hering, on the other, are not mutually contradictory as they were once thought to be; rather, they reflect different stages in the processing of color by the visual system.

B. Hue

Color has three main perceptual dimensions (surface colors can also have such perceptual properties as luster). Hue is the term used for the dimension described in casual conversation by names such as red, yellow, green, and purple. The physical variable that corresponds most closely to the dimension of hue is wavelength for a monochromatic light. The wavelengths that we see as light form a continuum from about 400 to 700 nm, and the peak sensitivities of the cone photopigments are at about 430, 530, and 560 nm. One might well expect, therefore, that the colors we perceive in the spectrum would be arranged in a line across the spectrum, with the hue of the shortest wavelengths being most different from that of the longest wavelengths. That is not the case; rather, the shortest and longest visible wavelengths resemble each other, and the perceptual arrangement of the colors is not one-dimensional, along a line, but two-dimensional, as if around a circle. Related to this is the fact that certain colors are complementary, so that when added together their hues cancel, producing an achromatic color.

The fact that colors form a circle has been known at least from the time of Newton, but the explanation for it was not obvious. A Helmholzian organization, with three color receptors feeding separately to the brain, would lead to a one-dimensional, linear arrangement of the different hues. That hues instead appear to be organized as a circle reflects the fact that the receptor outputs are not separately projected but rather compared in two opponent organizations. The initial opponent-color organization, as we have seen, is between cone types in the retina, L versus M, and S versus L+M. At the striate cortex there is a further interaction in which the outputs of the S-opponent cells are combined with that of the LM opponent cells (Cottaris & De Valois, 1998). The color system related to the very longest wavelengths (specifying red) thus also receives an input from receptors sensitive to the very shortest wavelengths, and the system specifying blue receives input both from the receptors sensitive to the shortest and from those sensitive to the longest wavelengths.

Many studies have determined how hue varies as a function of the wavelength of monochromatic light (e.g., Abramov, Gordon, & Chan, 1990; Sternheim & Boynton, 1966; Werner & Wooten, 1979), using a hue-scaling procedure. The observer is typically asked to scale the hue of each monochromatic light in terms of how much red, yellow, green, or blue she or he perceives in it. These studies agree in finding that the very long wavelengths are reported to be predominantly red, often with a small admixture of yellow. The red shades into a more equal mixture of red and yellow, eventually becoming uniquely yellow at wavelengths around 575–585 nm, then yellow-green at still shorter wavelengths. The spectral region identified as uniquely green varies considerably across studies and among subjects, ranging from about 500 nm to 525 nm. As the wavelength is lowered further, green becomes green-blue and finally unique blue, which appears for most subjects at about 475–480 nm. Lights of still shorter wavelengths are perceived as a combination of blue and red. To produce a color that is identified as unique red, it is usually necessary to add short-wavelength light to a long wavelength, producing an extraspectral color.

To compare the hues of different stimuli directly with the underlying cone, LGN opponent cell, and striate cortex cell responses, De Valois, De Valois, Switkes, and Mahon (1997) had observers scale the hues of the same isoluminant stimuli that had been used in single-cell recording experiments. The results (see Figure 9) show clearly that the hues seen as red, yellow, green, and blue do not coincide with the outputs of the various LGN opponent cell types, but are in each case rotated in MBDKL color space off these axes. This rotation was predicted by the De Valois

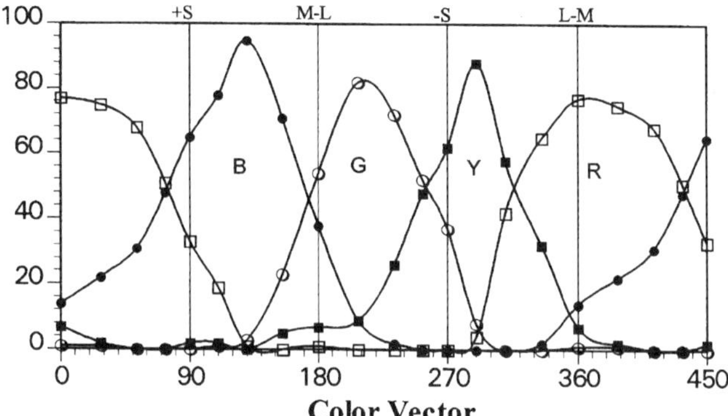

FIGURE 9 Scaling of the color appearance of various isoluminant stimuli. Plotted for each color vector is the percentage of times that the given stimulus was called each of the four permissible color names, red (R), yellow (Y), green (G), or blue (B). If the color names directly reflected the lateral geniculate nucleus (LGN) cell responses shown in Figure 5, B would coincide with +S (90°), G with M-L (180°), and so forth. Note that the way in which the perceptual responses are shifted from the geniculate axes is as predicted to occur with a further stage of color processing by the De Valois and De Valois (1993) color model.

and De Valois (1993) model, and is accounted for by the combination at the striate cortex of inputs from the LM-opponent and the S-opponent cells to form the various primary hue systems. Most striate cells are found to receive inputs from all the different LGN opponent cell types, just as was postulated (De Valois, Cottaris, & Elfar, 1997).

One might suppose that the colored lights that we describe as, say, red, simply reflect the way in which we had been taught to use the English term "red." Our breaking up color space into different hues could just reflect a linguistic convention rather than any underlying physiological property of the visual system. However, the evidence suggests otherwise. Extensive studies of the color categorization of people of many different languages and cultures (Berlin & Kay, 1969; Kay, Berlin, Maffi, & Merrifield, 1997) show a surprising agreement in how they divide up the colors into different hue categories. In some languages there are only words for light and dark, but if there are specific hue terms in the language, the color regions covered by particular color terms agree very closely with ours. Thus if asked to sort multiple colored chips into different color categories, people across dozens of different languages (even among isolated tribes in New Guinea, for instance) will group together in one category all the chips that we see as reddish, and will identify as the best exemplar of that color the same chip that we might describe as unique red.

C. Saturation

The second chromatic perceptual dimension, saturation, refers to the degree to which a given stimulus differs from achromatic. It describes the amount of color (or hue) in a stimulus as compared to the amount of white, black, or gray. Thus, both pastel blue and navy blue are less saturated than royal blue, and pink and maroon are both less saturated versions of red. A highly saturated light can be desaturated by the addition of white or by the addition of black (produced, for example, by surrounding the patch by a brighter annulus, thus inducing blackness into the patch itself). The physical measure that corresponds most closely to the perceptual variable of saturation is purity, the relative amount of monochromatic light in a mixture of a monochromatic light and a reference white. (White is produced by the superposition of multiple monochromatic lights. Two appropriately chosen wavelengths added in proper proportions can produce white, but whites more commonly contain many, often all, the visible wavelengths). For any given photopic light under otherwise invariant conditions, increasing purity results in an increase in saturation. Above we discussed the purity discrimination function, which shows a sharp minimum at about 570 nm. This part of the spectrum, which appears greenish-yellow under neutral adaptation, appears most similar to an achromatic stimulus.

D. Brightness or Lightness

The third perceptual dimension of color is brightness or lightness. A light of fixed hue and saturation in an invariant surround can be made brighter or darker, respectively, by increasing or decreasing its radiance. Brightness refers to the perceptual dimension corresponding most closely to a change in radiometric intensity of a light viewed in isolation, a condition termed aperture viewing. In this circumstance, the light appears almost to float in space that is otherwise empty. When the stimulus patch is viewed in the presence of other stimuli, such as an annular surround, its appearance is affected by the presence of the other stimuli, and it is more likely to look like a reflective surface rather than a disembodied light. Under these conditions, the term lightness is more appropriate, and the stimulus may be referred to as having surface color. In this mode, changing the intensity of the object's surround can dramatically affect its lightness, even when the stimulus patch is itself invariant. For example, greatly decreasing the intensity of the surround can produce a significant increase in the lightness of the test stimulus. With both aperture and surface colors, if all other factors remain constant, increasing the radiometric intensity of the light will result in an increase in its brightness or lightness, and decreasing the intensity produces a decrease in brightness or lightness.

Each of the three chromatic perceptual dimensions of hue, saturation, and brightness is associated most closely with a single physical dimension (wavelength, purity, and intensity, respectively), but the relationships are not exclusive. Hue, for example, can be affected by intensity and by purity, as well as by wavelength. When the intensity of a photopic monochromatic light is increased over a range of perhaps two log units, the associated hue is invariant in certain spectral regions, particularly those around the unique hues. At other wavelengths, however, as the light becomes increasingly intense, it appears to shift in hue towards blue or yellow. This is known as the Bezold-Brücke Effect (see Purdy, 1931, or Boynton & Gordon, 1965, for representative data). Similarly, the Abney Effect is a change in hue associated with a change in purity.

E. Similitude and Contrast

The hue, saturation, and lightness of a particular region in visual space are determined not just by the stimulation within that region at that instant, but by stimuli in neighboring regions and at previous times as well. These lateral interactions between two spatial or temporal regions can be in either of two opposite directions, depending on the stimulus conditions. In the **contrast** direction, two regions appear more different from each other than if they were seen in isolation. In the **similitude** direction, they appear more similar to each other than if each were seen in isolation. Simultaneous contrast and similitude refer to interactions between an area and its surround or other objects in the field of view; successive contrast and similitude refer to interactions between a region and what had been present there previously.

Similitude is also known as assimilation or the spreading effect of von Bezold (von Bezold, 1876). Although several factors can influence whether and how strongly similitude occurs (e.g., relative luminance, de Weert & Spillman, 1995), the most significant determining factor is probably the size of the test target (Fach & Sharpe, 1986). Optical or neural processes that lead to summation in space or time produce spatial or temporal similitude. Blur in the optics of the eye produces spatial similitude, by smearing the light from adjacent regions in the retinal image. The limit of resolution is that point at which there is complete similitude, with the black and white, or red and green lines in a grating pattern appearing the same uniform color. Neural summation produces the same effect: a bipolar cell that sums the outputs of a group of receptors may just average out any difference between the outputs of the individual receptors to produce spatial similitude within that small region; a cortical cell that sums together the outputs of several LGN cells would produce similitude over a somewhat larger area. Thus, a thin red line on a large white background would appear desaturated, and on a large blue background it would appear slightly bluish. Both of these changes could have been produced by either optical or neural spreading from the background.

The slow random nature of the cascade of reactions within a receptor similarly smears out temporal differences to produce temporal similitude (e.g., the overhead lights in a room may change from very bright to dark 60 times a second, but they appear to be a uniform intermediate brightness). Any temporal smearing (or low-pass filtering) that occurs at later synaptic levels would have the same effect as the slow cascade within the receptors.

Changes in color appearance in the contrast direction depend on inhibitory interactions in space or time. The responses in two regions with mutually inhibitory connections will be more different from each other than they would otherwise be. The antagonism between the center and surround within the RFs of LGN cells for luminance-varying patterns, and that between different subregions of cortical cells, are examples of interactions that produce spatial contrast over short distances. Spatial color contrast effects that require longer distance interactions take place at prestriate cortical loci, such as V4 (Schein & Desimone, 1990).

One factor that produces temporal color contrast is neural rebound in a spectrally opponent cell. Consider a cell that fires to long wavelengths and inhibits to middle wavelengths. After prolonged firing to a red stimulus, the cell will rebound into inhibition at the termination of the stimulus. Since inhibition in this cell may signal "green," this could produce a momentary appearance of a green afterimage, thus temporal contrast. Another major factor producing temporal contrast effects is receptor-specific adaptation, as discussed below.

Contrast and similitude effects can be related to the spatial and temporal contrast sensitivity functions. High-contrast sensitivity means that the different bars in the grating appear very different from each other, that is, in the contrast direction. In a region of low contrast sensitivity, the bars appear similar to each other, thus in the similitude direction. Similitude corresponds to the attenuation of the luminance CSF at very high and low temporal and spatial frequencies, and of the color CSF at high temporal and spatial frequencies. Color and brightness contrast corresponds to the increased sensitivity to middle spatial and temporal frequencies in the luminance CSF, and at low spatial and temporal frequencies in the color CSF. The differing color and luminance CSFs account for the fact that there are many situations in which we see color similitude but brightness contrast. The explanation for the different CSFs for color and luminance was discussed earlier.

F. Adaptation and Afterimages

Both the presence of other stimuli in the field of view and the observer's state of adaptation can dramatically affect the hue of a stimulus. The intensity of the illuminant in visual scenes varies over a huge range, and the visual system has several adaptational mechanisms that adjust the sensitivity of the system to the ambient illumination level. The average chromaticity of the world does not change so dramatically, but nonetheless the visual system must adjust for it in order to keep color appearance at least approximately constant across a day, a result known as color constancy. An adaptational system that is cone-type-specific would go far towards accomplishing this. It has been shown, for instance by Werner and Walraven (1982), that a wide range of desaturated colors all appear white when one adapts to them. Consider a shift from uniform white light that stimulated all the cone types equally to a yellowish background light. When the yellow light first appeared it would activate the L more than the M cones, and one would see it as quite yellowish. But the L cones would adapt more than the M cones, and after a brief period, the two cone types would again be responding equally to the light. The formerly yellowish light would now look white.

Another familiar example of the effects of adaptation can be found in many introductory psychology textbooks. The viewer is asked to adapt for a minute or so while fixating a point on a vividly colored picture. Immediately after the end of the adaptation, the viewer is instructed to look at a neutral, unpatterned surface such as a white wall, on which she or he will see an image of the object in colors complementary to those of the adaptation stimulus. Such negative afterimages reflect the effects of localized receptor adaptation as well as neural rebound.

V. THE ROLE OF COLOR IN SPATIAL VISION

The traditional separation between studies of color vision and studies of spatial vision might be taken to imply that color plays little role in visual pattern analysis. That assumption is reinforced by the fact that we can clearly capture much of the important information in a scene with an image that contains only luminance variations, such as a black-and-white photograph. Nonetheless, color differences can be used to analyze the spatial pattern in a scene. Indeed, in some cases color may be more useful for this purpose than luminance differences.

In considering the role of color in spatial vision, an obvious question is how well the visual system can discriminate patterns that differ along the basic spatial dimensions of spatial frequency and orientation when only color differences are present. Webster, De Valois, and Switkes (1990) determined the minimum differences in both orientation and spatial frequency for gratings defined along the three fundamental MBDKL axes. They found that when all gratings were equated in terms of equal multiples of their respective detection thresholds, spatial discrimination thresholds for the two isoluminant chromatic axes were very similar but were always somewhat higher than those for the luminance axis. The critical observation, however, was that discrimination was still very good even at isoluminance. Thus, spatial vision based solely upon color differences should be respectable, though not as precise as that supported by luminance variations.

A related question concerns the organization of spatial information in the color system. There is now a wealth of evidence demonstrating the presence of multiple parallel spatial channels in the luminance system (see De Valois & De Valois, 1988, and Geisler & Albrecht, chapter 3, this volume). The spatial channels are selective for, or bandpass along, the dimensions of spatial frequency and orientation. It is not obvious that the color system should be organized in the same manner as the luminance system, but it appears to be remarkably similar. The presence and characteristics of the spatial frequency channels in the luminance system were initially demonstrated by adaptation and masking experiments. Adaptation to a luminance grating of a particular spatial frequency produces a short-term reduction in contrast sensitivity for test gratings near in frequency to the adaptation grating. The loss in sensitivity decreases as the difference between adaptation and test frequencies increases, producing a bandpass function with an average spatial frequency bandwidth of a little more than an octave at half amplitude (Pantle & Sekuler, 1968; Blakemore & Campbell, 1969), though it may also depend upon factors such as spatial frequency and contrast. Similarly, adaptation to a grating of a single orientation produces an orientation-selective loss in contrast sensitivity (Blakemore & Campbell, 1969; Gilinsky, 1968), with no loss in sensitivity when adaptation and test gratings differ by about 45° or more.

Adaptation to an isoluminant color-varying grating also produces losses in contrast sensitivity that are bandpass in both spatial frequency and orientation (Bradley, Switkes, & De Valois, 1988). Along both dimensions, the spread of the adaptation effect is somewhat greater for isoluminant color-varying patterns than for comparable patterns that vary in luminance. The noteworthy observation, however, is that both adaptation functions are clearly bandpass, suggesting that the color system, like the luminance system, analyzes patterns using a set of tuned filters that are selective on the dimensions of spatial frequency and orientation. Far from merely reporting locally on color, the color vision system is capable of analyzing and characterizing the spatial patterns it encounters.

In nature, of course, color differences rarely occur in isolation from luminance differences. Most commonly, color and luminance changes are highly, though not perfectly, correlated. This observation raises several questions of interest. One is how, if at all, color and luminance differences interact when both are present. Does the existence of color contrast, for example, affect an observer's ability to detect luminance contrast? It can. Under some circumstances, the presence of a color-varying pattern can make the detection of a superimposed luminance-varying pattern dramatically more difficult, whereas a similar luminance-varying pattern can make a color pattern more detectable (De Valois & Switkes, 1983; Switkes, Bradley, & De Valois, 1988). The interactions between color and luminance variations can be complex (Cole, Stromeyer, & Kronauer, 1990; Mullen, Cropper, & Losada, 1997), however, and not easily predictable.

Another question of interest is whether luminance-varying stimuli are analyzed in a strictly color-blind fashion. Heterochromatic flicker photometry and other measures that show linear additivity between lights that differ in hue are tasks in which the visual system operates in a strictly color-blind fashion. As long as two lights are equated in sensation luminance, one can be substituted for the other without disturbing the effective intensity of a flickering light, for example. There is evidence that retinal ganglion cells in the Mc pathway exhibit the indifference to stimulus hue and the spectral luminous efficiency function that would be expected of the mechanism that underlies heterochromatic flicker photometry, but that the neurons in the Pc pathway do not (Lee, Martin, & Valberg, 1988). Although Pc pathway neurons respond vigorously to luminance contrast, they do so in a manner that is dependent upon the hue of the stimulus. To the extent that these cells are involved in the analysis of luminance-varying patterns, then, one might well expect color-selective responses even when the pattern is defined by luminance differences. There is evidence for the existence and operation of hue-selective, intensity-coding mechanisms (Rovamo, Hyvaerinen & Hari, 1982; Virsu & Haapasalo, 1973; Yamamoto, 1997).

A. Color Motion

In the natural world, objects typically differ from their surroundings in both chromaticity and luminance. In the laboratory, however, it is possible to produce a stimulus in which luminance remains invariant across a pattern defined only by color differences. As noted above, spatial and temporal contrast sensitivity functions for such stimuli are markedly different from those for patterns that contain luminance variations. There are certain striking perceptual anomalies associated with isoluminant patterns, as well. The most dramatic of these is the peculiar appearance of moving isoluminant patterns. Imagine an extended vertical sinusoidal grating that contains luminance variations (black and white, say) over the lower half of its extent, then turns into an isoluminant pattern (red and green, perhaps) over the upper half. The bars that are black in the lower half become red in the upper half, and those that are white in the lower half become green in the upper half. If such a grating is made to drift in a horizontal direction (so the bars move smoothly to the right, say), a strange perceptual dissociation occurs. The black–white half of the grating will appear to move smoothly to the right at a speed that is a function of the actual speed of the pattern. The red-green half, however, may appear not to move at all, to move only by occasional shifts in its position, or to move but exceedingly slowly (Cavanaugh, Tyler, & Favreau, 1984; Teller & Lindsey, 1993). This occurs despite the fact that the red bars clearly abut the black bars, and the green bars abut the white bars at every moment and across the entire grating. There is no point at which the attachment between the two seems to break, yet the two halves appear clearly to be moving at markedly different speeds. The perceptual slowing of moving isoluminant stimuli can be observed with discrete objects, as well as with drifting gratings (Troscianko & Fahle, 1988). It appears to be a ubiquitous feature of moving stimuli that are defined only by color differences. We have also observed that isolated moving gaussian blobs that differ from the background only in color may not appear to move along a smooth trajectory. From when their real movement path is straight, they may appear to move along some more complex trajectory.

To explain the perceptual slowing of color motion, it is necessary first to have a model of the way in which the visual system encodes speed. Despite the large number of models aimed at explaining direction selectivity in the visual system, there are relatively few models of speed encoding. An interesting and useful attempt to model the slowing of perceived speed at isoluminance has been presented by Metha and Mullen (1997).

The peculiarities associated with isoluminance should not blind us to the important role color can play. For example, color differences can strongly influence the way in which an observer perceptually segregates the objects in a complex scene, such as determining whether a moving plaid pattern is seen as a coherent whole or as separate components moving transparently (Kooi, De Valois, Switkes, & Grosof, 1992).

References

Abramov, I. (1968). Further analysis of the responses of LGN cells. *Journal of the Optical Society of America, 58,* 574–579.

Abramov, I., Gordon, J., & Chan, H. (1990). Using hue scaling to specify color appearance and to derive color differences. *Perceiving, measuring, and using color. Proceedings of the SPIE, 1250,* 40–51.

Anhelt, P. K., & Kolb, H. (1994). Horizontal cells and cone photoreceptors in human retina: a Golgi-electron microscope study of spectral connectivity. *Journal of Comparative Neurology, 343,* 406–427.

Anhelt, P. K., Kolb, H., & Pflug, R. (1987). Identification of a subtype of cone photoreceptor, likely to be blue-sensitive, in the human retina. *Journal of Comparative Neurology, 255,* 18–34.

Baylor, D., Nunn, B., & Schnapf, J. (1987). Spectral sensitivity of cones of the monkey *Macaca fascicularis. Journal of Physiology, 390,* 145–60.

Bedford, R. E., & Wyszecki, G. W. (1958). Luminosity functions for various field sizes and levels of retinal illuminance. *Journal of the Optical Society of America, 48,* 406–411.

Berlin, B., & Kay, P. (1969). *Basic color terms, their universality and evolution.* Berkeley: University of California Press.

Blakemore, C., & Campbell, F. W. (1969). On the existence of neurones in the human visual system selectively sensitive to the orientation and size of retinal images. *Journal of Physiology (London), 203,* 237–260.

Boynton, R. M., & Gordon, J. (1965). Bezold-Brücke hue shift measured by color-naming technique. *Journal of the Optical Society of America, 55,* 78–86.

Boynton, R. M., & Kaiser, P. K. (1968). Vision: The additivity law made to work for heterochromatic photometry with bipartite fields. *Science, 161,* 366–368.

Bradley, A., Switkes, E., & De Valois, K. K. (1988). Orientation and spatial frequency selectivity of adaptation to color and luminance gratings. *Vision Research, 28,* 841–856.

Cavanaugh, P., Tyler, C. W., & Favreau, O. E. (1984). Perceived velocity of moving chromatic gratings. *Journal of the Optical Society of America A, 1,* 893–899.

Cavonius, C. R., & Estévez, O. (1975). Contrast sensitivity of individual colour mechanisms of human vision. *Journal of Physiology (London), 248,* 649–662.

Cole, G., & Hine, T. (1992). Computation of cone contrasts for color vision research. *Behavioral Research Methods, Instruments, & Computers, 24,* 22–27.

Cole, G. R., Stromeyer, C. F., & Kronauer, R. E. (1990). Visual interactions with luminance and chromatic stimuli. *Journal of the Optical Society of America A, 7:* 128–140.

Cottaris, N. P., & De Valois, R. L. (1998). Temporal dynamics of chromatic tuning in macaque primary visual cortex. *Nature, 395,* 896–900.

Curcio, C. A., Sloan, K. R., Kalina, R. E., & Hendrickson, A. E. (1990). Human photoreceptor topography. *Journal of Comparative Neurology, 292,* 497–523.

Curcio, C. A., Allen, K. A., Sloan, K. R., Lerea, C. L., Hurley, J. B., Klock, I. B., & Milam, A. H. (1991). Distribution and morphology of human cone photoreceptors stained with anti-blue opsin. *Journal of Comparative Neurology, 312,* 610–624.

Dacey, D. M., & Lee, B. B. (1994). The 'blue-on' opponent pathway in primate retina originates from a distinct bistratified ganglion cell type. *Nature, 367,* 731–735.

de Monasterio, F. M. (1979). Asymmetry of on- and off-pathways of blue-sensitive cones of the retina of macaques. *Brain Research, 166,* 39–48.

de Monasterio, F. M., McCrane, E. P., Newlander, J. K., & Schein, S. J. (1985). Density profile of blue-sensitive cones along the horizontal meridian of macaque retina. *Investigative Ophthalmology and Visual Science, 26,* 289–302.

Derrington, A. M., Krauskopf, J., & Lennie, P. (1984). Chromatic mechanisms in lateral geniculate nucleus of macaque. *Journal of Physiology (London), 357,* 241–265.

De Valois, K. K., & Switkes, E. (1983). Simultaneous masking interactions between chromatic and luminance gratings. *Journal of the Optical Society of America, 73,* 11–18.

De Valois, R. L. (1965). Analysis and coding of color vision in the primate visual system. *Cold Spring Harbor Symposia on Quantitative Biology,* 567–579.

De Valois, R. L., Abramov, I., & Jacobs, G. H. (1966). Analysis of response patterns of LGN cells. *Journal of the Optical Society of America, 56,* 966–977.

De Valois, R. L., Cottaris, N. P., & Elfar, S. (1997). S-cone inputs to striate cortex cells. *Investigative Ophthalmology and Visual Science, 38,* S15.

De Valois, R. L., & De Valois, K. K. (1975). Neural coding of color. In E. C. Carterette & M. P. Friedman (Eds.), *Handbook of perception: Seeing* (Vol. 5, pp. 117–166). New York: Academic Press.

De Valois, R. L., & De Valois, K. K. (1988). *Spatial vision.* New York: Oxford University Press.

De Valois, R. L., & De Valois, K. K. (1993). A multi-stage color model. *Vision Research, 33,* 1053–1065.

De Valois, R. L., De Valois, K. K., Switkes, E., & Mahon, L. (1997). Hue scaling of isoluminant and cone-specific lights. *Vision Research, 37,* 885–897.

De Valois, R. L., Jacobs, G. H., & Abramov, I. (1964). Responses of single cells in visual system to shifts in the wavelength of light. *Science, 146,* 1184–1186.

De Valois, R. L., & Marrocco, R. T. (1973). Single cell analysis of saturation discrimination in the macaque. *Vision Research, 13,* 701–711.

De Valois, R. L., Morgan, H., Polson, M. C., Mead, W. R., & Hull, E. M. (1974). Psychophysical studies of monkey vision. I. Macaque luminosity and color vision tests. *Vision Research, 14,* 53–67.

De Valois, R. L., Snodderly, D. M., Yund, E. W., Jr., & Hepler, N. (1977). Responses of macaque lateral geniculate cells to luminance and color figures. *Sensory Processes, 1,* 244–259.

de Weert, C., & Spillmann, L. (1995). Assimilation: Asymmetry between brightness and darkness? *Vision Research, 35,* 1413–1419.

Ding, T., & Casagrande, V. A. (1997). The distribution and morphology of LGN K pathway axons within the layers and CO blobs of owl monkey. *Vision Neuroscience, 14,* 691–704.

Fach, C., & Sharpe, L. T. (1986). Assimilative hue shifts in color gratings depend on bar width. *Perception and Psychophysics, 40,* 412–418.

Famiglietti, E. V., & Kolb, H. (1976). Structural basis for On- and Off-center responses in retinal ganglion cells. *Science, 194,* 193–195.

Gilinsky, A. S. (1968). Orientation-specific effects of patterns of adapting light on visual acuity. *Journal of the Optical Society of America, 58,* 13–18.

Granger, E. M., & Heurtley, J. C. (1973). Visual chromaticity-modulation transfer function. *Journal of the Optical Society of America, 63,* 1173–1174.

Grassman, H. (1853). Zur Theorie der Farbenmischung. *Annals of Physics und Chemistry, 89,* 69–84; English translation: (1854). On the theory of compound colours. *Phil. Mag., 7,* 254–264.

Green, D. G. (1972). Visual acuity in the blue cone monochromat. *Journal of Physiology (London), 222,* 419–426.

Guth, S. L. (1967). Non-additivity and inhibition among chromatic luminances at threshold. *Vision Research, 7,* 319–328.

Hässler, R. (1967). Comparative anatomy of central visual systems in day- and night-active primates. In R. Hässler & H. Stephan (Eds.), *Evolution of the forebrain* (pp. 419–434). New York: Plenum Press.

Helmholtz, H. von (1867). *Handbuch der Physiologischen Optik* (1st ed.). Hamburg: Voss. English translation: J. P. C. Southall (Ed.). (1924). *Handbook of physiological optics* (3 vols.). Rochester, NY: Optical Society of America.

Hendry, S. H. C., & Yoshioka, T. (1994). A neurochemically distinct third channel in the macaque dorsal lateral geniculate nucleus. *Science, 264,* 575–577.

Hering, E. (1878). *Zur Lehre vom Lichtsinne.* Wien: Carl Gerolds Sohn. English translation: L. M. Hurvich & D. Jameson (Trans.). (1964). *Outlines of a theory of the light sense.* Cambridge, MA: Harvard University Press.

Hurvich, L. M., & Jameson, D. (1955). Some quantitative aspects of an opponent-colors theory. II. Brightness, saturation, and hue in normal and dichromatic vision. *Journal of the Optical Society of America, 45,* 602–616.

Hurvich, L. M., & Jameson, D. (1956). Some quantitative aspects of an opponent-colors theory. IV. A psychological color specifications system. *Journal of the Optical Society of America, 46,* 416–421.

Jacobs, G. H. (1981). *Comparative color vision.* New York: Academic Press.

Jameson, D., & Hurvich, L. M. (1955). Some quantitative aspects of an opponent-colors theory. 1. Chromatic responses and spectral saturation. *Journal of the Optical Society of America, 45,* 546–552.

Jameson, D., & Hurvich, L. M. (1956). Some quantitative aspects of an opponent-colors theory. III. Changes in brightness, saturation, and hue with chromatic adaptation. *Journal of the Optical Society of America, 46,* 405–415.

Kaiser, P. K. (1988). Sensation luminance: A new name to distinguish CIE luminance from luminance dependent on an individual's spectral sensitivity. *Vision Research, 28,* 455–456.

Kaiser, P. K., & Boynton, R. M. (1997). *Human color vision.* Washington, DC: Optical Society of America.

Kay, P., Berlin, B., Maffi, L., & Merrifield, W. (1997). Color naming across languages. In C. L. Hardin & L. Maffi (Eds.), *Color categories in thought and language* (pp. 21–56). Cambridge, UK: Cambridge University Press.

Kelly, D. H. (1983). Spatio-temporal variations of chromatic and achromatic contrast thresholds. *Journal of the Optical Society of America, 73,* 742–750.

Kolb, H., Boycott, B. B., & Dowling, J. E. (1969). Primate retina: Light microscopy. (Appendix). A second type of midget bipolar cell in the primate retina. *Philosophical Transactions of the Royal Society of London (Biology), 255,* 177–184.

Kooi, F., De Valois, K. K., Switkes, E., & Grosof, D. (1992). Higher-order factors influencing the perception of sliding and coherence of a plaid. *Perception, 21,* 583–598.

Kouyama, N., & Marshak, D. W. (1992). Bipolar cells specific for blue cones in the macaque retina. *Journal of Neuroscience, 12,* 1233–1252.

Lee, B. B., Martin, P. R., & Valberg, A. (1988). The physiological basis of heterochromatic flicker photometry demonstrated in the ganglion cells of the macaque retina. *Journal of Physiology (London), 404,* 323–347.

Lennie, P., Haake, P. W., & Williams, D. R. (1991). The design of chromatically opponent receptive fields. In M. S. Landy & J. A. Movshon (Eds.), *Computational models of visual processing* (pp. 71–82). Cambridge, MA: MIT Press.

Lennie, P., Krauskopf, J., & Sclar, G. (1990). Chromatic mechanisms in striate cortex of macaque. *Journal of Neuroscience, 10,* 649–669.

MacLeod, D. I. A., & Boynton, R. M. (1979). Chromaticity diagram showing cone excitation by stimuli of equal luminance. *Journal of the Optical Society of America, 69,* 1183–1186.

Malpeli, J. G., & Schiller, P. H. (1978). Lack of blue off-center cells in the visual system of the monkey. *Brain Research, 141,* 385–389.

Mariani, A. P. (1981). A diffuse, invaginating cone bipolar cell in primate retina. *Journal of Comparative Neurology, 197,* 661–671.

Mariani, A. P. (1984). Bipolar cells in monkey retina selective for the cones likely to be blue-sensitive. *Nature, 308,* 184–186.

Martin, P. R., White, A. J. R., Goodchild, A. K., Wilder, H. D., & Sefton, A. E. (1997). Evidence that blue-on cells are part of the third geniculocortical pathway in primates. *European Journal of Neuroscience, 9,* 1536–1541.

Maxwell, J. C. (1860). On the theory of compound colours, and the relations of the colours of the spectrum. *Philosophical Transactions of the Royal Society (London), 150,* 57–84.

Meadows, J. C. (1974). Disturbed perception of colours associated with localized cerebral lesions. *Brain, 97,* 615–632.

Metha, A. B., & Mullen, K. T. (1997). Red-green and achromatic temporal filters: A ratio model predicts contrast-dependent speed perception. *Journal of the Optical Society of America A, 14,* 984–996.

Missotten, L. (1965). *The ultrastructure of the human retina.* Bruxelles: Arscia.

Mullen, K. T. (1985). The contrast sensitivity of human colour vision to red-green and blue-yellow chromatic gratings. *Journal of Physiology (London), 359,* 381–400.

Mullen, K. T., Cropper, S. J., & Losada, M. A. (1997). Absence of linear subthreshold summation between red-green and luminance mechanisms over a wide range of spatio-temporal conditions. *Vision Research, 37,* 1157–1165.

Nagy, A. L., MacLeod, D. I. A., Heyneman, N. E., & Eisner, A. (1981). Four cone pigments in women heterozygous for color deficiency. *Journal of the Optical Society of America, 71,* 719–722.

Nathans, J., Thomas, D., & Hogness, D. S. (1986). Molecular genetics of human color vision: the genes encoding blue, green and red pigments. *Science, 232,* 193–202.

Neitz, J., & Jacobs, G. H. (1990). Polymorphism in normal human color vision and its mechanism. *Vision Research, 30,* 621–636.

Neitz, J., & Neitz, M. (1998). Molecular genetics and the biological basis of color vision. In W. G. K. Backhaus, R. Kliegl, & J. S. Werner (Eds.), *Color vision* (pp. 101–119). Berlin: De Gruyter.

Neitz, M., Neitz, J., & Jacobs, G. H. (1991). Spectral tuning of pigments underlying red-green color vision. *Science, 252,* 971–974.

Østerberg, G. (1935). Topography of the layer of rods and cones in the human retina. *Acta Ophthalmologic Kbh., Suppl. 6,* 1–102.

Palmer, G. (1777). *Theory of colours and vision.* London: S. Leacroft.

Pantle, A., & Sekuler, R. (1968). Size-detecting mechanisms in human vision. *Science, 162,* 1146–1148.

Parsons, J. H. (1915). *An introduction to the study of colour vision.* Cambridge, UK: Cambridge University Press.

Priest, I. G., & Brickwedde, F. G. (1938). The minimum perceptible colorimetyric purity as a function of dominant wavelength. *Journal of the Optical Society of America, 28,* 133–139.

Purdy, D. McL. (1931). Spectral hue as a function of intensity. *American Journal of Psychology, 43,* 541–559.

Reid, R. C., & Shapley, R. M. (1992). Spatial structure of cone inputs to receptive fields in primate lateral geniculate nucleus. *Nature, 356,* 716–718.

Rodieck, R. W., Binmoeller, K. F., & Dineen, J. (1985). Parasol and midget ganglion cells of the human retina. *Journal of Comparative Neurology, 233,* 115–132.

Rovamo, J., Hyvaerinen, & Hari, R. (1982). Human vision without luminance-contrast system: selective recovery of the red-green colour-contrast system from acquired blindness. *Documenta Ophthalmologica. Proceedings Series, 33,* 457–466.

Schein, S. J., & Desimone, R. (1990). Spectral properties of V4 neurons in the macaque. *Journal of Neuroscience, 10,* 3369–3389.

Schein, S. J., Marrocco, R. T., & de Monasterio, F. M. (1982). Is there a high concentration of color-selective cells in area V4 of monkey visual cortex? *Journal of Neurophysiology, 47,* 193–213.

Schiller, P. H. (1993). The effects of V4 and middle temporal (MT) lesions on visual performance in the rhesus monkey. *Vision Neuroscience, 10,* 717–746.

Schiller, P. H., & Malpeli, J. G. (1978). Functional specificity of lateral geniculate nucleus laminae of the rhesus monkey. *Journal of Neurophysiology, 41,* 788–797.

Schnapf, J. L., Kraft, T. W., & Baylor, D. A. (1987). Spectral sensitivity of human cone photoreceptors. *Nature, 325,* 439–441.

Schnapf, J. L., Kraft, T. W., Nunn, B. J., & Baylor, D. A. (1988). Spectral sensitivity of primate photoreceptors. *Visual Neuroscience, 1,* 255–261.

Smith, V. C., & Pokorny, J. (1975). Spectral sensitivity of the foveal cone photopigments between 400 and 500 nm. *Vision Research, 15,* 161–171.

Sperling, H. G., & Harwerth, R. S. (1971). Red-green cone interactions in the increment-threshold spectral sensitivity of primates. *Science, 172,* 180–184.

Sternheim, C. E., & Boynton, R. M. (1966). Uniqueness of perceived hues investigated with a continuous judgmental technique. *Journal of Experimental Psychology, 72,* 770–776.

Swanson, W. H., Ueno, T., Smith, V. C., & Pokorny, J. (1987). Temporal modulation sensitivity and pulse-detection thresholds for chromatic and luminance perturbations. *Journal of the Optical Society of America A, 4,* 1992–2005.

Switkes, E., Bradley, A., & De Valois, K. K. (1988). Contrast dependence and mechanisms of masking interactions among chromatic and luminance gratings. *Journal of the Optical Society of America A, 5,* 1149–1162.

Teller, D. Y., & Lindsey, D. T. (1993). Motion at isoluminance: Motion dead zone in three-dimensional color space. *Journal of the Optical Society of America A, 10,* 1324–1331.

Thorell, L. G., De Valois, R. L., & Albrecht, D. G. (1984). Spatial mapping of monkey V1 cells with pure color and luminance stimuli. *Vision Research, 24,* 751–769.

Tootell, R. B. H., Hadjikhani, N. K., Liu, A. K., & Cavanagh, A. M. (1998). Color and retinopathy in human visual cortical area V8. *Investigations in Ophthalmologic Vision Science, 39,* S1129.

Troscianko, T,. & Fahle, M. (1988). Why do isoluminant stimuli appear slower? *Journal of the Optical Society of America A, 5,* 871–880.

Valberg, A., Lee, B. B., & Tidwell, D. A. (1986). Neurones with strong inhibitory S-cone inputs in the macaque lateral geniculate nucleus. *Vision Research, 26,* 1061–1064.

Valberg, A., Lee, B. B., & Tryti, J. (1987). Simulation of responses of spectrally-opponent neurones in the macaque lateral geniculate nucleus to chromatic and achromatic light stimuli. *Vision Research, 27,* 867–882.

van der Horst, G. J. C., & Bouman, M. A. (1969). Spatiotemporal chromaticity discrimination. *Journal of the Optical Society of America, 59,* 1482–1488.

van der Horst, G. J. C., de Weert, C. M. M., & Bouman, M. A. (1967). Transfer of spatial chromaticity-contrast at threshold in the human eye. *Journal of the Optical Society of America, 57,* 1260–1266.

Virsu, V., & Haapasalo, S. (1973). Relationships between channels for colour and spatial frequency in human vision. *Perception, 2,* 31–40.

von Bezold, W. (1876). *The theory of colour* (American edition). Boston: Prang.

van Kries, J. (1905). Die Gesichtsempfindungen. In W. Nagel (Ed.), *Handbuch der Physiologie des Menschen* (pp. 109–282). Braunschweig: Vieweg.

Vos, J. J., & Walraven, P. L. (1971). On the derivation of the foveal receptor primaries. *Vision Research, 11,* 799–818.

Wässle, H., Boycott, B. B., & Röhrenbeck, J. (1989). Horizontal cells in monkey retina: Cone connections and dendritic network. *European Journal of Neuroscience, 1,* 421–435.

Wässle, H., Grünert, U., Martin, P. R., & Boycott, B. B. (1994). Immunocytochemical characterization and spatial distribution of midget bipolar cells in the macaque monkey retina. *Vision Research, 34,* 561–579.

Webster, M. A., De Valois, K. K., & Switkes, E. (1990). Orientation and spatial-frequency discrimination for luminance and chromatic gratings. *Journal of the Optical Society of America A, 7,* 1034–1049.

Werner, J. S., & Walraven, J. (1982). Effect of chromatic adaptation on the achromatic locus: the role contrast, luminance and background color. *Vision Research, 22,* 929–943.

Werner, J. S., & Wooten, B. R. (1979). Opponent chromatic mechanisms: Relation to photopigments and hue naming. *Journal of the Optical Society of America, 69,* 422–434.

Wright, W. D., & Pitt, F. H. G. (1934). Hue discrimination in normal colour vision. *Proceedings of the Physics Society (London), 46,* 459–473.

Wright, W. D., & Pitt, F. H. G. (1937). The saturation-discrimination of two trichromats. *Proceedings of the Physics Society (London), 49,* 329–331.

Yamamoto, T. L. (1997). Color-selective spatial tuning. Unpublished doctoral dissertation, University of California, Berkeley, CA.

Young, T. (1802). On the theory of light and colours. *Philosophical Transactions of the Royal Society (London), 92,* 12–48.

Zeki, S. M. (1973). Colour coding in rhesus monkey prestriate cortex. *Brain Research, 53,* 422–427.

CHAPTER 5

Binocular Vision

Clifton Schor

I. PERCEIVED VISUAL DIRECTION

A. Oculocentric Direction

Under binocular viewing conditions we perceive a single view of the world as though seen by a single cyclopean eye. Singleness results from a mapping of the two visual fields onto a common binocular space. The topography of this map will be described subsequently as the horopter, which is an analytical tool that provides a reference for quantifying retinal image disparity. Stimulation of binocularly corresponding points by targets on the horopter results in percepts by each eye in identical visual directions (i.e., directions in reference to the point of binocular fixation). This eye-referenced description of direction (oculocentric) can be transformed to a head-referenced description (egocentric direction) by including information about eye position as well as a reference point in the head from which the two eyes can judge direction.

B. The Cyclopean Eye

If we only had one eye, direction could be judged from the nodal point of the eye, a site where viewing angle in space equals visual angle in the eye, assuming the nodal point is close to the radial center of the retina. However, two eyes present a problem for a system that operates as though it only has a single cyclopean eye. The two eyes have viewpoints separated by approximately 6.5 cm. When the two eyes converge accurately on a near target placed along the midsagittal plane, the target appears straight ahead of the nose, even when one eye is occluded. In order for perceived egocentric direction to be the same when either eye views the near target monocularly, there needs to be a common reference point. This reference point is called the cyclopean locus or egocenter, and is located midway on the interocular axis. The location of the egocenter is found empirically by the site where perceptually aligned points at different depths in space are perceived to intersect the face. Thus the egocenter is the percept of a reference point for judging visual direction with either eye alone or under binocular viewing conditions. The validity of the egocenter is supported by sighting behavior in young children (< 2 years of age). When asked to sight targets through a tube, they place it between the eyes (Barbeito, 1983).

It is interesting to compare how visual directions are computed by animals with binocular visual systems that obey Hering's law of ocular movements (ambiocular systems) and animals such as the chameleon that have independent eye movements (utrocular systems). The utrocular system computes visual directions separately with each eye. Because the eye is displaced from the head center, information about eye position and retinal image location for one eye is insufficient to specify direction with respect to the head. In the utrocular system, additional information about target distance is also needed to compute head-centric direction. In the absence of binocular disparity or convergence cues, utrocular animals use accommodation to specify target distance (Ott & Schaeffel, 1995). Accommodation, combined with eye position and retinal image locus, could provide sufficient information to compute head-centric direction.

C. Egocentric Direction

Direction and distance can be described in polar coordinates as the angle and magnitude of a vector originating at the egocenter. For targets imaged on corresponding points, this vector is determined by the location of the retinal image and by the direction of gaze that is determined by versional or conjugate eye position. The angle the two retinal images form with the visual axes is added to the conjugate rotational vector component of binocular eye position (the average of right and left eye position). This combination yields the perceived egocentric direction. Convergence of the eyes, which results from disconjugate eye movements, has no influence on perceived egocentric direction. Thus, when the two eyes fixate near objects to the left or right of the midline in asymmetric convergence, only the version or conjugate component of the two eyes' positions contributes to perceived direction. These facets of egocentric direction were summarized by Hering (1879) as five laws of visual direction, and they have been restated by Howard (1982). The laws are mainly concerned with targets imaged on corresponding retinal regions (i.e., targets on the horopter).

D. Visual Directions of Disparate Images

How are visual directions judged for disparate targets (i.e., targets located nearer or farther than the horopter)? When target disparity is small and within Panum's fusional area, such that the target appears single, egocentric direction is based upon the average retinal image locus of the two eyes, and it deviates from either monocular perceived direction of the disparate target by half the angular disparity. The consequence of averaging monocular visual directions of disparate targets is that binocular visual directions are mislocalized by half their retinal image disparity. Binocular visual directions can only be judged accurately for targets lying on the horopter. When retinal image disparity becomes large, disparate targets appear diplopic (i.e., they are perceived in two separate directions). The directions of monocular components of the diplopic pair are perceived as though each one was stimulated by a target on the horopter (i.e., the diplopic images are seen as though both had paired images on corresponding points in their respective contralateral eye).

E. Visual Direction of Partially Occluded Objects

There are ambiguous circumstances where a target in the peripheral region of a binocular field is only seen by one eye because of occlusion by the nose. The monocular target could lie at a range of viewing distances; however, its direction is judged as though it was at the distance of the horopter, such that if it were seen binocularly, its images would be formed on corresponding retinal points (Barbeito & Simpson, 1991).

F. Violations of Hering's Laws of Visual Direction

The rules suggested by Hering for computing visual direction apply in many circumstances. However, several violations of Herings' rules for visual direction have been observed in both abnormal and normal binocular vision. In violation of Hering's rules, unilateral-constant strabismics can have constant diplopia, and they use the position of their preferred fixation eye to judge visual direction regardless of whether they fixate a target with their preferred or deviating eye. Alternating strabismics use the position of whichever eye is fixating to judge direction of objects (Mann, Hein, & Diamond, 1979). Both classes of strabismus use the position of only one eye to judge direction, whereas nonstrabismics use the average position of the two eyes to judge direction by either eye alone.

Two violations in normal binocular vision involve monocular images, and a third involves judgment of direction of binocular-disparate targets. Hering's rules predict that if a target is fixated monocularly, it will appear to move in the temporalward direction if the eyes accommodate, even if monocular fixation remains accurate. The temporalward movement results from the nasalward movement of the covered eye caused by the synkinesis between accommodation and convergence (Müller, 1843). Hering predicts that the average position of the eyes determines the egocentric direction of the foveated target. The first violation occurs when the apparent temporalward motion is greater during monocular fixation by one eye than the other. This violation resembles the perception of egocentric direction in constant-unilateral strabismus, and it may be related to an extreme form of eye dominance.

The second violation of Hering's rules occurs when monocular targets are viewed in close proximity to disparate binocular targets, as might occur naturally in the periphery or in the vicinity of a proximal surface that occludes a portion of the background in the central visual field. The direction of the monocular target is judged as though it was positioned at the same depth as the disparate binocular target rather than at the horopter. The visual system might assume there is an occluded counterpart of the monocular line in the contralateral eye that has the same disparity as the nearby binocular target, even though the image is seen only by one eye. The behavioral observation that is consistent with this hypothesis is that alignment of a monocular and binocular line is based on information presented only to the eye seeing both targets (Erkelens & van de Grind, 1994; Erkelens & Van Ee, 1997).

A third violation of Hering's rules is demonstrated by the biasing of the visual direction of a fused disparate target when its monocular image components have unequal contrast (Banks, van Ee, & Backus, 1997). Greater weight is given to the retinal locus of the image that has the higher contrast. The average location in the cyclopean eye of the two disparate retinal sites is biased toward the monocular direction of the higher-contrast image. These are minor violations that mainly occur for targets lying nearer or farther from the plane of fixation or distance of convergence. Since visual directions of off-horopter targets are mislocalized, even when Hering's rules of visual direction are obeyed, the violations have only minor consequences.

II. BINOCULAR CORRESPONDENCE

We perceive space with two eyes as though they were merged into a single cyclopean eye. This merger is made possible by a sensory linkage between the two eyes that is facilitated by the anatomical superposition of homologous regions of the two retinae in the visual cortex. This is achieved by partial decussation that is a characteristic of visual systems with overlapping visual fields. The Newton Mueller-Sudden law states that the degree of hemi-decussation is proportional to the amount of binocular overlap.

Why are the two retinal images matched at all? Primarily the matching allows us to reconstruct a 3-D world percept from a flat 2-D image. Three-dimensional space can be derived geometrically by comparing the small differences between the two retinal images that result from the slightly different vantage points of the two eyes caused by their 6.5-cm separation. Each eye sees slightly more of the temporal than nasal visual field, and they also see more of the ipsilateral than the contralateral side of a binocularly viewed object. This yields stereopsis but comes at a price of a reduced visual field from 360° to 190°. The binocular overlapping region is 114° and the remaining monocular portion is 37° for each eye.

A. Binocular Disparity

Binocular disparity results from the projection of 3-D objects onto two 2-D retinal surfaces that face the objects from slightly different angles and views or vantage points. The regions of the visual cortex that receive input from each eye are sensitive to various perspective differences or disparities of the two retinal images. These disparities take the form of horizontal, vertical, torsional, and distortion or shear differences between the two images. The disparities result from surface shape and depth as well as the direction and distance of gaze, and the torsion of the eyes (van Ee & Erkelens, 1996). These disparities are used to judge the layout of 3-D space and to sense the solidness or curvature of surfaces. Disparities are also used to break through camouflage in images such as seen in tree foliage.

Description and quantification of binocular disparity requires a coordinate system that is primarily for our convenience, as many types of coordinate systems could accomplish this task, and we are uncertain what system is used to encode disparity by the visual system. The coordinate system requires a reference point from which to describe distance and direction. Because we are describing disparities of the two retinal images, a coordinate system that is typically chosen is retinal based rather than one that is head or world based. The reference point is the fovea, and distance from the fovea is traditionally described in Cartesian x and y components of azimuth and elevation, but a polar description could and has also been used (Liu, Stevenson, & Schor, 1994a).

Since retinal locations are described by the position of targets in space that are imaged on them, a transformation is needed to link retinal and visual space. The optical transformation is described above by visual direction. In computations of visual direction, retinal images are projected or sighted out through the nodal point of the eye, so that directions from objects in spaces to an image on the retina do not deviate from straight lines. As long as the eyes remain stationary, differences in visual directions correspond to differences in retinal locations.

B. Corresponding Retinal Points

Hering (1879) defined binocular correspondence by retinal locations in the two eyes, which when stimulated, resulted in a percept in identical visual directions. For a fixed angle of convergence, some of these identical visual directions converged upon real points in space. In other cases, corresponding points have visual directions that do not intersect in real space. Accordingly, some corresponding regions of the two retinae might only be stimulated simultaneously by a real object under limited circumstances. We shall see that this unique stimulus only occurs at infinite viewing distances and that at finite viewing distances, only a small portion of corresponding points can be stimulated by real targets in space.

C. The Horizontal Horopter

The horopter is the locus in space of real objects or points whose images can be formed on corresponding retinal points. To appreciate the shape of the horopter, consider a theoretical case in which corresponding points are defined as homologous locations on the two retinae. Begin first by considering binocular matches between the horizontal meridians or equators of the two retinae. Under this circumstance, corresponding retinal loci lie equidistant from their respective foveas, and the intersection of their visual directions in space defines the longitudinal horopter.

A geometric theorem states "any two points on a circle subtend equal angles at any other two points on the same circle." Consider a circle that passes through the fixation point and the two nodal points of the eyes. Let two points be the two nodal points and let two other points be the fixation point and any other point on the circle. The theorem predicts that angles formed by the two nodal points and the other two points in space are equal. Because the angles pass through the nodal points they are also equal in the two eyes. One of the points is imaged on the two foveas, and the other point will be imaged at retinal loci that are equidistant from their respective foveas. By definition, these nonfoveal points are geometrically corresponding points. From this you can generalize that any point on this circle will be imaged at equal eccentricities from the two foveas on corresponding points in the two eyes except for the small arc of the circle that lies between the two eyes. This is the theoretical or geometric horopter. It was described by Alhazen (1989), Aguilonius (1613), and finally by Vieth and Muller and it bears their name (the Vieth-Muller [V-M] circle) (Figure 1).

The empirical horopter differs from the theoretical horopter in two ways. It can be skewed or tilted about a vertical axis (as shown in Figure 2), and its curvature can be flatter or steeper than the V-M circle (as shown in Figure 3). These two effects are described by fitting a conic section such as an ellipse through the empirical data, the fixation point, and the nodal points of the eyes. At the fixation point, the curvature variation of the best-fit conic from a circle is referred to as the Hering-Hillebrand deviation. The skew or tilt of the fit is described by an overall magnification of an array of points along the retinal equator in one eye that correspond to an array of points along the equator of the other eye. These deviations cause parts of the empirical horopter to lie either distal or proximal from the theoretical horopter. When this occurs, the points on the horopter no longer subtend equal angles at the two eyes. The spatial plot of the horopter shown in Figure 2 illustrates that points on the empirical horopter that are closer than the theoretical horopter subtend a smaller angle in the ipsilateral than contralateral eye. When this occurs, empirically measured corresponding points are not equidistant from their respective foveas.

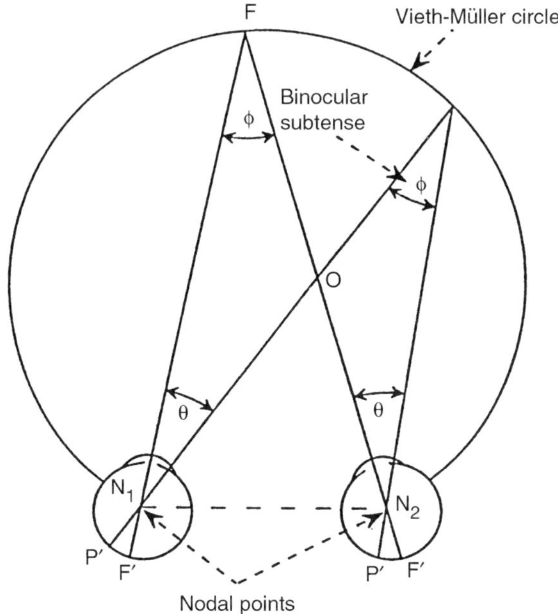

FIGURE 1 Spatial plot of the horizontal horopter. When the eyes are converged on point F, the images, F′, fall on the foveas and have zero disparity. Let ϕ be the binocular subtense of point F and let a circle pass through F and the nodal points of the eyes (the Vieth-Müller circle). The fixation point F and any other point P on the circle subtend equal angles at the nodal points of the two eyes, and P is imaged at equal eccentricities on the two retinae. (From BINOCULAR VISION AND STEREOPSIS by Ian P. Howard and Brian J. Rogers, Copyright © 1995 by Oxford University Press, Inc. Used by permission of Oxford University Press, Inc., and the authors.)

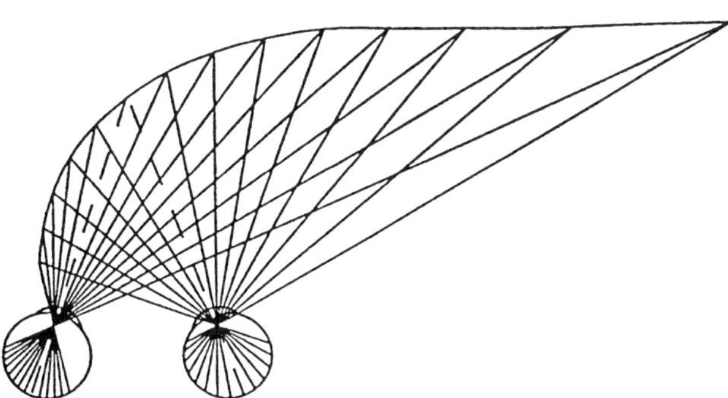

FIGURE 2 Horopter slant produced by uniform magnification of corresponding points in one eye. A uniform magnification of corresponding points in the right eye, relative to the left eye causes the horizontal horopter to be skewed about a vertical axis away from the right (magnified) eye. (From BINOCULAR VISION AND STEREOPSIS by Ian P. Howard and Brian J. Rogers, Copyright © 1995 by Oxford University Press, Inc. Used by permission of Oxford University Press, Inc., and the authors.)

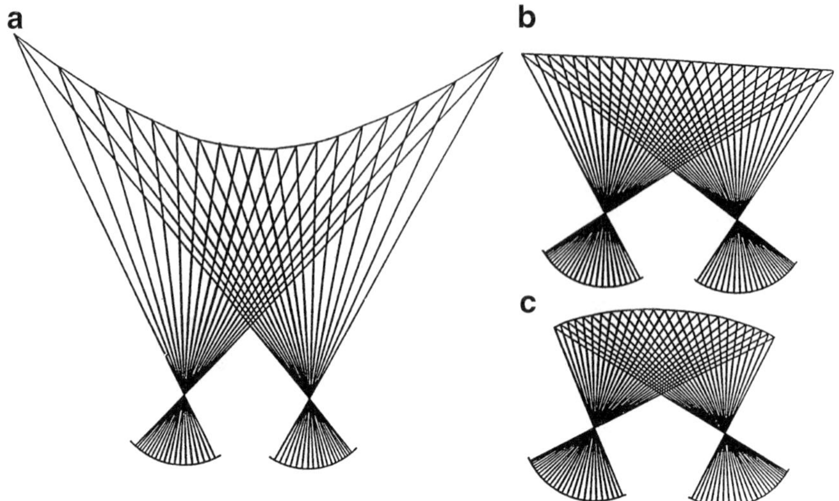

FIGURE 3 Changes in horopter curvature produced by nonuniform magnification of corresponding points in the temporal retinas relative to those in the nasal retinas. Nonuniform magnification of corresponding points of the nasal hemi-retinae flatten the horopter relative to the Vieth-Muller circle. The absolute curvature varies with viewing distance and becomes flatter as distance increases from concave at near (c) to convex at far (a). At an intermediate distance (b), the horopter coincides with the fronto-parallel plane when the Hering–Hillebrand deviation (H) equals the interpupillary distance/the viewing distance (Abathic Distance). All three empirical curves correspond to the same Hering–Hillebrand deviation, and the apparent curvature changes result from spatial geometry. (From BINOCULAR VISION AND STEREOPSIS by Ian P. Howard and Brian J. Rogers, Copyright © 1995 by Oxford University Press, Inc. Used by permission of Oxford University Press, Inc., and the authors.)

The horopter can also be represented analytically by a plot of the ratio of longitudinal angles subtended by empirical horopter points (Right/Left) on the y axis as a function of retinal eccentricity of the image in the right eye (Figure 4). Changes in curvature from a circle to an ellipse result from nonuniform magnification of retinal points in one eye. If the empirical horopter is flatter than the theoretical horopter, corresponding retinal points are more distant from the fovea on the nasal than temporal hemi retina (see Figure 3). A tilt of the horopter around a vertical axis results from a uniformly closer spacing of corresponding points to the fovea in one eye than the other eye (uniform magnification effect) (see Figure 2).

D. The Vertical Horopter

The theoretical vertical point-horopter for a finite viewing distance is limited by the locus of points in space where homologous visual directions will intersect real

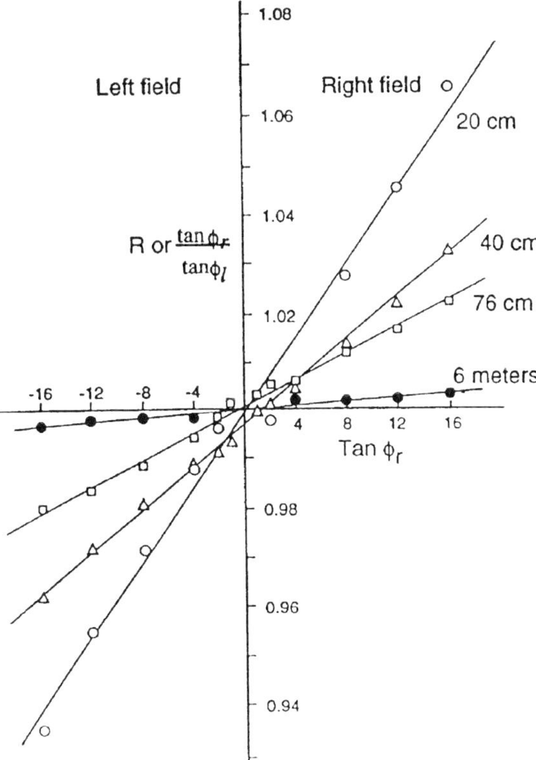

FIGURE 4 Analytical plot of horopter data. The tangent of the angular subtense of the right eye image (tan or) is plotted on the x axis, and the tangent ratio of the angle of subtense of the two images (R) for each point along the empirical horopter is plotted on the y axis. H is the slope of the resulting linear function, and it quantifies horopter curvature (Hering–Hillebrand deviation), where a slope of zero equals the curvature of the Vieth-Muller circle.

objects and is described by a vertical line that passes through the fixation point in the midsagittal plane (Figure 5). Eccentric points in tertiary gaze (points with both azimuth and elevation) lie closer to one eye than the other eye. Because they are imaged at different vertical eccentricities from the two foveas, tertiary points cannot be imaged on theoretically corresponding retinal points. However, all points at an infinite viewing distance can be imaged on homologous retinal regions, and at this viewing distance the vertical horopter becomes a plane.

The empirical vertical horopter is declinated in comparison to the theoretical horopter (Figure 6). Helmholtz (1909) reasoned this was because of a horizontal shear of the two retinae, which causes a real vertical plane to appear inclinated or a real horizontal plane, such as the ground, to lie close to the empirical vertical horopter.

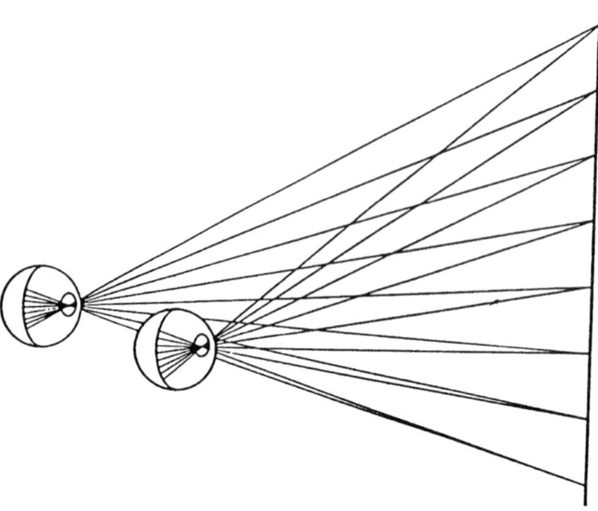

FIGURE 5 The theoretical vertical horopter. Corresponding visual lines from the midvertical meridians of the two eyes intersect in a vertical line in the median plane of the head. With near convergence, visual lines from any other pair of corresponding vertical meridians do not intersect, since the image of any eccentric vertical line in one eye is larger than the image of that line in the other eye. With parallel convergence, the horopter is a plane at infinity, orthogonal to the visual axes. (From BINOCULAR VISION AND STEREOPSIS by Ian P. Howard and Brian J. Rogers, Copyright © 1995 by Oxford University Press, Inc. Used by permission of Oxford University Press, Inc., and the authors.)

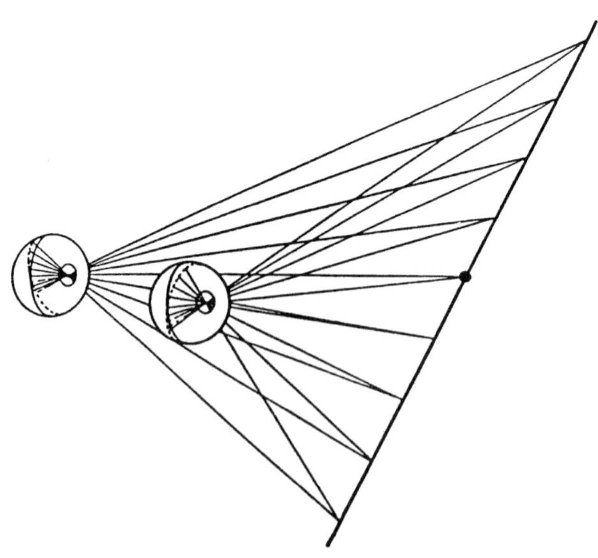

E. Coordinate Systems for Binocular Disparity

All coordinate systems for binocular disparity use the same theoretical horopter as a reference for zero retinal image disparity. Targets not lying on the horopter subtend nonzero disparities, and the magnitudes of these nonzero disparities depend on the coordinate system used to describe them. Howard and Rogers (1995) describe five coordinate systems (their Table 2.1), and these correspond to the oculomotor coordinate systems of Polar, Helmholtz, Fick, Harms, and Hess (Schor, Maxwell, & Stevenson, 1994). Howard and Rogers and most vision scientists use the Harms system. The different coordinate systems will quantify vertical and horizontal disparity equally for targets at optical infinity, as all points subtend zero disparity at this distance, but their disparity will change at finite viewing distances. This is because the visual axes and retinal projection screens are not parallel or coplanar at near viewing distances associated with convergences of the two eyes. Each of the five coordinate systems may be suitable for only one aspect of vision, and apparently none of them is adequate to describe binocular disparity as processed by the visual system.

Corresponding points can be described in terms of Cartesian coordinates of constant azimuth and elevation. Contours in space that appear at identical constant horizontal eccentricities or constant heights by the two eyes are, by Hering's definition of identical visual directions, imaged on binocular corresponding points. The theoretical retinal regions that correspond to constant azimuth and elevation can be described with epipolar geometry. Retinal division lines are retinal loci that give rise to the sense of constant elevation or azimuth. Regions in space that lie along the perspective projection of these retinal division lines are derived with transformations from the spherical retinal space to isopters in a planar Euclidean space. Isopters are contours on a tangent screen that appear to be straight and horizontal (or vertical). The relationship between the retinal division lines and isopters is a perspective projection through a projection center. The choice of retinal division lines (major or minor circles) and projection center (nodal point or bulbcenter) determines the coordinate system (Figure 7) (Tschermak-Seysenegge, 1952). The theoretical case is simplified by assuming the projection point and nodal point of the eye both lie at the center of curvature of the retinal sphere (bulbcenter). As shown in Figure 7, there are several families of theoretical retinal division lines. There are great circles, such as in the Harms system, which resemble lines of longitude on the globe (Schor et al., 1994). Their projections all pass through the bulbcenter as planes and form straight-line isopters on a tangent screen. There could also be a family of

FIGURE 6 The empirical vertical horopter. For near convergence, the vertical horopter is a straight line inclined top away in the median plane of the head. The dotted lines on the retinas indicate the corresponding vertical meridians. The solid lines indicate the true vertical meridian. (From BINOCULAR VISION AND STEREOPSIS by Ian P. Howard and Brian J. Rogers, Copyright © 1995 by Oxford University Press, Inc. Used by permission of Oxford University Press, Inc., and the authors.)

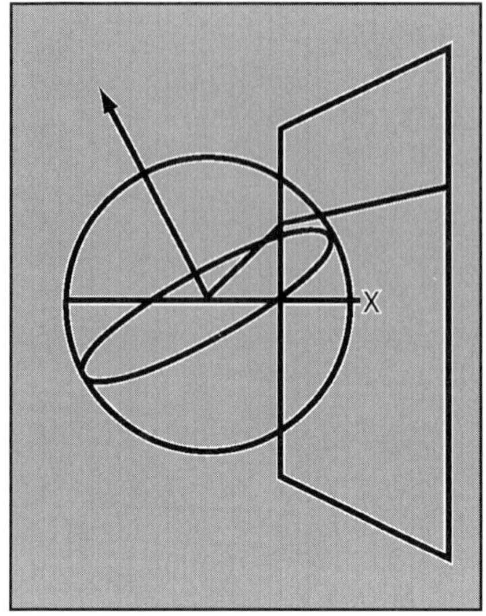

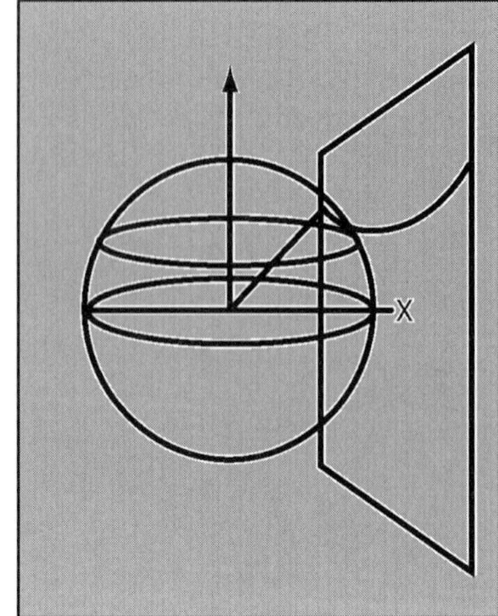

FIGURE 7 Epipolar geometry. Projection of great circles retinal division lines through the nodal point intersect the planar surfaces in space as straight lines. Projection of minor circles scribed on the retina through the nodal point intersect the planar surface in space as Parabolas. The minor circle retinal division lines closely approximate the retinal loci of perceived constant elevation isopters on the planar surface in space. The projections through the nodal point represent a transformation from spherical coordinates in the eye to Euclidean coordinates in space. (Reprinted from *Ophthalmic and Physiological Optics, 14,* Schor, C. M., Maxwell, J., & Stevenson, S. B. (1994). Isovergence surfaces: the conjugacy of vertical eye movements in tertiary positions of gaze. 279–286, with kind permission from Elsevier Science Ltd., The Boulevard, Langford Lane, Kidlington, OX5 1GB, United Kingdom.)

minor circles, such as in the Hess coordinate system, which resembles lines of latitude on the globe (Schor et al., 1994). Their projections also pass through the bulb-center as conic sections and form parabolic isopters on a tangent screen. None of these necessarily represents the set of retinal division lines used by the visual system, because retinal division lines, by definition, must produce a sense of equal elevation or equal azimuth. As will be discussed below, empirical measures of iso-elevation indicate that the projection point actually lies in front of the nodal point, such that it produces barrel distortions of the visual field (Liu & Schor, 1997).

The tangent plane projections represent a map of constant or iso-elevation and iso-azimuth contours. The only viewing distance at which projection maps of the two eyes can be superimposed is at optical infinity. At finite viewing distances, the eyes converge and the retinal projection screens are no longer parallel or coplanar such that a single tangent plane will make different angles with the axes of the two eyes. Because the coordinate systems describing binocular disparity are retinal based, their origins (the lines of sight) move with the eyes so that they project relative to the direction of the visual axis. In eye movements, the reference systems are head-centric at the primary position of gaze so that the coordinate systems do not change during convergence. The consequence of having a retinal-based coordinate system is that the projected tangent planes of the two eyes are not coplanar in convergence. This problem is solved by mapping both eyes onto a common tangent plane that is parallel to the face (fronto-parallel plane), which results in trapezoidal distortion of the projected isopters (Liu & Schor, 1997).

When the fronto-parallel maps of the two eyes isopters are superimposed, they only match along the primary vertical and horizontal meridians, and they are disparate elsewhere. Consequently, the theoretical horopter is not a surface but rather it is made up of a horizontal (V-M) circle and vertical line in the midsagittal plane (Figure 5). All coordinate systems yield the same pure horizontal or vertical disparity along these primary meridians, but they will compute different magnitudes of combined vertical and horizontal disparities in tertiary field locations.

The separations of the two eye's iso-elevation and iso-azimuth isopters describe vertical and horizontal misalignment of visual directions originating from corresponding retinal division lines (binocular discrepancy). Binocular discrepancy is distinguished from binocular disparity, which refers to the binocular misalignment of retinal images of any object in space from corresponding retinal points. Binocular discrepancy provides the objective reference points of each eye in the fronto-parallel plane for zero binocular disparity (Liu & Schor, 1997). Binocular discrepancy and disparity are related, as the discrepancy map also describes the pattern of binocular disparities subtended by points lying in the fronto-parallel plane.

F. Monocular Spatial Distortions and the Empirical Binocular Disparity Map

The mismatch of the projection fields of iso-elevation and iso-azimuth isopters at near viewing distances results in a binocular discrepancy map or field on the fronto-parallel plane. An empirically derived map needs to take into account the horizontal shear of the two monocular image spaces, described by Helmholtz, as well as other monocular spatial distortions. For example, horizontal contours that are viewed eccentrically above or below the point of fixation are seen as bowed or convex relative to the primary horizontal meridian (barrel distortion). Horizontal lines must be adjusted to a pincushion distortion to appear straight (Helmholtz, 1909). The retinal division lines corresponding to the pincushion adjustments needed to make horizontal lines appear at a constant or iso-elevation resembles the minor circles of the Hess coordinate system (Liu & Schor, 1997). These retinal division lines have been used to predict an empirical binocular discrepancy map for finite viewing distances.

The discrepancy map is derived from the combination of horizontal shear with empirically measured iso-elevation and iso-azimuth retinal division lines. Their projection from the two eyes onto isopters in a common fronto-parallel plane centered

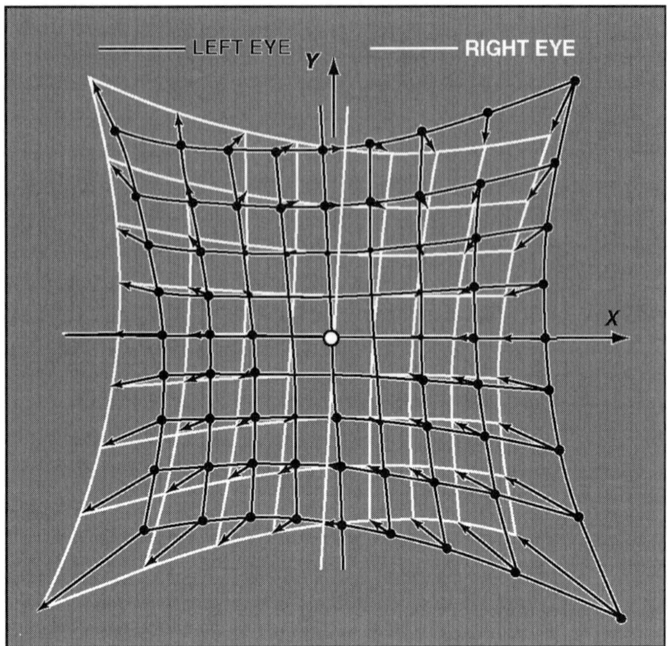

FIGURE 8 Binocular discrepancy map of isoelevation and iso-azimuth lines. Projection of the minor circle retinal division lines of the two eyes form intersecting iso-elevation and iso-azimuth grid in space. The grid is distorted by the horizontal shear of the retina that causes declination of the empirical vertical horopter shown in Figure 6. The grid is a complex pattern of horizontal and vertical disparities that are greater in the lower than upper field as a result of the horizontal shear of the two retinae. (Reprinted from Liu, L. & Schor, C. M. Monocular spatial distortions and binocular correspondence. *Journal of the Optical Society of America: Vision Science, 7,* 1740–55, Copyright © 1998. With kind permission from the Optical Society of America, and the authors.)

along the midsagittal axis produces a complex pattern of vertical discrepancies that are greater in the lower than upper visual field, as is illustrated in Figure 8 (Liu & Schor, 1998). Because the pincushion distortions vary dramatically between observers (Liu & Schor, 1977), it is impossible to generalize these results and predict the vertical discrepancy map for individuals and the magnitude of vertical disparities that are quantified relative to this map.

The general pattern of the binocular discrepancy distribution is the direct consequence of the basic monocular distortions (horizontal shear and vertical trapezoid) and therefore should be valid for most cases. However, the quantitative details of the map may vary among observers because Liu and Schor (1997) have demonstrated that different observers have different amounts of monocular pincushion distortion. It is important to realize the idiosyncrasy of binocular correspondence when designing experiments that involve manipulating large disparities in the periphery. Several theoretical models suggested that vertical disparity may carry information that is necessary for scaling stereoscopic depth (Gillam & Lawergren, 1983; Mayhew & Longuet-Higgins, 1982). Because vertical disparity is much smaller in magnitude compared to horizontal disparity, the empirical verification of the above theoretical speculations usually involves manipulating vertical disparities in the far periphery (Cumming, Johnston, & Parker, 1991; Rogers & Bradshaw, 1993). In such studies, accurate knowledge about the status of vertical correspondence across the visual field becomes critical because the discrepancy between geometric stimulus correspondence and empirical retinal correspondence may be large enough in the periphery to actually affect the amount of vertical disparity delivered by the stimulus.

III. BINOCULAR SENSORY FUSION

A. Panum's Fusional Areas

Binocular correspondence is described above as though there was an exact point-to-point linkage between the two retinal images. However, Panum (1858) observed that corresponding points on the two retinae are not points at all, but regions. He reported that in the vicinity of the fovea, the fusional system would accept two disparate contours as corresponding if they fell within a radius of 0.026 mm of corresponding retinal loci. This radius corresponds to a visual angle of approximately $\frac{1}{4}$ degrees. The consequence of Panum's area is that there is a range of disparities that yield binocular singleness. The horizontal extent of Panum's area gives the horopter a thickness in space (Figure 9). The vertical extent also contributes to single binocular vision when targets are viewed eccentrically in tertiary directions of gaze. Spatial geometry dictates that because these tertiary targets are closer to one eye than the other, they form unequal image sizes in the two eyes which subtend different heights and accordingly vertical disparities. Binocular sensory fusion of these targets is a consequence of Panum's areas.

Panum's area functions as a buffer zone to eliminate diplopia for small disparities near the horopter. Stereopsis could exist without singleness, but the double images near the fixation plane would be a distraction. The depth of focus of the human eye serves a similar function. Objects that are nearly conjugate to the retina appear as clear as objects focused precisely on the retina. The buffer for the optics of the eye is much larger than the buffer for binocular fusion. The depth of focus of the eye is approximately 0.75 diopters. Panum's area can be expressed in equivalent units and is only 0.08-meter angles or approximately one-tenth the magnitude of the depth of focus. Thus we are more tolerant of focus errors than we are of convergence errors.

Both accommodation and stereo-fusion are sensitive to differences in distance within their respective buffer zones. Accommodations can respond to defocus that is below our threshold for blur detection (Kotulak & Schor, 1986), and the eyes can sense small depth intervals (<10 arc sec) and converge in response to disparities (3 arc min) (Riggs & Niehl, 1960) that are smaller than Panum's area. Thus Panum's

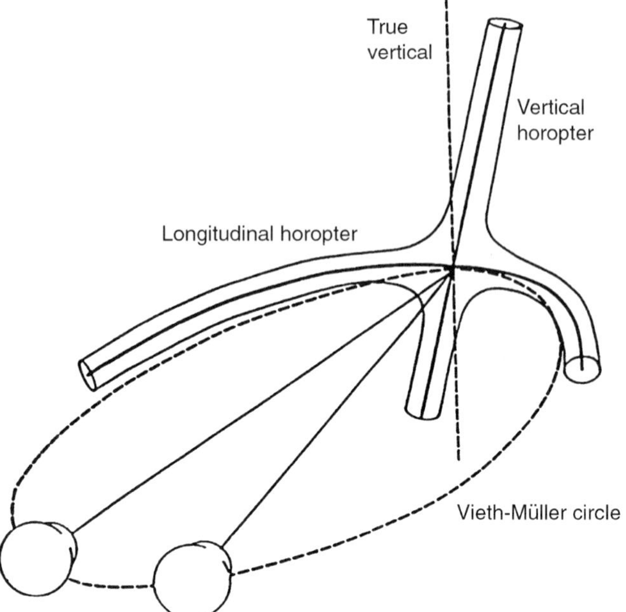

FIGURE 9 Panum's area gives the horopter volume. The lines depicting the theoretical horizontal and vertical horopters shown in Figures 1 and 5 become volumes when measured empirically with a singleness horopter, where a range of retinal points in one eye appear fused with a single point in the contralateral eye (Panum's area). (From BINOCULAR VISION AND STEREOPSIS by Ian P. Howard and Brian J. Rogers, Copyright © 1995 by Oxford University Press, Inc. Used by permission of Oxford University Press, Inc., and the authors.)

area is not a threshold or limit-to-depth sensitivity, nor is it limited by the minimal noise or instability of the binocular vergence system. However, it does allow the persistence of single binocular vision in the presence of constant changes in retinal image disparity caused by various oculomotor disturbances. For example, considerable errors of binocular alignment (>15 arc min) may occur during eye tracking of dynamic depth produced either by object motion or by head and body movements (Steinman & Collewijn, 1980).

B. Allelotropia

The comparison between the depth of focus and Panum's area suggests that single binocular vision is simply a threshold or resolution limit of visual direction discrimination (Le Grand, 1953). Although this is partially true, as will be described below, Panum's area also provides a combined percept in 3-D space that can be different in shape than either of its monocular components. The averaging of monocular shapes and directions is termed allelotropia. For example, it is possible to fuse two horizontal lines curved in opposite directions and perceive a straight line binocularly. There are limits to how dissimilar the two monocular images can be to support fusion, and when these limits are exceeded, binocular rivalry suppression occurs in which only one eye perceives in a given visual direction at one time. Clearly, fusion is not a simple summation process or a suppression process (Blake & Camisa, 1978) or one of rapid alternate viewing as proposed by Verhoeff (1935). The combination of the two retinal images follows many of the rules of binocular visual direction as described by Hering (Ono, 1979).

Allelotropia is not restricted to fused images. Dichoptically viewed stimuli subtending large disparities, beyond the fusion limit, are perceived in separate directions. The separation of these diplopic images is less than what is predicted by their physical disparity (Rose & Blake, 1988), demonstrating that visual directions can differ under monocular and binocular viewing conditions even when fusion is absent. This observation suggests that allelotropia may be an independent process from binocular sensory fusion.

C. Spatial Constraints

The range of singleness or size of Panum's area and its shape are not a constant. It is not a static zone of fixed dimension; it varies with a wide variety of parameters. The classical description of the fusional area, as described by Panum, is an ellipse with the long axis in the horizontal meridian (Mitchell, 1966; Ogle & Prangen, 1953; Panum, 1858). The horizontal radius is $\frac{1}{4}$ degree, whereas the vertical radius is $\frac{1}{20}$ degree. The elliptical shape indicates that we have a greater tolerance for horizontal than vertical disparities. Perhaps this is because vergence fluctuations associated with accommodation are mainly horizontal, and because the range of horizontal disparities presented in a natural environment is far greater for vertical disparities.

D. Spatial Frequency

Both the shape and size of Panum's area vary. Panum's area increases in size as the spatial frequency of the fusion target decreases (Schor, Wood, & Ogawa, 1984a) (Figure 10). The horizontal extent increases with spatial frequencies below 2.5 cpd. Panum's fusional area, centered about the fovea, has a range from 10–400-arc min as spatial frequency is decreased to 0.075 cpd (cycles per degree). At these lower spatial frequencies, the fusion range approaches the upper disparity limit for static stereopsis. The variation of the horizontal fusion range may be interpreted as two subcomponents of the fusion mechanism that process the position and phase of disparity. The fusion limit is determined by the least sensitive of the two forms of disparity. The fusion range at high spatial frequencies can be attributed to a 10-arc min positional limit, and the range at low spatial frequencies can be attributed to a 90° phase disparity. At high spatial frequencies, the 90° phase limit corresponds to a smaller angle than the 10-arc min positional disparity, and consequently fusion is

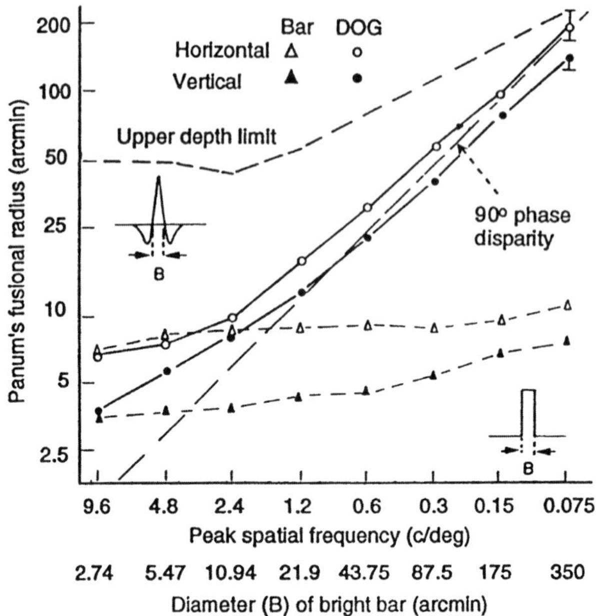

FIGURE 10 Fusion limits and spatial frequency. The diplopia threshold (radius of the fusional area) as a function of the peak spatial frequency of two Gaussian patches (spatial bandwidth 1.75 octaves) and of the width of two bright bars. For patches with a spatial frequency below about 1.5 c/deg, the diplopia threshold corresponds to a 90° phase shift of the stimulus, indicated by the dotted line. The fusion limit for the bars remains the same as that of the high spatial frequency patch. (Reprinted from *Vision Research, 24,* Schor, C. M., Wood, I. C., & Ogawa, J. Binocular sensory fusion is limited by spatial resolution, pp. 661–665, Copyright © 1984, with kind permission from Elsevier Science Ltd., The Boulevard, Langford Lane, Kidlington, OX5 1GB, United Kingdom.)

limited by the larger 10-arc min positional disparity. At low spatial frequencies, the 10-arc min positional disparity is smaller than the 90° phase disparity, and consequently the fusion range rises at a rate fixed by the constant 90° phase limit (Schor et al., 1984a). DeAngelis, Ohzawa, and Freeman (1995) have proposed a physiological analogue of this model that is supported by their observations of phase and position encoding disparity processing units in cat striate cortex.

The shape of Panum's area also changes when spatial frequency is decreased to 2.5 cpd. Panum's area changes from an elliptical shape at high frequencies to a circular shape at frequencies lower than 2.5 cpd. This is because the vertical dimension continues to decrease as spatial frequency is increased above 2.5 cpd, but the horizontal dimension remains constant at higher spatial frequencies. Interestingly, vertical disparity limits for fusion are only constrained by the phase limit. Their dimension is not limited at high spatial frequencies by a constant positional disparity.

E. Retinal Eccentricity

Panum's area also increases with retinal eccentricity of fusion stimuli (Crone & Leuridan, 1973; Hampton & Kertesz, 1983; Mitchell, 1966; Ogle, 1952). The increase in the fusion range is approximately 7% of the retinal eccentricity. These measures of fusion range have been made with broad-band spatial frequency stimuli. When fusion ranges are measured with narrow-band spatial frequency stimuli, such as the difference of Gaussian, (Schor, Wesson, & Robertson, 1986; Wilson, Blake, & Pokorny, 1988), the range of fusion does not change with retinal eccentricity. Fusion ranges remain small with spatial frequencies above 2.5 cpd as retinal eccentricity increases, as long as the fusion stimulus can be resolved. Eventually, when visual resolution decreases below 2.5 cpd (at 10° retinal eccentricity), lower spatial frequencies than 2.5 cpd must be used to stimulate fusion and Panum's area increases. However, the fusion range is the same as it would be at the fovea when measured with the same low spatial frequency. When measured with a broad-band stimulus, the highest resolvable spatial frequency will limit the fusion range (Schor, Heckman, & Tyler, 1989). Higher spatial frequency components are processed from the broad-band stimulus when imaged in the central retina, and the sensory fusion range will begin to increase when the peripheral retina is not able to resolve frequencies above 2.5 cpd and fusion is limited by the remaining lower spatial frequencies. These results and other studies of the independence of fusion limits and image contrast and luminance (Mitchell, 1966; Schor et al., 1989; Siegel & Duncan, 1960) suggest that binocular fusion is based on information in independent spatial-frequency channels rather than on the overall luminance distribution of a broad-band stimulus.

F. Disparity Gradient Limits

Fusion ranges are also reduced by the presence of other nearby stimuli that subtend different disparities (Braddick, 1979; Helmholtz, 1909; Schor & Tyler, 1981). As a rule of thumb, two adjacent targets of unequal disparity cannot be fused simultaneously when their disparity difference is greater than their separation (Burt & Julesz, 1980). This disparity gradient limit, defined as the ratio of disparity difference over separation, is 1.0. For example, the two dots pairs of unequal disparity shown in Figure 11 can be fused as long as their vertical separation is greater than their disparity difference.

The interaction between nearby targets is also influenced by their spatial frequency content. The disparity gradient limit is very strong when a small high spatial frequency-crossed disparity stimulus is presented adjacent to a slightly lower spatial frequency background (2 octaves lower) subtending zero disparity. However, a much lower spatial frequency background (4 octaves lower) or a higher spatial frequency background has less or no influence on the fusion range with the same foreground stimulus (Scheidt & Kertesz, 1993; Wilson, Blake, & Halpern, 1991). This coarse-to-fine limit demonstrates how low-frequency stimuli can constrain the

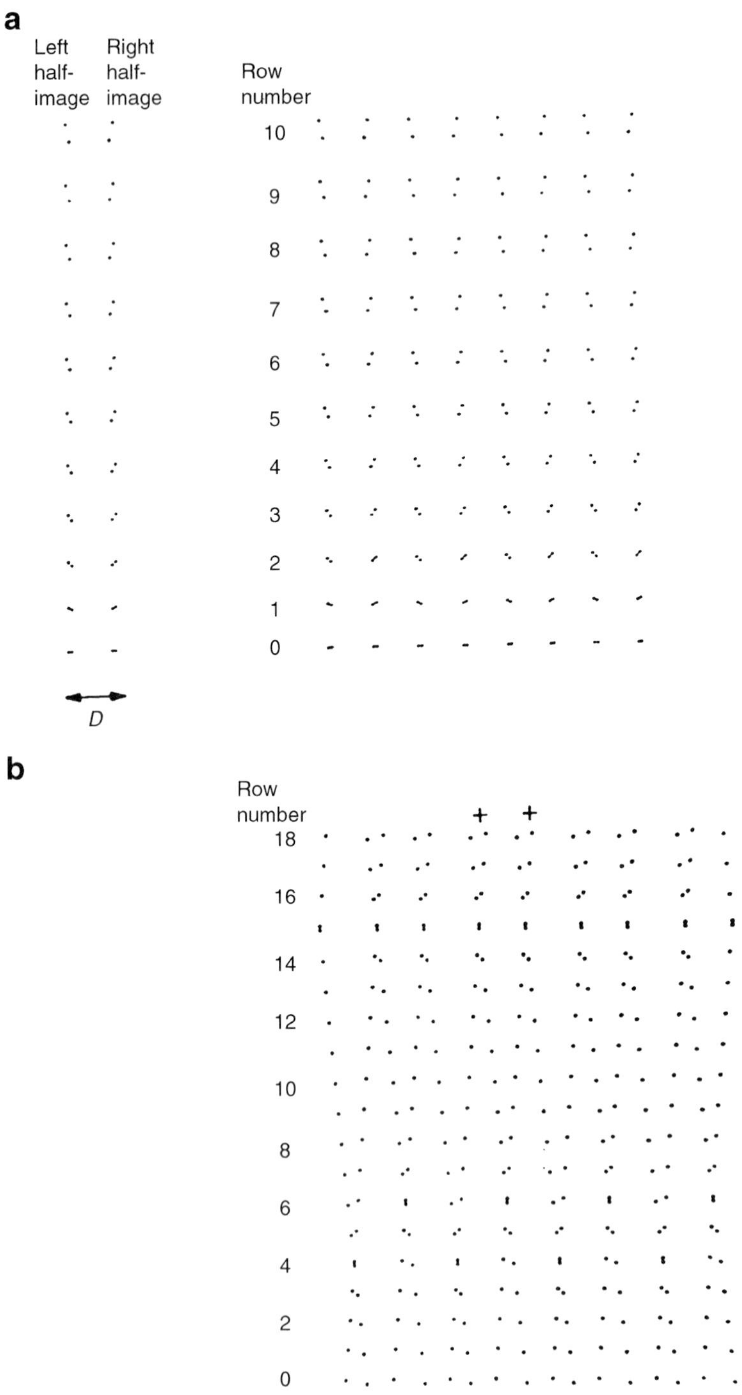

a

Left half-image
Right half-image
Row number
10
9
8
7
6
5
4
3
2
1
0
D

b

Row number
18
16
14
12
10
8
6
4
2
0

matches of higher spatial frequency stimuli. This can be beneficial in large textured surfaces that contain coarse and fine spatial frequency information. The coarse features have fewer ambiguous matches than the high-frequency features, and the disparity gradient limit helps to bias matches in ambiguous stimuli, such as tree foliage, to solve for smooth surfaces rather than irregular depth planes.

G. Temporal Constraints

The size and dimensions of Panum's area also depend upon the exposure duration and velocity at which disparity increases. The horizontal radius of Panum's area increases from 2 to 4 arc min as exposure of pulsed disparities increased from 5 to 100 ms and remains constant for longer durations (Woo, 1974). The horizontal dimension of Panum's area also increases as the velocity of slow continuous variations of disparity decreases, while the vertical dimension is unaffected by disparity velocity (Schor & Tyler, 1981). Thus at low velocities (2 arc min/sec), Panum's area extends beyond the static disparity limit to 20 arc min horizontally and has an elliptical shape. At higher velocities (> 10 arc min/sec) the horizontal dimension shrinks to equal the size of the vertical dimension (8 arc min) and has a circular shape. This velocity dependence of the fusion range may contribute to the small hysteresis of fusion in which the amplitude of Panum's area is larger when measured with slowly increasing disparities than with decreasing large disparities (Erkelens, 1988; Fender & Julesz, 1967; Piantanida, 1986).

H. Color Fusion

When narrow-band green (530 mμ) and red (680 mμ) are viewed dichoptically in a small field, a binocular yellow percept occurs (Prentice, 1948). Color fusion is facilitated by small fields that have textured patches, low luminance, desaturated colors, and flicker. Dichoptic color fusion or mixture suggests that a cortical process is involved (Hovis, 1989).

IV. ENCODING DISPARITY: THE MATCHING PROBLEM

The lateral separation of our eyes, which gives us two vantage points to view scenes, produces small differences or disparities in the two retinal images from which we

FIGURE 11 The disparity-gradient limit for binocular fusion. (a) Diverge or converge to fuse neighboring columns of dots, as shown in the inset on the left. If the lower pair of dots is fused in each set of four dots, the upper pair fused only if the disparity gradient is not higher than about 1. The disparity gradient increases down the rows and may be calibrated for a given viewing distance. The disparity-gradient limit of fusion can then be determined by reading off the row number at which fusion of the upper pair of dots fails. (From Burt, P., & Julesz, J. (1980). Modifications of the classical notion of Panum's fusional area. *Perception, 9,* 671–682. Pion, London, reprinted with permission.)

derive stereoscopic depth. Disparities of the two retinal images could be analyzed in various ways. In a local analysis, individual perceived forms or images could be compared to derive their disparity and sense their depth. In this local analysis, form perception would precede depth perception (Helmholtz, 1909). In a global analysis, luminance properties of the scene, such as texture and other token elements, could be analyzed to code a disparity map from which depth was perceived. The resulting depth map would yield perceptions of form. In this analysis, depth perception would precede form perception. In the local analysis it is clear which monocular components of the perceived binocular images are to be compared because of their uniqueness. The global analysis is much more difficult, as many similar texture elements, such as in tree foliage, must be matched, and the correct pairs of images to match are not obvious. An example of our prowess at accomplishing this feat is the perception of depth in the autostereogram shown in Figure 12. Free fusion of the two random-dot patterns yields the percept of a checkerboard. There are thousands of similar texture elements (dots), yet we can correctly match them

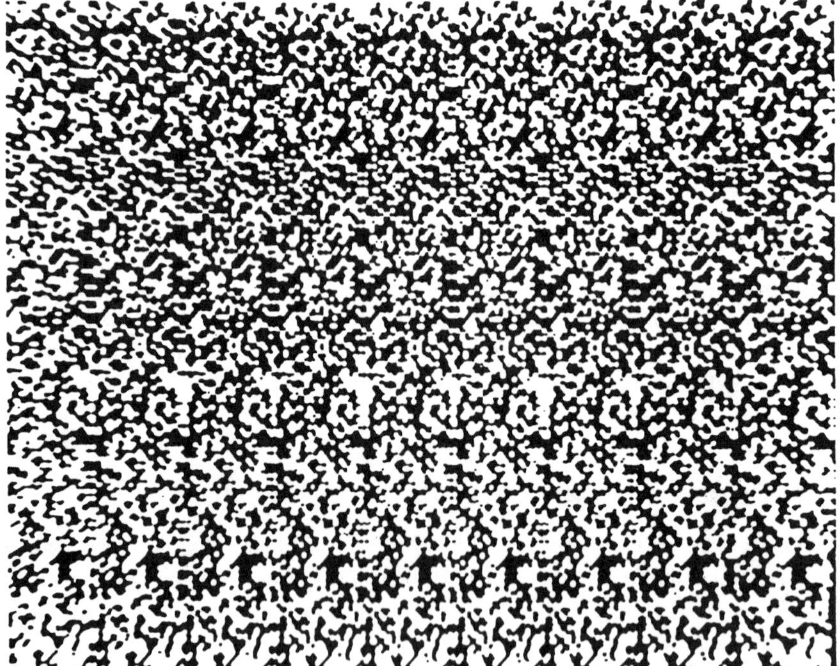

FIGURE 12 Random-dot stereogram of a checkerboard generated by the autostereogram technique. At 40-cm viewing distance, hold a finger about 10 cm above page and fixate finger continuously. The stereoscopic percept of a checkerboard will gradually emerge in the plane of the finger, which can then be removed for free viewing within the stereo space (From C. M. Schor & K. Ciuffreda, 1983. Vergence eye movements, basic and clinical aspects. In C. W. Tyler (Ed.), *Sensory processing of binocular disparity* (p. 241). Woburn, MA: Butterworth. Reproduced with permission of the author.)

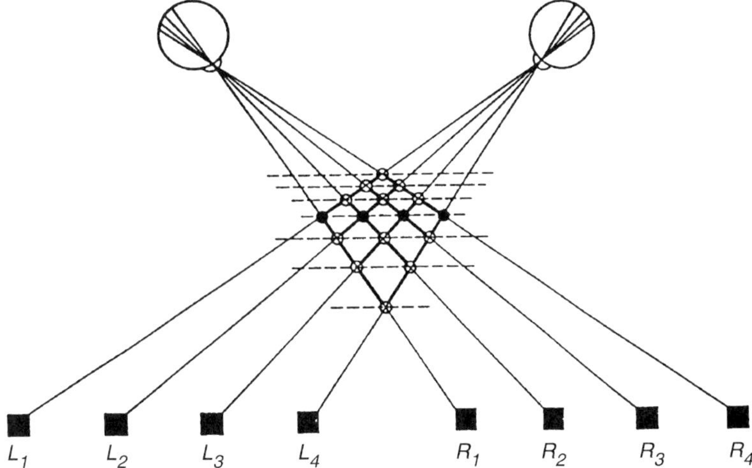

FIGURE 13 Each of the four points in one eye's view could match any of the four projections in the other eye's view. Of the 16 (*N*!) possible matches, only 4 are correct (filled circles); the remaining 12 are false targets (open circles). Without further constraints based on global consideration, such ambiguities cannot be resolved. (Reprinted with permission from Marr, D., & Poggio, T. (1976). Cooperative computation of stereo disparity. *Science, 194,* 283–287. Copyright © 1976, American Association for the Advancement of Science.)

to derive the disparity map necessary to see a unique form in depth. An important question is how does the visual system identify corresponding monocular features? This problem is illustrated in Figure 13, which shows a schematic of four dots imaged on the two retinae. This pair of retinal images could arise from many depth-dot patterns, depending on which dots were paired in the disparity analysis. The number of possible depth patterns that could be analyzed is *N*!, where *N* is the number of dots. Thus for 10 dots there are 3,628,800 possible depth patterns that could be yielded from the same pair of retinal images. How does the visual system go about selecting one of these many possible solutions? Clearly the problem must be constrained or simplified by limiting the possible number of matches. This is done by restricting matches to certain features of texture elements (types of primitives or tokens) and by prioritizing certain matching solutions over others. In addition, there is certainly an interaction between the local and global analysis, which simplifies the process. Local features are often visible within textured fields. For example, there are clumps of leaves in foliage patterns that are clearly visible prior to sensing depth. Vergence eye movements may be cued to align these unique monocular patterns on or near corresponding retinal points and thereby reduce the overall range of disparity subtended by the stimulus (Marr & Poggio, 1976). Once this has been done, the global system can begin to match tokens based upon certain attributes and priority solutions.

A. Classes of Matchable Tokens

There are many possible image qualities that are easily seen under monocular conditions, such as size, color, orientation, brightness, and contrast. These attributes are processed early in the visual system by low-level filters, and they could be used to pair binocular images. Marr and Poggio (1979) proposed that the most useful tokens would be invariant (i.e., reliable) under variable lighting conditions, and that perhaps the visual system had prioritized these invariant features. For example, contrast is a more reliable feature than brightness in the presence of variations in lighting conditions caused by shadows, station point of each eye, and variable intensity of the light source. Zero-crossings, or the maximum rate of change in the luminance distribution would be a locus in the retinal image that would not change with light level. Similarly, color and locations of uniquely oriented line segments or contours would be other stable features that varied slightly with station point. Points of peak contrast and patterns of contrast variation are other local cues that could also be used to match binocular images (Frisby & Mayhew, 1978; Hess & Wilcox, 1994).

When tested individually, none of these local tokens has been found to provide as much information as theoretically possible. Zero crossings predict better performance on stereo tasks at high spatial frequencies (>2 cpd) than observed empirically (Schor, Wood, & Ogawa, 1984b). Contour orientation contributes to matching when the line segments are longer than 3 arc min (Mitchell & O'Hagan, 1972). Contrast polarity is a very important token for the matching process. As shown in Figure 14, sustained stereoscopic depth is impossible in patterns containing coarse detail of opposite polarity (Krol & van de Grind, 1983). However, stereoscopic depth can be seen in line drawings of opposite contrast principally as a result of misalignment of convergence to bring like contrast edges (Mach bands) into alignment. Similarly, contrast variation within a patch can be used in matching to perform stereo-tasks near the upper disparity limits. Using Gabor patches, these studies show that the upper disparity limit for stereopsis is not limited by carrier spatial frequency but rather it increases with the size of the envelope or Gabor patch (Hess & Wilcox, 1994). These results could be attributed to contrast coding of disparity resulting from a nonlinear extraction of the stimulus contrast envelope (Wilcox & Hess, 1995; Schor, Edwards, & Pope, 1998; Pope, Edwards, & Schor, 1999a).

The upper disparity limit could increase with the size of first-order binocular receptive fields that encode luminance, or it could increase with the size of second-order binocular receptive fields that encode contrast. In the former case, stereopsis would require that similar spatial frequencies be presented to the two eyes, whereas in the latter case stereopsis would occur with very different spatial frequencies presented to the two eyes as long as the envelope in which they were presented was similar. Second order or contrast coding requires that information be rectified such that contrast variations could be represented by changes in neural activity, and this information could be used for binocular matching. Color has been investigated with stereo-performance using isoluminance patterns and found to only support stere-

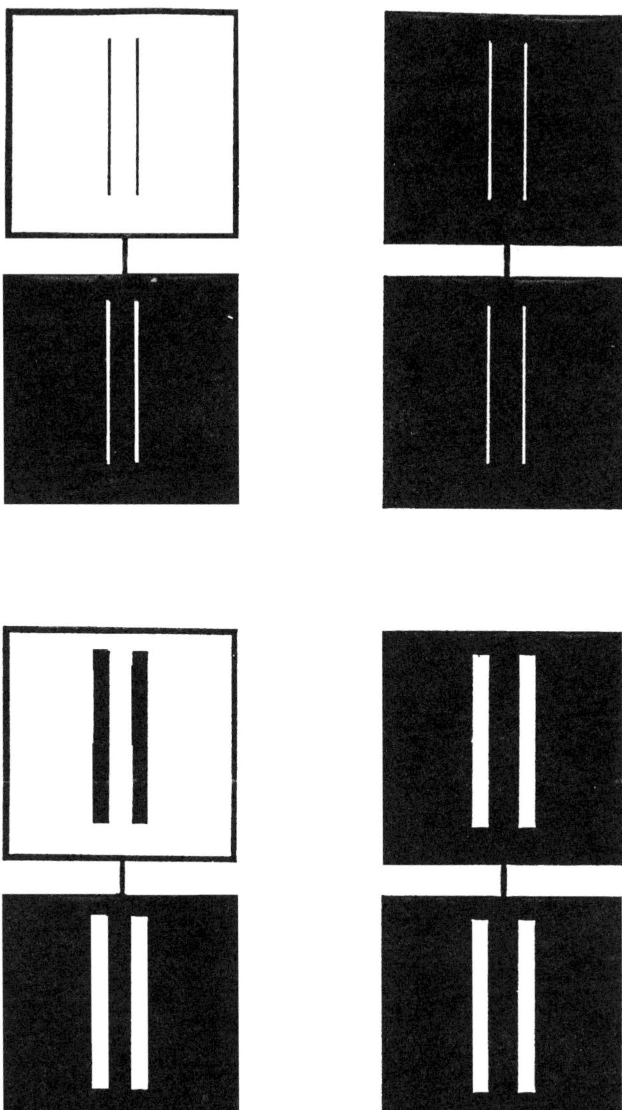

FIGURE 14 Reversed luminance polarity and line width. (left) Fusion of the narrow luminance-reversed fine lines in the upper stereogram produces depth, like that produced by the same-polarity images in the lower stereogram. (right) Luminance-reversed broad lines in the upper stereogram do not produce depth. The same-polarity images in the lower stereogram do produce depth. (From Krol, J. D., & van de Grind, W. A., 1983. Depth from dichoptic edges depends on vergence tuning. *Perception, 12,* 425–438. Pion, London, reprinted with permission.)

opsis with coarse detail (de Weert & Sadza, 1983). However, color can disambiguate binocular matches in conditions such as depth transparency when combined with other cues (Jordan, Geisler, & Bovik, 1990). Clearly, the visual system does not simply match one class of tokens. Redundant information present in several classes of tokens improves binocular matching performance.

B. Matching Constraints

Because we are able to perceive form in textured scenes such as tree foliage by virtue of stereo-depth, the binocular matching process must be constrained to simplify the task of choosing between the extreme number of possible solutions to the matching problem. When matching targets in a fixation plane that is parallel to the face, two rules can completely specify correct binocular matches. The *nearest-neighbor rule* specifies that matches are made between tokens that subtend the smallest disparity (a bias for precepts along the horopter), and the *unique-match rule* specifies that each individual token may only be used for a single match. Once a feature is matched it cannot have double duty and be matched to other features as well. Without this restriction, the number of possible matches in a random-dot field would greatly exceed $N!$. The nearest neighbor rule is demonstrated in the double nail illusion (Figure 15). Two nails are placed in the midsagittal plane and convergence is adjusted to an intermediate distance between them. There are two possible matches, one corresponding to the true midsagittal depth and one corresponding to two nails located at the same depth in the fixation plane to the left and right in the point of convergence. The former solution is one of two different disparities, and the latter solution is one of two very small equal or zero disparities. The visual system chooses the latter solution and the two nails appear side by side even though they are really at different depths in the midsagittal plane. These two matching rules can be applied over a wide range of viewing distances when accompanied by convergence eye movements that can bring depth planes at any viewing distance into close proximity with the horopter.

The unique match rule appears to be violated by the phenomenon known as Panum's limiting case. It can be demonstrated by aligning two nails along one eye's line of sight (Figure 16) such that a single image is formed on one retina and two images, corresponding to the two nails, are imaged on the other retina. Hering believed that the vivid appearance of depth of the two nails resulted from multiple matches of the single image in the aligned eye with the two images in the unaligned eye. However, Nakayama and Shimojo (1992) have accounted for the illusion as the result of a monocular or partial occlusion cue (DaVinci stereopsis) rather than a violation of the unique match rule.

Other rules account for our ability to match the images of targets that subtend non-zero disparities because they lie at different depths from the horopter and fixation plane. Usually these matches result in a single percept of the target. However, when disparities become too large they exceed a diplopia threshold and are seen as

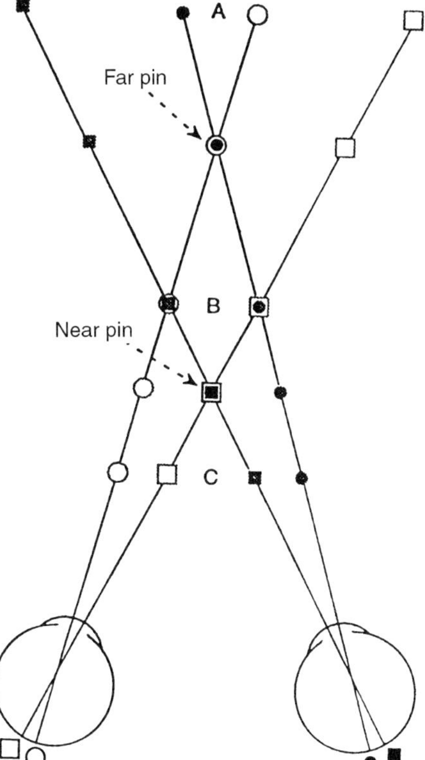

FIGURE 15 The double-nail illusion. Two pins are held in the median plane about 30 cm from the eyes, with one pin about 2 cm farther away than the other. Four images are seen when the eyes are converged at distance A or C. When the far pin is fixated, its images are fused and the near pin is seen with a crossed disparity. When the near pin is fixated, the far pin is seen with an uncrossed disparity. When convergence is a B, about halfway between the pins, the two pairs of images are matched inappropriately to form an impression of two pins side by side. A third pin between the other two helps bring the point of fixation to the intermediate position. (From BINOCULAR VISION AND STEREOPSIS by Ian P. Howard & Brian J. Rogers, Copyright © 1995 by Oxford University Press, Inc. Used by permission of Oxford University Press, Inc.

double. Diplopic targets, especially those subtending small amounts of disparity, can still be seen in stereoscopic depth, which suggests that some form of binocular matching is occurring for nonfused percepts. As noted by Hering, however, depth of diplopic and even monocular images can also be judged on the basis of monocular cues such as hemi-retinal locus (Harris & McKee, 1996; Kaye, 1978), in which case binocular matching would not be required.

Irrespective of whether the percept is diplopic or haplopic, several rules are needed to simplify the matching of images subtending retinal disparities. One of these is the smoothness or similarity constraint. Clearly, it is much easier to fuse and

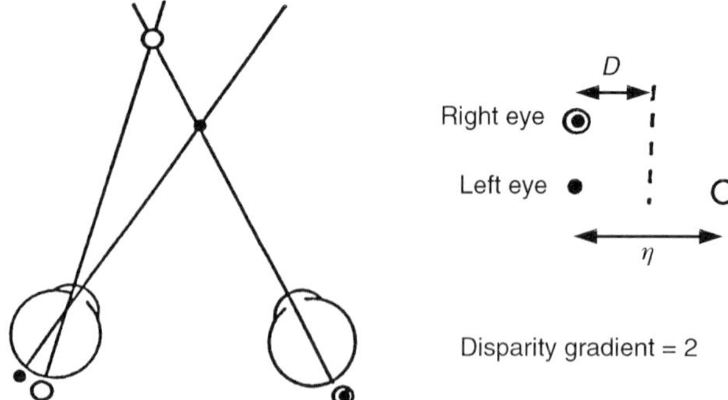

FIGURE 16 Panum's limiting case. Two objects on a visual line of one eye are fused with a single point imaged on the fovea of the other eye. The resulting stereo-percept has a disparity gradient of 2, which exceeds the disparity gradient limit described in Figure 11. (From BINOCULAR VISION AND STEREOPSIS by Ian P. Howard and Brian J. Rogers, Copyright © 1995 by Oxford University Press, Inc. Used by permission of Oxford University Press, Inc.

see depth variations in a gravel bed than it is to see the form of the leafy foliage on a tree. If the matching process assumes that surfaces and boundary contours in nature are generally smooth, then matches will be biased to result in similar disparities between adjacent features. This rule is enforced by a disparity-gradient limit of stereopsis and fusion. Figure 11 is a stereogram that illustrates how two points lying at different depths are both fused if they are widely separated, and only one can be fused at a time if they are crowded together. This effect is summarized by the rate of change of disparity as a function of the two target's separation (disparity gradient). When the difference in disparity between the two targets is less than their separation (disparity gradient less than one), both targets can be fused. When the change in disparity is equal to or greater than their separation (disparity gradient equal to or greater than one), the targets can no longer be fused (Burt & Julesz, 1980). Thus the bias helps to obtain the correct match in smooth surfaces but interferes with obtaining matches in irregular surfaces. Edge continuity might be considered as a corollary of the smoothness constraint. Matching solutions that result in continuous edges or surface boundaries are not likely to result from chance and are strong indicators that the correct binocular match has been made. Furthermore, subsequent matches along the same boundary contour will be biased to converge on the same solution.

Finally, the number of potential matches can be reduced dramatically by restricting matches to retinal meridians that lie in epipolar planes. The retinal locus of epipolar images lie in a plane that contains the target in space and the two nodal points of the eyes. Assuming that the nodal point lies very near the center of curvature of the retina, this plane intersects the two retinae and forms great circles whose radius of curvature equals the radius of the eye-globe. When presented with multiple images, matching would be greatly simplified if searches were made along these epipolar lines. Because the eyes undergo cyclovergence when we converge or elevate our direction of gaze, the epipolar planes will intersect different coplanar retinal meridians depending on gaze. Thus utilization of the epipolar constraint requires that eye position and torsion information be used to determine which retinal meridians lie in the earth-referenced epipolar plane. If matching is unconstrained, such as is the case with long oblique lines, it is completely ambiguous (aperture problem). Under these conditions matching is restricted to a small vertical disparity range (10 arc min) about epipolar lines (Van Ee & Schor, 1999). The matching solution in this case equals the vector average of all possible matches. The vertical extent of the operating range for binocular matching can be extended when matches are constrained by image primitives such as end or crossing points. For example, Stevenson and Schor (1997) have shown that a wide range of binocular matches can be made between random-dot targets containing combinations of large horizontal and vertical disparities (>1°). The epipolar constraint would, however, be ideal for artificial vision systems in which the orientation of two cameras could be used to determine which meridians in the two screen planes were coplanar and epipolar.

C. Computational Algorithms

In addition to the constraints listed above, several computational algorithms have been developed to solve the correspondence problem. Some of these algorithms exhibit global cooperativety in that the disparity processed in one region of the visual field influences the disparity solution in another region. Matches for different tokens are not made independently of one another. These algorithms are illustrated with a Keplarian grid, which represents an array of disparity detectors that sense depth over a range of distances and eccentricities in the visual plane from the point of convergence. Biological analogs to the nodes in this array are the binocularly innervated cortical cells in the primary visual cortex that exhibit sensitivity to disparity of similar features imaged in their receptive fields (Hubel & Wiesel, 1970; Poggio, Gonzalez, & Krause, 1988). Notice that the many possible matches of the points in Figure 17 fall along various nodes in the Keplarian grid. Cooperative models enforce the smoothness and disparity gradient constraints by facilitating activity of nodes stimulated simultaneously in the fronto-parallel plane (dashed lines) and inhibiting activity of nodes stimulated simultaneously in the orthogonal depth planes (e.g., midsagittal) (solid lines). The consequence is different disparity detectors inhibit one another and like disparity detectors facilitate one another (Dev, 1975; Nelson, 1975). This general principle has been elaborated upon in other models that extend the range of facilitation to regions falling outside the intersection of the visual axes and areas of inhibition to areas of the Keplarian grid that lie between the two visual axes (Marr & Poggio, 1976). For a review of other cooperative models see Blake and Wilson (1991).

Several serial processing models have also been proposed to optimize solutions to the matching problem. These serial models utilize the spatial filters that operate at the early stages of visual processing. Center-surround receptive fields and simple

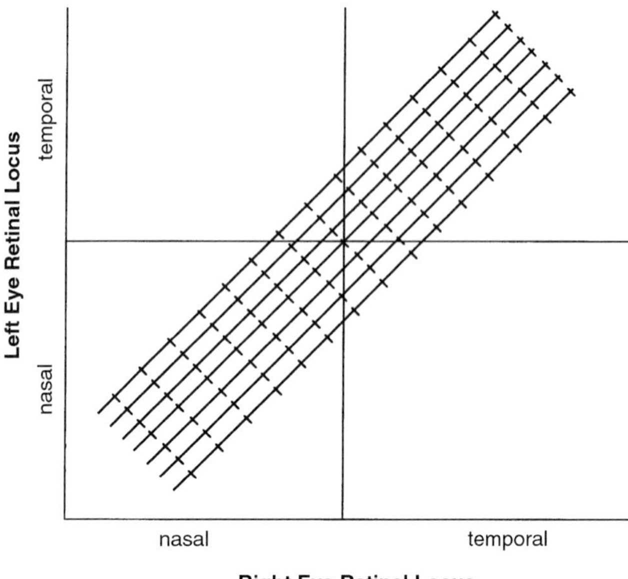

FIGURE 17 The Keplarian grid shown above represents some of the possible matches of points imaged on various retinal loci described along the horizontal position along the left retina and horizontal position along the right retina. Midsagittal targets are imaged along the long axis at 45° and frontoparallel objects are imaged along the dashed short axis at 135°. Several of the cooperative stereo-algorithms that have been proposed include just one set of inhibitory connections between detectors of different disparities (along the long 45° axis) at the same retinal position.

and complex cells in the visual cortex have optimal sensitivity to limited ranges of luminance periodicity that can be described in terms of spatial frequency. The tuning or sensitivity profiles of these cells have been modeled with various mathematical functions (difference of Gaussian, Gabor patches, Kauche functions, etc.) all of which have band-pass characteristics. They are sensitive to a limited range of spatial frequencies referred to as a channel, and there is some overlap in the sensitivity range of adjacent channels. These channels are also sensitive or tuned to limited ranges of different orientations. Thus they encode both the size and orientation of contours in space. There is both psychophysical and neurophysiological evidence that disparities or binocular matches are formed within spatial channels. These filters serve to decompose a complex image into discrete ranges of its spatial frequency components. In the Pollard Mayhew and Frisby (PMF) model (Frisby & Mayhew, 1980) three channels tuned to different spatial scales filter different spatial scale image components. Horizontal disparities are calculated between the contours having similar orientation and matched contrast polarities within each spatial scale. Matches are biased to obtain edge continuity. In addition, matches for contours of the same orientation and disparity are biased that agree across all three spatial scales. Most of these models employ both mutual facilitation and inhibition; however, several stereo-phenomenon suggest a lesser role for inhibition. For example, we are able to see depth in transparent planes, such as views of a stream bed through a textured water surface, or views of a distant scene through a spotted window or intervening plant foliage. In addition, depth of transparent surfaces can be averaged, seen as filled in or as two separate surfaces as their separation increases (Stevenson, Cormack, & Schor, 1989). Inhibition between dissimilar disparity detectors would make these precepts impossible.

Another serial model reduces the number of potential solutions with a coarse to fine strategy (Marr & Poggio, 1976). Problems arise in matching the high- and low-frequency components in a complex image when the disparity of the target exceeds one-half period of the highest frequency component. A veridical match can be made for any spatial frequency for any disparity that is less than a half the period (180° phase shift between binocular image components). However, there are unlimited matches that could be made once disparity exceeds the half period of a high-frequency component. False matches in the high-frequency range sensed by a small-scale channel could be reduced by first matching low-frequency components that have a larger range within their 180° phase limit for unambiguous matches in a large-scale channel. The large-scale solution constrains the small-scale (high-frequency component) solution. Indeed, Wilson et al. (1991) have shown that a low-frequency background will bias the match of a high-frequency pattern in the foreground to a solution that is greater than its half period unambiguous match. A phase limit of 90° rather than 180° for the upper disparity limit for binocular matches has been found empirically using band-pass targets (Schor et al., 1984b). The 90° phase limit results from the two-octave bandwidth of the stimulus as well as the spatial channels that process spatial information. Phase is referenced to the midfrequency of the channel rather than its upper frequency range, and the 180° phase limit still applies to the upper range of these channels.

The matching task could be facilitated by vergence responses to the large-scale component of the image. This would reduce overall disparity and bring the small-scale components within the unambiguous phase range of a small-scale channel (Marr & Poggio, 1979). Through iterations, a common disparity solution will eventually be found for all spatial frequency components. A similar result could be obtained in a parallel process with a single broadly tuned spatial channel that could be constrained to find a common match for all spatial frequency components of the image, as long as they had a wide enough range of spatial frequencies. When the frequency range is too narrow, then the nearest neighbor match will prevail, regardless of the real disparity of the target. This is seen in the wallpaper illusion in which a repetitive patter of vertical lines can be fused at any horizontal vergence angle. The depth of the grating is always the solution that lies nearest to the point of convergence, irrespective of the real distance of the wallpaper pattern.

The serial models or any spatial model of binocular matching that rely on the 180° phase limit for unambiguous disparity are not supported by empirical observations of fusion limits and stereopsis (Schor et al., 1984a,b). The theories predict that stereo threshold and binocular fusion ranges should become progressively lower as spatial frequency is increased. This prediction is born out as spatial frequency increases up to 2.5 cpd; however, both stereo acuity and horizontal fusion ranges are constant at frequencies above 2.5 cpd. As a result, disparities are processed in the high spatial scales that greatly exceed the 180° phase limit. This is a clear violation of theories of disparity sensitivity based upon phase sensitivity within spatial channels. In addition to phase sensitivity, there may be other limits of disparity resolution, such as a disparity position limit. Given the presence of both a phase and a position limit, the threshold would be set by whichever of these two limits was least sensitive. For large disparities, the constant position limit would be smaller than the phase limit, and the converse would be true for high spatial frequencies.

D. Interocular Correlation

Computational algorithms and matching constraints described above rely upon a preattentive mechanism that is capable of making comparisons of the two retinal images for the purpose of quantifying the strength of the many possible binocular matches. Ideally, all potential matches could be quantified with a cross-correlation or interocular correlation (IOC) function. This is represented mathematically as the convolution integral of the two retinal images.

$$\mathrm{IOC(d)} = \int f(x)h(x+d)\,dx,$$

where $f(x)$ and $h(x)$ represent the intensity profiles (or some derivative of them) along the horizontal meridian of the right and left eye's retinae. The IOC can be thought of as the degree to which the two retinal images match one another.

This nonlinear operation represents the strength of various matches with products between the two eyes images as a function of retinal disparities along epipolar lines. A random-dot stereogram (RDS) is an ideal target to test the binocular matching process in human vision because it is devoid of clear monocular forms that are only revealed after stereoscopic depth is perceived (Julesz, 1964). IOC of a RDS equals the proportion of dots in one eye's image that match dots in the other eye's image with the same contrast at the same relative location. The middle RDS shown in Figure 18 has 50% density and is composed of only black and white dots. Those dots that do not match correspond to images of opposite contrast. If all dots match, the correlation is +1. If no dots match, that is they all have paired opposite contrasts, the correlation is −1. If half the dots match, the correlation is zero.

FIGURE 18 Random-dot stereograms of varying degrees of correlation. (a) The two images are correlated 100%. They fuse to create a flat plane. (b) The interocular correlation is 50%. A flat plane is still perceived but with some dots out of the plane. (c) The correlation is zero and a flat plane is not perceived. Subjects had to detect transitions between different states of correlation. (Reprinted from *Vision Research, 31,* Cormack, L. K., Stevenson, S. B., & Schor, C. M. Interocular correlation, luminance contrast and cyclopean processing, pp. 2195–2207, Copyright © 1991, with kind permission from Elsevier Science Ltd., The Boulevard, Langford Lane, Kidlington, OX5 1GB, United Kingdom, and the authors.)

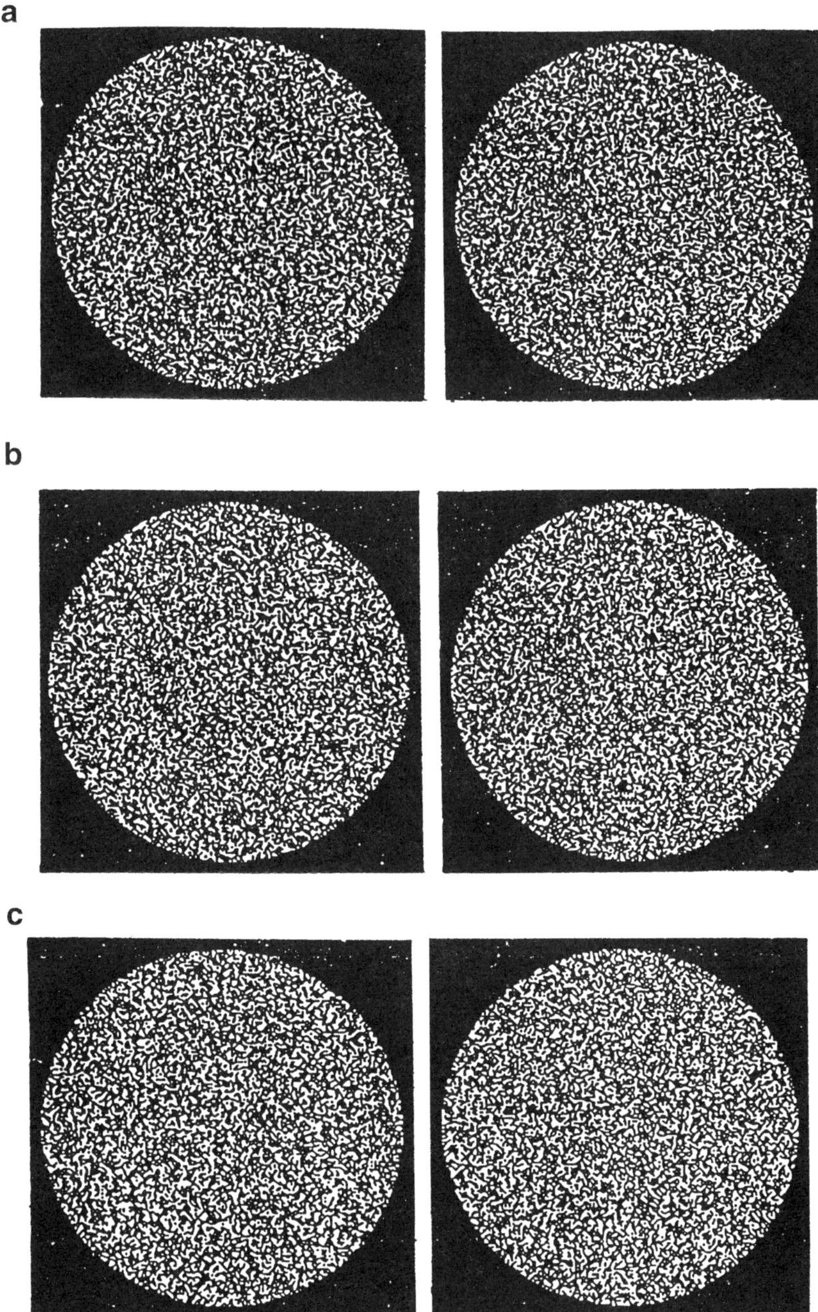
a
b
c

The image correspondence of the RDS can be quantified by a cross-correlation analysis of the luminance or contrast profile of the random-dot pattern. Figure 18 illustrates three patterns of random-element stereograms whose correlation varies from +1 at the top where all dots match, to zero at the bottom, where left and right image contrasts are randomly related. Note the variation in flatness of the fused images. Figure 19 illustrates the cross-correlation function of the previous autostereogram images, where the peak of each function represents the stimulus correlation at the disparity of the match, and the average amplitude of the surrounding noise represent a zero correlation composed of 50% matched dots. The noise fluctuations result from spurious matches that vary at different disparities. The negative side lobes about the peak result from the use of edge contrast rather than luminance in computing the cross-correlation function. With only two dot contrasts, the IOC equals the percent matched dots in the stimulus minus 50% divided by percent.

$$\text{IOC} = 2P_d - 1,$$

where P_d is the proportion of matching dots. The IOC is analogous to contrast in the luminance domain. At threshold, the IOC is analogous to a Weber fraction. The IOC represents stimulus disparity (signal) in the presence of a mean background correlation of zero with 50% matches (noise). At threshold, the cross-correlation provides a means of quantifying the visibility of the disparity much like contrast threshold quantifies the visibility of a luminance contour in the presence of a background luminance.

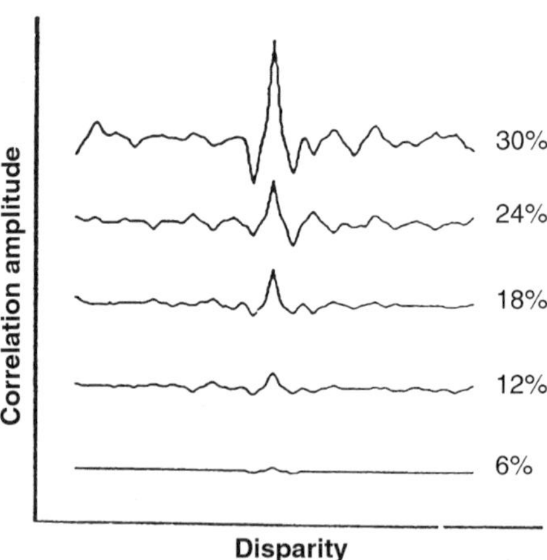

FIGURE 19 A family of cross-correlation functions for a random-dot stereogram with 80% interocular correlation but decreasing contrast (indicated by numbers on the right). The curves are vertically separated on the *y* axis. The signal (peak in the correlation function) and the extrinsic noise (lesser peaks due to spurious matches in the display) both vary with the square of contrast. The functions are displaced vertically. (Reprinted from *Vision Research, 31,* Cormack, L. K., Stevenson, S. B., & Schor, C. M. Interocular correlation, luminance contrast and cyclopean processing, pp. 2195–2207, Copyright © 1991, with kind permission from Elsevier Science Ltd., The Boulevard, Langford Lane, Kidlington, OX5 1GB, United Kingdom, and the authors.)

E. Off-Horopter Interocular Correlation Sensitivity

The RDS has been used to measure the sensitivity of the binocular system to correlation at different standing disparities with respect to the horopter. This is analogous to extrahoropteral studies of stereopsis by Blakemore (1970), Badcock and Schor (1985), and Siderov and Harwerth (1993), which measured stereopsis as a function of distance in front or behind the fixation plane, only here we are measuring correlation detection as opposed to differential disparity detection. The task with the RDS is for the subject to identify which of two intervals presents a partially correlated surface as opposed to one having zero correlation, where 50% of the dots match. Surprisingly, we are extremely good at this task, and under optimal conditions, some subjects can detect as little as 5% increment in correlation, whereas others can only detect 10%. Thus for a 10% correlation threshold, the latter subject is able to discriminate between 50 and 55% matching dots.

Figure 20 illustrates the off-horopter correlation thresholds for three subjects measured as a function of the disparity subtended by the correlated dots. Sensitivity falls off abruptly away from the horopter until 100% correlation is needed to discriminate between a zero correlated field at a one degree disparity on either side of the horopter. Beyond that distance, all correlations appear the same as zero. The

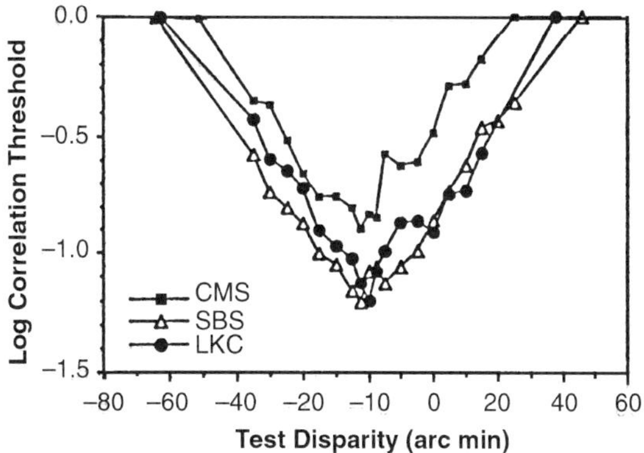

FIGURE 20 Baseline correlation thresholds for three subjects as a function of disparity pedestal amplitude. The log of interocular correlation at threshold is plotted against horizontal disparity of the test surface relative to fixation. Negative values of disparity indicate near (crossed) disparity. A value of 0.0 on the vertical axis represents a correlation of 1.0, the maximum possible. The intersection of each subject's curve with the line at 0.0 indicates the upper disparity limits for correlation detection in our task. Correlation thresholds were measured for each subject out to +/−35 arc min disparity, with each point representing the mean of five runs. Upper disparity limits were measured in a separate experiment. The general trend can be characterized as being symmetric about 0 disparity, with an exponential relationship between correlation threshold and disparity. Each subject showed idiosyncratic departures from this exponential trend, such as the bumps at 0 disparity for subject SBS, at +5 arc min for CMS and at +10 for subject LKC. (Reprinted from *Vision Research, 32,* Stevenson, S. B., Cormack, L. K., Schor, C. M., & Tyler, C. W. Disparity tuning mechanisms of human stereopsis, pp. 1685–1694, Copyright © 1992 with kind permission from Elsevier Science Ltd., The Boulevard, Langford Lane, Kidlington, OX5 1GB, United Kingdom, and the authors.)

range can be extended to two degrees by increasing the number of visible dots by increasing field size or reducing dot size. There is improvement as the number of dots is increased up to 10,000 dots (Cormack, Stevenson, & Schor, 1994) and then performance remains static, demonstrating the limited efficiency of the visual system. The function shown in Figure 20 illustrates that the horopter is to binocular vision as the fovea is to spatial resolution. It is the locus along the depth axis where correlation sensitivity is highest.

F. Extrinsic and Intrinsic Noise and Interocular Correlation

The matching problem is basically one of detecting a signal in the presence of noise. The peak of the cross-correlation function could represent the signal that is to be detected in the presence of various sources of noise. One extrinsic noise source results from the spurious matches in the stimulus at nonoptimal disparities. These are seen as the ripples in the flanks surrounding the peak of the IOC distribution. There are also intrinsic sources of noise that could result from the variable responses of physiological disparity detectors. The influence of these two noise sources can be revealed by measuring the correlation threshold of a RDS as a function of contrast. The IOC threshold is most sensitive at high contrasts and remains constant as contrast is reduced to 10 times the contrast threshold (approximately 16% contrast) for detecting the RDS. Figure 21 illustrates that at lower contrasts, the threshold

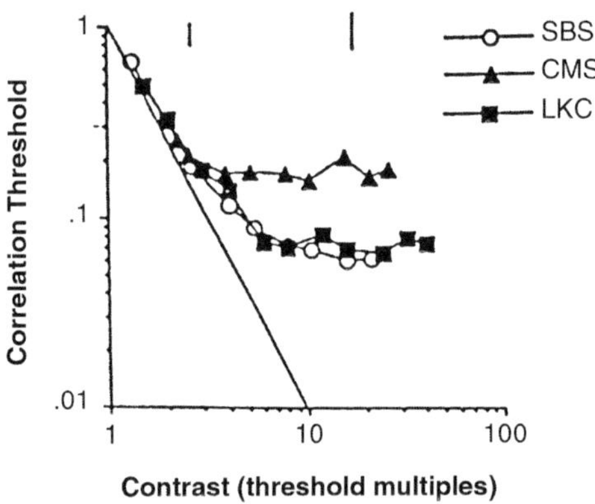

FIGURE 21 Correlation thresholds as a function of luminance contrast. Threshold for the detection of interocular correlation as a function of luminance contrast, expressed in threshold multiples, for the three subjects. Both axes are logarithmic. The data asymptote to a log-log slope of 0 at high contrasts and −2 at low contrasts. A line of slope −2, indicating a trading relation between interocular correlation and the square of contrast, is plotted for reference. The left- and right-hand vertical lines at the top of the figure represent typical SD for low and high contrast judgments respectively. (Reprinted from *Vision Research, 31,* Cormack, L. K., Stevenson, S. B., & Schor, C. M. Interocular correlation, luminance contrast and cyclopean processing, pp. 2195–2207, Copyright © 1991, with kind permission from Elsevier Science Ltd., The Boulevard, Langford Lane, Kidlington, OX5 1GB, United Kingdom, and the authors.)

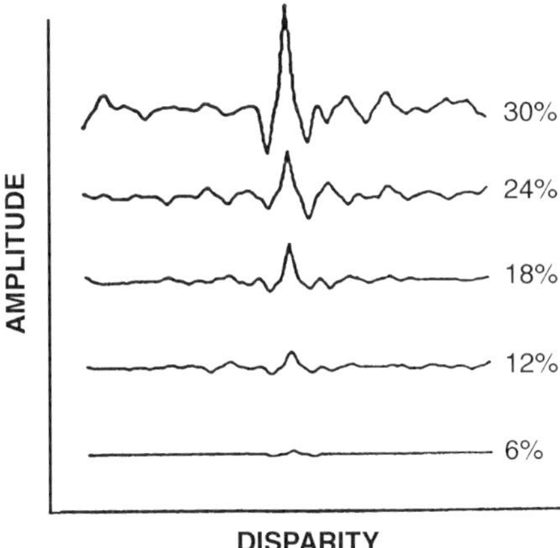

FIGURE 22 Effect of reduced contrast on signal to noise ratio for a stimulus noise source. As the contrast of an image pair with some fixed interocular correlation is reduced, both the signal amplitude and the noise level are decreased by the square of contrast. Shown in this figure is a family of cross-correlation functions, the members of which differ in the contrast of the input image pair. The particular contrast of each input image pair is displayed to the right of the corresponding function. The interocular correlation of the input image pair was 80% in all cases, and the functions are displaced vertically for clarity. (Reprinted from *Vision Research, 31,* Cormack, L. K., Stevenson, S. B., & Schor, C. M. Interocular correlation, luminance contrast and cyclopean processing, pp. 3195–2207, Copyright © 1991, with kind permission from Elsevier Science Ltd., The Boulevard, Langford Lane, Kidlington, OX5 1GB, United Kingdom, and the authors.)

increased proportionally with the square of the reduction (i.e., slope of −2 on a log-log scale). For example, if contrast is lowered by a factor of two, the correlation threshold for perception of a plane increases by a factor of four. Figures 22 and 23 illustrate the variation of signal-to-noise ratio that account for the flat and root 2 regions of the contrast function. In Figure 22, assume the noise results from spurious matches in the stimulus. Accordingly, as the contrast of an image pair with some fixed interocular correlation is reduced, both the signal amplitude and the noise level are decreased by the square of contrast. The square relationship reflects the product between the left and right images during the cross-correlation. The covariation of signal and noise with contrast results in a constant signal-to-noise ratio. Figure 23 assumes the noise results from an intrinsic source that is independent of the stimulus and that this intrinsic noise is greater than the extrinsic noise of the stimulus when the image contrast has been reduced below 10 times detection threshold. As contrast is reduced below a value of 10 times detection threshold, the signal is still reduced with the square of contrast; however, the intrinsic noise remains constant. Accordingly, signal-to-noise ratio decreased abruptly with the square of contrast causing a rapid rise in IOC threshold. These results illustrate the presence of intrinsic and extrinsic noise sources as well as a nonlinearity, which can be described as a binocular cross-correlation or product of the two monocular images.

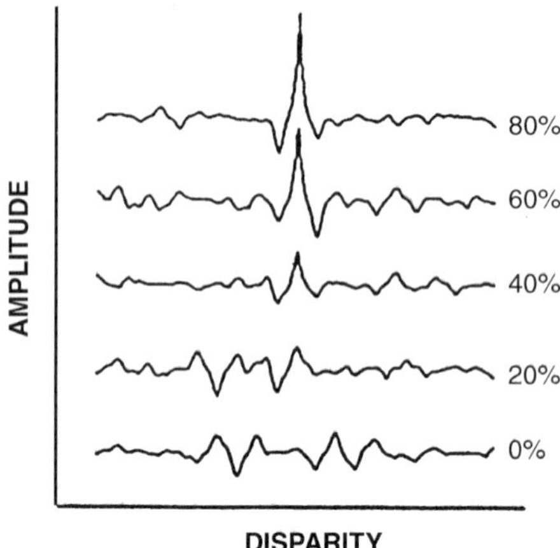

FIGURE 23 Effect of reduced contrast on signal-to-noise ratio for an intrinsic noise source. As the interocular correlation of an image pair with some fixed contrast is reduced, the signal amplitude is decreased proportionally while the noise level remains constant. Shown in this figure is a family of cross-correlation functions, the members of which differ in the interocular correlation of the input image pair. The particular interocular correlation of each input image pair is displayed to the right of the corresponding function. The contrast of the input image pair was 20% in all cases, and the functions are displaced vertically for clarity. (Reprinted from *Vision Research, 31,* Cormack, L. K., Stevenson, S. B., & Schor, C. M. Interocular correlation, luminance contrast and cyclopean processing, pp. 2195–2207, Copyright © 1991, with kind permission from Elsevier Science Ltd., The Boulevard, Langford Lane, Kidlington, OX5 1GB, United Kingdom, and the authors.)

G. Estimating Disparity Magnitude

Once features have been matched in the two eyes, the resulting disparities must be quantified and scaled with viewing distance in order to obtain a veridical quantitative sense of depth. Lehky, Pouget, and Sejnowski (1990) have summarized three classes of general mechanisms that have been proposed to quantify disparity. These include an array of narrowly tuned units with nonoverlapping sensitivity, which have sensitivities distributed over the range of disparities that stimulate stereopsis. The spatial layout of binocular receptive fields for these multiple local channels forms the nodes described in a Keplarian grid (Marr & Poggio, 1976; Mayhew & Frisby, 1980). The value of a disparity determines which channel is stimulated. A second process uses rate encoding to specify disparity with a single channel. Firing rate increases as disparity increases as suggested by models by Julesz (1971) and Marr and Poggio (1979). The third and most physiologically plausible means of disparity quantification utilizes a distribution of multiple channels with partially overlapping sensitivity to disparity. Because there is overlapping sensitivity, the activity of a single channel is ambiguous; however, disparity amplitude can be computed from the activity of all channels by such methods as averaging (Stevenson, Cormack, Schor, & Tyler, 1992) or by spectrum representation (Lehky & Sejnowski, 1990).

In all cases, if the disparity analysis is localized to a small region of space, there is little problem with confounding the analysis with multiple disparity stimuli. This only occurs in dense random-depth scenes, such as close-up views of tree foliage. In these circumstances, averaging mechanisms would have difficulty in resolving the separation of closely spaced depth planes, whereas spectral representations would have unique distributions for multiple disparities that could be analyzed with templates (Lehky et al., 1990). Our ability to solve the correspondence problem suggests, however, that there is some interaction between adjacent stimuli as described above in cooperative-global models. This is thought to involve inhibitory interactions between disparity detectors that have been described as inhibitory side-lobes of disparity tuned channels (Cormack, Stevenson, & Schor, 1993; Lehky et al., 1990; Poggio et al., 1988; Stevenson et al., 1992). This produces a band-pass sensitivity to periodic spatial variations of disparity, such as is seen in a depth-corrugated surface like a curtain (Tyler, 1975).

Our ability to perceive depth transparency is often cited as a phenomenon that is inconsistent with many models of stereopsis. However, if single values of depth are analyzed along discrete directions of space, some patches of space will be coded as near and some are far. These regions could be interpolated at a higher level to perceive that the near and far surfaces are actually continuous. The alternative is that the visual system processes the multiple matches in every visual direction, resulting in true transparency.

Finally, there is the question of the metric used to quantify disparity. Disparity has been described either as a positional offset of the two retinal images from corresponding points (measured in angular units) or as a phase offset, where phase describes the disparity as a proportion of the luminance spatial period to which the disparity is optimally tuned (Schor et al., 1984a). Thus a $\frac{1}{4}$-degree disparity would be a phase disparity of 180° for a unit tuned to 2 cycles/deg. Positional disparity could be encoded by the relative misalignment of two receptive fields that have the same distribution of excitatory and inhibitory zones in the two eyes (Barlow, Blakemore, & Pettigrew, 1967). Phase disparity could be encoded by receptive fields that are arranged in quadrature. These cells are not offset in the two eyes. They have relative phase offsets between excitatory and inhibitory zones within the monocular receptive fields, such that one cell could have a peak sensitivity centered in cosine phase and the other a displaced peak in sine phase (Figure 24) (DeAngelis, Ohzawa, & Freeman, 1991; Freeman & Ohzawa, 1990).

These models and physiological measures suggest several questions about stereopsis. These include (a) what is the minimum number of disparity channels that could account for stereo acuity? (b) what are the crowding limits on stereo-resolution for adjacent stimuli? (c) are multiple depths averaged or biased toward one another? (d) is there evidence supporting the existence of inhibitory interactions in stereo-processing mechanisms? and (e) is disparity coded by phase or position?

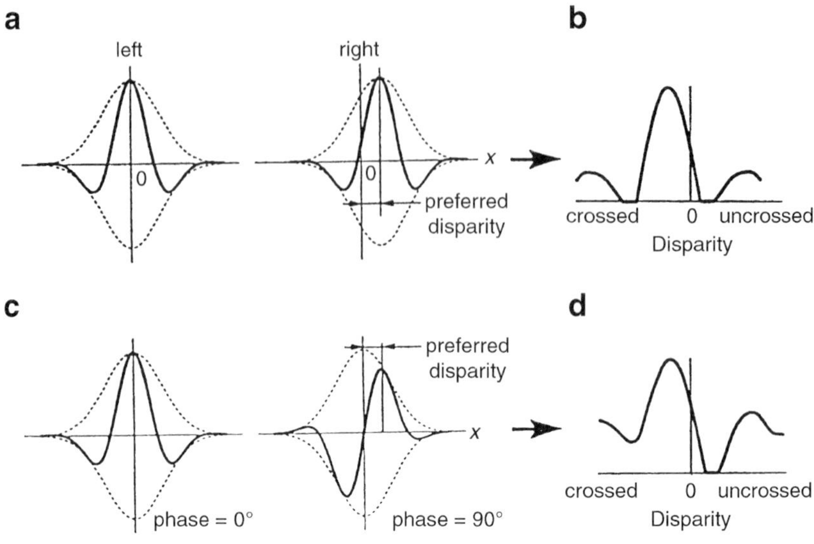

FIGURE 24 Position and phase encoding of disparity. Two possible schemes of disparity encoding by binocular simple cells. (a) The traditional model. Solid curves show Gabor functions that represent receptive field (RF) profiles of a simple cell for the left and right eyes. The abscissa (x) for each curve gives retinal position, and the ordinate represents sensitivity to a luminance increment, such that downward deflections of the curve correspond to dark-excitatory (or OFF) subregions and upward deflections correspond to bright-excitatory (or ON) subregions. Dashed curves show the Gaussian envelopes of the idealized RFs. In this conventional scheme, the two RF profiles are identical in shape, but their centers (the centers of the Gaussian envelopes) are located at noncorresponding points (i.e., they are binocularly disparate). (b) Disparity-tuning prediction is based on the conventional scheme shown in (a). The abscissa is binocular disparity, and the ordinate represents response strength. The cell is tuned to a particular (crossed) disparity by virtue of spatial offset of the RFs from the point of retinal correspondence. (c) An alternative scheme for disparity encoding, in which the left and right RF profiled may differ in shape (or phase), but are centered at corresponding retinal location (i.e., the centers of the Gaussian envelopes are at zero disparity). (d) Disparity tuning predicted by the phase-encoding scheme shown in (c). The optimal disparity for the cell is determined by the different in phase between the two RF profiles, and by the size (or spatial frequency) of the fields. Note that the two schemes shown here produce differently shaped disparity-tuning curves [(b) and (d)], but the optimal disparities are the same. (From DeAngelis, G. C., Ohzawa, I., & Freeman, R. D. [1995]. Neuronal mechanisms underlying stereopsis: How do simple cells in the visual cortex encode binocular disparity? *Perception, 24,* 3–31. Pion, London. Reprinted with permission of the publisher and authors.)

H. Disparity Pools or Channels

As will be discussed below, stereopsis has both a transient component that senses depth of very large (up to 12 degrees), briefly presented (<200 ms) disparities (Ogle, 1952; Westheimer & Tanzman, 1956) and a sustained component that senses small disparities (<1 degree) (Ogle, 1952) near the plane of fixation. Behavioral studies suggest that different channel structures underlie these two forms of stereopsis. Many individuals are unable to perceive transient depth to any disparity magnitude presented in one depth direction, either far or near, from the fixation plane while they are able to perceive it in response to a wide range of disparities presented in the opposite depth direction (Richards & Regan, 1973). This condition is referred to as stereo-anomalous (Richards, 1971). Stereo-anomalous subjects have normal stereo-acuity when measured with static (sustained) disparities in both the crossed and uncrossed directions. The stereo-anomalous observations have been used as evidence for three classes of disparity pools (crossed, uncrossed and zero) that sense transient disparities. Depth aliasing by the transient-stereo system also supports the three channel model (Edwards & Schor, 1999). Jones (1977) also observed a transient disparity-vergence deficit in stereo-anomalous subjects that was consistent with the three-pool model.

Simulations with the three-pool model indicate that the model has insufficient resolution to account for the static (sustained) stereo-acuity of 5- to 10-arc sec (Lehky et al., 1990). Correlation detection studies employing depth adaptation (Stevenson et al., 1992) and subthreshold summation (Cormack et al., 1993) revealed multiple sustained-disparity tuned mechanisms with peak sensitivities along approximately a 2° disparity continuum that had opponent center-surround organization. The width of these disparity-tuned functions varied from 5-arc min at the horopter to 20-arc min at a distance of 20-arc min from the fixation plane. Models of the sustained-stereo system that are based upon these data, and measures of stereo-depth sensitivity obtained in front and behind the fixation plane (Badcock & Schor, 1985), indicate that a minimum of approximately 20 disparity-tuned channels is necessary to account for the sensitivity of the sustained-stereo system (Lehky et al., 1990; Stevenson et al., 1992).

V. STEREOSCOPIC DEPTH PERCEPTION

A. Depth Ordering and Scaling

A variety of cues are used to interpret a 3-D space from the 2-D retinal images. Static monocular cues rely upon some familiarity with the absolute size and shape of targets in order to make quantitative estimates of their relative distance and surface curvature. Monocular cues such as overlap do not require any familiarity with objects. They only give qualitative information about depth ordering; however, they do not provide depth-magnitude information. Stereopsis and dynamic motion parallax cues do yield a quantitative sense of relative depth and 3-D shape, and they do not depend upon familiarity with size and shape of objects. Depth from stereo and motion parallax can be calculated from geometrical relationships (triangulation) between two separate views of the same scene, taken simultaneously in stereopsis or sequentially in motion parallax.

Three independent variables involved in the calculation stereo-depth are retinal image disparity, viewing distance, and the separation in space of the two viewpoints (i.e., the baseline). In stereopsis, the relationship between the linear depth interval between two objects and the retinal image disparity that they subtend is approximated by the following expression:

$$\Delta d = \eta \star d^2 2a,$$

where η is retinal image disparity in radians, d is viewing distance, 2a is the interpupillary distance, and Δd is the linear depth interval. 2a, d, and Δd are all expressed in the same units (e.g., meters). The formula implies that in order to perceive depths in units of absolute distance (e.g., meters), the visual system utilizes information about the interpupillary distance and the viewing distance. Viewing distance could be sensed from the angle of convergence (Foley, 1980) or from other retinal cues, such as oblique or vertical disparities. These disparities occur naturally with targets in tertiary directions from the point of fixation (Garding, Porrill, Mayhew, & Frisby, 1995; Mayhew & Longuet-Higgins, 1982; Gillam & Lawergren, 1983; Liu et al., 1994a; Rogers & Bradshaw, 1993; Westheimer & Pettet, 1992).

The equation illustrates that for a fixed retinal image disparity, the corresponding linear depth interval increases with the square of viewing distance and that viewing distance is used to scale the horizontal disparity into a linear depth interval. When objects are viewed through base-out prisms that stimulate additional convergence, perceived depth should be reduced by underestimates of viewing distance. Furthermore, the pattern of zero retinal image disparities described by the curvature of the longitudinal horopter varies with viewing distance. It can be concave at near distances and convex at far distances in the same observer (Figure 3) (Ogle, 1964). Thus, without distance information, the pattern of retinal image disparities across the visual field is insufficient to sense either depth ordering (surface curvature) or depth magnitude (Garding et al., 1995). Similarly, the same pattern of horizontal disparity can correspond to different slants about a vertical axis presented at various horizontal gaze eccentricities (Ogle, 1964). Convergence distance and direction of gaze are important sources of information used to interpret slant from disparity fields associated with slanting surfaces (Banks & Backus, 1998). Clearly, stereo-depth perception is much more than a disparity map of the visual field.

There are lower and upper limits of retinal image disparity that can be coded by the nervous system and used to interpret relative depth. The region of useful disparities is illustrated in Figure 25 (Tyler, 1983), which plots perceived depth as a function of binocular disparity. The lower left-hand corner of the function represents the lower disparity limit or stereo-acuity. The lower right-hand corner represents the upper disparity limit for stereopsis, beyond which no stereo depth is perceived. The upper disparity limit for stereopsis (approximately 1000 arc min) is much greater than for singleness or Panum's fusional area, indicated by the vertical line at 6 arc min (Ogle, 1952). When evaluated with narrow band sustained stimuli, however, the upper disparity limit is only slightly greater than the fusion limit (Figure 10). The largest upper disparity limit for stereopsis occurs at low spatial fre-

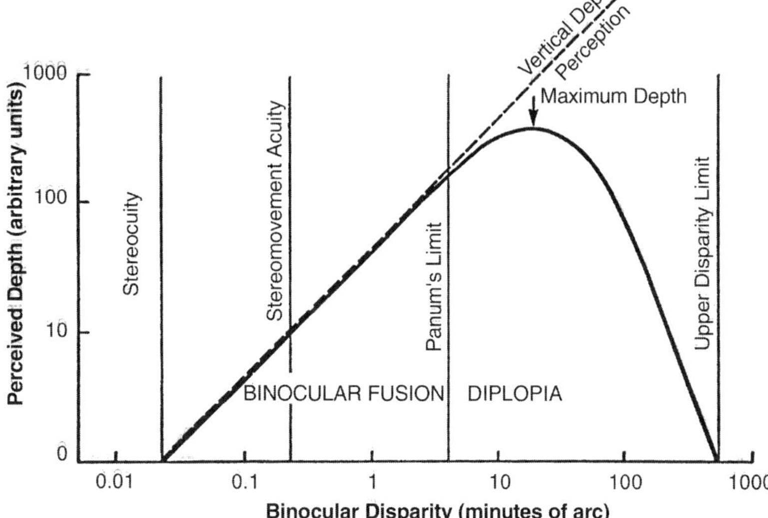

FIGURE 25 Sensory limits imposed by disparity. Schematic of some stereoscopic limits of perceived depth and fusion as a function of binocular disparity [From Tyler, C. W. (1983). Sensory processing of binocular disparity. In C. M. Schor & K. Ciuffreda (Eds.), *Vergence eye movements: Clinical and basic aspects*. Boston: Butterworth.]

quencies. It corresponds to the large upper stereo limit shown at the right side of the horizontal axis in Figure 25. Below Panum's limit, targets are seen singly and in depth, whereas above Panum's limit they are seen as double and in depth for a limited range. Between the upper and lower limits there is a region where there is a veridical match between perceived depth and actual depth. The maximum perceived depth occurs just beyond the fusion limit. Then perceived depth actually diminishes as disparity is increased to the upper disparity limit. The rising limb of this function describes quantitative stereopsis, in which perceived depth increases monotonically with retinal image disparity. The falling limb describes stereopsis with nonveridical depth equal to that perceived with smaller disparities.

B. Hyperacuity, Superresolution, and Gap Resolution

There are three classes of visual-direction acuity described by Westheimer (1979, 1987). They are referred to as Hyperacuity, Super-Resolution Acuity, and Gap Resolution Acuity (Figure 26). Hyperacuity tasks involve detection of a small relative displacement of targets in space or time. The term *hyperacuity* refers to extremely low thresholds that are less than the width of a single photoreceptor in the retina. A classic example is Vernier acuity, in which misalignment is detected between adjacent targets that are separated along a meridian that is orthogonal to the axis of their misalignment. Superresolution involves size discrimination between sequentially

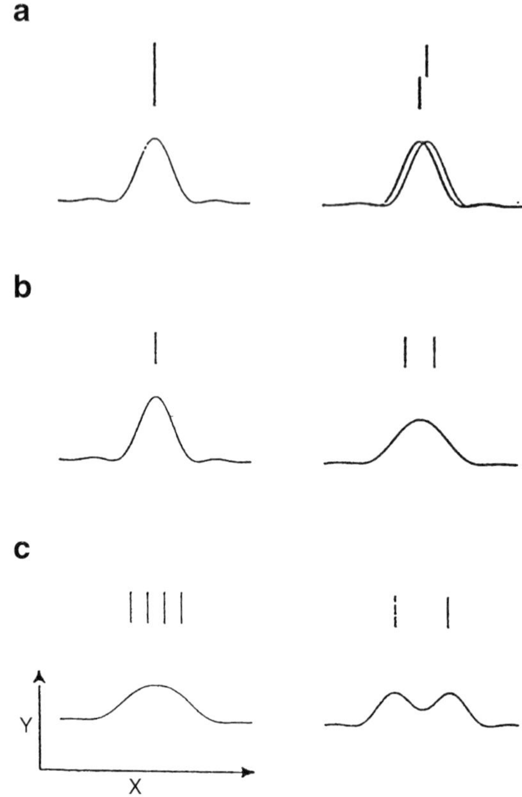

FIGURE 26 Hyperacuity, superresolution, and gap resolution tasks. Schematic diagram of targets and corresponding spread functions used to measure (a) hyperacuity, (b) superresolution, and (c) gap resolution. The left and right panels show alternatives given in a forced-choice procedure. A comparison of (a) single unbroken target and broken target measures offset hyperacuity; (b) single target and two parallel targets measures width or thickness superresolution acuity, (c) two parallel, separated targets and four targets of equal overall separation (approximating a filled area) measure gap resolution acuity. For luminance domain acuity measures, the targets could be thin lines; in these stereoscopic acuity measures, the targets were random-dot planes, with all offsets and separations occurring along the depth, or z-axis. The spread functions under each target represent hypothetical distributions produced in the nervous system on viewing the targets: presumably, the information on which the subject bases his or her choice in the task. The axes at lower left refer to these spread functions: for stereoacuity estimates, x is retinal disparity and Y could be some measure of interocular correlation or matching probability. (Reprinted from *Vision Research, 29,* Stevenson, S. B., Cormack, L. K., & Schor, C. M. Hyperacuity, superresolution and gap resolution in human stereopsis, pp. 1597–1605, Copyright © 1989, with kind permission from Elsevier Science Ltd., The Boulevard, Langford Lane, Kidlington, OX5 1GB, United Kingdom, and the authors.)

viewed targets. Width discrimination is a superresolution task. Gap-resolution represents our ability to resolve space between two separate targets that produces a dip in the combined target luminance profile. It is a judgment based upon something like a Raleigh criterion. Measures of visual acuity with a Snellen E or Landolt C are examples of gap-resolution.

There are forms of stereo-acuity that are analogous to the three forms of monocular acuity (Stevenson et al., 1989). As shown in Figure 27, stereo-hyperacuity tasks involve discrimination of depth between adjacent targets. Stereo-superresolution involves discriminating between the depth-axis thickness of surfaces (pykno-stereopsis) (Tyler, 1983). Stereo-gap-resolution tasks require discrimination between a single thick surface and two overlaying separate surfaces. Stereo-gap perception of

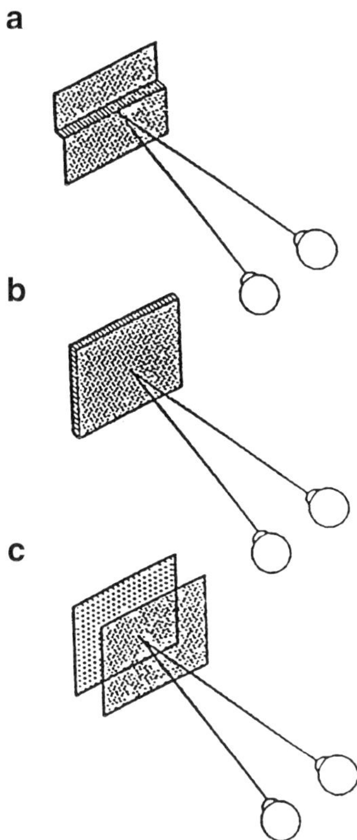

FIGURE 27 Schematic illustration of the suprathreshold appearance of stereo tasks of hyperacuity, superresolution, and gap resolution. The panel depicts a perspective view of the targets in Figure 26. (a) Hyperacuity stimulus appeared as a fronto-parallel plane of dynamic random dots split across the middle, with the bottom half closer in depth than the top. (b) Superresolution stimulus appeared as a thick random-dot slab, yield "pykno-stereopsis." (c) Gap resolution stimulus appeared as two distinct, overlapped random-dot surfaces with empty space between them, yielding diastereopsis. (Reprinted from *Vision Research, 29,* Stevenson, S. B., Cormack, L. K., & Schor, C. M. Hyperacuity, superresolution and gap resolution in human stereopsis, pp. 1597–1605, Copyright © 1989, with kind permission from Elsevier Science Ltd., The Boulevard, Langford Lane, Kidlington, OX5 1GB, United Kingdom, and the authors.)

two overlapping depth surfaces is referred to as dia-stereopsis (Tyler, 1983). The thresholds for these three stereo tasks are similar to their monocular counterparts. Thresholds for stereo-hyperacuity range from 3 to 6 arc sec. Threshold for stereo-super resolution ranges from 15 to 30 arc sec and threshold for stereo-gap resolution is approximately 200 arc sec. These distinct thresholds demonstrate that stereopsis can subserve different types of acuity tasks, and performance on these tasks follows performance on analogous visual direction acuity tasks. The thresholds are modeled from the spread functions depicted in Figure 28. The spread functions represent the combined noise produced by optical filtering, oculomotor vergence noise, and neural filtering. Acuity limits for stereo and visual direction tasks could be attributed to a 3-D ellipsoid of positional uncertainty formed by the spread functions on each spatial dimension.

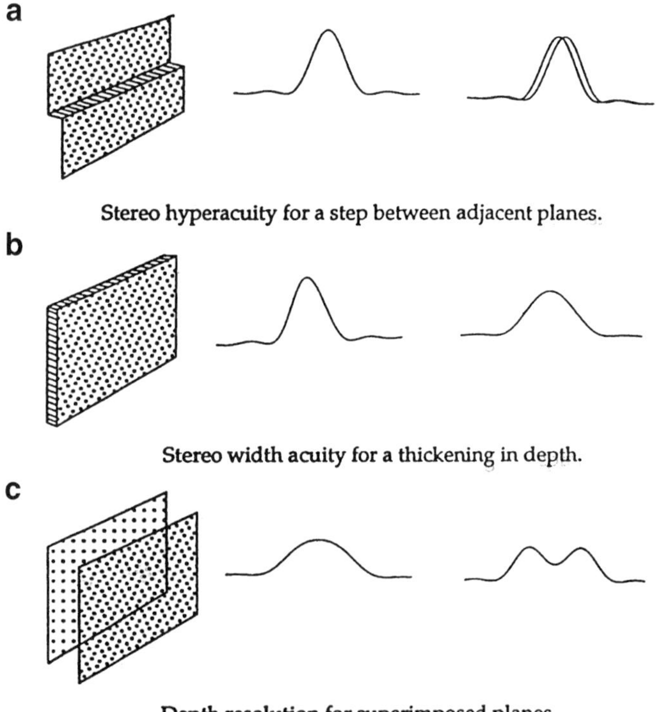

a
Stereo hyperacuity for a step between adjacent planes.
b
Stereo width acuity for a thickening in depth.
c
Depth resolution for superimposed planes

FIGURE 28 Neural activity associated with three types of stereo-acuity. Hypothetical distributions of neural activity corresponding to zero-disparity and the threshold stimulus for each task are on the right. Reprinted from *Vision Research, 29,* Stevenson, S. B., Cormack, L. K., & Schor, C. M. Hyperacuity, superresolution and gap resolution in human stereopsis, pp. 1597–1605, Copyright © 1989, with kind permission from Elsevier Science Ltd., The Boulevard, Langford Lane, Kidlington, OX5 1GB, United Kingdom, and the authors.)

C. Stereo-Acuity

Under optimal conditions we are able to resolve depth differences as small as 3 to 6 sec of arc. This performance level can be achieved with foveal fixation of targets located at the plane of fixation (on the horopter). Stereo-threshold is measured with two spatial offsets in each eye, such as is illustrated in Figure 29. It is remarkable that the spatial offset in each eye at the stereo-threshold is smaller than the minimum spatial offset that can be detected by one eye alone (Vernier threshold) (Berry, 1948; McKee & Levi, 1987; Schor & Badcock, 1985; Westheimer & McKee, 1979). This observation poses problems for ideal detector models of hyperacuity that attempt to explain limitations of vernier-acuity with retinal factors (Banks, Sekuler, & Anderson, 1991).

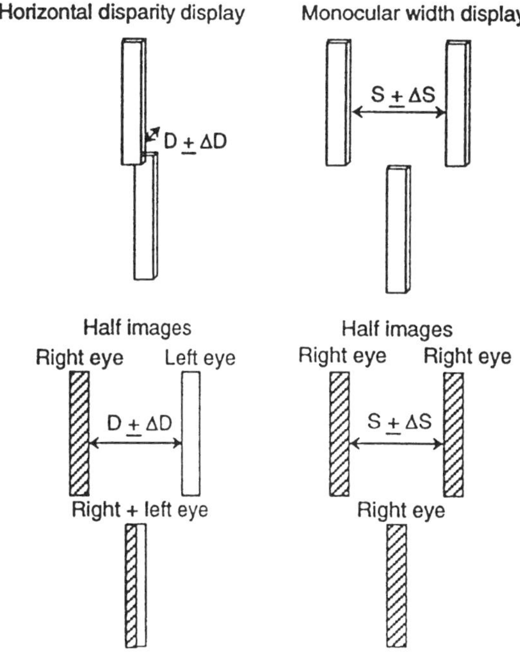

FIGURE 29 Stereo acuity and width discrimination. Diagram of displays used to compare a stereo-increment task with a monocular width-increment task. In the stereo task subjects fixated a line and detected a change in depth of a second line placed above it, about each of several depth pedestals. In the monocular task subjects fixated a line and detected a change in the distance between two other lines about each of several initial separations. (Reprinted from *Vision Research, 30,* McKee, S. P., Levi, D. M., & Bowne, S. F. The imprecision of stereopsis, pp. 1763–1779, Copyright © 1990, with kind permission from Elsevier Science Ltd., The Boulevard, Langford Lane, Kidlington, OX5 1GB, United Kingdom, and the authors.)

D. Relative Disparity

Stereopsis is our ability to detect relative depth between two objects, and relative depth could be computed in several ways. Each eye has an image of the two objects, and relative disparity could be computed as the difference in the image separations formed in the two eyes. Alternatively, each of the compared objects subtends an absolute disparity at the horopter, and relative depth could be computed from the difference in these absolute disparities. It has been argued that relative disparities for stereo-perception are computed from differences in absolute disparity rather than from comparisons of spatial offsets of the two monocular images (Westheimer & McKee, 1979). Although absolute disparity provides only a vague sense of depth, which is supplemented by oculomoter convergence (Foley, 1980) and monocular depth cues, depth could be discriminated with hyperresolution by comparing activity of two separate detectors of absolute disparity (Regan, 1982).

E. Stereo-Depth Contrast

Veridical space perception requires that the visual system does not confuse a disparity generated by object surfaces in our environment and disparities produced by errors of viewpoint caused, for example, by body sway or errors of gaze direction or eye alignment (Enright, 1990). For example, errors of cyclovergence and of gaze direction would produce disparity maps that would correspond to inclination and slant of real surfaces in space. Fortunately, the visual system is relatively insensitive to whole field disparity gradients (uniform and shear) (Gillam, Flag, & Findley, 1984; Mitchison & Westheimer, 1984, 1990; Shipley & Hyson, 1972; Stevens & Brookes, 1987, 1988; van Ee & Erkelens, 1996). This avoids confusion between real surface depth variations and surface slant distortions caused by viewpoint errors. In part, our insensitivity to whole field disparity gradients results from a global process that normalizes continuous variations of disparity (disparity gradients) so that an abrupt depth variation between a small surface within a background disparity gradient is perceived as a depth change relative to a normalized fronto-parallel background. The result is that the small object within a background composed of a disparity gradient will appear as though it were on a zero-disparity or fronto-parallel background field.

Depth contrast (Werner, 1937, 1938) is a specific class of a general category of percepts referred to as simultaneous contrast. Examples of simultaneous contrast in other visual-sensory modalities include luminance contrast (Helmholtz, 1909), induced motion such as the moon and moving cloud illusion (Duncker, 1929), color contrast (Kirschmann, 1890), tilt or orientation contrast as seen in the rod-and-frame illusion (Gibson, 1937), spatial frequency and size contrast (MacKay, 1973) and curvature contrast (Gibson, 1937). These various forms of simultaneous contrast allow a constancy of space perception in the presence of luminance and spectral changes in overall lighting, optical distortion caused by atmospheric thermals or optical aberrations of the eye, and motion caused by passive movements of the body and eyes. Figures 30 and 31 are illustrations of brightness and depth contrast illusions produced

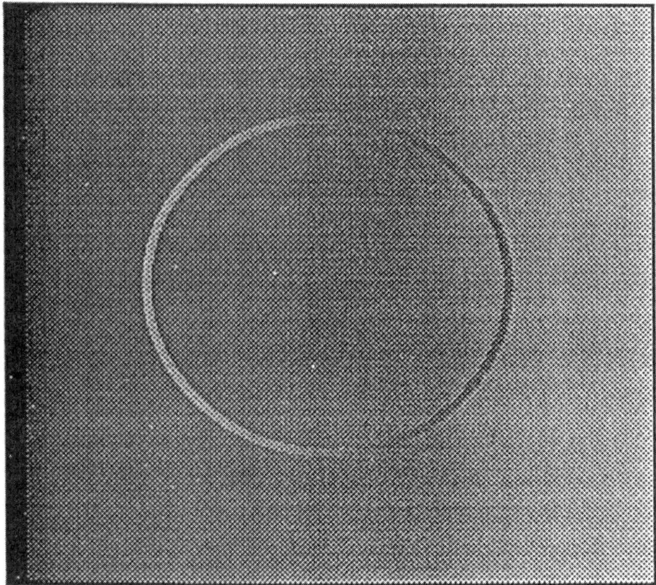

FIGURE 30 Kofka's ring and simultaneous luminance contrast. Kofka's ring is a ring of constant luminance embedded in a background of constant luminance gradient. Simultaneous luminance contrast is demonstrated by the perceived variation of the ring's brightness.

by a background gradient and a ring figure of either constant luminance (Koffka's ring) (Koffka, 1935) or zero disparity (Brookes & Stevens, 1989).

Local and global effects include simultaneous contrast between adjacent or overlapping targets, which is referred to as a local effect if the contrast results from

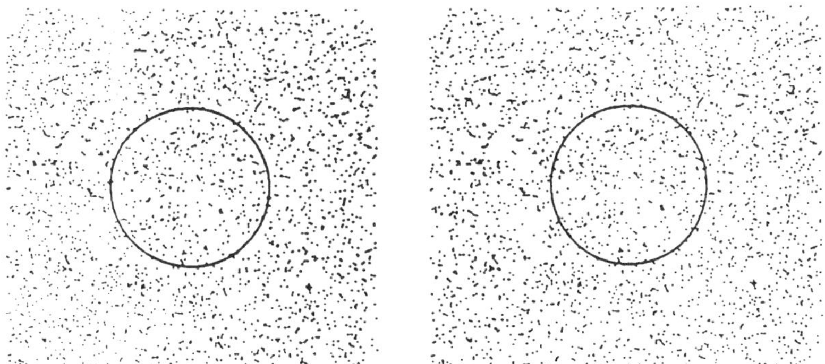

FIGURE 31 Simultaneous stereo-depth contrast. The stereo analog of Kofka's ring is a ring of constant disparity embedded in a background of constant disparity gradient. Stereo-depth contrast is demonstrated by the apparent slant of the ring. [From Brookes, A., & Stevens, K. A. (1989). The analogy between stereo depth and brightness. *Perception, 18,* 601–614, Pion, London, reprinted with permission.]

interactions between individual nearby disparities. Simultaneous depth contrast also operates globally over long ranges or large separations (Fahle & Westheimer, 1988). The global effect describes the referencing of all depth variations to the overall background disparity that has been normalized to appear as the fronto-parallel plane. The local effects are relative depth contrasts between adjacent objects or surfaces, all of which are seen with respect to the normalized background disparity. The magnitude of long-range global interactions varies with background disparity, contrast, and size (Kumar & Glaser, 1991). Local or short-range simultaneous contrast between two disparity gradients is greater when they are separated along a common slant axis (van Ee & Erkelens, 1996). These effects are enhanced by short exposure durations (10 ms) (Werner, 1937) and are dramatically reduced with several seconds of exposure (Kumar & Glaser, 1992).

F. Position and Phase Limits

As with sensory fusion, stereo-acuity depends upon spatial scale. When tested with a narrow-band luminance stimulus (1.75 octaves) such as produced by a difference of Gaussians (DOG), stereo-threshold becomes elevated when tested with spatial frequencies below 2.5 cycles/deg (Schor & Wood, 1983; Schor et al., 1984b; Smallman & MacLeod, 1994). The luminance spatial frequency dependence of stereopsis and fusion suggest that disparity is processed early in the visual system within a broad range of linear channels with band-limited tuning for luminance spatial frequency. Interocular differences in spatial frequency also influence sensitivity to binocular disparity (Schor et al., 1984b). Figure 32 illustrates that sensitivity to depth of a small patch, composed, for example, by DOG or Gabor patches with moderate bandwidths (1.75 octaves), is reduced when the patch is tilted about its vertical axis. Tilt is produced by horizontal disparities between patches of unequal size and spatial frequency. Stereo-sensitivity becomes reduced when center spatial frequencies of the patches differ by more than three octaves over a frequency range from 0.075 to 2 cpd. At higher spatial frequencies (2–19 cpd), stereoscopic depth thresholds of tilted patches remain acute over a much wider range of interocular differences in target width and corresponding spatial frequencies. The broad range of interocular differences in spatial frequency that support stereopsis suggest that disparity can also be encoded from disparities subtended by contrast features defined by the edges of the stimulus (envelope). Pattern size and location could be encoded from a nonlinear extraction of the overall contrast envelope that defines the spatial extent (overall size) of the target, independent of its luminance spatial frequency content (surface texture) (Wilcox & Hess, 1995; Schor et al., 1998; Edwards, Pope, & Schor, 1999).

Variations of fusion limits and stereo-threshold with luminance spatial frequency (Figure 10) may be related to the position and phase limits for disparity processing described previously for binocular sensory fusion. Physiologically, binocular receptive fields have two fundamental organizational properties. The receptive fields that represent binocular disparity can be offset from a point of zero retinal correspon-

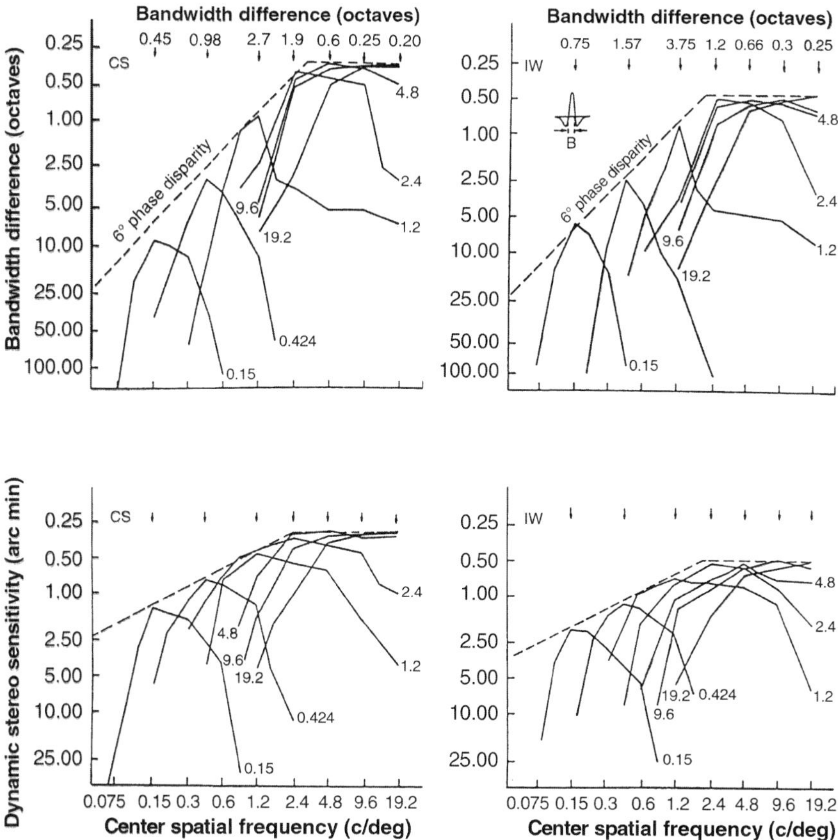

FIGURE 32 Static and dynamic stereo-spatial tuning functions. Spatial tuning functions are shown for static (top) and dynamic (bottom) stereopsis measured with seven standard width difference of Gaussian functions (DOGS), whose center spatial frequencies are indicated by the arrows along the upper edge of the figure. Bandwidths are greater for spatial functions tuned about high than low spatial frequencies. The dashed line is a maximum sensitivity envelope that describes stereo-sensitivity measure with equal width DOGS presented to the two eyes. The slopes of the sensitivity envelope differ for static and dynamic stereopsis. Numbers above arrows along the top margin of the figure quantify the increase of the spatial frequency range of tuning functions (in octaves) for dynamic compared with static stereopsis. The luminance profile of the DOG function is inset at the upper left side of the graph. (Reprinted from *Vision Research, 24,* Schor, C. M., Wood, I. C., & Ogawa, J. Spatial tuning of static and dynamic local stereopsis, pp. 573–578, Copyright © 1984, with kind permission from Elsevier Science Ltd., The Boulevard, Langford Lane, Kidlington, OX5 1GB, United Kingdom.)

dence (position disparity). They can also have zero positional disparity combined with a quadrature organization in which there is a 90° phase shift of the areas of excitation and inhibition in one eye's receptive field compared to the other (phase disparity) (Figure 24) (DeAngelis et al., 1995). The position limit at high spatial frequencies could result from positional jitter in all binocular receptive field sizes that has a minor influence on the sensitivity of large receptive fields. The same jitter is large relative to the phase-coding ability of small (high-frequency) receptive fields. The outcome is a breakdown of the size-disparity correlation at high spatial frequencies such that threshold remains constant above 2.5 cpd. Other models assume that disparity processing is based solely upon positional information in spatial channels tuned to frequencies above 2.5 cpd (Kontsevich & Tyler, 1994). In this model, elevated stereo-thresholds at low spatial frequencies (below 2.5 cpd) result from reduced effective contrast of low spatial frequencies passed by the lowest binocular spatial channel that is tuned to 2.5 cpd. The band-pass stereo tuning characteristics observed with interocular differences in low spatial frequencies (<2.5 cpd) (Schor et al., 1984b) could result from the differences in effective contrast of these stimuli and interocular inhibition (Kontsevich & Tyler, 1994).

A variety of factors influence stereo-threshold, and conditions which yield peak stereo-acuity are fairly specific. Geometrically, relative disparities, or differences in the absolute disparity subtended by two objects in depth, depends upon the distance of the targets from the eyes, but is independent of the distance of the two targets from the fixation plane (point of convergence) (Figure 33). The same pattern of relative retinal disparities remains if the eyes converge to a nearer point or diverge to a farther point of fixation. However, our stereo-sensitivity to relative disparity varies

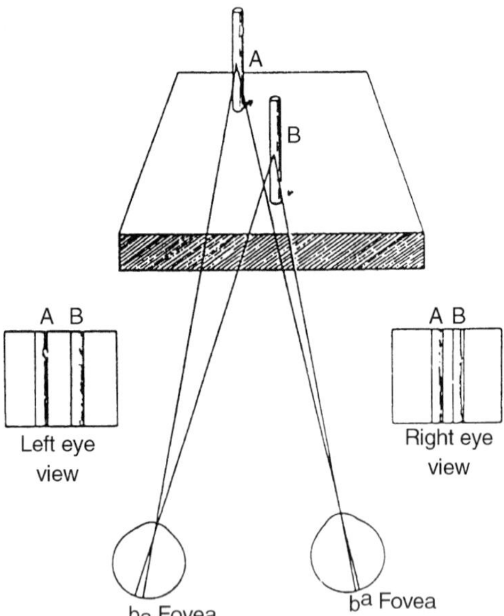

FIGURE 33 Relative disparity is independent of viewing distance. Retinal image disparity based on horizontal separation of the two eyes, target distance from the eyes, and target separation in depth. The relative disparity is independent of the convergence state of the eyes, so that it remains constant when the eyes converge proximal to or diverge distal to the targets. (From Moses, R. A., & Hart, W. M. (1987). *Adler's physiology of the eye [8th ed.]*. St. Louis, MO: Mosby-Year Book, Inc., Reprinted with permission.)

dramatically with distance of these targets from the horopter or plane of fixation. The distance of the two targets from the fixation plane is described as a depth pedestal. Depth discrimination thresholds, measured as a function of the depth pedestal, describe a depth-discrimination threshold function that is summarized by a Weber fraction (stereo-threshold/depth pedestal). The empirical measures of depth discrimination shown in Figure 34 indicate that the noise or variability of the

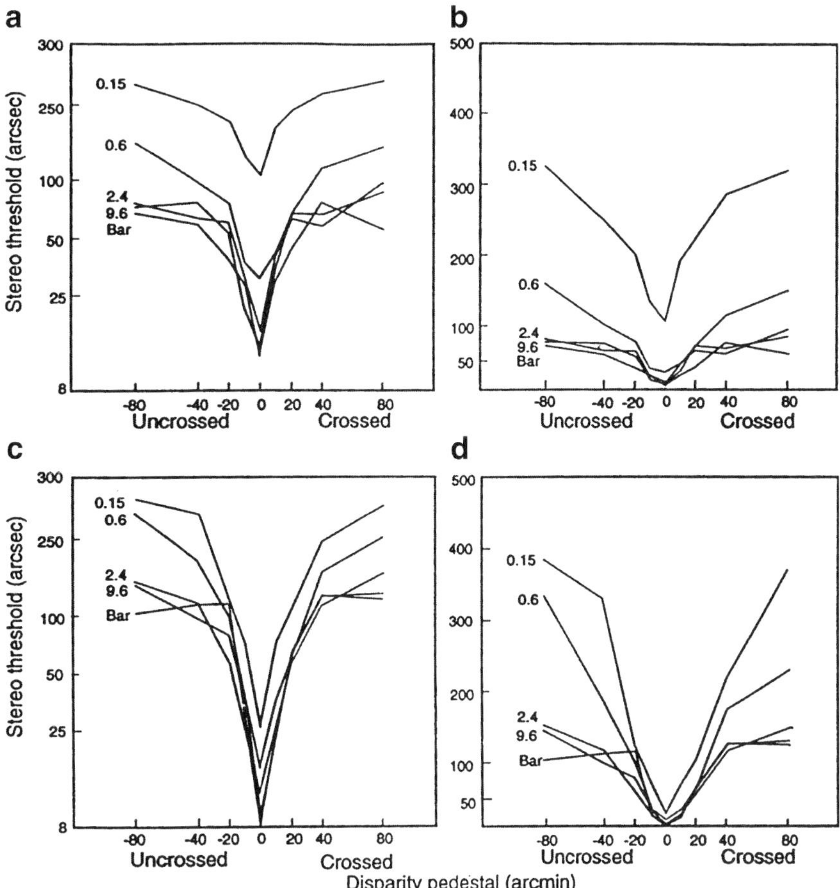

FIGURE 34 The threshold for discrimination of depth between a test stimulus and a comparison stimulus as a function of the disparity of the standard stimulus. Each curve shows the results of stimuli (DOG patches) of a specific center spatial frequency (indicated by the number by the curve). Panels A and B show the results when test and comparison stimuli were DOGs. Panels C and D are results when the comparison stimulus was a thin bright bar and the test stimulus was a DOG. Panels B and D show the same data as panels A and C, with the stereo-thresholds plotted on linear scales. Results for one subject. (From Badcock, D. R., & Schor, C. M. (1985). Depth-increment detection function for individual spatial channels. *Journal of the Optical Society of America, 2A,* 1211–1215. Reprinted with permission from the publisher and authors.)

absolute disparities subtended by the two targets is less than 5% over a range of disparity pedestals up to 0.5° (Badcock & Schor, 1985). Judgments of depth beyond this range of pedestals is clouded by the appearance of diplopia, which can be overcome by jittering the magnitude of the pedestal (Blakemore, 1970) and interleaving crossed and uncrossed disparity pedestals (Siderov & Harwerth, 1993). When these precautions are taken, the stereo-threshold grows exponentially with disparity pedestal when the targets contain high spatial frequency components (Figure 35). Stereo depth perception with the diplopic images may be due in part to depth sensed monocularly from the hemiretinal locus of the diplopic targets (Harris & McKee, 1996; Kaye, 1978). Stereo-threshold based on binocular disparity tends to level off at pedestals that exceed the singleness or fusion range. Stereo-threshold is elevated more for low than high spatial frequencies, for targets located on or off of the horopter. The similar dependence of stereo-acuity upon spatial frequency for targets located on or off the fixation plane suggests that relative disparity is processed on and off the horopter by the same range of spatial frequency channels.

G. Off-Horopter and Eccentric Depth Discrimination

The reduction of stereo-acuity with off-horopter stimuli is not the result of retinal image eccentricity produced by the pedestals. Stereo-acuity is extremely robust with

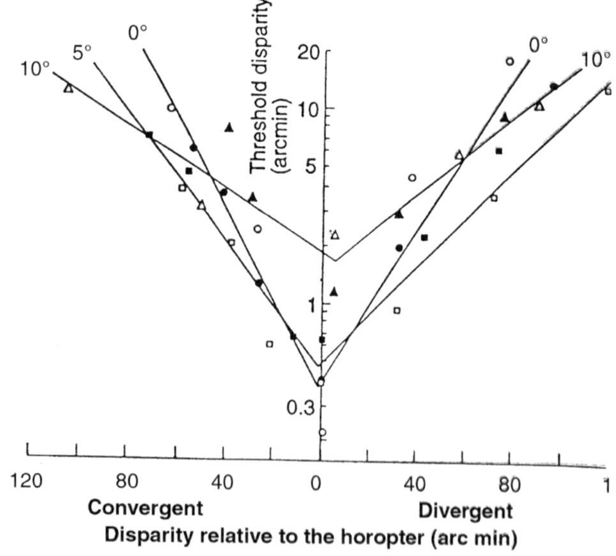

FIGURE 35 Stereo-acuity and absolute disparity. The disparity threshold for detecting relative depth between two vertical lines as a function of the absolute disparity in the image of the lines (depth pedestal). The three plots are for central placed stimuli (circles) and for stimuli at 5° (squares) and 1° (triangles) of eccentricity. Filled symbols for subject 1, closed symbols for subject 2. (From Blakemore, C., 1970. The range and scope of binocular depth discrimination in man. *Journal of Physiology, 211*, 599–622. Reprinted with permission of the author and publisher.)

retinal eccentricity along the horopter or fixation plane. Thus the stereo-threshold is lower at an eccentricity of 5° than it is with a disparity pedestal of only 80 arc min centered in the midsagittal plane (Krekling, 1974). Differences between stereo- and vernier acuity described above are highlighted when tested in the retinal periphery. Stereo-acuity remains constant with horizontal retinal eccentricities of up to 40 arc min, whereas vernier acuity rises by nearly an order of magnitude over the same range of retinal eccentricities (Schor & Badcock, 1985). Stereo-thresholds are elevated slightly with equivalent retinal eccentricities along the vertical meridian (McKee, 1983). At larger horizontal eccentricities, stereo-thresholds increase gradually up to 6° at a retinal eccentricity of 8° (Rawlings & Shipley, 1969).

H. Spatial Interactions

Stereo-sensitivity can either be enhanced or reduced by nearby targets. The threshold for detecting depth corrugations of a surface such as the folds in a hanging curtain decreases with depth-modulation frequency (reciprocal of spacing between the folds) up to 0.3 cycles per degree where it is lowest (Tyler, 1975). At depth-modulation frequencies lower than 0.3 cpd, the threshold for stereopsis is elevated and appears to be limited by a disparity gradient or minimal rate of change of depth/degree of target separation. At depth-modulation frequencies higher than 0.3 cpd, stereo-threshold is elevated as a result of depth averaging. Similar effects are seen with separations between point stimuli for depth (Westheimer & McKee, 1979; Westheimer, 1986; Westheimer & Levi, 1987).

When a few isolated targets are viewed foveally, changes in the binocular disparity of one introduces suprathreshold depth changes or biases in others when their separation is less than 4 min arc. This depth attraction illustrates a pooling of disparity signals. When targets are separated by more than 4–6 arc min, the bias is in the opposite direction, and features appear to repel one another in depth. Attraction and repulsion also occurs with cyclopean targets (Stevenson, Cormack, & Schor, 1991), showing that they are not based simply on positional effects at the monocular level. The enhancement of depth differences by repulsion might be considered a depth-contrast phenomenon that is analogous to Mach bands in the luminance domain that are thought to result form lateral inhibitory interactions. Depth distortions that are analogous to Mach bands have been demonstrated with horizontal disparity variations between vertically displaced contours (Lunn & Morgan, 1996), demonstrating analogous spatial interactions in the horizontal disparity domain and the luminance-contrast domain.

I. The Contrast Paradox

The luminance-contrast of targets also influences stereo-acuity. Cormack, Stevenson, and Schor (1991) demonstrated that both correlation thresholds and stereo-acuity were degraded as contrast was reduced below 16%. Both thresholds were proportional to the square of the contrast reduction (e.g., reducing the contrast by a factor of two caused a fourfold elevation of the thresholds). This marked reduction of disparity sensitivity results from intrinsic noise in the disparity-processing mechanism that exceeds the noise in low-contrast stimuli caused by spurious matches.

Curiously, when the contrast of the two eye's stimuli is reduced unequally, stereo-acuity is reduced more than if the contrast of both targets is reduced equally (Cormack, Stevenson, & Landers, 1997; Halpern & Blake, 1988; Legge & Gu, 1989; Lit, 1959; Rady & Ishak, 1955; Schor & Heckman, 1989). Stereo-acuity is reduced twice as much by lowering contrast in one eye than by lowering contrast in both eyes. This *contrast paradox* only occurs for stereopsis and is not observed for other disparity-based phenomenon, including correlation-detection thresholds (Cormack, Stevenson, & Landers, 1997), Panum's fusional limits (Schor & Heckman, 1989), or transient disparity-induced vergence (Schor et al., 1998). The contrast paradox occurs mainly with low spatial frequency stimuli (<2.0 cycles/degree) (Cormack et al., 1997; Halpern & Blake, 1988; Schor & Heckman, 1989). Several factors could account for this contrast tuning, including different amplitude noise sources in the two monocular signals that was uncancelled (Legge & Gu, 1989), an interocular inhibitory process (Kontsevich & Tyler, 1994; Schor & Heckman, 1989), or a temporal asynchrony between the transmission times for the two eyes signals to the visual cortex (Howard & Rogers, 1995). Contrast tuning might serve to reduce the possibility of false matches of off-horopter targets subtending large visual angles (Cormack et al., 1997).

J. Temporal Constraints

The duration and synchronization of monocular components of disparity signals greatly influence our stereo-sensitivity. Although depth in a stereogram may be perceived with just a spark of illumination (Dove, 1841), stereo-depth detection threshold decreases with exposure durations longer than 100 ms up to 3 sec with line (Langlands, 1926) and random dot (Harwerth & Rawlings, 1977) patterns. Critical duration for perceiving depth in random-dot stereograms can take several seconds in some individuals, whereas depth perception is almost immediate with line stereograms for the same individuals. The prolonged exposures needed for random-dot stereograms can be shortened by presenting monocular cues that guide vergence eye alignment to the depth plane of the stereogram (Kidd, Frisby, & Mayhew, 1979). This suggests that the extra time needed for perception of depth in the RDS results from the inability of the binocular system to resolve ambiguous matches for disparities exceeding 1° (Stevenson, Cormack, & Schor, 1994). In effect, vergence must search blindly until the disparity of the correct match is reduced to <1°, within the operating range of the binocular cross-correlation process.

Depending upon the luminance spatial frequency of a target, stereo-threshold also varies with target velocity. Stereosensitivity for dynamic or moving targets is greater than with static targets composed of low spatial frequencies (Schor et al.,

1984b; Morgan & Castet, 1995). Comparison of stereo-thresholds in Figure 32 illustrates that stereo-thresholds for target spatial frequencies lower than 2.4 cycles/deg were five times more sensitive with dynamic than static targets, whereas the thresholds were very similar for static and dynamic stimuli at higher spatial frequencies (Schor et al., 1984b). Sensitivity to dynamic depth is limited in part to sensitivity to interocular time delays. Sensing the depth of moving targets requires both spatial and temporal tuning. A nonzero binocular disparity stimulated by a target that is moving at a constant velocity parallel to the horopter is equivalent to a zero disparity of a target moving along the horopter, with a time delay to corresponding retinal points. The more sensitive the temporal resolution of a binocular neuron the better is its sensitivity to binocular disparity or interocular spatial phase shifts of the two ocular images. The minimum detectable spatial phase difference between the eyes for dynamic targets is about 5° and an interocular temporal delay as small as 450 μs (Morgan & Castet, 1995). These results suggest that stereopsis for moving targets is accomplished by neurons having a spatial-temporal phase shift in their receptive fields between the eyes.

Stereo-acuity is optimal with simultaneous presentation of both eyes' stimuli. It remains high with interocular delays shorter than 25 ms (Ogle, 1964) or as long as visual persistence allows some overlap of the two monocular stimuli (Engel, 1970). Optimal stereo-acuity with thresholds of 3 arc sec also requires simultaneous presentation of at least two targets that define the stereo-depth interval. When foveally viewed targets of different depth are presented sequentially, with no time gap between them, stereo-threshold can be elevated by an order of magnitude (22–52 arc sec) (Westheimer, 1979). When time gaps are introduced between the two successive views that exceed 100 ms, the stereo-threshold increases dramatically to 0.5°, presumably because of noise in the vergence system and a loss of memory of the vergence position of the first stimulus (Foley, 1976). Interestingly, sequential stereopsis is approximately the same for wide spatial separations (10°) between sequentially foveally fixated targets and narrow ones (Enright, 1991; Wright, 1951). This is surprising because the wide separation target requires saccades between the first and second target, and these introduce a small time interval between the two targets equal to the duration of the saccade (approximately 50 ms). One would also expect that vergence errors introduced by saccades would introduce a noise source that would elevate the sequential stereo-threshold. Enright reports that eye movements are also unstable with sequential stereo-measures between adjacent stimuli and perhaps they are as variable as the disconjugacy of large saccades to widely spaced stimuli. It is also clear that eye movements are not entirely responsible for the reduction of sequential stereo-acuity (Enright, 1991) and that perhaps temporal masking may contribute to the elevated sequential-stereo threshold. The small interval during the saccade between sequential stimuli might diminish the temporal masking between widely separated sequential stimuli compared to that associated with no time delay between adjacent sequential stimuli.

K. Upper Disparity Limit for Stereopsis

The upper disparity limit (UDL) for stereopsis describes the maximum disparity at which a particular target can be perceived with stereo-depth. As with the lower disparity limit or stereo-acuity, the upper limit is criterion dependent. It can describe the upper limit for the quantative perception of depth that is typical of sustained stimuli or the more vague qualitative seen with large-diplopic transient images (Ogle, 1952). The UDL also varies with several stimulus parameters, including exposure duration (Blakemore, 1970; Ogle, 1952; Richards & Foley, 1971; Westheimer & Tanzman, 1956), spatial frequency and size of the stimulus (Hess & Wilcox, 1994; Schor & Wood, 1983; Schor et al., 1984a), and spacing between depth targets (Schor, Bridgeman, & Tyler, 1983; Tyler, 1975).

As described in the prior section, sustained stereo-depth is optimal with long viewing durations. When measured with broad-band stimuli, the UDL for quantitative stereo ranges from 30–50 arc min (Schor & Wood, 1983; Schor et al., 1984a). However, when measured with narrow-band stimuli that present a limited range of spatial frequencies (e.g., 1.75 octaves) the UDL for quantitative stereopsis increases with the spatial period of the stimulus when a fixed number of cycles of the pattern are used (Schor & Wood, 1983; Schor et al., 1984a). The UDL ranges from 0.5 to 4° as spatial frequency is reduced from 2 cpd to 0.1 cpd. If, however, the size or envelope of the stimulus patch is varied independently of the number of cycles it contains, the upper disparity limit for sustained stereopsis varies primarily with stimulus size (envelope) and not stimulus spatial frequency content (Wilcox & Hess, 1995). This result suggests possible nonlinear operations that could determine the UDL, such as contrast coding prior to the derivation of the binocular disparity. Rectification or any power function would transform a narrow-band limited stimulus into a low-pass broad-band stimulus, such that stereopsis could be derived between dichoptic stimuli composed of different textures or spatial frequencies (Schor et al., 1998).

The UDL of the sustained stereo-system also varies with target separation. The UDL increases linearly with the vertical separation of targets whose depth is discriminated (Tyler, 1973). This is similar to the upper disparity gradient limit for Panums' fusional area (Burt & Julesz, 1980). The dependence of UDL on target separation undoubtedly serves the same function for stereo and fusion, which is to reduce the likelihood of false matches that are often associated with abrupt changes in disparity between nearby features.

L. Sustained and Transient Stereopsis

Stereoscopic-depth perception appears to be mediated by at least two mechanisms that differ in terms of their temporal (Pope et al., 1999a) and spatial disparity tuning (Schor et al., 1998) as well as their operating range of disparity processing (Cormack & Landers, 1999). The transient system processes diplopic images of briefly presented stimuli. For example, when the UDL is measured with transient or brief stimuli with durations of less than 0.5 sec, the UDL for stereoscopic depth reaches magnitudes of more than 10° of disparity (Blakemore, 1970; Richards & Foley, 1971; Westheimer & Tanzman, 1956). Perceived depth increases quantitatively with transient disparity magnitude up to 4° (Richards & Kaye, 1974), but it becomes vague or qualitative with larger disparities (Ogle, 1952). When large disparities remain visible for longer periods of time (>0.5 sec), the depth perceived by the sustained system fades (Landers & Cormack, 1999). The responses to transient disparity stimuli frequently have large biases, such that depth sensitivity is greater for crossed or uncrossed disparities (Richards, 1971). Depth can be evoked from the transient system with dichoptic stimuli that have different orientations (Edwards, Pope, & Schor, 1999), spatial frequencies (Schor, Edwards, & Pope, 1998), and opposite contrast polarities (Pope, Edwards, & Schor, 1999a). The lower limits for the disparity range of transient and sustained stereo partially overlap one another. Tests of transient stereopsis with opposite contrast (Pope et al., 1999a) and orthogonal stimuli (Edwards, Pope, & Schor, 1999) reveal that both systems yield depth for disparities lying within Panum's fusional area. The transient system has been described by Ogle (1964) as qualitative or latent and by Julesz (1978) as local or coarse stereopsis.

The sustained system mainly processes stimuli that appear fused (the disparities lie within Panum's area). The magnitude of perceived depth increases quantitatively with disparity magnitude, and the depth percept improves with exposure durations up to 1 sec (Harwerth & Rawlings, 1977). Depth can only be evoked from this system with dichoptic targets that have very similar orientations, spatial frequency, and contrast polarity. This system or systems have been described by Ogle (1964) as quantitative or patent and by Julesz (1978) as global or fine stereopsis.

The transient stereo system can be isolated behaviorally by measuring stereoperformance with opposite contrast stimuli (Pope et al., 1999a). Ability to perceive depth from opposite-contrast stereograms depends upon the temporal-frequency content of a stimulus. Stereo-depth can be perceived with opposite-contrast stimuli presented in a low-contrast long-duration (4 sec) temporal-pulse stimulus, but not a low-contrast long-duration temporal-raised cosine stimulus. However, transient stereo is possible if the luminance contrast of the long-duration temporal-cosine stimulus is very high. Stereo performance with reversed contrast stimuli improves as the duration of the raised cosine stimulus is reduced to 200 ms. Reduced duration increases the high temporal frequency content of the short-duration stimulus and increased contrast raises the energy of its high temporal frequency components of the long-duration stimulus. Clearly it is the visibility of high temporal-frequency content rather than the stimulus duration that is the defining difference between stimuli for qualitative and quantitative stereopsis as defined by Ogle (1952). Given this distinction, stereopsis can be classified according to the transient and sustained nature of effective disparity stimuli.

Transient stereopsis does not appear to have the high degree of spatial selectivity that is renown for sustained stereopsis. Large differences in shape or orientation between dichoptic stimuli can be tolerated by the transient stereo system (Mitchell,

1970) and transient vergence eye movements can be initiated by these shape-disparate stimuli (Jones & Kerr, 1972). The transient stereo system does, however, have a limited degree of spatial selectivity. When tested with dichoptic matched spatial frequencies, presented briefly (140 ms) as carrier in narrow-band Gabor patches, transient stereo responds to large 6° disparities. The visibility of the stereo-depth decreases as spatial frequency is increased from 0.5 cpd to 5 cpd, and the response is markedly attenuated with small (half-octave) interocular differences in spatial frequency (Schor et al., 1998). Binocularly pairing a low and a high spatial frequency results in a performance level that is lower than that obtained with paired high frequencies.

When different spatial frequencies are dichoptically paired (using Gabor patches), performance for transient stereopsis is improved when the stimulus strength is matched by reducing contrast of the lower spatial frequency. For example, stereo responses to a 6° transient disparity between 1 and 5 cpd Gabor patches improves when the contrast of a 1 cpd Gabor is reduced to 40%, while the contrast of the 5 cpd Gabor remains at 100% (Schor et al., 1998). These results suggest that disparity detectors for transient stereopsis have broad spatial frequency tuning that could be described as a low-pass filter. The contrast tuning of the stereo system reduces performance when the two ocular images have dissimilar stimulus strength or energy (contrast paradox) (Kontsevich & Tyler, 1994; Schor et al., 1998).

The spatial tuning of the transient system depends on the orientation of the dichoptic stimulus features (Edwards et al., 1999). When dichoptic stimuli have a parallel orientation, transient stereo has a low-pass response (i.e., it is possible to binocularly match a high and low frequency by lowering the contrast of the low frequency). When the dichoptic stimulus features are orthogonal, transient stereo has a multiple band-pass response (i.e., it is possible binocularly to match a high and low frequency by lowering the contrast of either the high or low frequency image). Current linear matching models that compute binocular disparities cannot account for the broad spatial tuning of the transient stereo system. However second-order nonlinear mechanisms that extract low frequency pattern contrast variations from the envelope (e.g., with a full-wave rectification) could combine dissimilar pattern stimuli to form binocular disparities (Wilcox & Hess, 1995; Schor et al., 1998).

The broad spatial frequency and orientation tuning for the transient stereo system results in a matching ambiguity with complex textured surfaces. The problem is which surface points should be matched without guidance from size, orientation, and contrast polarity? Accordingly, the ability to perform transient stereo tasks decreases as the number of texture surface elements increases when the texture elements have opposite contrast (Cogan, Lomakin, & Rossi, 1993) or different spatial frequencies in the two eyes (Ziegler & Hess, 1999). The problem of surface perception is exacerbated by a strong crowding effect, in which proximity of different amplitude transient disparities makes it difficult to perceive disparity-defined shapes or curvature of textured surfaces.

The sustained and transient components of stereopsis function as focused attention and surveillance mechanisms, respectively. Sustained stereo is used to interpret the depth and shape of targets near the horopter in the vicinity of the point of convergence. Transient stereo is a preattentive process that is used to roughly localize the sudden appearance or depth changes of targets that lie away from the point of fixation. The transient stereo system has an early nonlinearity that allows it to respond to both first-order (luminance stimuli) and second-order (contrast and texture stimuli), whereas the sustained stereo system is primarily responsive to first-order (luminance) stimuli. The transient nonlinearity is described mathematically as a full or half-wave rectification. The transient and sustained stereo systems process disparity in a coarse-to-fine sequence. The transient system serves to match coarse features, such as object boundaries, defined by either first- or second-order information. The operating range of the transient system includes small disparities within Panum's fusion limit, where it guides or constrains subsequent matches of finer first-order detail by the sustained stereo system. Transient stereo also matches larger disparities to stimulate transient vergence that initiates binocular alignment, and it also provides a preattentive sense of depth that is used to avoid obstacles subtending large disparities during locomotion.

M. Transient Vergence

Although the classification of transient stereopsis is new, a transient disparity vergence has been recognized for some time (Jones & Kerr, 1972). This transient process initiates vergence eye movements that are completed by sustained fusional vergence. To what degree do transient stereopsis and transient vergence share the same input or disparity stimulus? Like the transient stereo system, transient vergence is broadly tuned to spatial frequency, orientation, and contrast polarity (transient vergence responds to opposite polarity stimuli) (Edwards et al., 1998; Pope, Edwards, & Schor, 1999b). Unlike the transient stereo system, lowering the spatial frequency of either eye's stimulus facilitates transient vergence, and mixed low and high contrasts produce the same result as when contrasts are matched at the high level. Thus the main distinction between the transient stereopsis and transient vergence is that the performance of transient vergence is not reduced by dichoptic mixed contrasts (no contrast paradox or contrast tuning). These observations suggest that there is a single broad-band spatial channel that encodes disparity for initiating vergence eye movements and that vergence is not affected by a contrast paradox (Edwards et al., 1998). The low-pass channel could result from a nonlinear extraction of the envelope as a result of cortical image rectification.

VI. OCCLUSION STEREOPSIS

Prior to Wheatstone's hallmark publication in 1838, depth perception was thought to be based on monocular vision. Euclid (300 B.C.), Galen (175 A.D.), and Leonardo

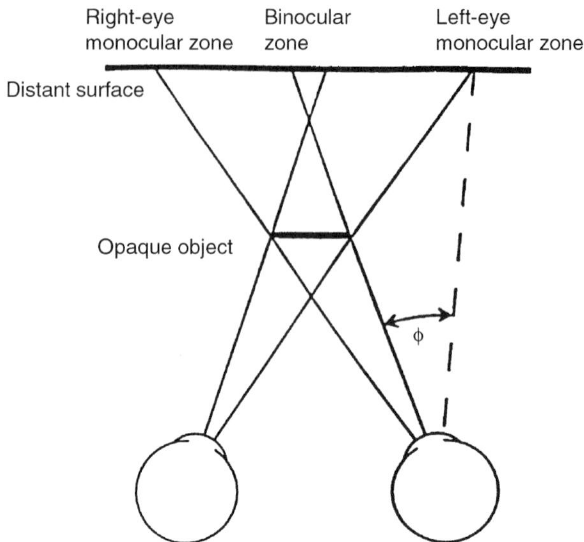

FIGURE 36 Occlusion geometry. When the occluding object is shorter than the interocular distance, both eyes see some or all of the region between the occlusion zones.

da Vinci (1452) all noted that monocular information resulting from partial occlusion of the visual field could be used as a strong depth cue. Each eye has a unique view of the background on the temporal side of an occluder, and these monocular views provide depth information (Figure 36). Usually, these monocular zones are regarded as problematic for solving the correspondence problem, however they provide a useful source of information for the extraction of depth and direction (Anderson & Nakayama, 1994). Matching the two eye's images requires judgments about what images are seen monocularly and binocularly. Most matching theories attempt to explain how the binocular images are matched, and the monocular images are considered as a secondary problem. However, recent results show that the monocular images result in depth percepts similar to those produced by binocular disparity cues to stereopsis (Shimojo & Nakayama, 1990, 1992; Liu, Stevenson, & Schor, 1994b; Anderson, 1994) (Figure 37). Thus the matching process needs to segregate monocular and binocular images to utilize these two different sources of depth information.

A. Discriminating between Monocular and Binocular Features

Computationally, occlusion geometry is consistent with an abrupt depth discontinuity (Gillam & Borsting, 1988). Monocular features could be identified by searching in the vicinity of either depth discontinuities or steep disparity gradients between binocular images. Conversely, depth discontinuities could be searched for

FIGURE 37 Convergent fusion of the six stereograms creates the display at the bottom, in which a white rectangle appears to stand out when cross-fused. The depth and nonius offset increase down the set. (From BINOCULAR VISION AND STEREOPSIS by Ian P. Howard and Brian J. Rogers. Copyright © 1995 by Oxford University Press, Inc. Used by permission of Oxford University Press, Inc. and the authors. Adapted from Liu, Stevenson, & Schor [1994b].)

in regions containing monocular images. The monocular region of the partially occluded background would be surrounded by binocular regions of the occluder and background, and two adjacent left–right eye monocular regions would never occur in natural viewing (Geiger, Landendorf, & Yuille, 1995). In addition, a partially occluded region would always be seen on the temporalward side of the binocularly viewed occluding surface (Shimojo & Nakayama, 1990).

B. Occlusion Geometry

The visual system is very adept at discriminating between monocular regions that meet and violate these geometric constraints. For example, Figure 38 illustrates a

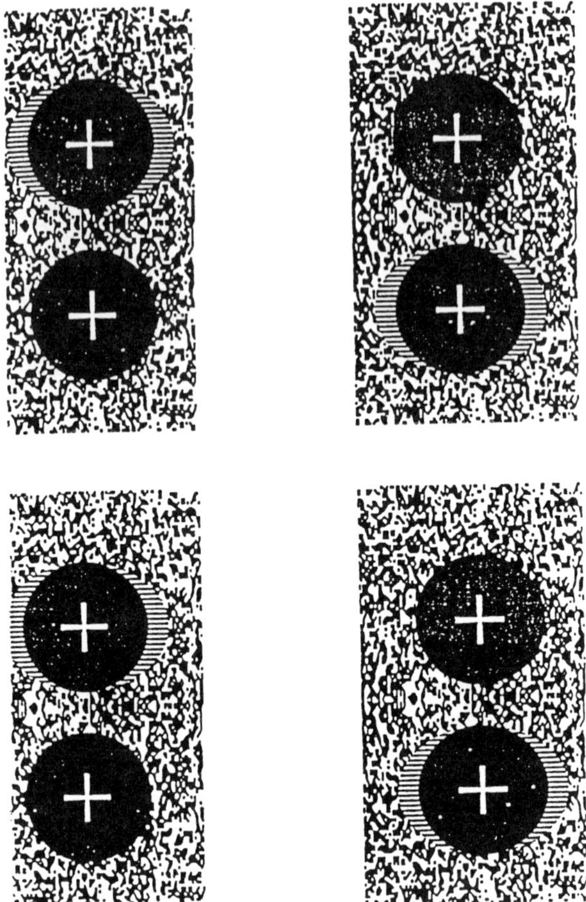

FIGURE 38 Normal and anomalous occlusion zones. When the fused image is seen as a black disc in front of the background, the occlusion zone on the appropriate (temporal) side is suppressed, whereas that on the inappropriate (nasal) side remains visible. When the fused image is seen as a disc beyond the background, both occlusion zones are inappropriate, and both are visible. (Reprinted from *Vision Research, 30,* Shimojo, S., & Nakayama, K. Real world occlusion constraints and binocular rivalry, pp. 69–80, Copyright © 1990, with kind permission from Elsevier Science Ltd., The Boulevard, Langford Lane, Kidlington, OX5 1GB, United Kingdom, and the authors.

display that presents a binocularly viewed occluding disk whose image in one eye is surrounded on the left and right by monocular regions that are either geometric-valid or geometric-invalid occluders. Valid monocular regions are seen on the temporal side of the occluder, and invalid monocular regions are seen on the nasal side of the occluder. When the stereogram is fused, a stable background is seen in the geometric-valid temporal-monocular region, and rivalry occurs between the background and geometric-invalid nasal-monocular region.

C. Depth Ambiguity

Just as retinal image disparity provides insufficient information to make quantitative judgments of distance, shape, and orientation of surfaces, the monocular image provides incomplete or ambiguous information regarding the depth-magnitude of targets in space. This problem is similar to the correspondence problem presented by Marr and Poggio (1979). The monocular image could be of a target lying at many possible depths and directions in space. Although the depth magnitude is ambiguous, it is not unlimited. It is bounded by the line of sight of the occluded eye, and depth of the monocular image appears to lie at this boundary (Nakayama & Shimojo, 1990). Other depth solutions could be reached with other constraining factors, including proximity to other targets in the visual field (adjacency principle) (Gogel, 1965; Hakkinen & Nyman, 1996), vergence and version state of the eyes (Hering, 1861; Howard & Ohmi, 1992; Howard & Rogers, 1995), monocular cues to perceived distance (Helmholtz, 1909), sharpness or focus of the occluder and background texture and their boundary (Marshall, Burbeck, Ariely, Rolland, & Martin, 1996), and the hemi-retinal location of the image (Harris & McKee, 1996; Hering, 1861; Kaye, 1978). Figure 37 is a unique demonstration of quantitative variations of depth resulting from occlusion cues because it lacks a reference binocular disparity of both the occluder and the background, and it also lacks any of the above-mentioned constraints. It is possible that binocular disparities of the foreground and background are derived from matches between dissimilar shapes seen by the two eyes that share a subset of common features (Liu, Stevenson, & Schor, 1997). However, if conventional positional disparity detectors are responsible for extracting depth in partially occluded scenes, then this kind of stimulus should be equally efficient in driving vergence eye movements in both horizontal and vertical directions because both horizontal and vertical vergence show robust tracking responses to conventional positional disparities. When vergence responses were compared between conventional disparities and horizontal and vertical occlusion cues, Liu et al. (1998) found that vertical occlusion failed to drive vertical vergence, whereas horizontal occlusion did drive horizontal vergence. These results indicate that depth-from-occlusion, or Da Vinci stereopsis (Nakayama & Shimojo, 1990) may play an important role in depth perception without corresponding binocular features.

VII. BINOCULAR SUPPRESSION

In a complex 3-D scene, binocular information can be described in three categories. Some information is coherent, such as images formed within Panum's fusional areas. Some information is fragmented, such as partially occluded regions of space resulting in visibility to only one eye. Finally, some information is uncorrelated, because it is either ambiguous or in conflict with other information, such as the superimposition of separate diplopic images arising from objects seen by both eyes behind or in front of the plane of fixation. One objective of the visual system is to preserve as much information from all three sources as possible to make inferences about objective space without introducing ambiguity or confusion of space perception. In some circumstances, conflicts between the two eyes are so great that conflicting percepts are seen alternatively, or in some cases, one image is permanently suppressed. For example, the two ocular images may have unequal clarity or blur, such as in asymmetric convergence, or large unfusable disparities originating from targets behind or in front of the fixation plane may appear overlapped with other large diplopic images. In the latter case the matching problem is exacerbated, particularly for transient stereopsis and vergence, which do not have selective feature specificity (Edwards, Pope, & Schor, 1998; Schor, Edwards, & Pope, 1998). The former case is dispensed with by permanent suppression of the blurred image, whereas the latter condition is resolved with alternating views of unfusable targets. As demonstrated in Figure 38, occlusion geometry may constrain the solution to one of these two outcomes.

Four classes of stimuli evoke what appear to be different interocular suppression mechanisms. The first is unequal contrast or blur of the two retinal images, which causes interocular blur suppression. The second is physiologically diplopic images of targets in front of or behind the singleness horopter, which result in suspension of one of the redundant images (Cline, Hofstetter, & Griffin, 1989). The third is targets of different shape presented in identical visual directions. Different size and shape result in an alternating appearance of the two images referred to as either binocular retinal rivalry or percept rivalry suppression. The fourth is partial occluders that obstruct the view of one eye, such that the portions of the background are only seen by the unoccluded eye, and the overlapping region of the occluder that is imaged in the other eye is permanently suppressed.

A. Interocular Blur Suppression

There are a wide variety of natural conditions that present the eyes with unequal image contrast. These include naturally occurring anisometropia, unequal amplitudes of accommodation, and asymmetric convergence on targets that are closer to one eye than the other. This blur can be eliminated in part by a limited degree of differential accommodation of the two eyes (Marran & Schor, 1998) and by interocular suppression of the blur. The latter mechanism is particularly helpful for a type of contact lens patient who can no longer accommodate (presbyopes) and prefer to wear a near contact lens correction over one eye and a far correction over the other (Monovision) rather than wearing bifocal spectacles. For most people, all of these conditions result in clear, nonblurred, binocular percepts with a retention of stereopsis (Schor, Landsman, & Erickson, 1987), albeit with the stereo-threshold elevated by approximately a factor of two (see section above on unequal contrast and stereo-acuity). Interocular blur suppression is reduced for high-contrast targets composed of high spatial frequencies (Schor et al., 1987). There is an interaction between interocular blur suppression and binocular rivalry suppression. Measures of binocular rivalry reveal a form of eye dominance defined as the eye that is suppressed least when viewing dichoptic forms of different shape. When the dominant eye for rivalry and aiming or sighting is the same, interocular blur suppression is more effective than when there is crossed sighting and rivalry dominance (Collins & Goode, 1994).

B. Suspension

Although binocular alignment of the eyes provides us with the opportunity to derive depth information from binocular disparities near the horopter, it has the disadvantage of producing large disparities for objects far in front and behind the plane of fixation. These disparities contribute weakly to sustained depth perception, and they introduce errors in perceived direction. Even though these disparities are well beyond the limits of Panum's fusional areas, they rarely evoke the perception of diplopia under normal casual viewing conditions; however, their suppression is not obligatory, and physiological diplopia can be evoked by calling attention to the disparate target. The suppression of physiological diplopia is referred to as suspension (Cline, Hofstetter, & Griffin, 1989) because this form of suppression does not alternate between the two images. Instead, only one image is continually suppressed, favoring visibility of the target imaged on the nasal hemi-retina (Crovitz & Lipscomb, 1963; Fahle, 1987; Kollner, 1914). This mechanism may be involved in the permanent suppression of pathological diplopia in the deviating eye of individuals with strabismus (Fahle, 1987; Harrad, 1996; Schor, 1977, 1978).

C. Binocular Retinal Rivalry

Binocular rivalry is stimulated by nonfusable or uncorrelated ocular images that are formed in the vicinity of corresponding retinal regions, such that they appear in identical visual directions. For example, when fusing two orthogonal gratings shown in Figure 39, rivalry suppression takes on several forms. At times only one set of

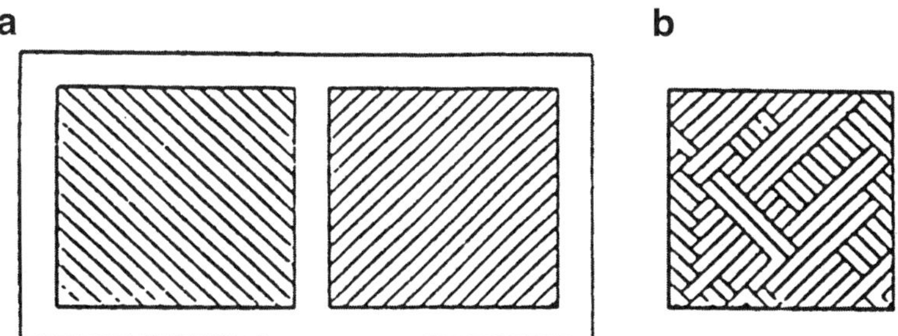

FIGURE 39 Binocular rivalry. (a) represents a rivalry stimulus composed of orthogonal grids to be seen by the left and right eye, and (b) illustrates the piece-wise rivalry percept.

FIGURE 40 The Helmholtz cross. The left and central figure represent lines viewed by the left and right eye, and the right figure illustrates the rivalry percept of the suppression halo at the point of intersection of the dichoptically viewed horizontal and vertical bars. (From BINOCULAR VISION AND STEREOPSIS by Ian P. Howard and Brian J. Rogers. Copyright © 1995 by Oxford University Press, Inc. Used by permission of Oxford University Press, Inc., and the authors.)

lines is seen, and after several seconds the image of the other set of lines appears to wash over the first. At other times the two monocular images become fragmented into small interwoven retinal patches from each eye that alternate independently of one another. In the latter case, suppression is regional and localized to the vicinity of the contour intersections. The spread of suppression is demonstrated by the Helmholtz cross figure, which when fused produces a halo percept about the points of intersection of the vertical and horizontal line (Figure 40). Following a technique developed by Kaufman (1963), Liu and Schor (1994) presented two band-pass spatially filtered lines with the same orientation to one eye and a single orthogonal line with the same spatial filtering to the other eye. The separation of the two

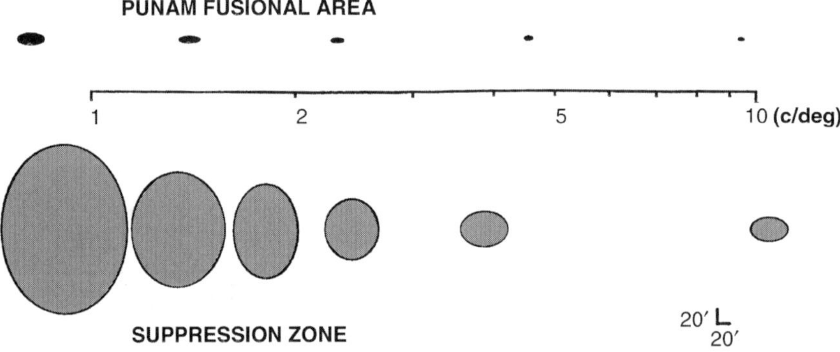

FIGURE 41 Comparison of Panum's fusional area and binocular suppression zones. Black ellipses above the spatial frequency scale were taken from Schor et al. (1984a). Gray ellipses below represent the horizontal and vertical extent of rivalry suppression measured as a function of the central spatial frequency of narrow-band filtered bars in the Helmholtz-cross configuration. Clearly the suppression zones are an order of magnitude larger than the range of binocular sensory fusion. (Reprinted from *Vision Research, 34,* Liu, L., & Schor, C. M. The spatial properties of binocular suppression zone, pp. 937–947, Copyright © 1994, with kind permission from Elsevier Science Ltd., The Boulevard, Langford Lane, Kidlington, OX5 1GB, United Kingdom, and the authors.)

parallel lines was increased to measure the largest gap that would totally suppress the overlapped region of the single line. Both the vertical and horizontal extents of the suppression zone increase with the spatial period or size of the lines, and the resulting suppression areas shown in Figure 41 were much greater than Panum's fusional area measured with the same targets. The difference in size of rival zones and Panum's area suggests that fusion is not likely to result from alternate suppression of the two ocular images, as proposed by Verhoeff (1935) and others. The zone of rivalry also increases with image contrast up to about 30%. As image contrast is lowered to near threshold values, rivalry ceases and there is complete summation of the two ocular images (Figure 42) (Liu, Tyler, & Schor, 1992).

The rivalrous patches alternate between the two ocular images approximately once every 4 sec. The rate of oscillation and its duty cycle vary with the degree of difference between the two ocular images and the stimulus strength. The rate of rivalry increases as the orientation difference increases beyond 22° between the targets (Fahle, 1982; Schor, 1977), indicating that rivalry is not likely to occur within the tuned range for cortical orientation columns. Levelt (1968) has formulated a series of rules describing how the on-and-off phases of rivalry vary with stimulus strength variables such as brightness, contrast, and motion. His basic observation is that the duration that a stimulus is suppressed decreases as its visibility or strength increases. If the strength of both-eyes stimuli is increased, the off-time is decreased

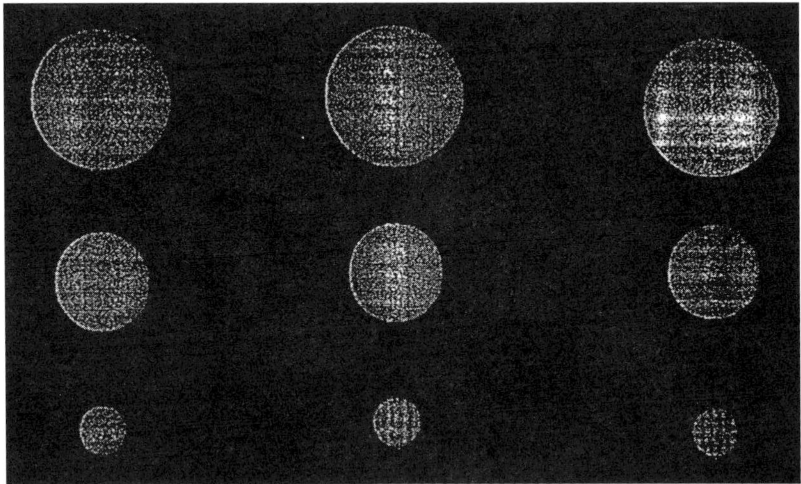

FIGURE 42 Dichoptic superimposition of low-contrast edges. Fusion of the images in the two left-hand columns results in superimposition of orthogonal edges. At high contrast these edges rival but at low contrast they appear superimposed for several seconds and create the impression of plaids, as depicted in the right-hand column. (Reprinted from *Vision Research, 32,* Liu, L., Tyler, C. W., & Schor, C. M. Failure of rivalry at low contrast: Evidence of a suprathreshold binocular summation process, pp. 1471–1479, Copyright © 1992, with kind permission from Elsevier Science Ltd., The Boulevard, Langford Lane, Kidlington, OX5 1GB, United Kingdom, and the authors.)

for both eyes, and the rate of rivalry increases. For example, reducing contrast of both-eyes stimuli reduces the rate of rivalry. Interestingly, rivalry ceases at very low contrast levels, and there is a binocular summation of nonfusable targets (Liu, Tyler, & Schor, 1992). Rivalry has a latency of approximately 200 ms so that briefly presented nonfusable patterns appear superimposed (Hering, 1920); however, rivalry occurs between dichoptic patterns that are alternated rapidly at 7 Hz or faster, indicating an integration time for at least 150 ms (Wolfe, 1983).

When rivalrous and fusable stimuli are presented simultaneously, fusion takes precedence over rivalry (Blake & Boothroyd, 1985), and the onset of a fusable target can terminate suppression, although the fusion mechanism takes time (150–200 ms) to become fully operational (Wolfe, 1986; Harrad, McKee, & Yang, 1994). Suppression and stereo-fusion appear to be mutually exclusive outcomes of binocular stimuli presented in a given retinal location (Timney, Wilcox, & St. John, 1989; Blake & O'Shea, 1988). However, it is possible to perceive them simultaneously when their respective stimuli are presented in different spatial frequency bands (Julesz & Miller, 1975), with different shaped targets (Figure 43) (Ogle & Wakefield, 1967; Wolfe, 1986) or with unequal contrast produced by monocular blur (Schor et al., 1987).

D. Binocular Percept Rivalry

Most theories model binocular rivalry as a competition between monocular images (see review by Fox, 1991). It is not clear, however, if it is the retinal images or the ocular percepts that rival. As described above, in conventional rivalry between orthogonal grids, such as shown in Figure 40, rivalrous images can appear as coherent alternations of each eye's view or mixed complementary fragments of the two images. Both of these percepts may occur in response to a natural condition in which images of objects that lie in separate directions appear in the same visual

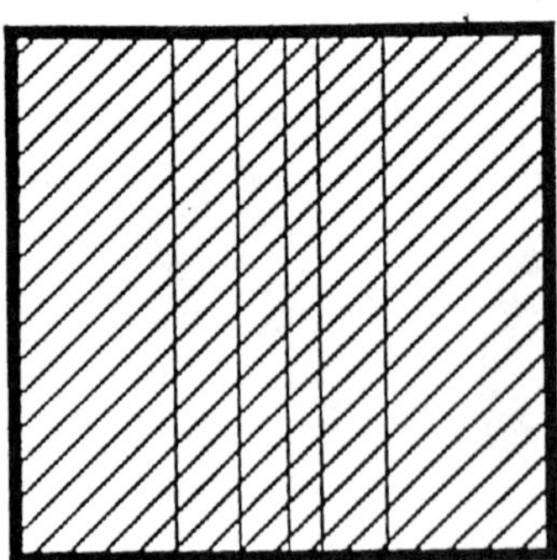

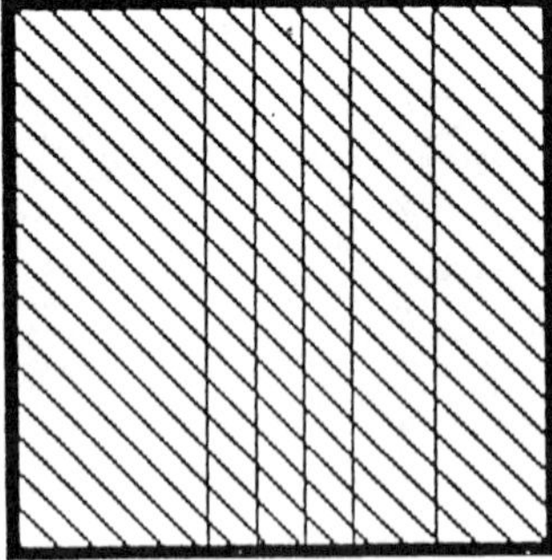

FIGURE 43 Stereopsis with rivalry. Depth is apparent in the nonrivalrous vertical lines superimposed on the background of rivalrous lines. (Reprinted from *Vision Research,* 7, Ogle, K. N., & Wakefield, J. M. Stereoscopic depth and binocular rivalry, pp. 89–98, Copyright © 1967, with kind permission from Elsevier Science Ltd., The Boulevard, Langford Lane, Kidlington, OX5 1GB, United Kingdom.)

direction, such as occurs when viewing extended objects lying behind the fixation plane. Under these conditions, the overlap of the disparate image components presents a conflict or "confusion" to the visual system that is solved by taking sequential-rivalrous views of the two images that appear in the same visual direction. When each eye's image can be perceived as a separate coherent form, the full ocular images can alternate or rival (Levelt, 1968; Walker, 1978). When the monocular images appear fragmented, they can rival as a piecemeal alternation between the fragments. Factors that determine image coherency versus fragmentation include contour continuity, orientation, texture, color, and depth (Nakayama, Shimojo, & Silverman, 1989; Treisman & Gelade, 1980; Crick, 1984). Thus depending on the composition of the two ocular images, it is possible for either whole images or fragmented images to rival.

The rivalry could either be guided by eye-of-origin information or by perceptual grouped attributes. These two factors can be uncorrelated by presenting a complementary interocular mixture or patchwork of two coherent images to the two eyes (Le Grand, 1967; Kovacs, Papathomas, Yang, & Feher, 1997). Free fusion of the two half-images in Figure 44 illustrates the same rivalry percept in the conventional stimulus at the top and mixed half-images of the bottom pair. In both cases, rivalry only affects parts of each ocular image in order to reconstruct a coherent figure, such that neither a monocular image nor one related to a particular cerebral hemisphere is dominant. If rivalry resulted exclusively from a competition between eyes, then the lower image pair would always appear piecemeal; however, it appears that rivalry can be between percepts and not always the individual retinal images. As discussed by Kovacs et al. (1997), the illustration demonstrates that perceptual grouping can be derived interocularly as long as precise vergence aligns coherent image components on corresponding retinal points. There are also periods where the images do appear as fragmented combinations of the two percepts, especially when vergence becomes inaccurate, indicating that eye-of-origin information also influences perceptual dominance.

Interocular grouping of dichoptic images has also been demonstrated with rivalry for contour (Le Grand, 1967; Whittle, Bloor, & Pocock, 1968), for motion (Beusmans, 1997), and for color (Treisman, 1962; Kulikowski, 1992). Blurring edges of the monocular image fragments facilitates the demonstration (Kovacs et al., 1997) by increasing the size of potentially binocularly fragmented rival zones or patches (Liu & Schor, 1994), which reduces the likelihood that they will disrupt the larger image percepts.

Additional evidence supporting the existence of perceptual rivalry is presented by Logothetis, Leopold, and Sheinberg (1996). During rivalry between orthogonal grids (as shown in Figure 40), he interchanged the two ocular images every 330 ms during 2–3-sec periods of on-time or visibility for one image. This procedure did not alter the longer dominance phase of a particular image orientation. Furthermore, increasing the contrast to one image orientation decreased its off-time even when it was rapidly switched between eyes. Thus the rivalry suppression followed the image percept, rather than a particular eye.

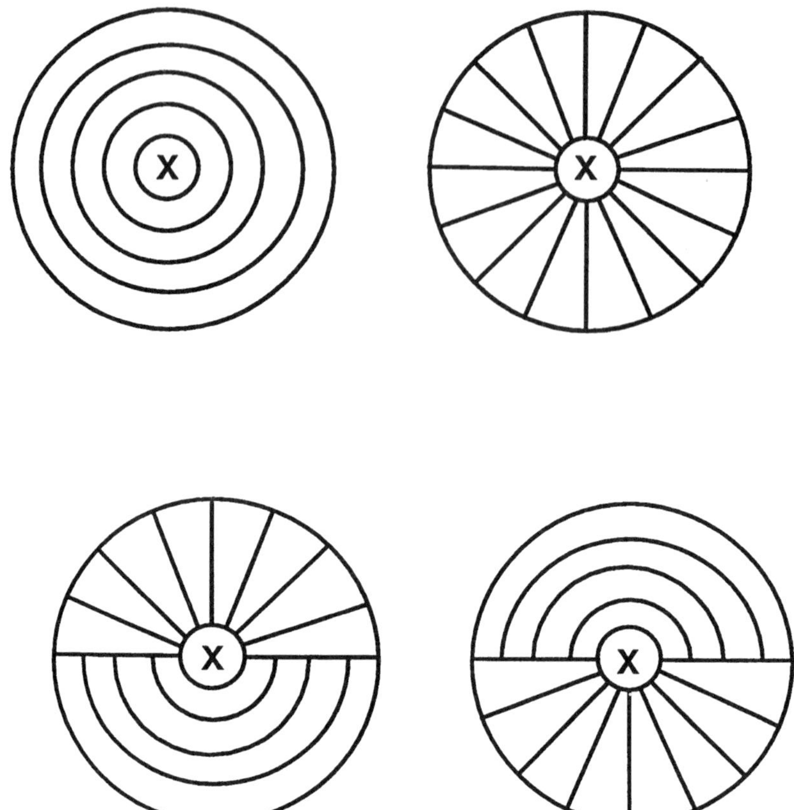

FIGURE 44 Binocular percept rivalry. Fusion of the left and right half images of the patterns above yields similar binocular percepts. Frequently both pairs of stimuli result in the percept of concentric circles or radial lines instead of the mixed percept that characterizes piece-wise rivalry. (Adapted from LeGrand, Y. (1967). *Form and shape vision*. Bloomington: Indiana University Press, p. 198.)

Both piecemeal and whole-image rivalry could both result from a perceptual competition that could occur after the point of binocular combination in the striate cortex. This is suggested by the phenomenon of monocular rivalry in which orthogonal components of a grid seen by one eye appear to alternate in time (Breese, 1899; Bradley & Schor, 1988). There could also be at least two rivalry mechanisms in which dominance was determined by either eye-of-origin information or perceptual grouping. Rivalry that is based on eye of origin, however, cannot explain the results presented in studies of whole-percept rivalry.

E. Permanent-Occlusion Suppression

There are many occasions in which the two eyes see dissimilar forms as a result of a partial occluder in the near visual field. Most often these are encountered when one eye's view of a distal target is partially obstructed by a nearby occluder, such as our own nose or the condition of viewing distal objects through a narrow aperture. Under these ecological or naturally occurring conditions we tend to consistently suppress the occluder and retain a constant view of the background. A striking demonstration of this is to hold a cylindrical tube before the right eye and face the palm of your hand before the left eye near the end of the tube. The combined stable percept is a hole in the hand. The hand is seen as the region surrounding the aperture through which the background is viewed. This is a generic or ecologically valid example of occlusion which gives priority to the background seen through the aperture as described above in the section of occlusion stereopsis. This stable or *permanent* suppression of the center of the hand is unlike rivalry suppression in that it produces different changes in the increment-threshold spectral sensitivity function (Ridder, Smith, Manny, Harwerth, & Kato, 1992). Other natural conditions, such as the overlap of diplopic images of several objects behind the plane of fixation, do not conform to partial occlusion geometry, and they do undergo rivalry. The dominance of the background may be influenced by low-pass blur of the out-of-focus occluder and the relative brightness of the background compared to the occluder. It remains to be seen what other depth-ordering information, in addition to overlap, might result in *permanent* as opposed to rivalry suppression.

References

Aguilonius, F. (1613). *Opticorum libri sex.* Antwerp: Plantin.

Alhazen, I. (1989). Book of optics. In *The optics of Ibn Al-Haytham* (2 vol.). A. I. Sabra (Trans.). London: Warburg Institute, University of London.

Anderson, B. L. (1994). The role of partial occlusion in stereopsis. *Nature, 367,* 365–367.

Anderson, B. L., & Nakayama, K. (1994). Towards a general theory of stereopsis: Binocular matching, occluding contours, and fusion. *Psychological Review, 101,* 414–45.

Badcock, D. R., & Schor, C. M. (1985). Depth-increment detection function for individual spatial channels. *Journal of the Optical Society of America, 2A,* 1211–1215.

Banks, M. S., Sekuler, A. B., & Anderson, S. J. (1991). Peripheral spatial vision: limits imposed by optics photoreceptors and receptor pooling. *Journal of the Optical Society of America. Optics and Image Science, 8*(11), 1775–1787.

Banks, M. S., van Ee, R., & Backus, B. T. (1997). The computation of binocular visual direction: A re-examination of Manfield and Legge (196). *Vision Research, 37*(12), 1605–1613.

Banks, M. S., Backus, B. T. (1998). Extra-retinal and perspective cues cause the small range of the induced effect. *Vision Research, 38*(2), 187–194.

Barbeito, R. (1983). Sighting from the cyclopean eye: The cyclops effect in preschool children. *Perception and Psychophysics, 33,* 561–564.

Barbeito, R., & Simpson, T. L. (1991). The relationship between eye position and egocentric visual direction. *Perception and Psychophysics, 50,* 373–382.

Barlow, H. B., Blakemore, C., & Pettigrew, J. D. (1967). The neural mechanism of binocular depth discrimination. *Journal of Physiology, 193,* 327–342.

Berry, R. N. (1948). Quantitative relations among vernier, real depth, and stereoscopic depth acuities. *Journal of Experimental Psychology, 38,* 708–721.

Beusmans, J. (1997). Evidence for striate cortex for binocular rivalry. Abstracts, *Society for Neuroscience Annual Meeting, 22,* 349.8.

Blake, R., & Boothroyd, K. (1985). The precedence of binocular fusion over binocular rivalry. *Perception and Psychophysics, 37,* 114–124.

Blake, R., & Camisa, J. (1978). Is binocular vision always monocular? *Science, 200,* 1497–1499.

Blake, R., & O'Shea, R. P. (1988). "Abnormal fusion" of stereopsis and binocular rivalry. *Psychological Review, 95,* 151–154.

Blake, R., & Wilson, H. R. (1991). Neural models of stereoscopic vision. *Trends in Neuroscience, 14*(10), 445–452.

Blakemore, C. (1970). The range and scope of binocular depth discrimination in man. *Journal of Physiology, 211,* 599–622.

Braddick, O. J. (1979). Binocular single vision and perceptual processing. *Proceedings of the Royal Society of London, 204,* 503–512.

Bradley, A., & Schor, C. (1988). The role of eye movements and masking in monocular rivalry. *Vision Research, 28,* 1129–1137.

Breese, B. (1899). Series of monograph supplements. On inhibition. *Psychology Review, 3,* 1–65.

Brookes, A., & Stevens, K. A. (1989). The analogy between stereo depth and brightness. *Perception, 18,* 601–614.

Burt, P., & Julesz, B. (1980). A disparity gradient limit for binocular fusion. *Science, 208,* 615–617.

Cline, D., Hofstetter, H. W., & Griffin, J. R. (1989). *Dictionary of visual science* (4th ed.). Radnor, PA: Chilton.

Cogan, A. L., Lomakin, A. J., & Rossi, A. F. (1993). Depth in anticorrelated stereograms: Effects of spatial density and interocular delay. *Vision Research, 33,* 1959–1975.

Collins, M. J., & Goode, A. (1994). Interocular blur suppression and monovision. *Acta Ophthalmologica, 72,* 376–380.

Cormack, L. K., Stevenson, S. B., & Landers, D. D. (1997). Interactions of spatial frequency and unequal monocular contrasts in stereopsis. *Perception, 26*(9), 1121–1136.

Cormack, L. K., Stevenson, S. B., & Schor, C. M. (1991). Interocular correlation, luminance contrast and cyclopean processing. *Vision Research, 31,* 2195–2207.

Cormack, L. K., Stevenson, S. B., & Schor, C. M. (1993). Disparity-tuned channels of the human visual system. *Visual Neuroscience, 10,* 585–596.

Cormack, L. K., Stevenson, S. B., & Schor, C. M. (1994). An upper limit to the binocular combination of stimuli. *Vision Research, 34,* 2599–2608.

Cormack, L. K., & Landers, D. D. (1999). Sustained and transient mechanisms in human stereopsis. *Vision Research,* submitted.

Crick, F. (1984). Function of the thalamic reticular complex: The searching hypothesis. *Proceedings of the National Academy of Science, 81,* 4586–4590.

Crone, R. A., & Leuridan, O. M. A. (1973). Tolerance for aniseikonia. I. Diplopia thresholds in the vertical and horizontal meridians of the visual field. *Albrecht v. Graefes Archiv für Opthalmologie, 188,* 1–16.

Crovitz, H. F., & Lipscomb, D. B. (1963). Dominance of the temporal visual fields at a short duration of stimulation. *American Journal of Psychology, 76,* 631–637.

Cumming, B. G., Johnston, E. B., & Parker, A. J. (1991). Vertical disparities and the perception of three-dimensional shape. *Nature, 349,* 411–413.

da Vinci, L. (1452). Trattato della pittura. [A treatise on painting] London: Rigaud.

DeAngelis, G. C., Ohzawa, I., & Freeman, R. D. (1991). Depth is encoded in the visual cortex by a specialized receptive field structure. *Nature, 352,* 156–159.

DeAngelis, G. C., Ohzawa, I., & Freeman, R. D. (1995). Neuronal mechanisms underlying stereopsis: How do simple cells in the visual cortex encode binocular disparity? *Perception, 24,* 3–31.

Dev, P. (1975). Perception of depth surfaces in random-dot stereograms: A neural model. *International Journal of Man-Machine Studies, 7,* 511–528.

de Weert, C. M. M., & Sadza, K. J. (1983). New data concerning the contribution of colour differences to stereopsis. In J. D. Mollon & L. T. Sharpe (Eds.), *Colour vision* (pp. 553–562). New York: Academic Press.

Dove, H. W. (1891). Die Combination der Eindrücker beider Ohren und beider Angen bu einem Eindruck. *Monatsberichte der Berliner Akademie,* 251–252.

Duncker, K. (1929). Uber induzierte Bewegung. *Psychologische Forschung, 22,* 180–259.

Edwards, M., Pope, D. R., & Schor, C. M. (1998). Luminance contrast and spatial-frequency tuning of the transient-vergence system. *Vision Research, 38,* 705–717.

Edwards, M., Pope, D. R., & Schor, C. M. (1999). Orientation tuning of the transient-stereopsis system. *Vision Research, 39,* 2717–2727.

Edwards, M., & Schor, C. M. (1999). Depth aliasing by the transient-stereopsis system. *Vision Research, 39,* 4333–4340.

Engel, G. R. (1970). An investigation of visual responses to brief stereoscopic stimuli. *Quarterly Journal of Experimental Psychology, 22,* 148–166.

Enright, J. T. (1991). Exploring the third dimension with eye movements: Better than stereopsis. *Vision Research, 28,* 925–930.

Enright, J. T. (1990). Stereopsis, cyclotorsional "noise" and the apparent vertical. *Vision Research, 30,* 1487–1497.

Erkelens, C. J. (1988). Fusional limits for a large random-dot stereogram. *Vision Research, 28,* 345–353.

Erkelens, C. J., & van de Grind, W. A. (1994). Binocular visual direction. *Vision Research, 34,* 2963–2969.

Erkelens, C. J., & van Ee, R. (1997). Capture of the visual direction of monocular objects by adjacent binocular objects. *Vision Research, 37*(9), 1193–1196.

Euclid. (300 B.C./1945). *Optics.* H. E. Burton (Trans.). *Journal of the Optical Society of America, 35,* 357–372.

Fahle, M. (1987). Naso-temporal asymmetry of binocular inhibition. *Investigative Ophthalmology and Visual Science, 28,* 1016–1017.

Fahle, M. (1982). Binocular rivalry: Suppression depends on orientation and spatial frequency. *Vision Research, 22,* 787–800.

Fahle, M., & Westheimer, G. (1988). Local and global factors in disparity detection of rows of points. *Vision Research, 28,* 171–178.

Fender, D., & Julesz, B. (1967). Extension of Panum's fusional area in binocularly stabilized vision. *Journal of the Optical Society of America, 57*(6), 819–830.

Foley, J. M. (1976). Binocular depth mixture. *Vision Research, 16,* 1263–1267.

Foley, J. M. (1980). Binocular distance perception. *Psychology Review, 87*(5), 411–434.

Fox, R. (1991). Binocular rivalry. In D. Regan (Ed.), *Vision and vision dysfunction.* Vol 9: *Binocular Vision* (pp. 93–110). London: Macmillan Press.

Freeman, R. D., & Ohzawa, I. (1990). On the neurophysiological organization of binocular vision. *Vision Research, 30,* 1661–1676.

Frisby, J. P., & Mayhew, J. E. W. (1978). Contrast sensitivity function for stereopsis. *Perception, 7,* 423–429.

Frisby, J. P., & Mayhew, J. E. W. (1980). Spatial frequency tuned channels: Implications for structure and function from psychophysical and computational studies of stereopsis. *Philosophical Transactions of the Royal Society of London, 290,* 95–116.

Galen, C. (175 A.D.). De usa partium croppers humani. Ithaca, NY: Cornell University Press.

Garding, J., Porrill, J., Mayhew, J. E. W., & Frisby, J. P. (1995). Stereopsis, vertical disparity and relief transformations. *Vision Research, 35*(5), 703–722.

Geiger, D., Ladendorf, B., & Yuille, A. (1995). Occlusion and binocular stereo. *International Journal of Computer Vision, 14,* 211–226.

Gibson, J. J. (1937). Adaptation, aftereffect, and contrast in the perception of tilted lines. II. Simultaneous contrast and the areal restriction of the aftereffect. *Journal of Experimental Psychology, 20,* 553–569.

Gillam, B., & Lawergren, B. (1983). The induced effect, vertical disparity, and stereoscopic theory. *Perception and Psychophysics, 34,* 121–130.

Gillam, B., Flagg, T., & Findlay, D. (1984). Evidence for disparity change as the primary stimulus for stereoscopic processing. *Perception and Psychophysics, 36,* 559–564.

Gogel, W. C. (1965). Equidistance tendency and its consequences. *Psychological Bulletin, 64,* 153–163..

Hakkinen, J., & Nyman, G. (1996). Depth asymmetry in da Vinci stereopsis. *Vision Research, 36,* 3815–3819.

Halpern, D. L., & Blake, R. (1988). How contrast affects stereoacuity. *Perception, 17,* 3–13.

Hampton, D. R., & Kertesz, A. E. (1983). Fusional vergence response to local peripheral stimulation. *Journal of the Optical Society of America, 73*(1), 7–10.

Harrad, R. (1996). Psychophysics of suppression. *Eye, 10,* 270–273.

Harrad, R. A., McKee, S. P., Blake, R., & Yang, Y. (1994). Binocular rivalry disrupts stereopsis. *Perception, 23,* 15–28.

Harris, J. M., & McKee, S. P. (1996). Monocular location provides a signed 'depth signal' for discriminating the sign of large disparities. *Investigative Ophthalmology & Visual Science, 37*(3), S283.

Harwerth, R. S., & Rawlings, S. C. (1977). Viewing time and stereoscopic threshold with random-dot stereograms. *American Journal of Optometry and Physiological Optics, 54,* 452–457.

Helmholtz, H. V. (1909). *3rd German edition of Handbuch der Physiologischen Optik* (1962) J. P. C. Southall (Trans.). New York: Dover Publications.

Hering, E. (1879). *Spatial sense and movements of the eye.* C. A. Radde (Trans.). Baltimore: American Academy of Optometry.

Hering, E. (1861). *Beitrage zur Physiologie* (Vol. 5). Leipzig: Engelmann.

Hess, R. F., & Wilcox, L. M. (1994). Linear and non-linear filtering in stereopsis. *Vision Research, 34,* 2431–3438.

Hovis, J. K. (1989). Review of dichoptic color mixing. *Optometry and Vision Science, 66,* 181–190.

Howard, I. P. (1982). *Human visual orientation.* Chichester: Wiley.

Howard, I. P., & Ohmi, M. (1992). A new interpretation of the role of dichoptic occlusion in stereopsis. *Investigative Ophthalmology & Visual Science, 33,* ARVO Suppl. Abs# 1370.

Howard, I. P., & Rogers, B. J. (1995). *Binocular vision and stereopsis.* Oxford: Oxford University Press.

Hubel, D. H., & Wiesel, T. N. (1970). Stereoscopic vision in macaque monkey. Cells sensitive to binocular depth in area 18 of the macaque monkey cortex. *Nature, 225*(227), 41–42.

Jones, R. (1977). Anomalies of disparity detection in the human visual system. *Journal of Physiology, 264,* 621–640.

Jones, R., & Kerr, K. W. (1972). Vergence eye movements to pairs of disparity stimuli with shape selection cues. *Vision Research, 12,* 1425–1430.

Jordan, J. R., Geisler, W. S., & Bovik, A. C. (1990). Color as a source of information in the stereo correspondence process. *Vision Research, 30,* 1955–1970.

Julesz, B. (1964). Binocular depth perception without familiarity cues. *Science, 145,* 356–362.

Julesz, B. (1971). *Foundations of cyclopean perception.* Chicago: University of Chicago Press.

Julesz, B., & Miller, J. E. (1975). Independent spatial frequency tuned channels for binocular fusion and rivalry. *Perception, 4,* 125–143.

Julesz, B. (1978). Global stereopsis: Cooperative phenomena in stereoscopic depth perception. In R. Held, H. W. Leibowitz, H.-L. Teuber (Eds.), *Handbook of sensory physiology.* Vol. VII: Perception. Berlin: Springer-Verlag.

Kaufman, L. (1963). On the spread of suppression and binocular rivalry. *Vision Research, 3,* 401–415.

Kaye, M. (1978). Stereopsis without binocular correlation. *Vision Research, 18,* 1013–1022.

Kidd, A. L., Frisby, J. P., & Mayhew, J. E. W. (1979). Texture contours can facilitate stereopsis by initiating vergence eye movements. *Nature, 280,* 829–832.

Kirschmann, A. (1890). Uber die quantitativen Verhaltnisse des simultanen Helligkeits-und Farbencontrastes. *Philosophische Studien, 6,* 417–491.

Koffka, K. (1935). *Principles of Gestalt psychology.* New York: Harcourt Brace.

Kollner, H. (1914). Das funktionelle Uberwiegen der nasalen Netzhauthalften im gemeinschaftlichen Schfeld. *Archiv Augenheilkunde, 76,* 153–164.

Kontsevich, L. L., & Tyler, C. W. (1994). Analysis of stereo thresholds for stimuli below 2.5 c/deg. *Vision Research, 34*(17), 2317–2329.

Kotulak, J. C., & Schor, C. M. (1986). A computational model of the error detector of human visual accommodation. *Biological Cybernetics, 54,* 189–194.

Kovacs, I., Papathomas, T. V., Yang, M., & Feher, A. (1997). When the brain changes its mind: Interocular grouping during binocular rivalry. *Proceedings of the National Academy of Science of the USA, 93*(26), 15508–15511.

Krekling, S. (1974). Stereoscopic threshold within the stereoscopic range in central vision. *American Journal of Optometry Physiological Optics, 51*(9), 626–634.

Krol, J. D., & van de Grind, W. A. (1983). Depth from dichoptic edges depends on vergence tuning. *Perception, 12,* 425–438.

Kulikowksi, J. J. (1992). Binocular chromatic rivalry and single vision. *Ophthalogy and Physiology Optics, 12,* 168–170.

Kumar, T., & Glaser, D. A. (1991). Influence of remote objects on local depth perception. *Vision Research, 31,* 1687–1699.

Kumar, T., & Glaser, D. A. (1992). Shape analysis and stereopsis for human depth perception. *Vision Research, 32,* 499–512.

Landers, D., & Cormack, L. K. (1999). Stereoscopic depth fading is disparity and spatial frequency dependent. Investigative Opthalogy & Visual Science, 40/4. [ARVP abstracts #2194 S416.]

Langlands, N. M. S. (1926). Experiments on binocular vision. *Transactions of the Optical Society* (London), *28,* 45–82.

Legge, G. E., & Gu, Y. (1989). Stereopsis and contrast. *Vision Research, 29*(8), 989–1004.

Le Grand, Y. (1953). Etudes binoculaires I: L'inexistence dis "aires di fusion de Panum." *Atti Fon. Giorgio Ronchi, 8,* 423–428.

Le Grand, Y. (1967). *Form and shape vision.* Bloomington, Indiana University Press.

Lehky, S. R., Pouget, A., & Sejnowski, T. J. (1990). Neural models of binocular depth perception. *Cold Spring Harbor Symposia on Quantitative Biology, 55,* 765–777.

Lehky, S. R., & Sejnowski, T. J. (1990). Neural model of stereoacuity and depth interpolation based on a distributed representation of stereo disparity. *Journal of Neuroscience, 10*(7), 2281–99.

Levelt, W. (1968). *Psychological studies on binocular rivalry.* The Hague: Mouton.

Lit, A. (1959). Depth-discrimination thresholds as a function of binocular differences of retinal illuminance at scotopic and photopic levels. *Journal of the Optical Society of America, 49*(8), 746–752.

Liu, L., & Schor, C. M. (1997). Functional division of human retina. In V. Lakshminarayanan (Ed.), *Basic and Clinical Applications of Vision Science. The Professor Jay M. Enoch Festschrift Volume.* Kluwer Academic Publishers. *Documenta Ophthalmologica Proceedings Series, 60,* 295–298.

Liu, L., & Schor, C. M. (1998). Monocular spatial distortions and binocular correspondence. *Journal of the Optical Society of America: Vision Science,* July 15 (7), 1740–1755.

Liu, L., & Schor, C. M. (1994). The spatial properties of binocular suppression zone. *Vision Research, 34,* 937–947.

Liu, L., Stevenson, S. B., & Schor, C. M. (1994a). A polar coordinate system for describing binocular disparity. *Vision Research, 34*(9), 1205–1222.

Liu, L., Stevenson, S. B., & Schor, C. M. (1994b). Quantitative stereoscopic depth without binocular correspondence. *Nature, 369,* 66–69.

Liu, L., Stevenson, S. B., & Schor, C. M. (1997). Binocular matching of dissimilar features in phantom stereopsis. *Vision Research, 37,* 633–644.

Liu, L., Stevenson, S. B., & Schor, C. M. (1992). Vergence eye movements elicited by stimuli without corresponding features. *Perception, 27,* 7–20.

Liu, L., Tyler, C. W., & Schor, C. M. (1992). Failure of rivalry at low contrast: evidence of a suprathreshold binocular summation process. *Vision Research, 32,* 1471-1479.

Logothetis, N. K., Leopold, D. A., & Sheinberg, D. L. (1996). What is rivalling during binocular rivalry. *Nature, 380,* N6575:621–624.

Lunn, P. D., & Morgan, M. J. (1996). The analogy between stereo depth and brightness. *Perception, 24,* 901–904.

MacKay, D. M. (1973). Lateral interaction between neural channels sensitive to texture density. *Nature, 245,* 159–161.

Mann, V. A., Hein, A., & Diamond, R. (1979). Localization of targets by strabismic subjects: Contrasting patterns in constant and alternating suppressors. *Perception and Psychophysics, 25,* 29–34.

Marr, D., & Poggio, T. (1976). Cooperative computation of stereo disparity. *Science, 194,* 283–287.

Marr, D., & Poggio, T. (1979). A computational theory of human stereo vision. *Proceedings of the Royal Society of London, 204,* 301–328.

Marran, L., & Schor, C. M. (1997). Lens induced aniso-accommodation. *Vision Research, 38*(27), 3601–19.

Marshall, J. A., Burbeck, C. A., Ariely, D., Rolland, J. P., & Martin, K. E. (1996). Occlusion edge blur: a cue to relative visual depth. *J Opt Soc of Am A, 13*(4), 681–688.

Mayhew, J. E. W., & Frisby, J. P. (1980). The computation of binocular edges. *Perception, 9,* 69–86.

Mayhew, J. E. W., & Longuet-Higgins, H. C. (1982). A computational model of binocular depth perception. *Nature, 297,* 376–378.

McKee, S. P. (1983). The spatial requirements for fine stereoacuity. *Vision Research, 23*(2), 191–198.

McKee, S. P., & Levi, D. M. (1987). Dichoptic hyperacuity: the precision of nonius alignment. *Journal of the Optical Society of America, 4*(6), 1104–1108.

Mitchell, D. E. (1966). A review of the concept of "Panum's fusional areas". *American Journal of Optometry and Archives of American Academy of Optometry, 43,* 387–401.

Mitchell, D. E. (1970). Properties of stimuli eliciting vergence eye movements and stereopsis. *Vision Research, 10,* 145–162.

Mitchell, D. E., & O'Hagan, S. (1972). Accuracy of stereoscopic localization of small line segment that differ in size or orientation for the two eyes. *Vision Research, 12,* 437–454.

Mitchison, G. J., & Westheimer, G. (1990). Viewing geometry and gradients of horizontal disparity. In C. Blakemore (Ed.), *Vision: Coding and efficiency,* pp. 302–309. Cambridge, UK: Cambridge University Press.

Mitchison, G. J., & Westheimer, G. (1984). The perception of depth in simple figures. *Vision Research, 24,* 1063–1073.

Morgan, M. J., & Castet, E. (1995). Stereoscopic depth perception at high velocities. *Nature,* Nov 23, *378*(6555), 380–383.

Müller, J. (1843). *Elements of physiology.* W. Baly (Trans.). London: Tayler and Walton.

Nakayama, K., & Shimojo, S. (1990). DaVinci stereopsis: Depth and subjective occluding contours from unpaired image points. *Vision Research, 30,* 1811–1825.

Nakayama, K., & Shimojo, S. (1992). Experiencing and perceiving visual surfaces. *Science, 257,* 1357–1363.

Nakayama, K., Shimojo, S., & Silverman, G. H. (1989). Stereoscopic depth: Its relation to image segmentation, grouping, and the recognition of occluded objects. *Perception, 18,* 55–68.

Nelson, J. I. (1975). Globality and stereoscopic fusion in binocular vision. *J Theor Biol, 49*(1), 1–88.

Ogle, K. N. (1952). On the limits of stereoscopic vision. *Journal of Experimental Psychology, 44,* 253–259.

Ogle, K. N. (1964). *Research in binocular vision.* New York: Hafner.

Ogle, K. N., & Prangen, A. D. H. (1953). Observations on vertical divergences and hyperphorias. *AMA Archives of Ophthalmology, 49,* 313–334.

Ogle, K. N., & Wakefield, J. M. (1967). Stereoscopic depth and binocular rivalry. *Vision Research, 7,* 89–98.

Ono, H. (1979). Axiomatic summary and deductions from Hering's principles of visual direction. *Perception & Psychophysics, 25,* 473–477.

Ott, M., & Schaeffel, F. (1995). A negatively powered lens in the chameleon. *Nature, 373*(6516), 692–694.

Panum, P. L. (1858). *Physiologische Untersuchungen über das Sehen mit zwei Augen.* Keil: Schwers.

Piantanida, T. P. (1986). Stereo hysteresis revisited. *Vision Research, 26,* 431–437.

Poggio, G. F., Gonzalez, F., & Krause, F. (1988). Stereoscopic mechanisms in monkey visual cortex: Binocular correlation and disparity selectivity. *Journal of Neuroscience, 8*(12), 4531–4550.

Pope, D. R., Edwards, M., & Schor, C. M. (1999a). Extraction of depth from opposite-contrast stimuli: Transient system can, sustained system can't. *Vision Research, 39,* 4010–4017.

Pope, D. R., Edwards, M., & Schor, C. M. (1999b). Orientation and luminance polarity tuning of the transient-vergence system. *Vision Research, 39,* 575–584.

Prentice, W. C. H. (1948). New observations of binocular yellow. *Journal of Experimental Psychology, 38,* 284–288.

Rady, A. A., & Ishak, I. G. H. (1955). Relative contributions of disparity and convergence to stereoscopic acuity. *Journal of the Optical Society of America, 45*(7), 530–534.

Rawlings, S. C., & Shipley, T. (1969). Stereoscopic acuity and horizontal angular distance from fixation. *Journal of the Optical Society of America, 59*(8), 991–993.

Regan, D. (1982). Comparison of transient and steady-state methods. *Annals of the New York Academy of Science, 388,* 45–71.

Richards, W. (1971). Anomalous stereoscopic depth perception. *Journal of the Optical Society of America, 61,* 410–414.

Richards, W., & Foley, J. M. (1971). Interhemispheric processing of binocular disparity. *Journal of the Optical Society of America, 61,* 419–421.

Richards, W., & Regan, D. (1973). A stereo field map with implications for disparity processing. *Investigative Ophthalmology & Visual Science, 12,* 904–909.

Richards, W. H., & Kaye, M. G. (1974). Local versus global stereopsis: Two mechanisms? *Vision Research, 14,* 1345–47.

Ridder, W. H., Smith, E. L., Manny, R. E., Harwerth, R. S., & Kato, K. (1992). Effects of interocular suppression on spectral sensitivity. *Optometry and Vision Science, 69,* 171–256.

Riggs, L. A., & Niehl, E. W. (1960). Eye movements recorded during convergence and divergence. *Journal of the Optical Society of America, 50*(9), 913–920.

Rogers, B. J., & Bradshaw, M. F. (1993). Vertical disparities, differential perspective and binocular stereopsis. *Nature, 361,* 253–255.

Rose, D., & Blake, R. (1988). Mislocalization of diplopic images. *Journal of the Optical Society of America, A, 5,* 1512–1521.

Scheidt, R. A., & Kertesz, A. E. (1993). Temporal and spatial aspects of sensory interactions during human fusion response. *Vision Research, 33*(9), 1259–1270.

Schor, C. M. (1977). Visual stimuli for strabismic suppression. *Perception, 6,* 583–593.

Schor, C. M., & Badcock, D. R. (1985). A comparison of stereo and vernier acuity within spatial channels as a function of distance from fixation. *Vision Research, 25*(8), 1113–1119.

Schor, C., Bridgeman, B., & Tyler, C. W. (1983). Spatial characteristics of static and dynamic stereoacuity in strabismus. *Investigative Ophthalmology & Visual Science, 24*(12), 1572–1579.

Schor, C. M., Edwards, M., & Pope, D. (1998). Spatial-frequency tuning of the transient-stereopsis system. *Vision Research, 38,* 3057–3068.

Schor, C. M., & Heckman, T. (1989). Interocular differences in contrast and spatial frequency: Effects on stereopsis and fusion. *Vision Research, 29,* 837–847.

Schor, C. M., Heckman, T., & Tyler, C. W. (1989). Binocular fusion limits are independent of contrast, luminance gradient and component phases. *Vision Research, 29,* 821–835.

Schor, C. M., Landsman, L., & Erikson, P. (1987). Ocular dominance and the interocular suppression of blur in monovision. *American Journal of Optometry and Physiological Optics, 64,* 723–730.

Schor, C. M., Maxwell, J., & Stevenson, S. B. (1994). Isovergence surfaces: The conjugacy of vertical eye movements in tertiary positions of gaze. *Ophthalmic and Physiological Optics, 14,* 279–286.

Schor, C. M., & Tyler, C. W. (1981). Spatio-temporal properties of Panum's fusional area. *Vision Research, 21,* 683–692.

Schor, C. M., Wesson, M., & Robertson, K. M. (1986). Combined effects of spatial frequency and retinal eccentricity upon fixation disparity. *American Journal of Optometry and Physiological Optics, 63,* 619–626.

Schor, C. M., & Wood, I. (1983). Disparity range for local stereopsis as a function of luminance spatial frequency. *Vision Research, 23*(12), 1649–54.

Schor, C. M., Wood, I. C., & Ogawa, J. (1984a). Binocular sensory fusion is limited by spatial resolution. *Vision Research, 24,* 661–665.

Schor, C. M., Wood, I. C., & Ogawa, J. (1984b). Spatial tuning of static and dynamic local stereopsis. *Vision Research, 24,* 573–578.

Schor, C. M. (1978). Zero retinal image disparity: A stimulus for suppression in small angle strabismus. *Documenta Ophthalmologica, 46,* 149–160.

Shimojo, S., & Nakayama, K. (1990). Real world occlusion constraints and binocular rivalry. *Vision Research, 30,* 69–80.

Shipley, T., & Hyson, M. (1972). The stereoscopic sense of order—a classification of stereograms. *American Journal of Optometry and Archives of America Academy of Optometry, 49,* 83–95.

Siderov, J., & Harwerth, R. S. (1993). Precision of stereoscopic depth perception from double images. *Vision Research, 33*(11), 1553–1560.

Siegel, H., & Duncan, C. P. (1960). Retinal disparity and diplopia vs. luminance and size of target. *American Journal of Psychology, 73,* 280–284.

Smallman, H. S., & MacLeod, D. I. (1994). Size-disparity correlation in stereopsis at contrast threshold. *Journal of the Optical Society of America A, 11*(8), 2169–83.

Steinman, R. M., & Collewijn, H. (1980). Binocular retinal image motion during active head rotation. *Vision Research, 20,* 415–429.

Stevens, K. A., & Brookes, A. (1987). Depth reconstruction in stereopsis. *Proceedings of the First IEE International Conference on Computer Vision, London,* 682–686.

Stevens, K. A., & Brookes, A. (1988). Integrating stereopsis with monocular interpretations of planar surfaces. *Vision Research, 28,* 371–386.

Stevenson, S. B., Cormack, L. K., & Schor, C. M. (1989). Hyperacuity, superresolution and gap resolution in human stereopsis. *Vision Research, 29,* 1597–1605.

Stevenson, S. B., Cormack, L. K., & Schor, C. M. (1991). Depth attraction and repulsion in random dot stereograms. *Vision Research, 31,* 805–813.

Stevenson, S. B., Cormack, L. K., & Schor, C. M. (1994). The effect of stimulus contrast and interocular correlation on disparity vergence. *Vision Research, 34*(3), 383–396.

Stevenson, S. B., Cormack, L. K., Schor, C. M., & Tyler, C. W. (1992). Disparity tuning mechanisms of human stereopsis. *Vision Research, 32,* 1685–1694.

Stevenson, S. B., & Schor, C. M. (1997). Human stereo matching is not restricted to Epipolar lines. *Vision Research, 37,* 2717–2723.

Timney, B., Wilcox, L. M., & St. John, R. (1989). On the evidence for a 'prue' binocular process in human vision. *Spatial Vision, 4,* 1–15.

Treisman, A. (1962). Binocular rivalry and stereoscopic depth perception. *Quarterly Journal of Experimental Psychology, 14,* 23–37.

Treisman, A., & Gelade, G. (1980). A feature integration theory of attention. *Cognitive Psychology, 12,* 97–136.

Tschermak-Seysenegg, A. V. (1952). Introduction to Physiological Optics. P. Boeder (Trans.). Springfield, IL: Charles C. Thomas Pub.

Tyler, C. W. (1973). Stereoscopic vision: cortical limitations and a disparity scaling effect. *Science, 181,* 276–278.

Tyler, C. W. (1975). Spatial organization of binocular disparity sensitivity. *Vision Research, 15,* 583–590.

Tyler, C. W. (1983). Sensory processing and binocular disparity. In C. M. Schor & K. Ciuffreda (Eds.), *Vergence eye movements: Clinical and basic aspects.* Boston: Butterworth.

van Ee, R., & Erkelens, C. J. (1996). Anisotropy in Werner's binocular depth-contrast effect. *Vision Research, 36,* 2253–2262.

van Ee, R., & Erkelens, C. J. (1996). Temporal aspects of binocular slant perception. *Vision Research, 36,* 43–51.

van Ee, R., & Erkelens, C. J. (1996). Stability of binocular depth perception with moving head and eyes. *Vision Research, 36,* 3827–3842.

van Ee, R., & Schor, C. M. (1999). Unconstrained stereoscopic matching of lines. *Vision Research.* In press.

Verhoeff, F. H. (1935). A new theory of binocular vision. *AMA Archives of Ophthalmology, 13,* 151-175.

Vieth, G. A. U. (1818). Uber die Richtung der Augen. *Annalen der Physik, 28,* 233–253.

Walker, P. (1978). Binocular rivalry: central or peripheral selective processes? *Psychiatry Bulletin, 85,* 376–389.

Werner, H. (1937). Dynamical theory of depth perception. *Psychological Monographs 49,* 1–127.

Werner, H. (1938). Binocular depth-contrast and the conditions of the binocular field. *American Journal of Psychology, 51,* 489–497.

Westheimer, G. (1979a). Cooperative neural processes involved in stereoscopic acuity. *Experimental Brain Research, 36,* 585–597.

Westheimer, G. (1979b). The spatial sense of the eye. *Investigative Ophthalmology and Visual Science, 18,* 893–912.

Westheimer, G. (1986). Spatial interaction in the domain of disparity signals in human stereoscopic vision. *Journal of Physiology, 370,* 619–629.

Westheimer, G. (1987). Visual acuity and hyperacuity: Resolution, localization, form. *American Journal of Optometry and Physiological Optics, 64,* 567–574.

Westheimer, G., & Levi, D. M. (1987). Depth attraction and repulsion of disparate foveal stimuli. *Vision Research, 27*(8), 1361–1368.

Westheimer, G., & McKee, S. P. (1979). What prior uniocular processing is necessary for stereopsis? *Investigative Ophthalmology & Visual Science, 18*(6), 614–621.

Westheimer, G., & Petet, M. W. (1992). Detection and processing of vertical disparity by the human observer. *Proceedings of Royal Society of London, B, Biological Science,, 250*(1329), 243–247.

Westheimer, G., & Tanzman, I. J. (1956). Qualitative depth localization with diplopic images. *Journal of the Optical Society of America, 46,* 116–117.

Wheatstone, C. (1838). Contributions to the physiology of vision—Part the first. On some remarkable, and hitherto unobserved, phenomena of binocular vision. *Philosophical Actions of the Royal Society, 128,* 371–394.

Whittle, P., Bloor, D. C., & Pocock, S. (1968). Some experiments on figural effects in binocular rivalry. *Perception and Psychophysics, 4,* 183–188.

Wilcox, L. M., & Hess, R. F. (1995). Dmax for stereopsis depends on size, not spatial frequency content. *Vision Research, 35*(8), 1061–1069.

Wilson, H. R., Blake, R., & Halpern, D. L. (1991). Coarse spatial scales constrain the range of binocular fusion on fine scales. *Journal of the Optical Society of America A, 8,* 229–236.

Wilson, H. R., Blake, R., & Pokorny, J. (1988). Limits of binocular fusion in the short wave sensitive ("blue") cones. *Vision Research, 28*(4), 555–562.

Wolfe, J. M. (1983). Afterimages, binocular rivalry, and the temporal properties of dominance and suppression. *Perception, 12,* 439–445.

Wolfe, J. M. (1986). Stereopsis and binocular rivalry. *Psychological Review, 93,* 269–282.

Woo, G. C. S. (1974). The effect of exposure time on the foveal size of Panum's area. *Vision Research, 14,* 473–480.

Wright, W. D. (1951). The role of convergence in stereoscopic vision. *The Proceedings of the Physical Society, Section B. 64,* (376B), 289–297.

Ziegler, L. R., & Hess, R. F. (1999). Stereoscopic depth but not shape perception from second-order stimuli. *Vision Research, 39,* 1491–1507.

CHAPTER 6

Seeing Motion

Andrew Derrington

I. OVERVIEW

Motion is central to the business of seeing. At one level motion provides us with information. It informs us about changes in our world as we move about or as objects move around us. At a more fundamental level, motion makes vision possible. Often it is only by virtue of an object's motion that we can see at all; motion may also assist us by making an object stand out from its stationary background or from other objects moving in different directions or at different speeds. At the simplest level, if all motion and temporal change are removed from the visual image, the image itself will rapidly fade and become invisible.

In this chapter I shall deal only with analyzing motion and only with the simplest kind of motion, translation within the retinal image plane, motion at right angles to the line of sight. I shall concentrate on the problem of how very different attributes of the stimulus may be processed to reveal the same information. A more extensive discussion of a wider range of motions, how they are sensed and how the information derived from them is put to use, can be found elsewhere (Smith & Snowden, 1994).

Before we begin, it is important to point out that there is another respect in which motion is a fundamental aspect of seeing. In principal we could derive the motion of an object from an analysis of changes in its position with time. In this case, the analysis of motion would be secondary to analyses of time and position.

Seeing

However, there are clear cases where the presentation of two stimuli in quick succession elicits a clear sensation of motion along the axis that connects the locations of the two stimuli in the direction that leads from the position of the first stimulus to the position of the second stimulus. We can be quite sure that the motion analysis is not derived from analyses of position and time because the positions of the two stimuli are indistinguishable if they are presented with a time delay that is too long to allow motion to be seen, or if they are presented simultaneously (Thorson, Lange, & Biederman-Thorson, 1969). Thus motion is fundamental in that it is not, or, at any rate, need not be synthesized from more elementary aspects of our visual sense: we can extract information about motion directly from the image.

In this chapter, I shall begin by discussing and illustrating the various ways in which motion may conveniently be represented on paper and show how the different kinds of moving stimuli commonly used in research are represented. I shall then use the same kinds of representation to illustrate how the different kinds of hypothetical motion analyzes extract information about motion from moving images. Finally, I shall discuss whether the available experimental data constrain the possibilities for modeling visual motion.

II. REPRESENTING IMAGE MOTION

A full representation of the motion in a two-dimensional (2-D) image requires three dimensions (x, y, and t), which makes it impossible to represent any but the most stylized moving image on paper. This problem can be addressed in several different ways. Perhaps the most straightforward is to sample the moving image in time and present it as a series of spatial images like the frames in a movie. An alternative that works well for simple motions or simple images is to sacrifice one of the spatial dimensions and present the temporal dimension and one of the spatial dimensions of the image on a 2-D space–time plot.

Just as the time axis can be sampled repeatedly to give the frames of a movie, the spatial axes can be sampled to yield a series of sections through the spatiotemporal image. For simple linear motion, a rotation of the spatial axis to align it with the axis of motion will usually yield an informative space–time plot.

Moving images can also be represented in the frequency domain. Again the complete representation requires 3-D plots to show two dimensions of spatial frequency and one of temporal frequency, and again the range of images that can be represented on paper is limited. Two-dimensional plots showing one dimension of spatial frequency and one of temporal frequency are fine for 1-D moving stimuli. Fortunately, the early stages of motion analysis in the mammalian visual system appear to be one-dimensional so these simple representations take us a long way.

Finally, 2-D motion can be represented as vector plots in 2-D velocity space.

Each of these ways of representing image motion makes explicit one or more of the cues that may be used by visual mechanisms to extract motion information from the image.

A. Movies

Figure 1 shows eight snapshots, taken 0.125 sec apart, of a patch of sinusoidal grating of spatial frequency five cycles per image. The grating is moving within the static patch at a speed of 0.1 image frames per second. The patch has a smooth spatial profile provided by a 2-D Gaussian spatial window. The contrast of the grating changes smoothly over time, governed by a Gaussian temporal envelope.

The speed and direction of motion of the grating can be estimated from the sequence of images by monitoring the change in position of any feature of the grating's luminance profile, such as a peak or a trough or the edge between a dark and a bright bar, either with respect to some fixed reference point in the image or in terms of its absolute position. The white spot in each image tags one such feature, the peak of the darkest bar in the image, as it moves from frame to frame. Ullman (1979) has described how the visual system might analyze motion by measuring the displacements between such corresponding features in successive images. This approach, which is known as "correspondence-based" motion analysis or as "feature-tracking," will be discussed later.

Feature tracking is probably the most reliable way of analyzing motion, and it can be applied directly to a sequence of video frames. The change in spatial position of an image feature divided by the time it takes to undergo that displacement gives the velocity. Other ways of displaying the same moving stimulus, however, show that the spatiotemporal image contains features that encode the motion more directly.

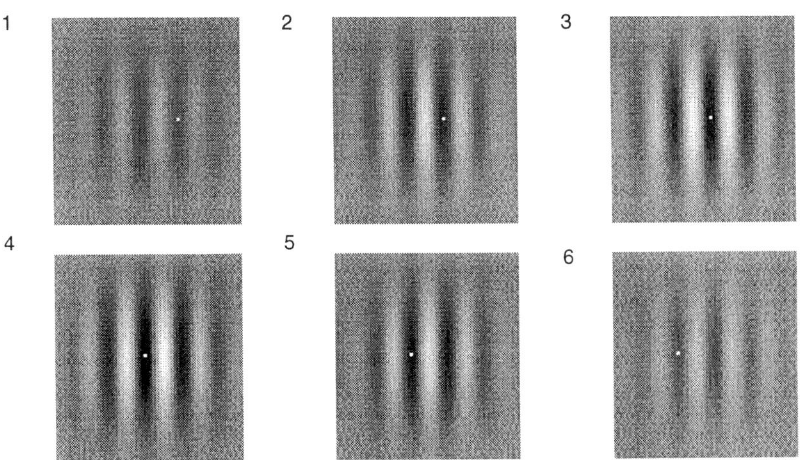

FIGURE 1 Six snapshots taken at intervals of 0.125 sec showing a sinusoidal grating moving at 0.5 image frames/sec. The spatial and temporal profiles of the grating are shaped by Gaussian functions of position and time. The white spot in each image marks the peak of a dark bar as it changes position through the sequence.

B. Space–Time Images

Figure 2 shows a space–time image made from a horizontal slice through the imoving image that gives rise to the sequence of samples shown in Figure 1. It shows how the luminance profile along a horizontal line through the center of the image changes over time. The horizontal axis is spatial position; the vertical axis is time.

In this representation the moving grating appears to be oriented in space–time. Moving up the time axis shows the horizontal displacement of the bars as they move. The speed of the grating—its displacement over time—is directly shown as the tangent of the angle between the bars of the spatiotemporal grating and the vertical. Accordingly, all stationary image features would be vertical in this plot, and moving features make the angle given by the arctangent of their velocity with the vertical. The axes of this representation are space and time, which gives the tangent units of velocity.

Adelson and Bergen (Adelson & Bergen, 1985) pointed out that motion analysis can conveniently be thought of as the identification of the orientation of features in such a space–time image and that motion detectors can be represented as

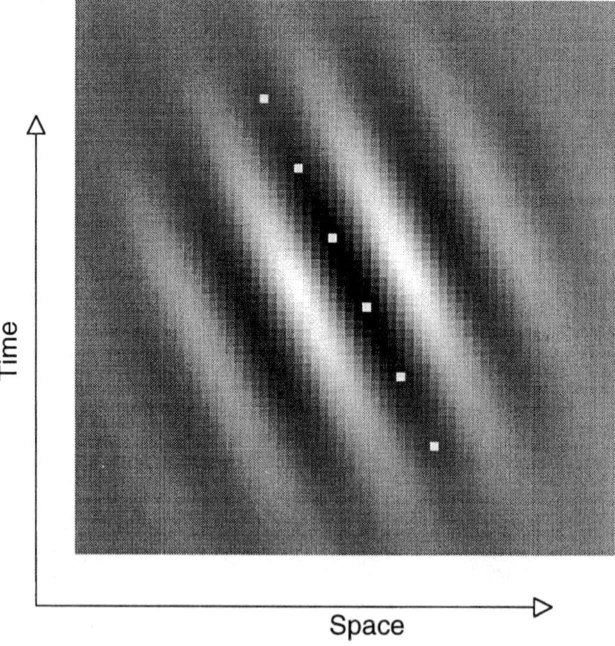

FIGURE 2 Space–time plot of a horizontal slice through the moving pattern that generated the image sequence shown in Figure 1. The white spots correspond to the markers in each frame of the image sequence. The velocity is given by the horizontal separation between the markers divided by the vertical separation (distance/time). The vertical axis represents 1 sec.

filters oriented in space and time. This makes it clear that motion is represented directly in the spatiotemporal image, rather than being an attribute of the stimulus that only emerges from the comparison of the locations of objects in successive spatial images.

It is important to be clear that spatiotemporal filtering and feature tracking are simply different strategies designed to achieve the same goal. Feature tracking can be represented in Figure 2 as locating the horizontal positions of the same image feature at two different vertical positions in the figure. The white dots in Figure 2 show the trajectory of the feature signaled in Figure 1. The angle that the line through two (or more) spatiotemporal points makes with the vertical axis defines the velocity in exactly the same way as does the orientation of spatiotemporal features.

C. Frequency Domain Representations

The frequency domain representation of the same moving stimulus (shown in Figure 3) illustrates how motion becomes explicit in the spatiotemporal frequency domain and reveals another possible strategy for visual motion analysis (Watson &

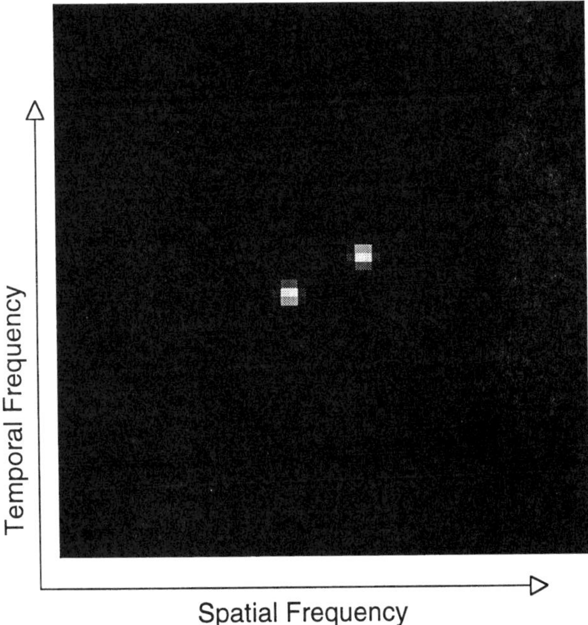

FIGURE 3 Spatiotemporal frequency content of Figure 2. Zero is in the center of the picture. The two clusters of spatiotemporal frequency components are symmetrically located in the first and third quadrants. The velocity is given by the ratio of the temporal frequency to the spatial frequency.

Ahumada, 1983, 1985). The axes of Figure 3 are spatial frequency and temporal frequency. Moving components of the image have a temporal frequency that is given by their velocity divided by their temporal frequency. Thus the components of an extended moving image will fall on a straight line whose gradient is the image velocity. This means that the velocity in one spatial dimension of an image can be estimated by a combination of spatial frequency filtering and temporal frequency estimation (Watson & Ahumada, 1985).

In a more general sense, the direction (sign) of the motion determines the sign of the temporal frequencies generated by different spatial frequencies. Motion to the left (negative velocities) generates positive temporal frequencies from positive spatial frequencies and negative temporal frequencies from negative spatial frequencies, whereas motion to the right generates the opposite pairs of sign combinations. Accordingly, the direction of motion is signaled by whether the spatiotemporal frequency components it generates lie in the first and third or second and fourth quadrants of the spatiotemporal frequency diagram.

Because it is truncated in space and time, our moving grating is spread out in spatial and temporal frequency. Its spatiotemporal frequency components form a 2-D Gaussian pulse centered on the line that corresponds to its notional velocity. In a 3-D plot they would also be spread slightly in orientation about the nominal orientation of the original grating (vertical). The components of an extended two-dimensional object occupy a plane tilted in temporal frequency. Again, image motion can be estimated by using the outputs of filters selective for spatial frequency, orientation, and temporal frequency to estimate the azimuth and elevation of this plane (Heeger, 1987).

D. Second-Order Motion

In the moving image we have considered so far, a moving grating is seen through a stationary window, and the motion is signaled directly by the spatiotemporal variations in the luminance profile of the stimulus. However, it is also important to consider other kinds of moving stimuli in which luminance patterns remain stationary, but higher order attributes of the patterns move. One example of this is the contrast-modulated grating, shown in Figures 4a and b, which consists of a carrier pattern, usually a high spatial frequency sinusoid or a random 1-d or 2-d noise pattern, whose contrast is modulated by a spatial envelope of lower spatial frequency. As Figure 4b and c show, the envelope can be made to move while leaving the carrier stationary. This is an example of *second-order,* or *non-Fourier* motion.

The human visual system can discriminate the motion of a contrast envelope even when the motion of the luminance signals that make it up is undetectable (Badcock & Derrington, 1985). This makes it important to consider how such motion may be represented and how it may be processed. When these second-order patterns are made to move, the luminance pattern itself remains static and the contrast modulation moves. This is made clear in Figure 4c and d, which shows a space–

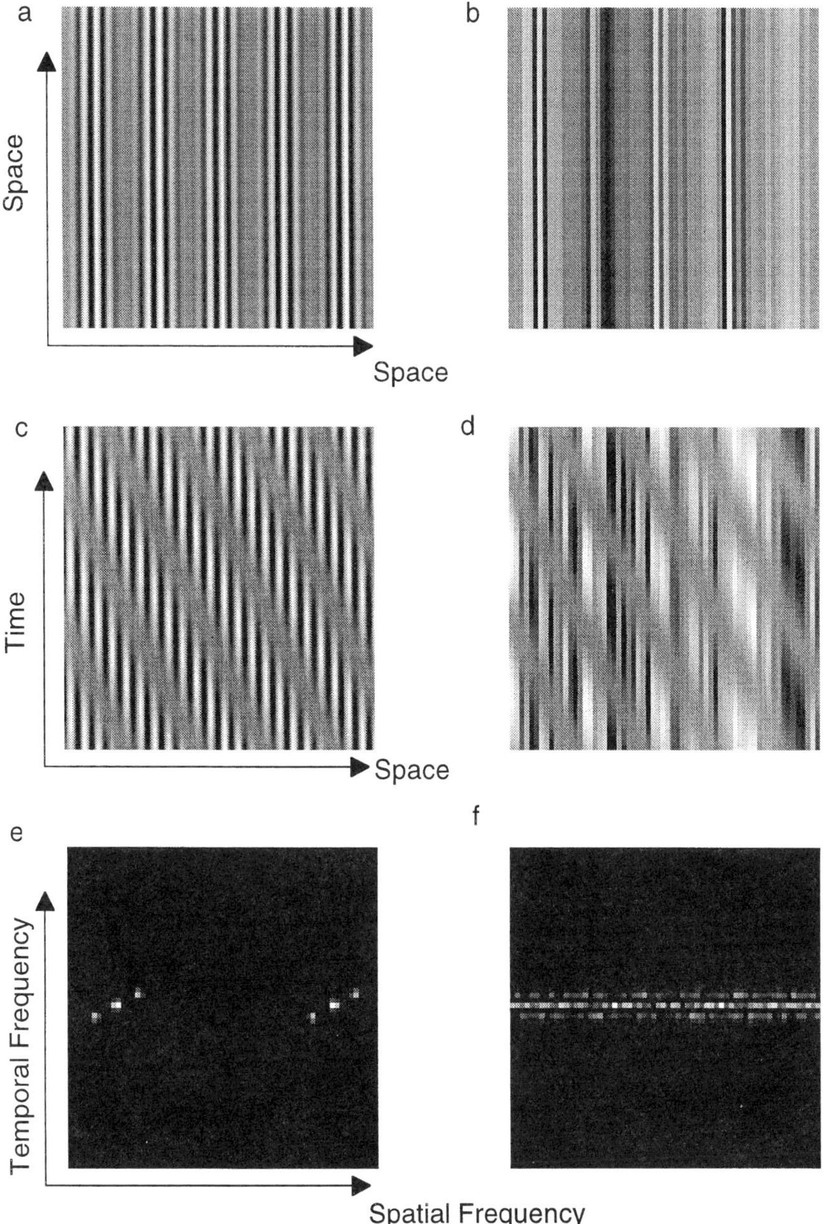

FIGURE 4 Second-order patterns and representations of their motion. (a) A contrast-modulated sinusoidal grating and (b) a contrast-modulated 1-D random-noise pattern. The modulation frequency (expressed in cycles/picture) is the same as in Figures 1 and 2. Space–time plots of the same two patterns moving at 0.5 image frames/sec are shown in (c) and (d). Note that the carriers are stationary: their bars are vertical, only the contrast-envelope is tilted. (e), (f) The spatiotemporal frequency representations of (c) and (d).

time plot of a slice through the middle of each of the second-order patterns from Figure 4, moving at a speed of 0.1 image frames per second.

In each case the luminance variation is marked by dark and light lines that run vertically through the figure, giving it a local horizontal profile that is either sinusoidal (4c) or random (4d). The fact that the lines representing the luminance profiles run vertically through the plot indicates that the carriers themselves are stationary. But the horizontal sinusoidal contrast envelope that modulates each carrier pattern is clearly moving: the contrast envelope shifts gradually towards the left as one moves up the time axis.

The motion of a contrast-modulated sine wave also has a signature in the frequency domain. This comes from the fact that modulating a sinusoidal carrier of frequency f_c at some modulation frequency f_m is the same as adding sidebands of frequencies $f_c + f_m$ and $f_c - f_m$ to it

$$\{1 + m\sin 2\pi(f_m x + \omega t)\}\sin(2\pi f_c x) = \sin(2\pi f_c x) + \frac{m}{2}\{\sin 2\pi(f_c x + f_m x + \omega t) + \sin 2\pi(f_c x - f_m x - \omega t)\}. \quad (1)$$

The higher frequency sideband moves in the same direction as the contrast modulation, and the lower frequency sideband moves in the opposite direction. This means that, as with moving luminance patterns, the motion is represented by a group of spatiotemporal frequency components that lie along a line whose slope gives the velocity of the motion. However, unlike the situation with a moving luminance pattern, the line does not pass through the origin. Instead it crosses the x axis at a location corresponding to the spatial frequency of the carrier. If the carrier is itself a complex pattern containing many spatial frequency components, then each component has oppositely moving sidebands of higher and lower spatial frequencies added to it.

Figure 4e and f show spatiotemporal frequency representations of the patterns whose motion is represented as S-T plots in Figure 4c and d. In Figure 4e, in which the carrier is a simple sinusoid, the two extra components corresponding to the sidebands are easily seen. When the carrier contains a large number of static spatial frequency components, as in the case in Figure 6f, the signature is less obvious.

E. Representing Motion in 2-D Velocity Space

As we shall see, the visual system's early analysis of motion appears to rely on orientation-selective analyzers, each performing an analysis in one spatial dimension of the motion along a particular axis in the 2-D image. Such analyses can conveniently be represented as 2-D space–time plots or spatiotemporal frequency plots; however, to show how analyses from two differently oriented spatial axes can be represented and combined to calculate an unambiguous 2-D motion, we need to represent motion in two spatial dimensions.

This can be done by representing motions as vectors in a space that has horizontal and vertical velocity as its cardinal axes. Some convention is needed to distinguish between vectors that represent 1-D motion along some predetermined axis, and those that represent truly 2-D motions.

In this chapter I shall use the terms *1-D vector* to refer to a component of a 2-D motion along some predetermined axis, such as the motion of an oriented feature of a moving object or pattern which must necessarily appear to move along an axis perpendicular to its orientation. The motion is 1-D in that each oriented feature is constrained to move along the axis perpendicular to its orientation, although the axes of the 1-D motions of differently oriented features have different directions in 2-D velocity space. We use the term *2-D vector* to refer to the motion of a 2-D pattern that is necessarily 2-D.

Figure 5 shows an example of the reconstruction of 2-D vectors from several 1-D vectors. Each 1-D vector constrains the 2-D vector of the object containing the feature that gave rise to it to lie along a line orthogonal to the 1-D vector and passing through its end point. Where features of several different orientations are present, the constraint lines that they specify will intersect at the same point unless they belong to more than one object moving with more than one velocity. If there are multiple velocities in a pattern they will give rise to multiple intersection points.

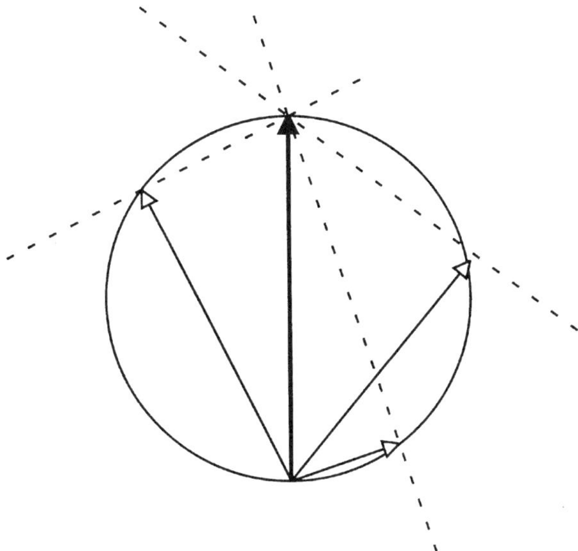

FIGURE 5 Velocity space representation of the intersection of constraints construction for resolving the 2-D motion (solid-headed arrow) consistent with several 1-D motion vectors (empty-headed arrows). The dashed lines passing through the tip of each 1-D vector shows the constraint line, the range of 2-D velocities consistent with that 1-D velocity. The three constraint lines intersect, indicating that they are all consistent with a single 2-D velocity.

III. ANALYZING DIRECTION OF MOTION ALONG A GIVEN AXIS

A. Principles and Approaches

Theoretical models of detectors that would be selectively sensitive to one direction of motion along a predetermined axis have been inspired by a broad range of motion analyzing problems from physiology, psychophysics, and machine vision. Perhaps the earliest motion detector that is still current was inspired by analysis of the optomotor response in the beetle (Reichardt, 1961). Reichardt's motion detector derives a motion signal by spatiotemporal correlation of luminance signals from neighboring points in the image. The same principle has been applied both to luminance signals and to second-order signals to account for aspects of human motion perception, and to explain the physiological properties of direction-selective neurones.

Other models of human motion detection have been derived from analysis of the signature that motion in a particular direction leaves in the spatiotemporal frequency domain (Watson & Ahumada, 1985), from analyses of contrast energy (Adelson & Bergen, 1985) and from comparison of the spatial and temporal variations in luminance in moving images (Fennema & Thompson, 1979; Johnston, McOwan, & Buxton, 1992). In the following sections I shall introduce examples of the different detectors that have been derived from these approaches and discuss their similarities. In each case I start by considering the motion-detector as a device designed to respond selectively to one of the representations of motion shown in Figures 2–4.

1. Correlation

Reichardt's model of the motion detectors that process the signals from the insect's compound eye exploits the fact that, when an image moves along a line between two receptors, the two receptors receive time-shifted versions of the same temporal signal. This is illustrated in Figure 6a, which shows vertical slices through the space–time image of Figure 2a. These show the temporal profile of the moving image measured at horizontal positions 0.25 grating periods apart. The two profiles show similar temporal waveforms shifted slightly in time.[1]

The time shift between the two profiles is simply the time it takes for any part of the image to move through the distance between the two points at which the profile is measured. It can be calculated as the spatial separation between the two points divided by the velocity of the image motion.

Reichardt's model of the insect motion-detector consists of two stages. The first stage correlates signals from two neighboring receptors by multiplying the signal from one of them by a temporally filtered version of signal from its neighbor. The temporal filter introduces a time shift, so the multiplier's output for any given

[1]There is a slight difference in the profile caused by the fact that the moving grating does not have uniform contrast throughout the whole image but is spatially shaped by a stationary Gaussian window.

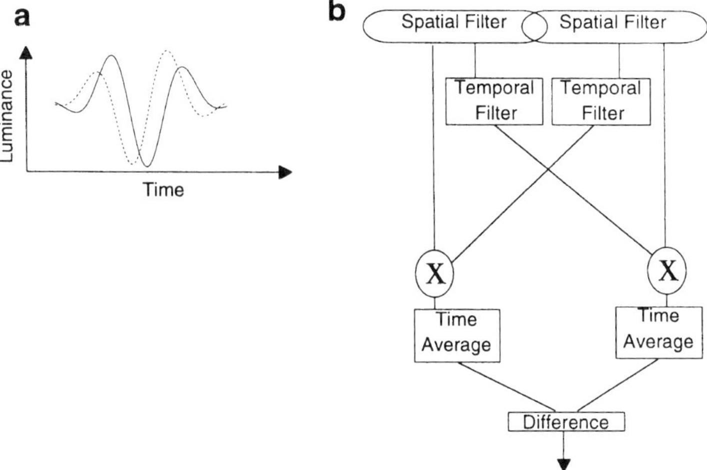

FIGURE 6 (a) Temporal profiles of the stimulus in Figure 2 at two points 0.25 spatial periods apart. (b) Elaborated Reichardt motion detector. Each side multiplies the output of one spatial filter by the delayed output from the other, thereby selecting stimuli moving in the direction from the delayed to the nondelayed filter. Consequently the two multipliers select opposite directions of motion. By taking the difference between the time-averaged outputs of the two multipliers the detector produces an output that indicates the direction of motion by its sign.

moving image is greatest when velocity of the motion is such that the time shift within the temporal filter matches the time taken for the image to move the distance between the two receptors. Each first stage has a symmetrical partner that differs from it only in that it time-shifts the signal from the second receptor instead of the first, in order to sense motion in the opposite direction. The second stage of the detector simply subtracts the signals of the two first stages.

Reichardt's motion detector has been developed in order to apply it to human psychophysics (van Santen & Sperling, 1984, 1985). Figure 6b shows an elaborated version that differs from the original in that it has additional filtering stages. Spatial filters at the input restrict the range of spatial frequencies passed by the detector in order to prevent it from responding to high spatial frequencies moving in the opposite direction. Temporal filters at the output integrate the response over time. The spatial filters shown in Figure 6b are identical to each other and spatially offset. To prevent a response to high spatial frequency patterns moving in the opposite direction (spatial aliasing), the filters should remove spatial frequencies above $1/(2d)$ cycles per degree, where d is the separation between the centers of the input receptive fields (van Santen & Sperling, 1984). An alternative way of arranging the filters is for the two input spatial filters to be superimposed on one another, but to give them spatial profiles that differ in a way that causes a phase shift between them of $\pi/2$ for all spatial frequencies in their passband (van Santen & Sperling, 1984).

2. Linear Spatiotemporal Frequency Filters

Watson and Ahumada (1985) took a different approach to designing a motion-sensor. They sought to design a spatiotemporal frequency filter that was selective for the characteristic distribution of spatiotemporal frequency components into opposite quadrants, which is the signature of motion in a particular direction.

Their approach was very straightforward. The sensor achieved its selectivity for direction of motion by linearly combining the outputs of component filters that were nondirectional but that had different spatial and temporal phase characteristics. The component filters' phase characteristics were designed so that signals representing the preferred direction of motion would give rise to outputs that reinforced each other, whereas those representing the opposite direction of motion would give rise to outputs that would cancel each other.

The main components of the sensor were a quadrature pair of spatial filters and a quadrature pair of temporal filters that were connected together so that signals took two parallel paths through the sensor. Each path contained one of the quadrature pair of spatial filters and one of the quadrature pair of temporal filters in series. The effect was that spatiotemporal frequencies from adjacent quadrants, which represent opposite directions of motion, generate outputs from the two pathways through the sensor that are opposite in sign. Consequently, adding or subtracting the signals in the two pathways generates variants of the sensor that are identical except that they respond selectively to opposite directions of motion. All the components representing the nonpreferred direction of motion within each sensor are canceled by the addition or subtraction of the first-stage filters.

Figure 7a and b shows plots of the sensitivity profiles of spatial and temporal filters that can be combined to produce a motion sensor of the type devised by Watson and Ahumada (1985).[2] The products of these spatial and temporal filters produce four different filters with spatiotemporal profiles that are not oriented in space–time (Figure 7c–f). The lack of orientation in space–time means that the filters are not selective for either direction of movement, although they may be selective for high temporal frequency and thus respond better to moving images than to static images. However, the sums and differences of the separable filters, shown in Figure 7 g–k, are oriented to the left or to the right in space time and consequently are selective for that direction of image motion.

The motion sensors shown in Figure 7 g–k are linear in spatial and temporal summation. An image sequence that represents motion in its preferred direction gives rise to the same total output as it would if it were played in reverse to give motion in the opposite direction. The difference is that although the mean level is the same for both directions, motion in the preferred direction modulates the detector output more strongly. For example, sinusoidal gratings moving in different directions all give rise to sinusoidal outputs that have a mean level of zero, but the

[2]In fact the temporal filters used here are not a quadrature pair; they have the form proposed by Adelson and Bergen (1985).

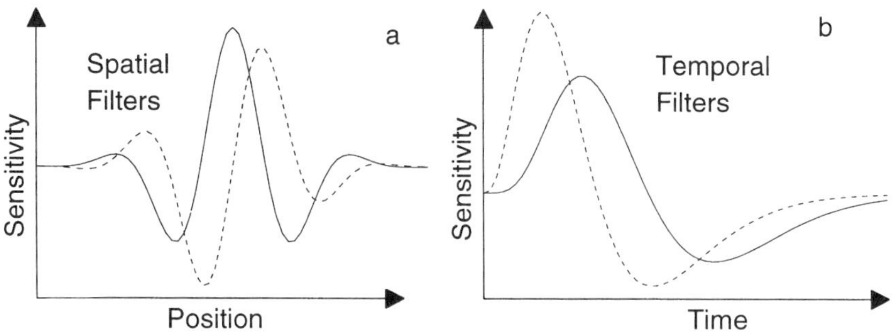

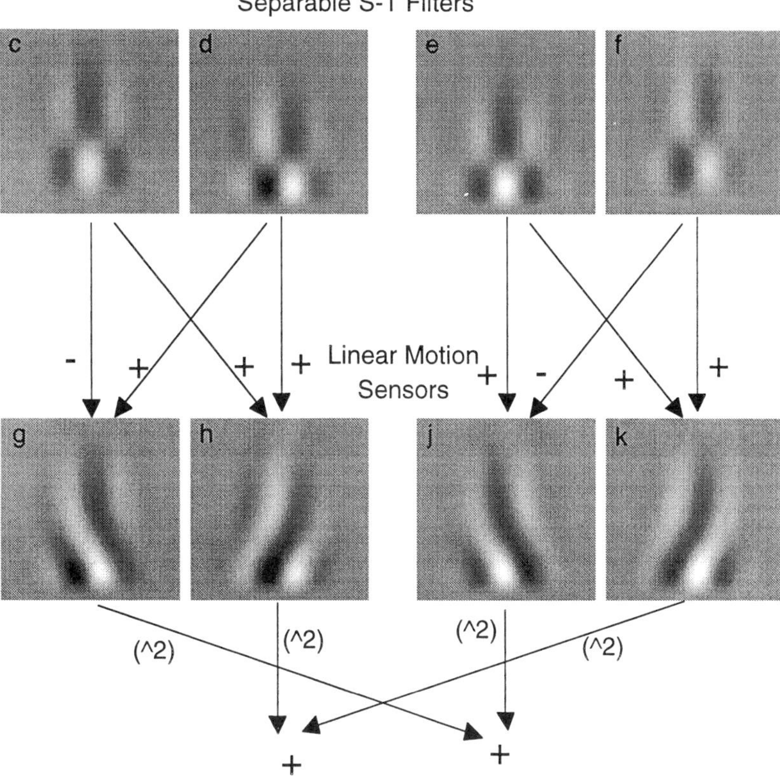

FIGURE 7 Spatiotemporal filtering operations leading to linear motion sensors and motion-energy filters. (a) Spatial filters for the front-end of a linear motion sensor. The two functions are an even-symmetric and an odd-symmetric Gabor function. (b) Two physiologically plausible temporal filters with different time-courses (Adelson & Bergen, 1985). (c,d,e,f) Space–time plots of the spatiotemporal impulse responses of four spatiotemporal filters formed from the products of the spatial and temporal filters in a and b. None of these filters is oriented in space/time. (g,h,j,k) Space–time plots of the spatiotemporal impulse responses of linear motion sensors produced from the sums and differences of the filters c–f as indicated. These filters are oriented in space–time; g and j are selective for leftward motion, and h and k are selective for rightward motion. The pairs of filters selective for each direction of motion for spatial quadrature pairs. Consequently the summed squares of the outputs of the filters tuned to each direction of motion constitute the motion energy signal. The difference between the two motion energy signals (not indicated) would be an opponent motion-energy signal.

amplitude of the sinusoid varies with direction of motion, being greatest for motion in the sensor's preferred direction and zero for motion in the opposite direction.

Watson and Ahumada (1985) exploit the oscillations in the output of their motion sensor to derive an estimate of image velocity. Because the sensor is selective for spatial frequency, the temporal frequency of the oscillations in its output in response to a spatially broad-band input depends on the speed of the input. Image velocity is estimated by metering the temporal frequency of the outputs of direction-detectors tuned to different axes of motion and fitting a sinusoid.

3. Motion Energy Filtering

The outputs of linear motion sensors can be combined to make a filter selective for oriented contrast energy in the s-t image (Adelson & Bergen, 1985) (shown in Figure 7). The motion energy is constructed by taking the outputs of quadrature pairs of motion sensors tuned to the same direction and speed of motion, squaring them, and summing them. The resulting direction-selective detector is nonlinear: it gives a nonoscillating response to a moving sinusoid. An optional final stage of the motion energy filter (not shown in Figure 7) subtracts the responses of the symmetrical stages tuned to opposite directions of motion and gives an output whose sign signals the direction of motion.

The motion energy filter and the linear motion sensor contain very similar linear spatiotemporal filters that extract a direction-selective signal. The essential difference between the detectors is in the nonlinear processing that follows the direction-selective filtering. Whereas the linear motion sensor uses the temporal frequency of variations in the output from the filter to extract a velocity signal, the energy detector squares and sums the outputs from different filters to produce a smoothly changing output. Van Santen and Sperling (1985) have shown that relatively minor modifications make the Reichardt motion detector exactly equivalent to the opponent motion energy detector and have argued that the three motion-detecting schemes are equivalent; however, this argument ignores the stages of Watson and Ahumada's model of motion sensing that measure velocity.

The motion energy filter gives no direct information about velocity. The filter's output depends on contrast, on spatial frequency, and on temporal frequency; however, the effects of contrast and spatial frequency can be discounted by comparing the output of two energy filters tuned to the same spatial frequency but to different temporal frequencies. Adelson and Bergen suggest that in order to estimate velocity the output of the motion energy filter could be divided by the output of a contrast energy filter tuned to zero temporal frequency.

4. Spatiotemporal Gradients

The spatial variations in luminance in a moving image give rise to temporal variations at different points in space when the image moves. If we make the assumption that all the temporal variation in a space–time image is caused by movement, it becomes possible to use the relation between spatial and temporal variations at any position to infer the nature of the motion rather exactly. Figure 8 illustrates this for a simple luminance gradient in an image. As the gradient moves past a point in space, the luminance at that point rises at a rate that is proportional to the product of steepness of the spatial gradient and the velocity of translation. This can be expressed exactly in the form

$$V_x \partial L/\partial x = -\partial L/\partial t, \tag{2}$$

where V_x is the velocity along an axis x in the image, L is luminance at any point in the image, x is distance along the axis x in the image, and t is time. The velocity is given by dividing the temporal derivative by the spatial derivative

$$V_x = -(\partial L/\partial t)/(\partial L/\partial x). \tag{3}$$

This approach has been used successfully to derive local velocity signals from a sequence of television images and to segment the image on the basis of the different velocities present (Fennema & Thompson, 1979). This approach, however, does suffer from the problem that the expression for the velocity is a fraction with the spatial luminance gradient as its denominator. When the luminance gradient is small or zero, that is, in parts of the image where the luminance is spatially uniform, the velocity computation will be very noisy.

There are several possible solutions to this problem. The simplest, which was adopted by Fennema and Thompson and has also been incorporated into a specific biological model of motion detection (Marr & Ullman, 1981) is only to make the motion calculation at locations where the spatial luminance gradient has already been identified as being sufficiently steep to produce a reliable result. An alternative is to include higher spatial derivatives in the velocity calculation, which has a stabilizing effect because it is rare for all the derivatives to be zero simultaneously (Johnson et al., 1992).

5. Similarity between the Spatiotemporal Gradient Approach and Motion Energy Filtering

Although on the face of it the computation of velocity as the ratio of the local temporal and spatial luminance derivatives in an image seems very different from the filtering approach, in fact there are ways of expressing the two approaches that bring them

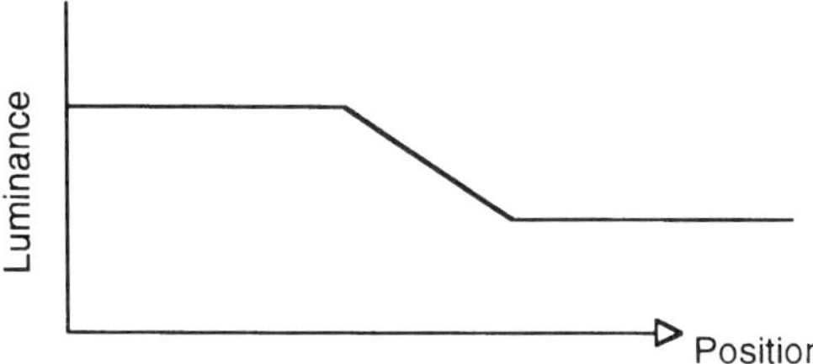

FIGURE 8 Spatial luminance gradient. When it moves to the left the luminance at any point on the gradient will decrease at a rate proportional to the velocity and vice versa.

together. When the differentiation that calculates the spatial and temporal gradients is combined with filtering, as it generally is in any biologically plausible motion-detecting model, it is possible to express the two approaches in very similar ways.

There are two reasons for this. First, differentiating an image and then filtering it with a linear filter gives exactly the same result as differentiating the filter and then using it to filter the original image. Second, differentiating a filter converts an even filter into an odd filter, introducing the same phase shifts as exist between the quadrature pairs of filters in the linear motion sensor. Differentiation also changes the amplitude spectrum of the filter, making it more high pass. One consequence of this is that combining a low-pass or mildly band-pass blurring function, such as might be produced by retinal processing, with differentiation produces a band-pass filter that becomes narrower with subsequent differentiation operations.

Mark Georgeson has shown that the motion energy computation can be done using input filters that have these spatial and temporal profiles and that the motion energy velocity computation, which is done by dividing the output of the motion energy stage by the output of a spatially matched static contrast energy stage, is identical to the velocity computation based directly on spatial and temporal derivatives (Bruce, Green, & Georgeson, 1996). This blurs the distinction between the multi-channel gradient model and energy models of motion analyzers.

B. Experimental Data

The preceding section shows that, although the various approaches to analyzing the direction of motion have different starting points, most of them can be brought to a common end point by appropriate choice of filter characteristics and of subsequent processing. This overlap between the different models has the consequence that psychophysical experiments may not reveal which of the approaches described in the previous section provides the most appropriate description of the mechanisms that enable us to see motion.

In this section we shall see that psychophysical experiments allow us not only to demonstrate that some motion percepts cannot be derived from analysis of the correspondence between image features over time and so must result from some sort of filtering operation applied to the raw spatiotemporal luminance profile but also to infer the spatial and temporal characteristics of the filters involved. They may yet allow us to distinguish between the different nonlinear operations that follow the filtering stages in the models outlined in the previous section. We shall also see that physiological experiments on single neurones can determine which of the different classes of model best applies to the neurone in question.

1. Psychophysics

a. Filtering versus Correspondence

In order to demonstrate that a motion percept does not depend on an analysis of how features or objects in the image change their position with time, it is sufficient to show either that motion is perceived when features are not displaced or do not appear to be displaced, or that the perceived motion and the perceived feature displacement may have different speeds or go in different directions. I shall discuss three clear demonstrations of this kind of dissociation between perceived motion and the perceived displacement of features, indicating that some motion percepts must be extracted directly from the image. In most images, however, motion analysis by tracking of features and by filtering gives the same result, and special techniques are necessary to distinguish motion percepts based on filtering from those based on correspondence.

Perhaps the most straightforward demonstration of a dissociation between perceived motion and the perceived positions of objects arises in the motion aftereffect, or waterfall illusion, first described in the modern literature in the nineteenth century (Addams, 1834). If, after looking at an object or pattern in continuous motion for some time, the motion is stopped or the gaze is shifted, motion in the opposite direction to that which had actually been occurring is seen in the same part of the visual field. However, static objects in that part of the visual field do not appear to change their positions with time.

The fact that the motion aftereffect does not involve any changes in perceived position is clear evidence that the perception of motion can be dissociated from any changes in the position (or the perceived position) of image features, and thus must result from activity in special-purpose mechanisms for the perception of motion. Barlow and Hill suggested that the motion aftereffect arises because the perception of motion in a given direction arises when there is an excess of activity in neurones selective for motion in that direction, relative to those selective for motion in the opposite direction. They illustrated the point by showing recordings from a direction-selective neurone recorded in the retina of the rabbit. Prolonged stimulation with motion in the preferred direction was followed by a depression of its firing rate below the normal resting level (Barlow & Hill, 1963). Although it is unlikely that direction-selective mechanisms in the human visual system are exactly the same as those in the rabbit retina, the motion aftereffect does point to the existence of motion-sensors in the human visual system that do not depend on changes in position.

A second situation in which motion and position changes are dissociated occurs when subjects attempt to detect oscillating relative motion in random-dot fields (Nakayama & Tyler, 1981). The stimulus consists of a rectangular field of random dots in which each row of dots oscillates to and fro along a horizontal path. The horizontal velocity of each dot is given by the product of a sinusoidal function of its vertical position and a sinusoidal function of time. If the motion of such a pattern were sensed by a mechanism that sensed changes in the horizontal positions of dots, one would expect that the motion would be detectable whenever the amplitude of the oscillating displacement exceeded the smallest detectable displacement.

In fact, as Figure 9 shows, for temporal frequencies up to about 2 Hz, the threshold displacement in an oscillating random-dot display declines almost exactly in

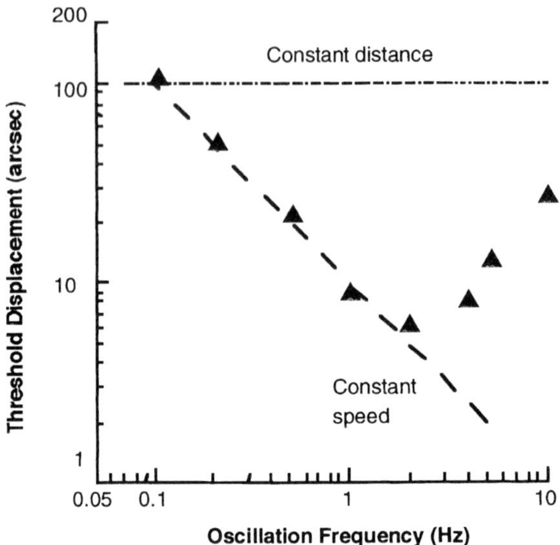

FIGURE 9 Displacement thresholds for detecting oscillatory shearing motion in a pattern of random dots. From approximately 0.1 Hz to 2 Hz the threshold declines in proportion to the temporal frequency of oscillation which indicates that, expressed as a velocity, it is unchanging over this range. (Reprinted from *Vision Research, 21,* Nakayama, K., & Tyler, C. W. Psychophysical isolation of movement sensitivity by removal of familiar position cues, pp. 427–433. Copyright 1981, with permission of Elsevier Science and the author.)

proportion to the temporal frequency, indicating that threshold is reached at a constant velocity rather than at a constant displacement. Although it is not possible *a priori* to define how the sensitivity of motion detectors of different types should vary with temporal frequency, it seems likely that in this case the limit is not set by a mechanism that tracks displacements since one would expect the performance of such a mechanism to be limited by displacement, and to decline rapidly at high temporal frequency, since one might expect that the encoding of each position displacement would take a more or less fixed time.

A third situation in which motion judgments and displacement judgments are dissociated arises when human subjects are asked to discriminate the direction of motion of complex grating patterns that contain a high spatial-frequency (about 3 cycles/deg) moving sinusoid added to a low spatial-frequency (1 cycle/deg) sinusoid that does not move. At long durations the motion of such a pattern is seen correctly, but when it is presented for less than about 100 ms the pattern appears to move in the opposite direction to the actual motion of the 3 cycle per degree component, both when the motion is continuous and when it is part of a two-frame apparent motion sequence (Derrington & Henning, 1987b; Henning & Derrington, 1988). However, if subjects are asked to discriminate the direction of vernier offset between the two frames of the apparent motion sequence presented one above the other, they perform correctly both at short durations and at long durations, as shown in Figure 10.

It is not clear what makes this pattern appear to move in the wrong direction when it is presented for a short duration; however, the fact that it reverses its direction of motion without reversing the offset in perceived position indicates that the motion signal is derived independently of any sense of spatial position. It does not depend on a correspondence-based mechanism.

If we make the assumption that the reversal of the motion percept at short durations is some intrinsic property of the motion filters, such as an interaction between filters tuned to different spatial frequencies, it follows that the most likely explanation for the recovery in performance at long durations is that the correspondence-based mechanism for sensing motion is able to provide a veridical signal at long durations that overcomes the erroneous signal derived from motion filters. From this it is tempting to infer that the stimulus duration at which veridical motion is first seen, about 200 ms, represents a lower limit on the operation of the correspondence-based motion-sensing mechanism. It suggests that one way to isolate motion mechanisms based on spatiotemporal filters is to use stimuli shorter in duration than this.

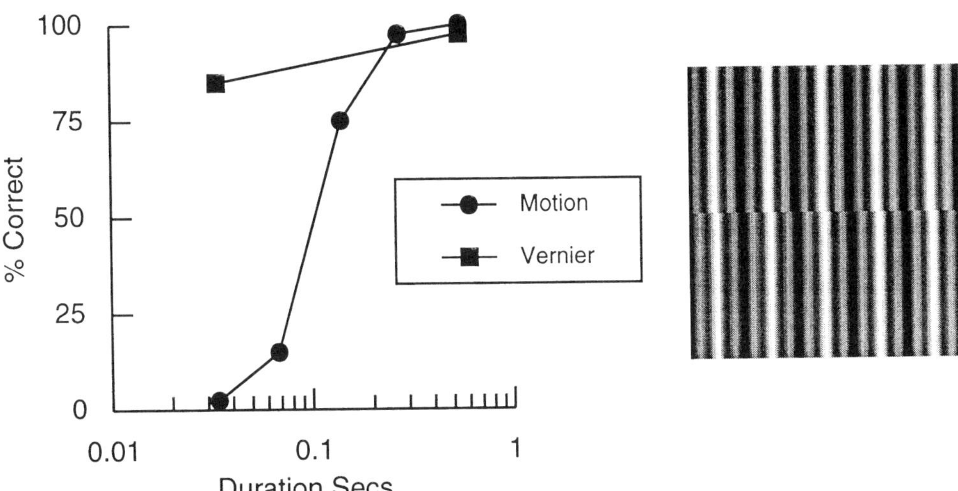

FIGURE 10 Performance in judging direction of motion and direction of vernier offset in a pattern that consisted of the sum of a 3 cycle/degree grating that was displaced either between frames (in the motion task) or between the top of the frame and the bottom of the frame (in the vernier task) and a 1 cycle/degree grating that was not displaced. The motion discrimination is reliable but incorrect (i.e., observers see reversed motion) at short durations and correct at long durations. The vernier discrimination is correct at long and short durations. (Reprinted from *Vision Research, 27,* Derrington, A. M., & Henning, G. B. Errors in direction-of-motion discrimination with complex stimuli, 61–75. Copyright 1987, with permission of Elsevier Science.)

Motion discriminations that depend on correspondence-based mechanisms can be identified by adding to the stimulus a mask that prevents a correspondence-based mechanism from extracting a motion signal but does not affect the motion filter. Lu and Sperling (1995) have shown that adding a *pedestal,* a high-contrast static replica of itself, to a moving sinusoidal grating should have no effect on an elaborated Reichardt detector, while making it impossible for a correspondence-based analysis to extract a motion signal.

The logic of the pedestal test is straightforward. First, the elaborated Reichardt detector is immune to the pedestal because its response to the sum of several different temporal frequencies is the sum of the responses to the individual temporal frequencies (Lu & Sperling, 1995). The pedestal simply adds an extra temporal frequency component—0 Hz, which generates no output from the Reichardt detector—to the moving stimulus. Accordingly, the pedestal should not affect the response of the Reichardt detector. In fact, we can expect that when the contrast of the pedestal is high it will reduce sensitivity by activating gain-control mechanisms, but this should not happen until it is several times threshold contrast.

On the other hand, even if the pedestal is only slightly higher in contrast than the moving pattern, it will prevent features from moving consistently in any one direction. Instead, as Figure 11 illustrates, the features oscillate backwards and forwards over a range that depends on the relative contrasts of the moving pattern and the pedestal. In the presence of the pedestal any mechanism that depends solely on changes in the positions of features in the image to compute a motion signal will be prevented from extracting a consistent motion signal.

Psychophysical measurements of contrast thresholds show that pedestals of moderate contrast do not affect thresholds for judgments of direction of motion of simple luminance patterns, but several more complex motion stimuli are affected. Adding a pedestal to the moving stimulus raises the contrast required to discriminate direction of motion of patterns defined by variations in binocular disparity or direction of motion (Lu & Sperling, 1995).

These results raise the possibility that we may be able to divide motion stimuli into two classes according to whether or not they are susceptible to pedestals. How-

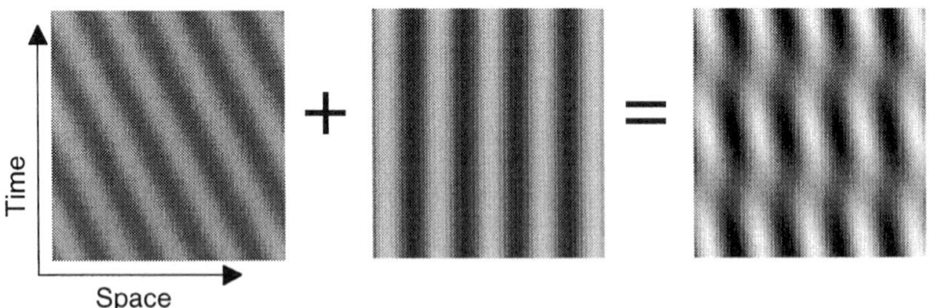

FIGURE 11 Space–time plots of a moving sinusoidal grating, a static pedestal of twice its contrast, and their sum. Adding the pedestal to the grating prevents the continuous displacement of features that occurs during movement. Instead the features oscillate and change their contrast over time.

ever, although such a classification is attractive, it is not necessarily as straightforward to interpret as Lu and Sperling (1995) suggest. In fact, there are three specific reasons that we should not leap to the conclusion that all motion stimuli that are immune to pedestals are analyzed by correspondence-based mechanisms (feature trackers) and those that are not vulnerable are analyzed by motion filters.

First, the Reichardt detector's immunity to pedestals depends on an assumption that the detector's response is integrated over time. The space–time plot in Figure 15 shows that the addition of a pedestal to a moving sinusoidal grating gives rise to a stimulus that moves backwards and forwards over time. When the motion is forwards (i.e., in the same direction as when there is no pedestal) the contrast is higher; however, the grating spends almost half its time moving in the reverse direction. Brief stimuli, or stimuli that are not integrated over time could well give rise to a motion signal in the opposite direction resulting in a deterioration in performance in the presence of the pedestal. Thus relatively minor variations in the detailed architecture of the Reichardt motion detector might make it vulnerable to pedestals. In addition, Lu and Sperling (1995) suggest that high-contrast pedestals are likely to impair the performance of a Reichardt motion analyzer simply by activating a contrast gain-control mechanism.

Second, the assertion that correspondence-based or feature-tracking motion analyzers are vulnerable to pedestals depends on an assumption that the contrast of a feature has no effect on the ability to analyze its location or to track it. It might well be that when different features signal opposite directions of motion, or when the same feature signals opposite directions of motion at different times, the features with higher contrast are more likely to determine the perceived direction of motion. If this were to happen we would expect that feature-tracking motion analyzing mechanisms would be resistant to pedestals.

Third, even if all feature-tracking motion mechanisms are vulnerable to pedestals and all motion filters are resistant to them, we should acknowledge that in principle any feature can be tracked, whether or not its motion is normally analyzed by a motion filter or Reichardt detector. Thus many moving stimuli will be analyzed by both types of mechanisms and the effect of interfering with one or other mechanism will depend on which is the more sensitive.

It follows that the discovery that under a particular set of circumstances our ability to analyze the motion of a particular stimulus is resistant to a pedestal does not mean that under normal circumstances feature tracking may not make an important contribution to the analysis of the motion of that particular stimulus. In my own lab we have found that the same sinusoidal grating moving at the same speed can become vulnerable to a pedestal simply by making its motion less smooth by causing it to move in jumps of $\frac{3}{8}$ period (Derrington & Ukkonen, unpublished observations).

This change can easily be explained by assuming that when the grating moves in smaller steps, spatiotemporal filters are more sensitive than the feature-tracking mechanism, and when it moves in large steps, the reverse is true. This kind of change in relative sensitivities seems quite reasonable in two respects. First, as the jump size increases and the average speed remains constant, tracking features should become easier because the features spend more time stationary in between jumps. Second, changing the jump size while keeping the speed constant affects the responsiveness of motion detectors based on quadrature pairs of spatial filters because the temporal frequency spectrum of the stimulus becomes contaminated by sampling artifacts (Watson, 1990).

In sum, although the pedestal test represents a promising potential technique for distinguishing between different types of motion mechanisms, it is appropriate to be cautious both in interpreting the results and in extrapolating from them.

b. Characteristics of Motion Filters

The spatial and temporal frequency selectivity of the mechanisms subserving motion perception can be analyzed by the same techniques as have been used to study the mechanisms of spatial vision (Braddick, Campbell, & Atkinson, 1978). The most widely used techniques are adaptation (also known as habituation), in which the aftereffect of viewing a moving stimulus is a selective elevation of threshold for subsequently presented stimuli that are moving in the same direction, and masking, in which a high-contrast moving "mask" selectively elevates the threshold of concurrently presented stimuli that are similar to the mask. One of the most complete descriptions of the spatial and temporal frequency selectivity of mechanisms responsible for the detection of moving stimuli comes from a study in which observers adjusted the contrast of a moving grating until it was just visible (Burr, Ross, & Morrone, 1986). High-contrast masking gratings that flickered in temporal counterphase but did not move were added to the test and elevated its threshold.[3] When plotted as a function of spatial frequency, the threshold elevation curves always peaked at the spatial frequency of the test grating. When plotted as functions of temporal frequency, however, the threshold elevation function peaked at a frequency close to that of the test when the test had high temporal frequency (8 Hz) regardless of the spatial frequency, and were low-pass with constant height from 10 Hz down to 0.3 Hz when the test grating had a low temporal frequency (0.3 Hz).

By measuring how threshold elevation varied with the contrast of the mask, Burr et al. (1986) were able to infer the threshold sensitivity of the mechanisms responsible for detecting the test. They made the assumption that detection was determined by a linear filter, which was followed by a compressive nonlinearity. Consequently, by using the way threshold elevation changes with mask contrast to factor out the nonlinearity, they were able to calculate the spatiotemporal frequency sensitivity of the filter; they were also able to calculate its profile in space–time. Figure 12 shows space–time profiles of the filters responsible for detecting test stimuli of 0.1, 1, and 5 cycles/deg moving at 8 Hz, and 5 cycles/deg moving at 0.3 Hz. In the first three cases the characteristics of the filter are well matched both to the spa-

[3] A counterphase flickering grating is the sum of two sinusoidal gratings of the same spatial frequency and contrast moving in opposite directions.

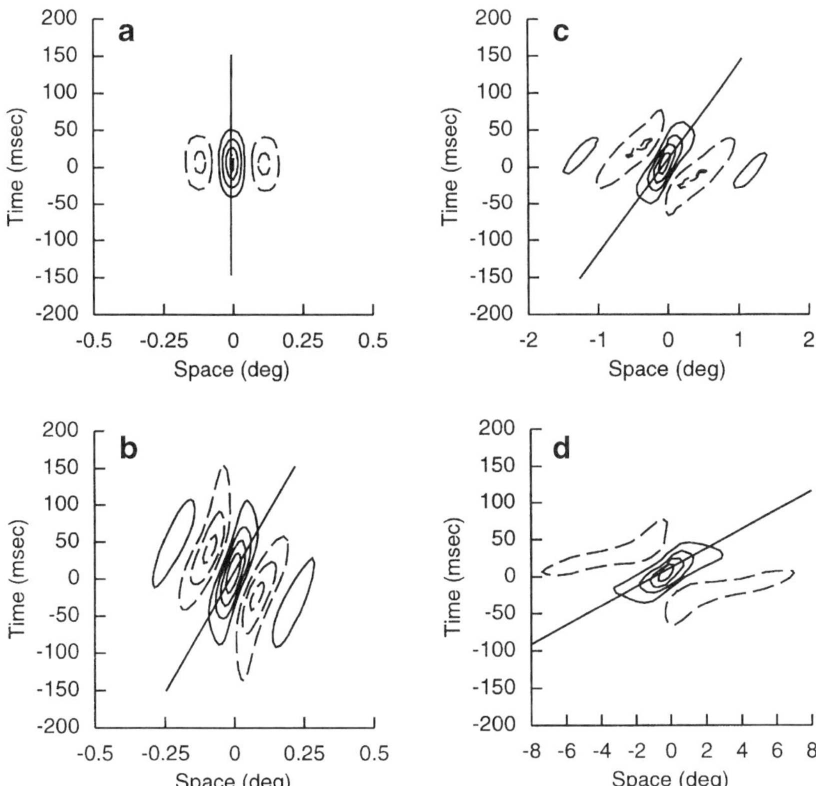

FIGURE 12 Space–time contour plots of the spatiotemporal impulse responses of motion-detectors in the human visual system inferred from masking experiments. Areas of opposite sign are indicated by dashed and continuous lines respectively. The straight line through the center of each plot represents the speed of the test pattern. Note that the horizontal scale changes by factors of 4 from b to c and again from c to d. (Data from Burr et al., 1986, Figure 6 with permission of the Royal Society of London and authors.)

tial structure of the stimulus and to the changes over time as it moves. In the last case, where the stimulus moves at 0.3 Hz, the spatial structure of the filter matches that of the grating, but its temporal structure shows no selectivity either for moving stimuli against static stimuli or for one direction of motion against the other.

Burr and his colleagues suggested that it is the combined spatial and temporal selectivity of the motion-selective filters that allows us to analyze the spatial structure of moving objects and to integrate the energy from a moving spot without smearing it; however, the relationship between the outputs of such filters and our perception of the motion of complex patterns is not straightforward. When a simple, briefly presented, moving grating is added to a static grating of lower spatial frequency, the resulting stimulus appears to move in the opposite direction from that in which it actually moves. Subjects are perfectly reliable in discriminating between opposite directions of motion, but consistently wrong in their decision about which direction is which. This illusory reversed motion is at its strongest when the contrast of the moving pattern and that of the static pattern are roughly equal, and well above threshold (Derrington & Henning, 1987a). This suggests that there is some kind of nonlinear interaction between the filters tuned to different spatial frequencies that creates a motion metamer, that is, a stimulus that is moving in one direction but appears as if it is moving in the opposite direction.

2. Physiology

The fact, discussed in section III.A, that different schemes for generating direction selectivity can be rendered exactly equivalent to one another makes it difficult to conceive of psychophysical experiments that would reveal the principles of operation of direction-selective mechanisms. Part of the difficulty here is that in a typical psychophysical experiment, the observer makes a single, usually binary, decision based on a large number of mechanisms. There is no access to the outputs of individual mechanisms. However, in physiological experiments on the mammalian visual cortex, it is possible to record the outputs of single cells that can be represented as direction-selective spatiotemporal frequency filters (Cooper & Robson, 1968; Movshon, Thompson, & Tolhurst, 1978a, 1978b).

Emerson et al. (1987) have shown that the responses of a complex cell to spatiotemporal sequences of bars flashed in different parts of the receptive field can be used to distinguish between different nonlinear filtering operations that might give rise to direction selectivity. Figure 13 shows an example of the responses of a complex cell in cat striate cortex. The pattern of these responses is consistent with what would be produced by the nonopponent level of the motion energy filter, but not the Reichardt detector.

A plausible physiological implementation of the motion energy filter in the complex cell receptive field uses two direction-selective subunits with receptive fields of opposite sign to represent each direction-selective filter in the quadrature pair (Emerson, 1997). Each subunit has a nonlinear output stage that half-wave rectifies and then squares the signal (Heeger, 1991), so that adding together the two complementary subunits gives the effect of a linear filter followed by a squarer. A second pair of filters in quadrature spatial and temporal phase relationship to the first pair complete the model and render the receptive field model formally identical to the motion-energy filter (Adelson & Bergen, 1985; Emerson, 1997).

Simple cells respond to a moving grating with a modulated response whose temporal frequency matches the temporal frequency of the moving grating (Movshon et al., 1978b), so direction-selective simple cells could not possibly be based on the motion energy filter which gives an unmodulated response to a moving grating (Adelson & Bergen, 1985). However, a number of features of the responses of simple cell receptive field suggest that its selectivity for direction of motion could be based, at least in part, on linear filtering like that underlying the motion energy filter.

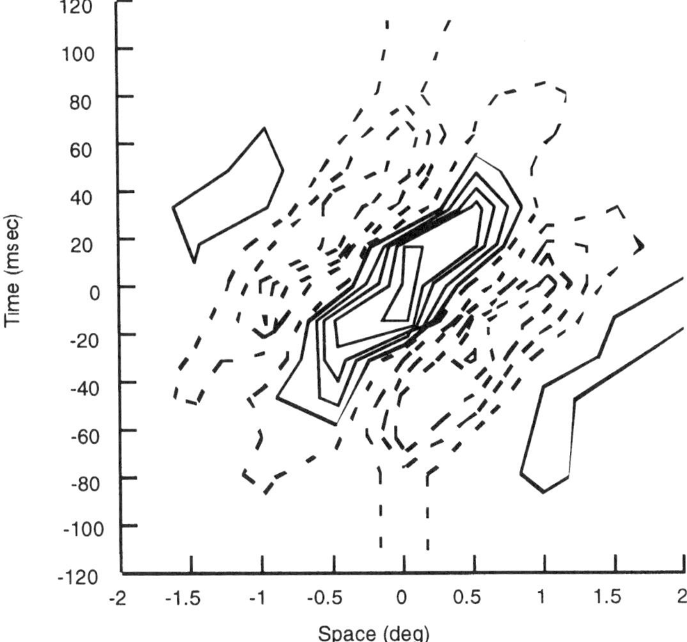

FIGURE 13 Space–time contour plot of nonlinear motion-selective spatiotemporal interactions in the receptive field of a cortical cell. The plot is produced by measuring the increase (continuous line) or decrease (dashed line) in the response to a conditioning flash produced by a test flash that is presented at a different time and position. The interaction is plotted as a function of the spatial and temporal separation between the test flash and the conditioning flash. The spatiotemporal pattern of facilitation and inhibition represent a nonlinear contribution to direction-selectivity. (Replotted from Emerson, Citron, Vaughn, & Klein, 1987, with permission from the American Psychological Society.)

The temporal phase of a simple cell's response to a flickering sinusoidal grating varies with the spatial phase of the grating, and the temporal impulse response varies with the location of the stimulus in the receptive field in a way that suggests that the linear receptive field is oriented in space–time like the linear motion sensor (Albrecht & Geisler, 1991). Detailed nonlinear analyses of simple cell responses to flickering gratings and to flashing bars in different parts of the receptive field suggest that in fact the simple-cell receptive field may contain a single pair of linear motion filters that have a quadrature spatial and temporal phase relationship with one another (Emerson, 1997; Emerson & Huang, 1997). The resulting receptive fields are very similar to those of the single subunits in linear receptive-field models, except that they give a more sustained response to a stimulus moving in the preferred direction.

The receptive field model of the simple cell contains exactly half the components from the model of the complex receptive field. Missing from the simple cell model are the complementary negative replicas of each motion-filtering subunit which, by generating a positive response when the subunit's response would be negative, convert the ensemble from a half-wave rectified squarer to a full squarer. This difference provides a simple explanation of the fact that the simple cell possesses and the complex cell lacks a quasi-linear receptive field wherein the response to simple stimuli readily predicts the main features of the response to more complex and larger stimuli (Hubel & Wiesel, 1962, 1968). The fact that the complex cell's output contains only terms that correspond to the squares of the outputs of quasi-linear filters means that the linear component of its output is zero.

Another way of expressing the difference between the models is to say that the direction-selective complex cell receptive field model can be decomposed into two simple cell receptive fields. The simple cell receptive fields are aligned so that the linear components of their responses cancel one another and the nonlinear components reinforce one another. Consequently, the linear response of the complex cell receptive field should be zero; it should give the same response to increments and to decrements of luminance throughout its receptive field.

Although the qualitative similarity between the responses of direction-selective cortical neurones and those of the motion-energy filter is encouraging, the number of cells that have been examined in detail is small. At this stage it would be premature to exclude other model motion-detectors; however, one qualitative feature of motion-selective neurones in striate cortex that has been very widely confirmed is that cells are selective for the orientation and direction of motion of elongated contours. Experiments with random 2-D textures, which inevitably contain large numbers of components of different spatial frequency and orientation, have yielded confusing results, which at least in some cases can be explained by the mixture of excitatory and inhibitory effects of the different orientation and spatial-frequency components of the random pattern (Morrone, Burr, & Maffei, 1982). When they are stimulated with simpler 2-D patterns composed by summing only two sinusoidal components, cells in monkey striate cortex respond when the pattern is orientated so that one of its components falls within the range of orientations to which the cell is sensitive and moves in the cell's preferred direction, even when, as is inevitably the case when a pattern consists of two differently oriented components both of which are moving, the pattern moves along a different axis of motion to the component.

Cortical area middle temporal (MT), which is the destination of some of the projections from striate cortex and which appears to be specialized for analyses of motion (Dubner & Zeki, 1971) contains cells that respond selectively to the axis of motion of a pattern, regardless of the orientations and axes of motion of its components (Movshon, Adelson, Gizzi, & Newsome, 1985). In the conscious monkey, cells in area MT respond to the motion of patterns of dots in which the direction of motion perceived is determined by a small proportion of the dots that move coherently in a consistent direction while the directions of motion of the remaining dots are randomly distributed. The proportion of dots that must move coherently in order to excite a neurone is comparable to the proportion needed to reach the monkey's behavioral threshold for reporting motion in a particular direction (Britten, Shadlen, Newsome, & Movshon, 1992), supporting the idea that visual area MT is crucially implicated in the business of seeing motion.

Consideration of the early processing of moving stimuli in the mammalian visual cortex supports the idea that the motion of 2-D stimuli is analyzed in two stages. In the first stage the motion of orientated components, which will not, in general, be moving along the same axis as the stimulus, is analyzed by a range of sensors, each selective for motion along an axis orthogonal to its preferred orientation. In the second stage, the signals from these oriented 1-D sensors are combined to compute the axis and speed of motion of the stimulus as a whole. Two-stage analyses of motion have also been used in analyzing television pictures of objects in motion. In the first stage the speed of motion of luminance gradients in the image, in each case measured along the axis along which the gradient is steepest, is computed; in the second stage the signals from different parts of the image that constitute the same object are combined to compute the correct 2-D axis of motion and the speed of motion (Fennema & Thompson, 1979). The next section deals with the relationships between 1-D and 2-D analyses of the motion of 2-D patterns.

IV. INTEGRATING MOTION SIGNALS FROM DIFFERENT AXES: TWO-DIMENSIONAL VECTORS

A. What Is the Problem in Going from 1-D to 2-D Motion?

The problem the visual system faces in calculating the axis and speed of motion of a 2-D pattern or object from the 1-D signals generated by mechanisms that sense the motion of its oriented spatial frequency components or features has been exemplified in at least three different ways: (a) as a problem of viewing a stimulus through an aperture that only reveals some of its features; (b) as a problem of calculating the motion of an object from the motions of its oriented features; and (c) as a problem of interpreting signals from orientation-selective motion sensors or receptive fields. Each of these approaches emphasizes different aspects of the general problem, so I shall deal with each of them briefly before discussing the problem in general terms.

The aperture problem presents the 1-dimensional motion signal as a consequence of viewing an extended object through an aperture that only shows a small part of the object in which there is only one orientation present. Naturally, the only motion that can be seen through this aperture is orthogonal to the orientation of the visible feature. Apertures that reveal features that have different orientations but are part of the same object will, of course, reveal motions in different directions. Figure 14a and b show two examples of the aperture problem. Apertures on each of the sides of a moving rectangle show features moving in different directions, neither of which coincides with the true axis of motion of the rectangle unless the axis of motion is parallel to one of its sides.

Localized analyses of motion carried out on an entire image can also produce a phenomenon very similar to the aperture problem. In the absence of features, there

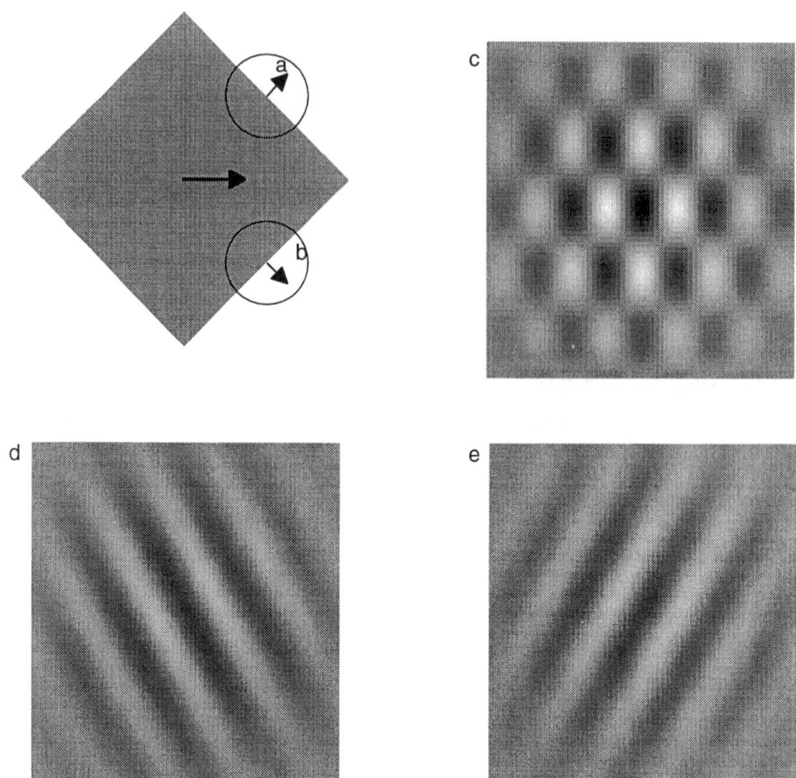

FIGURE 14 (a,b) The edges of the tilted square appear to move along an axis orthogonal to their orientation even though the square is moving in a different direction. (c) The plaid has horizontally and vertically oriented features but its components (d & e) are obliquely oriented gratings.

is no motion signal and where features are present the local motion signal tends to be strongest along an axis orthogonal to the local orientation of the feature. When speed is computed from local spatial and temporal gradients, the computation is most easily carried out along the axis of steepest spatial gradient, in which case it computes the motion along the axis orthogonal to the feature that generates the gradient (Fennema & Thompson, 1979). Each of the (minuscule) areas over which the spatial and temporal gradients are analyzed constitutes an aperture with its attendant aperture problem.

Orientation-selective motion filters operate on limited regions of the image, which means that they are susceptible to the aperture problem. In addition they are selective for orientation: each filter senses only features of its preferred orientation and consequently only signals motion along an axis orthogonal to that orientation. The fact that each filter is orientation-selective means that it can sense the motion of oriented spatial frequency components that do not themselves give rise to image features, as when two sinusoidal gratings of different orientations are added together to produce a plaid pattern. In the example shown in Figure 14c, the two components that make up the plaid pattern are oblique, 30° either side of vertical, but all the features—edges, dark and light lines—are either vertical or horizontal. Motion of the pattern would potentially give rise to motion signals in sensors tuned to all these orientations. The visual system then has the problem of computing the true motion of the pattern from the signals generated in the various filters.

In all three cases outlined above, the problem is that the local motion measurements give estimates of velocity along the axis of the oriented motion detector or along the axis orthogonal to the local feature. Consequently, the magnitude of these 1-D motion vectors is given by the product of the true motion vector and the cosine of the angle between the true 2-D motion vector and the 1-D motion vector. So

$$\nu_\theta = V\cos(\Theta - \theta), \tag{4}$$

where ν_θ is the magnitude of the 1-D vector along the axis θ, V is the magnitude, and Θ is the direction of the 2-D vector. The problem for the visual system is to estimate V and Θ from measurements of ν_θ along different axes, that is, for different values of θ. The values of θ are given by the local orientation of the features in the image (or are inherent properties of the oriented motion filters), the values of ν_θ are measured from the moving image. Equation 4 shows that one measurement of ν_θ constrains the relationship between V and Θ. Two measurements along different axes (i.e., with different values of θ) are sufficient to specify both V and Θ by the intersection of constraints, as illustrated graphically in Figure 5.

Thus although 1-D motion vectors are ambiguous cues to a pattern's true (2-D) velocity because each 1-D vector is consistent with a range of 2-D vectors, any two 1-D vectors give enough information to resolve the 2-D velocity (Fennema & Thompson, 1979). The 1-D vectors can be derived from spatial frequency components in the pattern or from features produced by local or global analyses of different sorts (Adelson & Movshon, 1982; Derrington & Badcock, 1992; Derrington, Badcock, & Holroyd, 1992; Movshon et al., 1985; Wilson, Ferrera, & Yo, 1992). The next section deals with experiments aimed at showing which 1-D vectors are used by the visual system and how they are combined.

B. How Does the Visual System Compute 2-D Motion from 1-D Motion Vectors?

1. Plaid Pattern Experiments and the Intersection of Constraints

Arguably the simplest 2-D pattern with which to compare 1-D and 2-D motion analysis is the plaid pattern, made by summing two sinusoidal gratings, which has been extensively used in vision research since its introduction by Adelson and Movshon (1982). When the two component gratings are very different in contrast, spatial frequency, or temporal frequency, they are seen as separate patterns that slide over one another. However, when their spatial frequency, temporal frequency, and contrast are similar, the gratings cohere perceptually to form a rigidly moving pattern whose speed and direction of motion is determined from the speeds and directions of motion of the component gratings by the intersection of constraints.

The motion of the plaid pattern could also be derived in other ways. Local features in the plaid, gradients, peaks, and troughs in its luminance profile can be used to derive 1-D motion vectors. Any two different 1-D vectors allow the 2-D vector to be calculated through the intersection of constraints (Figure 5) (Adelson & Movshon, 1982). Another possibility is that correspondence-based mechanisms could be used to track plaid features in two dimensions (Adelson & Movshon, 1982). However two sets of experiments in which the motion processing of plaid patterns can be predicted from the way in which the plaids' component gratings are processed suggests that the visual system calculates the motion of the plaid from the motion signals generated by its component gratings.

First, the precision with which subjects can estimate the speed of motion of a plaid appears to be predicted from the speed discrimination thresholds for its component gratings rather than from speed discrimination thresholds for other patterns superficially more similar to the plaid (Welch, 1989). Welch used a plaid made from gratings of the same spatial and temporal frequency. The speed of such a plaid relative to the speed of its component gratings increases with the angle between the gratings. This can be seen from the fact that the component speed is related to the plaid speed by the cosine of the angle between the plaid axis of motion and that of the component (equation 4).

Figure 15 shows Weber fractions for speed discrimination (discrimination threshold divided by speed) obtained with a plaid that moves approximately five times faster than its components compared with thresholds obtained with a grating of the same spatial frequency as the components. When plotted against the velocity of the component grating, both sets of Weber fractions show a distinctive dip at a speed of about 2°/sec.

When the data are plotted against the speed of the pattern, the dip for the plaid occurs at a speed five times higher. Welch argues that the fact that the data coincide when they are plotted as a function of component speed suggests that the visual system analyzes the plaid's speed by analyzing the speeds of its components. In an ingenious control experiment, she showed that if the angle between the plaid's components varies randomly from trial to trial, it is very difficult to discriminate the speed of its components when they are presented together in the form of a plaid, but not if they are presented alone. This suggests that although the visual system's estimate of the speed of the plaid may depend on its estimates of the speeds of its components, the speeds of the components cannot be used directly to make perceptual discriminations (Welch, 1989).

Another piece of evidence that the motion of plaid patterns is computed by the visual system from the perceived motions of their components comes from experiments in which the perceived speed of one of the components of a plaid pattern is reduced either by presenting it with lower contrast (Stone, Watson, & Mulligan,

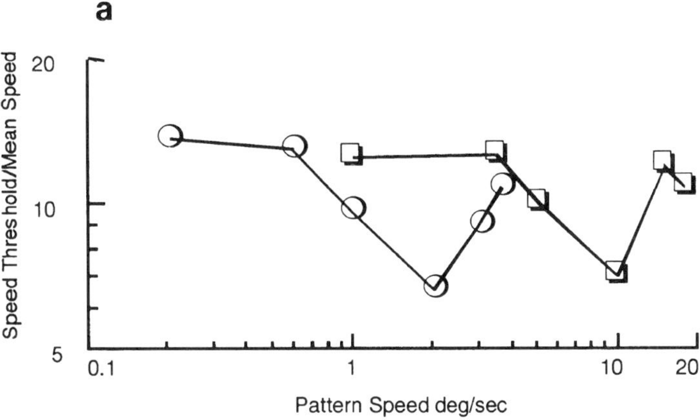

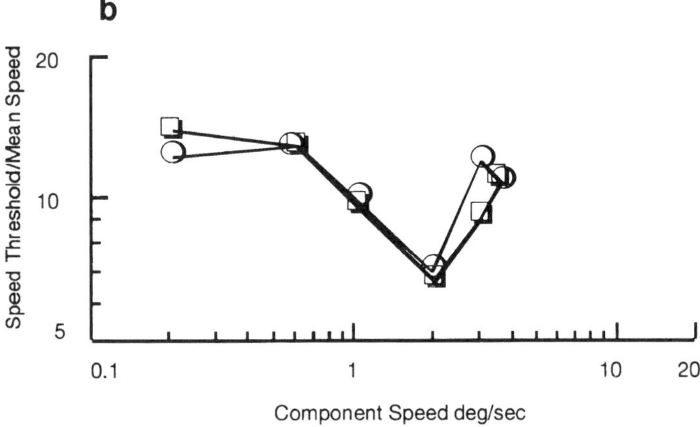

FIGURE 15 (a) The Weber fraction for speed discrimination of a plaid is plotted against the speed with which the pattern moves; there is a clear minimum at about 10 deg/sec. When the Weber pattern for a grating is plotted it reaches a minimum at 10 deg/sec. (b) The Weber fraction of the grating and the plaid are plotted in against the speed of the sinusoidal components. The minima for the two patterns now coincide at 2 deg/sec. (Data replotted with permission of the author and from *Nature, 337,* Welch, L., The perception of moving plaids reveals two motion-processing stages, 734–736. Copyright, 1989, MacMillan Magazines Limited.)

1990) or by adapting to a moving grating of the same spatial frequency and orientation presented in the same retinal position. The reduction in the perceived speed of the plaid's component changes the perceived axis of motion in the same way that it would have changed if the real speed of the component had been reduced. As Figure 16 shows, a plaid in which one of the components has its apparent velocity reduced by a motion aftereffect appears to move in its original direction if the actual

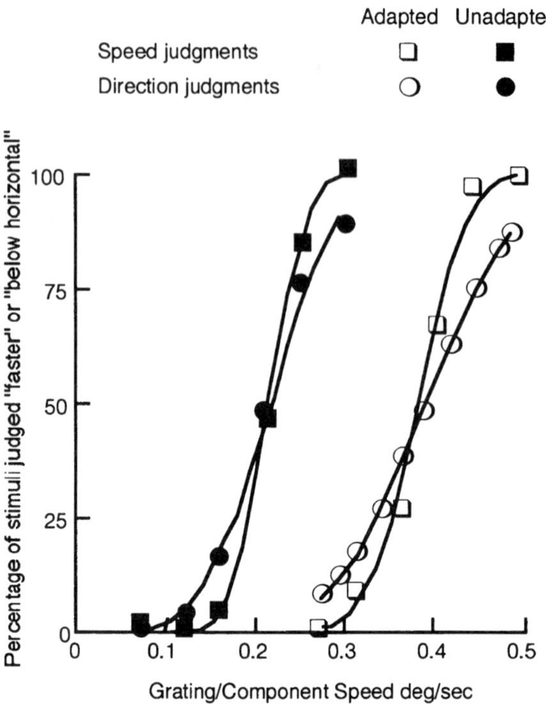

FIGURE 16 Aftereffect of viewing a moving grating on the perceived speed of a 2 c/deg grating and on the perceived direction of motion of a plaid pattern. The squares show the percentage of trials on which a test grating was judged to be moving faster than a standard grating moving at a speed of 0.38 deg/sec, plotted as a function of the speed of the test grating. Open squares show results obtained without adaptation; filled squares show results obtained while the patch of retina on which the standard grating was presented was being adapted to a grating moving in the same direction at 0.5 deg/sec. The circles show the percentage of trials on which a plaid pattern containing a 2 c/deg grating moving 45° upwards at 0.38 deg/sec and a 2 c/deg grating moving 45° downwards at variable speed was judged to be moving downwards as a function of the speed of the downward-moving component. Empty circles show results obtained without adaptation; the plaid is judged to be moving horizontally when the two components have equal speed. Filled circles show results obtained during adaptation to a grating moving 45° upwards at 0.5 deg/sec; the plaid appears to move horizontally when the upward-moving grating has its speed reduced to match the perceived speed of the upward-moving grating. (Data replotted from *Vision Research, 31,* Derrington, A. M., & Suero, M. Motion of complex patterns is computed from the perceived motions of their components, 139–149. Copyright 1991, with permission of Elsevier Science.)

speed of the other component of the plaid is reduced to match the perceived speed of the component whose perceived speed has been reduced (Derrington & Suero, 1991). This is absolutely consistent with the idea that the visual system computes the motion of the plaid from the motions of its component gratings.

Although these studies are consistent with the idea that the visual system computes the motion of plaid patterns from the motions of their sinusoidal components using the intersection of constraints, they do not exclude alternative hypotheses. For example, one weakness of Welch's study is the absence of comparison measurements for a grating with the same spatial period as the plaid along its axis of motion. It could be that the dip in the Weber fractions in Figure 19 depends on the temporal frequency of the pattern, which inevitably matches the temporal frequency of the components, rather than on its speed. Similarly, the studies in which the apparent speed of one component was reduced, used symmetrical plaids for which the intersection of constraints algorithm predicts qualitatively the same results as other simpler alternatives, such as a vector sum (Derrington & Suero, 1991; Stone et al., 1990; Wilson et al., 1992). In the next section we consider some results that are not consistent with the simple version of the intersection of constraints model.

2. Experiments That Contradict the Simple Version of the IOC

Two sets of experimental results, which will be dealt with in this section, are inconsistent with the hypothesis that the visual system computes the motion of plaid patterns from the motions of their component gratings using the intersection of constraints algorithm. First, thresholds for discriminating the direction of motion of plaid patterns suggest that in computing the direction of motion of plaid patterns the visual system is likely to use 1-D motion vectors derived from local features such as edges and from second-order analyses of the plaid, although the computation could be carried out using the intersection of constraints algorithm, and it could also use 1-D vectors derived from the component gratings (Derrington & Badcock, 1992; Derrington et al., 1992). Second, the perceived axes of motion of some types of plaid pattern deviate systematically from the axis predicted by the intersection of constraints, which has led to the proposal that the visual system uses a different algorithm, based on summing 1-D motion vectors, to compute the axis of motion of 2-D patterns (Wilson et al., 1992).

a. Plaid and Component Motion Identification Thresholds

Subjects are able to discriminate correctly between leftward and rightward motion of a horizontally moving plaid pattern when it is moving so slowly that the motion of its component gratings cannot be discriminated (Derrington & Badcock, 1992). This threshold difference probably occurs because the plaid moves faster than the component gratings, but even so, it could not happen if the visual system computed the motion of the plaid from the motions of its component gratings, because that would make the threshold for discriminating the motion of the component gratings the lower limit on the threshold for discriminating the motion of the plaid. Analysis of thresholds for identifying axes of motion over vertical and oblique directions shows that when spatial frequency or contrast is high it is easier to discriminate the motion of the plaid than to discriminate the direction of motion of its component gratings (Cox & Derrington, 1994).

These observations lead inescapably to the conclusion that in detecting the motion of plaid patterns the visual system must use something other than, or in addition to, the motion vectors derived from the component gratings. Two obvious sets of oriented features that would give rise to 1-D motion vectors with the same magnitude as the plaid pattern's 2-D vector would be the plaid's local vertical and horizontal edges and the vertical and horizontal second-order features associated with the plaid's contrast envelope (Derrington & Badcock, 1992).

It is difficult to demonstrate unequivocally that the visual system uses local features, but it is possible to show that it uses motion vectors derived from a second-order analysis of the plaid's contrast envelope. The test uses a moving plaid stimulus in which first-order and second-order analyses signal opposite directions of motion. The test stimulus and the results are shown in Figure 17 (Derrington et al., 1992).

The test takes advantage of the fact that the horizontal spatial period of the contrast envelope is half the horizontal spatial period of the luminance profile. Thus when the pattern is made to move in jumps of increasing size, Figure 17a shows that the direction of motion of the contrast envelope reverses when the jump size is between 0.25 and 0.5 periods of the luminance profile. Figure 17b and d show the test stimulus and its horizontal luminance profile. The horizontal contrast envelope (Figure 17c) is a rectified version of the luminance profile and so has half the spatial period. Figure 17e and f show space–time plots of the luminance profile and the contrast profile jumping repeatedly leftwards in jumps of 0.375 of the period of the luminance profile. The luminance profile appears to be jumping leftwards, and the contrast profile appears to be jumping rightwards.

Figure 17a shows that when the jump size exceeds 0.25 cycles the percentage of trials on which the observer is correct drops below chance (0.5), indicating that the observer systematically reports reversed motion, suggesting that the motion percept is derived from the contrast envelope rather than from first-order features. We also know that first-order features are important because even in this special case where first-order and second-order analyses signal opposite directions of motion, the observer reports motion in the first-order direction at high temporal frequencies and at high spatial frequencies. Thus, the data in Figure 17a suggest very strongly that observers use second-order motion signals in analyzing the motion of plaids.

b. Errors in the Perceived Axis of Motion: The Vector Sum Model

When a plaid pattern consists of two gratings whose axes of motion make an acute angle and whose speeds are very different from one another, the axis of motion of the plaid falls outside the angle formed by the axes of the components. Such a plaid is known as a Type II plaid (Ferrera & Wilson, 1987). An example of the intersection of constraints diagram for a type II plaid is shown in Figure 18a. The axis of motion of type II plaids is systematically misperceived: it appears to be closer to the axes of motion of its components than it actually is (Ferrera & Wilson, 1987). The misperception is more extreme for type II plaids presented for short durations or in peripheral vision. If they are presented for only 60 ms, type II plaids appear to move approximately along the axis predicted by summing the 1-D vectors of their component gratings, and if they are presented in the periphery, the perceived axis of motion may deviate by 40° from the true axis of motion (Yo & Wilson, 1992).

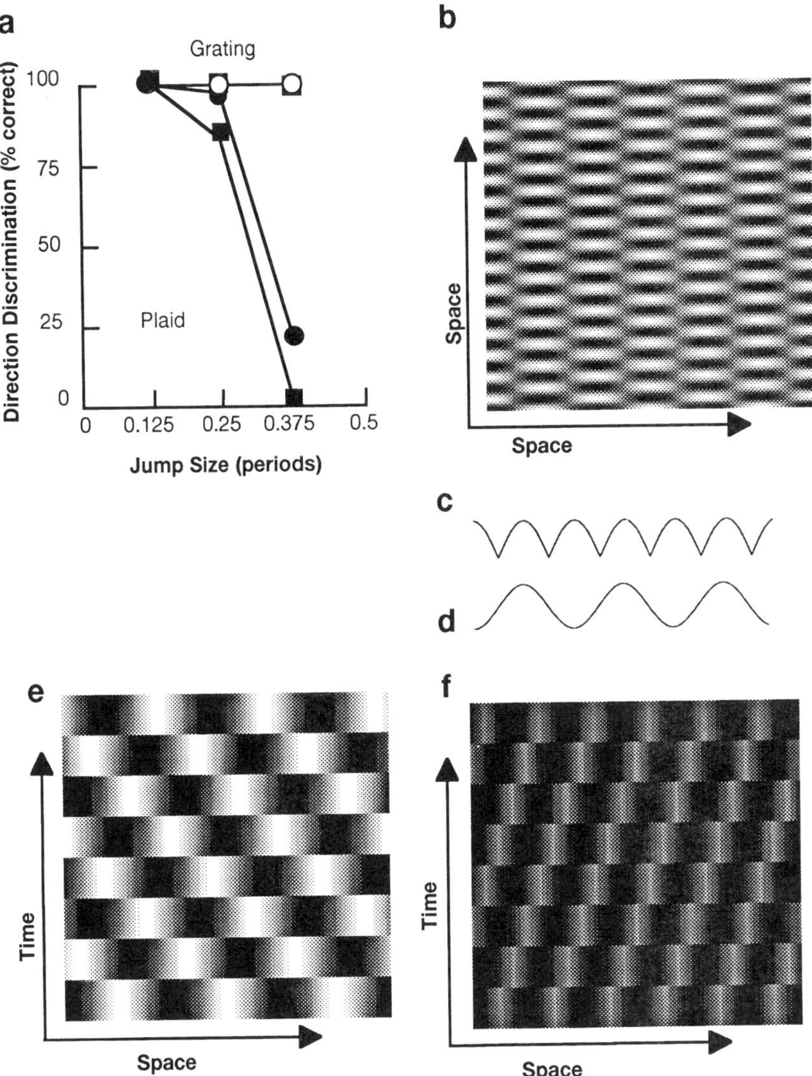

FIGURE 17 (a) Performance of two observers discriminating the direction of motion of a plaid pattern or a grating pattern that jumped either to the left or to the right in jumps of different sizes. The percentage of trials on which the subject was correct is plotted against the jump size, expressed as a fraction of the period of the pattern. Performance with the grating pattern is essentially perfect at all jump sizes; performance with the plaid pattern reverses when the jump size exceeds 0.25 periods. (Data replotted from *Vision Research, 32,* Derrington, A. M., Badcock, D. R., & Holroyd, S. A. Analysis of the motion of 2-dimensional patterns: evidence for a second-order process, 699–707. Copyright 1992, with permission of Elsevier Science.) (b) the plaid pattern, (c) its contrast profile, and (d) luminance profile. (e) A space–time plot of a section through the luminance profile jumping to the left in jumps of 0.375 periods. It looks as if it is jumping leftwards. (f) A space–time plot if the contrast profile of the same stimulus. It looks as if it is jumping rightwards.

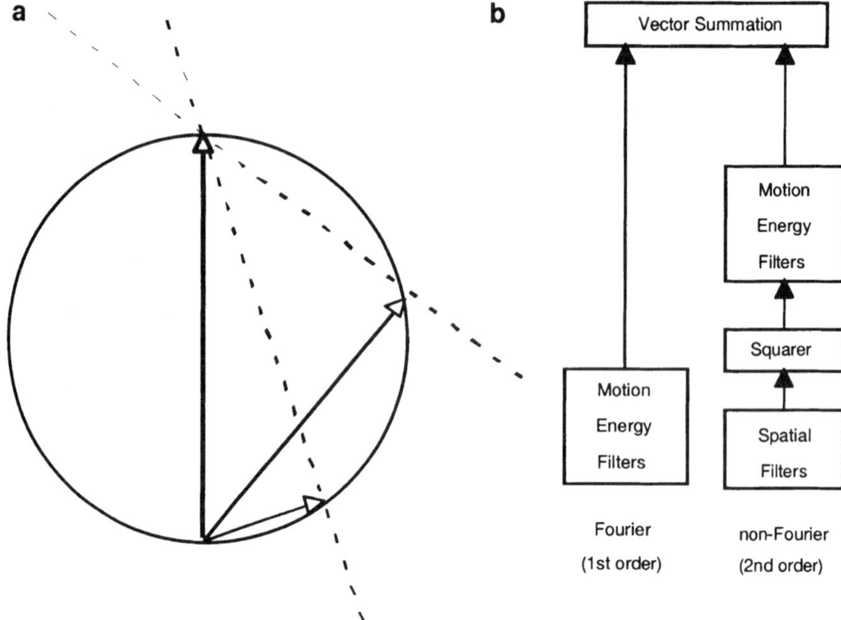

FIGURE 18 (a) The intersection of constraints diagram for a type II plaid. Both components are moving to the right of vertical but the intersection of constraints is vertical. (b) A block diagram of Wilson et al.'s (1992) model of 2-D direction-of-motion analysis. Direction of motion is computed by summing the outputs of orientation-selective motion-energy filters operating directly on the spatiotemporal image and those of motion-energy filters that operate on the squared outputs of linear spatial-frequency-selective filters.

These perceptual properties of type II plaids can be explained by a model, outlined in Figure 18b, which proposes that the visual system computes the axis of motion of a 2-D pattern by summing its 1-D motion vectors rather than by computing the intersection of constraints. In addition to the 1-D vectors provided by the sinusoidal grating components of the plaid pattern, the model also uses 1-D vectors provided from extra frequency components, generated in the so-called non-Fourier pathway through the model by first filtering the image then squaring it and filtering it again at a lower spatial frequency (Wilson et al., 1992).

The model accounts for the fact that the perceived axis of motion of a plaid pattern lies further from its true axis if the pattern is presented in the periphery rather than in the center of the visual field by assuming that the relative weight assigned to the non-Fourier motion signals is lower in the peripheral visual field (Wilson et al., 1992). The aspect of the model that accounts for the way the perceived axis of motion of a type II plaid changes with its presentation duration is that the non-Fourier pathway operates more slowly than the direct pathway (there is independent evidence in support of this that will be reviewed in section V.B). Consequently, in short presentations the only 1-D vectors that contribute to the vector-sum computation are those derived from the grating components of the plaid; hence the plaid appears to move in the vector-sum direction. At longer presentation durations the non-Fourier 1-D motion vectors become available and the perceived axis of motion moves closer to the true axis of motion. In simulations the model can replicate the effects of varying duration and eccentricity (Wilson et al., 1992).

Although the vector-sum model accounts satisfactorily for changes in the perceived direction of motion of Type II plaid stimuli, it is not without its problems. Perhaps the most serious is that although the delay in the non-Fourier pathway accounts nicely for the improvement, with increasing presentation duration, in the accuracy with which observers perceive the axis of motion of a type II plaid, it is unlikely to be a complete explanation of this phenomenon. As Figure 19 shows, a similar improvement in performance occurs although over a somewhat longer time course, with type II plaid stimuli whose components are non-Fourier gratings (Cropper, Badcock, & Hayes, 1994). It may be that the increase over time in the accuracy with which we perceive the axis of motion occurs because the precision with which motion vectors can be estimated, and the sensitivity with which motion

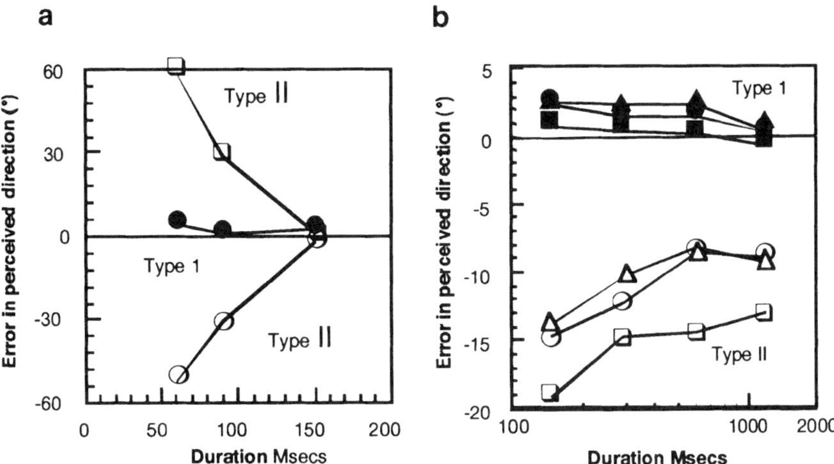

FIGURE 19 Perceived axes of motion of type I and type II plaids presented for different durations. (a) Results obtained with plaids made by summing sinusoidal luminance gratings. (Data replotted from *Vision Research, 32,* Yo, C., & Wilson, H. R. Perceived direction of moving two-dimensional patterns depends on duration, contrast and eccentricity, 135–147. Copyright 1992, with permission of Elsevier Science.) (b) Results obtained with plaids made by summing second-order gratings. (Data replotted from *Vision Research, 34,* Cropper, S. J., Badcock, D. R., & Hayes, A. On the role of second-order signals in the perceived motion of type II plaid patterns, 2609–2612. Copyright 1994, with permission of Elsevier Science.) In both cases the perceived direction of motion of type II plaids is initially incorrect and gradually improves with time. The time course of the improvement is much slower when the plaids are made from second-order grating patterns.

components can be detected, improve with time, both for first-order and for second-order motion stimuli. Consistent with this we have found that the accuracy with which subjects estimate the motion of type I plaids—even when the plaid components are at orientations 90° apart so that vector sum, non-Fourier vector sum, and intersection of constraints computations all give exactly the same result—improves with stimulus duration.

Thus although the vector-sum model makes a number of successful predictions, it seems clear that the errors in the perceived direction of motion of type II plaids are not solely due to a difference in the time it takes to process second-order motion signals.

V. SECOND-ORDER MOTION MECHANISMS

One unusual aspect of the vector-sum model is that it seeks to integrate first-order and second-order motion analysis mechanisms. It exploits the fact that in most normal situations the two mechanisms act in harmony, providing alternative ways of deriving the same information from the same image. However, in order to investigate second-order mechanisms in isolation, it is necessary to devise stimuli in which first-order and second-order cues are either isolated or set into conflict with one another, since this is the only way in which one can isolate second-order mechanisms to assess their properties. It is worth pointing out that the same caveat applies to investigations designed to reveal the properties of first-order mechanisms, although it is usually ignored.

A. Importance of Second-Order Motion Signals

When the signals provided by first-order mechanisms are inadequate, second-order mechanisms may occasionally come to the rescue. For example, if a large textured object consists mainly of very high spatial frequency components, its motion may induce such large phase changes in its visible spatial frequency components that their direction of motion is ambiguous. In the limit, the spatial frequency of the components may be too high to allow any reliable motion analysis, in which case second-order analysis of the motion of the contrast envelope is the only possible way of sensing motion. In the natural world, striped animals like zebras and tigers may have this property; in the laboratory, a pattern composed by adding together two sinusoidal gratings of the same orientation and contrast and slightly different spatial frequencies makes an excellent substitute.

Figure 20 shows that second-order motion may be perceived when the first order motion that gives rise to it is invisible. The first order stimulus was a sinusoidal grat-

FIGURE 20 Discriminating the direction of a sudden jump of a high spatial frequency grating when it is presented alone or added to a stationary grating of similar spatial frequency so that it forms a low spatial frequency beat that jumps much farther than the high spatial frequency grating; if the stationary grating has higher spatial frequency, the beat moves in the opposite direction. (a) Space–time plots of the

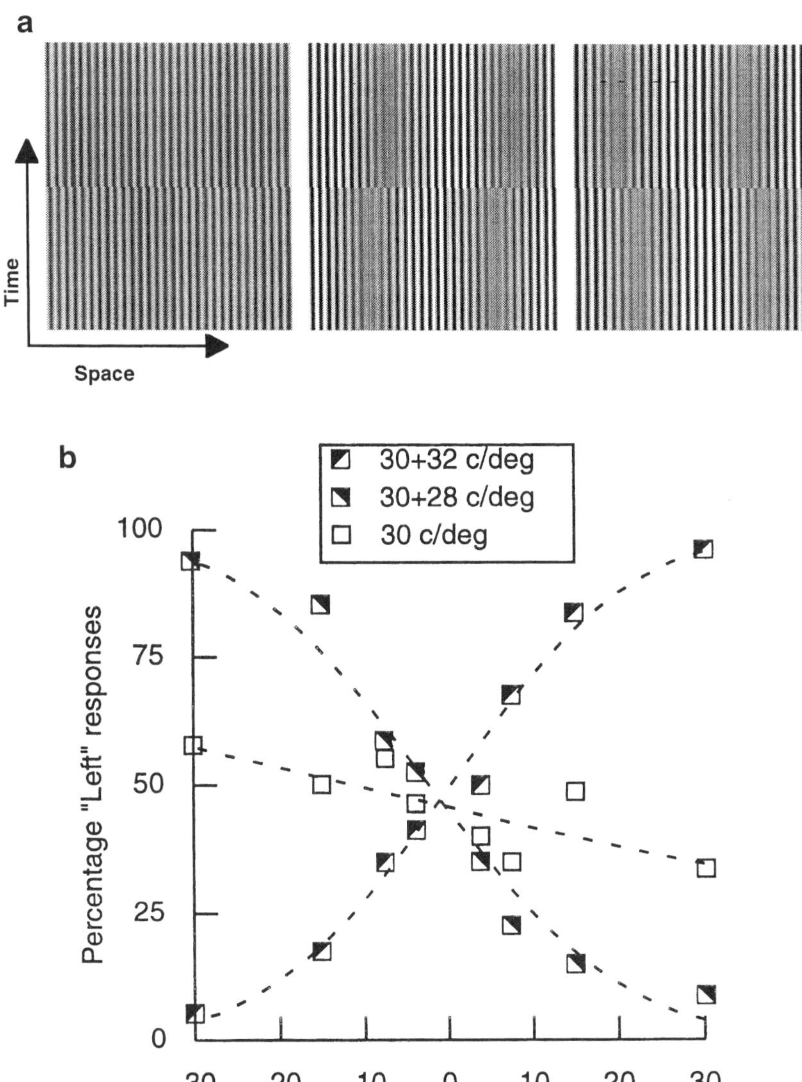

stimuli; the 30 c/deg grating is shown on its own on the left, added to the 32 c/deg grating in the center and added to the 28 cycle/deg grating on the right. Note that the beat in the center panel moves to the left and the beat in the right-hand panel moves to the right. (b) Direction-discrimination performance of a human observer. Performance is close to chance with the lone 30 c/deg grating; when a stationary grating is added to the moving grating the observer reports the pattern to move in the direction of the beat: this is the same as the moving grating when the static grating has spatial frequency 28 c/deg and the opposite direction when the static grating has spatial frequency 32 c/deg. (Data replotted from *Vision Research, 25,* Badcock, D. R., & Derrington, A. M. Detecting the displacement of periodic patterns, 1253–1258. Copyright 1985, with permission of Elsevier Science.)

ing of spatial frequency 30 cycles/degree that underwent a phase shift half-way through its presentation. A space-time plot is shown in Figure 20a. The data in Figure 20b show that a subject was unable reliably to discriminate the direction of motion of this very high spatial frequency pattern. However, adding a second stationary grating of 28 or 32 cycles per degree to the stimulus introduces a second-order pattern, a spatial variation in contrast known as a beat, that can be seen clearly in the space-time plots in Fig 20a.

The beat moves much further than the grating, and its direction of motion depends on the spatial frequency of the added grating. Observers are able to discriminate its motion without difficulty. The fact that the direction of their responses reverses when the stationary grating has higher spatial frequency than the moving grating indicates that they are responding to the motion of the beat. Thus the human visual system is clearly able to analyze the motion of contrast modulations, the question is, how does it do it?

B. What Sort of Mechanism Analyzes the Motion of Contrast Variations?

Before considering how the visual system analyses the motion of contrast patterns it is important to establish what are the minimum requirements for such an analysis, since these set a limit on the ways in which it might be carried out. The model outlined in Figure 18 makes the point that a combination of filtering and squaring will turn a non-Fourier motion signal into a signal that can be analyzed by a standard motion filter. This is true of a wide range of non-Fourier motion stimuli (Chubb & Sperling, 1988, 1989). A general model of non-Fourier motion analysis would combine sets of filters to extract spatial variations in the motion carrier, followed by standard motion analysis based on one of the possible spatio-temporal comparators described earlier (Cavanagh & Mather, 1989).

When the second-order motion signal is carried by contrast variations the situation is much simpler. There is no need for filtering. Squaring, or any of a wide range of nonlinearities in transduction or transmission will turn a contrast signal into a luminance signal (Burton, 1973).[4] Thus one possibility is that a nonlinearity very early in the visual pathway could cause the contrast signal to act in exactly the same way as a luminance signal (Burton, 1973; Derrington, 1987; Henning et al., 1975; Sekiguchi, Williams, & Packer, 1991) and to stimulate exactly the same motion-selective filters, there would be no need for a separate pathway to extract the motion of contrast envelopes. It is important to exclude this possibility before

[4]The simplicity with which the contrast signal can be transformed into the same form as a luminance signal brings complications. The range of nonlinearities that will produce the required transform is immense and includes the typical nonlinear relationship between luminance and driving voltage of a cathode-ray-rube monitor (Henning, Hertz, & Broadbent, 1975). This means that great care must be taken in generating and displaying contrast patterns in order to avoid inadvertently supplementing the contrast signal with a luminance signal before it enters the visual pathway.

proposing the existence of a special mechanism for analyzing the motion of contrast patterns, whether it be based on filtering, like that shown in Figure 23, or on tracking features in the contrast waveform.

Thus the limits imposed by the processing required to extract the motion of contrast patterns are extremely broad, and suggest three main possibilities. First, nonlinear distortion early in the visual pathway could cause the contrast pattern to generate exactly the same signal in exactly the same neural elements as would be generated by a luminance pattern, so the motion would be analyzed by the standard motion pathway. There is some evidence that this is what happens when contrast is very high. Second, the motion could be analyzed by a separate set of motion filters dedicated to the analysis of contrast patterns. Finally, the motion might be analyzed by tracking features in the contrast waveform, either with a dedicated mechanism or simply by paying attention (Cavanagh, 1992). Since features can be tracked in any type of pattern, we must be able to analyze the motion of contrast patterns by tracking features too. The big question is whether there is any kind of dedicated mechanism for analyzing contrast motion or whether we always accomplish this task by tracking features.

1. Psychophysics

A number of psychophysical experiments show differences between our ability to discriminate the motion of contrast patterns and our ability to discriminate the motion of luminance patterns. These differences are of the sort that we would expect if there were no special-purpose mechanism for analyzing the motion of second-order contrast patterns: temporal resolution is worse with contrast patterns than with luminance patterns, and motion discriminations with contrast patterns are more vulnerable to pedestals than are motion discriminations with luminance patterns. However, temporal resolution improves with contrast, as one would expect if a nonlinearity early in the visual pathway were to cause contrast patterns to generate signals in the visual mechanisms that normally respond only to luminance patterns (Burton, 1973). Unfortunately, there are some differences between results obtained in different laboratories and between results obtained using different carriers which cloud the issue slightly.

Figure 21 shows the highest and lowest temporal frequencies at which observers could discriminate the direction of motion of a luminance pattern (a 1 c/deg grating) and a contrast pattern (a 1 c/deg beat between gratings of 9 c/deg and 10 c/deg) plotted as functions of contrast. Lower thresholds of motion are not very different; thresholds are slightly lower for the grating than for the beat at all except the lowest contrast. This is possibly a reflection of the fact that at low spatial and temporal frequencies the high spatial frequency components of the beat are more visible than the 1 c/deg grating. However, the resolution limits, the maximum temporal frequencies at which direction of motion can be discriminated, show clear differences between the grating and the beat. The limit for the grating changes only

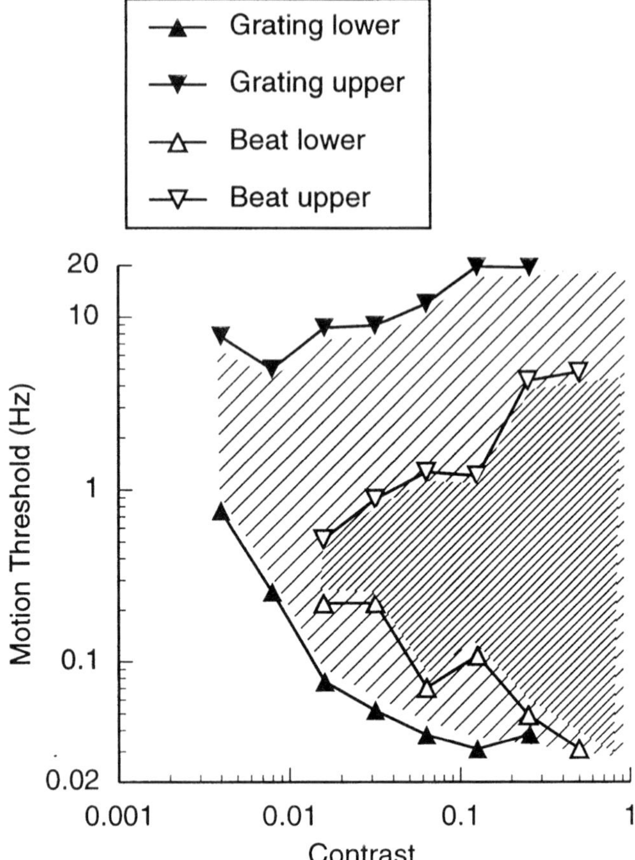

FIGURE 21 Upper and lower thresholds for discriminating the direction of motion of smoothly moving luminance patterns (1 c/deg sinusoidal gratings) and contrast patterns (1 c/deg beats between gratings of 9 and 10 c/deg) plotted as functions of the contrast of the pattern. At all contrasts the range of temporal frequencies over which the motion of the beat pattern can be discriminated (fine hatching) is smaller than the range of temporal frequencies over which the motion of the luminance pattern (coarse hatching). (Data replotted from *Vision Research, 25,* Derrington, A. M., & Badcock, D. R. Separate detectors for simple and complex grating patterns?, 1869–1878. Copyright 1985, with permission of Elsevier Science.)

slightly with contrast, increasing by about a factor of two, from about 8 Hz to about 20 Hz, over about two log units of contrast. The limit for the beat is generally much lower and increases much more sharply with contrast, rising from about 0.5 Hz at the lowest contrast to about 5 Hz 2 log units higher.

There is other evidence that mechanisms detecting the motion of contrast patterns are more sluggish. It is impossible to discriminate the direction of motion of beat patterns that are presented for less than about 200 ms, whereas the motion of luminance or color patterns can be distinguished at durations down to 20 ms or less (Cropper & Derrington, 1994; Derrington, Badcock, & Henning, 1993). The reversed motion of plaid patterns shown in Figure 21, which is attributed to the intrusion of second-order mechanisms, only occurs at low temporal frequencies (Derrington et al., 1992).

There is a suggestion in Figure 21 that the increase in temporal resolution for the beat pattern is not a gradual change, but that it occurs suddenly. When the contrast reaches about 0.2 resolution jumps from around 1 Hz to around 5 Hz, as if there were two different mechanisms involved, a high temporal resolution mechanism active at high contrast and a low temporal resolution one active at low contrast.

In the beat patterns used to collect the data in Figure 21, the contrast was always modulated between zero and the maximum possible, which makes it impossible to distinguish between changes in sensitivity and changes in resolution. Figure 22 shows sensitivity measurements made with contrast-modulated gratings. Direction discrimination performance was measured as a function of the depth of modulation of a contrast envelope of fixed mean contrast, and the reciprocal of the threshold was plotted as a function of the temporal frequency.

The resulting temporal modulation sensitivity functions show clearly that raising the contrast improves the relative sensitivity as well as the resolution of the mechanisms that detect the motion of contrast waveforms. When the mean contrast is 0.1, sensitivity falls rapidly for frequencies above 2 Hz. Raising the mean contrast to 0.5 produces a slight improvement in overall sensitivity and a huge improvement in temporal resolution: sensitivity remains high up to 16 Hz. At high mean contrast the temporal resolution in discriminating the direction of motion of contrast modulations is comparable to that shown when the task is simply to detect the motion of the envelope. Temporal resolution of sinusoidally amplitude-modulated 2-D noise patterns with high mean contrast is also extremely good (Lu & Sperling, 1995).

The most likely explanation for the excellent temporal resolution that occurs at high contrasts is that under these circumstances the moving contrast patterns are processed by mechanisms similar or identical to those that normally process moving luminance patterns. There are several ways that this could happen.

One possibility is that the visual system contains an array of second-order motion sensors that process the motion of contrast-modulated patterns and that have identical temporal resolution to first-order motion sensors (Lu & Sperling, 1995). Although this represents an attractive possibility, it is surprising that this array of sensors should be completely insensitive to contrast patterns with sinusoidal carriers of low or moderate mean contrast. It is also slightly suspicious that sensitivity varies in exactly the same way with changes in temporal frequency as in the mechanisms that process luminance patterns. Consequently, it is worth considering the possibility that the motion sensors that support this high temporal resolution are in fact the same ones that process moving luminance patterns. There are three ways in which this could come about.

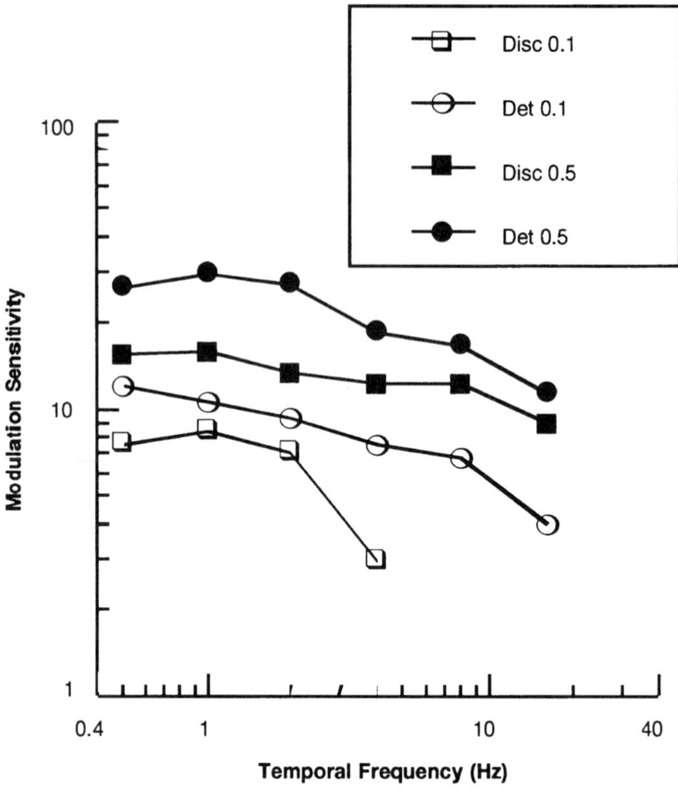

FIGURE 22 Modulation-sensitivity functions for detecting (circles) and discriminating the direction of motion (squares) of moving contrast-modulation envelopes of sinusoidal gratings of different contrast. Modulation sensitivity (the reciprocal of the modulation depth at which performance in the task reaches 75% correct) is plotted as a function of temporal frequency. When the carrier contrast is 0.1 (open symbols) sensitivity in the direction-discrimination task falls off rapidly at temporal frequencies above 2 Hz and was too low to measure at 8 Hz; sensitivity in the detection task, which could be performed simply by detecting the slight first-order flicker associated with the second-order motion, falls off very slowly and is still measurable at 16 Hz. When the carrier contrast is raised to 0.5 (solid symbols), the two tasks show very similar, shallow declines in sensitivity with temporal frequency, as though the direction of motion of the contrast envelope were being signaled by a standard motion filter, although performance is still better in the detection task than in the discrimination task.

First, in the case of modulated random-noise patterns, the display itself is likely to contain local patches of moving luminance patterns. These should arise because the noise carrier contains a very wide range of spatial frequencies, so we should expect that within relatively large local patches of the pattern there will be slight deviations from the mean luminance, although these will average out over large areas. When the noise is multiplied by the moving sinusoidal envelope, the areas of higher or lower mean luminance will generate local patches of moving luminance grating. Motion sensors that integrate over large areas would not sense these signals, but ones that integrate over small areas would. It is difficult to be certain whether such local luminance signals could account for the high temporal resolution that occurs with moving contrast-modulated noise patterns (Lu & Sperling, 1995). On the one hand, resampling the noise on every frame, which should remove any systematic local luminance signals, reduces temporal resolution (Smith & Ledgeway, 1998) on the other, a computer simulation of a motion-energy sensor failed to detect any systematic motion signal in contrast-modulated noise (Benton & Johnston, 1997).

A second possibility is that the same motion sensor might be sensitive both to luminance patterns and to contrast patterns. The multichannel gradient motion sensor can be implemented in a way that makes it sensitive both to first-order and to second-order motion (Johnston et al., 1992). This is an attractive possibility, but it does not explain why temporal resolution for contrast patterns should be so much worse when carrier contrast is low, unless the multichannel gradient sensor is sensitive only when carrier contrast is high.

A third possibility is that distortion within the visual pathway causes the contrast pattern to generate a signal (a "distortion product") in the luminance pathway. There is independent evidence for nonlinearities early in the visual pathway that would have exactly this effect (MacLeod, Williams, & Makous, 1992). Scott-Samuel (1999) found that observers were able to discriminate consistent motion when a contrast-modulated grating flickers in alternation with a sinusoidal grating of the same spatial frequency as the envelope. The direction of motion of the compound stimulus suggests that an internal luminance-like signal (a distortion product) is generated from the contrast-modulated grating by a compressive nonlinearity (Scott-Samuel, 1999). The magnitude of the distortion product should grow in proportion to the product of the carrier contrast and the modulation depth. This accelerated growth would explain why it is only when contrast is high that second-order contrast patterns support good temporal resolution in motion discriminations: high contrast is needed to ensure that the distortion product is large enough to be processed by the "standard" motion processing filters. How then is the motion of these patterns processed when contrast is low?

The simplest assumption is that the visual system does not have a motion filter that analyzes the motion of contrast patterns and that their motion is simply inferred from the displacement of features over time. Indirect evidence for this is that these patterns do not support a normal motion aftereffect (Derrington & Badcock, 1985) and they do not give rise to optokinetic nystagmus (Harris & Smith, 1992).

More direct evidence comes from the fact, illustrated in Figure 23, that the contrast needed to discriminate the direction of motion of a beat pattern increases when a stationary pedestal is added to the moving pattern. The impairment of motion discrimination performance by the addition of a pedestal is an indication that the motion discrimination depends on feature-tracking rather than on filtering (Lu & Sperling, 1995). Figure 23 also confirms that motion discrimination of

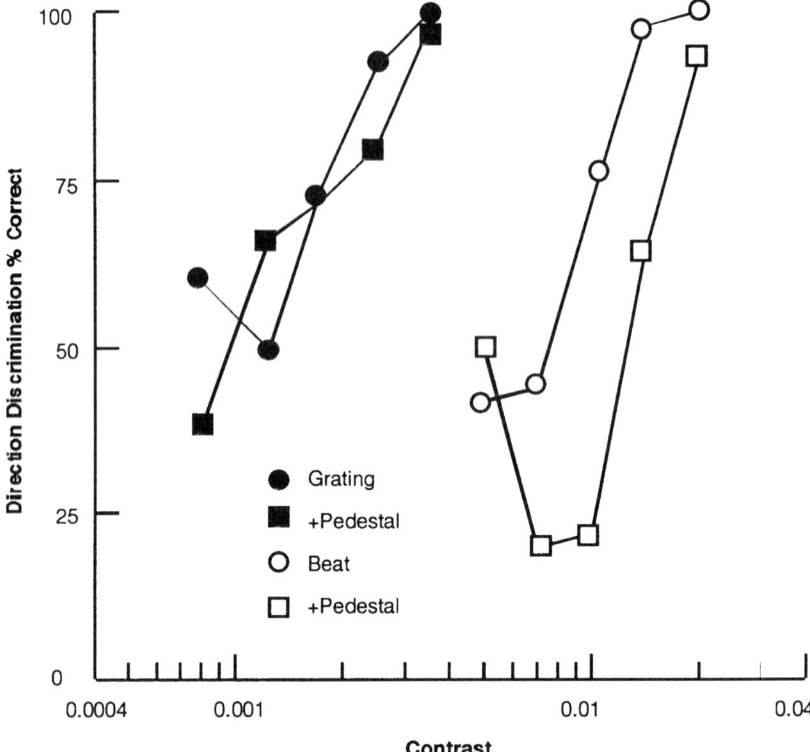

FIGURE 23 Effect of a pedestal on direction-of-motion discrimination tasks using luminance patterns and contrast patterns. The filled symbols show performance in discriminating the direction of motion of a sinusoidal 1 c/deg luminance grating as a function of its contrast. When a pedestal—a stationary pattern identical to the moving pattern but with twice the contrast that the moving pattern has at threshold—is added to the moving grating (filled squares), performance is just the same as when the moving pattern is presented on its own (filled circles). When a pedestal is added to the moving beat the performance at threshold contrast falls to below chance, and the threshold rises by almost a factor of 2.

luminance patterns is not affected by the addition of a pedestal (Lu & Sperling, 1995).

When the carrier contrast is high, motion discrimination performance with contrast-modulated patterns—both with sinusoidal carriers and with random-noise carriers—is not impaired by adding a stationary pedestal (Lu & Sperling, 1995, 1996; Ukkonen & Derrington, 1997). This result is also consistent with the suggestion that these patterns are processed by the same motion filters as luminance patterns. Motion discrimination of contrast-modulated noise patterns is unaffected by the addition of a pedestal. This would be consistent with other evidence showing that motion can be detected in contrast-modulated high-contrast noise patterns without tracking features (Smith, 1994).

On the other hand Seiffert and Cavanagh (Seiffert & Cavanagh, 1998) found, using a range of different second-order motion stimuli, that over a range of temporal frequencies the threshold at which oscillating motion can be detected depends on the distance moved, whereas (as shown in Figure 13) thresholds for detecting the motion of luminance patterns depends on velocity. The range of patterns used by Seiffert and Cavanagh included contrast-modulated noise, contrast-modulated gratings, orientation-modulated gratings, and disparity-modulated noise, but in all the contrast patterns the mean contrast was below 30%. These results are consistent with the idea that motion of all these second-order attributes is normally detected by a feature-tracking mechanism.

In summary, the psychophysical data show that, when average contrast is low, the motion-of-contrast patterns is processed by a mechanism that has poor temporal resolution, that does not support a motion aftereffect, whose sensitivity is limited by the distance an object travels rather than by the speed it moves, and that is disrupted by a static pedestal. These are all attributes to be expected of a feature-tracking mechanism. When contrast is high, contrast patterns are detected by a mechanism that has high temporal resolution and is resistant to pedestals. There is also some evidence that it treats luminance and contrast patterns in exactly the same way. These are all characteristics of the mechanism that normally processes the motion of simple luminance patterns. If it is the same mechanism we would expect high-contrast amplitude-modulated gratings to produce a motion aftereffect.

Physiological results only support part of this view. The most complete study of direction-selective responses to contrast patterns, which was carried out in the cat's visual cortex, shows a number of differences between cells' characteristics when tested with luminance patterns and their characteristics when tested with contrast patterns (Mareschal & Baker, 1998; Zhou & Baker, 1993, 1996).

First, the cells usually prefer different frequencies of spatial modulation in contrast patterns than in luminance patterns, although they always prefer the same direction of motion for the two types of patterns. This suggests that the inputs to the cell that cause it to respond to contrast-patterns are organized differently from the inputs that cause it to respond to luminance patterns, although it might be possible, for example, that the response to contrast patterns is determined by a subset of the inputs that give rise to the luminance response.

Second, cells preferred contrast patterns made from spatial frequencies that were too high to elicit a response as luminance patterns. This also suggests that the signals that cause the cell to respond to contrast patterns may originate in a separate pathway.

Finally not all cells—fewer than 20% of cells in area 17 and about 60% of cells in area 18—respond to contrast patterns. This suggests that not all cells receive signals from the pathway that generates responsiveness to contrast patterns. This is consistent with the hypothesis that the responses to contrast patterns are generated in a special second-order pathway rather than arising as an accidental by-product of nonlinear distortion.

One hypothesis that would be consistent with all this evidence is that the response to contrast-modulated patterns originates in Y-cells, and the cells that respond to contrast-modulation envelopes are those that have substantial input from Y-cells in the lateral geniculate nucleus. Y-cell receptive fields contain nonlinear subunits that respond to higher spatial frequencies than does the receptive field center. The subunits are distributed over a much larger area than the receptive field center (Hochstein & Shapley, 1976). These two properties could be sufficient to ensure that the cortical targets of Y-cells responded to contrast-modulated patterns in the way described by Zhou and Baker (1993, 1996).

VI. CONCLUSIONS

There is a consensus that motion of simple luminance patterns can be extracted from the image by local spatiotemporal filters. So far there is no consensus on which of the available models best describes the filters. Physiological data from the cat favor the motion-energy detector.

The perceived motion of 2-D patterns appears to be synthesized from the perceived motions of their 1-D components, but it is not clear either how big is the region over which 1-D measurements are made, or whether the measurements are combined by an intersection of constraints or a vector-sum rule.

Psychophysical data suggest that, at low and medium contrasts, the motion of contrast-modulation waveforms is detected by a mechanism that tracks features and is relatively insensitive to high temporal frequencies. At high contrasts, temporal resolution improves and motion appears to be extracted by filtering rather than feature tracking. There is some evidence that this filter is also sensitive to luminance modulations.

Some neurones in cat visual cortex respond selectively to the motion both of luminance modulations and contrast modulations. There is no information about how contrast affects the sensitivity or temporal resolution of responses to different types of patterns.

Acknowledgments

This work was supported by research grants from the Leverhulme Trust, The Wellcome Trust, The Medical Research Council, and the Biotechnology and Biological Sciences Research Council.

References

Addams, R. (1834). An account of a peculiar optical phaenomenon seen after having looked at a moving body etc. *London and Edinburgh Philosophical Magazine and Journal of Science,* 3rd Series, *5,* 373–4.

Adelson, E. H., & Bergen, J. R. (1985). Spatiotemporal energy models for the perception of motion. *Journal of the Optical Society of America A, 2*(2), 284–299.

Adelson, E. H., & Movshon, J. A. (1982). Phenomenal coherence of moving visual patterns. *Nature, 300*(5892), 523–525.

Albrecht, D. G., & Geisler, W. S. (1991). Motion selectivity and the contrast-response function of simple cells in the visual cortex. *Visual Neuroscience, 7,* 531–546.

Badcock, D. R., & Derrington, A. M. (1985). Detecting the displacement of periodic patterns. *Vision Research, 25*(9), 1253–1258.

Barlow, H. B., & Hill, R. M. (1963). Evidence for a physiological explanation of the waterfall phenomenon and figural after-effects. *Nature, 200,* 1345–1347.

Benton, C. P., & Johnston, A. (1997). First-order motion from contrast-modulated noise? *Vision Research, 37*(22), 3073–3078.

Braddick, O., Campbell, F. W., & Atkinson, J. (1978). Channels in vision: Basic aspects. In R. Held, H. W. Leibowitz, & H. L. Teuber (Eds.), *Handbook of sensory physiology* (pp. 3–38). Springer Verlag.

Britten, K. H., Shadlen, M. N., Newsome, W. T., & Movshon, J. A. (1992). The analysis of visual motion: A comparison of neuronal and psychophysical performance. *Journal of Neuroscience, 12*(12), 4745–4765.

Bruce, V., Green, P. R., & Georgeson, M. A. (1996). *Visual perception, physiology, psychology, and ecology* (2 ed.). Hove, UK: Psychology Press.

Burr, D. C., Ross, J., & Morrone, M. C. (1986). Seeing objects in motion. Proceedings of the Royal Society London B *227,* 249–265.

Burton, G. J. (1973). Evidence for non-linear response processes in the human visual system from measurements on the thresholds of spatial beat frequencies. *Vision Research, 13,* 1211–1225.

Cavanagh, P. (1992). Attention-based motion perception. *Science, 257,* 1563–1565.

Cavanagh, P., & Mather, G. (1989). Motion: The long and short of it. *Spatial Vision, 4*(2/3), 103–129.

Chubb, C., & Sperling, G. (1988). Drift-balanced random stimuli: A general basis for studying non-Fourier motion perception. *Journal of the Optical Society of America A, 5*(11), 1986–2006.

Chubb, C., & Sperling, G. (1989). Second-order motion perception: Space/time separable mechanisms. In *IEEE, Proceedings: Workshop on Visual Motion* (pp. 126–138). Irvine, CA: IEEE Computer Society Press.

Cooper, G. F., & Robson, J. G. (1968). Successive transformations of spatial information in the visual system. In I.E.E./N.P.L. Conference on Pattern Recognition (pp. 134–143). *I.E.E. Conference* Publication no. 47.

Cox, M. J., & Derrington, A. M. (1994). The analysis of motion of two-dimensional patterns: Do Fourier components provide the first stage? *Vision Research, 34*(1), 59–72.

Cropper, S. J., Badcock, D. R., & Hayes, A. (1994). On the role of second-order signals in the perceived motion of type II plaid patterns. *Vision Research, 34*(19), 2609–2612.

Cropper, S. J., & Derrington, A. M. (1994). Motion of chromatic stimuli: First-order or second-order? *Vision Research, 34*(1), 49–58.

Derrington, A. M. (1987). Distortion products in geniculate X cells: A physiological basis for masking by spatially modulated gratings? *Vision Research, 27,* 1377–1386.

Derrington, A. M., & Badcock, D. R. (1985). Separate detectors for simple and complex grating patterns? *Vision Research, 25*(12), 1869–1878.

Derrington, A. M., & Badcock, D. R. (1992). Two-stage analysis of the motion of 2-dimensional patterns, what is the first stage? *Vision Research, 32*(4), 691–698.

Derrington, A. M., Badcock, D. R., & Henning, G. B. (1993). Discriminating the direction of second-order motion at short stimulus durations. *Vision Research, 33*(13), 1785-1794.

Derrington, A. M., Badcock, D. R., & Holroyd, S. A. (1992). Analysis of the motion of 2-dimensional patterns: evidence for a second-order process. *Vision Research, 32*(4), 699–707.

Derrington, A. M., & Henning, G. B. (1987a). Errors in direction-of-motion discrimination with complex stimuli. *Vision Research, 27*(1), 61–75.

Derrington, A. M., & Henning, G. B. (1987b). Further observations on errors in direction-of-motion discrimination. *Investigative Ophthalmology and Visual Science, 28,* 298.

Derrington, A. M., & Suero, M. (1991). Motion of complex patterns is computed from the perceived motions of their components. *Vision Research, 31*(1), 139–149.

Dubner, R., & Zeki, S. (1971). Response properties and receptive fields in an anatomically defined area of the superior temporal sulcus in the monkey. *Brain Research, 35,* 528–532.

Emerson, R. C. (1997). Quadrature subunits in directionally selective simple cells: spatiotemporal interactions. *Visual Neuroscience, 14,* 357–371.

Emerson, R. C., Citron, M. C., Vaughn, W. J., & Klein, S. A. (1987). Nonlinear directionally selective subunits in complex cells of cat striate cortex. *Journal of Neurophysiology, 58*(1), 33–65.

Emerson, R. C., & Huang, M. C. (1997). Quadrature subunits in directionally selective simple cells: Counterphase and drifting grating responses. *Visual Neuroscience, 14,* 373–385.

Fennema, C. L., & Thompson, W. B. (1979). Velocity determination in scenes containing several moving objects. *Computer Graphics and Image Processing, 9,* 301–315.

Ferrera, V. P., & Wilson, H. R. (1987). Direction specific masking and the analysis of motion in two dimensions. *Vision Research, 27*(10), 1783–1796.

Harris, L. R., & Smith, A. T. (1992). Motion defined exclusively by second-order characteristics does not support optokinetic nystagmus. *Visual Neuroscience, 9,* 565–570.

Heeger, D. J. (1987). Model for extraction of image flow. *Journal of the Optical Society of America A, 4*(8), 1455–1471.

Heeger, D. J. (1991). Nonlinear model of neural responses in cat visual cortex. In M. S. Landy & J. A. Movshon (Eds.), *Computational models of visual processing.* MIT Press, Cambridge, Mass. (pp. 119–133).

Henning, G. B., & Derrington, A. M. (1988). Direction-of-motion discrimination with complex patterns: Further observations. *Journal of the Optical Society of America A, 5*(10), 1759–1766.

Henning, G. B., Hertz, B. G., & Broadbent, D. E. (1975). Some experiments bearing on the hypothesis that the visual system analyses spatial patterns in independent bands of spatial frequency. *Vision Research, 15,* 887–897.

Hochstein, S., & Shapley, R. M. (1976). Linear and nonlinear spatial subunits in Y cat retinal ganglion cells. *Journal of Physiology, 262,* 265–284.

Hubel, D. H., & Wiesel, T. N. (1962). Receptive fields, binocular interactions, and functional architecture in cat's visual cortex. *Journal of Physiology, 160,* 106–154.

Hubel, D. H., & Wiesel, T. N. (1968). Receptive fields and functional architecture of monkey striate cortex. *Journal of Physiology, 195,* 215–243.

Johnston, A., McOwan, P. W., & Buxton, H. (1992). A computational model of the analysis of some first-order and second-order motion patterns by simple and complex cells. *Proceedings of the Royal Society of London B, 250,* 297–306.

Lu, Z. L., & Sperling, G. (1995). The functional architecture of human visual motion perception. *Vision Research, 35*(19), 2697–2722.

Lu, Z. L., & Sperling, G. (1996). Contrast gain control in first- and second-order motion perception. *Journal of the Optical Society of America A, 13,* 2305–2318.

MacLeod, D. I. A., Williams, D. R., & Makous, W. (1992). A visual non-linearity fed by single cones. *Vision Research, 32,* 347–363.

Mareschal, I., & Baker, C. L. (1998). Temporal and spatial response to second-order stimuli in cat area 18. *Journal of Neurophysiology, 80*(6), 2811–2823.

Marr, D., & Ullman, S. (1981). Directional selectivity and its use in early visual processing. *Proceedings of the Royal Society of London,* B 211, 151–180.

Morrone, M. C., Burr, D. C., & Maffei, L. (1982). Functional implications of cross-orientation inhibition of cortical visual cells. I. Neurophysiological evidence. *Proceedings of the Royal Society,* B *216,* 335–354.

Movshon, J. A., Adelson, E. H., Gizzi, M. S., & Newsome, W. H. (1985). The analysis of moving visual patterns. In C. Chagas, R. Gatass, & C. Gross (Eds.), *Pattern recognition mechanisms* (pp. 117–151). New York: Springer Verlag.

Movshon, J. A., Thompson, I. D., & Tolhurst, D. J. (1978a). Receptive field organization of complex cells in the cat's striate cortex. *Journal of Physiology, 283,* 79–99.

Movshon, J. A., Thompson, I. D., & Tolhurst, D. J. (1978b). Spatial summation in the receptive fields of simple cells in the cat's striate cortex. *Journal of Physiology, 283,* 53–77.

Nakayama, K., & Tyler, C. W. (1981). Psychophysical isolation of movement sensitivity by removal of familiar position cues. *Vision Research, 21,* 427–433.

Reichardt, W. (1961). Autocorrelation, a principle for the evaluation of sensory information by the central nervous system. In W. A. Rosenblith (Eds.), *Sensory communication* (pp. 303–317). New York: Wiley.

Scott-Samuel, N. E. (1999). Does early non-linearity account for second-order motion? *Vision Research, 39*(17), 2853–2865.

Seiffert, A. E., & Cavanagh, P. (1998). Position displacement not velocity is the cue to motion detection of second-order patterns. *Vision Research, 38,* 3569–3582.

Sekiguchi, N., Williams, D. r., & Packer, O. (1991). Nonlinear distortion of gratings at the foveal resolution limit. *Vision Research, 31*(5), 815–832.

Smith, A. T. (1994). Correspondence-based and energy-based detection of second-order motion in human vision. *Journal of Optical Society of America A, 11*(7), 1940–1948.

Smith, A. T., & Ledgeway, T. (1998). Sensitivity to second-order motion as a function of temporal frequency and viewing eccentricity. *Vision Research, 38*(3), 403–411.

Smith, A. T., & Snowden, R. J. (Ed.). (1994). *Visual detection of motion.* London: Academic press.

Stone, L. S., Watson, A. B., & Mulligan, J. B. (1990). Effect of contrast on the perceived direction of a moving plaid. *Vision Research, 30*(7), 1049–1067.

Thorson, J., Lange, G. D., & Biederman-Thorson, M. (1969). Objective measure of the dynamics of a visual movement illusion. *Science, 164,* 1087–1088.

Ukkonen, O. I., & Derrington, A. M. (1997). A pedestal blocks the perception of non-Fourier motion. *Perception, 26* (suppl), 83–84.

Ullman, S. (1979). *The interpretation of visual motion.* Cambridge, MA: MIT Press.

van Santen, J. P. H., & Sperling, G. (1984). Temporal covariance model of human motion perception. *Journal of the Optical Society of America A, 1*(5), 451–473.

van Santen, J. P. H., & Sperling, G. (1985). Elaborated Reichardt detectors. *Journal of the Optical Society of America A, 2*(2), 300–321.

Watson, A. B. (1990). Optimal displacement in apparent motion and quadrature models of motion sensing. *Vision Research, 30*(9), 1389–1393.

Watson, A. B., & Ahumada, A. J. (1983). A look at motion in the frequency domain. In J. Tsotsos (Eds.), *Motion: Perception and representation.* New York: Association for Computing Machinery. Pages 1–10.

Watson, A. B., & Ahumada, A. J. J. (1985). Model of human visual-motion sensing. *Journal of the Optical Society of America A, 2*(2), 322–342.

Welch, L. (1989). The perception of moving plaids reveals two motion-processing stages. *Nature, 337,* 734–736.

Wilson, H. R., Ferrera, V. P., & Yo, C. (1992). A psychophysically motivated model for two-dimensional motion perception. *Visual Neuroscience, 9,* 79–97.

Zhou, Y. X., & Baker, C. L. (1996). Spatial properties of envelope-responsive cells in area 17 and 18 neurons of the cat. *Journal of Neurophysiology, 75*(3), 1038–1050.

Zhou, Y. X., & Baker, C. L. J. (1993). A processing stream in mammalian visual cortex for non-Fourier responses. *Science, 261,* 98–101.

CHAPTER 7

The Neural Representation of Shape

Jack L. Gallant

I. INTRODUCTION

When we open our eyes we instantly recognize the shapes of familiar objects and understand the structure of our visual environment. The effortless nature of vision is impressive given the computational complexity of the problem. Natural scenes typically contain many objects, each of which might be composed of several parts, and the retinal images of these shapes vary with changes in lighting and viewpoint. In addition, the interpretation of a natural scene depends on the goals of the observer, and any scene can be interpreted in many different ways. Our visual system can instantly segment shapes from the background and group the disparate parts of single objects together, and these processes can be altered to suit our immediate needs.

In primates, visual processing is accomplished by a system composed of several dozen distinct subcortical and cortical visual areas, organized into both parallel and hierarchical pathways (Felleman & Van Essen, 1991; Van Essen & Gallant, 1994). This chapter reviews the cortical ventral form pathway, which is concerned with shape processing and object recognition. The dorsal pathway is more concerned with motion and spatial position. We will focus on four aspects of the ventral system: the anatomical organization of the constituent areas and their interconnections; the physiological responses of the various areas and their influences upon one another; the effects of extraretinal factors such as attention, learning and memory,

Seeing

and motor control; and the computational principles underlying processing in each area, to the extent that such principles are known. Our understanding of these issues varies widely across the visual system. We will not discuss these issues with respect to visual areas for which we currently have little information.

II. ORGANIZATION OF THE VENTRAL PATHWAY

The organization of the primate visual system has been most thoroughly studied in the macaque monkey. The macaque is an excellent model system for vision because it is accessible to experiments using histological markers, anatomical tracers, and physiological mapping of the visual field across the cortical surface. The macaque visual system occupies almost half of the entire neocortex, and includes over 30 distinct cortical areas that are either entirely or predominantly visual, in addition to several subcortical structures dedicated to visual processing (Felleman & Van Essen, 1991). The organization of the human visual system is similar in many respects to that of the macaque, but of course humans have a much larger cortical surface. Human data have come from studies of brain lesions, anatomical tracer studies in postmortem tissue, and more recently from human cortical mapping studies using functional magnetic resonance imaging (fMRI) (Hadjikhani, Liu, Dale, Cavanagh & Tootell, 1998).

Figure 1 illustrates several of the most important cortical areas of the macaque visual system, as well as their primary interconnections (Van Essen & Gallant, 1994). The first and largest processing stage is area V1, which receives input from the retina via the lateral geniculate nucleus (LGN). The LGN input is reorganized in V1 so that form, motion, and color dimensions are processed in anatomically distinct but overlapping modules. These modules project to higher cortical areas via two distinct cortical pathways. The dorsal pathway predominantly processes information about motion and the position of objects in space. From V1 it projects to the cytochrome-oxidase (CO) thick stripes of V2, then on to area MT, MST, and several subsequent stages of processing in the dorsal portions of cortex.

The ventral pathway, which is the primary focus of this chapter, is more concerned with shape processing and object recognition (Ungerlieder & Mishkin, 1982). From V1 it projects primarily to the CO-thin stripes and the interstripes of area V2 (Felleman & Van Essen, 1991; Van Essen & Gallant, 1994). The CO interstripes are selective for dimensions related to form, while cells in the thin stripes emphasize wavelength and color information (Levitt, Kiper, & Movshon, 1994; Livingstone & Hubel, 1984, 1988; Van Essen & Gallant, 1994). From area V2 the ventral processing stream continues into area V4. Evidence from optical imaging (Ghose & Ts'o, 1997) as well as physiological data (Gallant, Connor, Rakshit, Lewis, & Van Essen, 1996; DeYoe, Glickman, & Wieser, 1992; Zeki, 1983) suggest that area V4 is also modularly organized, and that the modular emphasis on form versus color information is retained.

Area V4 projects primarily to posterior inferotemporal (PIT) cortex (corres-

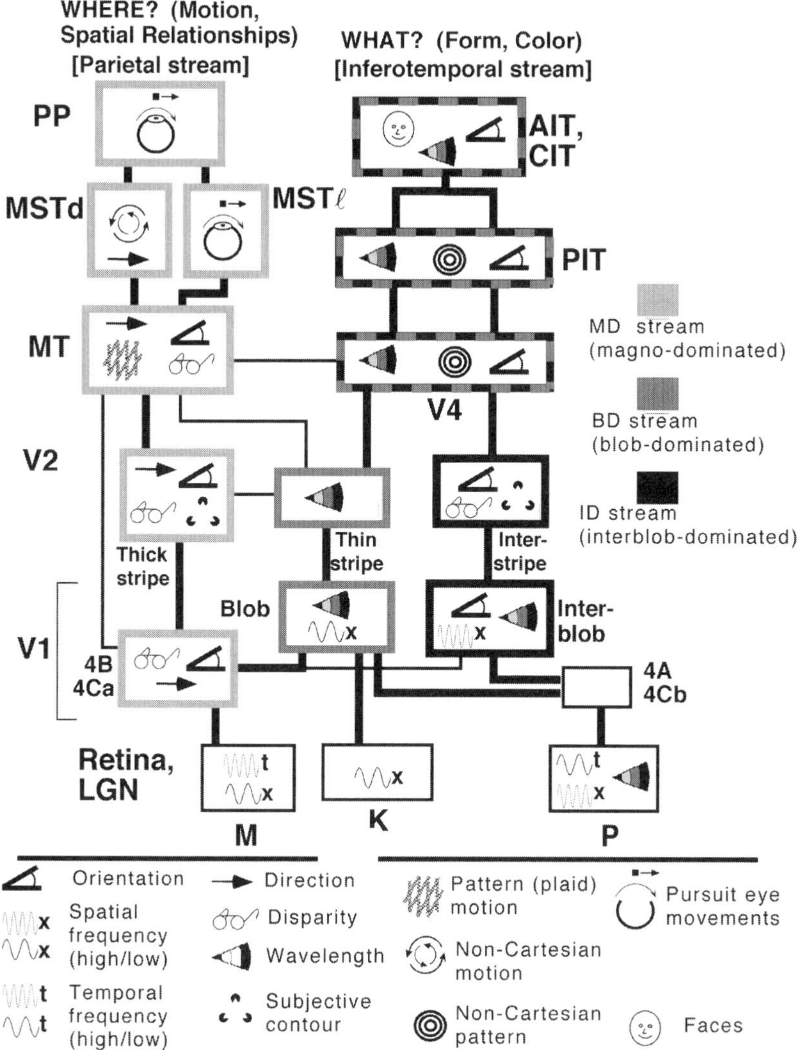

FIGURE 1 Hierarchical organization of concurrent processing streams in the macaque (from Van Essen & Gallant, 1994). Boxes represent visual areas, compartments within an area, and subcortical centers; solid lines represent major connections between structures (usually reciprocal pathways); and icons represent characteristic neurophysiological properties. Subcortical streams in the retina and lateral geniculate nucleus (LGN) include the magnocellular (M), koniocellular (K), and parvocellular (P) streams. Cortical streams at early and intermediate stages include the magno-dominated (MD), blob-dominated (BD), and interblob-dominated (ID) streams (light gray, dark gray, and black, respectively). The posterior parietal complex (PP) includes the ventral intraparietal area (VIP), the lateral intraparietal area (LIP), and area 7a. The inferotemporal complex includes posterior inferotemoporal areas (PIT) that are components of the BD and ID streams plus central and anterior areas (CIT and AIT).

ponding roughly to a commonly cited anatomical subdivision known as area TEO (Felleman & Van Essen, 1991). Evidence from anatomical tracer studies suggests that PIT is modularly organized, and this modularity is probably related to that observed in earlier areas (DeYoe, Felleman, Van Essesn, & McClendan, 1994). From PIT information passes to the final purely visual destination of the ventral processing stream, the inferotemporal cortex (IT). IT is a collection of several distinct areas that have been difficult to distinguish using anatomical and physiological methods; based on general functional criteria they have been grouped into central (CIT) and anterior (AIT) regions. Beyond IT visual information is routed to a variety of cortical and subcortical structures that process information from a variety of sensory modalities.

Each of the pathways and processing stages plays a unique role in vision, although there is significant functional overlap between them. In addition to the major connections between adjacent stages of processing, there are also extensive connections between the various pathways, between nonadjacent processing stages, and between each cortical area and a variety of subcortical structures. These connections permit cross-talk between pathways and allow a substantially more complex flow of information than would be possible in a purely hierarchical, feedforward system.

There are several systematic changes that occur between earlier and later stages of the ventral processing pathway. First, the size of the classical receptive field (CRF) grows significantly from earlier to later stages. The CRF is defined as the region of space which, when stimulated appropriately, evokes a response from a given cell. In area V1, each CRF is typically smaller than a half degree in diameter. Visual space is mapped systematically across the cortical surface in terms of these CRFs, forming a retinotopic map. In contrast, the CRF of an IT cell can encompass almost the entire visual field. In this case there is no retinotopic map, because each cell can represent stimuli from any location in visual space. The absence of a retinotopic map in higher cortical areas has made it particularly difficult to identify their boundaries using either anatomical or physiological methods, and this is the primary reason that the highest cortical stages of visual processing have only been divided into broad regions that may each contain several functionally distinct areas.

Second, extraretinal factors become more important at higher stages of processing. The responses of area V1 neurons are determined largely by retinal input. However, the responses of cells in higher cortical areas are modulated by several nonretinal factors, such as attention, memory, and eye movements. Because it can be difficult to manipulate and control variables that reflect behavioral and intentional states, these extraretinal factors increase the difficulty of characterizing higher visual areas.

Third, responses become increasingly nonlinear in higher areas. The linearity of a cortical system has a large influence on our ability to understand its function. If a system is linear then its responses to complex stimuli can be predicted entirely from its responses to simple stimuli. This allows us to characterize the system using relatively simple tools. Early stages of visual processing such as the LGN and area V1 are quasilinear, and under many conditions they can be treated as linear systems. In contrast, if a system is nonlinear, then its responses to a complex stimulus cannot be explained by, and are not predictable from their responses to simple stimuli. This is true for most extrastriate and higher visual areas. For example, IT cells that are highly selective for faces (see below) may give no response to simpler stimuli, such as the components of faces (Desimone, Albright, Gross, & Bruce, 1984). Because we lack a rigorous analytical framework for characterizing nonlinear systems, it has been particularly difficult to understand how shape is represented in higher visual areas.

III. PHYSIOLOGICAL PROPERTIES

As noted earlier, cells in early visual areas are activated by stimuli occurring in a specific region of the visual field (known as the CRF). These cells are typically selective for several other stimulus properties as well. For example, a V1 cell might respond to a narrow range of orientations and spatial frequencies, and a different cell might respond to a particular color. These stimulus properties can be viewed as separate dimensions, analogous to the two dimensions of space that define the CRF. Therefore, each cell can be viewed as a multidimensional filter that responds to a range of stimuli that fall within its multidimensional passband. Different cells within an area respond to different values of each dimension (e.g., in V1 they respond to different spatial locations, orientations, and spatial frequencies). Because each neural filter can pass a range of information, the specific identity of a stimulus must be determined by comparing the output of multiple cells.

Cells in different visual areas appear to respond to different stimulus dimensions, suggesting that the various areas represent different aspects of visual scenes. Any specific representation will make some types of information explicit. Explicit information can be decoded directly and so is immediately accessible to other processes. Other information will be represented implicitly and must undergo further processing before it can be used. If none of the cells in a visual area represent a dimension either explicitly or implicitly, then the information is lost and cannot be recovered by further processing.

A. Area V1

Almost all input to higher visual cortical areas of primates passes through V1 (Felleman & Van Essen, 1991), also known as area 17 or striate cortex. Therefore this area represents, either explicitly or implicitly, nearly all the visual information needed for higher processing. Form processing in area V1 is mediated by cells that are highly selective for the position, orientation, and spatial frequency (or scale) of local contours (DeValois & DeValois, 1990; Field, 1994; Hubel & Wiesel, 1968). V1 cells are often viewed as quasilinear filters. This linearity assumption is convenient because a great deal is known about linear systems, and many tools have been developed precisely to characterize these systems (Victor, 1992). In addition, linearity implies that a cell's responses to complex stimuli can be predicted from its responses to simple stimuli.

When stimuli have moderate contrast and are confined to the CRF, V1 cells are indeed quasilinear. However, these cells also have several nonlinear characteristics that may be particularly important for form processing. For example, many V1 cells (called complex cells) do not preserve information about the spatial phase of sinusoidal gratings presented in the CRF (DeValois, Albrecht, & Thorell, 1982). This loss of phase information is the first stage of a progressive loss of absolute retinal position information that continues throughout the ventral pathway. Another important V1 nonlinearity comes from the nonclassical receptive field (nCRF), which surrounds the CRF of V1 cells (other visual areas such as V2 and V4 also have nCRFs—Allman, Miezin, & McGuiness, 1985). Stimuli falling within the nCRF do not drive a V1 cell directly, but rather modulate the response to stimuli falling within the CRF. This modulation is most often suppressive; responses obtained with CRF stimulation alone are usually larger than when the same CRF stimulation is paired with stimulation of the nCRF (Knierim & Van Essen, 1992; Gallant, Connor, & Van Essen, 1998). However, in some cases nCRF stimulation can also increase response magnitude (Kapadia, Ito, Gilbert, & Westheimer, 1995).

B. Area V2

One of the most striking changes between areas V1 and V2 concerns the representation of contour information. Cells in V1 respond primarily to changes in luminance; responses to second-order cues such as texture borders are weaker and more variable. In contrast, some area V2 cells appear to be selective for contours defined by a range of nonluminance cues, such as texture borders and stereoscopic depth (von der Heydt, Zhou, & Friedman, 1998). Some V2 cells also respond to illusory contours, borders that are perceptually distinct but that have no physical counterpart (Peterhans & von der Heydt, 1987). Lesion results provide further support that V1 encodes luminance borders, whereas V2 encodes borders defined by higher order cues. Animals with V2 lesions can easily discriminate shapes defined by luminance borders, but are severely impaired in discriminating shapes defined by texture borders (Merigan, Nealey, & Maunsell, 1993). Taken together, the evidence suggests that the representation of edge information in area V2 is relatively form-cue invariant (Albright, 1992); the defined shape is important, but the defining cue is not.

Another dimension that may first be represented in area V2 is local curvature. The CRF of V1 cells encodes information about a single orientation. In contrast, many cells in area V2 are selective for curved contours or luminance gradients that contain significant curvature energy (Hegde & Van Essen, 1997). The curvature data obtained thus far from V2 are similar to the more extensive observations made previously in area V4 (Gallant et al., 1996; Pasupathy & Connor, 1997), so this issue will be discussed further in the next section.

Several nonlinear properties that are first observed in area V1 are enhanced in

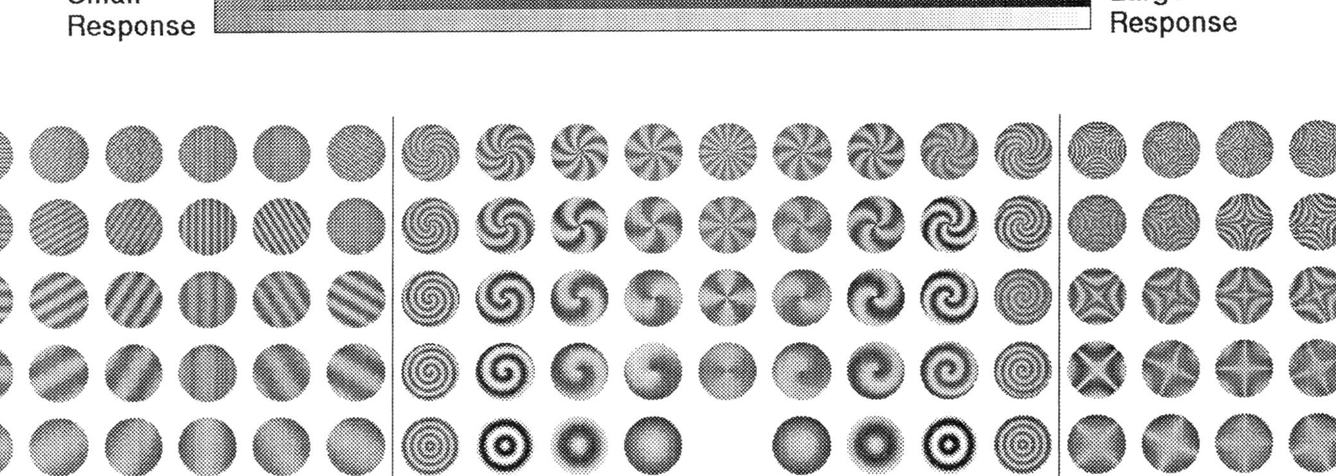

FIGURE 2 Response of a single V4 cell to a variety of Cartesian, polar, and hyperbolic (non-Cartesian) sinusoidal gratings. Each icon represents a particular stimulus, and its contrast represents the mean response obtained with that stimulus over several repetitions, relative to the spontaneous firing rate of the cell. This cell was highly selective for a narrow range of concentric and spiral gratings.

area V2. In area V1, simple cells preserve phase information, whereas complex cells are insensitive to spatial phase. In area V2 almost all cells are insensitive to phase (Hubel & Livingstone, 1985; Levitt et al., 1994), suggesting that these cells receive substantial input from V1 complex cells. In area V1, end-stopped cells are suppressed by bars that extend beyond the boundaries of the CRF. In area V2 many cells are tuned for lengths that are substantially smaller than the diameter of the CRF (von der Heydt & Peterhans, 1989; Levitt et al., 1994), perhaps reflecting the influence of end-stopped cells in V1. More generally, the existence of form–cue invariance suggests that nonlinear processes are important for shaping V2 responses.

C. Area V4

Area V4 appears to play an important role in processing both color and form information. Many V4 cells are tuned for particular colors, though the pattern of tuning can be fairly complex (Schein & Desimone, 1990). Consistent with this, lesions of V4 in humans may produce achromotopsia, in which visual experience is reduced to shades of gray (Zeki, 1990). (Some researchers have suggested that achromotopsia is not caused by lesions of area V4, but rather by lesions of a later stage of processing (Hadjikhani et al., 1998; Heywood, Gadotti, & Cowey, 1992). The color selectivity of area V4 also suggests that it may play a central role in color constancy, the perception that colors do not change even during changes in illumination that can drastically alter the spectral signature of a surface (Zeki, 1983).

Area V4 appears to encode more complex aspects of form than those that are represented in earlier areas. Many V4 cells are selective for curved contours with a specific radius of curvature (Kobatake & Tanaka, 1994; Pasupathy & Connor, 1997), and they are tuned within a non-Cartesian, polar coordinate system whose axes specify radial and concentric frequency (Gallant, Braun, & Van Essen, 1993; Gallant et al., 1996). Figure 2 illustrates the responses of one V4 cell to sinusoidal gratings modulated in Cartesian (left), polar (center), and hyperbolic (right) coordinate systems (response strength is represented by the contrast of the gratings). A V1 cell with classical orientation tuning would be well tuned in the Cartesian stimulus space, but would respond weakly to most of the polar stimuli. In contrast, the cell shown in Figure 2 is selective for concentric and high-frequency spiral gratings, and responds quite poorly to Cartesian and hyperbolic gratings. Some V4 cells are selective for other classes of non-Cartesian patterns, such as hyperbolic gratings (Gallant et al., 1996), corners (Pasupathy & Connor, 1997) and other moderately complex configurations of straight contours (Kobatake & Tanaka, 1994). These cells may be distinct from the subpopulation of V4 cells that encode curvature information (Gallant et al., 1996).

Non-Cartesian stimuli evoke responses in area V4 neurons that are both larger and more selective than those produced by conventional Cartesian gratings (Gallant et al., 1996). V4 cells selective for curvature probably respond to both curved lines and curved gratings, though this has only been assessed in V2, not V4 (Hedge & Van Essen, 1997). Thus area V4 may explicitly represent information about the curvature and orientation of contours and surfaces in a scene. This information might in turn be used to segment a scene and to determine the spatial distribution of local surface patches (Freeman & Adelson, 1991).

The nonlinearities first observed in earlier areas are enhanced in area V4. Tuning for the length and width of bars and gratings is common, but the optimal length or width may be significantly smaller than the diameter of the CRF, and the position of the optimal bar within the CRF is not critical (Desimone and Schein 1987). Changes in stimulus position may change the absolute response level, but tuning curves remain remarkably stable across moderate shifts in spatial position (Desimone & Schein, 1987; Gallant et al., 1996). Thus V4 cells are quite sensitive to the shape, size, and configuration of stimuli within the CRF, but they are much less sensitive to absolute spatial position.

D. Posterior Inferotemporal Cortex

We currently know much less about the function of PIT than area V4. PIT receptive fields are somewhat larger than V4, though this area retains a clear retinotopic map of space. The optimal stimuli for driving PIT cells appear to be somewhat more complex than those that are most effective in area V4 (Kobatake & Tanaka, 1994). However, little is really known about the representation of form in PIT because PIT is too nonlinear to permit quantitative estimation of filtering properties using current methods.

One clear difference between PIT and V4 concerns the perceptual effects of lesions in the two areas. While area V4 lesions cause relatively mild form discrimination deficits, PIT lesions cause profound deficits of form vision and an inability to learn new visual discriminations (see Farah, 1990). These differences suggest that areas PIT and V4 play quite different roles in form processing. However, it is unclear to what extent PIT lesions directly affect the representation of objects *per se* versus merely reflecting learning and memory deficits that are known to result from lesions of the IT complex.

E. Central and Anterior Inferotemporal Cortex

Based on general physiological and anatomical criteria, IT has been subdivided into CIT and AIT (Felleman & Van Essen, 1991); however, IT is actually a collection of several areas that are difficult to distinguish physiologically; the large CRFs of IT cells preclude the identification of a visual topographic map (if one exists), and their receptive field properties are relatively complex and do not clearly fall into distinct classes.

IT cells are sensitive to a wide variety of stimulus attributes, such as shape, color, and texture (Gross, Rocha-Miranda, & Bender, 1972). These cells appear to have more complex shape tuning than cells at any earlier stage of processing (Desimone et al., 1984; Gross et al., 1972), yet they still respond quite well to shapes that are much simpler than those that typically occur in the natural world (Tanaka, Saito, Fukada, & Moriya, 1991). IT cells are often selective for configurations of several simple shapes with a specific spatial relationship (Gross, 1994; Kobatake & Tanaka, 1994; Tanaka et al., 1991), and this may reflect coding for complex objects that have several distinct parts. Some IT cells are selective for complex ethologically important patterns, such as faces and hands (Gross et al., 1972; Perrett, Rolls, & Caan, 1982). In some cases, these cells may be tuned for a particular head orientation (Desimone et al., 1984), direction of gaze (Perrett et al., 1985), or facial expression (Perrett et al., 1984).

Different shapes may be stored in different anatomical modules or columns within IT. Face-selective cells appear to be concentrated in specific anatomical subdivisions within IT in both humans and other primates (Hasselmo, Rolls, Baylis, & Nalwa, 1989; Kanwisher, McDermott, & Chun, 1997; McCarthy, Puce, Gore, & Allison, 1997; Perrett et al., 1985). There is also some evidence that different cortical columns in IT may be selective for different attributes of shape (Fujita & Tanaka, 1992; Fuster & Jervey, 1981).

The nonlinear response characteristics first observed in earlier areas, such as position invariance, form–cue invariance, and complex shape selectivity, are much more pronounced in IT. These cells maintain stimulus selectivity regardless of the position of stimuli within the CRF, even though their CRFs span most of the visual field (Sato, Kawamura, & Iwai, 1980; Schwartz, Desimone, Albright, & Gross, 1983). In addition, many IT cells will respond to a specific shape regardless of the cues that define the borders of the shape (Sary, Vogels, Kovacs, & Orban, 1995). Finally, IT cells that are tuned for complex, multipart shapes respond poorly to a subset of the features that make up the critical shape (Desimone et al., 1984; Kobatake & Tanaka, 1994; Tanaka, 1993). Thus IT cells are sensitive to the presence and arrangement of critical shape attributes, but are insensitive to absolute position and to the specific cues to shape.

As one might expect from its physiological responses to shape, the IT complex appears to be particularly important for object recognition. Lesions of IT have even greater effects on learning and memory for objects than they do on simple pattern-matching tasks (Farah, 1990; Logothetis, Pauls, & Poggio, 1995). Many researchers have focused on how IT enables object recognition regardless of viewpoint. One current idea is that the visual system stores many different views of each object (Poggio, 1990; Tarr & Pinker, 1989), and each object is represented in a viewer-centered coordinate system. This scheme only requires a subset of the views to be stored because the intermediate views can be estimated by interpolating between several stored views. As new objects are seen they are identified by comparing them to those in the stored library. Support for this position comes from a study in which animals were trained to discriminate completely novel objects from specific views (Logothetis & Pauls, 1995). Recordings were made in area AIT, and a small subset of the recorded cells were selective for specific views of the trained objects. Some of these cells were selective for trained views, while others were tuned for intermediate views that did not exist in the training set. In addition, some face-selective cells in IT appear to be sensitive to the direction from which faces are displayed (Perrett et al., 1984), suggesting that faces might also be stored as a collection of views.

An alternative idea is that the visual system stores a single representation of each object in an object-centered coordinate system that is invariant to viewpoint (Marr & Nishihara, 1978). In this case the visual system would have to map incoming objects into a canonical reference frame in order to permit comparison with the stored library of objects. Evidence in favor of viewpoint-invariant theories comes from the demonstration that some IT cells (in a different location than those described above) are selective for faces regardless of viewpoint (Hasselmo et al., 1989). The contradictory nature of these data illustrates the limitations of our current understanding of shape coding in IT. In reality, both views are probably oversimplifications. If IT contains several distinct representations of shape, then both single-view and viewpoint-invariant representations could exist in different populations of cells.

IV. ATTENTION, LEARNING, MEMORY, AND MOTOR SIGNALS

Most if not all cortical visual areas are affected by extraretinal factors, such as attention, learning, memory, and motor control. However, these effects are generally larger at later stages of processing. The most commonly observed effect of attention is to change the responsiveness or gain of cells that share the attended dimension. Attention can also modulate the interactions of neighboring cells, which can have fairly complex effects on filtering properties. At the highest stages of visual processing, responses can also reflect memory processes and task demands. Finally, many cells in the visual system are affected by eye movements or eye position. In some cases, this modulation is probably due to a motor signal from the eyes that encodes eye position, while in others it may reflect attentional reallocation associated with eye movements. In general, extraretinal influences modulate the way information is represented in the various visual areas by changing information flow or altering filtering properties.

A. Area V1

Attentional effects in V1 are quite modest, and they have been relatively difficult to demonstrate using single-cell recording techniques. Two types of attentional effects have now been observed neurophysiologically. First, attention can preferentially weight the responses of cells. For example, when attention is directed toward a specific color, the responses of V1 cells that are tuned to unattended colors are suppressed (Motter, 1993). Suppression of cells tuned to unattended dimensions will favor those whose filtering properties are best suited to the current perceptual task.

Second, attention can modulate the interactions between neighboring cells. For example, when attention is directed toward the CRF of a cell it can reduce the normally suppressive effect of surrounding stimuli in the nCRF (Press, Knierim, & Van Essen, 1994). Changes in nCRF suppression also alter the filtering properties of a cell. In both cases attention appears to alter the representation of information at higher stages of processing by enhancing attended attributes while suppressing unattended information (Van Essen, Olshausen, Anderson, & Gallant, 1991). If we conceptualize the CRF as a multidimensional filter, then attention appears to warp the filter to sharpen it along the attended dimension.

B. Area V4

A variety of attentional effects have been observed in area V4. Many of these affect processing within the CRF. Without attention, the response of a V4 cell to an effective stimulus can be suppressed by placing a second, ineffective stimulus (one which, by itself, does not evoke a response) inside the CRF (Moran & Desimone, 1985). However, attention to the effective stimulus can rescue the response, reducing the inhibitory effects of the second stimulus (Moran & Desimone, 1985). Thus, attention may increase the selectivity of a V4 cell by preserving its responses to effective stimuli while suppressing the effects of irrelevant information. Attention to a specific color regardless of spatial position produces responses similar to those observed in earlier areas; the responses to unattended colors are suppressed, while attended colors continue to be processed (Motter 1994).

Few models of intermediate form vision address attentional effects like those found in V4 (Olshausen, Anderson, & Van Essen, 1993). From a functional point of view, attention to stimuli within the CRF could affect responses in several ways. If attention increased the gain of responses, then we would expect to see changes in firing rate and a broadening of tuning curves. If attention sharpened (or narrowed) tuning curves, then we would expect to see an increase in stimulus selectivity with attention. If it shifted tuning curves, then attention could completely alter the selectivity of a cell. This issue has not been resolved definitively, but current evidence suggests that attention to stimuli within the CRF alters the gain and perhaps the width of V4 tuning curves, but does not shift their tuning curves (McAdams & Maunsell, 1997).

When attention is directed just outside the CRF, the spatial profile of a V4 cell can actually shift toward the focus of attention (Connor, Gallant, Preddie, & Van Essen, 1996; Connor, Preddie, Gallant, & Van Essen, 1997). The shift can be on the order of degrees, which is a substantial fraction of the size of a V4 CRF. These shifts probably reflect attentional modulation of neural connections both within area V4 and between V4 and other extrastriate visual areas (Salinas & Abbott, 1997). V4 cells can also show more complex effects that depend on the spatial relationship between the driving stimulus and the attentional focus. In the experiment depicted in Figure 3, ring-shaped target stimuli were positioned above, below, to the right, and to the left of the cell's receptive field. On each trial the animal had to attend to one of

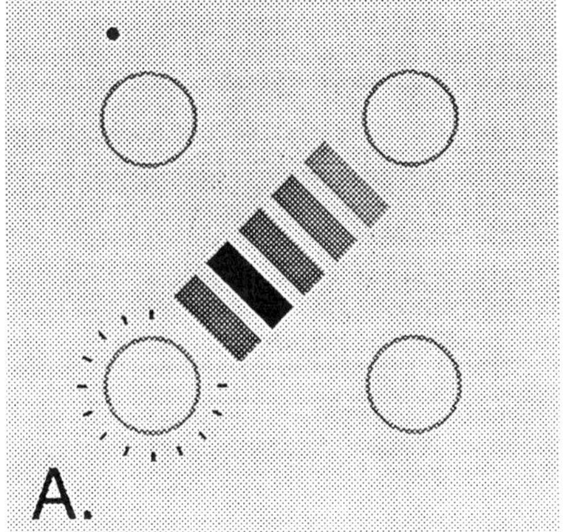

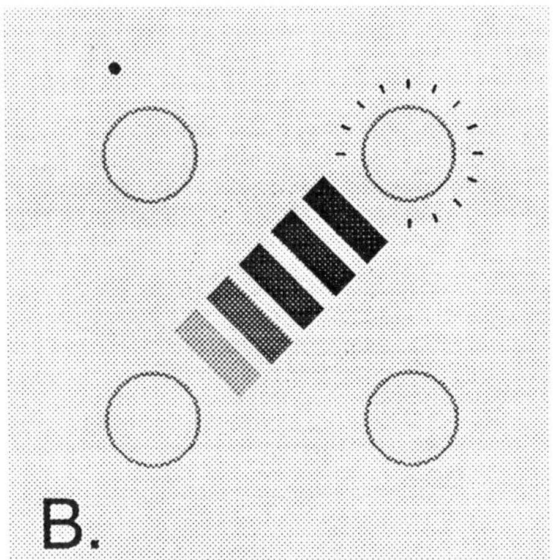

FIGURE 3 Shifts in V4 CRF profiles with attention. (A) The small dot represents the fixation point, and the dashed circle represents the location of the CRF (which was not visible on the display). The animal was cued to pay attention to the ring in the lower left of the display, and it had to maintain attention on the ring for several seconds without breaking fixation. During this time bars flashed at five positions spanning the CRF, but only one position was tested at a time. The brightness of the bars represents the strength of the corresponding response. Under these conditions the cell gave a vigorous response to bars near the bottom of the CRF. (B) Results obtained from the same cell shown in (A) when the animal has to attend to the ring in the upper right of the display. Under these conditions responses declined overall, and the peak response shifted up towards the top of the CRF.

the rings (denoted by highlight rays) while bars were flashed in five locations spanning the CRF (response strength is coded by the brightness of the bars). When attention was directed below the CRF, the cell responded vigorously, and the peak response was shifted toward the bottom of the CRF. When attention was directed above the CRF, response strength declined and the peak response shifted toward the top of the CRF. Most cells in V4 show such asymmetric response modulation with attention, suggesting that it creates a local reference frame for specifying the positions of individual features (Connor et al., 1997). Thus attention may act not only to boost the signal but also to organize the local positional information critical for shape processing (Hinton, 1981).

C. Central and Anterior Inferotemporal Cortex

Cells in CIT and AIT show attentional effects much like those observed in earlier areas, but they are also highly modulated by other extraretinal factors, such as short-term and long-term memory, and eye movements. IT cells also show strong adaptation effects that reflect recent perceptual history. Novel stimuli produce the largest responses, and these are reduced when stimuli are presented repeatedly (Miller, Li, & Desimone, 1993). Many of the extraretinal effects observed in IT are related to cueing and expectation. Several labs have investigated these effects using a match-to-sample task, where stimuli function either as cues, irrelevant distracters, or as the target (Miyashita, 1993). IT cells often give much larger responses to the cue and the target than they do to the distracters (Miller & Desimone, 1994). Finally many IT cells, particularly those in AIT, show significant learning effects after training on a specific set of visual patterns (Logothetis & Pauls, 1995). All of these observations indicate that IT plays a critical role, not only in the representation of objects, but in object learning, recognition, and visual memory.

V. COMPUTATIONAL PRINCIPLES

Anatomical and physiological data provide important clues about form vision, but a complete understanding of visual function requires us to work backward from the neural implementation to the computational principles involved. Experiments describe the tuning profiles of cells in a particular area and, in some cases, the anatomical distribution of cells with similar response properties. Computational considerations must be invoked to address the underlying representation and its functional role in vision.

A. Area V1

As discussed earlier, many V1 cells are jointly tuned for position, orientation, and scale. This tuning suggests that early vision employs some variant of the Gabor wavelet transform (Daugman, 1990). In this coding scheme, an image is decomposed into many localized elements known as basis functions. The basis functions are two-dimensional Gaussian-modulated sinusoids that vary in spatial position, orientation, size, and phase. The Gabor transform is an especially useful representation for vision because it efficiently encodes many types of information that are important for visual processing, such as edges, luminance gradients, and texture (Navarro, Tabernero, & Cristobal, 1996). Most importantly, this representation may allow later stages of processing to efficiently extract the higher order structure of complex objects from visual scenes.

As discussed earlier, the responses of V1 cells are also affected by stimuli falling within the nCRF. These nCRF effects are diverse, and cells with similar CRF profiles can vary widely in their nCRF profiles (DeAngelis, Robson, Ohzawa, & Freeman, 1992; Knierim & Van Essen, 1992). Thus, the nCRF effectively increases the diversity of neural filters in area V1. One effect of this expansion of filter types is to decorrelate the responses of nearby cells with similar CRFs. This would also have the effect of making the representation in V1 more sparse, which could increase visual processing efficiency (Olshausen & Field, 1997).

Gabor filters are fairly broadband, and any single filter can respond to many patterns in visual scenes. Compound filters composed of a Gabor CRF and a nonlinear nCRF will necessarily be more selective, and so will respond to fewer patterns in a visual scene. This is consistent with observations made in area V1. For example, some cells give a larger response to a contour extending beyond the CRF than to one that is confined to the CRF (Kapadia et al., 1995). Because long contours are likely to correspond to the edges of solid objects, facilitation of responses to long contours might help cells reliably code this important aspect of natural scenes.

B. Area V2

A computational model of V2 must account for responses to illusory borders (von der Heydt & Peterhans, 1989) and for more general form–cue invariant responses. It should also encode curvature (Hedge & Van Essen, 1997). One mechanism that might produce all of these responses is a linear-nonlinear-linear (LNL) filter (Wilson, 1993). As illustrated in Figure 4, an LNL filter consists of a linear filtering stage followed by a nonlinearity and then by a second linear filter (Graham, Beck, & Sutter, 1992; Wilson, 1993). The nonlinearity can alter the representation of an illusory or texture border, adding information that would be consistent with the existence of a real border at the same location (Pelli, 1987). LNL filters can also be constructed so as to be selective both for curved contours and for luminance gradients with appropriate curvature energy (Wilson, 1999). Note that a strictly linear filter cannot produce form–cue invariant responses.

An LNL mechanism might be implemented in area V2 by linear filtering of the rectified output of area V1. LNL filters constructed in this way should respond to the modulation frequency of an amplitude-modulated sinusoidal grating, and such responses have now been observed in V2 (Zhou & Baker, 1994, 1996). Because V1 complex cells receive some rectified input from V1 simple cells we might also expect to see some LNL behavior in area V1. These effects have also been observed, though they are much smaller than in V2 (Grosof, Shapley, & Hawken, 1993; Zhou & Baker, 1994).

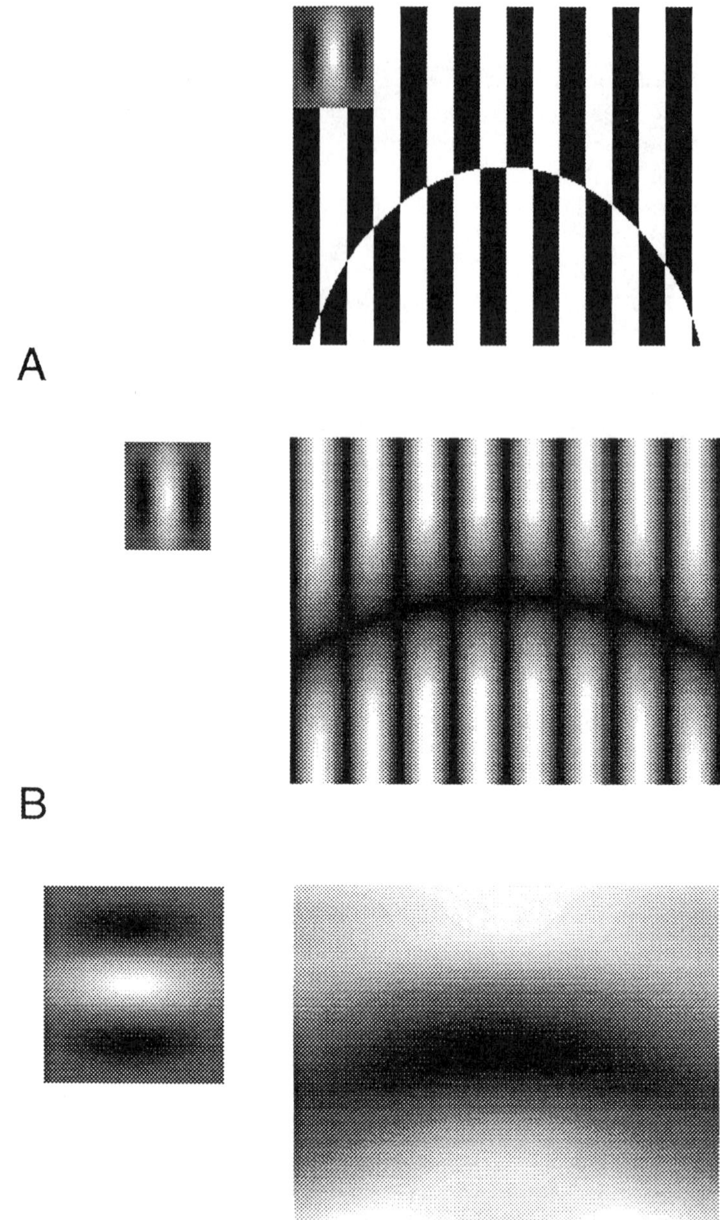

FIGURE 4 Demonstration of LNL filtering at a texture boundary (from the model proposed by Wilson, 1993). (A) A texture boundary generated by a phase shift of a square wave grating. The vertical filter shown in panel B has been superimposed in the upper left corner. (B) A vertically oriented filter similar to a simple cell (left) and the result of filtering the texture pattern shown in (A) with a bank of similar linear filters, followed by rectification (right). The filtering and rectification operation is sensitive to the grating, but it does not explicitly encode the boundary. (C) A second horizontally oriented filter (left) and the result of filtering the filtered, rectified pattern shown in (B) with a bank of similar secondary linear filters. The texture boundary is easily detected at this stage of processing.

C. Area V4

The tuning for curved and polar grating responses observed in area V4 can be interpreted using a computational framework that is an extension of the LNL framework discussed above for area V2 (Wilson, 1999; Wilson & Wilkenson, 1998; Wilson, Wilkenson & Asaad, 1997). According to this view, V4 cells integrate the output of several smaller LNL filters in order to represent the curvature energy of the input. The small LNL filters encode local curvature by virtue of their limited spatial extent and simple orientation tuning. V4 cells encode more complex curvature energy by integrating across several LNL filters at different positions and orientations. Integrated LNL filters such as these can respond equally to many different types of curved stimuli, such as curved contours, curved textures, or curved shadows, as long as the stimuli have similar curvature energy (Wilson, 1999). In principle the responses of V4 hyperbolic cells could be described using a similar framework.

The application of quantitative nonlinear filtering models to area V4 is still in its infancy, so we do not know how much of the physiological data can be explained within this framework. Some V4 cells can be extremely tightly tuned for particular non-Cartesian stimuli (Gallant et al., 1996), and it is unclear whether LNL integration models can account for these tuning curves. Mechanisms based on LNL filters are insensitive to spatial phase, so they may fail to account for the selectivity some cells show for surface contrast polarity (Pasupathy & Connor, 1997). It is also unclear whether LNL integration models can account for the entire diversity of shape responses that have been observed in area V4 (Kobatake & Tanaka, 1994).

Both physiological and lesion results suggest that V4 also plays an important role in representing shapes within an invariant reference frame that can facilitate object recognition. The asymmetric shifts of V4 CRFs resulting from shifts of visual attention (Connor et al., 1997) suggest that single V4 cells might encode information relative to the focus of attention. On the other hand, V4 lesions impair the ability to discriminate three-dimensional (3-D) shapes that are shown from different viewpoints, but they have little effect on direct matching of shapes shown from the same viewpoint (Merigan & Phan, 1998). Thus the reference frame in V4 may represent information about 3-D pose.

D. Central and Anterior Inferotemporal Cortex

As discussed above, modern theories of form processing in early visual areas generally adopt a filtering framework; however, cells in IT cortex are highly nonlinear and their response characteristics are unclear. Because the filtering framework assumes linearity, it has been difficult to apply this framework to IT cortex. For example, the face-selective cells discussed earlier appear to respond to a constellation of facial features, and they can be entirely unresponsive to a subset of these features (Perrett et al., 1985; Rolls, Baylis, & Hasselmo, 1987; Young & Yamane, 1992). Thus IT cells usually cannot be characterized in terms of their responses to simple features.

Current computational models of higher vision attempt to generalize the linear filter framework in order to account for these nonlinear response characteristics (e.g., Poggio & Edelman, 1990). This requires two basic modifications to the framework. First, the cells are assumed to encode information in a space that is closer to our perceptual ideas about object structure than to the simple dimensions represented in earlier areas. For example, cells that are selective for faces might encode information in a space defined by the principle components of human faces (Atick, Griffin, & Redlich, 1996). Such cells would still function as filters with well-defined tuning curves, but their coding properties would be better suited to higher vision. Second, the cells are assumed to encode information in a high-dimensional space in which their nonlinear responses are computationally tractable. This may seem counterintuitive, but in fact this procedure is commonly used in engineering and statistics to enable quasilinear analysis of nonlinear signals.

The available evidence suggests that IT does indeed implement a higher order filtering scheme. Most importantly, many IT cells have clear tuning curves within relevant stimulus spaces. For example face-selective cells in and near IT do not respond to a single face, but rather to a range of faces that are similar in appearance to the optimal face (Young & Yamane, 1992). These cells may encode faces within an abstract space that represents the various dimensions along which faces differ (e.g., Atick et al., 1996). In this case the cells would be equivalent to a set of filters that are each selective for a local region of this multidimensional face space. A single face would then be represented by the joint activity of many such cells.

Computational models of the IT complex have also addressed how the representation of a shape might be indexed into memory. One of the central problems that the visual memory system has to solve is how to recognize shapes regardless of viewpoint. Two possibilities have been proposed. First, the visual system might transform perceived shapes into a unique and consistent reference frame (Biederman, 1987; Marr & Nishihara, 1978). This would make memory access simple because each shape could be referred to a single canonical representation in memory, but it would require active processes that continuously normalize objects in the visual scene (perhaps involving earlier visual areas; see Olshausen et al., 1993). The second possibility is that the visual system stores multiple representations of each object as seen from different viewpoints (Tarr & Pinker, 1989; Poggio & Edelman, 1990). In this case incoming shapes would be compared to several stored representations of each object. This scheme eliminates the complexities of achieving viewpoint invariance but requires more template-matching operations and more memory capacity. The physiological evidence is still too weak to decide which if either of these schemes is actually implemented by the visual system. Some cells in IT and STP show consistent tuning for faces across changes in viewpoint (Hasselmo et al., 1989), but it is unclear whether this reflects a viewpoint-invariant representation or an interpolation process. Some support for interpolation comes from a study that suggested that some AIT cells were tuned for specific views of learned 3-D stimuli (Logothetis & Pauls, 1995), but this effect was only observed in a small proportion of cells.

VI. CURRENT RESEARCH IN THE NEUROBIOLOGY OF FORM VISION

There are many aspects of form processing in the ventral visual pathway that we are only beginning to understand. This is due to several factors, including limitations in the available data, limited understanding of the computational constraints on shape representation, and analytical difficulties inherent in assessing highly nonlinear systems. The problem of shape representation is currently being addressed in several ways.

Most experiments on shape have traditionally used geometrical patterns that are much simpler than those typically found in natural scenes (Field 1987, 1994). The nonlinearities found throughout the visual system suggest that responses to simple shapes probably do not fully account for responses to natural scenes, but research in this area is still in its infancy (Baddeley et al., 1997; Gallant et al., 1998; Vinje & Gallant, 1998). Regular geometrical patterns such as bars and gratings also fail to capture the rich interactions between the various aspects of natural shape, such as bounding contours, texture, shading, and volumetric properties. We are only beginning to understand how these attributes might be represented and how they are organized in the representation of 3-D objects (Edelman & Duvdevani-Bar, 1997).

Finally, although visual attention may be critical for many aspects of natural vision, researchers have only begun to integrate research on the neural basis of attention with that on shape (Connor et al., 1997). Future advances in all these areas should bring a much richer conceptualization of shape representation in vision. Because vision is an excellent model system for many brain functions, these findings should be applicable to many aspects of systems and cognitive neuroscience.

Acknowledgments

I thank Charles Connor for substantial contributions to this chapter and William Vinje, James Mazer, and David Moorman for helpful comments. Preparation was supported by the University of California, Berkeley.

References

Albright, T. D. (1992). Form-cue invariant motion processing in primate visual cortex. *Science, 255,* 1141–1143.

Allman, J., Miezin, F., & McGuiness, E. (1985). Stimulus-specific responses from beyond the classical receptive field: neurophysiological mechanisms for local-global comparisons on visual neurons. *Annual Review of Neuroscience, 8,* 407–430.

Atick, J. J., Griffin, P. A., & Redlich, A. N. (1996). The vocabulary of shape: principle shapes for probing perception and neural response. *Network: Computation in Neural Systems, 7,* 1–5.

Baddeley, R., Abbott, L. F., Booth, M. C. A., Sengpiel, F., Freeman, R., Wakeman, E. A., & Rolls, E. T. (1997). Responses of neurons in primary and inferior temporal visual cortices to natural scenes. *Proceedings of the Royal Society of London B, 264,* 1775–1783.

Biederman, I. (1987). Recognition by components: a theory of human image understanding. *Psychological Review, 94,* 115–147.

Connor, C. E., Gallant, J. L., Preddie, D. C., & Van Essen, D. C. (1996). Responses in area V4 depend on the spatial relationship between stimulus and attention. *Journal of Neurophysiology, 75,* 1306–1308.

Connor, C. E., Preddie, D. C., Gallant, J. L., & Van Essen, D. C. (1997). Spatial attention effects in macaque area V4. *Journal of Neuroscience, 17,* 3201–3214.

Daugman, J. G. (1990). An information-theoretic view of analog representation in striate cortex. In E. L. Schwartz (Ed.), *Computational Neuroscience* (pp. 403–423). Cambridge, MA: MIT Press.

DeAngelis, G. C., Robson, J. G., Ohzawa, I., & Freeman, R. D. (1992). Organization of suppression in receptive fields of neurons in cat visual cortex. *Journal of Neurophysiology, 68,* 144–163.

Desimone, R., Albright, T. D., Gross, C. G., & Bruce, C. (1984). Stimulus-selective properties of inferior temporal neurons in the macaque. *Journal of Physiology, 357,* 219–240.

Desimone, R., & Schein, S. J. (1987). Visual properties of neurons in area V4 of the macaque: Sensitivity to stimulus form. *Journal of Neurophysiology, 57,* 835–868.

DeValois, R. L., Albrecht, D. G., & Thorell, L. G. (1982). Spatial frequency selectivity of cells in macaque visual cortex. *Vision Research, 22,* 545–559.

DeValois, R. L., & DeValois, K. K. (1990). *Spatial Vision.* New York, NY: Oxford.

DeYoe, E. A., Felleman, D. J., Van Essen, D. C., & McClendon, E. (1994). Multiple processing streams in occipitotemporal visual cortex. *Nature, 371*(151–154).

DeYoe, E. A., Glickman, S., & Wieser, J. (1992). *Clustering of visual response properties in cortical area V4 of macaque monkeys.* Paper presented at the Society for Neuroscience Abstracts.

Edelman, S., & Duvdevani-Bar, S. (1997). Similarity, connectionism, and the problem of representation in vision. *Neural Computation, 9,* 701–720.

Farah, M. J. (1990). *Visual Agnosia.* Cambridge, MA: MIT Press.

Felleman, D. J., & Van Essen, D. C. (1991). Distributed hierarchical processing in the primate cerebral cortex. *Cerebral Cortex, 1,* 1–47.

Field, D. J. (1987). Relations between the statistics of natural images and the response properties of cortical cells. *Journal of the Optical Society of America A, 4,* 2379–2394.

Field, D. J. (1994). What is the goal of sensory coding? *Neural Computation, 6,* 559–601.

Freeman, W. T., & Adelson, E. H. (1991). The design and use of steerable filters. *IEEE Transactions on pattern analysis and machine intelligence, 13,* 891–906.

Fujita, I., & Tanaka, K. (1992). Columns for visual features of objects in monkey inferotemporal cortex. *Nature, 360,* 343–346.

Fuster, J. M., & Jervey, J. P. (1981). Inferotemporal neurons distinguish and retain behaviorally relevant features of visual stimuli. *Science, 212,* 952–955.

Gallant, J. L., Braun, J., & Van Essen, D. C. (1993). Selectivity for polar, hyperbolic, and Cartesian gratings in macaque visual cortex. *Science, 259,* 100–103.

Gallant, J. L., Connor, C. E., Rakshit, S., Lewis, J. W., & Van Essen, D. C. (1996). Neural Responses to Polar, Hyperbolic, and Cartesian Gratings in Area V4 of the Macaque Monkey. *Journal of Neurophysiology, 76,* 2718–2739.

Gallant, J. L., Connor, C. E., & Van Essen, D. C. (1998). Neural Activity in Areas V1, V2 and V4 During Free Viewing of Natural Scenes Compared to Controlled Viewing. *NeuroReport, 9*(2153–2158).

Ghose, G. M., & Ts'o, D. Y. (1997). Form processing modules in primate area V4. *Journal of Neurophysiology, 77,* 2191–2196.

Graham, N., Beck, J., & Sutter, A. (1992). Nonlinear processes in spatial-frequency channel models of perceived texture segregation: Effects of sign and amount of contrast. *Vision Research, 32*(4), 7 19–743.

Grosof, D. H., Shapley, R. M., & Hawken, M. J. (1993). Macaque V1 neurons can signal 'illusory' contours. *Nature, 365,* 550–552.

Gross, C. G. (1994). How inferior temporal cortex became a visual area. *Cerebral Cortex, 4,* 455–469.

Gross, C. G., Rocha-Miranda, C. E., & Bender, D. B. (1972). Visual properties of neurons in inferotemporal cortex of the macaque. *Journal of Neurophysiology, 35,* 96–111.

Hadjikhani, N., Liu, A. K., Dale, A. M., Cavanagh, P., & Tootell, R. B. H. (1998). Retinotopy and color sensitivity in human visual cortical area V8. *Nature Neuroscience, 1,* 235–247.

Hasselmo, M. E., Rolls, E. T., Baylis, G. C., & Nalwa, V. (1989). Object-centered encoding of face-selective neurons in the cortex in the superior temporal sulcus of the monkey. *Experimental Brain Research, 75,* 417–429.

Hegde, J., & Van Essen, D. C. (1997). Selectivity for complex contour stimuli in visual area V2. *Inv. Opth. Vis. Sci. Supp., 38,* 969.

Heywood, C. A., Gadotti, A., & Cowey, A. (1992). Cortical area V4 and its role in the perception of color. *Journal of Neuroscience, 12,* 4056–4065.

Hinton, G. F. (1981). *Shape representation in parallel systems.* Paper presented at the 7th Internat. Joint Conf. on Art. Intell.

Hubel, D. H., & Livingstone, M. S. (1985). Complex-unoriented cells in a subregion of primate area 18. *Nature, 315,* 325–327.

Hubel, D. H., & Wiesel, T. N. (1968). Receptive fields and functional architecture of monkey striate cortex. *Journal of Physiology (London), 195,* 215–243.

Kanwisher, N., McDermott, J., & Chun, M. M. (1997). The fusiform face area: A module in human extrastriate cortex specialized for face perception. *Journal of Neuroscience, 17,* 4302–4311.

Kapadia, M. K., Ito, M., Gilbert, C. D., & Westheimer, G. (1995). Improvement in visual sensitivity by changes in local context: Parallel studies in human observers and in V1 of alert monkeys. *Neuron, 15,* 843–856.

Knierim, J., & Van Essen, D. C. (1992). Neural responses to static texture patterns in area V1 of the alert macaque monkey. *Journal of Neurophysiology, 67,* 961–980.

Kobatake, E., & Tanaka, K. (1994). Neuronal selectivities to complex object features in the ventral visual pathway of the macaque cerebral cortex. *Journal of Neurophysiology, 71,* 856–867.

Levitt, J. B., Kiper, D. C., & Movshon, J. A. (1994). Receptive fields and functional architecture of macaque V2. *Journal of Neurophysiology, 71,* 2517–2542.

Livingstone, M., & Hubel, D. H. (1984). Anatomy of physiology of a color system in the primate visual cortex. *Journal of Neuroscience, 4,* 309–356.

Livingstone, M., & Hubel, D. H. (1988). Segregation of form, color, movement, and depth: Anatomy, physiology, and perception. *Science, 240,* 740–749.

Logothetis, N. K., & Pauls, J. (1995). Psychophysical and physiological evidence for viewer-centered object representations in the primate. *Cerebral Cortex, 3,* 270–288.

Logothetis, N. K., Pauls, J., & Poggio, T. (1995). Shape representations in the inferior temporal cortex of monkeys. *Current Biology, 5*(5), 552–563.

Marr, D., & Nishihara, H. K. (1978). Representation and recognition of the spatial organization of three-dimensional shapes. *Proceedings of the Royal Society of London B, 200,* 269–294.

McAdams, C. J., & Maunsell, J. H. R. (1997). *Spatial attention and feature-directed attention can both modulate neuronal responses in macaque area V4.* Paper presented at the Society for Neuroscience Abstracts.

McCarthy, G., Puce, A., Gore, J. C., & Allison, T. (1997). Face-specific processing in the human fusiform gyrus. *Journal of Cognitive Neuroscience, 9,* 605–610.

Merigan, W. H., Nealey, T. A., & Maunsell, J. H. R. (1993). Visual effects of lesions of cortical area V2 in macaques. *Journal of Neuroscience, 13,* 3180–3191.

Merigan, W. H., & Phan, H. A. (1998). V4 lesions in macaques affect both single- and multiple-viewpoint shape discriminations. *Visual Neuroscience, 15,* 359–367.

Miller, E. K., & Desimone, R. (1994). Parallel neuronal mechanisms for short-term memory. *Science, 263,* 520–522.

Miller, E. K., Li, L., & Desimone, R. (1993). Activity of neurons in anterior inferior temporal cortex during a short-term memory task. *Journal of Neuroscience, 13,* 1460–1478.

Miyashita, M. (1993). Inferior temporal cortex: Where visual perception meets memory. *Annual Review of Neuroscience, 16*(369–402).

Moran, J., & Desimone, R. (1985). Selective attention gates visual processing in the extrastriate cortex. *Science, 229*(782–784).

Motter, B. C. (1993). Focal attention produces spatially selective processing in visual cortical areas V1, V2 and V4 in the presence of competing stimuli. *Journal of Neurophysiology, 70,* 1–11.

Motter, B. C. (1994). Neural correlates of attentive selection for color or luminance in extrastriate area V4. *Journal of Neuroscience, 14,* 2178–2189.

Navarro, R., Tabernero, A., & Cristobal, G. (1996). Image representation with Gabor wavelets and its applications. In P. W. Hawkes (Ed.), *Advances in Imaging and Electron Physics* (Vol. 97, pp. 1–84). New York: Academic Press.

Olshausen, B. A., Anderson, C. E., & Van Essen, D. C. (1993). A neural model of visual attention and invariant pattern recognition. *Journal of Neuroscience, 13,* 4700–4719.

Olshausen, B. A., & Field, D. J. (1997). Sparse coding with an overcomplete basis set: A strategy employed by V1? *Vision Research, 23,* 3311–3325.

Pasupathy, A., & Connor, C. E. (1997). Feature synthesis in macaque area V4. *Society for Neuroscience Abstracts, 23,* 2016.

Pelli, E. (1987). Perception of high-pass filtered images. *Proceedings of SPIE, 845,* 140–146.

Perrett, D. I., Rolls, E. T., & Caan, W. (1982). Visual neurons responsive to faces in the monkey temporal cortex. *Experimental Brain Research, 47*(329–342).

Perrett, D. I., Smith, P. A. J., Potter, D. D., Mistlin, A. J., Head, A. S., Milner, A. D., & Jeeves, M. A. (1984). Visual cells in the temporal cortex sensitive to face view and gaze direction. *Proceedings of the Royal Society of London B, 223,* 293–317.

Perrett, D. I., Smith, P. A. J., Potter, D. D., Mistlin, A. J., Head, A. S., Milner, A. D., & Jeeves, M. A. (1985). Neurones responsive to faces in the temporal cortex: Studies of functional organization, sensitivity to identity and relation to perception. *Human Neurobiology, 3,* 197–208.

Peterhans, E., & von der Heydt, R. (1987). Mechanisms of contour perception in monkey visual cortex. II. Contours bridging gaps. *Journal of Neuroscience, 9,* 1749–1763.

Poggio. (1990). A theory of how the brain might work. *Cold Spring Harbor Symposium on Quantitative Biology, 55,* 899–910.

Poggio, T., & Edelman, S. (1990). A network that learns to recognize three-dimensional objects. *nATURE, 343,* 263–266.

Press, W. A., Knierim, J. J., & Van Essen, D. C. (1994). Neuronal correlates of attention to texture patterns in macaque striate cortex. *Society for Neuroscience Abstracts, 20,* 838.

Rolls, E. T., Baylis, G. C., & Hasselmo, M. E. (1987). The responses of neurons in the cortex in the superior temporal sulcus of the monkey to band-pass spatial frequency filtered faces. *Vision Research, 27,* 311–326.

Salinas, E., & Abbott, L. F. (1997). Invariant visual responses from attentional gain fields. *Journal of Neurophysiology, 77,* 3267–3272.

Sary, G., Vogels, R., Kovacs, G., & Orban, G. A. (1995). Responses of monkey inferior temporal neurons to luminance-, motion-, and texture-defined gratings. *Journal of Neurophysiol, 73,* 1341–1354.

Sato, T., Kawamura, T., & Iwai, E. (1980). Responsiveness of inferotemporal single units to visual pattern stimuli in monkeys performing discrimination. *Experimental Brain Research, 38,* 313–319.

Schein, S. J., & Desimone, R. (1990). Spectral properties of V4 neurons in the macaque. *Journal of Neuroscience, 10,* 3369–3389.

Schwartz, E. L., Desimone, R., Albright, T. D., & Gross, C. G. (1983). Shape recognition and inferior temporal neurons. *Proceedings of the National Academy of Sciences USA, 80,* 5776–5778.

Tanaka, K. (1993). Neuronal mechanisms of object recognition. *Science, 262,* 685–688.

Tanaka, K., Saito, H., Fukada, Y., & Moriya, M. (1991). Coding of visual images of objects in the inferotemporal cortex of the macaque monkey. *Journal of Neurophysiology, 66,* 170–189.

Tarr, M. J., & Pinker, S. (1989). Mental rotation and orientation-dependence in shape recognition. *Cognitive Psychology, 21,* 233–282.

Underlieder, L. G., & Mishkin, M. (1982). Two cortical visual systems. In D. G. Ingle, M. A. Goodale, & R. J. Q. Mansfield (Eds.), *Analysis of Visual Behavior* (pp. 549–586). Cambridge, MA: MIT Press.

Van Essen, D. C., & Gallant, J. L. (1994). Neural mechanisms of form and motion processing in the primate visual system. *Neuron, 13,* 1–10.

Van Essen, D. C., Olshausen, B., Anderson, C. H., & Gallant, J. L. (1991). Pattern recognition, attention, and information bottlenecks in the primate visual system. *Proc. SPIE Conf. on Visual Information Processing: From Neurons to Chips, 1473,* 17–28.

Victor, J. D. (1992). Nonlinear systems analysis in vision: Overview of kernel methods. In R. B. Pinter & B. Nabet (Eds.), *Nonlinear vision: Determination of neural receptive fields, function, and networks* (pp. 1–38). Boca Raton: CRC Press.

Vinje, W. E., & Gallant, J. L. (1998). Modeling complex cells in an awake macaque during natural image viewing. In M. I. Jordan, M. J. Kearns, & S. A. Solla (Eds.), *Advances in Neural Information Processing Systems 10* (pp. 236–242). Cambridge, MA: MIT Press.

von der Heydt, R., & Peterhans, E. (1989). Mechanisms of contour perception in monkey visual cortex. I. Lines of pattern discontinuity. *Journal of Neuroscience, 9,* 1731–1748.

von der Heydt, R., Zhou, H., & Friedman, H. S. (1998). Cells of monkey visual cortex signal contours in random-dot stereograms., submitted.

Wilson, H. R. (1993). Nonlinear processes in visual pattern discrimination. *Proceedings of the National Academy of Sciences, 90,* 9785–9790.

Wilson, H. R. (1999). Non-Fourier cortical processes in texture, form and motion perception. In A. Peters & E. G. Jones (Eds.), *Cerebral Cortex: Models of Cortical Circuitry.* New York, NY: Plenum.

Wilson, H. R., & Wilkinson, F. (1998). Detection of global structure in Glass patterns: implications for form vision. *Vision Research, 38,* 2933–2947.

Wilson, H. R., Wilkinson, F., & Asaad, W. (1997). Concentric orientation summation in human vision. *Vision Research, 37,* 2325–2330.

Young, M. P., & Yamane, S. (1992). Sparse population coding of faces in the inferotemporal cortex. *Science, 256,* 1327–1331.

Zeki, S. M. (1983a). Colour coding in the cerebral cortex: The reaction of cells in monkey visual cortex to wavelengths and colours. *Neurosciences, 9,* 741–765.

Zeki, S. M. (1983b). The distribution of wavelength and orientation selective cells in different areas of monkey visual cortex. *Proceedings of the Royal Society of London B, 217,* 449–470.

Zeki, S. M. (1990). A century of cerebral achromatopsia. *Brain,* 1721–1777.

Zhou, Y. X., & Baker, C. L. (1994). Envelope-responsive neurons in areas 17 and 18 of cat. *Journal of Neurophysiology, 72*(5), 2134–2150.

Zhou, Y. X., & Baker, C. L. (1996). Spatial properties of envelope-responsive cells in area 17 and 18 of the cat. *Journal of Neurophysiology, 75*(3), 1038–1050.

CHAPTER 8

Visual Attention

Jeremy M. Wolfe

What a piece of work is man, how noble in reason, how infinite in faculties . . .
—*Hamlet,* 2:2:312–313

I. INTRODUCTION

Hamlet was wrong. We are dramatically limited in our faculties. Look at the center of Figure 1 and find a big black circle surrounding a small white square.

Now look for a black triangle surrounding a white square. The patterns in Figure 1 are deliberately large to circumvent the decline in visual resolution with eccentricity. You can see all of these patterns. Nevertheless, because your ability to process visual stimuli is limited, you do not immediately know that the first requested item is present at the lower left location and that the second requested item is not present at all. In order to perform the requested task, you had to restrict your visual processing to one item at a time. If you obeyed the instructions and kept your eyes on the central fixation point, you changed your processing of the visual input over time without changing the actual input.

Such acts of *visual attention* are the subject of this chapter. Because we cannot process everything, we must attend to something if we are to act on the basis of visual input.

Attention is a thriving area of research. The goal of this chapter is to introduce the reader to those aspects of the field most relevant to vision research. In many cases, that introduction is quite cursory, with the text serving as an annotated bibliography pointing the reader to the relevant papers. The chapter is divided into four sections:

Seeing

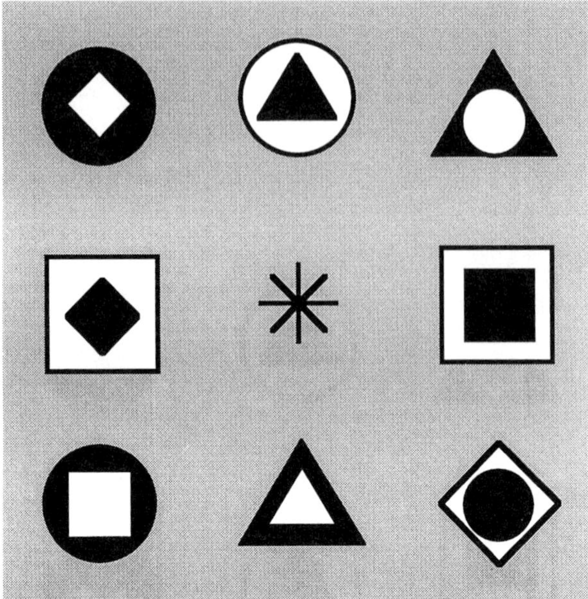

FIGURE 1 To see *and* not to see, that is the question.

1. Vision before attention—Looking at Figure 1, you saw something before you knew if that something included a black triangle surrounding a white square. What visual information is available "preattentively," before attention is directed to a locus or an object?

2. Vision with attention—Most of vision research involves vision with attention, since subjects are generally asked to perform some task while attending to some visual stimulus. How does attention alter a preattentive visual representation?

3. Vision after attention—Assuming that attention is restricted in space and time, does it leave any marks of its passage once it has been deployed away from a stimulus?

4. Vision without attention—In some situations it is meaningful to ask about the fate of stimuli that are never attended. This is related to, but not identical to, the question of vision before attention.

A. Other Resources

As noted, attention has become a very large topic in the past decade. This chapter, for instance, will introduce the reader to a substantial portion of the literature dealing with the "visual" side of visual attention. Other sources provide coverage of other aspects of the field. Pashler (1997) has written an excellent book for those interested in attention in its own right. Also recommended are Shiffrin's (1988) chapter in the 1988 edition of Steven's *Handbook of Experimental Psychology,* and *Annual Review* chapters by Kinchla (1992), and Egeth and Yantis (1997). Bundesen (1996) offers a concise review of formal models in a book that contains a considerable amount of useful information (Kramer, Cole, & Logan, 1996). Reviews of specific topics can be found in Pashler (1998).

II. VISION BEFORE ATTENTION

Neisser (1967) introduced the idea of a "preattentive" stage of visual processing—vision before attention. Preattentive vision would be vision without capacity limitations. At the preattentive stage, everything could be processed at once across the entire visual field. What aspects of vision might have this property? Answering this question is not trivial, because any time an experimenter asks a subject to respond to some visual stimulus, the subject will direct attention to that stimulus. It is probably impossible to get an explicit response from a subject based exclusively on the preattentive representation of a stimulus (see section V, Vision without Attention, for more on this issue).

A. The Uses and Interpretation of Visual Search Experiments

In trying to understand vision before attention, a more common strategy has been to look for the marks of preattentive processing in a task that requires both preattentive and attentive processing. One of the most useful methods is the *visual search* experiment. In a standard visual search experiment, the observer is looking for one target item in a display containing some number of distracting items. One of the attractions of this paradigm is that it brings a very common real-world visual behavior into the lab. In our day-to-day life, we frequently look for keys, socks, the can opener, or any of a host of visual targets in the cluttered visual display that is our world. The efficiency of a visual search can be assessed by looking at changes in performance; generally reaction time (RT) or accuracy, as a function of changes in the "set size"; the number of items in the display. These changes, in turn, can be used to make inferences about vision without attention. The slope of the RT × Set-Size Function is the most commonly used measure of the efficiency of visual search. Specifically, the deployment of visual attention can be "guided" with varying degrees of efficiency by the results of preattentive visual processing (Egeth, Virzi, & Garbart, 1984; Hoffman, 1979; Wolfe, Cave, & Franzel, 1989). As an example, consider a search for a red "F" among a number of other letters that can be either red or green. How is attention guided in such a search? For starters, preattentive processes are able to direct attention to objects so attention will not be deployed to random locations. It will be deployed to letters. Second, as will be discussed below, preattentive processes can guide attention on the basis of color information, so attention will be directed to red letters and not to green (Egeth et al., 1984). However, preattentive processes probably cannot read letters, so attention will be randomly deployed through the set of red letters.

1. "Pop-out" and Search Asymmetries

As noted, different levels of preattentive guidance are reflected in the slope of RT × Set-Size Functions. If preattentive processing can be used to direct attention to a target without fail on every target-present trial, then there will be no effect of set size on search performance. In Neisser's terms, an item that can be detected on the basis of preattentive processing should "pop-out" of the display. An intuitively clear example would be a search for a red item among green distractors. The red target pops out and summons attention with minimal interference from the distractors. The slope of the RT × Set-Size Function will be near zero.

The phenomenal experience of "pop-out" has a rather subjective quality to it, but RT and/or accuracy measures serve to operationalize it in visual search experiments. If the amount of time required to perform a visual search does not change as a function of the number of items in the display (the set size), then it is reasonable to propose that all items were processed at one time. Figure 2 shows an example of a task that would produce evidence of this sort along with hypothetical data.

Most examples of pop-out occur in searches in which the target is defined by a single basic feature. A limited set of basic features exists. The evidence for specific features in this set is found in section II.D.

An important characteristic of many feature searches is that they are asymmetrical. That is, if a search for A among B is efficient, it is not necessarily the case that a search for B among A is efficient (Treisman & Souther, 1985). In orientation, for example, it is easier to find a tilted line among vertical lines than vice versa. This can be understood in various ways. Treisman has argued that it is easier to find a deviation from a canonical stimulus (here, presumably, vertical) than it is to find a canonical stimulus among deviants (Treisman, 1985; Treisman & Souther, 1985). Another possibility, also introduced by Treisman, is that it is easier to find the presence of something than to find its absence. Continuing with the orientation example, visual search seems to treat all orientations as steep or shallow and as left or right tilted (Wolfe, Friedman-Hill, Stewart & O'Connell, 1992). Consequently, a right-tilted item would be readily found among verticals because it has a unique categorical attribute (right tilt). A vertical target among right-tilted distractors is defined by the absence of tilt (if all items are "steep"); consequently, it would be harder to find (Wolfe, 1994). Foster holds that search asymmetries in orientation are the by-product of broadly tuned channels subserving orientation feature search (Foster & Ward, 1991a). There need not be a single account for all search asymmetries, nor must these accounts be thought of as mutually exclusive. For instance, the orientation categories proposed by Wolfe et al. (1992) might be implemented as Foster's broadly tuned channels.

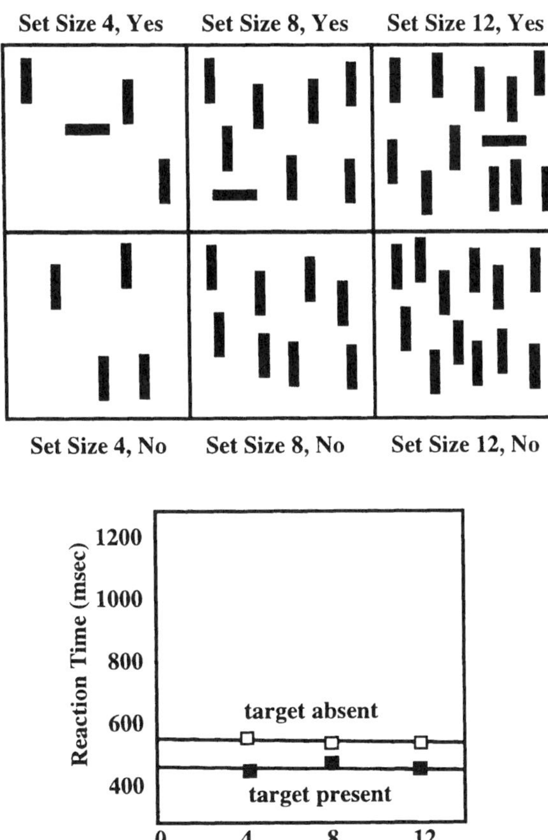

FIGURE 2 Sample trials and hypothetical data for a search task that produces reaction times that are independent of set size. In a real experiment, the order of trials would be random.

2. Inefficient "Serial" Searches

By contrast, if preattentive processing can do nothing more than segregate the items from the background, then attention will be deployed without further guidance over the set of items. As a result, performance will be strongly dependent on the set size. RT will increase and accuracy will decrease with set size. A search for a single target letter in a diverse set of distractor letters will probably proceed without preattentive guidance (but see Caerwinski, Lightfoot, & Shiffrin, 1992; Schneider & Shiffrin, 1977; Shiffrin & Schneider, 1977). As a rough rule of thumb, such unguided searches will produce target-present slopes of 20–30 ms/item and target-absent slopes of at least twice that magnitude. Such data are roughly consistent with a serial, self-terminating search through the items, but there are limited-capacity parallel accounts of the same data (Palmer, 1995; Townsend, 1971, 1976, 1990; Van Zandt & Townsend, 1993). See Wolfe 1998b for a more detailed look at data of this sort.

3. Conjunction Searches

Between pop-out and a complete absence of guidance are cases, like the red "F" example given above, where preattentive processing provides imperfect guidance. The efficiency of search will be intermediate in these cases. As noted, search for a red F will be more efficient if half the letters are red and half are green than if all are red (Carter, 1982; Green & Anderson, 1956; Smith, 1962). In these cases, the deployment of attention can be restricted to a subset of items that preattentive processing can identify as likely to be targets.

The most important class of search tasks producing slopes of intermediate efficiency are conjunction searches. In conjunction tasks, subjects look for a target defined by a combination of basic features among distractors that share some but not all features with the target. An example might be a Color × Orientation conjunction search for a red vertical target among red horizontal and green vertical distractors. In her original Feature Integration Theory, Anne Treisman proposed that all conjunction searches were serial, self-terminating searches through all items that shared *any* features with the target (Treisman & Gelade, 1980). Subsequent research made it clear that this claim was too strong. First, as noted earlier, there were studies that showed that search could be restricted to subsets of the items—subsets defined by features like color (Egeth et al., 1984). Later studies showed that more than one feature at a time could contribute to the guidance of conjunction search (e.g., Alkhateeb, Morland, Ruddock, & Savage, 1990; McLeod, Driver, Dienes, & Crisp, 1991; Nakayama & Silverman, 1986; Treisman & Sato, 1990; Wolfe, 1992b). The differences between Treisman's experiments and the later findings are discussed in Wolfe et al. (1989).

In an effort to explain efficient conjunction searches, it has been argued that some features are special in their ability to group distractors, segregate depth planes, or otherwise guide attention. This type of claim has been made for motion (McLeod et al., 1991; Nakayama & Silverman, 1986), stereopsis (Nakayama & Silverman, 1986), luminance polarity (Theeuwes & Kooi, 1994), and color, among others. As data have accumulated, it has become increasingly clear that efficient conjunction search is not restricted to searches involving only a few basic features. There is good evidence for efficient conjunction searches involving orientation, curvature (Wolfe, Yee, & Friedman-Hill, 1992), and, indeed, almost any feature that has been tested. Rather than invoking special attention-guiding abilities for one feature or the other, it might be better to assume that all the preattentive features discussed in the next section have some ability to guide attention, but that some features provide better guidance than others. The ability to guide attention in a conjunction search seems to be related to the salience of the stimulus differences involved (Wolfe et al., 1989). That is, red items are easier to segregate from green items than from orange (Duncan & Humphreys, 1989). To make claims for the special status of one type of feature, stimulus salience would need to be equated across features. Nothdurft (1993c) has provided a useful method to do this, but the issue has not been pursued in conjunction search studies.

While guidance of visual search can be used as evidence for preattentive processing of the guiding attribute, the reverse is not true. Failure to find guidance, in the form of efficient visual search, is not definitive evidence that a property is *not* processed preattentively. It is theoretically possible to have a preattentive process capable of responding to some stimulus property but unable to provide guidance for the subsequent deployment of attention. As an analogy, consider trying to describe a sunset to a friend on the other side of the country. Your description can never quite capture the richness and detail of your perception. Your inability to convey the exact shading of the sky does not mean that you did not see it. The same logical possibility exists in inferences about preattentive vision based on visual search. If a search experiment produces RT × Set-Size slopes near zero, as in Figure 2, that is evidence that preattentive processes are sensitive to the differences between targets and distractors. If the slopes are not near zero, that is evidence that preattentive processes cannot direct attention based on the differences between targets and distractors. Those differences might still be registered preattentively but be unavailable for export.

B. Typical Conditions and Pitfalls in Visual Search Tasks

That cautionary note notwithstanding, there is a great deal to be learned about preattentive processing from visual search experiments. In this section, I will address a few methodological issues before turning to the results of search studies.

In a typical visual search task, subjects would run several hundred trials of the sort shown in Figure 2. A range of set sizes would be tested with the set size on each trial chosen randomly. Target presence or absence would also vary from trial to trial. Usually targets are presented on 50% of trials. Items are positioned at random in the visual field with target position, likewise, random. Reaction time and accuracy are measured. Subjects are usually instructed to keep error rates low in these experiments where "low" means something like "below 10%." The slope of the RT × Set Size function is the main measure of interest, though the mean RT and/or the *y*-intercepts of RT × Set Size function may also be useful. In our lab, we have found that the statistical reliability of slopes from individual subjects running 300 or 400 trials is quite low (P. O'Neill & J. M. Wolfe, personal communication). Consequently, statements about slopes should be based on data from multiple subjects (ten is a reasonable sample) or on quite massive amounts of data from single subjects (thousands, not hundreds of trials).

The linearity of RT × Set Size functions is often asserted with more vigor than data. Typical search experiments use three or four set sizes. Regression coefficients based on linear fits of three points will be high for almost any set of three monotonically increasing values. Moreover, linearity over a relatively small range of set sizes (typical in search experiments) does not guarantee linearity over a large range (for a clear illustration of this point see Carrasco, Evert, Chang, & Katz, 1995).

The distribution of RTs for a single set size are generally not normally distributed. Most commonly, the distributions are positively skewed. Therefore, slopes based on simple means may be somewhat misleading because the RT means may be poor representatives of the central tendency of the data. Common solutions to this problem include using median RTs and using the mean of log transformed RTs, but examination of the actual distributions seems preferable to blind application of any solution.

Probably the greatest opportunities for error in visual experiments lie in the creation of the stimuli rather than the analysis of the data. Efficient, preattentively guided search can be masked by several factors. The most basic of these involve issues of resolution and eccentricity. If items need to be foveated before targets can be discriminated from distractors, then slopes are going to be steep. Indeed, any time slopes of RT × Set Size functions approach 100–150 ms/item for target-present trials and twice that for target absent, one should suspect an eye movement artifact. If the stimuli are of an adequate size, then it should be possible to identify a single item as target or distractor in a brief (e.g., 200 ms) exposure at any location in the display. Given adequately large stimuli, it is probably not necessary to tightly restrict eye movements. Zelinsky and Sheinberg (1997) have shown that the pattern of RTs is very similar under conditions of both free eye movement and rigorous fixation.

Even with large stimuli, there are very substantial effects of eccentricity on RT (Carrasco et al., 1995; Chun & Wolfe, 1996; Sanders, 1993; Wolfe, O'Neill, & Bennett, 1998). In some cases, these can be eliminated by scaling stimuli with a cortical magnification factor (Carrasco & Frieder, 1997). There is evidence that eccentricity effects are not isotropic. Unfortunately, the literature is not clear on the nature of the anisotropy. Right field superiority has been found (Efron & Yund, 1996; Yund, 1996; Yund, Efron, & Nichols, 1990), as have lower field (He, Cavanagh, & Intriligator, 1996) and upper field superiority (Previc, 1996; Previc & Blume, 1993). The topic is interesting in its own right, but for purposes of standard search experiments, the message is that the distribution of target locations should be the same as the distribution of distractor locations in order to avoid systematic errors.

In search experiments, multiple items are presented at one time. This raises the possibility of lateral interactions between items, notably mutual interference (Berger & McLeod, 1996; Cohen & Ivry, 1991). These effects of crowding are more marked in the periphery than they are near the fovea (He et al., 1996). This becomes a methodological problem in visual search experiments because, as a general rule, density increases with set size (Cohen & Ivry, 1991). One can hold density constant, but then it becomes necessary to allow mean eccentricity to increase with set size (clearly undesirable) or to position regions of uniform density at different locations in the visual field from trial to trial. This latter method is useful when the stimuli are briefly exposed, precluding eye movements. Otherwise, the eyes have a tendency to move to the center of gravity of the display (Findlay, 1995; Zelinsky, Rao, Hayhoe, & Ballard, 1996). This introduces an eccentricity artifact as if all displays were centered on fixation. In a generic search task, it is probably wise to space items so widely that crowding effects are unimportant even at the highest set sizes and densities.

C. Texture Segmentation and Visual Search

Done correctly, visual search experiments can be used to identify properties of the visual input that are processed prior to attention. The properties have been called "basic" or "preattentive features." As shown in Figure 2, highly efficient search (RT × Set Size slopes near zero) is the mark of preattentive processing. However, a slope near zero, by itself, is not definitive evidence that the target differs from distractors on the basis of a preattentive feature. Evidence from some converging operation is desirable before enrolling a feature in the ranks of the preattentive (Garner, Hake, & Eriksen, 1956). One of the most useful converging methods is texture segmentation (Beck, 1966a, 1966b, 1982; Julesz, 1981; Treisman & Gelade, 1980; see also Trick & Enns, 1997). In texture segmentation tasks, a target ***region*** of items differs from the background items. That region either does or does not "pop-out," as shown in Figure 3.

In 3a, a difference in orientation causes the lower left region to clearly segment. In Figure 3b, the difference between and is much less evident. To quantify the degree of texture segmentation, the usual methods involve brief presentation of the patterns in order to prevent item-by-item scrutiny. Subjects are asked to make a forced-choice localization of the target region or, perhaps, an identification of the shape of the region (vertical, horizontal, etc.) (Bergen & Julesz, 1983).

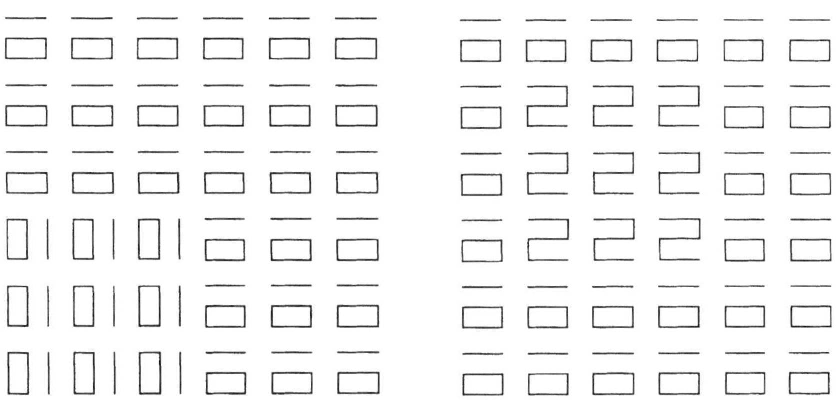

FIGURE 3 Texture segmentation. (After Julesz, 1981.)

Search and texture segmentation sound very similar, but they are not identical, as Figure 4 illustrates.

In Figure 4a, the targets are tilted 15° and 45° to the right of vertical among distractors tilted 15° to the left and 75° to the right. It is not hard to see that there is a vertical texture patch, but a quite laborious search is required to find the isolated 15° and 75° targets (row 4, column 3 for one, row 9, column 10 for the other). In Figure 4b, the targets are white horizontal and black verticals. Isolated examples of these are found quite efficiently, but it will take considerable scrutiny to determine the orientation of the texture region defined by the appropriate conjunctions of color and orientation. Stimulus properties that produce both efficient search and effortless texture segmentation are good candidates for preattentive features (Donk & Meinecke, 1997; Nothdurft, 1994; Wolfe, 1992a).

D. Preattentive Features

This section will review the data supporting specific preattentive features. A somewhat more extensive review of this topic can be found in Wolfe (1998a).

1. Color

Color has long been accepted as a preattentive feature (Bundesen & Pedersen, 1983; Carter, 1982; Farmer & Taylor, 1980; Green & Anderson, 1956; Smith, 1962; Williams, 1966a). Search for a target color among homogeneous distractors is efficient as long as the target and distractor colors are not too similar (Nagy & Sanchez, 1990; Nagy, Sanchez, & Hughes, 1990). With multiple distractor colors, search is efficient if a line can be drawn through color space separating the target

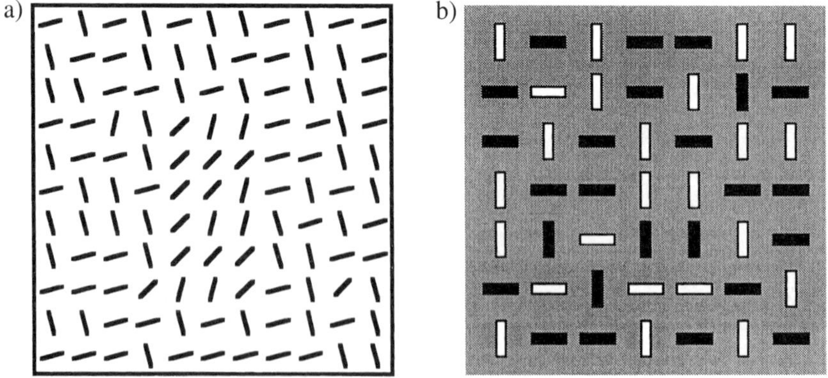

FIGURE 4 (a) An example of good texture segmentation with difficult search, (b) efficient search without good texture segmentation. (After Wolfe, 1992a.)

and distractors colors (linear separability Bauer, Jolicœur, & Cowan, 1996; Bauer, Jolicœur, & Cowan, 1996; D'Zmura & Lennie, 1988) or if the colors are widely separated (Duncan, 1988; Smallman & Boynton, 1990; Wolfe et al., 1990). With widely separated colors, some colors may be more basic than others. Thus, for instance, purple may be represented as red and blue in the preattentive guidance of attention (Moraglia, Maloney, Fekete, & Al-Basi, 1989; Treisman, 1985; Treisman & Gormican, 1988). Color space is three-dimensional. There is some evidence that the achromatic dimension is treated differently in visual search (Theeuwes & Kooi, 1994).

Preattentively processed color information is readily used to select items for subsequent, attentional processing (Egeth et al., 1984; Kaptein, Theeuwes, & Van der Heijden, 1994; Poisson & Wilkinson, 1992; Wolfe et al., 1989; Zohary, Hochstein, & Hillman, 1988). This selection can be seen physiologically in, for example, area V4 (Motter, 1994a). Because it is so effective, selection by color is common in the design of visual displays (e.g., Backs & Walrath, 1995; Van Orden, 1993). Shih and Sperling (1996) have argued that this selection is a selection of colored locations (or objects) rather than a selection of color in some more abstract sense.

In general, it is difficult to use two colors to guide attention simultaneously (Wolfe et al., 1990). There are some exceptions to this rule (Grabowecky & Khurana, 1990; Heathcote & Mewhort, 1993). Notably, search for items defined by the conjunction of two colors may improve markedly with practice (Ponte, Rechea, Sampedro, & Carrasco, 1997). In addition, while it may be hard to find the item that is "red and yellow," it is substantially easier to find a red "object" surrounding a yellow "part" (Bilsky & Wolfe, 1995; Wolfe, Friedman-Hill, & Bilsky, 1994).

Finally, there is mixed evidence for a preattentive ability to detect a change in color. D'Zmura and Mangalick (1993) find that subjects can search efficiently for a target that is undergoing a smooth color change different from that of the distractors. However, Theeuwes (1995) finds that subjects cannot search efficiently for an abrupt change in color. The meaning of these differences is presently unclear, though D'Zmura and Mangalick (1993) were simulating conditions of changing illumination, and that more natural situation may be critical here.

2. Orientation

Orientation differences can guide the deployment of attention. A target will pop-out of a field of homogeneous distractors if the difference between target and distractor orientations is large enough (15° is a good rule of thumb). Foster and his colleagues have collected the most systematic data on this point (Foster & Ward, 1991a, 1991b). Work by Moraglia (1989a) and, much more extensively, by Nothdurft makes it clear that local differences in orientation are critical in these cases (Luschow & Nothdurft, 1993; Nothdurft, 1991b, 1992, 1993a, 1993b, 1993c) (see also Bravo & Blake, 1992; Landy & Bergen, 1991). Converging evidence for the featural status of orientation is readily available from texture segmentation studies (e.g., Landy & Bergen, 1991; Nothdurft, 1991b).

When more than one distractor orientation is present, several factors determine the efficiency of search (Alkhateeb, Morris, & Ruddock, 1990). One of these is the categorical status of the items. For the purpose of guiding attention, orientations seem to be categorized as "steep," "shallow," "left-tilted," and "right-tilted." It appears to be quite easy to search for a target if it is categorically unique and quite difficult if it is not. For example, search for a 10° target among +/− 50 deg distractors is quite efficient. With vertical defined as 0°, the 10° target is the only "steep" item in the display. Search for the same 10° target among +70 and −30° distractors in less efficient because −30° items share "steepness" with the target, and the +70° items share "rightness" (Wolfe et al., 1992). Foster's group has proposed a set of broadly tuned filters that perform operations similar to the proposed categorization of orientations (Foster & Ward, 1991b; Foster & Westland, 1995, but see Mannan, Ruddock, & Wright, 1995).

These results can be thought of in terms of target–distractor and distractor–distractor similarity. Duncan and Humphreys (1989) argue that search efficiency increases with distractor–distractor similarity. The more homogeneous the distractors, the more efficient the search. Search efficiency decreases with target–distractor similarity. The Wolfe et al.'s (1992) results show that similarity is modulated by categorical status as well as by angular separation. The similarity of orientations is also modulated by symmetry relations. In visual search, symmetrical orientations are more similar than their simple angular separations would suggest (Wolfe & Friedman-Hill, 1992a). Additionally, efficient orientation search can be based on unique angular relationships between items (Wolfe & Friedman-Hill, 1992b). (Asymmetries in orientation search were discussed in section II.A.1.)

Efficient orientation search can be performed with items that are created from a wide range of different surface media. The items can be defined by luminance, color, texture, motion, or other, smaller oriented lines (Bravo & Blake, 1990; Cavanagh, Arguin, & Treisman, 1990; Luschow & Nothdurft, 1993). All of this suggests that the preattentive representation that supports orientation search comes relatively late in visual processing. Physiological evidence suggests that early processing (primary visual cortex) can represent luminance-defined orientation but not the other methods of stimulus generation (Von der Heydt, Peterhans, & Baumgartner, 1984).

There are some oriented items that will not support efficient search. For example, Gilchrist, Jane, and Heiko (1997) found that subjects could search efficiently for an oriented target defined by two white circles or by two black circles. However, if the item was defined by circles of different polarity, one white and one black, then search was inefficient. Interestingly, if the circles were replaced by squares, efficient search became possible. Apparently, the colinearity of the edges of the squares could overcome the preattentive resistance to polarity reversal (see also Enns & Kingstone, 1995).

It does not seem to be possible to guide attention to two orientations at the same time (Bilsky & Wolfe, 1995; Wolfe et al., 1990). Finally, there is some indication that the preattentive coding of orientation and size (or spatial frequency) may not be independent (Sagi, 1988).

3. Curvature

Curvature has been proposed as a preattentive feature (Foster, 1983; Treisman, 1986). Search for curve among straight is efficient, as is search for a curve among its 180° rotation (left vs. right, up vs. down). The claim of featural status has support from texture segmentation experiments (Simmons & Foster, 1992). Curvature may not be a terribly robust feature. If the curves form the mouths of schematic happy and sad faces, efficient search does not appear to be possible (Nothdurft, 1993d), possibly because the other components of the face mask the curvature cue.

The status of curvature as a visual feature has been a matter of debate for many years in other contexts (Blakemore & Over, 1974; Riggs, 1973; Stromeyer & Riggs, 1974). The heart of the argument concerns whether curvature is coded by the visual system as curvature *per se* or merely as a local change in orientation. In visual search, it appears that curvature is more than just local orientation change (Wolfe, Yee, & Friedman-Hill, 1992).

4. Size

In thinking about size as a basic feature, there are several different but related senses of the term that must be considered. In visual search, size can refer to the spatial extent of an item. There is good evidence for the featural status of size in this sense. Search for the biggest item is particularly efficient (Bilsky, Wolfe, & Friedman-Hill, 1994; Dehaene, 1989; Stuart, 1993; Williams, 1966b). In unpublished work, we have found that searches for the biggest and smallest items are efficient enough, but search for the medium-sized target among big and small distractors is inefficient. Again there is support from texture segmentation (Wolfe, Chun, & Friedman-Hill, 1993).

Size can also refer to spatial frequency. Efficient search can be based on patches of the same angular subtense if they contain gratings of different spatial frequency (Verghese & Nakayama, 1994). As with size, the extremes of coarsest and finest are relatively easy to find, whereas an intermediate frequency is hard to find among coarser and finer distractors (M. Bost and J. M. Wolfe, unpublished). As noted above, it may be difficult to treat spatial frequency and orientation as independent features (Moraglia, 1989b; Sagi, 1988). There is support from texture segregation for a preattentive role for spatial frequency (Julesz & Papathomas, 1984).

Spatial scale is the final sense in which size enters into research on spatial attention. It is intuitively clear that scale can be an important factor. If you are looking at someone, you can attend to the person, the face, the nose, or the spot on the end of the nose, all while having the same visual stimulus present in the field and all while having attention centered on the same location in that stimulus. In the laboratory, work on spatial scale has rarely involved such natural stimuli. More commonly, the stimuli have been forms composed of other forms, as shown in Figure 5.

Navon (1977) proposed that processing of such stimuli proceeds from the global to the local level (see also Paquet, 1992). That appealing simple story gave way to the more complicated realization that so-called "global precedence" could be modulated by the size and spatial frequency content of the stimuli (Kinchla & Wolfe,

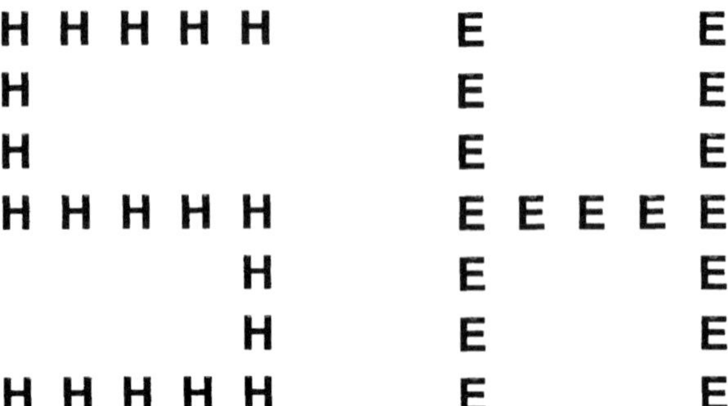

FIGURE 5 Global/local stimuli. (After Navon, 1977.)

1979; LaGasse, 1993; Lamb & Robertson, 1990; Lamb & Yund, 1993) as well as by attentional factors (e.g., cueing—Robertson, Egly, Lamb, & Kerth, 1993). In visual search experiments, Enns and Kingstone (1995) found relatively efficient search for local forms with less efficient search for global. They argued that an "attention-demanding grouping stage" was required to put together global stimuli of the sort shown in Figure 5. Saarinen (1994) reported a global precedence effect with globally oriented stimuli composed of locally oriented stimuli; however, this result may be an artifact of the particular orientations used (Durgin & Wolfe, 1997). Completing this somewhat confused picture, there is evidence that attention can be directed to two scales at once but with some cost (Farell & Pelli, 1993; Verghese & Pelli, 1994; but see Saarinen, 1995).

This global-local literature (pre-1992) has been well reviewed by Kimchi (1992). For present purposes, perhaps the safest conclusion to be drawn from these experiments is that, since attention can be directed on the basis of scale, scale must be represented preattentively. This would be consistent with our finding that visual search can be modified by the hierarchical structure of items (Wolfe et al., 1994). It is less reasonable to conclude that attention must be directed to one level in a display before another. The findings are simply too diverse.

5. Motion

Moving targets pop-out of a field of stationary distractors (Dick, Ullman, & Sagi, 1987). In recent, as yet unpublished work, my colleagues and I have looked simple feature search in five conditions with results as shown in Table 1. Individual spots could move in a single direction throughout a trial, or their motion could change randomly from frame to frame. Search for random or linear motion among stationary distractors was very efficient. Search for the absence of motion is less efficient. This asymmetry was most marked when the distractor motion was random. This probably reflects the fact that attention is attracted to points of local change (Nothdurft, 1991a, 1993c), and the random-distractor motion creates the greatest quantity of irrelevant local motion contrast.

TABLE 1 Results of Simple Motion Search Experiments

Target	Distractors	Target-present slope (ms)	Target-absent slope (ml)
Linear motion	Stationary	−1.2	−1.4
Brownian motion	Stationary	−0.7	−0.4
Stationary	Linear one direction	6.5	10.5
Stationary	Linear multiple directions	12.9	25.6
Stationary	Brownian motion	13.0	18.7

There have been some investigations of visual search using other motion displays, notably optic flow displays that simulate observer motion through a stationary world (Royden, Wolfe, Konstantinova, & Hildreth, 1996, 1997). In these studies, subjects were able to search with reasonable efficiency for spots that were stationary in the stimulus, even though multiple directions of motion were present in the distractors. At least two interpretations of these data suggest themselves. If the display was interpreted as a stationary world seen by a moving observer, then the physically stationary target would represent a moving, attention-grabbing stimulus in the world. Alternatively, since motion in optic flow stimuli is locally quite homogeneous, the stationary item might simply represent the locus of the greatest local change in motion. Control experiments seem to favor the latter account, but the issue is not settled.

In optic flow, the entire field moves in a coherent manner. It is also possible to create items that each have their own pattern of expansion or contraction. With these localized flow patterns, we can ask if an expanding item pop-outs from a collection of contracting items or vice versa. (Obviously, it is necessary to control for uninteresting size artifacts.) It had been argued that all such searches were inefficient (Braddick & Holliday, 1991). However, more recent work finds that two-dimensional patterns of expansion are found efficiently among contracting distractors, while contracting targets remain hard to find among expanding distractors (Takeuchi, 1997).

There is an asymmetry in speed detection with fast stimuli among slow found more efficiently than slow among fast (Ivry, 1992). Driver, McLeod, & Dienes (1992a) report on a series of experiments revealing the rather complex relationship of speed and direction in visual search. In apparent motion, short-range apparent motion (or whatever one cares to call it—Cavanagh & Mather, 1989) supports efficient search while long-range does not (Dick et al., 1987; Horowitz & Treisman, 1994; Ivry & Cohen, 1990). Motion defined by equiluminant stimuli does not support efficient search (Luschow & Nothdurft, 1993), nor does motion with bicontrast dot (Horowitz & Treisman, 1994).

When it comes to guiding attention toward more complex targets, motion is one of the most effective of the preattentive features. Knowing the motion of a target speeds search (Berbaum, Chung, & Loke, 1986). Most of the evidence for the guiding power of motion comes from conjunction searches (McLeod, 1993; McLeod, Driver, & Crisp, 1988; McLeod et al., 1991; Nakayama & Silverman, 1986; see also Kawahara, 1993). A number of studies have concentrated on the tendency of moving stimuli to form coherent groups (Driver, McLeod, & Dienes, 1992b; Duncan, 1995). Some of the complexities of the relationships between features are revealed in series of papers on Orientation × Motion conjunctions. In one task, the target might be a moving item of orientation A among stationary items of orientation A and moving items of orientation B. In another task, the target could be stationary A among moving A and stationary B, and so forth. Control conditions assessed the efficiency of the relevant orientation features searches (orientation A among B and vice versa, moving among stationary and vice versa). Driver and McLeod (1992) found that if the orientation feature search was efficient, then the conjunction task was easier if target was in motion. If orientation task was inefficient, then the conjunction task was easier if the target was stationary. Müller and Maxwell (1994) failed to replicate this search asymmetry. Berger and McLeod (1996) argued that this was due to differences in item density, though Müller and Found (1996) disagreed. This somewhat arcane disagreement is worth pausing over because it illustrates the fact that the finer details of preattentive processing are hard to infer from single experiments. Visual search is a signal-detection problem with the properties of the target providing the signal and the properties of the distractors and their interrelationships providing the noise (e.g., see discussion in Eckstein, Thomas, Palmer, & Shimozaki, 1996; Hübner, 1993; Verghese & Nakayama, 1994; Wolfe, 1994). Seemingly simple changes in something like the orientation of half of the items may have complex consequences. Firm conclusions may require evidence from a series of experiments using different stimuli, though, in some case, the definitive answer may not be worth the effort.

6. Depth Cues

The third dimension of space is represented in preattentive vision. This can be seen in the ability of various depth cues to guide and modulate the deployment of attention. Stereopsis will support efficient search (Nakayama & Silverman, 1986). In fact, Julesz's classic random-dot stereograms can be seen as texture segmentation evidence for the preattentive calculation of disparity (Julesz, 1962, 1964, 1971). Some of the details of preattentive processing of disparity are worked out in the visual search experiments of O'Toole and Walker (1997) (see also Chau & Yei-Yu, 1995). These studies used stimuli in the frontal plane—one disparity per stimulus. Search experiments also reveal preattentive sensitivity to changes in depth within a stimulus. When targets and distractors differ in the tilt out of the frontal plane, efficient search is possible (Holliday & Braddick, 1991) (see also Epstein & Babler, 1990; Epstein, Babler, & Bownds, 1992).

Depth relationships within items are at the heart of most other demonstrations of preattentive processing of the third dimension. Preattentive processes seem to be able to distinguish objects that appear concave from those that appear convex using shading as the cue to depth (Kleffner & Ramachandran, 1992; Ramachandran, 1988; Snyder & Barlow, 1988) (see also Aks & Enns, 1992; Braun, 1993). These studies use circular patches filled with a grayscale gradient, brighter on top and dimmer on bottom (or vice versa). Left–right gradients do not work as well, suggesting a bias to assume a light source shining from above (Sun & Perona, 1996b). Step changes that do not look like shading at all will also support reasonably efficient search (Heathcote & Mewhort, 1993; Kleffner & Ramachandran, 1992). This could cause one to wonder if shading is, indeed, the cue in these experiments. In other contexts, shading information does seem to be unambiguously useful in distinguishing targets and distractors (Enns & Rensink, 1990a; Sun & Perona, 1996a), and there is evidence that preattentive processes are sensitive to the physical properties of shadows (Rensink & Cavanagh, 1993).

Enns and Rensink have done a series of experiments showing that the preattentive processes can interpret line drawings as simple 3D shapes (cubes, etc.) and can base visual search performance on properties like the orientation of a bar in depth (Enns, 1992; Enns & Rensink, 1990b, 1991, 1993). They used RT measures. Sun and Perona (1996a) used accuracy measures to confirm and extend these results. Like other features, preattentive processing of depth cues produces search asymmetries. For example, finding an upward tilted cube among downward tilted cubes is easier than downward among upward (Von Grünau & Dubé, 1994).

Evidence for preattentive processing of occlusion comes from interesting work by Rensink and Enns (1995), showing that preattentive processes cannot ignore the results of occlusion. Thus, a 1° long line is treated as a 1° long line even if a portion of the middle of that line is occluded.

Further evidence for the preattentive processing of depth information comes from experiments on the deployment and spread of attention. Several experiments show an ability to allocate attention to locations cued in depth (e.g., Andersen, 1990; Downing & Pinker, 1985). Other experiments show restriction of attention to surfaces defined by stereodisparity (He & Nakayama, 1992, 1994a, 1994b).

7. Vernier

Fahle has shown that vernier offsets can be found efficiently and that this ability is not reducible to a form of orientation search (Fahle, 1990, 1991).

8. Lustre

Wolfe and Franzel (1988) have shown that binocular lustre could be found efficiently. Binocular lustre, produced by putting a dark field in one eye and a light field at the corresponding location in the other (Helmholtz, 1924; Tyler, 1983), is just one way of making a surface appear to be shiny. Presumably, the preattentive feature is the surface property of shininess and not something specific to binocular visual processing, though this has not been tested. Other dichoptic properties like binocular rivalry (Blake, 1989; Wolfe, 1986) do not support efficient search (Wolfe & Franzel, 1988).

9. Aspects of Shape

Shape is the holy grail of preattentive features. Like the grail of myth, it seems clearly present yet frustratingly illusive. Some aspects of spatial configuration are available to preattentive processes, but it has proven rather difficult to specify exactly which ones. Terms like shape and form are often used rather loosely. For instance, a study could involve search for a moving *X* among stationary *X*s and moving *O*s. This task might be described as a search for a conjunction of motion and form (McLeod et al., 1988) but *X*s differ from *O*s in a number of ways. *O*s are curved, closed, and without terminators. *X*s are composed of straight lines, they do not form closed regions, and they have four terminators. Which of these aspects is available preattentively?

Julesz and his colleagues tried to account for shape effects with an argument that preattentive vision could only sense differences in the first-order statistics of patterns. Texture segmentation could not be supported by texture elements that differed only in second order or higher properties (Caelli, Julesz, & Gilbert, 1978; Julesz, Gilbert, Shepp, & Frisch, 1973). Exceptions to this rule gave rise to Julesz's texton theory (Bergen & Julesz, 1983; Julesz, 1981, 1984, 1986; Julesz & Bergen, 1983). Here he argued for a limited set of shape primitives, like line termination, whose presence could be detected preattentively.

a. Terminators

There is good support for the preattentive processing of line termination (Bergen & Julesz, 1983; Julesz, 1984). For some pairs of target and distractor, it can be a little difficult to decide if line termination or closure is the critical feature in a search. For example, consider the difference between an *O* and a *C*. Is the *O* closed or does the *C* have a pair of line terminators? If we accept Treisman's analysis of search asymmetries, then, in the case of *C*s and *O*s, the evidence comes down in favor of line termination. Treisman has argued that it is easier to find the presence of a feature than to detect its absence (Treisman & Gormican, 1988). Thus, given the finding that it is easier to find a *C* among *O*s than vice versa, it follows that the *C* must carry the feature. In this case, that would appear to be line termination.

While the presence of a terminator may be easy to detect among its absence, the quantity of terminators is not as useful in guiding deployment of attention. Taylor and Badcock (1988) found that search was inefficient when a target with seven terminators was presented among distractors with only two. The data of Cheal and Lyon (1992) complicate the picture further. They obtained shallower target trial slopes for an *S* among *E*s (two vs. three terminators) than for an *E* among *S*'s (three vs. two terminators). When Enns (1986) used elongated stimuli, the ability to search for terminators was impaired.

b. Intersection and Filter Models of Texture Segmentation

Julesz proposed that intersections served as textons. The classic demonstration is shown in Figure 6. Each of the elements in the figure is composed of a pair of orthogonal lines of equal length, yet it is clear that the "+"s form a discrete region while the border between the *T*s and the *L*s is not easy to see. Bergen and Adelson (1988) questioned the need to explain these texture segmentations by invoking texture primitives like textons. Like others, they suggested that spatial filters of the sort found in early vision would do the job (see also Graham, Venkatesan, & Sutter, 1993; Gurnsey & Browse, 1989; Keeble & Morgan, 1993; Malik & Perona, 1990). Julesz and Krose (1988) created textures that they argued could not be explained with standard filtering models. He and Nakayama (1994b) argued a similar point with a different set of experiments. The debate has a certain similarity to the old debate about whether vision was a matter of feature detectors or channels—one of those either-or debates where later generations find it a bit difficult to see exactly what the argument was about (Weisstein, 1973). If we take as given that spatial filters/channels are the front end of the visual system, then, if a "T" is to be discriminated from a "+," that information must be present in some form in those channels. For our purposes, the question is whether intersections are represented preattentively and the evidence is equivocal.

c. Closure

The preattentive processing of closure is seen less in its ability to support efficient search in its own right and more in its ability to make other searches efficient. For example, consider the searches in Figure 7, derived from the work of Elder and Zucker (1993, 1994, 1998). The search for brackets pointing in at each other among brackets pointing out is made easier if the brackets are clearly part of the same object. A similar point is made by Donnelly, Humphreys, and Riddoch (1991).

d. Topology

Chen and his colleagues have argued that the topological status of objects is available preattentively. For instance, targets with holes can be found efficiently among

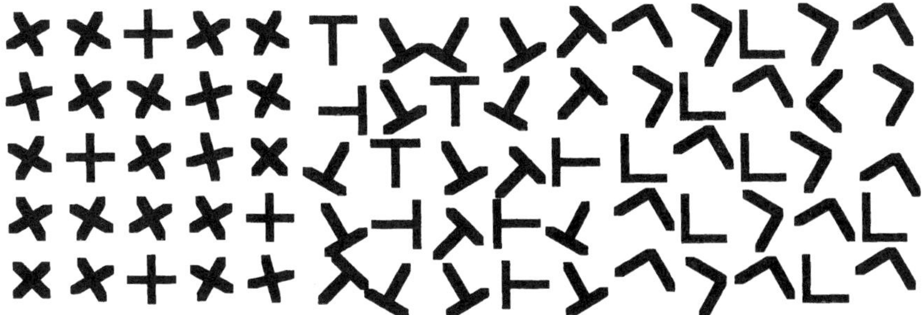

FIGURE 6 The border between + and T is clearer than that between T and L.

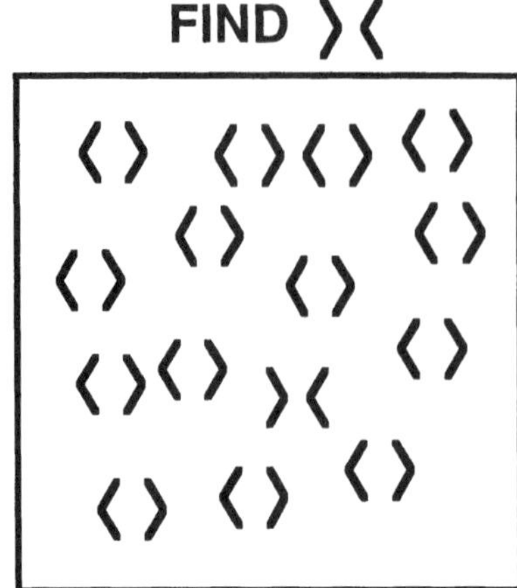

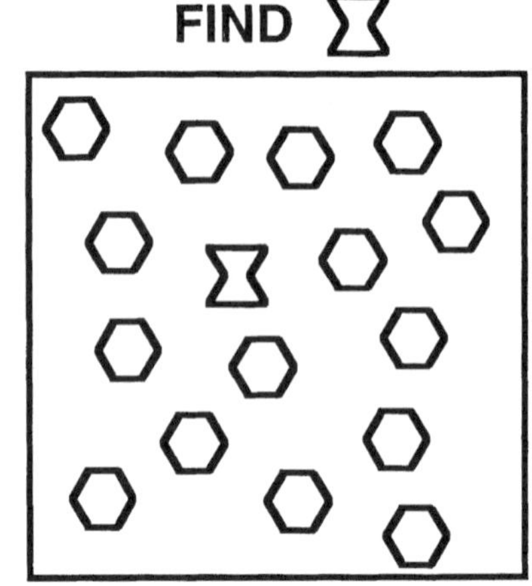

FIGURE 7 It is easier to determine the relationship between two local elements if they are part of the same object. (After Elder & Zucker, 1993.)

distractors without holes (Chen, 1982, 1990; Chen & Zhou, 1997; but see Rubin & Kanwisher, 1985).

E. The Preattentive Processing of Objects

The status of closure and topology raise the more general issue of the role of objects in preattentive vision. In visual search, there is a good case to be made that attention is deployed from object to object rather than from location to location or feature to feature. In most laboratory search tasks, this is an idle distinction since objects and their features occupy unique locations. However, the distinction becomes important in the real world where objects and observers move. These real-world considerations make an *a priori* argument for attention to objects. It is hard to imagine that it would be useful to have an attentional system that deployed attention to the location of a toddler at one moment but then left attention at that location while the toddler toddled off. A substantial number of experiments have been devoted to the ability to use attention to track target objects among distractor objects while all are moving (e.g., Culham & Cavanagh, 1994; Intriligator, Nakayama, & Cavanagh, 1991; Pylyshyn & Storm, 1988; Yantis, 1992).

Evidence for the preattentive status of objects comes from experiments that show that object status modulates visual search or some other attention-demanding task. For instance, it is much easier to determine the relationship of two properties if they are part of the same object than if they are not (Duncan, 1984, 1993; see also Lavie & Driver, 1996; Vecera & Farah, 1994). In these experiments, features maintain the same spatial relationships whether they are one object or two. This suggests that attention is directed to objects and that it can be spread across a pair of objects only with difficulty. If attention is being directed to an object, it follows that the object was represented preattentively in some fashion. The work of Baylis and Driver (1993) makes a similar point, using figures rather like those shown in Figure 8. In this case, the task was to determine if the left vertex was above or below the right. He found that this task was much easier if the vertices were part of the same object (for further discussion of these issues see Baylis, 1994; Gibson, 1994).

Evidence that attention is directed to objects should not be read as evidence that attention cannot be directed to locations. Both types of deployment are possible. One line of evidence for this comes from studies of "inhibition of return" (Nakayama & Mackeben, 1989; Posner & Cohen, 1984). Once attention has been withdrawn it is harder to return attention to whatever was previously attended. A number of studies show that inhibition of return can be space-based or object-based (Gibson & Egeth, 1994; Tipper & Weaver, 1996; Tipper, Weaver, Jerreat, & Burak, 1994; see also Müller & von Muhlenen, 1996). For a theoretical treatment of this aspect of the data see Logan (1996).

Treisman and Kahneman introduced the idea "object files" that would be created through the agency of attention (Kahneman & Treisman, 1984; Kahneman, Treisman, & Gibbs, 1992; Treisman, 1982). The evidence that attention is directed to objects suggests that some sort of object must exist preattentively. Wolfe and Bennett (1997) have called these "preattentive object files." When attention is directed to a preattentive object (or object file, if one prefers), the processing of the associated features of that object seems to have a mandatory flavor to it. Recent data show that all the features of an object enter memory as a group (Luck & Vogel, 1997). Wolfe and Bennett (1997) found that the automatic attachment of features to objects can make apparently simple searches quite difficult. This is illustrated in Figure 9.

Even though each array contains 10 gray lines and 10 black lines, it is easier to find the black horizontal line (or the gray vertical line) in the array on the right. On the right, each item has a single color and a single orientation. On the left, the items are all "black" and "gray" and "vertical" and "horizontal." Preattentive vision

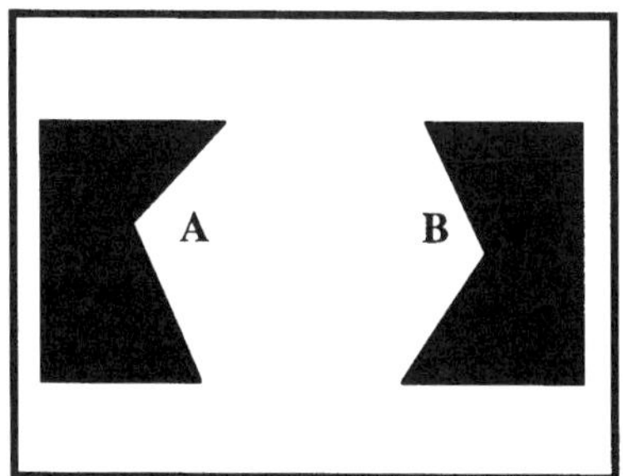

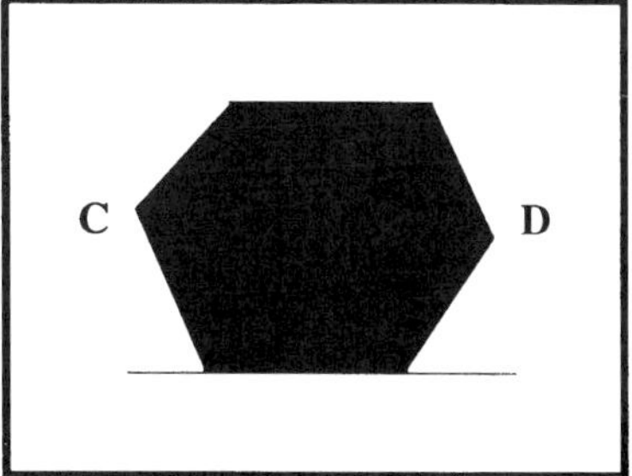

FIGURE 8 It is easier to determine that vertex C is above D than to determine that A is above B. (After Baylis & Driver, 1993.)

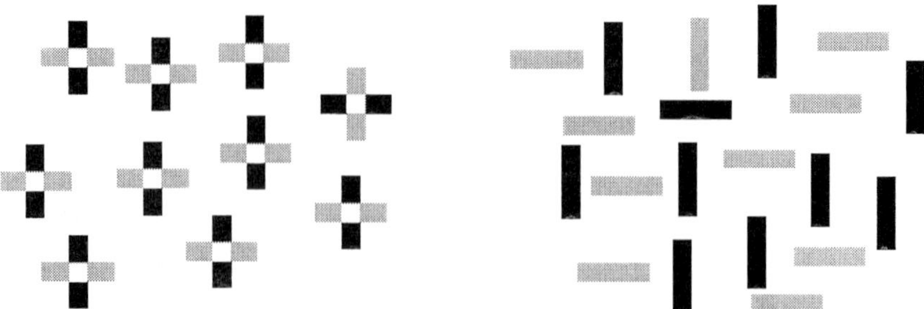

FIGURE 9 You will probably find it easier to locate the black horizontal in the array on the right than in the array on the left. (After Wolfe & Bennett, 1997.)

seems mandated to treat each "plus" as an object and seems unable to bind color to orientation in parallel.

1. Shape of Entire Objects

The work just reviewed shows that the preattentive world is parsed into some sort of objects prior to the arrival of attention. What do we know about the preattentive representation of the shape of whole objects?

When other features are controlled for, shape of an object does not appear to be available for the preattentive guidance of attention. Wolfe and Bennett (1997) performed a series of experiments with meaningful and meaningless stimuli, and in all cases search for one shape among other shapes proved to be very inefficient. This does not mean that no aspect of shape is processed preattentively. For instance, grouping and good continuation make some sets of line segments into good, closed-curve objects, while other sets do not form good objects (Figure 10). Donnelly et al. (1991) showed that visual search is sensitive to the object-forming processes.

Looking at Figure 10, searches for stimulus A among B are efficient because the 4 Ls group into a larger object. It may be that the identifying shape of an object is not available preattentively to guide attention. However, the basic processes of object formation are clearly occurring preattentively. Various other experiments could be used to make the same point including Pomerantz and Pristach (1989) and the work of Elder and Zucker (1993).

2. Letters and Words

A great deal of work in the study of visual attention has used letters as stimuli. This produces a degree of confusion in the analysis of the visual aspects of visual attention because letters are not a simple set of stimuli. Letters can differ from each other in basic features like the orientation of their line segments (e.g., A vs. H) or line termination (X vs. O). Letters that do not differ in basic features (e.g., L vs. T) must still be discriminable or they would be of little use as members of an alphabet. Are those letters preattentively discriminable, and if so, is that discriminability based on

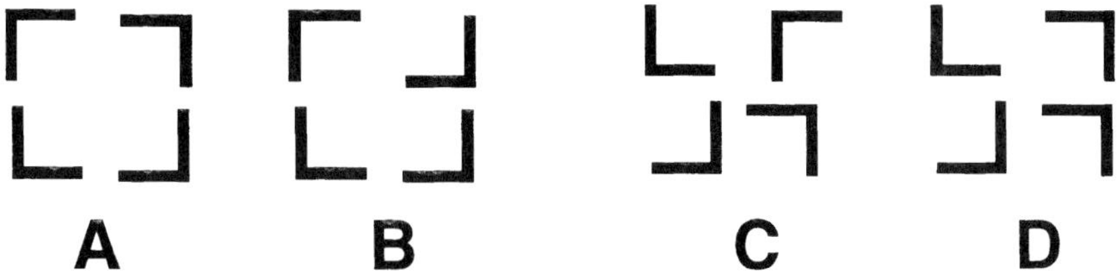

FIGURE 10 It is much easier to tell A from B than C from D. (After Donnelly et al., 1991.) A forms an object, B forms a broken object, whereas C and D are merely collections of Ls.

learned preattentive processing? There is evidence for efficient processing of letters (e.g., Schneider & Shiffrin, 1977; Shiffrin & Schneider, 1977), but the visual properties of the letters were not a particular concern in this work. Wang and his colleagues (Wang, Cavanagh, & Green, 1994) argued for a preattentive distinction between overlearned letters and unlearned but related figures (like a mirror-reversed "N") (see also Wang & Cavanagh, 1993). Their notion that novelty pops-out is related to similar claims on behalf of novel words by Johnston and his colleagues (Hawley, Johnston, & Farnham, 1994; Johnston, Hawley, & Farnham, 1993; but see Christie & Klein, 1994).

There has been some suggestion that the categorical status of overlearned items like letters is available preattentively. For instance, some experiments seem to show that the character "0" is treated differently when it is thought of as an "oh" as opposed to "zero" (Brand, 1971; Egeth, Jonides, & Wall, 1972). Subsequent work casts doubt on the robustness of this phenomenon (Duncan, 1983; Krueger, 1984).

Words and nonword letter strings behave differently as visual stimuli; however, with the exception of the novel pop-out claims of Johnston and his colleagues (Hawley et al., 1994; Johnston et al., 1993), the evidence suggests that these effects occur after attention has been directed to the stimulus (Bundesen, Kyllingsbaek, Houmann, & Jensen, 1997; Flowers & Lohr, 1985; LaBerge, 1983).

3. Faces

Beyond basic features, there are two broad classes of complex stimuli that are repeatedly offered as candidates for preattentive processing. Letters and words were discussed above. The other class consists of faces and related stimuli. There is no doubt that search among upright faces is more efficient than search among inverted or scrambled faces (Suzuki & Cavanagh, 1995) (see also Levin, 1996; Reinitz, Morrissey, & Demb, 1994), but these differences are between inefficient search for faces and *really* inefficient search through inverted or scrambled faces (Nothdurft, 1993d). Real or schematic faces behave the same way. A similar story holds for eye position. Von Grünau and Anston (1995) found that search for a straight-ahead gaze was more efficient than search for gaze left or gaze right, but this was a modulation of a basically inefficient search. Claims for efficient search for an angry face (Hansen & Hansen, 1988) have been challenged as artifactual (Purcell, Stewart, & Skov, 1996).

F. Preattentive Summary

Evidence suggests that visual attention can be guided by the preattentive processing of a limited set of basic features. These include color, orientation, motion, size, curvature, various cues to depth, and several aspects of form (e.g., line termination). The case for preattentive processing of more complex properties like object shape, letters, or faces is weak, though there is some evidence for efficient search for some overlearned stimuli. Conjunctions of features are implicitly available. For instance, color and orientation in the same place at the same time will produce an orientation-contingent color aftereffect (the McCollough effect, Houck & Hoffman, 1986; see also Mordkoff, Yantis, & Egeth, 1990); however, those conjunctions do not seem to be explicitly available (see, for instance, Lavie, 1996).

III. VISION WITH ATTENTION

A. Attention Enables Other Visual Processes

If preattentive vision is a world of visual features loosely parsed into unidentified objects, then what is the role of attention when it arrives in that world? If we are going to attempt to encapsulate the role of attention in a single phrase, perhaps it would be best to say that attention serves as an *enabler* rather than an actor in its own right. Rather than saying that attention binds features, we would say that attention enables binding to occur. Rather than saying that attention somehow identifies an object, we would say that attention enables object-recognition processes to work on a single item at a time. Indeed, attention enables a vast array of perceptual abilities. Consider that virtually all of vision research involves judgments about visual stimuli that are scrutinized with all available attention. Outside of those working on preattentive or inattentive vision, no one would design an experiment in which subjects were intended to make fine perceptual assessments of one stimulus while attending to another. This we may take as *prima facie* evidence that attention is required for many aspects of routine visual processing.

B. How and What Does Attention Enable?

Attention enables visual processing in a wide variety of ways. The purpose of the next section is to catalog these various modes of attention. The items on this list should not be seen as mutually exclusive.

1. Selection in Space

Stimulus selection is one of the most critical functions of attention. There are many visual processes that simply cannot operate on the entire retinal image at once. Attention acts as a gatekeeper, passing a relevant subset of the stimuli to one or more limited-capacity processes. Face perception is a clear example. As discussed above, face identification occurs one face at a time. The problem would seem to be that the face identifier wants to operate on one set of eyes, nose, mouth, and so on. Presented with multiple faces, this limited-capacity process suffers from a version of the *binding problem* (e.g., Treisman, 1986). It does not know which eyes go with which nose, and so forth. Selective attention allows just one face to reach the face processor at one time.

In the 19th century, Helmholtz (1924) noted that one could selectively attend to stimuli away from the focus of attention. James (1890) put forth an early version of a spotlight metaphor in which attention acts like a mental flashlight, moving around the scene. The literature on the selective powers of attention is vast, and this review can only point at some of its more salient features (for a much more extensive review see chapters 2 and 5 of Pashler, 1997; see also Kahneman & Treisman, 1984; Lavie & Tsal, 1994a). Chapter 4 of Styles (1997) is devoted to the spotlight issue (see also Castiello & Umilta, 1992). As a metaphor for attentional selection, the spotlight needs substantial modification. First, there is the matter of the movement of the spotlight. If a real spotlight sweeps across a scene from point A to point B, it illuminates the space in between. When the spotlight of attention goes from A to B, this redeployment is probably better understood as attention withdrawing from one location and reappearing at another without necessarily illuminating intermediate locations (e.g., Sagi & Julesz, 1985; Sperling & Weichselgartner, 1995) (but see Tsal, 1983). Second, a standard spotlight is directed to a location in space. The attentional spotlight is directed to objects. Space-based models by themselves are inadequate to handle the data on objects (e.g., Schneider, 1993), though cueing of specific spatial locations can modulate the object-based effects (Lavie & Driver, 1996). Things get more complicated if a subject is asked to attend to items based on some feature (e.g., color). We found that subjects could process specific subsets of the stimuli in parallel in visual search tasks even when the relevant and irrelevant items were intermixed (Friedman-Hill & Wolfe, 1995). As noted above, many others have found evidence for serial processing of subsets of stimuli (Egeth et al., 1984). This could be seen as evidence that attention can be directed to multiple locations at one time, but perhaps this should be seen as a stage prior to the deployment of an attentional spotlight. Color (or some other basic feature) can be used to prioritize the subsequent deployment of attention. This is consistent with claims from several labs that selection by color is, in fact, selection of location based on color information (Cave & Pashler, 1995; Kim & Cave, 1995; Tsal & Lavie, 1993). Presumably, the same would hold for selection by other features.

Third, to the extent that attentional selection can be seen as a spotlight, its size is adjustable (Broadbent, 1982). A zoom lens has been offered as a metaphor (Eriksen & St. James, 1986) (cf. Richards, 1968). This, in turn, leads to the idea that attention and processing capacity can be spread over multiple objects, maybe over the entire scene, and that attentional load is the critical determinant of the size of the spotlight (Lavie & Cox, 1996; Lavie & Tsal, 1994a, 1994b) (see also Nakayama, 1990).

Fourth, there is an ongoing debate about the ability to divide the spotlight into multiple, noncontiguous regions. It is probably the case that attention can select one object even if that object is broken into noncontiguous regions. For this point, the relevant experiments are those showing that attention can be attached to some group of items while apparently not spilling over on to intervening space or intervening items. For instance, Driver and Baylis (1989) showed more flanker interference (see below) with items that moved together, but see Kramer, Tham, and Yeh (1991). Perhaps more striking are the experiments on multielement tracking (Intriligator et al., 1991; Pylyshyn & Storm, 1988; Yantis, 1992) (see also Culham & Cavanagh, 1994). In these studies, subjects are asked to attend to *N* out of *M* moving items. They can keep track of three to six of these. Pylyshyn's FINST theory accomplishes this by proposing that there is a preattentive, limited-capacity mechanism devoted to spatially indexing objects. These indexes allow attention to be efficiently guided to members of a desired subset of a set of moving objects as if they had blinking lights attached to them (Pylyshyn, 1989, 1994, 1998). Alternatively, attention might be used to hold 3–6 bits in some sort of virtual object (see Cavanagh's idea of attentional "sprites"—Cavanagh, 1999). In either case, as Driver and Baylis (1989) note, data of this sort make it clear that the spotlight metaphor cannot be taken in any literal sense. The spotlight of attention is doing things that no light source can do.

Fifth, control of selection is not perfect. One of the classic illustrations of this fact is the Eriksen flanker task (Eriksen & Eriksen, 1974; Eriksen & Hoffman, 1973). In a flanker task, one might see three letters in a row. The instructions might be to push one key if the central letter was an *A* and another if it was a *B*. The basic finding is that RTs for {A A A} are faster than for {C A C} which are, in turn, faster than {B A B}. The flanking letters, even though they are utterly irrelevant to the task, exert an influence on the response. They cannot be ignored. The effect varies with the spatial properties of the display (distance to the flankers, etc., Miller, 1991) and with load (Lavie, 1995).

Though this is not a review of the physiological literature on attention, it is worth mentioning that there are physiological correlates of selection by location and object (Moran & Desimone, 1985) and by feature (Motter, 1994a, 1994b). For a review, see Desimone and Duncan (1995).

2. Selection in Time

Attention is involved in the selection of items in time as well as in space. The "attentional blink" is an important example of this aspect of attention (Raymond, Shapiro, & Arnell, 1992; Shapiro, 1994). In a standard attentional blink experiment, subjects monitor a stream of items appearing at a rate of around 10 Hz. Most often these would be alphanumeric characters, presented at fixation. Items can be monitored at this speed for the presence of a target element (Sperling, Budiansky, Spivak, & Johnson, 1971), even for quite complex scene properties (Intraub, 1985; Potter, 1975, 1993; Potter & Levy, 1969). However, if subjects detect a first target, they will tend to be unable to respond to a second target presented within 200–500 ms of the first (e.g., Chun & Potter, 1995; Ward, Duncan, & Shapiro, 1996, 1997). The fate of the "blinked" stimuli will be discussed when we talk about vision in the absence of attention (section V).

"Inhibition of return," mentioned above, is another example of attentional selection in time (Posner & Cohen, 1984). Attention to an object at one moment in time makes it harder to re-attend to the same object in the next second or so. Inhibition of return would seem like an obviously useful mechanism, preventing subjects from revisiting useless locations or objects during visual search tasks (Klein, 1988), but it has proven difficult to confirm a role for inhibition of return (Horowitz & Wolfe, 1997; Wolfe & Pokorny, 1990; see Pratt & Abrams, 1995; Tipper, Weaver, & Watson, 1996, for a similar controversy).

3. Vigilance

Faced with the impossibility of processing everything all of the time, attention enables resources to be devoted to important new events. Vigilance can be thought of as an attentional state in which a display is monitored for something worthy of focal attention. In typical *vigilance* tasks, subjects might be monitoring a display for the appearance of a designated target (e.g., Baker, 1958; Koelega, Brinkman, Hendriks, & Verbaten, 1989). These tasks mimic important real-world tasks like the monitoring of air control displays or industrial equipment. (For reviews see Mackie, 1977; Parasuraman, 1986.)

Vigilance implies an ability to spread some processing resource across a substantial portion of the visual field. It is possible to design tasks where vigilance in peripheral vision coexists with focal attention to some foveal tasks. This suggests that these are separate mechanisms of attention. Separate or not, focal attention does influence the ability to deploy resources to more peripheral locations. As a general rule, as foveal load increases, peripheral processing decreases in a form of attentional tunnel vision (Ikeda & Takeuchi, 1975; Williams, 1985, 1989). Rossi and Paradiso (1995) report an interesting wrinkle on this effect. The reduction of sensitivity to a peripheral grating depends on the relationship between the properties of that grating and the stimuli producing the central load.

Sanders (1970) talked about a "useful field off view." Roughly speaking this is the region within which attention can be effectively deployed. In addition to shrinking as load increases, the useful field of view also shrinks as age increases (Ball, Beard, Roenker, Miller, & Griggs, 1988; Owsley, Ball, & Keeton, 1995; Sekuler & Ball, 1986). This effect is separable from any changes in perimetric visual field (Ball, Owsley, & Beard, 1990) and may be related to real-world problems, such as car accidents in the elderly (Ball, Owsley, Sloane, Roenker, & Bruni, 1993; see also Weltman & Egstrom, 1966).

There is also a bottom-up, stimulus-driven aspect to attentional vigilance. Initially, it was proposed that abrupt onsets automatically attracted focal attention

(Remington, Johnston, & Yantis, 1992; Yantis & Johnson, 1990; Yantis & Jonides, 1990; see also Miller, 1989). Theeuwes (1991, 1994, 1995) argued for mandatory capture by onset stimuli, but this is probably too strong a claim (Bacon & Egeth, 1994; Wolfe, 1996). All else being equal, abrupt onsets will capture attention, but this can be modulated by top-down task demands.

More recently, Yantis and his colleagues have argued that it is not an onset *per se* that is critical. In a series of experiments, they have made a case for attentional deployment to new objects (Hillstrom & Yantis, 1994; Yantis, 1993; Yantis & Hillstrom, 1994). This seems reasonable. It would be useful to have a mechanism that automatically took note of new objects in the field. A mechanism that wanted to direct attention to any visual transient would be less useful, since many uninteresting events in the world can produce such transients.

4. Reduction of Uncertainty

Consider the problem faced by a central decision-making process with the task of determining if a signal is present in a visual display. In the absence of any other information, that signal could be in any spatial location. Worse, if we do not know the nature of the signal, it could be found in any channel (Braddick et al., 1978). It could be low spatial frequency or red or moving or whatever. The decision maker is left in a state of great uncertainty. Attention enables uncertainty to be reduced. In most standard psychophysical experiments, the experimenter tells the subject where to look, when to look, and what to look for—all in an effort to reduce uncertainty. This implicit assumption about the role of attention has been explicitly tested several times (e.g., Davis, Kramer & Graham, 1983; Krupinski, Nodine, & Kundel, 1993; Kurylo, Reeves, & Scharf, 1996; Solomon, Lavie, & Morgan, 1997). Inevitably, reduction of uncertainty makes tasks easier. This is often discussed in terms of signal-detection theory (e.g., Swensson, 1980; Swensson & Judy, 1981).

These effects also serve to underline a point made earlier. Attention is not a term that is used to describe a single thing operating at a single locus. Reduction of uncertainty in space probably involves a different mechanism than reduction of uncertainty in a feature space or in time. Consider a search for a salient feature singleton. This is a very efficient search, producing RT × Set Size slopes near zero. Nevertheless, RTs are shorter if the subject is certain about the feature space in which the singleton will appear (i.e., will it be an oddball in color or orientation or size?) (Müller, Heller, & Ziegler, 1995; see also Bacon & Egeth, 1994).

5. Enhancement

Given that it is easier to detect or identify a stimulus when one is paying attention to that stimulus, several authors have wondered if attention acts to enhance the signal produced by that stimulus. There is evidence for such an enhancement at both the neural (Spitzer, Desimone, & Moran, 1988) and the behavioral level (Sagi & Julesz, 1986; Urbach & Spitzer, 1995). In the context of signal-detection theory, efforts have been made to separate detectability effects (d′) from changes in response criterion. Evidence for changes in d′ has been found (Downing, 1988; Hawkins et al., 1990). Sometimes both d′ and criterion effects are found (e.g., Müller & Findlay, 1987). Sometime only criterion effects are seen (Palmer, Ames, & Lindsey, 1993).

Many discriminations can be made only when attention is directed to a stimulus. As a general rule, preattentive processes such as those mediating "pop-out" require rather large differences between stimuli. Thus, in orientation, it is not possible to search efficiently for small orientation differences that can easily be discriminated with attention (Foster & Ward, 1991b; Wolfe, Friedman-Hill et al., 1992). Similar statements can be made about color (Nagy & Sanchez, 1990) or, indeed, about any basic feature.

There are two senses in which attention might enable fine perceptual discrimination. It could be that attention can be used to select small, preattentively generated signals. These signals might be present but unable to govern behavior without attention. Alternatively, attention might be required to sharpen or enhance the processing of a perceptual attribute. In this case, the signal would not exist prior to the application of attention.

6. Speed of Processing

Some phenomena suggest that attention to an object or location actually speeds processing, even quite basic processing. For example, Shimojo and his colleagues flashed a horizontal line on a screen and asked subjects to say if the line appeared to be drawn from the left or the right end. An isolated line produces no systematic bias for either direction. However, if one end of the line is cued, in any of a variety of ways, that line will appear to be drawn from the cued end to the uncued end (Hikosaka, Miyauchi, & Shimojo, 1993; Hikosaka, Miyauchi, Takeichi, & Shimojo, 1996; Hikosaka, Satoru, Hiroshige, & Shinsuke, 1996; Shimojo, Miyauchi, & Hikosaka, 1992). They argued that the attended end of the line reaches awareness before the unattended end (see also Stelmach, Herdman, & MacNeil, 1994). Some aspects of the effect may be better explained as versions of apparent motion (Downing & Treisman, 1997; Tse, Cavanagh, & Nakayama, 1998; Von Grünau, Dubé, & Kwas, 1996; Von Grünau & Faubert, 1992). However, it does seem clear that the apparent motion of line can be modulated by attention.

7. Modulation of Visual Processing

The line motion effects can be seen as evidence for the ability of attention to alter the perception of simple visual stimuli. Other evidence comes from studies of the attentional modulation of the effects of adaptation. Attention to the adapting stimuli is not a prerequisite for the production of aftereffects (He et al., 1996; Houck & Hoffman, 1986). However, attention does modulate aftereffects. For example, when two conflicting sources of adaptation are available, attention can select one and, thus, select the direction of adaptation (motion, Lankheet & Verstraten, 1995;

Necker cube resolution, Shulman, 1993b; see also Chaudhuri, 1990; Shulman, 1991, 1993a). Attending away from the adapting stimulus reduces figural aftereffects (Shulman, 1992; Yeh, Chen, DeValois, & DeValois, 1996). Prism adaptation is also modulated by attention (Redding & Wallace, 1985). Physiological underpinnings of these effects may have been seen in single cells of macaques (Treue & Maunsell, 1996) and in human fMRI data (O'Craven, Rosen, Kwong, & Treisman, 1997; Rees, Frith, & Lavie, 1997).

8. Feature Binding

Treisman has long argued that attention is needed to accurately bind features together (Treisman, 1986, 1988; Treisman & DeSchepper, 1996; Treisman & Gelade, 1980; Treisman & Sato, 1990). This is a central pillar of her important Feature Integration Theory. (For some arguments with that pillar see Duncan & Humphreys, 1989, 1992; Navon, 1990a, 1990b; Treisman, 1990, 1991, 1992). In the first formulations of this idea, Treisman argued that features like color and orientation could float freely through the preattentive perceptual world. Illusory conjunctions, erroneously reported combinations of features, were one consequence of the failure to accurately bind features (Treisman & Schmidt, 1982). More recent formulations hold that features are at least roughly associated with locations and even with objects, but the relationship of features to their objects and to each other is not known in the absence of attention (see also Wolfe & Bennett, 1997). Thus, in Figure 8, shown earlier, a preattentive object might have black, gray, vertical, and horizontal features, but only with attention would these features be bound into a "plus" composed of black vertical and gray horizontal bars. Keele, Cohen, Ivry, and Liotti (1988) asked if spatial or temporal synchrony was critical to binding and found that it was important that the features to be bound should occupy the same part of space.

Illusory conjunctions have generated an interesting body of research in their own right (e.g., Cohen & Ivry, 1989; Prinzmetal, Henderson, & Ivry, 1995; Prinzmetal & Keysar, 1989). Some of this work indicates that illusory conjunctions are possible between attributes that are quite clearly not basic features (words Treisman & Souther, 1986), (scene elements, Intraub, 1985), (elements of Chinese characters Fang & Wu, 1989). The meaning of the phenomenon remains controversial. In standard illusory conjunction paradigms, stimuli are briefly presented and the subject is queried about the appearance of those stimuli after they are gone. It is possible that the phenomenon shows that binding by attention is a fragile affair. As soon as the stimulus is gone, the explicit binding of the features ends and the possibility for error appears (Tsal, 1989a; Tsal, Meiran, & Lavie, 1994) (but see Briand & Klein, 1989; Tsal, 1989b).

IV. VISION AFTER ATTENTION

Postattentive vision, vision after attention, has been the subject of relatively little research to date. The visual percept of an object can be said to be preattentive before attention is directed to that object. The percept becomes attentive when attention is deployed to the object and postattentive when attention departs that object for some other object. By this definition, much of a percept of a scene must become postattentive over time. What is striking about the limited research on postattentive vision is that there is little evidence for any difference between postattentive and preattentive vision. That is, there is little evidence for persistent perceptual effects of attention.

A. Repeated Search

We have used a "repeated search" task to examine postattentive vision. In a standard visual search experiment, subjects might perform several hundred search trials. Each trial would involve a search through a different search display. In repeated search, subjects search multiple times through the same display as illustrated in Figure 11.

On each trial, the designated target is indicated at the center of the display. In Figure 11, the subject is first asked if a "white oblique" is present in the display. It is not. On the next trial, only the probe at the center of the display changes to "black vertical." The search display remains unaltered and the answer is "yes." With stimuli of this sort, a standard visual search experiment would produce inefficient target-present slopes of about 40 ms/item. It is inefficient because the search set is very heterogeneous and, perhaps more importantly, because the target changes from trial to trial. In repeated search, even though subjects are searching the same display over and over, search does not become more efficient (Wolfe, Klempen, & Dahlen, 1998). This failure to improve search efficiency holds over a wide range of variations on the repeated search theme. We have used letters, real objects, arbitrary closed curves, in addition to these compound conjunction stimuli. We have had subjects search

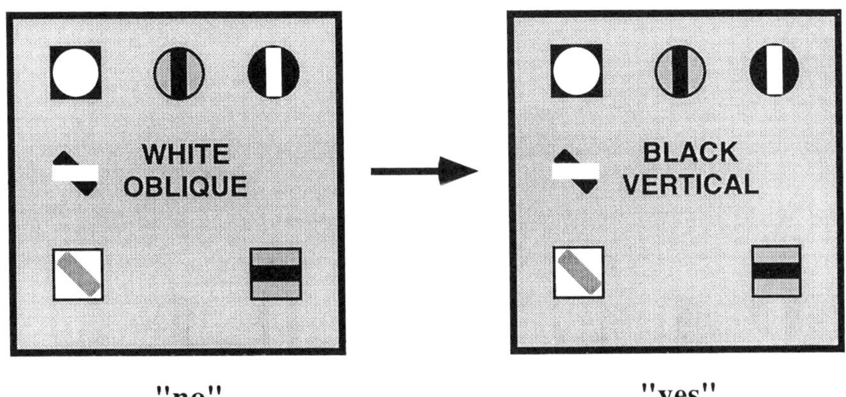

FIGURE 11 The Repeated Search Paradigm.

hundreds of times through the same few stimuli. If a search was inefficient on trial 1, it remains inefficient on trial N.

This is not to say that attention has no consequences. For instance, after multiple searches through the same set of letters, subjects certainly remember the letters. Subjects *know* more about attended stimuli. However, they do not seem to see more of those stimuli. In most real-world tasks, the encoding of a scene into memory would be useful ("Didn't I leave those keys by the back door?"). However, in our repeated search tasks, the best a subject could do with memory would be to replace a visual search through *N* items with a memory search through *N* items. Such a search would proceed at a rate equivalent to about 40 ms/item (McElree & Dosher, 1989; Sternberg, 1969)—no better than the inefficient visual search.

B. Change Blindness

The lack of lasting perceptual consequences of attention is dramatically illustrated by a phenomenon that Rensink (1996b) has dubbed "change blindness" (Simons & Levin, 1997a). Change blindness is illustrated in Figure 12. You may find that it takes a surprisingly long time to notice the difference between the two images. This is not a true example of change blindness because there are actually two images in two different places (Blackmore, Brelstaff, Nelson, & Troscianko, 1995).

However, subjects are just as blind to changes in a single scene as long as the change is made in a manner that does not produce an attention-grabbing visual transient. (Look at the cook if you still have not found the change in Figure 11.) Thus, subjects fail to notice substantial changes made during saccades (Grimes, 1996; see also Irwin, 1996; Irwin, Zacks, & Brown, 1989, 1990). Movie makers know that it is hard to detect changes when the camera moves away from a scene and then returns (Levin & Simons, 1997; Simons, 1996). They also miss changes between two versions of a scene if a blank screen is briefly presented between scenes to mask the transients (Pashler, 1988; Rensink, O'Regan, & Clark, 1995, 1996a), or if a salient transient is added to the scene to distract attention from the transient caused by the change (O'Regan, Rensink, & Clark, 1996). Finally, we cannot leave the topic of change blindness without mentioning the experiment of Simons and Levin (1997b). They engaged pedestrians in conversation and changed the identity of the experimenter/conversationalist during the conversation. To mask the change, they had two "workers" carry a door between the subject and experimenter. Under these conditions, 50% of subjects failed to notice the change to a new person.

The change blindness demonstrations are interesting because, in many cases, there is no question that observers have attended to the scene and to the objects in the scene. Nevertheless, substantial changes in the scene are missed. The changes are seen when the observer's attention remains with an object while it changes. Prior attention to the object is usually not enough, suggesting that the postattentive visual representation is quite sketchy. (For further discussion of these issues see Wolfe, 1997a; Wolfe et al., 1998.)

FIGURE 12 Change blindness: What is the difference between the two images?

V. VISION WITHOUT ATTENTION

A. The Problem

Finally, we should say something about the fate of visual stimuli that are never attended. As a general rule, studies of the effects of inattention try to force subjects to attend to one stimulus while other stimuli are presented. The subject is then queried, implicitly or explicitly, about the unattended stimulus. Experiments of this sort yield a very wide range of opinions about the fate of the unattended. At one extreme, Mack and her colleagues have argued for "inattentional blindness" (Mack & Rock, 1998; Mack, Tang, Tuma, & Kahn, 1992). At the other extreme are claims for semantic processing of unattended words (Hawley et al., 1994; Johnston et al., 1993). These debates about unattended stimuli are the latest version of the late versus early selection debates in the attention literature (well reviewed by Pashler, 1997). Models that hold that preattentive processing stops with the processing of basic features can be labeled as "early selection models." Models that hold that stimuli are much more thoroughly processed preattentively are late selection models. In early selection models, attention is needed to complete the act of perception. In late selection models, attention selects responses to fully processed stimuli.

B. How Unattended Can You Get?

Can any sense be made out of the divergent studies of the perception of unattended stimuli? Although the topic remains controversial, some headway can be made. First, we should consider what it means for a stimulus to be unattended. In a series of experiments, Braun and his colleagues had subjects perform a demanding visual search task at fixation and, at the same time, assessed their ability to perform other search tasks in the periphery. Simple visual search tasks for feature singletons like color and shape from shading were still possible (Braun, 1993; Braun & Julesz, 1998; Braun & Sagi, 1990, 1991). Other tasks like grouping were impaired (Ben-Av, Sagi, & Braun, 1992). This would seem to support a view that basic features are available in unattended stimuli but that more complicated properties are not. However, Joseph, Chun, and Nakayama (1997) did a rather similar experiment but tied up attention with the attentional blink (see section III.B). Now even a simple orientation pop-out task became impossible. It is possible that the Joseph et al. (1997) method ties up attention more completely than Braun's task. Lavie's work has shown that the fate of stimuli that are irrelevant to a task depends on the attentional load imposed by the relevant stimuli (Lavie, 1995; Lavie & Cox, 1996; Lavie & Tsal, 1994a).

It may be too simple to suggest that the attentional blink is a particularly effective way to capture attention. Consider, for example, that implicit measures show that subjects can extract meaning from words presented during an attentional blink (Luck, Vogel, & Shapiro, 1996; Shapiro, Driver, Ward, & Sorenson, 1997). Research on negative priming may help explain how it can be possible to read during a blink and still be unable to perform a simple search task. In a standard negative priming experiment, subjects are presented with two, partially overlapping stimuli. They are instructed to ignore one stimulus and make some report about the other. If the ignored stimulus is presented on the next trial as the to-be-attended stimulus, then subjects are somewhat slowed in their responses as compared to their responses to a neutral stimulus (Tipper, 1985; Tipper & Cranston, 1985; Tipper & Driver, 1988; Tipper & Weaver, 1996). It seems that the "unattended" stimulus was quite fully processed and had to be actively inhibited in order to be successfully ignored. Even novel objects can be inhibited (DeSchepper & Treisman, 1996), suggesting that the ignored object is coded into memory without being explicitly attended.

C. All Inattention Is Not Created Equal

These negative priming effects fail to occur when multiple items are ignored (Neumann & DeSchepper, 1992). That is, if you are instructed to respond to a red *A* and ignore a green *B,* it will be possible to measure inhibition with a subsequently presented *B.* However, if the irrelevant set is larger, *B C D E,* inhibition will not be seen. This strongly suggests that "ignored" is not quite the same as "unattended." With only a couple of stimuli, it may be impossible not to devote some processing resources to the irrelevant stimulus (again, see Lavie, 1995). The irrelevant stimulus is inhibited in order to keep it from interfering with the task at hand. With multiple stimuli, attention simply never reaches most of the irrelevant items. Evidence suggests that there is processing of the basic features of these items (e.g., Houck & Hoffman, 1986) but not of more complex properties (like letter identity Eriksen, Webb, & Fournier, 1990).

We run into definitional problems in the case of the "ignored" stimuli. They share some attributes with attentionally blinked stimuli and with stimuli lost to inattentional blindness. They cannot be explicitly reported. For instance, in the case of negative priming of novel shapes, there is no explicit recognition of the shapes (DeSchepper & Treisman, 1996). However, as already discussed, there is substantial implicit evidence for quite high-level processing of these stimuli. One possibility, put forth by Wolfe (1997a) is that these stimuli are seen but are removed without their being coded into explicit memory. Thus, subjects would be amnesic for these stimuli. Like any good amnesic, subjects would deny seeing the stimuli if queried after the stimuli were removed. It becomes a semantic point whether one wants to label such stimuli as "attended" or "unattended." The important point, for present purposes, is that stimuli can be divided into three broad categories. There are explicitly attended stimuli. These can be recognized and acted upon. There are stimuli that attention never reaches. These seem to leave marks of their preattentive features but probably not of their more complex properties. Finally, there are stimuli that receive some processing resources but fail to leave any lasting impression on the observer. These may be seen but instantly forgotten, leaving implicit but not explicit traces for the experimenter to measure.

VI. CONCLUSION

From the vantage point of vision research, the study of attention is rather sobering. The evidence suggests that focal attention can be directed to one or, perhaps, a few objects at any one time. The number of possible targets for attention in a visual scene is usually many times that number. Consequently, most of the visual stimuli that we see at any moment are represented either preattentively or postattentively. Most of what we know about vision, on the other hand, comes from studies in which the stimulus is the focus of attention. We have a detailed description of only a small part of visual experience. This is not meant as a criticism of vision research. If one was going to concentrate on any aspect of vision, the processing of attended stimuli would be a sensible place to focus one's energy. After all, most if not all of the visual control of behavior requires attention. In Patrick Cavanagh's (1999) felicitous phrase, attention is in the business of "exporting vision to the mind" (p. 129).

References

Aks, D. J., & Enns, J. T. (1992). Visual search for direction of shading is influenced by apparent depth. *Perception and Psychophysics, 52*(1), 63–74.

Alkhateeb, W. F., Morland, A. B., Ruddock, K. H., & Savage, C. J. (1990). Spatial, colour, and contrast response characteristics of mechanisms which mediate discrimination of pattern orientation and magnification. *Spatial Vision, 5*(2), 143–157.

Alkhateeb, W. F., Morris, R. J., & Ruddock, K. H. (1990). Effects of stimulus complexity on simple spatial discriminations. *Spatial Vision, 5*(2), 129–141.

Andersen, G. J. (1990). Focused attention in three-dimensional space. *Perception & Psychophysics, 47,* 112–120.

Backs, R. W., & Walrath, L. C. (1995). Ocular measures of redundancy gain during visual search of colour symbolic displays. *Ergonomics, 38*(9), 1831–1840.

Bacon, W. F., & Egeth, H. E. (1994). Overriding stimulus-driven attentional capture. *Perception and Psychophysics, 55*(5), 485–496.

Baker, C. H. (1958). Attention to visual displays during a vigilance task: I. Biasing attention. *British Journal of Psychology, 49,* 279–288.

Ball, K. K., Owsley, C., & Beard, B. (1990). Clinical visual field perimetry underestimates visual field problems in older adults. *Clinical Vision Science, 5*(2), 113–125.

Ball, K., Owsley, C., Sloane, M. E., Roenker, D. L., & Bruni, J. R. (1993). Visual attention problems as a predictor of vehicle crashes among older drivers. *Investigative Ophthalmology and Visual Science, 34*(11), 3110–3123.

Ball, K. K., Beard, B. L., Roenker, D. L., Miller, R. L., & Griggs, D. S. (1988). Age and visual search: expanding the useful field of view. *Journal of the Optical Society of America A, 5*(12), 2210–2219.

Bauer, B., Jolicœur, P., & Cowan, W. B. (1996). Visual search for colour targets that are or are not linearly-separable from distractors. *Vision Research, 36*(10), 1439–1466.

Bauer, B., Jolicœur, P., & Cowan, W. B. (1996b). Distractor heterogeneity versus linear separability in colour visual search. *Perception, 25*(1), 1281–1294.

Baylis, G. C. (1994). Visual attention and objects: Two object cost with equal convexity. *Journal of Experimental Psychology: Human Perception and Performance, 20*(1), 208–212.

Baylis, G. C., & Driver, J. (1993). Visual attention and objects: Evidence for hierarchical coding of location. *Journal of Experimental Psychology: Human Perception and Performance, 19*(3), 451–470.

Beck, J. (1966a). Effect of orientation and shape similarity on perceptual grouping. *Perception and Psychophysics, 1,* 300–302.

Beck, J. (1966b). Perceptual grouping produced by changes in orientation and shape. *Science, 154,* 538–540.

Beck, J. (1982). Textural segmentation. In J. Beck (Ed.), *Organization and representation in perception* (pp. 285–317). Hillsdale, NJ: Erlbaum.

Ben-Av, M. B., Sagi, D., & Braun, J. (1992). Visual attention and perceptual grouping. *Perception and Psychophysics, 52*(3), 277–294.

Berbaum, K., Chung, C., & Loke, W. (1986). Improved localization of moving targets with prior knowledge of direction of target motion. *American Journal of Psychology, 99*(4), 509–514.

Bergen, J. R., & Adelson, E. H. (1988). Early vision and texture perception. *Nature, 333,* 363–364.

Bergen, J. R., & Julesz, B. (1983). Rapid discrimination of visual patterns. *IEEE Trans on Systems, Man, and Cybernetics, SMC-13,* 857–863.

Berger, R. C., & McLeod, P. (1996). Display density influences visual search for conjunctions of movement and orientation. *Journal of Experimental Psychology: Human Perception and Performance, 2*(1), 114–121.

Bilsky, A. A., & Wolfe, J. M. (1995). Part-whole information is useful in size X size but not in orientation X orientation conjunction searches. *Perception and Psychophysics, 57*(6), 749–760.

Bilsky, A. A., Wolfe, J. M., & Friedman-Hill, S. F. (1994). Part-whole information is useful in size Z size but not in orientation X orientation conjunction searches. *Investigative Ophthalmology and Visual Science, 35*(4), 1622.

Blackmore, S. J., Brelstaff, G., Nelson, K., & Troscianko, T. (1995). Is the richness of our visual world an illusion? Transsaccadic memory for complex scenes. *Perception, 24,* 1075–1081.

Blake, R. (1989). A neural theory of binocular rivalry. *Psychology Review, 96,* 145–167.

Blakemore, C., & Over, R. (1974). Curvature detectors in human vision. *Perception, 3,* 3–7.

Braddick, O., Campbell, F. W., Atkinson, J., Held, R., Leibowitz, W. H., & Teuber, H.-L. (1978). Channels in vision: Basic aspects, *Perception: Handbook of Sensory Physiology,* (pp. 3–38). Berlin: Springer-Verlag.

Braddick, O. J., & Holliday, I. E. (1991). Serial search for targets defined by divergence or deformation of optic flow. *Perception, 20*(3), 345–354.

Brand, J. (1971). Classification without identification in visual search. *Quarterly Journal of Experimental Psychology, 23,* 178–186.

Braun, J. (1993). Shape-from-shading is independent of visual attention and may be a texton. *Spatial Vision,* 7(4), 311–322.

Braun, J., & Julesz, B. (1998). Dividing attention at little cost: detection and discrimination tasks. *Perception and Psychophysics, 60*(1), 1–23.

Braun, J., & Sagi, D. (1990). Vision outside the focus of attention. *Perception & Psychophysics, 48*(1), 45–58.

Braun, J., & Sagi, D. (1991). Texture-based tasks are little affected by second tasks requiring peripheral or central attentive fixation. *Perception, 20,* 483–500.

Bravo, M., & Blake, R. (1990). Preattentive vision and perceptual groups. *Perception, 19,* 515–522.

Bravo, M. J., & Blake, R. (1992). The contributions of figure and ground textures to segmentation. *Vision Research, 32*(9), 1793–1800.

Briand, K. A., & Klein, R. M. (1989). Has feature integration come unglued? A reply to Tsal. *J. Exp. Psychol. - Human Perception and Performance, 15*(2), 401–406.

Broadbent, D. E. (1982). Task combination and selective intake of information. *Acta Psychologica, 50,* 253–290.

Bundesen, C. (1996). Formal models of visual attention: A tutorial review. In A. Kramer, G. H. Cole, & G. D. Logan (Eds.), *Converging operations in the study of visual selective attention* (pp. 1–44). Washington, DC: American Psychological Association.

Bundesen, C., Kyllingsbaek, S., Houmann, K. J., & Jensen, R. M. (1997). Is visual attention automatically attracted by one's own name? *Perception and Psychophysics, 59*(5), 714–720.

Bundesen, C., & Pedersen, L. F. (1983). Color segregation and visual search. *Perception and Psychophysics, 33,* 487–493.

Caelli, T., Julesz, B., & Gilbert, E. (1978). On perceptual analyzers underlying texture discrimination. *Biological Cybernetics, 29,* 201–214.

Caerwinski, M., Lightfoot, N., & Shiffrin, R. (1992). Automatization and training in visual search. *American Journal of Psychology, 105*(2), 271–315.

Carrasco, M., Evart, D. L., Chang, I., & Katz, S. M. (1995). The eccentricity effect: Target eccentricity affects performance on conjunction searches. *Perception and Psychophysics, 57*(8), 1241–1261.

Carrasco, M., & Frieder, K. S. (1997). Cortical magnification neutralizes the eccentricity effect in visual search. *Vision Research, 37*(1), 63–82.

Carter, R. C. (1982). Visual search with color. *Journal of Experimental Psychology: Human Perception and Performance, 8*(1), 127–136.

Castiello, U., & Umilta, C. (1992). Splitting focal attention. *Journal of Experimental Psychology: Human Perception and Performance, 18*(3), 837–848.

Cavanagh, P. (1999). Attention: Exporting vision to the mind. In C. Taddei-Ferretti (Ed.), *Neuronal basis and psychological aspects of consciousness* (pp. 129–143). Singapore: World Scientific.

Cavanagh, P., Arguin, M., & Treisman, A. (1990). Effect of surface medium on visual search for orientation and size features. *J. Experimental Psychology: Human Perception and Performance, 16*(3), 470–492.

Cavanagh, P., & Mather, G. (1989). Motion: The long and the short of it. *Spatial Vision, 4,* 103–129.

Cave, K. R., & Pashler, H. (1995). Visual selection mediated by location: Selecting successive visual objects. *Perception & Psychophysics, 57*(4), 421–432.

Chau, A. W., & Yei-Yu, Y. (1995). Segregation by color and stereoscopic depth in three-dimensional visual space. *Perception & Psychophysics, 57*(7), 1032–1044.

Chaudhuri, A. (1990). Modulation of the motion aftereffect by selective attention. *Nature, 344*(6261), 60–62.

Cheal, M., & Lyon, D. (1992). Attention in visual search: Multiple search classes. *Perception and Psychophysics, 52*(2), 113–138.

Chen, L. (1982). Topological structure in visual perception. *Science, 218,* 699–700.

Chen, L. (1990). Holes and wholes: A reply to Rubin and Kanwisher. *Perception and Psychophysics, 47,* 47–53.

Chen, L., & Zhou, W. (1997). Holes in illusory conjunctions. *Psychonomic Bulletin and Review, 4*(4), 507–511.

Christie, J., & Klein, R. (1994, November). Novel popout: The true story. *Presented at the 35th annual meeting of the Psychonomic Society,* St. Louis, MO.

Chun, M. M., & Potter, M. C. (1995). A two-stage model for multiple target detection in RSVP. *Journal of Experimental Psychology: Human Perception & Performance, 21*(1), 109–127.

Chun, M. M., & Wolfe, J. M. (1996). Just say no: How are visual searches terminated when there is no target present? *Cognitive Psychology, 30,* 39–78.

Cohen, A., & Ivry, R. B. (1989). Illusory conjunction inside and outside the focus of attention. *Journal of Experimental Psychology: Human Perception and Performance, 15,* 650–663.

Cohen, A., & Ivry, R. B. (1991). Density effects in conjunction search: Evidence for coarse location mechanism of feature integration. *Journal of Experimental Psychology: Human Perception and Performance, 17*(4), 891–901.

Culham, J. C., & Cavanagh, P. (1994). Motion capture of luminance stimuli by equiluminous color gratings and by attentive tracking. *Vision Research, 34*(20), 2701–2706.

D'Zmura, M., & Lennie, P. (1988). Attentional selection of chromatic mechanisms. *Investigative Ophthalmology & Visual Science (suppl.), 29,* 162.

D'Zmura, M., & Mangalick, A. (1993). Detection of contrary chromatic change. *Journal of the Optical Society of America A, 11*(2), 543–546.

Davis, E., Kramer, P., & Graham, N. (1983). Uncertainty about spatial frequency, spatial position, or contrast of visual patterns. *Perception and Psychophysics, 33,* 20–28.

Dehaene, S. (1989). Discriminability and dimensionality effects in visual search for featural conjunctions: A functional pop-out. *Perception & Psychophysics, 46*(1), 72–80.

DeSchepper, B., & Treisman, A. (1996). Visual memory of novel shapes: Implicit coding without attention. *Journal of Experimental Psychology: Learning, Memory & Cognition, 22*(27–47).

Desimone, R., & Duncan, J. (1995). Neural mechanisms of selective visual attention. *Annual Review Neuroscience, 18,* 193–222.

Dick, M., Ullman, S., & Sagi, D. (1987). Parallel and serial processes in motion detection. *Science, 237,* 400–402.

Donk, M., & Meinecke, C. (1997, November). *The effects of retinal eccentricity in texture segmentation and element search.* Paper presented at the Annual Meeting of the Psychonomic Society, Philadelphia.

Donnelly, N., Humphreys, G. W., & Riddoch, M. J. (1991). Parallel computation of primitive shape descriptions. *Journal of Experimental Psychology: Human Perception & Performance, 17*(2), 561–570.

Downing, C. J. (1988). Expectancy and visual-spatial attention: Effects on perceptual quality. *Journal Experimental Psychology, 14,* 188–202.

Downing, C. J., & Pinker, S. (1985). The spatial structure of visual attention. In M. I. Posner & O. S. M. Marin (Eds.), *Mechanisms of attention: Attention and performance XI* (pp. 171–187). NY: Hillsdale, NJ: Erlbaum.

Downing, P. E., & Treisman, A. M. (1997). The line-motion illusion: Attention or impletion: *Journal of Experimental Psychology: Human Perception & Performance, 23*(3), 768–779.

Driver, J., & Baylis, G. C. (1989). Movement and visual attention: The spotlight metaphor breaks down. *Journal of Experimental Psychology: Human Perception and Performance, 15*(3), 448–456.

Driver, J., & McLeod, P. (1992). Reversing visual search asymmetries with conjunctions of movement and orientation. *Journal of Experimental Psychology: Human Perception and Performance, 18,* 22–33.

Driver, J., McLeod, P., & Dienes, Z. (1992a). Are direction and speed coded independently by the visual system? Evidence from visual search. *Spatial Vision, 6*(2), 133–147.

Driver, J., McLeod, P., & Dienes, Z. (1992b). Motion coherence and conjunction search: Implications for guided search theory. *Perception and Psychophysics, 51*(1), 79–85.

Duncan, J. (1983). Category effects in visual search: A failure to replicate the "oh-zero" phenomenon. *Perception and Psychophysics, 34*(3), 221–232.

Duncan, J. (1984). Selective attention and the organization of visual information. *Journal of Experimental Psychology: General, 113,* 501–517.

Duncan, J. (1988). Boundary conditions on parallel processing in human vision. *Perception, 17,* 358.

Duncan, J. (1993). Coordination of what and where systems in the visual control of behaviour. *Perception, 22,* 1261–1270.

Duncan, J. (1995). Target and non-target grouping in visual search. *Perception and Psychophysics, 57*(1), 117–120.

Duncan, J., & Humphreys, G. W. (1989). Visual search and stimulus similarity. *Psychological Review, 96,* 433–458.

Duncan, J., & Humphreys, G. W. (1992). Beyond the search surface: Visual search and attentional engagement. *Journal of Experimental Psychology: Human Perception and Performance, 18*(2), 578–588.

Durgin, F. H., & Wolfe, S. E. (1997). Global precedence in visual search? Not so fast: Evidence instead for an oblique effect. *Perception, 26,* 321–332.

Eckstein, M. P., Thomas, J. P., Palmer, J., & Shimozaki, S. S. (1996). Further predictions of signal detection theory on visual search accuracy: Conjunctions, disjunctions, and triple conjunctions. *Investigative Ophthalmology and Visual Science, 37*(3), S15.

Efron, R., & Yund, E. W. (1996). Spatial uniformities in visual search. *Brain & Cognition, 31*(3), 331–368.

Egeth, H., Jonides, J., & Wall, S. (1972). Parallel processing of multielement displays. *Cognitive Psychology, 3,* 674–698.

Egeth, H. E., Virzi, R. A., & Garbart, H. (1984). Searching for conjunctively defined targets. *Journal of Experimental Psychology: Human Perception and Performance, 10,* 32–39.

Egeth, H. E., & Yantis, S. (1997). Visual Attention: Control, representation, and time course. *Annual Review of Psychology, 48,* 269–297.

Elder, J., & Zucker, S. (1993). The effect of contour closure on the rapid discrimination of two-dimensional shapes. *Vision Research, 33*(7), 981–991.

Elder, J., & Zucker, S. (1994). A measure of closure. *Vision Research, 34*(24), 3361–3369.

Elder, J., & Zucker, S. (1998). Evidence for boundary-specific grouping. *Vision Research, 38*(1), 142–152.

Enns, J. (1986). Seeing textons in context. *Perception and Psychophysics, 39*(2), 143–147.

Enns, J. T. (1992). Sensitivity of early human vision to 3-D orientation in line-drawings. *Canadian Journal of Psychology, 46*(2), 143–169.

Enns, J. T., & Kingstone, A. (1995). Access to global and local properties in visual search for compound stimuli. *Psychological Science, 6*(5), 283–291.

Enns, J. T., & Rensink, R. A. (1990a). Scene based properties influence visual search. *Science, 247,* 721–723.

Enns, J. T., & Rensink, R. A. (1990b). Sensitivity to three-dimensional orientation in visual search. *Psychological Science, 1*(5), 323–326.

Enns, J. T., & Rensink, R. A. (1991). Preattentive recovery of three-dimensional orientation from line drawings. *Psychology Review, 98*(3), 335–351.

Enns, J. T., & Rensink, R. A. (1993). A model for the rapid discrimination of line drawing in early vision. In D. Brogan, A. Gale, & K. Carr (Eds.), *Visual search 2* (pp. 73–89). London, UK: Taylor & Francis.

Epstein, W., & Babler, T. (1990). In search of depth. *Perception and Psychophysics, 48*(1), 68–76.

Epstein, W., Babler, T., & Bownds, S. (1992). Attentional demands of processing shape in three-dimensional space: Evidence from visual search and precuing paradigms. *Journal of Experimental Psychology: Human Perception and Performance, 18*(2), 503–511.

Eriksen, B. A., & Eriksen, C. W. (1974). Effects of noise letters upon the identification of a target letter in a nonsearch task. *Perception & Psychophysics, 16,* 143–149.

Eriksen, C. W., & Hoffman, J. E. (1973). The extent of processing of noise elements during selective encoding from visual displays. *Perception & Psychophysics, 14,* 155–160.

Eriksen, C. W., & St. James, J. D. (1986). Visual attention within and around the field of focal attention: A zoom lens model. *Perception and Psychophysics, 40,* 225–240.

Eriksen, C. W., Webb, J. M., & Fournier, L. R. (1990). How much processing do nonattended stimuli receive? Apparently very little, but . . . *Perception & Psychophysics, 47*(5), 477–488.

Fahle, M. (1990). *Parallel, semi-parallel, and serial processing of visual hyperacuity.* Paper presented at the SPIE: Human Vision and Electronic Imaging: Models, Methods, and Applications, Santa Clara, CA.

Fahle, M. (1991). A new elementary feature of vision. *Investigative Ophthalmology and Visual Science, 32*(7), 2151–2155.

Fang, S. P., & Wu, P. (1989). Illusory conjunctions in the perception of Chinese characters. *Journal of Experimental Psychology: Human Perception and Performance, 15*(3), 434–447.

Farell, B., & Pelli, D. G. (1993). Can we attend to large and small at the same time? *Vision Research, 33*(18), 2757–2772.

Farmer, E. W., & Taylor, R. M. (1980). Visual search through color displays: Effects of target-background similarity and background uniformity. *Perception and Psychophysics, 27,* 267–272.

Findlay, J. M. (1995). Visual search: Eye movements and peripheral vision. *Optometry and Vision Science, 72,* 461–466.

Flowers, J. H., & Lohr, D. J. (1985). How does familiarity affect visual search for letter strings? *Perception and Psychophysics, 37,* 557–567.

Foster, D. H. (1983). Visual discrimination, categorical identification, and categorical rating in brief displays of curved lines: Implications for discrete encoding processes. *Journal of Experimental Psychology: Human Perception and Performance, 9*(5), 785–806.

Foster, D. H., & Ward, P. A. (1991a). Asymmetries in oriented-line detection indicate two orthogonal filters in early vision. *Proceedings of the Royal Society (London B), 243,* 75–81.

Foster, D. H., & Ward, P. A. (1991b). Horizontal-vertical filters in early vision predict anomalous line-orientation frequencies. *Proceedings of the Royal Society (London B), 243,* 83–86.

Foster, D. H., & Westland, S. (1995). Orientation contrast vs orientation in line-target detection. *Vision Research, 35*(6), 733–738.

Friedman-Hill, S. R., & Wolfe, J. M. (1995). Second-order parallel processing: Visual search for the odd-item in a subset. *Journal of Experimental Psychology: Human Perception and Performance, 21*(3), 531–551.

Garner, W. R., Hake, H. W., & Eriksen, C. W. (1956). Operationism and the concept of perception. *Psychological Review, 63,* 149–159.

Gibson, B. S. (1994). Visual attention and objects: One vs two or convex vs concave? *Journal of Experimental Psychology: Human Perception and Performance, 20*(1), 203–207.

Gibson, B. S., & Egeth, H. (1994). Inhibition of return to object-based and environment-based locations. *Perception and Psychophysics, 55*(3), 323–339.

Gilchrist, I. D., W., H. G., Jane, R. M., & Heiko, N. (1997). Luminance and edge information in grouping: A study using visual search. *Journal of Experimental Psychology: Human Perception & Performance, 23*(2), 464–480.

Grabowecky, M., & Khurana, B. (1990). Features were meant to be integrated. *Investigative Ophthalmology and Visual Science, 31*(4), 105.

Graham, N., Venkatesan, C., & Sutter, A. (1993). Spatial-frequency- and orientation-selectivity of simple and complex channels in region segregation. *Vision Research, 33*(14), 1893–1911.

Green, B. F., & Anderson, L. K. (1956). Color coding in a visual search task. *Journal of Experimental Psychology, 51,* 19–24.

Grimes, J. (1996). On the failure to detect changes in scenes across saccades. In K. Akins (Ed.), *Perception* (pp. 89–110). New York: Oxford University Press.

Gurnsey, R., & Browse, R. A. (1989). Asymmetries in visual texture discrimination. *Spatial Vision, 4*(1), 31–44.

Hansen, C. H., & Hansen, R. D. (1988). Finding the face in the crowd: An anger superiority effect. *Journal of Personality & Social Psychology, 54*(6), 917–924.

Hawkins, H. L., Hillyard, S. A., Luck, S. J., Mouloua, M., Downing, C. J., & Woodward, D. P. (1990). Visual attention modulates signal detectability. *Journal of Experimental Psychology: Human Perception and Performance, 16*(4), 802–811.

Hawley, K. J., Johnston, W. A., & Farnham, J. M. (1994). Novel popout with nonsense string: Effects of predictability of string length and spatial location. *Perception and Psychophysics, 55,* 261–268.

He, J. J., & Nakayama, K. (1994a). Perceived surface shape not features determines correspondence strength in apparent motion. *Vision Research, 34*(16), 2125–2135.

He, J. J., & Nakayama, K. (1994b). Perceiving textures: Beyond filtering. *Vision Research, 34*(2), 151–162.

He, S., Cavanagh, P., & Intriligator, J. (1996). Attentional resolution and the locus of visual awareness. *Nature, 383,* 334–337.

He, Z. J., & Nakayama, K. (1992). Surfaces versus features in visual search. *Nature, 359,* 231–233.

Heathcote, A., & Mewhort, D. J. K. (1993). Representation and selection of relative position. *Journal of Experimental Psychology: Human Perception and Performance, 19*(3), 488–516.

Helmholtz, H. v. (1924). *Treatise on physiological optics* (J. P. Southall, Trans.). (Trans. from 3rd German ed. of 1909, ed.). Rochester, NY: The Optical Society of America.

Hikosaka, O., Miyauchi, S., & Shimojo, S. (1993). Focal visual attention produces illusory temporal order and motion sensation. *Vision Research, 33*(9), 1219–1240.

Hikosaka, O., Miyauchi, S., Takeichi, H., & Shimojo, S. (1996). Multimodal spatial attention visualized by motion illusion. In T. Inui & J. L. McClelland (Eds.), *Attention and performance 16: Information integration in perception and communication. Attention and performance* (Vol. 16, pp. 237–261). Hillsdale, NJ: Lawrence Erlbaum.

Hikosaka, O., Satoru, M., Hiroshige, T., & Shinsuke, S. (1996). Multimodal spatial attention visualized by motion illusion. In T. Inui & J. L. McClelland (Eds.), *Attention and performance 16: Information integration in perception and communication. Attention and performance* (Vol. 16, pp. 237–261). Hillsdale, NJ: Lawrence Erlbaum.

Hillstrom, A. P., & Yantis, S. (1994). Visual motion and attentional capture. *Perception & Psychophysics, 55,* 399–411.

Hoffman, J. E. (1979). A two-stage model of visual search. *Perception and Psychophysics, 25,* 319–327.

Holliday, I. E., & Braddick, O. J. (1991). Pre-attentive detection of a target defined by stereoscopic slant. *Perception, 20,* 355–362.

Horowitz, T., & Treisman, A. (1994). Attention and apparent motion. *Spatial Vision, 8*(2), 193–219.

Horowitz, T. S., & Wolfe, J. M. (1997). Is visual search lost in space? *Investigative Ophthalmology and Visual Science, 38*(4), S688.

Houck, M. R., & Hoffman, J. E. (1986). Conjunction of color and form without attention. Evidence from an orientation-contingent color aftereffect. *Journal of Experimental Psychology: Human Perception and Performance, 12,* 186–199.

Hübner, R. (1993). On possible models of attention in signal detection. *Journal of Mathematical Psychology, 37*(2), 266–281.

Ikeda, M., & Takeuchi, T. (1975). Influence of foveal load on the functional visual field. *Perception and Psychophysics, 18,* 255–260.

Intraub, H. (1985). Visual dissociation: An illusory conjunction of pictures and forms. *J. Experimental Psychology: Human Perception and Performance, 11,* p431–442.

Intriligator, J., Nakayama, K., & Cavanagh, P. (1991). Attention tracking of multiple moving objects at different scales. *Investigative Ophthalmology and Visual Science, 32*(4), S1040.

Irwin, D. E. (1996). Integrating information across saccadic eye movements. *Current Directions in Psychological Science, 5*(3), 94–100.

Irwin, D. E., Zacks, J. L., & Brown, J. S. (1989). Absence of spatiotopic interaction across saccades. *Investigative Ophthalmology & Visual Science (suppl), 39,* 457.

Irwin, D. E., Zacks, J. L., & Brown, J. S. (1990). Visual memory and the perception of a stable visual environment. *Perception and Psychophysics, 47,* 35–46.

Ivry, R. B. (1992). Asymmetry in visual search for targets defined by differences in movement speed. *Journal of Experimental Psychology: Human Perception & Performance, 18*(4), 1045–1057.

Ivry, R. B., & Cohen, A. (1990). Dissociation of short- and long-range apparent motion in visual search. *Journal of Experimental Psychology: Human Perception and Performance, 16*(2), 317–331.

James, W. (1890). *The principles of psychology.* New York: Henry Holt and Co.

Johnston, W. A., Hawley, K. J., & Farnham, J. M. (1993). Novel popout: Empirical boundaries and tentative theory. *Journal of Experimental Psychology: Human Perception and Performance, 19*(1), 140–153.

Joseph, J. S., Chun, M. M., & Nakayama, K. (1997). Attentional requirements in a "preattentive" feature search task. *Nature, 387,* 805.

Julesz, B. (1962). Visual pattern discrimination. *International Radio Engineering: Transactions in Information Theory, IT-8,* 84–92.

Julesz, B. (1964). Binocular depth perception without familiarity cues. *Science, 45,* 356–362.

Julesz, B. (1971). *Foundations of cyclopean perception.* Chicago: University of Chicago.

Julesz, B. (1981). A theory of preattentive texture discrimination based on first order statistics of textons. *Biological Cybernetics, 41,* 131–138.

Julesz, B. (1984). A brief outline of the texton theory of human vision. *Trends in Neuroscience,* 7(Feb), 41–45.

Julesz, B. (1986). Texton gradients: The texton theory revisited. *Biological Cybernetics, 54,* 245–251.

Julesz, B., & Bergen, J. R. (1983). Textons, the fundamental elements in preattentive vision and perceptions of textures. *Bell Systems Technology Journal, 62,* 1619–1646.

Julesz, B., Gilbert, E. N., Shepp, L. A., & Frisch, H. L. (1973). Inability of humans to discriminate between visual textures that agree in second-order statistics—revisited. *Perception, 2,* 391–405.

Julesz, B., & Krose, B. (1988). Features and spatial filters. *Nature, 333,* 302–303.

Julesz, B., & Papathomas, T. V. (1984). On spatial-frequency channels and attention. *Perception and Psychophysics, 36*(4), 398–399.

Kahneman, D., & Treisman, A. (1984). Changing views of attention and automaticity. In R. Parasuraman & D. R. Davies (Eds.), *Varieties of attention* (pp. 29–61). New York: Academic Press.

Kahneman, D., Treisman, A., & Gibbs, B. (1992). The reviewing of object files: Object-specific integration of information. *Cognitive Psychology, 24,* 179–219.

Kaptein, N. A., Theeuwes, J., & Van der Heijden, A. H. C. (1994). Search for a conjunctively defined target can be selectively limited to a color-defined subset of elements. *Journal of Experimental Psychology: Human Perception and Performance, 21*(5), 1053–1069.

Kawahara, J. I. (1993). The effect of stimulus motion on visual search. *Japanese Journal of Psychology, 64*(5), 396–400.

Keeble, D. R., & Morgan, M. J. (1993). A linear systems approach to texture perception. *Investigative Ophthalmology and Visual Science, 34*(4), 1237.

Keele, S. W., Cohen, A., Ivry, R., & Liotti, M. (1988). Tests of a temporal theory of attentional binding. *Journal of Experimental Psychology: Human Perception & Performance, 14*(3), 444–452.

Kim, M., & Cave, K. R. (1995). Spatial attention in visual search for features and feature conjunctions. *Psychological Science, 6*(6), 376–380.

Kimchi, R. (1992). Primacy of wholistic processing and global/local paradigm: A critical review. *Psychological bulletin, 112*(1), 24–38.

Kinchla, R. A. (1992). Attention. *Annual Review of Psychology, 43,* 711–742.

Kinchla, R. A., & Wolfe, J. M. (1979). The order of visual processing: "Top-down," "bottom-up," or "middle-out." *Perception and Psychophysics, 25,* 225–231.

Kleffner, D. A., & Ramachandran, V. S. (1992). On the perception of shape from shading. *Perception and Psychophysics, 52*(1), 18–36.

Klein, R. (1988). Inhibitory tagging system facilitates visual search. *Nature, 334,* 430–431.

Koelega, H. S., Brinkman, J.-A., Hendriks, L., & Verbaten, M. N. (1989). Processing demands, effort, and individual differences in four different vigilance tasks. *Human Factors, 31*(1), 45–62.

Kramer, A., Cole, G. H., & Logan, G. D. (1996). *Converging operations in the study of visual selective attention.* Washington, DC: American Psychological Association.

Kramer, A. F., Tham, M.-P., & Yeh, Y.-Y. (1991). Movement and focused attention: A failure to replicate. *Perception and Psychophysics, 50*(6), 537–546.

Krueger, L. E. (1984). The category effect in visual search depends on physical rather than conceptual differences. *Perception and Psychophysics, 35*(6), 558–564.

Krupinski, E. A., Nodine, C. F., & Kundel, H. L. (1993). Perceptual enhancement of tumor targets in chest X-ray images. *Perception and Psychophysics, 53*(5), 519–526.

Kurylo, D. D., Reeves, A., & Scharf, B. (1996). Expectancy of line segment orientation. *Spatial Vision, 10*(2), 149–162.

LaBerge, D. (1983). Spatial extent of attention to letters and words. *J. Experimental Psychology: Human Perception and Performance, 9,* 371–379.

LaGasse, L. L. (1993). Effects of good form and spatial frequency on global precedence. *Perception and Psychophysics, 53*(1), 89–105.

Lamb, M. R., & Robertson, L. C. (1990). The effect of visual angle on global and local reaction times depends on the set of visual angles presented. *Perception and Psychophysics, 47*(5), 489–496.

Lamb, M. R., & Yund, E. W. (1993). The role of spatial frequency in the processing of hierarchically organized stimuli. *Perception and Psychophysics, 54*(6), 773–784.

Landy, M. S., & Bergen, J. R. (1991). Texture segregation and orientation gradient. *Vision Research, 31*(4), 679–691.

Lankheet, M. J., & Verstraten, F. A. (1995). Attentional modulation of adaptation to two-component transparent motion. *Vision Research, 35*(10), 1401–1412.

Lavie, N. (1995). Perceptual load as a necessary condition for selective attention. *Journal of Experimental Psychology: Human Perception & Performance, 21*(3), 451–468.

Lavie, N. (1996). Feature integration and selective attention: Response competition from unattended distractor features. *Perception and Psychophysics, 59*(4), 543–556.

Lavie, N., & Cox, S. (1996). On the efficiency of visual selective attention: Efficient visual search leads to inefficient distractor rejection. *Psychological Science, 8,* 395–398.

Lavie, N., & Driver, J. (1996). On the spatial extent of attention in object-based visual selection. *Perception and Psychophysics, 58,* 1238–1251.

Lavie, N., & Tsal, Y. (1994). Perceptual load as a major determinant of the locus of selection in visual attention. *Perception and Psychophysics, 56*(2), 183–197.

Levin, D. (1996). Classifying faces by race: The structure of face categories. *Journal of Experimental Psychology: Learning, Memory, & Cognition, 22*(6), 1364–1382.

Levin, D. T., & Simons, D. J. (1997). Failure to detect changes to attended objects in motion pictures. *Psychological Bulletin and Review, 4*(4), 501–506.

Logan, G. D. (1996). The CODE theory of visual attention: An integration of space-based and object-based attention. *Psychological Review, 103*(4), 603–649.

Luck, S. J., & Vogel, E. K. (1997). The capacity of visual working memory for features and conjunctions. *Nature, 390* (20 Nov), 279–281.

Luck, S. J., Vogel, E. K., & Shapiro, K. L. (1996). Word meanings can be accessed but not reported during the attentional blink. *Nature, 382,* 616–618.

Luschow, A., & Nothdurft, H. C. (1993). Pop-out of orientation but not pop-out of motion at isoluminance. *Vision Research, 33*(1), 91–104.

Mack, A., & Rock, I. (1998). Inattentional blindness: Cambridge, MA: MIT Press.

Mack, A., Tang, B., Tuma, R., & Kahn, S. (1992). Perceptual organization and attention. *Cognitive Psychology, 24,* 475–501.

Mackie, R. R. (1977). *Vigilance: Theory, operational performance and physiological correlates.* New York: Plenum.

Malik, J., & Perona, P. (1990). Preattentive texture discrimination with early vision mechanisms. *Journal of the Optical Society of America A,* 7(5), 923–932.

Mannan, S., Ruddock, K. H., & Wright, J. R. (1995). Eye movements and response times for the detection of line orientation during visual search. In J. M. Findlay, R. Walker, & Robert W. Kentridge (Eds.), *Eye movement research: Mechanisms, processes, and applications. Studies in visual information processing* (Vol. 6, pp. 337–348). Amsterdam, Netherlands: Elsevier Science Publishing Co, Inc.

McElree, B., & Disher, B. A. (1989). Serial position and set size in short-term memory: The time course of recognition. *Journal of Experimental Psychology: General, 118*(4), 346–373.

McLeod, P. (1993). Filtering and physiology in visual search: A convergence of behavioural and neurophysiological measures. In A. D. Baddeley & L. Weiskrantz (Eds.), *Attention: Selection, awareness, and control: A tribute to Donald Broadbent* (pp. 72–86). Oxford, UK: Clarendon Press/Oxford University Press.

McLeod, P., Driver, J., & Crisp, J. (1988). Visual search for conjunctions of movement and form is parallel. *Nature, 332,* 154–155.

McLeod, P., Driver, J., Dienes, Z., & Crisp, J. (1991). Filtering by movement in visual search. *Journal of Experimental Psychology: Human Perception and Performance,* 17(1), 55–64.

Miller, J. (1989). The control of visual attention by abrupt visual onsets and offsets. *Perception and Psychophysics, 45,* 567–571.

Miller, J. (1991). The flanker compatibility effect as a function of visual angle, attentional focus, visual transients, and perceptual load. *Perception and Psychophysics, 49*(3), 270–288.

Moraglia, G. (1989a). Display organization and the detection of horizontal lines segments. *Perception and Psychophysics, 45,* 265–272.

Moraglia, G. (1989b). Visual search: Spatial frequency and orientation. *Perceptual & Motor Skills, 69*(2), 675–689.

Moraglia, G., Maloney, K. P., Fekete, E. M., & Al-Basi, K. (1989). Visual search along the colour dimension. *Canadian Journal of Psychology, 43*(1), 1–12.

Moran, J., & Desimone, R. (1985). Selective attention gates visual processing in the extrastriate cortex. *Science, 229,* 782–784.

Mordkoff, J. T., Yantis, S., & Egeth, H. E. (1990). Detecting conjunctions of color and form in parallel. *Perception and Psychophysics, 48*(2), 157–168.

Motter, B. C. (1994a). Neural correlates of attentive selection for color or luminance in extrastriate area V4. *The Journal of Neuroscience, 14*(4), 2178–2189.

Motter, B. C. (1994b). Neural correlates of feature selective memory and pop-out in extrastriate area V4. *The Journal of Neuroscience, 14*(4), 2190–2199.

Müller, H. J., & Findlay, J. M. (1987). Sensitivity and criterion effects in the spatial cuing of visual attention. *Perception & Psychophysics, 42,* 383–399.

Müller, H., & Found, A. (1996). Visual search for conjunctions of motion and form: Display density and asymmetry reversal. *Journal of Experimental Psychology: Human Perception and Performance, 22*(1), 122–132.

Müller, H. J., Heller, D., & Ziegler, J. (1995). Visual search for singleton feature targets within and across feature dimensions. *Perception and Psychophysics, 57*(1), 1–17.

Müller, H., & Maxwell, J. (1994). Perceptual integration of motion and form information. *Journal of Experimental Psychology: Human Perception and Performance, 20,* 397–420.

Müller, H. J., & von Muhlenen, A. (1996). Attentional tracking and inhibition of return in dynamic displays. *Perception & Psychophysics, 58*(2), 224–249.

Nagy, A. L., & Sanchez, R. R. (1990). Critical color differences determined with a visual search task. *Journal of the Optical Society of America A, 7*(7), 1209–1217.

Nagy, A. L., Sanchez, R. R., & Hughes, T. C. (1990). Visual search for color differences with foveal and peripheral vision. *Journal of the Optical Society of America A, 7*(10), 1995–2001.

Nakayama, K. (1990). The iconic bottleneck and the tenuous link between early visual processing and perception. In C. Blakemore (Eds.), *Vision: coding and efficiency* (pp. 411–422). Cambridge, UK: Cambridge University Press.

Nakayama, K., & Mackeben, M. (1989). Sustained and transient components of focal visual attention. *Vision Research, 29*(11), 1631–1647.

Nakayama, K., & Silverman, G. H. (1986). Serial and parallel processing of visual feature conjunctions. *Nature, 320,* 264–265.

Navon, D. (1977). Forest before the trees: The precedence of global features in visual perception. *Cognitive Psychology, 9,* 353–383.

Navon, D. (1990a). Does attention serve to integrate features? *Psychology Review, 97*(3), 453–459.

Navon, D. (1990b). Treisman's search model does not require feature integration: Rejoinder to Treisman (1990). *Psychology Review, 97*(3), 464–465.

Neisser, U. (1967). *Cognitive psychology.* New York: Appleton, Century, Crofts.

Neumann, E., & DeSchepper, B. G. (1992). An inhibition-based fan effect: Evidence for an active suppression mechanism in selective attention. *Canadian Journal of Psychology, 46,* 1–40.

Nothdurft, H. C. (1991a). The role of local contrast in pop-out of orientation, motion and color. *Investigative Ophthalmology and Visual Science, 32*(4), 714.

Nothdurft, H. C. (1991b). Texture segmentation and pop-out from orientation contrast. *Vision Research, 31*(6), 1073–1078.

Nothdurft, H. C. (1992). Feature analysis and the role of similarity in pre-attentive vision. *Perception and Psychophysics, 52*(4), 355–375.

Nothdurft, H. C. (1993a). The role of features in preattentive vision: Comparison of orientation, motion and color cues. *Vision Research, 33*(14), 1937–1958.

Nothdurft, H. C. (1993b). Saliency effects across dimensions in visual search. *Vision Research, 33*(5/6), 839–844.

Nothdurft, H. C. (1993c). The conspicuousness of orientation and visual motion. *Spatial Vision, 7*(4), 341–366.

Nothdurft, H. C. (1993d). Faces and facial expression do not pop-out. *Perception, 22,* 1287–1298.

Nothdurft, H. C. (1994). Common properties of visual segmentation. In G. R. Bock & J. A. Goode (Eds.), *Higher-order processing in the visual system* (pp. 245–259). Chicester, UK: John Wiley & Sons.

O'Craven, K. M., Rosen, B. R., Kwong, K. K., & Treisman, A. (1997). Voluntary attention modulates fMRI activity in human MT-MST. *Neuron, 18*(April), 591–598.

O'Regan, J. K., Rensink, R., & Clark, J. J. (1996). "Mud splashes" render picture changes invisible. *Investigative Ophthalmology and Visual Science, 37*(3), S213.

O'Toole, A. J., & Walker, C. L. (1997). On the preattentive accessibility of stereoscopic disparity: Evidence from visual search. *Perception & Psychophysics, 59*(2), 202–218.

Owsley, C., Ball, K., & Keeton, D. M. (1995). Relationship between visual sensitivity and target localization in older adults. *Vision Research, 35*(4), 579–587.

Palmer, J. (1995). Attention in visual search: Distinguishing four causes of a set size effect. *Current Directions in Psychological Science, 4*(4), 118–123.

Palmer, J., Ames, C. T., & Lindsey, D. T. (1993). Measuring the effect of attention on simple visual search. *Journal of Experimental Psychology: Human Perception & Performance, 19*(1), 108–130.

Paquet, L. (1992). Global and local processing in nonattended objects: A failure to induce local processing dominance. *Journal of Experimental Psychology: Human Perception and Performance, 18*(2), 512–529.

Parasuraman, R. (1986). Vigilance, monitoring, and search. In K. R. Boff, L. Kaufmann, & J. P. Thomas (Eds.), *Handbook of human perception and performance* (1st ed., Vol. 2, pp. 43.1–43.39). New York: John Wiley and Sons.

Pashler, H. (1988). Familiarity and visual change detection. *Perception and Psychophysics, 44,* 369–378.

Pashler, H. (1997). *The psychology of attention.* Cambridge, MA: MIT Press.

Poisson, M. E., & Wilkinson, F. (1992). Distractor ratio and grouping processes in visual conjunction search. *Perception, 21,* 21–38.

Pomerantz, J. R., & Pristach, E. A. (1989). Emergent features, attention, and perceptual glue in visual form perception. *Journal of Experimental Psychology: Human Perception and Performance, 15*(4), 635–649.

Ponte, D., Rechea, C., Sampedro, M. J., & Carrasco, M. (1997). A color × color conjunction can be searched in 'parallel.' *Investigative Ophthalmology and Visual Science, 38*(4), S365.

Posner, M. I., & Cohen, Y. (1984). Components of attention. In H. Bouma & D. G. Bouwhuis (Eds.), *Attention and Performance X* (pp. 55–66). Hillside, NJ: Erlbaum.

Potter, M. C. (1975). Meaning in visual search. *Science, 187,* 965–966.

Potter, M. C. (1993). Very short-term conceptual memory. *Memory & Cognition, 21*(2), 156–161.

Potter, M. C., & Levy, E. I. (1969). Recognition memory for a rapid sequence of pictures. *Journal of Experimental Psychology, 81,* 10–15.

Pratt, J., & Abrams, R. A. (1995). Inhibition of return to successively cued spatial locations. *Journal of Experimental Psychology: Human Perception and Performance, 21*(6), 1343–1353.

Prević, F. H. (1996). Attentional and oculomotor influences on visual field anisotropies in visual search performance. *Visual Cognition, 3*(3), 277–301.

Previc, F. H., & Blume, J. L. (1993). Visual search asymmetries in three-dimensional space. *Vision Research, 33*(18), 2697–2704.

Prinzmetal, W., Henderson, D., & Ivry, R. (1995). Loosening the constraints on illusory conjunctions: the role of exposure duration and attention. *Journal of Experimental Psychology: Human Perception and Performance, 21*(6), 1362–1375.

Prinzmetal, W., & Keysar, B. (1989). Functional theory of illusory conjunctions and neon colors. *Journal of Experimental Psychology: General, 118*(2), 165–190.

Purcell, D. G., Stewart, A. L., & Skov, R. B. (1996). It takes a confounded face to pop out of a crowd. *Perception, 25*(9), 1091–1108.

Pylyshyn, Z. W. (1989). The role of location indexes in spatial perception: A sketch of the FINST spatial-index model. *Cognition, 32,* 65–97.

Pylyshyn, Z. W. (1994). Some primitive mechanisms of spatial attention. *Cognition, 50,* 363–384.

Pylyshyn, Z., & Storm, R. W. (1988). Tracking multiple independent targets: Evidence for a parallel tracking mechanism. *Spatial Vision, 3,* 179–197.

Ramachandran, V. S. (1988). Perception of shape from shading. *Nature, 331,* 163–165.

Raymond, J. E., Shapiro, K. L., & Arnell, K. M. (1992). Temporary suppression of visual processing in an RSVP task: An attentional blink? *Journal of Experimental Psychology: Human Perception and Performance, 18*(3), 849–860.

Redding, G. M., & Wallace, B. (1985). Cognitive interference in prism adaptation. *Perception and Psychophysics, 37,* 225–231.

Rees, G., Frith, C., & Lavie, N. (1997). Modulating irrelevant motion perception by varying attentional load in an unrelated task. *Science, 278*(5343), 1616–1619.

Reinitz, M. T., Morrissey, J., & Demb, J. (1994). Role of attention in face encoding. *Journal of Experimental Psychology: Learning, Memory, and Cognition, 20*(1), 161–168.

Remington, R. W., Johnston, J. C., & Yantis, S. (1992). Involuntary attentional capture by abrupt onsets. *Perception and Psychophysics, 51*(3), 279–290.

Rensink, R., & Cavanagh, P. (1993). Processing of shadows at preattentive levels. *Investigative Ophthalmology and Visual Science, 34*(4), 1288.

Rensink, R. A., & Enns, J. T. (1995). Pre-emption effects in visual search: Evidence for low-level grouping. *Psychological Review, 102*(1), 101–130.

Rensink, R., O'Regan, J. K., & Clark, J. J. (1995). Image flicker is as good as saccades in making large scene changes invisible. *Perception, 24* (suppl.), 26–27.

Rensink, R., O'Regan, J. K., & Clark, J. J. (1996a). To see or not to see: The need for attention to perceive changes in scenes. *Investigative Ophthalmology and Visual Science, 37*(3), S213.

Rensink, R., O'Regan, J. K., & Clark, J. J. (1996b). To see or not to see: The need for attention to perceive changes in scenes. *Psychological Science, 8,* 368–373.

Richards, W. (1968). Spatial remapping in the primate visual system. *Kybernetik, 4,* 146–156.

Riggs, L. A. (1973). Curvature as a feature of pattern vision. *Science, 181,* 1070–1072.

Robertson, L. C., Egly, R., Lamb, M. R., & Kerth, L. (1993). Spatial attention and curing to global and local levels of hierarchical structure. *Journal of Experimental Psychology: Human Perception and Performance, 19*(3), 471–487.

Rossi, A., & Paradiso, M. A. (1995). Feature-specific effects of selective visual attention. *Vision Research, 35* 621–634.

Royden, C. S., Wolfe, J. M., Konstantinova, E., & Hildreth, E. C. (1996). Search for a moving object by a moving observer. *Investigative Ophthalmology and Visual Science, 37*(3), S299.

Royden, C. S., Wolfe, J. M., Konstantinova, E., & Hildreth, E. C. (1997). *Search for a moving object by a moving observer: Locating a static object among moving distractors.* Paper presented at the Annual meeting of the Cognitive Neuroscience Society, Boston.

Rubin, J. M., & Kanwisher, N. (1985). Topological perception: Holes in an experiment. *Perception and Psychophysics, 37,* 179–180.

Saarinen, J. (1995). Visual search at different spatial scales. *Scandinavian Journal of Psychology, 36*(1), 1–9.

Saarinen, J. (1994). Visual search for global and local stimulus features. *Perception, 23, 2*(2), 237–243.

Sagi, D. (1988). The combination of spatial frequency and orientation is effortlessly perceived. *Perception and Psychophysics, 43,* 601–603.

Sagi, D., & Julesz, B. (1985). Fast noninertial shifts of attention. *Spatial Vision, 1,* 141–149.

Sagi, D., & Julesz, B. (1986). Enhanced detection in the aperture of focal attention during simple discrimination tasks. *Nature, 321,* 693–695.

Sanders, A. F. (1970). Some aspects of the selective process in the functional visual field. *Ergonomics, 13*(1), 101–117.

Sanders, A. F. (1993). Processing information in the function visual field. In G. d'Ydewalle & J. VanRensbergen (Eds.), *Perception and cognition* (pp. 3–22). Amsterdam: Elsevier Science.

Schneider, W. X. (1993). Space-based visual attention models and object selection: Constraints, problems, and possible solutions. *Psychological Research, 56,* 35–43.

Schneider, W., & Shiffrin, R. M. (1977). Controlled and automatic human information processing: I. Detection, search, and attention. *Psychological Review, 84,* 1–66.

Sekuler, R., & Ball, K. (1986). Visual localization: Age and practice. *Journal of the Optical Society of America - A, 3*(6), 864–868.

Shapiro, K., Driver, J., Ward, R., & Sorenson, R. E. (1997). Priming from the attentional blink. *Psychological Science, 8*(2), 95–100.

Shapiro, K. L. (1994). The attentional blink: The brain's eyeblink. *Current Directions in Psychological Science, 3*(3), 86–89.

Shiffrin, M. R., & Schneider, W. (1977). Controlled and automatic human information processing: II. Perceptual learning, automatic attending, and a general theory. *Psychological Review, 84,* 127–190.

Shiffrin, R. M. (1988). Attention. In R. Atkinson, R. J. Herrnstein, G. Lindzey, & R. D. Luce (Eds.), *Steven's handbook of experimental psychology* (2nd ed., Vol. 2, pp. 739–812). New York: John Wiley & Sons.

Shih, S. I., & Sperling, G. (1996). Is there feature-based attentional selection in visual search. *J. Experimental Psychology: Human Perception and Performance, 22*(3), 758–779.

Shimojo, S., Miyauchi, S., & Hikosaka, O. (1992). Voluntary and involuntary attention directed by the line-motion effect. *Perception, 22* (suppl. 2 (ECVP - Pisa), 12.

Shulman, G. L. (1991). Attentional modulation of mechanisms that analyze rotation in depth. *Journal of Experimental Psychology: Human Perception and Performance, 17*(3), 726–737.

Shulman, G. L. (1992). Attentional modulation of a figural aftereffect. *Perception, 21,* 7–19.

Shulman, G. L. (1993a). Attentional effects on adaptation of rotary motion in the plane. *Perception, 22,* 947–961.

Shulman, G. L. (1993b). Attentional effects on Necker cube adaptation. *Canadian Journal of Experimental Psychology, 47*(3), 540–547.

Simmons, D. R., & Foster, D. H. (1992). Segmenting textures of curved-line elements. In G. A. Orban & H. H. Nagel (Ed.), *Artificial and biological vision systems* (pp. 324–349). Berlin: Springer-Verlag.

Simons, D. J. (1996). In sight, out of mind. *Psychological Science, 7*(5), 301–305.

Simons, D. J., & Levin, D. T. (1997a). Change blindness. *Trends in Cognitive Sciences, 1*(7), 261–267.

Simons, D. J., & Levin, D. T. (1997b). Failure to detect changes to attended objects. *Investigative Ophthalmology and Visual Science, 38*(4), S707.

Smallman, H. S., & Boynton, R. M. (1990). Segregation of basic color in an information display. *J. Optical Society of America - A,* 7(10), 1985–1994.

Smith, S. L. (1962). Color coding and visual search. *Journal of Experimental Psychology, 64,* 434–440.

Snyder, A. W., & Barlow, H. B. (1988). Revealing the artist's touch. *Nature, 331,* 117–118.

Solomon, J. A., Lavie, N., & Morgan, M. J. (1997). The contrast discrimination function: spatial cuing effects. *Journal of the Optical Society of America, 14,* 2443–2448.

Sperling, G., Budiansky, J., Spivak, J., & Johnson, M. C. (1971). Extremely rapid visual search. The maximum rate of scanning letters for the presence of a numeral. *Science, 174,* 307–311.

Sperling, G., & Weichselgartner, E. (1995). Episodic theory of the dynamics of spatial attention. *Attention & Psychological Review, 102*(3), 503–532.

Spitzer, H., Desimone, R., & Moran, J. (1988). Increased attention enhances both behavioral and neuronal performance. *Science, 240,* 338–340.

Stelmach, L. B., Herdman, C. M., & MacNeil, K. R. (1994). Attentional modulation of visual processes in motion perception. *Journal of Experimental Psychology: Human Perception and Performance, 20*(1), 108–121.

Sternberg, S. (1969). High-speed scanning in human memory. *Science, 153,* 652–654.

Stromeyer, C. F., & Riggs, L. A. (1974). Curvature detectors in human vision? *Science, 184,* 1199–1201.

Stuart, G. W. (1993). Preattentive processing of object size: Implications for theories of size perception. *Perception, 22*(10), 1175–1193.

Styles, E. A. (1997). *The Psychology of Attention.* Hove, East Sussex, UK: The Psychology Press.

Sun, J., & Perona, P. (1996a). Preattentive perception of elementary three dimensional shapes. *Vision Research, 36*(16), 2515–2529.

Sun, J., & Perona, P. (1996b). Where is the sun? *Investigative Ophthalmology and Visual Science, 37*(3), S935.

Suzuki, S., & Cavanagh, P. (1995). Facial organization blocks access to low-level features: An object inferiority effect. *Journal of Experimental Psychology: Human Perception and Performance, 21*(4), 901–913.

Swensson, R. G. (1980). A two-stage detection model applied to skilled visual search by radiologists. *Perception and Psychophysics, 27*(1), 11–16.

Swensson, R. G., & Judy, P. F. (1981). Detection of noisy visual targets: Models for the effects of spatial uncertainty and signal-to-noise ratio. *Perception and Psychophysics, 29*(6), 521–534.

Takeuchi, T. (1997). Visual search of expansion and contraction. *Vision Research, 37*(5), 2083–2090.

Taylor, S., & Badcock, D. (1988). Processing feature density in preattentive perception. *Perception and Psychophysics, 44,* 551–562.

Theeuwes, J. (1991). Exogenous and endogenous control of attention: The effect of visual onsets and offsets. *Perception and Psychophysics, 49*(1), 83–90.

Theeuwes, J. (1994). Stimulus-driven capture and attentional set: Selective search for color and visual abrupt onsets. *Journal of Experimental Psychology: Human Perception and Performance, 20*(4), 799–806.

Theeuwes, J. (1995). Abrupt luminance change pops out; abrupt color change does not. *Perception & Psychophysics, 57*(5), 637–644.

Theeuwes, J., & Kooi, J. L. (1994). Parallel search for a conjunction of shape and contrast polarity. *Vision Research, 34*(22), 3013–3016.

Tipper, S. P. (1985). The negative priming effect: Inhibitory priming by ignored objects. *Quarterly Journal of Experimental psychology, 37A,* 571–590.

Tipper, S. P., & Cranston, M. (1985). Selective attention and priming: Inhibitory and facilitatory effects of ignored primes. *Quarterly Journal of Experimental Psychology, 37A,* 591–611.

Tipper, S. P., & Driver, J. (1988). Negative priming between pictures and words in a selective attention task: Evidence for semantic processing of ignored stimuli. *Memory and Cognition, 16*(1), 64–70.

Tipper, S. P., & Weaver, B. (1996). The medium of attention: Location-based, object-based, or scene-based? In R. Wright (Ed.), *Visual attention* (pp. 77–107). New York: Oxford University Press.

Tipper, S. P., Weaver, B., Jerreat, L. M., & Burak, A. L. (1994). Object-based and environment-based inhibition of return of visual attention. *Journal of Experimental Psychology: Human Perception & Performance, 20*(3), 478–499.

Tipper, S. P., Weaver, B., & Watson, F. L. (1996). Inhibition of return to successively cued spatial locations: Commentary on Pratt and Abrams (1995). *Journal of Experimental Psychology: Human Perception & Performance, 22*(5), 1289–1293.

Townsend, J. T. (1971). A note on the identification of parallel and serial processes. *Perception and Psychophysics, 10,* 161–163.

Townsend, J. T. (1976). Serial and within-stage independent parallel model equivalence on the minimum completion time. *Journal of Mathematical Psychology, 14,* 219–239.

Townsend, J. T. (1990). Serial and parallel processing: Sometimes they look like Tweedledum and Tweedledee but they can (and should) be distinguished. *Psychological Science, 1,* 46–54.

Treisman, A. (1982). Perceptual grouping and attention in visual search for features and for objects. *Journal of Experimental Psychology: Human Perception and Performance, 8,* 194–214.

Treisman, A. (1985). Preattentive processing in vision. *Computer vision, graphics, and image processing, 31,* 156–177.

Treisman, A. (1986). Properties, parts, and objects. In K. R. Boff, L. Kaufmann, & J. P. Thomas (Eds.), *Handbook of human perception and performance* (1 ed., Vol. 2, pp. 37.1–35.70). New York: John Wiley and Sons.

Treisman, A. (1988). Features and objects: The 14th Bartlett memorial lecture. *Quarterly Journal of Experimental Psychology, 40A,* 201–237.

Treisman, A. (1990). Variations on a theme of feature integration. Reply to Navon (1990). *Psychological Review, 97*(3), 460–463.

Treisman, A. (1992). Spreading suppression or feature integration? A reply to Duncan and Humphreys (1992). *Journal of Experimental Psychology: Human Perception and Performance, 18*(2), 589–593.

Treisman, A., & DeSchepper, B. (1996). Object tokens, attention, and visual memory. In T. Inui & J. McClelland (Eds.), *Attention and performance XVI: Information integration in perception and communication* (pp. 15–46). Cambridge, MA: MIT Press.

Treisman, A., & Gelade, G. (1980). A feature-integration theory of attention. *Cognitive Psychology, 12,* 97–136.

Treisman, A., & Gormican, S. (1988). Feature analysis in early vision: Evidence from search asymmetries. *Psychological Review, 95,* 15–48.

Treisman, A., & Sato, S. (1990). Conjunction search revisited. *Journal of Experimental Psychology: Human Perception and Performance, 16*(3), 459–478.

Treisman, A. M., & Schmidt, H. (1982). Illusory conjunctions in the perception of objects. *Cognitive Psychology, 14,* 107–141.

Treisman, A., & Souther, J. (1985). Search asymmetry: A diagnostic for preattentive processing of separable features. *Journal of Experimental Psychology: General, 114,* 285–310.

Treisman, A., & Souther, J. (1986). Illusory words: The roles of attention and of top-down constraints in conjoining letters to form words. *Journal of Experimental Psychology: Human Perception and Performance, 12,* 3–17.

Treue, S., & Maunsell, J. H. R. (1996). Attentional modulation of visual motion processing in cortical areas MT and MST. *Nature, 382,* 539–541.

Trick, L. M., & Enns, J. T. (1997). Measuring preattentive processes: When is pop-out not enough? *Visual Cognition, 4*(2), 163–198.

Tsal, Y. (1983). Movement of attention across the visual field. *Journal of Experimental Psychology: Human Perception & Performance, 9*(4), 523–530.

Tsal, Y. (1989a). Do illusory conjunctions support feature integration theory? A critical review of theory and findings. *Journal of Experimental Psychology: Human Perception and Performance, 15*(2), 394–400.

Tsal, Y. (1989b). Further comments on feature integration theory. A reply to Briand and Klein. *Journal of Experimental Psychology: Human Perception and Performance, 15*(2), 407–410.

Tsal, Y., & Lavie, N. (1993). Location dominance in attending to color and shape. *Journal of Experimental Psychology: Human Perception and Performance, 19,* 131–139.

Tsal, Y., Meiran, N., & Lavie, N. (1994). The role of attention in illusory conjunctions. *Perception and Psychophysics, 55*(3), 350–358.

Tse, P., Cavanagh, P., & Nakayama, K. (1998). The role of parsing in high-level motion processing. In T. Watanabe (Ed.), *High-level motion processing* (pp. 249–266). Cambridge, MA: MIT Press.

Tyler, C. W. (1983). Sensory processing of binocular disparity. In C. W. Schor & K. J. Ciuffreda (Eds.), *Vergence eye movements* (pp. 199–295). Boston: Butterworth.

Urbach, D., & Spitzer, H. (1995). Attentional effort modulated by task difficulty. *Vision Research, 35*(15), 2169–2177.

Van Orden, K. F. (1993). Redundant use of luminance and flashing with shape and color as highlighting codes in symbolic displays. *Human Factors, 35*(2), 195–204.

Van Zandt, T., & Townsend, J. T. (1993). Self-terminating versus exhaustive processes in rapid visual and memory search: An evaluative review. *Perception and Psychophysics, 53*(5), 563–580.

Vecera, S. P., & Farah, M. J. (1994). Does visual attention select objects or locations? *Journal of Experimental Psychology: General, 123*(2), 146–160.

Verghese, P., & Nakayama, K. (1994). Stimulus discriminability in visual search. *Vision Research, 34*(18), 2453–2467.

Verghese, P., & Pelli, D. G. (1994). The scale bandwidth of visual search. *Vision Research, 34*(7), 955–962.

Von der Heydt, R., Peterhans, E., & Baumgartner, G. (1984). Illusory contours and cortical neuron responses. *Science, 224,* 1260–1262.

Von Grunau, M., & Anston, C. (1995). The detection of gaze direction: A stare-in-the-crowd effect. *Perception, 24*(11), 1297–1313.

Von Grünau, M., & Dubé, S. (1994). Visual search asymmetry for viewing direction. *Perception and Psychophysics, 56*(2), 211–220.

Von Grünau, M., Dubé, S., & Kwas, M. (1996). Two contributions to motion induction: A preattentive effect and facilitation due to attentional capture. *Vision Research, 36,* 2447–2457.

Von Grunau, M., & Faubert, J. (1992). Interactive effects in motion induction. *Perception, 22*(suppl. 2 (ECVP - Pisa), 12.

Wang, Q., & Cavanagh, P. (1993). Acquired familiarity effects in visual search with chinese characters. *Investigative Ophthalmology and Visual Science, 34*(4), 1236.

Wang, Q., Cavanagh, P., & Green, M. (1994). Familiarity and pop-out in visual search. *Perception and Psychophysics, 56*(5), 495–500.

Ward, R., Duncan, J., & Shapiro, K. (1996). The slow time-course of visual attention. *Cognitive Psychology, 30*(1), 79–109.

Ward, R., Duncan, J., & Shapiro, K. (1997). Effects of similarity, difficulty, and nontarget presentation on the time course of visual attention. *Perception and Psychophysics, 59*(4), 593–600.

Weisstein, N. (1973). Beyond the yellow Volkswagen detector and the grandmother cell: A general strategy for the exploration of operations in human pattern recognition. In R. L. Solso (Ed.), *Contemporary issues in cognitive psychology: The Loyola Symposium.* Washington, DC: Winston/Wiley.

Weltman, G., & Egstrom, G. H. (1966). Perceptual narrowing in novice divers. *Human Factors, 8,* 499–506.

Williams, L. G. (1966a). The effect of target specification on objects fixated during visual search. *Perception & Psychophysics, 1,* 315–318.

Williams, L. G. (1966b). The effect of target specification on objects fixed during visual search. *Perception and Psychophysics, 1,* 315–318.

Williams, L. J. (1985). Tunnel vision induced by a foveal load manipulation. *Human Factors,* 27(2), 221–227.

Williams, L. J. (1989). Foveal load effects the functional field of view. *Human Performance,* 2(1), 1–28.

Wolfe, J. M. (1986). Stereopsis and binocular rivalry. *Psychological Review, 93,* 269–282.

Wolfe, J. M. (1992a). "Effortless" texture segmentation and "parallel" visual search are *not* the same thing. *Vision Research, 32*(4), 757–763.

Wolfe, J. M. (1992b). The parallel guidance of visual attention. *Current Directions in Psychological Science, 1*(4), 125–128.

Wolfe, J. M. (1994). Guided Search 2.0: A revised model of visual search. *Psychonomic Bulletin and Review, 1*(2), 202–238.

Wolfe, J. M. (1996). Extending Guided Search: Why Guided Search needs a preattentive "item map." In A. Kramer, G. H. Cole, & G. D. Logan (Eds.), *Converging operations in the study of visual selective attention.* (pp. 247–270). Washington, DC: American Psychological Association.

Wolfe, J. M. (1997a). Inattentional amnesia. *Abstracts of the Psychonomic Society, 2*(Nov), 18.

Wolfe, J. M. (1998a). Visual search. In H. Pashler (Ed.), *Attention* (pp. 13–74). Hove, UK: Psychology Press.

Wolfe, J. M. (1998b). What do 1,000,000 trials tell us about visual search? *Psychological Science, 9*(1), 33–39.

Wolfe, J. M., & Bennett, S. C. (1997). Preattentive Object Files: Shapeless bundles of basic features. *Vision Research, 37*(1), 25–44.

Wolfe, J. M., Cave, K. R., & Franzel, S. L. (1989). Guided Search: An alternative to the Feature Integration model for visual search. *Journal of Experimental Psychology—Human Perception and Performance, 15,* 419–433.

Wolfe, J. M., Chun, M. M., & Friedman-Hill, S. R. (1993). Making use of texton gradients: Visual search and texton grouping exploit the same parallel processes in different ways. *Spatial Vision,* 7(1), 90 (abstract only).

Wolfe, J. M., & Franzel, S. L. (1988). Binocularity and visual search. *Perception and Psychophysics, 44,* 81–93.

Wolfe, J. M., & Friedman-Hill, S. R. (1992a). On the role of symmetry in visual search. *Psychological Science, 3*(3), 194–198.

Wolfe, J. M., & Friedman-Hill, S. R. (1992b). Visual search for orientation: The role of angular relations between targets and distractors. *Spatial Vision, 6*(3), 199–208.

Wolfe, J. M., Friedman-Hill, S. R., & Bilsky, A. B. (1994). Parallel processing of part/whole information in visual search tasks. *Perception and Psychophysics, 55*(5), 537–550.

Wolfe, J. M., Friedman-Hill, S. R., Stewart, M. I., & O'Connell, K. M. (1992). The role of categorization in visual search for orientation. *Journal of Experimental Psychology: Human Perception and Performance, 18*(1), 34–49.

Wolfe, J. M., Klempen, N., & Dahlen, K. (1998). Post-attentive vision. *submitted 12/97.*

Wolfe, J. M., O'Neill, P. E., & Bennett, S. C. (1998). Why are there eccentricity effects in visual search? *Perception and Psychophysics, 60,* 1, 140–156.

Wolfe, J. M., & Pokorny, C. W. (1990). Inhibitory tagging in visual search: A failure to replicate. *Perception and Psychophysics, 48,* 357–362.

Wolfe, J. M., Yee, A., & Friedman-Hill, S. R. (1992). Curvature is a basic feature for visual search. *Perception, 21,* 465–480.

Wolfe, J. M., Yu, K. P., Stewart, M. I., Shorter, A. D., Friedman-Hill, S. R., & Cave, K. R. (1990). Limitations on the parallel guidance of visual search: Color X color and orientation X orientation conjunctions. *Journal of Experimental Psychology: Human Perception and Performance, 16*(4), 879–892.

Yantis, S. (1992). Multielement visual tracking: Attention and perceptual organization. *Cognitive Psychology, 24,* 295–340.

Yantis, S. (1993). Stimulus-driven attentional capture. *Current Directions in Psychological Science, 2*(5), 156–161.

Yantis, S., & Hillstrom, A. P. (1994). Stimulus-driven attentional capture: Evidence from equiluminant visual objects. *Journal of Experimental Psychology: Human Perception and Performance, 20*(1), 95–107.

Yantis, S., & Johnson, D. N. (1990). Mechanisms of attentional priority. *Journal of Experimental Psychology: Human Perception and Performance, 16*(4), 812–825.

Yantis, S., & Jonides, J. (1990). Abrupt visual onsets and selective attention: voluntary versus automatic allocation. *Journal of Experimental Psychology: Human Perception and Performance, 16*(1), 121–134.

Yeh, S.-L., Chen, I. P., De Valois, K. K., & De Valois, R. L. (1996). Figural aftereffects and spatial attention. *Journal of Experimental Psychology: Human Perception & Performance, 22*(2), 446–460.

Yund, E. W. (1996). Guided search: The effects of learning. *Brain and Cognition, 31*(3), 369–386.

Yund, E. W., Efron, R., & Nichols, D. R. (1990). Detectability gradients as a function of target location. *Brain and Cognition, 12,* 1–16.

Zelinsky, G. J., Rao, R. P. N., Hayhoe, M. M., & Ballard, D. H. (1996). Eye movements reveal the spatio-temporal dynamics of visual search. *Psychological Science, 8*(6), 448 453.

Zelinsky, G. J., & Sheinberg, D. L. (1997). Eye movements during parallel / serial visual search. *Journal of Experimental Psychology: Human Perception and Performance, 23*(1), 244–262.

Zohary, E., Hochstein, S., & Hillman, P. (1988). Parallel and serial processing in detecting conjunctions. *Perception, 17,* 416.

Index

D

E

F

G

H

I

K

L

M

N